Annual Editions:
Human Sexualities, 35/e
Elizabeth Schroeder

D1417440

http://create.mheducation.com

ISBN-10: 1259346137   ISBN-13: 9781259346132

Contents

Preface

Human sexuality is a complex construct that goes far beyond sexual behaviors. It is misunderstood and misconstrued, interpreted and misinterpreted, in cultures all around the world. It is frequently treated as an individual, isolated aspect of who we are as human beings, rather than integrated in the holistic understanding of human experience, growth, and development.

Over the years, our fascination with the myriad sexuality-related topics that exist and emerge has only grown. We have gone from never talking about sexuality because it was taboo to seeing it portrayed in mainstream news and entertainment media. We have expanded from defining heterosexual marriage as the only acceptable type of long-term, committed relationship and the only context within which it would be appropriate to raise children, to recognizing the wide range of committed relationship structures and the fact that people can be strong parents regardless of relationship status or structure.

We have gone from seeing non-heterosexual sexual orientations as psychological disorders and treating them with chemical castration and electroconvulsive therapy to the validation of lesbian, gay, bisexual, queer, and other individuals as equal to heterosexual members of society, parents, and caregivers, and in some states, legal spouses.

We have seen great progress in understanding diversity in biological sex and gender identity, and pressing for equal civil rights for all people. This includes moving far away from the disturbing historical practices of surgically altering infants with ambiguous genitalia and diverse chromosomal composition to the more common practice today of embracing this diversity and letting children grow up and determine for themselves whether or when they alter their bodies, if they so desire. We have seen great advances in rights for transgender individuals in terms of being able to legally change pronouns on identification documents and receiving legal protections in the workplace.

Yet in all of these cases, there is an important word missing: "Some." There has been great progress, yes—but for some people, not all. There have been some advances in legal standing and protections, but not nearly enough. There are some countries in which lesbian, gay, bisexual, and/or transgender people can openly identify themselves as such, and other countries in which doing so can result in jail sentences, beatings, and/or death sentences.

Those of us who live in the United States cannot forget for a moment that the world is not the West—nor can we think that the United States is what we see in our institutions of higher education, where critical thinking and exploration are expected, valued, and celebrated. Throughout the United States, there are individuals and groups who are deeply threatened and frightened by open discussions about sexuality; by the idea of equality between men and women, and they cannot begin to understand the idea of some people being transgender. There remain people who are so deeply homophobic and transphobic that they must bully, harass, or even physically assault people who are not heterosexual or cisgender. Some people believe that individuals who engage in less- traditional sexual behaviors or relationship structures threaten the stability of society. How striking that an aspect of our lives that can bring so many positive feelings and experiences can simultaneously be so feared and even reviled.

Granted, one reason for this is the knowledge that people do not always exercise their sexual freedoms responsibly or respectfully. Far too many people take advantage of and abuse others, or simply treat them as inferior to themselves. It is my sincere hope that the ongoing attention paid to this topic through books like "Annual Editions" will contribute, even in some small way, to changing attitudes and behaviors that are unhealthy or harmful to oneself or others.

In writing this preface, I was amazed to find that this is the 35th edition of the Annual Editions books on human sexualities. The enduring interest in this topic speaks volumes about the hunger we have to learn, talk, and debate about sex and sexuality. We want to understand who we are, how we feel, and how we behave regarding a topic that has had and continues to have such a conflictual relationship with many of the people for whom human sexuality is a key part of their lives.

The articles in the current edition are designed to be used flexibly to suit the needs of the instructor or course. Although grouped by topic, articles can be used individually and in any order the user wishes. In some cases, the subject matter of the articles will be considered fairly mainstream. The subjects of other articles may surprise or even shock you. Regardless, they all promise to make you think about how you feel about this aspect of our human experience.

Many, many thanks go to Mary Foust, Product Developer at McGraw-Hill, and possibly the most patient editor on the planet. More than being supportive, Mary literally made this book happen. I am equally grateful to McGraw-Hill for continuing to recognize the importance of human sexuality as a topic of study, and for not shying away from controversial or challenging topics. I would also like to thank Bobby Hutchison, the previous academic editor of *Annual Editions: Human Sexualities*, some of whose selections remain in this edition of the book. I also appreciate the many authors whose work appears here for challenging us to always think, learn, and grow.

Finally, and most importantly, I want to thank my 12-year-old son, Matthew, who, when I tell him what I'm working on, is never shocked, embarrassed—or, at this point, even surprised. I wish you a lifetime of health and happiness, my guy.

Thank you for taking the time to read and use this book in your work. We welcome your feedback on how these topics have worked for you and on what you'd like to see addressed in the future!

Elizabeth Schroeder, EdD, MSW
Editor

Editor

Elizabeth Schroeder, EdD., MSW., is an award-winning, internationally recognized educator, trainer, and author in the areas of sexuality education pedagogy, LGBTQ issues, working with adolescent boys and the use of technology and social media to reach and teach young people. She has provided consultation and direct education and training for schools, parent groups, and youth-serving organizations in countries around the world for more than 20 years.

She is the former executive director of Answer, a national sexuality education organization dedicated to providing and promoting unfettered access to comprehensive sexuality education to young people and the adults who teach them. She has also served as the associate vice president of education and training at Planned Parenthood of New York City, and, before that, manager of education and special projects at Planned Parenthood Federation of America.

Dr. Schroeder was a co-founding editor of the *American Journal of Sexuality Education*, and has authored or edited numerous publications, including the four-part book series, *Sexuality Education: Past, Present and Future* with Dr. Judy Kuriansky and *Sexuality Education: Theory and Practice* with Dr. Clint Bruess. She is a frequently

sought-out spokesperson and guest blogger in the news media on issues relating to sexual health education and youth development.

Dr. Schroeder provides national and international conference keynotes on sexuality and adolescent development, and has received numerous honors throughout her career, including the Healthy Teen Network Carol Mendez Cassell Award for excellence in leadership in sexuality education, the American Association of Sexuality Educators, Counselors and Therapists' Schiller Prize for her approaches to teaching Internet safety to youth, Widener University's William R. Stayton Award in recognition of outstanding contributions to the field of human sexuality, and the Planned Parenthood Mary Lee Tatum Award. She holds a Doctorate of Education in Human Sexuality Education from Widener University and a Master of Social Work from NYU, and teaches undergraduate courses at Montclair State University and graduate courses at Widener.

Academic Advisory Board

Members of the Academic Advisory Board are instrumental in the final selection of articles for the *Annual Editions* series. Their review of the articles for content, level, and appropriateness provides critical direction to the editor(s) and staff. We think that you will find their careful consideration reflected in this book.

Ben Anderson-Nathe
Portland State University

Janet Armitage
St. Mary's University

Harriet Bachner
Pittsburg State University

Janice I. Baldwin
University of California, Santa Barbara

John D. Baldwin
University of California, Santa Barbara

Anita P. Barbee
University of Louisville

Yvonne Barry
John Tyler Community College

Corinne Blackmer
Southern Connecticut State University

M. Jennifer Brougham
Arizona State University

Laurie Buchanan
Clark State Community College

Angela M. Butts
Rutgers University

Teresa Jean Byrne
Kent State University

Michael Calhoun
Elon University

Mike Calvert
Butler Community College

Amy Capwell Burns
University of Toledo

Bernardo J. Carducci
Indiana University Southeast

Dianne Catherwood
University of Gloucestershire

Jeffrey K. Clark
Ball State University

Maureen A. Clinton
Suffolk County Community College

Linda J. Coleman
Salem State University

Sandra Collins
Brown Mackie College

Carol Conaway
University of New Hampshire

Vanessa Cooke
Bowie State University

Clara Cosen-Woolfolk
Remington College, Memphis

Sheree Cox
Webster University, San Landro Center

Elizabeth Desnoyers-Colas
Armstrong Atlantic State University

Donald R. Devers
Northern Virginia Community College

Michael Drissman
Macomb Community College

Wilton Duncan
ASA College

Karen Edwards
University of Delaware

Brad Engeldinger
Sierra College

Harry F. Felton
Pennsylvania State University

Tony Fowler
Florence-Darlington Technical College

Bernard Frye
University of Texas, Arlington

Marilyn Gardner
Western Kentucky University

Rachel Gillibrand
University of the West of England

Kris Gowen
Portland State University

Marylou Hacker
Modesto Junior College

Marissa A. Harrison
Penn State Harrisburg

Robert A. Hayes
Lewis-Clark State College

Elizabeth Hegeman
John Jay College, CUNY

Bridget A. Hepner-Williamson
Sam Houston State University

Debby Herbenick
Indiana University, Bloomington

Sheri Hixon
Truckee Meadows Community College

Elizabeth Hodge
Gavilan College

Jennifer Hughes
Agnes Scott College

Loeen M. Irons
Baylor University

Kathleen Kaiser
California State University, Chico

Gary F. Kelly
Clarkson University

Charles Krinsky
Northeastern University

John T. Lambert
Mohawk College, Fennell

Bruce D. LeBlanc
Black Hawk College

Pat Lefler
Bluegrass Community and Technical College

Dennis A. Lichty
Wayne State College

Cynthia Mahaffey
Bowling Green State University

Jody Martin de Camilo
St. Louis Community College, Meramec

Danielle McAneney
Southwestern College

Mary McGinnis
Columbia College Chicago

Abi Mehdipour
Troy University

Holly Moyseenko-Kossover
Kent State University

Shan Parker
University of Michigan, Flint

Fred L. Peterson
University of Texas, Austin

Jane Petrillo
Kennesaw State University

Terry Pettijohn II
Coastal Carolina University

Doug Rice
California State University, Sacramento

Grant J. Rich
University of Alaska Southeast

Pamela Richards
Central College

Florence Sage
Clatsop Community College

Sadie B. Sanders
University of Florida, Gainesville

John G. Shiber
Big Sandy Community & Technical College

David Skiba
Niagara University

Leretta Smith
North Dakota State University

Michael Thomas
Arkansas State University

Glenda Warren
University of the Cumberlands

Casey Welch
Flagler College

Deitra Wengert
Towson University

Janis White
University of Phoenix

Karl Wielgus
Anoka Ramsey Community College

Virginia Wilson
Mountain State University

Charles Wood II
Southern W. Virginia Comm. and Tech College

Patricia Wren
Oakland University

Unit 1

UNIT

Prepared by: Elizabeth Schroeder, EdD, MSW,
Elizabeth Schroeder Consulting

Social and Cultural Foundations

There is not one culture in the world wherein human sexuality is seen as a neutral topic. All cultures have attitudes, values, and beliefs relating to human sexuality. These attitudes, values, and beliefs can be transmitted proactively through religious teachings, a country's or state's policies on what can and cannot be taught in school-based sex education courses, or the rating given to a film based on sexuality-related content that determines the age group for which the film is recommended. Cultural biases relating to sexuality are reflected in the gender makeup of a particular country's government, laws relating to same-sex marriage, and whether policies relating to sexual and reproductive healthcare are supportive or restrictive.

The United States, with its diversity of cultures, remains a fascinating and inconsistent place to live when it comes to sexuality. It boasts one of the most hypersexualized media markets, yet social conservatives try at every turn to keep young people from getting comprehensive sexuality education in schools.

Of all the sexuality-related topics that can be taught in a class or discussed within a culture, gender remains among the most complex, and simultaneously, most important. While progress has been made in some countries throughout the world on gender equity and human rights, quite a bit more needs to be done. This is because deeply held sexist beliefs pervade in many cultures. The more socially conservative a culture or a faction of a culture, the more invested that population will be in maintaining strict, binary gender lines and in keeping men in positions of power and superior to women. This unit explores some of these issues relating to gender, culture, and society.

At one extreme is the ongoing practice of infanticide—the vast majority of which involves killing female babies in favor of boys. In Pakistan, a social welfare organization called The Edhi Foundation, reported in 2014 that the number of dead babies that have been discarded in the trash and then picked up by their ambulances has increased by almost 20 percent each year since 2010. As one Pakistani man in an article reported on by Al Jazeera said, "In Pakistan, girls are considered bad fortune, and for this reason, many of the children killed are girls." Even when babies are born "illegitimate," or out-of-wedlock, which is considered an offense against Islam, exceptions are often made for boy babies, who may be raised by other family members as their own. Girl babies are much more likely to be killed or discarded.

At the other extreme are less nefarious, but still significant, cultural and social issues relating to gender that have an impact on people's overall well-being. Economic issues within relationships determine whether some women and men remain in long-term, committed relationships or marriages. Ongoing inequity in pay based on gender plays a role on whether women stay in relationships that may not be satisfying or healthy for them. And the ongoing dichotomy of how women are simultaneously seen as pure and then reviled for being sexual beings remains as confusing as it is misguided. One clear example of this is the ongoing debate relating to public breastfeeding. In a world in which women's breasts are barely concealed in even the most mainstream media, it is still mind boggling that people object to a woman feeding her baby.

Perhaps the most fascinating inconsistency within gender, culture, and society has to do with transgender, two-spirit, third gender, and gender non-conforming people. In the United States, progress has been made in recognizing the unique needs of transgender youth and adults as well as the legal protections they deserve—but there is far more work to be done here. The small country of Nepal was the first country to recognize a third gender on their census forms and passports in 2007 and then 2011. Other countries have since followed suit, although progress is slow.

Most recently in the United States, transgender rights within traditionally single-sex colleges and universities has come under scrutiny. Students who were assigned female at birth and who matriculate to these colleges and universities, only to come out as transgender or identify as male, raise several questions: do they belong at so-called all-women universities if they do not identify as female, regardless of what their biology was or is, or the status of any medical transition they may elect to have? Has the concept of, and need for, single-sex institutions of higher education become a thing of the past? There are strong feelings about this, with many students and alumnae pushing hard for maintaining an all-women educational environment while trying to figure out how to not penalize people for discovering their true genders. As of the writing of this book, the issue has not yet been resolved.

Although gender is different from sexual orientation, the two often get conflated. There are numerous reasons for this, not the least of which is the strong desire to keep people in categories or "boxes" in order to know how to interact with those people. A woman who is stereotypically masculine (a gender expression) will be simultaneously stereotyped as lesbian (a sexual orientation). Some people may react to that with fear and discomfort (homophobia), but a masculine presentation of a lesbian makes sense—especially if she were to be in a relationship with a stereotypically feminine woman. The idea of a same-sex relationship in which there is still the representation of a "man" and a "woman" still makes sense to many people. What is more challenging is two masculine women in a relationship; two masculine or feminine men, and so on.

Similarly, a transgender or gender nonconforming person who transitions from one gender binary to another makes sense for people trying to understand this experience. Yet many people do not "land" on one particular gender—many people identify as "trans," not male or female. There may be partial hormonal and surgical realignment, but no intention of full sex realignment surgery. Many people do not use male or female pronouns, instead opting for "zie," "hir," or simply a plural—"they." Most cultures are far less understanding or accepting of people who do not fit neatly into a gender box. This is at the heart of where society needs to progress—as understanding, compassion, and empathy builds, so will the support for equality.

Article

Prepared by: Elizabeth Schroeder, EdD, MSW,
Elizabeth Schroeder Consulting

Breastfeeding Is Not Obscene

CATHERINE MARSHALL

Learning Outcomes

After reading this article, you will be able to:

- Describe how female breasts are viewed in U.S. culture.

- Explain how the way in which we define breastfeeding culturally can affect the experience and benefits of breastfeeding.

- Identify at least one objection people who are opposed to public breastfeeding have.

Breasts are everywhere these days. They saturate our media in guises both trivial and sombre. Whether grotesquely augmented, stricken with cancer or tumbling unbidden from the frocks of soccer wives, breasts guarantee rapt attention and ongoing debate.

But never are these appendages more hotly debated than when they are being used according to their very purpose and design—that is, for the nourishment of babies.

Although the West's growing technological sophistication is inversely proportionate to its tolerance for organic activities such as breastfeeding, the negative attitudes are hardly new. History is littered with wet nurses to whom this distasteful activity was outsourced and modern mothers who dispensed with the biological process altogether in favour of Nestle's magical infant formula.

Buoyed by groups like the World Health Organisation, breastfeeding is creeping back into the public square, but western newborns still enter a world riven with dissent over their right to a ready meal.

It was refreshing to see the lactating Mexican actress and UNICEF ambassador Salma Hayek instinctively suckle a malnourished Sierra Leonean baby while visiting that country earlier this year. Hayek told reporters it was a compassionate act for a dying child, and that it came naturally to her to reach out to this baby when her own milk supply was plentiful. It was also an attempt to diminish the stigma of breastfeeding.

Not since Rose of Sharon breastfed a dying man in John Steinbeck's *The Grapes of Wrath* had breasts been used to commit such a revolutionary act. This Hollywood sex symbol wasn't just sharing her milk with a stranger's baby; she was doing so under the full public gaze.

How could it possibly be, then, that just last month in culturally diverse and thoroughly modern Australia a mother was asked by a flight attendant to conceal her breastfeeding activity from the puritanical eyes of fellow travellers? And that as recently as 2007 the NSW state government was forced to pass legislation making it illegal to discriminate against women breastfeeding in public?

Opinions around this issue are violently split between the supporters who believe babies should be allowed to feed wherever they please and the detractors who accuse nursing mothers of indecent exposure.

Could this really be happening in the same laissez-faire society where, not long before Kevin Rudd became prime minister, he was praised as being 'red-blooded' for visiting a New York strip club? Where young women flaunt their cleavages on city streets and semi-naked models stare out from the covers of men's magazines in service stations and news agencies across the country? Where prostitutes advertise their ware on the classified pages of suburban family newspapers?

Or, to put it more bluntly: is female nakedness culturally acceptable only when it is aimed exclusively at the arousal and satisfaction of men?

The reaction from some quarters to the Salma Hayek story seems to reinforce this hypothesis. As a presenter on the American talk show *The Young Turks* remarked, 'I wanted to be turned on by her breasts, but in that context I just couldn't do it.'

Of course, the reverse is true in traditional societies, where women tend to dress conservatively and the natural function of breasts is well-respected. In the many years I breastfed my own children, it never occurred to me that I might offend anyone. The fact that I lived in Africa contributed, no doubt, to the ease with which I was able to conduct this ritual.

In Africa, breasts exist primarily as vessels of nourishment rather than as sexual objects. Women breastfeed their children on trains, buses and taxis, in restaurants and on park benches, in church and at work. Mostly they do so discreetly, but it's hardly newsworthy when they don't.

Using these African mamas as role models, I fed my babies on demand, regardless of where we happened to be at the time. The only person to object was a friend's mother, who believed vehemently that breasts were for sex, not babies. As if the two were somehow mutually exclusive.

And herein, perhaps, lies the absurd conundrum facing Australian women, who live in a strangely dichotomous society which tolerates them lying topless on the beach but chokes on its collective latte when they expose their nursing bras. In its typically prurient way, Western culture has co-opted breasts and sexualised them so thoroughly that their basic function is no longer accommodated.

This primordial act, upon which every other mammal relies for survival, has been twisted from its nurturing premise into an act of awful obscenity.

Sadly, society's fixation on the 'perversion' of public breastfeeding obscures the inordinate benefits that flow from it: breast milk improves infants' health and intellectual outcomes and decreases their carbon footprints; its production results in elevated levels of oxytocin within the nursing mother's brain, contributing to her emotional equilibrium, and decreases her risk of developing ovarian and breast cancer.

Almost a decade into the new century, it's a disgrace that women are still made to feel uncomfortable while using their breasts to nourish their babies. Breastfeeding is neither primitive nor obscene; it is an act of love and generosity, a forward-thinking deposit into society's depleted bank account.

Critical Thinking

1. What social significance do the female breasts have in our culture?
2. How do social and cultural definitions of breastfeeding impact the experience and outcomes of breastfeeding?

Internet References

La Leche League International
http://www.llli.org
Nursing Freedom
http://www.nursingfreedom.org
United States Breastfeeding Committee
http://www.usbreastfeeding.org

Article   Prepared by: Elizabeth Schroeder, EdD, MSW,
                                                  Elizabeth Schroeder Consulting

When Women Become Men at Wellesley

Ruth Padawer

Learning Outcomes

After reading this article, you will be able to:

- Provide at least two reasons why Wellesley and other traditionally all-women colleges/universities have let students who identify as transgender men remain at their institutions.

- Explain how these traditionally all-women colleges and universities have responded to transgender women's applications.

- Describe how Mount Holyoke has adapted its policies relating to student admission and attendance and gender.

Hundreds of young women streamed into Wellesley College on the last Monday of August, many of them trailed by parents lugging suitcases and bins filled with folded towels, decorative pillows and Costco-size jugs of laundry detergent. The banner by the campus entranceway welcoming the Class of 2018 waved in the breeze, as if beckoning the newcomers to discover all that awaited them. All around the campus stood buildings named after women: the Margaret Clapp library, the Betsy Wood Knapp media and technology center, dorms, labs, academic halls, even the parking garage. The message that anything is possible for women was also evident at a fenced-in work site, which bore the sign "Elaine Construction," after a firm named for one woman and run by another.

It was the first day of orientation, and along the picturesque paths there were cheerful upper-class student leaders providing directions and encouragement. They wore pink T-shirts stamped with this year's orientation theme: "Free to Explore"— an enticement that could be interpreted myriad ways, perhaps far more than the college intended. One of those T-shirted helpers was a junior named Timothy Boatwright. Like every other matriculating student at Wellesley, which is just west of

Boston, Timothy was raised a girl and checked "female" when he applied. Though he had told his high-school friends that he was transgender, he did not reveal that on his application, in part because his mother helped him with it, and he didn't want her to know. Besides, he told me, "it seemed awkward to write an application essay for a women's college on why you were not a woman." Like many trans students, he chose a women's college because it seemed safer physically and psychologically.

From the start, Timothy introduced himself as "masculine-of-center genderqueer." He asked everyone at Wellesley to use male pronouns and the name Timothy, which he'd chosen for himself.

For the most part, everyone respected his request. After all, he wasn't the only trans student on campus. Some two dozen other matriculating students at Wellesley don't identify as women. Of those, a half-dozen or so were trans men, people born female who identified as men, some of whom had begun taking testosterone to change their bodies. The rest said they were transgender or genderqueer, rejecting the idea of gender entirely or identifying somewhere between female and male; many, like Timothy, called themselves transmasculine. Though his gender identity differed from that of most of his classmates, he generally felt comfortable at his new school.

Last spring, as a sophomore, Timothy decided to run for a seat on the student-government cabinet, the highest position that an openly trans student had ever sought at Wellesley. The post he sought was multicultural affairs coordinator, or "MAC," responsible for promoting "a culture of diversity" among students and staff and faculty members. Along with Timothy, three women of color indicated their intent to run for the seat. But when they dropped out for various unrelated reasons before the race really began, he was alone on the ballot. An anonymous lobbying effort began on Facebook, pushing students to vote "abstain." Enough "abstains" would deny Timothy the minimum number of votes Wellesley required, forcing a new election for the seat and providing an opportunity for other candidates to come forward. The "Campaign to Abstain" argument was simple: Of all the people at a multiethnic women's college who could hold the school's "diversity" seat, the least fitting one was a *white man*.

"It wasn't about Timothy," the student behind the Abstain campaign told me. "I thought he'd do a perfectly fine job, but it just felt inappropriate to have a white man there. It's not just about that position either. Having men in elected leadership positions undermines the idea of this being a place where women are the leaders."

I asked Timothy what he thought about that argument, as we sat on a bench overlooking the tranquil lake on campus during orientation. He pointed out that he has important contributions to make to the MAC position. After all, at Wellesley, masculine-of-center students *are* cultural minorities; by numbers alone, they're about as minor as a minority can be. And yet Timothy said he felt conflicted about taking a leadership spot. "The patriarchy is alive and well," he said. "I don't want to perpetuate it."

In the 19th century, only men were admitted to most colleges and universities, so proponents of higher education for women had to build their own. The missions at these new schools both defied and reinforced the gender norms of the day. By offering women access to an education they'd previously been denied, the schools' very existence was radical, but most were nevertheless premised on traditional notions: College-educated women were considered more likely to be engaging wives and better mothers, who would raise informed citizens. Over time, of course, women's colleges became more committed to preparing students for careers, but even in the early 1960s, Wellesley, for example, taught students how to get groceries into the back of a station wagon without exposing their thighs.

By the late 1960s, however, gender norms were under scrutiny. Amid the growing awareness of civil rights and women's liberation, academic separation based on gender, as with race, seemed increasingly outdated. As a vast majority of women opted for coed schools, enrollment at women's colleges tumbled. The number of women's colleges dropped to fewer than 50 today from nearly 300.

In response to shifting ideas about gender, many of the remaining women's colleges redefined themselves as an antidote to the sexism that feminists were increasingly identifying in society. Women's colleges argued that they offered a unique environment where every student leader was a woman, where female role models were abundant, where professors were far more likely to be women and where the message of women's empowerment pervaded academic and campus life. All that seemed to foster students' confidence. Women's colleges say their undergrads are more likely to major in fields traditionally dominated by men. Wellesley alumnae in particular are awarded more science and engineering doctorates than female graduates of any other liberal-arts college in the nation, according

to government data. Its alums have become two secretaries of state; a groundbreaking string theorist; a NASA astronaut; and Korea's first female ambassador.

As women's colleges challenged the conventions of womanhood, they drew a disproportionate number of students who identified as lesbian or bisexual. Today a small but increasing number of students at those schools do not identify as women, raising the question of what it means to be a "women's college." Trans students are pushing their schools to play down the women-centric message. At Wellesley, Smith, Mount Holyoke and others, they and their many supporters have successfully lobbied to scrub all female references in student government constitutions, replacing them with gender-neutral language. At Wellesley, they have pressed administrators and fellow students to excise talk of sisterhood, arguing that that rhetoric, rather than being uplifting, excludes other gender minorities. At many schools, they have also taken leadership positions long filled by women: resident advisers on dorm floors, heads of student groups and members of college government. At Wellesley, one transmasculine student was a dorm president. At Mills College, a women's school in California, even the president of student government identifies as male.

What's a women's college to do? Trans students point out that they're doing exactly what these schools encourage: breaking gender barriers, fulfilling their deepest yearnings and forging ahead even when society tries to hold them back. But yielding to their request to dilute the focus on women would undercut the identity of a women's college. While women in coed schools generally outpace men in enrollment and performance, the equation shifts after college: Recent female graduates working full time earn far less than their male counterparts, and more experienced women are often still shut out of corporate and political leadership—all of which prompts women's-college advocates to conclude that a four-year, confidence-building workshop still has its place.

"Sisterhood is why I chose to go to Wellesley," said a physics major who graduated recently and asked not to be identified for fear she'd be denounced for her opinion. "A women's college is a place to celebrate being a woman, surrounded by women. I felt empowered by that every day. You come here thinking that every single leadership position will be held by a woman: every member of the student government, every newspaper editor, every head of the Economics Council, every head of the Society of Physics. That's an incredible thing! This is what they advertise to students. But it's no longer true. And if all that is no longer true, the intrinsic value of a women's college no longer holds."

A few schools have formulated responses to this dilemma, albeit very different ones. Hollins University, a small women's college in Virginia, established a policy several years ago stating it would confer diplomas to only women. It also said that students who have surgery or begin hormone therapy to become men—or who legally take male names—will be "helped to transfer to another institution." Mount Holyoke and Mills College, on the other hand, recently decided they will not only continue to welcome students who become trans men while at school but will also admit those who identify on their applications as trans men, noting that welcoming the former and not the latter seemed unjustifiably arbitrary.

But most women's colleges, including Wellesley, consider only female applicants. Once individuals have enrolled and announced that they are trans, the schools, more or less, leave it to the students to work out how trans classmates fit into a women's college. Two of those students hashed it out last fall after Kaden Mohamed, then a Wellesley senior who had been taking testosterone for seven months, watched a news program on WGBH-TV about the plummeting number of women's colleges. One guest was Laura Bruno, another Wellesley senior. The other guest was the president of Regis College, a women's school that went coed in 2007 to reverse its tanking enrollment. The interviewer asked Laura to describe her experience at an "all-female school" and to explain how that might be diminished "by having men there." Laura answered, "We look around and we see only women, only people like us, leading every organization on campus, contributing to every class discussion."

Kaden, a manager of the campus student cafe who knew Laura casually, was upset by her words. He emailed Laura and said her response was "extremely disrespectful." He continued: "I am not a woman. I am a trans man who is part of your graduating class, and you literally ignored my existence in your interview. . . . You had an opportunity to show people that Wellesley is a place that is complicating the meaning of being an 'all women's school,' and you chose instead to displace a bunch of your current and past Wellesley siblings."

Laura apologized, saying she hadn't meant to marginalize anyone and had actually vowed beforehand not to imply that all Wellesley students were women. But she said that under pressure, she found herself in a difficult spot: How could she maintain that women's colleges would lose something precious by including men, but at the same time argue that women's colleges should accommodate students who identify as men?

Although it may seem paradoxical, Jesse Austin said he chose to attend Wellesley because being female never felt right to him. "I figured if I was any kind of woman, I'd find it there. I knew Wellesley would have strong women. They produce a ton of strong women, strong in all sorts of ways."

When Jesse arrived on campus in the fall of 2009, his name was Sara. Eighteen years old, Sara wore form-fitting shirts and snug women's jeans, because growing up in a small, conservative town in Georgia, she learned that that's what girls were supposed to do—even though she never felt like a girl. As a child, Sara had always chosen to be male characters in pretend plays,

and all her friends were boys. In middle school, those boys abandoned her because she was a social liability: not feminine enough to flirt with and not masculine enough to really be one of the guys. In high school, at the urging of well-intentioned female classmates, she started wearing her hair down instead of pulled back and began dressing like they did, even though people kept pointing out that she still acted and carried herself like a boy. "I had no idea that gender was something you could change," Jesse told me recently. "I just thought I needed to make myself fit into these fixed places: There are boys, and there are girls. I knew I didn't fit; I just didn't know what was wrong with me."

Around the middle of Sara's first year at Wellesley, she attended a presentation by trans alums, including one who was in the process of transitioning. As Sara listened, the gender dysphoria she'd always felt suddenly made sense. "It was all so clear to me," Jesse told me. "All I needed were the words." Sara spent the next two weeks scouring the Internet for videos and information on becoming a man. She learned that unlike previous generations, today's trans young adults don't consider physical transformation a prerequisite for identity. Some use hormones; some have their breasts removed in "top" surgery; some reject medical interventions altogether, as unnecessary invasions and expense. She discovered that sexual orientation is independent of gender: Some trans men are attracted to women, some to men, some to both. And she learned that trans men aren't necessarily determined to hide the fact they were raised as girls, or that they once attended a women's college.

Soon after, Sara cut her hair short and bought her first pair of men's jeans. Sara told friends she was a man. By second semester, he was using male pronouns and calling himself Jesse, the other name his mother had considered for her daughter. He also joined a tiny campus group for students who knew or suspected they were trans men. It was called Brothers, a counterweight to the otherwise ubiquitous message of sisterhood.

That summer, Jesse saw a gender therapist, and early in his sophomore year, he began injecting testosterone into his thigh every two weeks, making him one of the first students to medically transform into a man while at Wellesley. He became the administrator of Brothers. Though he felt supported, he also felt alone; all the other trans men on campus had graduated, and the other students in Brothers were not even sure they identified as men. Outside Brothers, everything at Wellesley was still sisterhood and female empowerment. Nevertheless, he said, "I thought of Wellesley as my home, my community. I felt fine there, like I totally belonged."

Jesse decided he wanted to have top surgery over winter break, and his parents agreed to pay for it. He returned for spring semester but only briefly, taking a sudden leave of absence to go home and help care for his ill father. When Jesse re-enrolled at Wellesley a year- and- a- half later, in fall 2012, much had changed in Jesse and at school. Having been on testosterone for two years at that point, Jesse no longer looked like a woman trying to pass as a man. His voice was deep. His facial hair was thick, though he kept it trimmed to a stubble. His shoulders had become broad and muscular, his hips narrow, his arms and chest more defined.

Wellesley was different, too. By then, a whole crowd of people identified as trans—enough for two trans groups. Brothers had officially become Siblings and welcomed anyone anywhere on the gender spectrum except those who identified as women. Meanwhile, Jesse and some transmasculine students continued to meet unofficially as Brothers, though Jesse was the only one on testosterone.

Over all, campus life had a stronger trans presence than ever. At least four of the school's 70 R.A.s did not identify as women. Student organizations increasingly began meetings by asking everyone to state preferred names and pronouns. Around campus, more and more students were replacing "sisterhood" with "siblinghood" in conversation. Even the school's oldest tradition, Flower Sunday—the 138-year-old ceremony that paired each incoming student with an upper-class Big Sister to support her—had become trans-inclusive. Though the school website still describes Flower Sunday as "a day of sisterhood," the department that runs the event yielded to trans students' requests and started referring to each participant as a Big or Little "Sister/Sibling"—or simply as Bigs and Littles.

And yet even with the increased visibility of trans students on campus, Jesse stood out. When he swiped his Wellesley ID card to get into friends' dorms, the groundskeepers would stop him and say, "You can't go in there without a woman to escort you." Residential directors who spotted him in the dorm stairwells told him the same thing. In his own dorm, parents who were visiting their daughters would stop him to ask why he was there. Because bathrooms in the dorms are not labeled "women" or "men" but rather "Wellesley only" and "non-Wellesley," students who didn't know Jesse would call him out for using the "Wellesley only" bathroom instead of the one for visitors. When he tried to explain he *was* a Wellesley student, people sometimes thought he was lying.

"Everything felt very different than it had before," he said of that semester. "I felt so distinctly male, and I felt extremely awkward. I felt like an outsider. My voice was jarring—a male voice, which is so distinct in a classroom of women—so I felt weird saying much in class. I felt much more aware of Wellesley as a women's place, even though the college was starting to change."

Once spring semester ended, Jesse withdrew. "I still think of Wellesley as a women's place, and I still think that's a wonderful idea," he said. "It just didn't encompass me anymore. I felt it was a space I shouldn't tread in."

Some female students, meanwhile, said Wellesley wasn't female enough. They complained among themselves and to the administration that sisterhood had been hijacked. "Siblinghood," they argued, lacked the warm, pro-women connotation of "sisterhood," as well as its historic resonance. Others were upset that even at a women's college, women were still expected to accommodate men, ceding attention and leadership opportunities intended for women. Still others feared the changes were a step toward coeducation. Despite all that, many were uneasy: As a marginalized group fighting for respect and clout, how could women justify marginalizing others?

"I felt for the first time that something so stable about our school was about to change, and it made me scared," said Beth, a junior that year, who asked to be identified by only her middle name because she was afraid of offending people she knew. "Changing 'sister' to 'sibling' didn't feel like it was including more people; it felt like it was taking something away from sisterhood, transforming our safe space for the sake of someone else. At the same time, I felt guilty feeling that way." Beth went to Kris Niendorf, the director of residential life, who listened sympathetically and then asked: Why does "sibling" take away from your experience? After thinking about it, Beth concluded that she was connected to her classmates not because of gender but because of their shared experiences at Wellesley. "That year was an epiphany for me. I realized that if we excluded trans students, we'd be fighting on the wrong team. We'd be on the wrong side of history."

Exactly how Wellesley will resolve the trans question is still unclear. Trans students say that aside from making sure every academic building on campus has a unisex bathroom, Wellesley has not addressed what gender fluidity means for Wellesley's identity. Last spring, Alex Poon won Wellesley's 131-year-old hoop-rolling race, an annual spirit-building competition among seniors. Alex's mother was the hoop-rolling champion of the Class of '82 and had long ago taught her daughters the ways of the hoop, on the assumption that they would one day attend her alma mater. (One of Alex's older sisters was Wellesley Class of '11; another went to Bryn Mawr.) Alex was a former Girl Scout who attended an all-girls high school. But unknown to his mother, he was using Google to search for an explanation for his confusing feelings. By the time Alex applied to Wellesley, he secretly knew he was trans but was nonetheless certain Wellesley was a good fit. For one thing, going there was a family tradition; for another, it was a place where gender could be reimagined. In his sophomore year at Wellesley, he went public with his transgender status.

On hoop-rolling day, Alex—wearing a cap backward on his buzz-cut hair—broke through the finish-line streamer. President H. Kim Bottomly took a selfie with him, each with a wide smile. A small local newspaper covered the event, noting that for the first time in the school's history, the winner was a man. And yet the page on Wellesley's website devoted to school traditions continues to describe the race as if it involves only women. "Back in the day, it was proclaimed that whoever won the Hoop Roll would be the first to get married. In the status-seeking 1980s, she was the first to be C.E.O. Now we just say that the winner will be the first to achieve happiness and success, whatever that means to her." But Alex isn't a her, and he told me that his happiness and success includes being recognized for what he is: a man.

That page is not the only place on the site where Wellesley markets itself as a school of only female students. Elsewhere, it crows that "all the most courageous, most provocative, most accomplished people on campus are women." The student body, it says, is "2,300 smart, singular women feeling the power of 2,300 smart, singular women together" on a campus where "our common identity, spirit and pride as Wellesley women" are celebrated. Those sorts of messages, trans students say, make them feel invisible.

"I just wish the administration would at least acknowledge our existence," said Eli Cohen, a Wellesley senior who has been taking testosterone for nearly a year. "I'd be more O.K. with 'We're not going to cater to you, because men are catered to everywhere else in life,' rather than just pretending we don't exist."

Some staff and faculty members, however, are acknowledging the trans presence. Women-and-gender-studies professors, and a handful of others, typically begin each semester asking students to indicate the names and pronouns they prefer for themselves. Kris Niendorf, director of campus and residential life, recruits trans students who want to be R.A.s, as she does with all minorities. Niendorf also initiated informational panels with trans students and alums. And before this school year began, at the urging of trans students, Niendorf required all 200 student leaders to attend a trans-sensitivity workshop focused on how to "create a more inclusive Wellesley College." For the last few years, orientation organizers have also included a trans student as one of the half-dozen upper-class students who stand before the incoming first-years and recount how they overcame a difficult personal challenge.

And yet many trans students feel that more needs to be done. They complain that too many professors assume all their students are women. Students provided numerous examples in courses across subject areas where they've been asked their viewpoint "as a woman." In a course on westerns two years ago, an essay assignment noted that western films and novels were aimed at male audiences and focused on masculinity. The professors asked students for their perspective "as a female reader or watcher"—wording that offended the three trans students in class. When a classmate pointed out the problematic wording to the professors, the instructors asked everyone instead "to explore how your own gender identity changes how you approach westerns."

At times, professors find themselves walking a fine line. Thomas Cushman, who has taught sociology at Wellesley for

the last 25 years, first found out about Wellesley's trans population five years ago, after a student in one of his courses showed up at Cushman's office and introduced himself as a trans male. The student pointed out that every example Cushman gave in class referred to women, and every generic pronoun he used was female, as in "Ask your classmate if she. . . . " He told Cushman that Wellesley could no longer call itself a "women's college," given the presence of trans men, and he asked Cushman to use male pronouns and male examples more often, so trans students didn't feel excluded. Cushman said he would abide by whatever pronoun individual students requested for themselves, but he drew the line at changing his emphasis on women.

"All my life here," Cushman told me, "I've been compelled to use the female pronoun more generously to get away from the sexist 'he.' I think it's important to evoke the idea that women are part of humanity. That should be affirmed, especially after being denied for so long. Look, I teach at a women's college, so whenever I can make women's identity central to that experience, I try to do that. Being asked to change that is a bit ironic. I don't agree that this is a 'historically' women's college. It is still a women's college."

On the second day of orientation this fall, Eli Cohen arrived on campus in a muscle T and men's shorts, with a carabiner full of keys hanging from his belt loop. He was elated to be back to the place that felt most like home. It was the first time in four years that Eli had not been part of orientation—first as a newcomer and then two years as an R.A. We hung out in the Lulu Chow Wang Campus Center, known affectionately as Lulu, and watched the excited first-years flutter by, clutching their orientation schedules and their newly purchased Wellesley wear.

Just 12 days earlier, Eli underwent top surgery, which he said gave him a newfound self-assurance in his projection of manhood. It had been nine months since he started testosterone, and the effects had become particularly noticeable over the three-month summer break. His jaw line had begun to square, his limbs to thicken and the hair on his arms and legs to darken. And of course now his chest was a flat wall. As his friends caught sight of him for the first time in months, they hugged him and gushed, "You look sooo good!"

Though Eli secretly suspected in high school that he was a boy, it wasn't until after he arrived at Wellesley that he could imagine he might one day declare himself a man. By his second year, he had buzz-cut his hair and started wearing men's clothes. He asked his friends to call him Beckett, which is similar to his female birth name, which he asked me not to mention. His parents live only 14 miles away and dropped by for short visits. He left his girl nameplate on his dorm door. His friends understood that whenever his parents arrived, everyone was to revert to his female name and its attendant pronouns. He was an R.A. at the time and decided not to reveal his male name to his first-year students, figuring it was too complicated to explain which name to use when.

Given how guarded he had to be, being Beckett was exhausting and anxiety-inducing. Demoralized, he eventually told his pals to just use his birth name. The summer after his sophomore year, he got an internship at a Boston health center serving the L.G.B.T. community, and many of his co-workers were trans. Their confidence gave him confidence. When the Wellesley office that coordinates internships sent out an email to all interns that began, "Good morning, ladies . . .," he emailed back to say he did not identify as a woman. The coordinator apologized and explained that all the names on her paperwork from Wellesley were female.

By summer's end, he began introducing himself as Eli, a name utterly unlike his birth name. Eli mustered the courage to tell his parents. It took a little while for his mother to accept that her only daughter was actually a son, but she came around.

When I asked Eli if trans men belonged at Wellesley, he said he felt torn. "I don't necessarily think we have a right to women's spaces. But I'm not going to transfer, because this is a place I love, a community I love. I realize that may be a little selfish. It may be a lot selfish." Where, he wondered, should Wellesley draw a line, if a line should even be drawn? At trans men? At transmasculine students? What about students who are simply questioning their gender? Shouldn't students be "free to explore" without fearing their decision will make them unwelcome?

Other trans students have struggled with these questions, too. Last December, a transmasculine Wellesley student wrote an anonymous blog post that shook the school's trans community. The student wrote to apologize for "acting in the interest of preserving a hurtful system of privileging masculinity." He continued: "My feelings have changed: I do not think that trans men belong at Wellesley . . . . This doesn't mean that I think that all trans men should be kicked out of Wellesley or necessarily denied admission." He acknowledged he didn't know how Wellesley could best address the trans question, but urged fellow transmasculine classmates to "start talking, and thinking critically, about the space that we are given and occupying, and the space that we are taking from women."

The reactions were swift and strong. "A lot of trans people on campus felt emotionally unsafe," recalled Timothy, a sophomore that year. "A place that seemed welcoming suddenly wasn't. The difficulty was that because it was a trans person saying it, people who don't have enough of an understanding to appreciate the nuance of this can say, 'Well, even a trans person says there shouldn't be trans people at Wellesley, so it's O.K. for me to think the same thing, too.'"

Students and alums—queer and straight, trans and not—weighed in, sometimes in agreement but other times in anger. Some accused the blogger of speaking on behalf of women as if they were unable to speak for themselves. Others accused him of betraying transmasculine students. (He declined to comment for this article.) But other students, including several transmasculine ones, were glad he had the courage to start a public discussion about Wellesley's deeply conflicted identity. "It's a very important conversation to have," Eli said. "Why can't we have this conversation without feeling hurt or hated?"

In some ways, students are already having that conversation, though perhaps indirectly. Timothy ended up easily winning his seat on the student government last spring, capturing two-thirds of the votes. Given that 85 percent of the student body cast ballots in that race, his victory suggests most students think that transmasculine students—and transmasculine leaders—belong at Wellesley.

Another difficult conversation about trans students touches on the disproportionate attention they receive on campus. "The female-identified students somehow place more value on those students," said Rose Layton, a lesbian who said she views trans students as competitors in the campus dating scene. "They flirt with them, hook up with them. And it's not just the hetero women, but even people in the queer community. The trans men are always getting this extra bit of acknowledgment. Even though we're in a women's college, the fact is men and masculinity get more attention and more value in this social dynamic than women do."

Jesse Austin noticed the paradox when he returned to campus with a man's build and full swath of beard stubble after nearly two years on testosterone. "That was the first time in my life I was popular! People were clamoring to date me."

Trans bodies are seen as an in-between option, Timothy said. "So no matter your sexuality, a trans person becomes safe to flirt with, to explore with. But it's not really the person you're interested in, it's the novelty. For lesbians, there's the safety of 'I may be attracted to this person, but they're "really" a woman, so I'm not actually bi or straight.' And for straight people, it's 'I may be attracted to a woman's body, but he's a male, so I'm not really lesbian or bi.'"

Kaden Mohamed said he felt downright objectified when he returned from summer break last year, after five months of testosterone had lowered his voice, defined his arm muscles and reshaped his torso. It was attention that he had never experienced before he transitioned. But as his body changed, students he didn't even know would run their hands over his biceps. Once at the school pub, an intoxicated Wellesley woman even grabbed his crotch and that of another trans man.

"It's this very bizarre reversal of what happens in the real world," Kaden said. "In the real world, it's women who get fetishized, catcalled, sexually harassed, grabbed. At Wellesley, it's trans men who do. If I were to go up to someone I just met and touch her body, I'd get grief from the entire Wellesley community, because they'd say it's assault—and it is. But for some reason, when it's done to trans men here, it doesn't get read the same way. It's like a free pass, that suddenly it's O.K. to talk about or touch someone's body as long as they're not a woman."

While trans men are allowed at most women's colleges if they identify as female when applying, trans women—people raised male who go on to identify as women—have found it nearly impossible to get through the campus gates. Arguably, a trans woman's identity is more compatible with a women's college than a trans man's is. But most women's colleges require that all of an applicant's documentation indicate the candidate is female. That's a high bar for a 17- or 18-year-old born and raised male, given that so few come out as trans in high school. (Admissions policies at private undergraduate schools are exempt from Title IX, which bans gender discrimination at schools receiving federal funds.) Two years ago, Calliope Wong, a high-school trans woman from Connecticut, applied to Smith College, but her application was returned because her federal aid form indicated she was male. She posted the rejection letter online, catalyzing a storm on the Internet and student rallies at Smith. Smith eventually agreed to require that the applicant be referred to as female only in the transcript and recommendation letters, but not on financial-aid documents; by then, however, Wong had decided to attend the University of Connecticut.

For its part, Wellesley has never admitted a trans woman, at least not knowingly. Many Wellesley students, including some who are uncomfortable having trans men on campus, say that academically eligible trans women should be admitted, regardless of the gender on their application documents.

Others are wary of opening Wellesley's doors too quickly—including one of Wellesley's trans men, who asked not to be named because he knew how unpopular his stance would be. He said that Wellesley should accept only trans women who have begun sex-changing medical treatment or have legally changed their names or sex on their driver's licenses or birth certificates. "I know that's a lot to ask of an 18-year-old just applying to college," he said, "but at the same time, Wellesley needs to maintain its integrity as a safe space for women. What if someone who is male-bodied comes here genuinely identified as female, and then decides after a year or two that they identify as male—and wants to stay at Wellesley? How's that different from admitting a biological male who identifies as a man? Trans men are a different case; we were raised female, we know what it's like to be treated as females and we have been discriminated against as females. We get what life has been like for women."

In May, Mills College became the first women's college to broaden its admissions policy to include self-identified trans women, even those who haven't legally or medically transitioned and even if their transcripts or recommendation letters refer to them as male. The new policy, which begins by affirming Mills's commitment to remaining a women's college, also welcomes biological females who identify anywhere on the gender spectrum, as long as they haven't become legally male. The change grew out of two years of study by a committee of faculty and staff, which noted that Mills has always fought gender-based oppression and concluded, "Trans inclusiveness represents not an erasure but an updating of this mission."

Mills also aims to educate students, staff and faculty members to be more trans inclusive, said Brian O'Rourke, who oversees enrollment at the college and was the president's liaison to the committee. I asked O'Rourke if that included reducing the focus on women in the classroom. "I honestly don't know," he said. "We had a national speaker on trans issues join us on campus about a year ago, and one of the things she suggested is that we stop referring to Mills as a women's college, because that concept is exclusionary. In the auditorium, there was an audible gasp. We've had a lot of conversations about how to stress women's leadership and women's empowerment and at the same time, include people who may not identify as women. The answer is: We don't know yet."

Last month, Mount Holyoke College announced a more far-reaching policy: It would admit all academically qualified students regardless of their anatomy or self-proclaimed gender, except for those biologically male at birth who still identify as male. In a list that reflects just how much traditional notions of gender have been upended, Mount Holyoke said eligible candidates now include anyone born biologically female, whether identified as woman, man, neither or "other" and anyone born biologically male who identifies as a woman or "other." The school president, Lynn Pasquerella, said she and her officers made the decision after concluding it was an issue of civil rights.

But Pasquerella said accommodations for trans students will not include changing the school's mission. "We're first and foremost committed to being a women's college," she told me. "I'm not going to stop using the language of sisterhood." She mentioned she taught a class in critical race theory two years ago and told her students, "When I use the term 'sisterhood,' I'm using it in a way that acknowledges the fact that not everybody here identifies as a woman. It is a rhetorical device . . . , but it is not intended to exclude anybody."

I said her explanation seemed like the one for using "he" as a generic pronoun for a male or female. She offered a different analogy, noting the parallel between women's colleges and historically black colleges and universities. "Isn't it still legitimate to speak of being a community of color even if you have half a dozen students who aren't individuals of color?" she asked. "The same might be said about women's colleges. Our mission was built upon education for women, and while we recognize that not everyone identifies this way, this is who we are and how we talk about things."

Meanwhile, Wellesley continues to struggle with its own identity. In August, Debra DeMeis, the dean of students, told me the administration had not yet worked out how to be a women's college at a time when gender is no longer considered binary. President H. Kim Bottomly and Jennifer C. Desjarlais, the dean of admissions, declined to talk to me. But a few days after Mount Holyoke's announcement, Bottomly released a statement saying that Wellesley would begin to think about how to address the trans question.

On the last Friday in May, some 5,000 parents, alumnae and soon-to-be graduates streamed onto the rolling field near Severance Hall, named after Elisabeth Severance, a generous 1887 alumna. It was a gorgeous, temperate morning for Wellesley's 136th annual commencement, and once the last baccalaureate degree was conferred, the audience was asked to stand. As is the school's tradition, two graduates led an uplifting rendition of "America, the Beautiful." The lyrics, for those who needed them, were printed in the commencement program, including the chorus: "And crown thy good, with brotherhood, from sea to shining sea!"

Those words were penned by Katharine Lee Bates, an 1880 graduate of Wellesley who defied the expectations of her gender, and not just by becoming a professor, published author and famous poet. A pastor's daughter, she never married, living instead for 25 years with Katharine Coman, founder of Wellesley's economics department, with whom she was deeply in love. When a colleague described "free-flying spinsters" as a "fringe on the garment of life," Bates, then 53, answered: "I always thought the fringe had the best of it."

As parents, professors and graduates joined in the singing of Bates's most famous poem, many felt an intense pride in their connection to the graduates and this remarkable college, which has sent forth so many women who leave impressive marks on the world. As the hundreds of voices rounded the curve on "And crown thy good with . . .," the unknowing parents continued to "brotherhood," the word that was always supposed to stand in for women too, but never really did. Wellesley women long ago learned that words matter, and for decades, this has been the point in the song when their harmonious choral singing abruptly becomes a bellow as they belt out "sisterhood," drowning out the word that long excluded them and replacing it with a demand for recognition. It's one of the most powerful moments of commencement, followed every year by cheers, applause and tears, evoked by the rush of solidarity with

women throughout time, and the thrill of claiming in one of the nation's most famous songs that women matter—even if the world they're about to enter doesn't always agree.

In the last few years, a handful of graduates have changed that word once again, having decided that "sisterhood," no matter how well intended, is exclusionary, and so they instead call out "siblinghood." A few trans men find even that insufficient, and in that instant, they roar the word that represents them best: "brotherhood," not as a sexist stand-in for all humankind, but as an appeal from a tiny minority struggling to be acknowledged.

In truth, it's difficult to distinguish in the cacophony each of the words shouted atop one another. What is clear is that whatever word each person is hollering is immensely significant as a proclamation of existence, even if it's hard to make out what anyone else is saying.

Critical Thinking

1. Should Wellesley let students who matriculated as biological women and transitioned to men or came to identify as transgender while they were attending the university continue to attend?
2. What are some of the reasons why single-sex institutions of higher education exist?
3. Some colleges and universities have a culture that reinforces gender role stereotypes, which makes transgender students feel uncomfortable or even unsafe. What would need to happen to make sure students of all genders feel safe wherever they attend?

Internet References

National Center for Transgender Equality
  http://transequality.org
Transgender Law Center
  http://transgenderlawcenter.org
Trans Student Educational Resources
  http://transstudent.org

RUTH PADAWER, an adjunct professor in the Columbia University Graduate School of Journalism, is also a contributing writer at *The New York Times Magazine,* focusing primarily on gender and social issues. She has freelanced for the radio show "This American Life," as well as *USA Today* and *MSNBC online.* Her work has also appeared in *The Guardian, The Week, Marie Claire France, Haaretz Magazine, Internazionale,* and *GEO.*

Prepared by: Elizabeth Schroeder, EdD, MSW,
Elizabeth Schroeder Consulting

Article

Gendercide

Killed, aborted or neglected, at least 100m girls have disappeared—and the number is rising.

Learning Outcomes

After reading this article, you will be able to:

- Discuss the extent of female infanticide within a global context.

- Assess the extent to which female infanticide remains a social problem and the effectiveness of any potential solutions.

- Describe at least two reasons why girls are devalued to such a dramatic extent in countries worldwide.

Imagine you are one half of a young couple expecting your first child in a fast-growing, poor country. You are part of the new middle class; your income is rising; you want a small family. But traditional *mores* hold sway around you, most important in the preference for sons over daughters. Perhaps hard physical labour is still needed for the family to make its living. Perhaps only sons may inherit land. Perhaps a daughter is deemed to join another family on marriage and you want someone to care for you when you are old. Perhaps she needs a dowry.

Now imagine that you have had an ultrasound scan; it costs $12, but you can afford that. The scan says the unborn child is a girl. You yourself would prefer a boy; the rest of your family clamours for one. You would never dream of killing a baby daughter, as they do out in the villages. But an abortion seems different. What do you do?

For millions of couples, the answer is: abort the daughter, try for a son. In China and northern India more than 120 boys are being born for every 100 girls. Nature dictates that slightly more males are born than females to offset boys' greater susceptibility to infant disease. But nothing on this scale.

For those who oppose abortion, this is mass murder. For those such as this newspaper, who think abortion should

be "safe, legal and rare" (to use Bill Clinton's phrase), a lot depends on the circumstances, but the cumulative consequence for societies of such individual actions is catastrophic. China alone stands to have as many unmarried young men—"bare branches", as they are known—as the entire population of young men in America. In any country rootless young males spell trouble; in Asian societies, where marriage and children are the recognised routes into society, single men are almost like outlaws. Crime rates, bride trafficking, sexual violence, even female suicide rates are all rising and will rise further as the lopsided generations reach their maturity.

It is no exaggeration to call this gendercide. Women are missing in the millions—aborted, killed, neglected to death. In 1990 an Indian economist, Amartya Sen, put the number at 100m; the toll is higher now. The crumb of comfort is that countries can mitigate the hurt, and that one, South Korea, has shown the worst can be avoided. Others need to learn from it if they are to stop the carnage.

The Dearth and Death of Little Sisters

Most people know China and northern India have unnaturally large numbers of boys. But few appreciate how bad the problem is, or that it is rising. In China the imbalance between the sexes was 108 boys to 100 girls for the generation born in the late 1980s; for the generation of the early 2000s, it was 124 to 100. In some Chinese provinces the ratio is an unprecedented 130 to 100. The destruction is worst in China but has spread far beyond. Other East Asian countries, including Taiwan and Singapore, former communist states in the western Balkans and the Caucasus, and even sections of America's population (Chinese- and Japanese-Americans, for example): all these have distorted sex ratios. Gendercide exists on almost every continent. It affects rich and poor; educated and illiterate; Hindu, Muslim, Confucian and Christian alike.

Wealth does not stop it. Taiwan and Singapore have open, rich economies. Within China and India the areas with the worst sex ratios are the richest, best-educated ones. And China's one-child policy can only be part of the problem, given that so many other countries are affected.

In fact the destruction of baby girls is a product of three forces: the ancient preference for sons; a modern desire for smaller families; and ultrasound scanning and other technologies that identify the sex of a fetus. In societies where four or six children were common, a boy would almost certainly come along eventually; son preference did not need to exist at the expense of daughters. But now couples want two children—or, as in China, are allowed only one—they will sacrifice unborn daughters to their pursuit of a son. That is why sex ratios are most distorted in the modern, open parts of China and India. It is also why ratios are more skewed after the first child: parents may accept a daughter first time round but will do anything to ensure their next—and probably last—child is a boy. The boy-girl ratio is above 200 for a third child in some places.

How to Stop Half the Sky Crashing Down

Baby girls are thus victims of a malign combination of ancient prejudice and modern preferences for small families. Only one country has managed to change this pattern. In the 1990s South Korea had a sex ratio almost as skewed as China's. Now, it is heading towards normality. It has achieved this not deliberately, but because the culture changed. Female education, anti-discrimination suits and equal-rights rulings made son preference seem old-fashioned and unnecessary. The forces of modernity first exacerbated prejudice—then overwhelmed it.

But this happened when South Korea was rich. If China or India—with incomes one-quarter and one-tenth Korea's levels—wait until they are as wealthy, many generations will

pass. To speed up change, they need to take actions that are in their own interests anyway. Most obviously China should scrap the one-child policy. The country's leaders will resist this because they fear population growth; they also dismiss Western concerns about human rights. But the one-child limit is no longer needed to reduce fertility (if it ever was: other East Asian countries reduced the pressure on the population as much as China). And it massively distorts the country's sex ratio, with devastating results. President Hu Jintao says that creating "a harmonious society" is his guiding principle; it cannot be achieved while a policy so profoundly perverts family life.

And all countries need to raise the value of girls. They should encourage female education; abolish laws and customs that prevent daughters inheriting property; make examples of hospitals and clinics with impossible sex ratios; get women engaged in public life—using everything from television newsreaders to women traffic police. Mao Zedong said "women hold up half the sky." The world needs to do more to prevent a gendercide that will have the sky crashing down.

Critical Thinking

1. Why is there such an imbalance between the numbers of male and female infants worldwide?

2. Why do some countries have a bigger problem with female infanticide?

3. What are the impacts of female infanticide at both the individual and societal levels?

Internet References

The Girl Effect
   http://www.girleffect.org

Women and Girls' Fund
   http://www.togetherforwomen.org

Women for Women International
   http://www.womenforwomen.org

Article

Prepared by: Elizabeth Schroeder, EdD, MSW,
Elizabeth Schroeder Consulting

Death by Gender

CYNTHIA FUCHS EPSTEIN

Learning Outcomes

After reading this article, you will be able to:

- Define what "honor killings" are and the reasons given for performing these crimes.

- Identify at least two countries in which honor killings still take place.

- Describe at least two actions, according to the article, that girls and women take in some cultures that can increase the likelihood of them being targeted for an honor killing.

Finally, the atrocity of gendercide—the murder and mutilation of victims selected by sex—is getting prominent attention in the press. Through feminist online activism, but more prominently through the efforts of *New York Times* columnist Nicholas Kristof (in his new book *Half the Sky,* written with his wife, Sheryl WuDunn, and in his *New York Times* column), a socially embedded and systematic assault on women and girls in much of the world has been brought to public consciousness. The crimes at issue range from the killing of girls and women—often by their fathers, brothers, or male cousins, acting for the "honor" of the family—to the trafficking of women as sex slaves and to their forced recruitment as suicide bombers.

I will focus in this article on honor killing because the act is so vile. Further, the concept is difficult to dislodge. The notion of "honor" is at the core of many conflicts within and between societies all over the world, although it has been substantially reduced in the West. But, notions of honor underpin the marriage system in the tribal societies that are common in the Middle East and many parts of Africa. The most important connections between tribes are based on kinship and marriage, and value in the marriage market depends on female "virtue"—so girls and women must be tightly controlled to assure the "purity" of these social connections. Girls' families

won't invest emotionally in them because they typically leave their birth families while very young and are brought into their husband's families as outsiders whose purpose is to bear children and take care of elderly family members. Without personal or social resources, they often are forced to be the servants or slaves of men in their birth families and then again in the families they enter by marriage. In "honor societies," which are characteristic of much of the developing world, girls and women are denied the protections that outside affiliations and affection might provide. Deviation from the rules imposed by male authorities may label a female as "contaminated" and elicit harsh sanctions. At its most serious, contamination is decreed when a women or girl is believed to have sought or had a sexual connection outside marriage—whether she acts from a desire to choose her own mate or is a victim of rape. Whether it has occurred within or outside the family, sexual contamination may be punished by murder. Thus, in some societies, the murder of girls and woman is justified by perceived social and moral infractions, and women are held in strict segregation to guard against these possibilities.

The belief that women are symbolic bearers of the honor of the clan or tribe is widely held, most often in Muslim countries but in others as well. And although Islamic law, or sharia, does not mandate honor killing as a punishment, it is practiced in many Islamic communities, openly so in some of them. It can be found also in some other groups, such as the Sikhs. There are lesser violations of honor for which girls and women are sometimes killed, like failing to comply with restrictive dress codes—wearing makeup or taking off the head scarf or hijab, for example—or for dating or merely appearing with unrelated boys or men in public. (According to the Al Arabia Web site, a Saudi father killed his daughter for chatting with a man on Facebook.) Trying to escape an arranged marriage is another important violation of traditional family norms that may merit death—as in the case of a young British woman who was stabbed to death by her father in London in 2002 when her family heard a love song dedicated to her on the radio and suspected that she had a boyfriend she had chosen for herself. A similar report comes from Turkey.

Women who protest forced marriage and abusive husbands can become targets of honor killings. And women and girls who have been raped can be doomed to death at the hands of a kinsman—or be forced to kill themselves to shield the rapist, if he himself is a kinsman, from punishment by the civil authorities. The dishonor of rape is so great that it can be used for political purposes. In January 2009, an Iraqi woman, Samira Ahmed Jassim, confessed to organizing the rapes of more than eighty women so that their shame would make them susceptible to recruitment as suicide bombers by al Qaeda. Twenty-eight of the women were said to have carried out suicide attacks.

The Turkish Human Rights Directorate reported in 2008 that in Istanbul alone there is one honor killing every week; more than one thousand occurred there in the preceding five years. UNICEF reported that in the Gaza Strip and the West Bank, according to 1999 figures, two-thirds of all murders were probably honor killings. In 2003, anthropologist/journalist James Emery of the Metropolitan State College of Denver stated that in the Palestinian communities of the West Bank, Gaza Strip, Israel, and Jordan, dishonored women were executed in their homes, in open fields, and occasionally in public before cheering crowds. Honor killings, Emery reported, account for virtually all recorded murders of Palestinian women. Although there are attempts by organizations such as the Women's Affairs Technical Committee (WATC) and other NGOs to provide education and practical services to protect and assist women, they have had little success so far.

Death because of gender is arguably a leading cause of female homicide in many societies, but gendercide occurs in other ways: in 1990 the Nobel laureate Amartya Sen wrote in the *New York Review of Books* that more than one hundred million women were missing from the world as a result of sex-selective abortion and ill treatment. No doubt, the number has increased as girls continue to be selectively pruned in such places as India and Pakistan—not only by the poor who undernourish their girl babies but also by members of the middle class who use sonograms to determine the sex of a fetus and then abort the females. The truth is that gender is regarded as a birth defect in much of the world, and this fact is neither analyzed nor addressed.

The officially reported estimates of the numbers of women who die in honor killings range from five thousand to ten thousand a year. (The UN Population Fund has estimated the total at five thousand a year, and that figure was reported by the secretary-general to the UN General Assembly in 2006.) But these numbers underestimate the actual toll because most honor murders are recorded as suicides or accidental deaths—or are not recorded at all. And the reports cannot begin to describe the terror girls and women must feel when they know that any

aberrant behavior might provoke their fathers or close kin to kill them. Commentators in the West who suggest that women freely choose to conform to restrictions on their behavior and dress are not sensitive to the lurking threat of deadly punishment for violations of the codes. It is ludicrous to suggest that Islamic women decide for themselves to wear restrictive clothing and head coverings, given the possible consequences of not doing so.

Surprisingly, the support for honor killings is not limited to tribal societies but exists also among individuals living in traditional communities in modern societies. Even there, women who "go astray" and violate the bonds of marriage or assume individual identities often face physical assault. A poll by the BBC's Asia network, for example, found that one in ten young British Asians believe that honor killings can be justified. And in a poll of five hundred Hindus, Sikhs, Christians, and Muslims reported in 2009 by the online Women's E-news, one-tenth said they would condone the murder of someone who "disrespected" their family's honor.

Honor killings are not identified as a critically important instance of women's degraded status in many societies, and the practice is rarely condemned by the educated and sophisticated members of the societies in which the killings occur—nor by the social activists or leaders of the "free world." Nicholas Cohen, a writer for *Standpoint* magazine, asks why the outrage against apartheid does not extend to the women who are segregated and locked in their own homes, forced into arranged marriages, or raped and stoned. Why, he asks, do the societies that tolerate such practices not face irate Western boycotts or demonstrations in front of their embassy buildings?

It is clear, however, that the practice and the reasoning behind it will be difficult to erase. The protection of women's honor is an important part of the symbolic glue of kin groups that are, in many societies, the essential political bodies that maintain social order. Sociologists like Roger Friedland and Mounira Charrad have argued that control over women and marriage ensures that tribal groups can fully regulate the relationships between clans. (This is not so different from the marriages negotiated between the royal houses and aristocratic families of many countries in the West up to the early twentieth century.) Young women have to have unsullied reputations, and of course, they have to be virgins. Offering the bloodied sheets of the marital bed to relatives of the bride and groom is still necessary in many countries of the world.

Friedland has criticized the lack of awareness by political scientists (to say nothing of the media experts) who attempt to understand societies such as Afghanistan and Pakistan without attending to the tribal alliances created by marriages engineered by tribal elders. The obedience of women (actually girls, because these marriages are typically of underage children) is essential, and so the discipline over them is intense. Charrad, a sociologist studying the tribal foundations of the former French colonies of Algeria, Morocco, and Tunisia, similarly points to the political importance of tribal alliances created through the exchange of women.

Of course, men also are affected by these exchanges, but the men stay in their families of origin and it is the exchanged women who are forced to leave their places of birth and childhood. Because girls are married off early and torn from their families, they are powerless in the new environments to which they come as strangers. They are virtual slaves in the women's quarters of their new families.

Why do some women and girls internalize these views of honor and defend the very practices that enslave them? Why do we hear accounts of mothers who hold down their daughters as their husbands plunge knives into them or who observe the stoning that kills them? Or who insist that their daughters be circumcised when they know the pain and future discomfort this practice will bring?

Taken as child brides into the homes of their husbands, the only power these women have comes later in life as the mothers of sons who may, or may not, support them—and as the mothers of daughters, whom they can help to control but can't protect. They have learned the costs of deviance, and they teach those costs to, and even impose them on, their daughters. The resistance to the education of girls in Afghanistan, by the Taliban and also, sometimes, by their own parents, is now well known, but girls' education is poor in many other regions where their "honor" is the most important thing about them—as in Pakistan, for example, and parts of India.

Are things getting better? Attempts by international human rights associations and women's rights organizations to impose penalties for honor killings have recently been undercut at the UN. According to ESCR-FEM, the online listserv for Women's Economic, Social and Cultural Rights, the UN Human Rights Council adopted a resolution in 2009 "promoting human rights and fundamental freedoms through a better understanding of *traditional* values of humankind . . ." [emphasis added]. The vote was twenty-six in favor, fifteen against, with six abstentions. The resolution was proposed by Russia and supported by the Arab League and the Organization of the Islamic Conference, a grouping of fifty-seven UN member states. Human Rights organizations across the globe strongly opposed it, declaring that its passage would set a destructive precedent by affirming a concept ("traditional values") often used to legitimize human rights abuses. The nongovernmental Cairo Institution for Human Rights Studies issued a statement expressing deep concern over the text. It declared that "such a concept has been used in the Arab region to justify treating women as second class citizens, female genital mutilation, honor crimes,

child marriage, and other practices that clearly contradict international human rights standards."

There are a number of organizations devoted to improving the conditions of girls' and women's lives in the countries where those lives are most at risk. They include the International Initiative on Maternal Mortality and Human Rights and the Association for Women's Rights in Development, the Center for Women's Global Leadership, and the International Women's Rights Action Watch–Asia Pacific. Some organizations devoted to improving the situation of women are connected to agencies of the United Nations. It is more than thirty years since 90 percent of the member countries of the United Nations signed on to the Convention on the Elimination of all forms of Discrimination Against Women, which proclaimed that women's rights are human rights. But many of the signatories are countries in which the worst practices are carried out against women. Ironically, the United States has not signed.

What is to be done? We know that individuals' hearts and minds are difficult to change, but we also know that with proper incentives and political will they can sometimes change swiftly. Perhaps it is time for world leaders to insist on basic standards of human rights as a precondition for full commercial and diplomatic relations regardless of a country's religion or traditional culture. And perhaps it is also time for the resurgence of a woman's movement in the United States that will connect with the fledgling women's movements in countries of the Global South to form an alliance that will act politically to insist that women's and girls' rights be on the agenda of every international meeting.

Critical Thinking

1. What is the purpose of honor killings?
2. Why would some women defend honor killings?
3. Other than murder, how else does death by gender occur?

Internet References

Honour-Based Violence Awareness Network
  http://hbv-awareness.com
Human Rights Watch
  http://www.hrw.org
International Rescue Committee
  http://www.rescue.org

CYNTHIA FUCHS EPSTEIN is Distinguished Professor of Sociology at The Graduate Center of the City University of New York. Among her books are *Woman's Place*, *Women in Law*, and *Deceptive Distinctions*.

From *Dissent*, Spring 2010, pp. 54–57. Copyright © 2005 by Foundation for Study of Independent Ideas, Inc. Reprinted by permission of University of Pennsylvania Press. www.dissentmagazine.org

Prepared by: Elizabeth Schroeder, EdD, MSW,
Elizabeth Schroeder Consulting

Article

Female Power

THE ECONOMIST

Learning Outcomes

After reading this article, you will be able to:

- Discuss how and in which arenas women have become more empowered.

- Explain the connection between politics, employment, and women's empowerment.

- Describe at least two cultural factors that enable women to be more or less empowered in various countries around the world.

Across the rich world more women are working than ever before. Coping with this change will be one of the great challenges of the coming decades.

The economic empowerment of women across the rich world is one of the most remarkable revolutions of the past 50 years. It is remarkable because of the extent of the change: millions of people who were once dependent on men have taken control of their own economic fates. It is remarkable also because it has produced so little friction: a change that affects the most intimate aspects of people's identities has been widely welcomed by men as well as women. Dramatic social change seldom takes such a benign form.

Yet even benign change can come with a sting in its tail. Social arrangements have not caught up with economic changes. Many children have paid a price for the rise of the two-income household. Many women—and indeed many men—feel that they are caught in an ever-tightening tangle of commitments. If the empowerment of women was one of the great changes of the past 50 years, dealing with its social consequences will be one of the great challenges of the next 50.

At the end of her campaign to become America's first female president in 2008, Hillary Clinton remarked that her 18m votes in the Democratic Party's primaries represented 18m cracks in the glass ceiling. In the market for jobs rather than votes the

ceiling is being cracked every day. Women now make up almost half of American workers (49.9% in October). They run some of the world's best companies, such as PepsiCo, Archer Daniels Midland and W.L. Gore. They earn almost 60% of university degrees in America and Europe.

Progress has not been uniform, of course. In Italy and Japan, employment rates for men are more than 20 percentage points higher than those for women. Although Italy's female employment rate has risen markedly in the past decade, it is still below 50%, and more than 20 percentage points below those of Denmark and Sweden. Women earn substantially less than men on average and are severely under-represented at the top of organisations.

The change is dramatic nevertheless. A generation ago working women performed menial jobs and were routinely subjected to casual sexism—as "Mad Men", a television drama about advertising executives in the early 1960s, demonstrates brilliantly. Today women make up the majority of professional workers in many countries (51% in the United States, for example) and casual sexism is for losers. Even holdouts such as the Mediterranean countries are changing rapidly. In Spain, the proportion of young women in the labour force has now reached American levels. The glass is much nearer to being half full than half empty.

What explains this revolution? Politics have clearly played a part. Feminists such as Betty Friedan have demonised domestic slavery and lambasted discrimination. Governments have passed equal-rights acts. Female politicians such as Margaret Thatcher and Mrs Clinton have taught younger women that anything is possible. But politics is only part of the answer: such discordant figures as Ms Friedan and Lady Thatcher have been borne aloft by subterranean economic and technological forces.

The rich world has seen a growing demand for women's labour. When brute strength mattered more than brains, men had an inherent advantage. Now that brainpower has triumphed the two sexes are more evenly matched. The feminisation of the workforce has been driven by the relentless rise of the service sector (where women can compete as well as men) and the equally relentless decline of manufacturing (where they could not). The landmark book in the rise of feminism was arguably not Ms Friedan's "The Feminine Mystique" but Daniel Bell's "The Coming of Post-Industrial Society".

Demand has been matched by supply: women are increasingly willing and able to work outside the home. The vacuum cleaner has played its part. Improved technology reduced the amount of time needed for the traditional female work of cleaning and cooking. But the most important innovation has been the contraceptive pill. The spread of the pill has not only allowed women to get married later. It has also increased their incentives to invest time and effort in acquiring skills, particularly slow-burning skills that are hard to learn and take many years to pay off. The knowledge that they would not have to drop out of, say, law school to have a baby made law school more attractive.

The expansion of higher education has also boosted job prospects for women, improving their value on the job market and shifting their role models from stay-at-home mothers to successful professional women. The best-educated women have always been more likely than other women to work, even after having children. In 1963, 62% of college-educated women in the United States were in the labour force, compared with 46% of those with a high school diploma. Today 80% of American women with a college education are in the labour force compared with 67% of those with a high school diploma and 47% of those without one.

This growing cohort of university-educated women is also educated in more marketable subjects. In 1966, 40% of American women who received a BA specialised in education in college; 2% specialised in business and management. The figures are now 12% and 50%. Women only continue to lag seriously behind men in a handful of subjects, such as engineering and computer sciences, where they earned about one-fifth of degrees in 2006.

One of the most surprising things about this revolution is how little overt celebration it has engendered. Most people welcome the change. A recent Rockefeller Foundation/Time survey found that three-quarters of Americans regarded it as a positive development. Nine men out of ten said they were comfortable with women earning more than them. But few are cheering. This is partly because young women take their opportunities for granted. It is partly because for many women work represents economic necessity rather than liberation. The rich world's growing army of single mothers have little choice but to work. A growing proportion of married women have also discovered that the only way they can preserve their households' living standards is to join their husbands in the labour market. In America, families with stay-at-home wives have the same

inflation-adjusted income as similar families did in the early 1970s. But the biggest reason is that the revolution has brought plenty of problems in its wake.

Production versus Reproduction

One obvious problem is that women's rising aspirations have not been fulfilled. They have been encouraged to climb onto the occupational ladder only to discover that the middle rungs are dominated by men and the upper rungs are out of reach. Only 2% of the bosses of Fortune 500 companies and five of those in the FTSE 100 stockmarket index are women. Women make up less than 13% of board members in America. The upper ranks of management consultancies and banks are dominated by men. In America and Britain, the typical full-time female worker earns only about 80% as much as the typical male.

This no doubt owes something to prejudice. But the biggest reason why women remain frustrated is more profound: many women are forced to choose between motherhood and careers. Childless women in corporate America earn almost as much as men. Mothers with partners earn less and single mothers much less. The cost of motherhood is particularly steep for fast-track women. Traditionally "female" jobs such as teaching mix well with motherhood because wages do not rise much with experience and hours are relatively light. But at successful firms wages rise steeply and schedules are demanding. Future bosses are expected to have worked in several departments and countries. Professional-services firms have an up-or-out system which rewards the most dedicated with lucrative partnerships. The reason for the income gap may thus be the opposite of prejudice. It is that women are judged by exactly the same standards as men.

This Hobson's choice is imposing a high cost on both individuals and society. Many professional women reject motherhood entirely: in Switzerland 40% of them are childless. Others delay child-bearing for so long that they are forced into the arms of the booming fertility industry. The female drop-out rate from the most competitive professions represents a loss to collective investment in talent. A study of graduates of the University of Chicago's Booth School of Business by Marianne Bertrand and her colleagues found that, ten years after graduating, about half of the female MBAs who had chosen to have children remained in the labour force. It also leaves many former high-flyers frustrated. Another American study, this time of women who left work to have children, found that all but 7% of them wanted to return to work. Only 74% managed to return, and just 40% returned to full-time jobs.

Even well-off parents worry that they spend too little time with their children, thanks to crowded schedules and the ever-buzzing BlackBerry. For poorer parents, juggling the twin demands of work and child-rearing can be a nightmare. Child care eats a terrifying proportion of the family budget, and many childminders are untrained. But quitting work to look after the children can mean financial disaster. British children brought up in two-parent families where only one parent works are almost three times more likely to be poor than children with two parents at work.

A survey for the Children's Society, a British charity, found that 60% of parents agreed that "nowadays parents aren't able to spend enough time with their children". In a similar survey in America, 74% of parents said that they did not have enough time for their children. Nor does the problem disappear as children get older. In most countries schools finish early in the afternoon. In America they close down for two months in the summer. Only a few places—Denmark, Sweden and, to a lesser extent, France and Quebec—provide comprehensive systems of after-school care.

Different countries have adopted different solutions to the problem of combining work and parenthood. Some stress the importance of very young children spending time with their mothers. Austria, the Czech Republic, Finland and Hungary provide up to three years of paid leave for mothers. Germany has introduced a "parent's salary", or Elterngeld, to encourage mothers to stay at home. (The legislation was championed by a minister for women who has seven children.) Other countries put more emphasis on preschool education. New Zealand and the Nordic countries are particularly keen on getting women back to work and children into kindergartens. Britain, Germany, Japan, Switzerland and, above all, the Netherlands are keen on mothers working part-time. Others, such as the Czech Republic, Greece, Finland, Hungary, Portugal and South Korea, make little room for part-time work for women. The Scandinavian countries, particularly Iceland, have added a further wrinkle by increasing incentives for fathers to spend more time caring for their children.

The world's biggest economy has adopted an idiosyncratic approach. America provides no statutory paid leave for mothers and only 12 weeks unpaid. At least 145 countries provide paid sick leave. America allows only unpaid absence for serious family illness. America's public spending on family support is low by OECD standards. It spends only 0.5% of its GDP on public support for child care compared with 1.3% in France and 2.7% in Denmark.

It is difficult to evaluate the relative merits of these various arrangements. Different systems can produce similar results: anti-statist America has roughly the same proportion of children in kindergartens as statist Finland. Different systems have different faults. Sweden is not quite the paragon that its fans imagine, despite its family-friendly employment policies. Only 1.5% of senior managers are women, compared with 11% in America. Three-quarters of Swedish women work in the public sector; three-quarters of men work in the private sector. But there is evidence that America and Britain, the countries that combine high female employment with reluctance to involve the state in child care, serve their children especially poorly. A report by UNICEF in 2007 on children in rich countries found that America and Britain had some of the lowest scores for "well-being".

A Woman's World

The trend towards more women working is almost certain to continue. In the European Union, women have filled 6m of the 8m new jobs created since 2000. In America, three out of four people thrown out of work since the recession began are men; the female unemployment rate is 8.6%, against 11.2% for men. The Bureau of Labour Statistics calculates that women make up more than two-thirds of employees in ten of the 15 job categories likely to grow fastest in the next few years. By 2011, there will be 2.6m more women than men studying in American universities.

Women will also be the beneficiaries of the growing "war for talent". The combination of an ageing workforce and a more skill-dependent economy means that countries will have to make better use of their female populations. Goldman Sachs calculates that, leaving all other things equal, increasing women's participation in the labour market to male levels will boost GDP by 21% in Italy, 19% in Spain, 16% in Japan, 9% in America, France and Germany, and 8% in Britain.

The corporate world is doing ever more to address the loss of female talent and the difficulty of combining work with child care. Many elite companies are rethinking their promotion practices. Addleshaw Goddard, a law firm, has created the role of legal director as an alternative to partnerships for women who want to combine work and motherhood. Ernst & Young and other accounting firms have increased their efforts to maintain connections with women who take time off to have children and then ease them back into work.

Home-working is increasingly fashionable. More than 90% of companies in Germany and Sweden allow flexible working. A growing number of firms are learning to divide the working week in new ways—judging staff on annual rather than weekly hours, allowing them to work nine days a fortnight, letting them come in early or late and allowing husbands and wives to share jobs. Almost half of Sun Microsystems's employees work at home or from nearby satellite offices. Raytheon, a maker of missile systems, allows workers every other Friday off to take care of family business, if they make up the hours on other days.

Companies are even rethinking the structure of careers, as people live and work longer. Barclays is one of many firms that allow five years' unpaid leave. John Lewis offers a six-month paid sabbatical to people who have been in the company for

25 years. Companies are allowing people to phase their retirement. Child-bearing years will thus make up a smaller proportion of women's potential working lives. Spells out of the labour force will become less a mark of female exceptionalism.

Faster change is likely as women exploit their economic power. Many talented women are already hopping off the corporate treadmill to form companies that better meet their needs. In the past decade, the number of privately owned companies started by women in America has increased twice as fast as the number owned by men. Women-owned companies employ more people than the largest 500 companies combined. Eden McCallum and Axiom Legal have applied a network model to their respective fields of management consultancy and legal services: network members work when it suits them and the companies use their scale to make sure that clients have their problems dealt with immediately.

Governments are also trying to adjust to the new world. Germany now has 1,600 schools where the day lasts until mid-afternoon. Some of the most popular American charter schools offer longer school days and shorter summer holidays.

But so far even the combination of public- and private-sector initiatives has only gone so far to deal with the problem.

The children of poorer working mothers are the least likely to benefit from female-friendly companies. Millions of families still struggle with insufficient child-care facilities and a school day that bears no relationship to their working lives. The West will be struggling to cope with the social consequences of women's economic empowerment for many years to come.

Critical Thinking

1. Describe how the power of women has changed over the past 50 years.

2. What have been the costs of these changes?

3. Is there a need for further changes in the relative status of women in developed societies?

Internet References

Ms. Foundation for Women
http://forwomen.org

Women's Global Empowerment Fund
http://wgefund.org

Women Thrive Worldwide
http://womenthrive.org

Article   Prepared by: Elizabeth Schroeder, EdD, MSW,
Elizabeth Schroeder Consulting

Estranged Spouses Increasingly Waiting out Downturn to Divorce

DONNA ST. GEORGE

Learning Outcomes

After reading this article, you will be able to:

- Identify at least two impacts the economy has on couples' decisions to remain legally married.

- Describe at least two effects that economic well-being has on an individual's social, emotional, and psychological well-being.

- Discuss whether economic factors have a similar or different impact on same-sex vs. different-sex marriages.

In the Great Recession, breaking up is hard to do.

With housing values depressed and jobs disappearing, divorce has become a luxury beyond the reach of some couples. There is often not enough money to pay for separate households or to hire lawyers, fight over children and go to court.

What has always been painful is now desperate and confounding, with a growing number of couples deciding to wait out the economic storm while others take new approaches—such as living together as they separate.

"I have lots of files sitting in the drawer, where people can't move forward," says David Goldberg, a divorce lawyer and mediator in Gaithersburg. He has been working in family law for 44 years and says he has never seen a time like this one.

Lately, he said, "I have a lot of clients who have ended up in bankruptcy."

The difficulties of divorce in the downturn are familiar to Paulene Foster, a 42-year-old federal worker from Olney, who says her precarious finances forced her to wait a year. If that wasn't enough, she also shared a house with her estranged husband—him in the basement, her upstairs. Strapped months went by as the couple were saddled with a suburban townhouse that would not sell.

"It was a mess," Foster said.

Her divorce, filed last month with a $105 check after going to a *self-help law clinic* in Montgomery County, comes as the national rate of failed marriages has declined slightly—not necessarily because divorce-minded couples are happier than before but, some experts suggest, because they don't have the money to call it quits.

At one Woodbridge law firm, 20 to 25 percent of clients seeking a divorce live under the same roof as their estranged spouse to save money as they await court action.

Other couples say they are stymied by the grim reality that they owe more on the family home than they could get if they sold it.

How do they start over if debt is all that's left to divide?

Heather Hostetter, who has a divorce practice in Bethesda, said that many couples used to divorce with enough equity in a house so that both spouses could re-create lives not so different from their old ones.

"It used to be you could go own another home," she said. "Maybe it's a little smaller, maybe it's not in the same neighborhood.

"Now you see people who go from homeowners to renters."

Divorce and Bankruptcy

Facing harsher circumstances, Marissa Fuller, who works in child care in Fairfax City, says her husband's job loss and then his underemployment had an accumulating impact. They had relationship troubles. They fell short on bills month after month. She tired of begging utility companies to turn back on the family's water and electricity.

In January, she filed both for bankruptcy and divorce, sure that the economic tension and the discord that came with it took a toll. "That really made the marriage crumble," she said. Fuller found housing through a nonprofit program and is saving for her own apartment, but she says the math of providing for two children on her salary seems nearly impossible.

Experts say that divorce claims slightly more than 40 percent of marriages. *Rates calculated by the National Marriage Project* show a modest decline in divorce during 2008, the first year of the recession, when 838,000 cases were granted in 44 states—at a time when growing economic strain might have produced a spike in divorce. A year earlier, 856,000 divorces were finalized. Scores of studies show a link between tough times and divorce.

W. Bradford Wilcox, director of the National Marriage Project at the University of Virginia, says some families are pulling together amid the economic turmoil, and others that want to split up are postponing until they see a rebound in the economy and in home values. A divorce can cost as little as $100 on a do-it-yourself basis with little in dispute and $10,000 to $20,000—or more—for a divorce that ends up in court.

Still, dividing into two households can prove the more daunting task—the same income being used to cover an extra housing payment, extra utility bills, separate groceries. This can be tricky when a home has no equity or line of credit to draw from.

In Manassas, lawyer Kirk Wilder says that in some cases, the house is so void of value that neither party wants to be stuck with it. "It used to be, 'Well, I want the house,'" he said. "Now it's, 'You take the house.' That's a huge change."

The economics of breaking up are a little better in the District and parts of Northern Virginia, where spouses can live in the same house during the required separation period, as long as they share little more than the space around them. No sex. No meals. No togetherness.

"They don't do each other's laundry, they don't eat together, they don't go to the kids' soccer game together," says Pat Hammond, a lawyer in Prince William County who advises clients with increasing frequency about how to get divorced without moving out of the house. "If they live in a three-bedroom townhouse, and they have four kids, it ain't going to work."

A Place to Sleep

Steve Halbert, an Arlington County resident who divorced in 2008, attests to the difficulty of the proposition.

His wife lived in one bedroom; he lived in another. He tried to work as much as possible to stay out of the house. "If you're in the same room, then a fight is waiting to happen," he said. For all of the struggle, his mortgage is still upside down 18 months later—and he still does not have a way to refinance his house and clear his ex-wife's name from the mortgage loan.

Halbert, a commercial real estate appraiser, says he earns half of what he did in the boom days and now pays alimony. "There used to be a lot of disposable income," he said, "and now it's, 'Be glad you have a place to sleep.'"

Prince William lawyer Larry Fabian says perhaps a quarter of his clients live together while they seek a divorce, which was almost unheard of five or so years ago. "It's really difficult," he says of their experiences. "It's pretty much the worst of all worlds."

Then again, some would say it is even harder in Maryland, which requires a full year of separate residences for mutual and voluntary divorce. That requirement is economically difficult for some; impossible for others.

Jesslyn Haskins, 42, a nurse and mother of three in Upper Marlboro, says a judge threw out her divorce case because she and her ex-husband had shared the same house during their separation. She says she then left, moving in with friends and ultimately getting an apartment, as relations grew more bitter and the mortgage went unpaid. Now divorced, she says she lives in the house and pays the mortgage but is in jeopardy of foreclosure because of missed back payments.

The National Marriage Project's Wilcox says working-class couples, who already have high rates of divorce, are especially vulnerable to a recession-related breakup because they are hit harder by unemployment, which is a significant predictor of divorce. Men, in particular, see themselves as breadwinners and are prone to feelings of worthlessness and depression during lengthy periods without a job, Wilcox says. "We would predict this recession is having a pretty big impact on working-class couples," he says.

In terms of divorce, the recession bears similarities to the Great Depression, says Johns Hopkins University sociologist Andrew Cherlin, noting that in the 1930s, divorce rates fell amid the worst of the economic crisis, only to rise as the country recovered. "Troubled economic times breed troubled marriages," he says. "But whether those marriages end in divorce right away is another thing."

Cherlin said the recession has probably created "a backlog of unhappy married couples who would like to get a divorce soon but can't afford it," and he predicted a surge in cases during the first several recovery years. "The longer this severe economic downturn continues," he said, "the larger the backlog will be."

Critical Thinking

1. What economic trends have impacted the decision to stay married vs. divorce for many couples?
2. How have social problems such as the housing market collapse and economic downturns impacted the relationship decisions people make?

3. What strategies have couples devised to deal with new challenges brought on by changes in global economic forces?

Internet References

American Association for Marriage and Family Therapy
http://www.aamft.org

The Relationship Foundation
http://www.therelationshipfoundation.org

Women's Institute for Financial Education
http://www.wife.org

Unit 2

UNIT

Prepared by: Elizabeth Schroeder, EdD, MSW,
Elizabeth Schroeder Consulting

Biological Foundations

This unit explores the biological influences on our sexual development, functioning, and decision-making. Understanding social and cultural processes that have an impact on human sexuality provides us with part of the picture in our attempt to understand sexuality in its broadest definition. Another essential part of the picture, explored here in this unit, is biology.

We are biological beings who may experience a range of sexual behaviors and reproductive experiences. Even though most people have the capacity for sexual reproduction, infertility issues are common in today's society. Just as common is the assumption that if two people are in a male-female long-term relationship or marriage, or if one is a woman of childbearing years, that there is a desire to parent. Some cannot comprehend why those who are biologically capable of causing a pregnancy or becoming pregnant would choose not to. Others cannot fathom why people who are able to reproduce would opt to adopt a child instead of, or in addition to, having one biologically.

While human reproduction is as old as humanity, many things in today's society are changing at an amazing pace. New technologies have had major impacts on reproductive capacities. Although carrying additional risks to both the fetus and pregnant woman, women have been able to become pregnant and give birth in their fifties and sixties. Embryos from one woman can be fertilized in a lab and implanted into another woman who has a healthy uterus but could not conceive without assistance; sperm from a man can be frozen and used later to inseminate his female partner. Two women in a relationship can opt for a known or anonymous sperm donor if one or both partners wants to become pregnant. Two men can engage a surrogate to become pregnant and carry their fetus to term. Just when individuals and couples think they have run out of reproductive choices, another type of assistive technology becomes available.

With so many advances in reproductive technologies, it is ironic and devastating that in less industrialized countries around the world childbirth is a life-threatening experience for far too many women. According to the World Health Organization (WHO), nearly all of the maternal deaths during childbirth occur in developing countries. The WHO estimates that nearly 300,000 women die during childbirth each year—a reduction from previous years, but still alarmingly too high. Those at highest risk are adolescent girls, particularly those who live in rural areas where access to reproductive health and support is either limited, far away, or nonexistent.

As an increasing number of options have become available for creating pregnancies, an equally increasing number of laws have been proposed and passed in states throughout the United States restricting women's access to abortion. By the first week of February 2015, states had already introduced over 100 bills designed to restrict access to abortion. Debates on reproductive freedom and access continue to rage nationwide and around the world. Equally passionate is the debate on an individuals' right to select the biological sex of their fetus for one of two reasons. One reason is to either diversify family composition (e.g, a parent or parents who already have a child of one sex and want a second of a different sex). The other reason is in countries where girls are devalued, the desire to avoid having a girl is strong. If people can afford (and it is legal) to select the sex chromosome composition of a fetus, they would; if they can find out early enough in the pregnancy that the fetus has XX chromosomes (biologically female) they may elect to terminate the pregnancy in order to try again for a male child. China has been stereotyped as the leading country in this type of sex selection due to its one-child policy (which was recently relaxed for some qualifying couples), but it is not the only country in which this is practiced—even if it is not a formal government policy. Even in China, couples are allowed to try for a second child if the first child is born a girl. One wonders what the impact of this cultural unwantedness is on girls in the many countries in which it still exists.

Matters of biology can quickly become social issues of urgent importance. Nowhere is this seen more clearly than in the advocacy for the rights of transgender people. We are a world that categorizes people based on their chromosomes and body parts, which works well for those people whose chromosomes and body parts match their inner sense of who they are. But when they don't, when a person's biology does not match their gender identity, which should win? Currently, in the dominant culture, biology wins—but that is slowly starting to change. Transgender people have started receiving the right to change the sex designation they were assigned at birth to the one they truly are on legal documents like birth certificates, passports, and driver's licenses. Colleges and universities are beginning to recognize the need for gender neutral accommodations, and governments are changing laws to work to eliminate workplace discrimination against trans people. A key word that must be added to these examples, however, is "some." These social and legal changes are exciting, but are far from over. Much more work still needs to be done to promote equality for all genders.

Prepared by: Elizabeth Schroeder, EdD, MSW,
Elizabeth Schroeder Consulting

Article

Women in Developing Countries 300 Times More Likely to Die in Childbirth

UN report reveals 500,000 women in developing world die each year as a result of pregnancy.

SARAH BOSELEY

Learning Outcomes

After reading this article, you will be able to:

- Name at least two countries where there is a high prevalence of women dying during childbirth.

- Explain the risk to a newborn baby's life soon after childbirth in less-developed countries around the world.

Women in the world's least developed countries are 300 times more likely to die during childbirth or because of their pregnancy than those in the UK and other similarly developed countries, a UN report says today.

The death toll is more than half a million women a year, according to Unicef, the UN children's emergency fund. Some 70,000 who die are girls and young women aged 15 to 19. Although it is the subject of one of the millennium development goals, the death toll is not going down.

The reasons are multiple, according to Unicef's annual state of the world's children report on maternal and newborn health. "The root cause may lie in women's disadvantaged position in many countries and cultures and in the lack of attention to, and accountability for, women's rights," it says.

"Saving the lives of mothers and their newborns requires more than just medical intervention," said Ann Veneman, Unicef's executive director. "Educating girls is pivotal to improving maternal and neonatal health and also benefits families and societies."

Women die as a result of infection and of haemorrhage. Some have obstructed labour and cannot get a caesarean section. Others die of preventable complications.

Both mothers and babies are vulnerable in the weeks after birth, the report points out. They need post-natal visits, proper hygiene and counselling about the danger signs for themselves and their baby.

Many developing countries have succeeded in reducing the death rate for children under five, but have failed to make much progress on mothers. Niger and Malawi, for example, cut under-five deaths by nearly half between 1990 and 2007.

In the developing world, a woman has a one-in-76 risk of dying because of pregnancy or childbirth in her lifetime. In developed countries, that risk is only one in 8,000.

Having a child in a developing country is one of the most severe health risks for women. For every woman who dies, another 20 suffer illness or injury, which can be permanent.

The 10 countries with the highest risk of maternal death, says Unicef, are Niger, Afghanistan, Sierra Leone, Chad, Angola, Liberia, Somalia, the Democratic Republic of Congo, Guinea-Bissau and Mali.

Deaths of newborns have also received too little attention, the report says. A child born in one of the least developed countries is nearly 14 times more likely to die within the first 28 days of life than one in an industrialised country such as the UK.

Critical Thinking

1. What actions could reduce the risk of illness or injury for women during childbirth? How about after childbirth?
2. What role does education play in preventing illness or injury?

Internet References

Marie Stopes International
http://mariestopes.org

Merck for Mothers
http://www.merckformothers.com

Pathfinder International
http://www.pathfind.org

Prepared by: Elizabeth Schroeder, EdD, MSW,
Elizabeth Schroeder Consulting

Article

Abstinence-Only Education and Teen Pregnancy Rates: Why We Need Comprehensive Sex Education in the U.S.

KATHRIN F. STANGER-HALL AND DAVID W. HALL

Learning Outcomes

After reading this article, you will be able to:

- Explain the difference between comprehensive sexuality education programs and abstinence-only-until-marriage programs.

- Explain at least two connections between the type of sexuality education offered to young people and risk of getting pregnant or causing a pregnancy as a teen.

- Name at least three states in the United States in which comprehensive sexuality education is mandated and at least three that would be considered to be abstinence-only states.

Introduction

The appropriate type of sex education that should be taught in U.S. public schools continues to be a major topic of debate, which is motivated by the high teen pregnancy and birth rates in the U.S., compared to other developed countries [1–4] (Table 1). Much of this debate has centered on whether abstinence-only versus comprehensive sex education should be taught in public schools. Some argue that sex education that covers safe sexual practices, such as condom use, sends a mixed message to students and promotes sexual activity. This view has been supported by the United States government, which promotes abstinence-only initiatives through the Adolescent Family Life Act (AFLA), Community-Based Abstinence Education (CBAE)

and Title V, Section 510 of the Personal Responsibility and Work Opportunity Reconciliation Act of 1996 (welfare reform), among others [5]. Funding for abstinence-only programs in 2006 and 2007 was $176 million annually (before matching state funds) [5,6]. The central message of these programs is to delay sexual activity until marriage, and under the federal funding regulations most of these programs cannot include information about contraception or safer-sex practices [5,7].

The federal funding for abstinence-only education expired on June 30, 2009, and no funds were allocated for the FY 2010 budget. Instead, a "Labor-Health and Human Services, Education and Other Agencies" appropriations bill including a total of $114 million for a new evidence-based Teen Pregnancy Prevention Initiative for FY 2010 was signed into law in December 2009. This constitutes the first large-scale federal investment dedicated to preventing teen pregnancy through research- and evidence-based efforts. However, despite accumulating evidence that abstinence-only programs are ineffective [6,8], abstinence-only funding (including Title V funding) was restored on September 29, 2009 [8] for 2010 and beyond by including $250 million of mandatory abstinence-only funding over 5 years as part of an amendment to the Senate Finance Committee's health-reform legislation (HR 3590, Amendment #2786, section 2954). This was authorized by the legislature on March 23, 2010 [9].

With two types of federal funding programs available, legislators of individual states now have the opportunity to decide which type of sex education (and which funding option) to choose for their state, while pursuing the ultimate goal of reducing teen

Table 1 U.S. Teenage Pregnancy and Birth Rates are High Compared to Other Developed Countries

International Data	U.S.	France	Germany	Netherlands	Canada	UK
Pregnancy rate (2002–5)	72.2	25.7	18.8	11.8	29.2	41.3^
Birth rate (2006)	41.9	7.8	10.1	3.8	13.3	26.7

Rates are listed as numbers per 1000 girls 15–19 years old,
^15–18 years old [1–4].
doi:10.1371/journal.pone.0024658.t001

pregnancy rates. This large-scale analysis aims to provide scientific evidence for this decision by evaluating the most recent data on the effectiveness of different sex education programs with regard to preventing teen pregnancy for the U.S. as a whole. We used the most recent teenage pregnancy, abortion and birth data from all U.S. states along with information on each state's prescribed sex education approach to ask "what is the quantitative evidence that abstinence-only education is effective in reducing U.S. teen pregnancy rates?" If abstinence education results in teenagers being abstinent, teenage pregnancy and birth rates should be lower in those states that emphasize abstinence more. Other factors may also influence teenage pregnancy and birth rates, including socio-economic status, education, cultural influences [10–12], and access to contraception through Medicaid waivers [13–15] and such effects must be parsed out statistically to examine the relationship between sex education and teen pregnancy and birth rates. It was the goal of this study to evaluate the current sex-education approach in the U.S., and to identify the most effective educational approach to reduce the high U.S. teen pregnancy rates. Based on a national analysis of all available state data, our results clearly show that abstinence-only education does not reduce and likely increases teen pregnancy rates. Comprehensive sex and/or STD education that includes abstinence as a desired behavior was correlated with the lowest teen pregnancy rates across states. In alignment with the *Precaution Adoption Process Model* advocated by the National Institutes of Health we suggest that comprehensive sex and HIV/STD education should be taught as part of the biology curriculum in middle and high school science classes, along with a social studies curriculum that addresses risk-aversion behaviors and planning for the future.

Materials and Methods
Level of Emphasis on Abstinence in State Laws

Data on abstinence education were retrieved from the Education Commission of the States [16]. Of the 50 U.S. states, only 38 states had sex education laws (as of 2007; Table 2). Thirty

of the 38 state laws contained abstinence education provisions; 8 states did not. Following the analysis of the Editorial Projects in Education Research Center [17], which categorizes the data on abstinence education into four levels (from least to most emphasis on abstinence: no provision, abstinence covered, abstinence promoted, abstinence stressed), we assigned ordinal values from 0 through 3 to each of these four categories respectively. A higher category value indicates more emphasis on abstinence with level 3 stressing abstinence only until marriage as the fundamental teaching standard (similar to the federal definition of abstinence-only education), if sex or HIV/STD education is taught (sex education is not required in most states) [16–18]. The primary emphasis of a level 2 provision is to promote abstinence in school-aged teens if sex education or HIV/STD education is taught, but discussion of contraception is not prohibited. Level 1 covers abstinence for school-aged teens as part of a comprehensive sex or HIV/STD education curriculum, which should include medically accurate information on contraception and protection from HIV/ STDs [16–18]. Level 0 laws on sex education and/or HIV education do not specifically mention abstinence.

Level of Emphasis on Abstinence in State Laws & Policies

States without sex education laws may nevertheless have policies regarding sex and/or HIV/STD education. These policies may be published as Health Education standards or Public Education codes [19]. These policies can also provide information on how existing sex education laws may be interpreted by local school boards. Information on the sex education laws and policies for all 50 US states was retrieved from the website of the Sexuality Information and Education Council of the US (SIECUS). We analyzed the 2005 state profiles on sex education laws and policy data for all 50 states [19] following the criteria of the Editorial Projects in Education Research Center [17] to identify the level of abstinence education (Table 2). The coding for the state laws (N = 38) and the coding for both laws and policies (N = 48) were more or less the same for the

Table 2 Abstinence Provisions and Levels of Abstinence Education in State Laws & Policies

State	Law: Abstinence[1]	Law Level[2]	Laws & Policy Level[3]
Alabama	Yes	3	3
Alaska	–	–	1
Arizona	Yes	2	3
Arkansas	Yes	2	3
California	Yes	1	1
Colorado	Yes	2	2
Connecticut	No	0	0
Delaware	–	–	3
Florida	Yes	3	3
Georgia	Yes	2	2
Hawaii	–	–	3
Idaho	No	0	0
Illinois	Yes	3	3
Indiana	Yes	3	3
Iowa	No	0	0
Kansas	–	–	0
Kentucky	–	–	3
Louisiana	Yes	3	3
Maine	Yes	1	1
Maryland	–	–	0
Massachusetts	No	0	1
Michigan	Yes	1	1
Minnesota	Yes	1	1
Mississippi	Yes	3	3
Missouri	Yes	2	2
Montana	–	–	0
Nebraska	–	–	2
Nevada	No	0	0
New Hampshire	No	0	0
New Jersey	Yes	1	1
New Mexico	–	–	3
New York	–	–	1
North Carolina	Yes	3	3
North Dakota	–	–	–
Ohio	Yes	3	3
Oklahoma	Yes	3	3
Oregon	Yes	1	1
Pennsylvania	Yes	2	3
Rhode Island	Yes	2	3
South Carolina	Yes	3	3
South Dakota	Yes	2	2

Table 2 *(continued)*

State	Law: Abstinence[1]	Law Level[2]	Laws & Policy Level[3]
Tennessee	Yes	3	3
Texas	Yes	3	3
Utah	Yes	3	3
Vermont	Yes	1	1
Virginia	Yes	2	2
Washington	Yes	2	2
West Virginia	No	0	0
Wisconsin	No	0	1
Wyoming	–	–	–

1 State laws with (yes) or without (no) an abstinence provision as of 2007 [16].
2 Level of Abstinence provision in state law as of 2007 [17].
3 Level of Abstinence provision in state law or other policy as of 2005 [19]; differences to laws 2 are noted in *italics*.
doi:10.1371/journal.pone.0024658.t002

states represented in both data sets with 6 exceptions (Table 2): the additional information on policies moved two states from a level 0 (abstinence not mentioned) to level 1 (abstinence covered), and four states from a level 2 abstinence provision (abstinence emphasized) to a level 3 (abstinence stressed). Only two states had neither a state law nor a policy regarding sex or STD/HIV education (as of 2005): North Dakota and Wyoming. Analyses of the two data sets gave essentially identical results. In this paper we present the analyses of the more extensive (48 states) law and policy data set.

Teen Pregnancy, Abortion and Birth Data

Data on teen pregnancy, birth and abortion rates were retrieved for the 48 states from the most recent national reports, which cover data through 2005 [11,12]. The data are reported as number of teen pregnancies, teen births or teen abortions per one thousand female teens between 15 and 19 years of age. In general, teen pregnancy rates are calculated based on reported teen birth and abortion rates, along with an estimated miscarriage rate [12]. We used these data to determine whether there is a significant correlation between level of prescribed abstinence education and teen pregnancy and birth rates across states. The expectation is that higher levels of abstinence education will be correlated with higher levels of abstinence behavior and thus lower levels of teen pregnancy.

Other Factors

Data on four possibly confounding factors were included in our analyses.

Socio-economics

To account for cost-of-living differences across the US, we used the adjusted median household income for 2006 for each state from the Council for Community and Economic Research: C2ER [20]. These data are based on median household income from the *Current Population Survey for 2006* from the U.S. Census Bureau [21] and the 2006 cost of living index (COLI).

Educational attainment

As an estimate of statewide education levels among teens, we used the percentage of high school graduates that took the SAT in 2005/2006 in each state [22].

Ethnic composition

We determined the proportion of the three major ethnic groups (white, black, Hispanic) in the teen population (15–19 years old) for each state [12], and assessed whether the teen pregnancy, abortion and birth rates across states were correlated with the ethnic composition of the teen population. To account for the ethnic diversity among the teen populations in the different states in a multivariate analysis of teen pregnancy and birth rates, we included only the proportion of white and black teens in the state populations as covariates, because the Hispanic teen population numbers were not normally distributed (see below).

Medicaid waivers for family planning

Medicaid-funded access to contraceptives and family planning services has been shown to decrease the incidence of unplanned pregnancies, especially among low-income women and teens [13]. According to the Guttmacher Institute, the national family planning program prevents 1.94 million unintended pregnancies, including almost 400,000 teen pregnancies each year by providing millions of young and low-income women access to voluntary contraceptive services [13]. Medicaid covered 71% of expenditures for these programs in 2006, and it is estimated that states saved $4 (associated with unintended births) for each $1 spent on contraceptive services [13]. Since the increasing role of Medicaid in funding family planning was mainly due to the efforts of 21 states to expand eligibility for family planning for low-income women who otherwise would not qualify for Medicaid, we analyzed whether these Medicaid waivers for family planning services (available in some states but not in others) could bias our results. We determined which states had received permission (as of 2005) from the Federal Medicaid program to extend Medicaid eligibility for family planning services to large numbers of individuals whose incomes are above the state-set levels for Medicaid enrollment [15]. We assessed whether the waivers (access to family planning services) had an effect on our analysis of teen pregnancy and birth rates across states, specifically whether they could bias our analysis with respect to the effects of the different levels of abstinence education.

Statistical Analyses
Sample statistics

Using JMP 8 software [23], we tested all variables for normality (Goodness of Fit: Shapiro Wilkes Test; JMP 8.0). Except for teen abortion rates and Hispanic teen population data, all variables were normally distributed. The distribution of the Hispanic teen population across states was not normal: most states had relatively small Hispanic teen populations, and a few states had a relatively large population of Hispanic teens. Teen pregnancy and birth rate distributions included outliers, but these outliers did not cause the distributions within abstinence education levels to differ significantly from normal; thus all outliers were included in subsequent analyses. For all further statistical analyses we used SPSS [24].

Correlations

We used non-parametric (Spearman) correlations to assess relationships between variables, and for normally distributed variables we also used parametric (Pearson) correlations, but these results showed the same trends and significance levels as the non-parametric correlations. As a result, we only report the results for the non-parametric correlations here.

Multivariate analyses

Only the two normally distributed dependent variables were included in the multivariate analysis (MANOVA and MANCOVA [24]): teen pregnancy and teen birth rates. We tested for homogeneity of error variances (Levene's Test) and for equality of covariance matrices (Box test) between groups. For MANCOVA we report the estimated marginal means of teen pregnancy and birth rates (i.e. means after the influence of covariates was removed). For pairwise comparison between abstinence levels, we used the Bonferroni adjustment for multiple comparisons.

Results

Among the 48 states in this analysis (all U.S. states except North Dakota and Wyoming), 21 states stressed abstinence-only education in their 2005 state laws and/or policies (level 3), 7 states emphasized abstinence education (level 2), 11 states covered abstinence in the context of comprehensive sex education (level 1), and 9 states did not mention abstinence (level 0) in their state laws or policies (Figure 1). In 2005, level 0 states had an average (± standard error) teen pregnancy rate of 58.78 (±4.96), level 1 states averaged 56.36 (±3.94), level 2 states averaged 61.86 (±3.93), and level 3 states averaged 73.24 (±2.58) teen pregnancies per 1000 girls aged 14–19 (Table 3). The level of abstinence education (no provision, covered, promoted, stressed) was positively correlated with both teen pregnancy (Spearman's *rho* = 0.510, p = 0.001) and teen birth

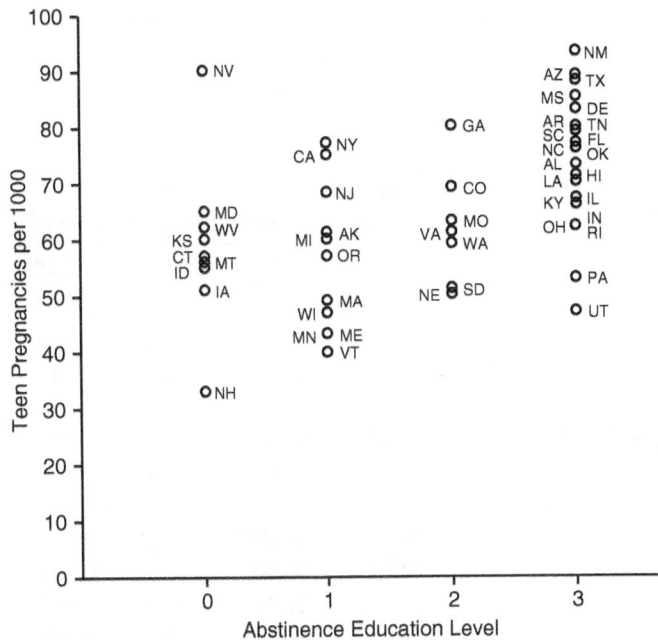

Figure 1 Abstinence education level prescribed in 2005 state laws or policies. All 48 states with state laws or policies on sex and/or HIV education are shown (North Dakota and Wyoming are not represented).

doi:10.1371/journal.pone.0024658.g001

($rho = 0.605$, $p < 0.001$) rates (Table 4), indicating that abstinence education in the U.S. does not cause abstinence behavior. To the contrary, teens in states that prescribe more abstinence education are actually more likely to become pregnant (Figure 2). Abortion rates were not correlated with abstinence education level ($rho = -0.136$, $p = 0.415$). A multivariate analysis of teen pregnancy and birth rates identified the level of abstinence education as a significant influence on teen pregnancy and birth rates across states (pregnancies $F = 5.620$, $p = 0.002$; births $F = 11.814$, $p < 0.001$). The significant pregnancy effect was caused by significantly lower pregnancy rates in level 0 (no abstinence provision) states compared to level 3 (abstinence stressed) states ($p = 0.036$), and level 1 (abstinence covered) states compared to level 3 states ($p = 0.005$); the significant birth effect was caused by significantly lower teen birth rates in level 0 states compared to level 3 ($p = 0.006$) states, and significantly lower teen birth rates in level 1 states compared to level 3 states ($p < 0.001$).

Socio-economic status, educational attainment, and ethnic differences across states exhibited significant correlations with some variables in our model (Table 4). We examined the influence of each possible confounding factor on our analysis by including them as covariates in several multivariate analyses. However, after accounting for the effects of these covariates, the effect of abstinence education on teenage pregnancy and birth rates remained significant (Figure 3).

Table 3 Teen Pregnancy, Abortion and Birth Rates (Per 1000 Girls Aged 14–19) by Level of Abstinence Education

Descriptive Statistics by Abstinence Education Level						95% Confidence Interval			
Outcomes	Level	N	Median	Mean	Std. Error	Lower Bound	Upper Bound	Minimum	maximum
Teen Pregnancies	0	9	57.0	58.78	4.966	47.43	70.23	33	90
	1	11	57.0	56.36	3.943	47.58	65.15	40	77
	2	7	61.0	61.86	3.931	52.24	71.47	50	80
	3	21	76.0	73.24	2.589	67.84	78.64	47	93
	Total	48	62.5	65.00	2.064	60.85	69.15	33	93
Teen Abortions	0	9	11.0	15.78	2.681	9.6	21.96	9	28
	1	11	16.0	20.27	3.069	13.43	27.11	10	41
	2	7	15.0	13.57	2.010	8.65	18.49	6	20
	3	21	12.0	14.86	1.306	12.13	17.58	6	27
	Total	48	15.00	16.08	1.096	13.88	18.29	6	41
Teen Births	0	9	35.2	34.82	3.316	22.8	41.5	18	50
	1	11	26.5	28.43	1.950	24.08	32.77	19	39
	2	7	40.0	39.29	2.765	32.52	46.05	31	53
	3	21	49.1	47.43	2.197	42.85	52.01	30	62
	Total	48	38.5	39.52	1.687	36.13	42.92	18	62

Based on 2005 data for all states except North Dakota and Wyoming, N = number of states.

doi:10.1371/journal.pone.0024658.t003

Table 4   Socioeconomics and Ethnic Diversity as Potential Influences on Teen Pregnancy, Abortion and Birth Rates in 48 States

Correlation Coefficients		Teen Rates per 1000 girls (14–19)			Adjusted median household income	% Teens in population[1]		
		Pregnancies	Abortions	Births		White	Black	Hispanic
Abstinence Education level	Spearman's rho	0.507**	−0.083	0.562**	−0.349*	−0.382**	0.419**	0.030
	p (2-tailed)	<0.001	0.577	<0.001	0.015	0.007	0.003	0.839
Teen Pregnancies per 1000 girls	Spearman's rho		0.329*	0.806**	−0.383*	−0.807**	0.597**	0.341*
	p (2-tailed)		0.022	<0.001	0.007	<0.001	<0.001	0.018
Teen Abortions per 1000 girls	Spearman's rho			−0.221	−0.116	−0.564**	0.263	0.557**
	p (2-tailed)			0.131	0.432	<0.001	0.071	<0.001
Teen Births per 1000 girls	Spearman's rho				−0.296*	−0.482**	0.393**	0.036
	p (2-tailed)				0.041	0.001	0.006	0.806
Adjusted median income	Spearman's rho					0.298*	−0.238	0.089
	p (2-tailed)					0.040	0.103	0.547
% white teens in population	Spearman's rho						−0.566**	−0.532**
	p (2-tailed)						<0.001	<0.001
% black teens in population	Spearman's rho							−0.014
	p (2-tailed)							0.925

Significant correlations are marked in bold type (*significant at p<0.05, **significant at p<0.01).

[1]The % teen population variables are measures of the ethnic diversity of the states. Please note the teen pregnancy, abortion and birth data (per 1000) reflect the behavior of all teens in each state: they are not limited to the behavior within that particular ethnic teen population (see Table 5).

doi:10.1371/journal.pone.0024658.t004

Socio-economic Status

There was a significant negative correlation between median household income (adjusted for cost of living) and level of abstinence education ($rho = -0.349$, p = 0.015; Table 4), indicating a socio-economic bias at the state level on state laws and regulations with regard to sex education. The adjusted median household income was negatively correlated with teen pregnancy ($rho = -0.383$, p = 0.007) and birth ($rho = -0.296$, p = 0.041) rates across states: pregnancy and birth rates tended to be higher in lower-income states. There was no correlation between household income and abortion rates ($rho = -0.116$, p = 0.432). When including the adjusted median household income as a covariate in a multivariate analysis (evaluated at \$45,892), income significantly influenced teen pregnancy (F = 5.427, p = 0.025) but not birth (F = 2.216, p = 0.144) rates. After accounting for socioeconomic status, the level of abstinence education still had a significant effect on teen pregnancy (F = 4.103, p = 0.012) and birth rates (F = 10.480, p<0.001).

Educational Attainment

There was no significant correlation between statewide teen education (percentage of high school graduates that took the SAT in 2005/2006) and level of abstinence education ($rho = -0.156$, p = 0.291). Education was not correlated with teen pregnancy rates ($rho = -0.014$, p = 0.925), but it was positively correlated with teen abortion rates ($rho = 0.662$, p < 0.001), and as a consequence, negatively correlated with teen birth rates ($rho = -0.412$, p = 0.004). There was no correlation between socio-economic status and teen educational attainment across states ($rho = -0.048$, p = 0.748), suggesting that these trends apply to both rich and poor states. When including education (% graduates taking the SAT) as a covariate in a multivariate analysis, education had a significant influence on teen birth (F = 8.308, p = 0.006), but not on teen pregnancy (F = 0.161, p = 0.690) rates, and after accounting for the influence of teen education (evaluated at 39.7% of graduates taking the SAT), the level of abstinence education still had a significant effect on

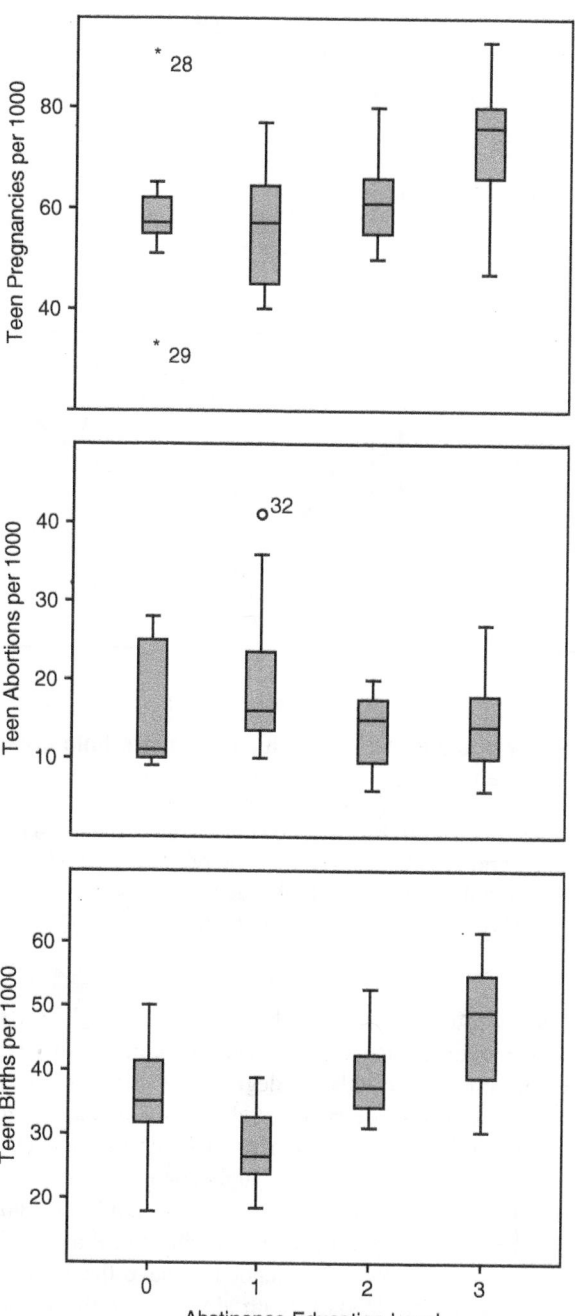

Figure 2   Mean teen pregnancy, abortion and birth rates by level of prescribed abstinence education. [Rates = numbers per 1000 girls 15–19 years old: shown are means 62 SE]. Top panel: Teen pregnancies [outliers: #28 Nevada and #29 New Hampshire]; Middle panel: Teen abortions [outlier: #32 New York]; Bottom panel: Teen births. All outliers were included in the statistical analyses. A multivariate analysis of teen pregnancy and birth rates identified the level of abstinence education as a significant influence on teen pregnancy and birth rates across states.

doi:10.1371/journal.pone.0024658.g002

both teen pregnancy (F = 5.527, p = 0.003) and teen birth rates (F = 10.772, p<0.001).

Ethnic Composition

For this analysis we focused on the three largest ethnic groups for which data are available: white, black, and Hispanic [12]. Teen pregnancy rates differ across these three ethnic groups. For the 48 states in this analysis, an ethnic breakdown (for all three ethnic groups) of teen pregnancy and abortion rates was available for 26 states, and of teen birth rates for 43 states. Across this reduced sample of states, 2005 teen pregnancy rates averaged 48.1 ($\pm$1.95) pregnancies per 1000 white teens, 103.7 ($\pm$5.38) pregnancies per 1000 black teens, and 141.6 ($\pm$8.55) pregnancies per 1000 Hispanic teens. Teen birth rates averaged 27.6 ($\pm$1.5) births per 1000 white teens, 59.2 ($\pm$2.58) births per 1000 black teens, and 96.1 ($\pm$5.39) births per 1000 Hispanic teens. Abstinence education levels were positively correlated with teen birth rates in all three ethnic groups (white: rho= 0.439, p = 0.002; black: rho= 0.328, p = 0.028; Hispanic: rho= 0.461, p = 0.001; Table 5).

Across all 48 states, abstinence education levels were significantly correlated with the proportions of white and black teens in the state populations (Table 4). In general, states with higher proportions of white teens tended to emphasize abstinence less (rho= −0.382, p = 0.007), and states with higher proportions of black teens tended to emphasize abstinence more (rho= 0.419, p = 0.003). When we included the proportion of white and black teens in the state populations as covariates in a multivariate analysis (evaluated at proportion white: 0.704 and proportion black: 0.138), only the proportion of white teens had a significant effect on teen pregnancy (F = 42.206, p<0.001) and teen birth rates (F = 5.894, p = 0.020). After accounting for this influence, the level of abstinence education still had a significant effect on teen pregnancy (F = 2.839, p = 0.049) and teen birth rates (N = 43 states: F = 7.782, p<0.001; Figure 3).

Medicaid Waivers

If Medicaid waivers contribute to the positive correlation between abstinence education and teen pregnancy at the state level, then states with waivers should have different teen pregnancy and birth rates than states without waivers. This was not the case. States with waivers (N = 17) were represented across all four abstinence education levels (Figure 4) and did not differ significantly in teen pregnancy rates from states without waivers (N = 21, Mann Whitney U = 237, p = 0.086), suggesting no significant effect of waivers (at the state level) on the correlation between abstinence levels and teen pregnancy rates. A recent study [14] found the same level of (non-)significance (0.05 < p < 0.1) for the effect of waivers on teen birth rates, but reported it as significant.

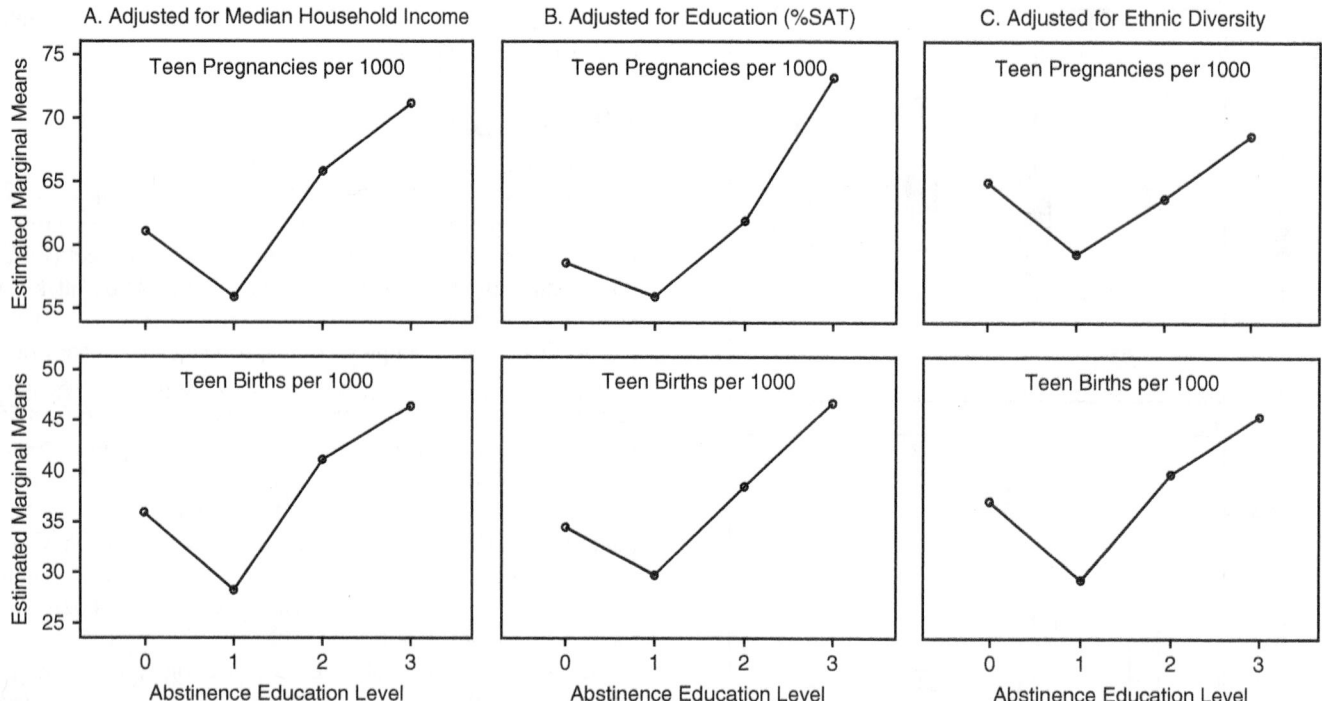

Figure 3 Trends in teen pregnancy and birth rates after accounting for socioeconomics, education and ethnic diversity.
(A) The adjusted median household income significantly influenced teen pregnancy and birth rates, but the level of abstinence education still had a significant influence on teen pregnancy and birth rates after accounting for socioeconomic status. (B) Education had a significant influence on teen birth, but not on teen pregnancy rates. After accounting for the influence of teen education, the level of abstinence education still had a significant influence on both teen pregnancy and teen birth rates. (C) The proportion of white teens (but not black teens) in the population had a significant influence on teen pregnancy and teen birth rates. After accounting for this influence, the level of abstinence education still had a significant influence on teen pregnancy and birth rates.

doi:10.1371/journal.pone.0024658.g003

Discussion

This study used a correlational approach to assess whether abstinence-only education is effective in reducing U.S. teen pregnancy rates. Correlation can be due to causation, but it can also be due to other underlying factors, which need to be examined. Several factors besides abstinence education are correlated with teen pregnancy rates. In agreement with previous studies, our analysis showed that adjusted median household income and proportion of white teens in the teen population both had a significant influence on teen pregnancy rates. Richer states tend to have a higher proportion of white teens in their teen populations, tend to emphasize abstinence less, and tend to have lower teen pregnancy and birth rates than poorer states. A recent study [25] found that higher teen birth rates in poorer states were also correlated with a higher degree of religiosity (and a lower abortion rate) at the state level. Medicaid waivers have previously been shown to reduce teen pregnancy rates [13], but our analysis shows that they do not explain our main result, the positive correlation between abstinence education level and teen pregnancy rates.

After accounting for other factors, the national data show that the incidence of teenage pregnancies and births remain positively correlated with the degree of abstinence education across states: The more strongly abstinence is emphasized in state laws and policies, the higher the average teenage pregnancy and birth rate. States that taught comprehensive sex and/or HIV education and covered abstinence along with contraception and condom use (level 1 sex education); also referred to as "abstinence-plus" [26], tended to have the lowest teen pregnancy rates, while states with abstinence-only sex education laws that stress abstinence until marriage (level 3) were significantly less successful in preventing teen pregnancies. Level 0 states present an interesting sample with a wide range of education policies and variable teen pregnancy and birth data [17–19]. For example, several of the level 0 states (as of 2007) did not mandate sex education, but required HIV education only (e.g. CT, WV) [19]. Only three of the level 0 states (IA, NH and NV) mandated both sex education and HIV education, but one of them (NV) did not require that teens learn about condoms and contraception. This state (NV) has the highest teen

Table 5   Ethnic Breakdown of Teen Pregnancy, Birth, and Abortion Rates and Their Relationship with Abstinence Education, Educational Attainment (Sat), Adjusted Income and Teen Diversity in the States

Correlation Coefficients for ethnic diversity in states		Pregnancy rates (per 1000 girls)			Abortion rates (per 1000 girls)			Birth rates (per 1000 girls)		
		White	Black	Hispanic	White	Black	Hispanic	White	Black	Hispanic
Abstinence Education level	Spearman's rho	0.360	0.029	**0.489***	0.024	−0.166	0.005	**0.463****	**0.332***	**0.437****
	p (2-tailed)	0.071	0.890	**0.011**	0.909	0.417	0.980	**0.002**	**0.030**	**0.003**
Percent of graduates taking SAT	Spearman's rho	−0.134	0.053	0.104	**0.723****	**0.461***	**0.613****	**−0.450****	**−0.504****	−0.258
	p (2-tailed)	0.514	0.796	0.614	**<0.001**	**0.018**	**0.001**	**0.002**	**0.001**	0.094
Adjusted median household income	Spearman's rho	−0.033	0.143	0.103	−0.348	−0.171	−0.240	**−0.335***	0.106	0.099
	p (2-tailed)	0.873	0.486	0.617	0.081	−0.404	0.238	**0.028**	0.500	0.529
Proportion of white teens in population	Spearman's rho	−0.307	0.054	−0.318	−0.376	−0.015	−0.256	−0.017	0.162	0.064
	p (2-tailed)	0.127	0.794	0.114	0.058	0.944	0.206	0.916	0.298	0.685
Proportion of black teens in population	Spearman's rho	**0.550****	**0.539****	**0.393***	0.113	0.086	0.031	0.282	**0.420****	0.215
	p (2-tailed)	**0.004**	**0.004**	**0.047**	0.584	0.675	0.880	0.067	**0.005**	0.166
Proportion of Hispanic teens in population	Spearman's rho	−0.366	−0.226	0.071	0.093	0.108	0.262	**−0.434****	**−0.347***	−0.140
	p (2-tailed)	0.066	0.267	0.730	0.652	0.600	0.196	**0.004**	**0.023**	0.370

Sample sizes for the analysis of ethnic breakdown (for all three ethnic groups) of teen pregnancy and abortion (N = 26 states) and birth rates (N = 43 states) are limited. Significant correlations are marked in bold type (*significant at p<0.05, **significant at p<0.01).

doi:10.1371/journal.pone.0024658.t005

pregnancy and birth rates in that group (Figure 1). Nevada is also one of only five states (with MD in level 0, CO in level 2, and AZ and UT in level 3) that required parental consent for sex education in public schools instead of an opt-out requirement that is present in all the other states [16,19].

The effectiveness of Level 1 (comprehensive) sex education in our nation-wide analysis is supported by Kirby's meta-analysis of individual sex education programs [8], Underwood et al.'s analysis of HIV prevention programs [27], and a recent review by the CDC taskforce on community preventive services [28]. All these studies suggest that comprehensive sex or HIV education that includes the discussion of abstinence as a recommended behavior, and also discusses contraception and protection methods, works best in reducing teen pregnancy and sexually transmitted diseases.

Individual Research Studies

Despite large differences between individual research studies that evaluate specific sex education programs (e.g. sample size, approaches to sex education studied, selection of participants,

choice of control groups, types of data, control for cross-talk between students outside of class), several case studies show that abstinence-only education rarely has a positive effect on teen sexual behavior [6,8,29]. One of the few exceptions is the recent study by Jemmott et al. [30] on black middle school students in low-income urban schools: after receiving 8 hours of abstinence education as 12 year olds, significantly more students (64/95) reported to be abstinent after 24 months when compared to (control) students who received 8 hours of health education (without any form of sex education: 47/88; Fishers exact test, p = 0.037), or students who received 8 hours of safe-sex education (without an abstinence component: 41/85; Fishers exact test, p = 0.007). However, there was no significant difference in abstinence behavior between students who had received abstinence education (64/95) and students who received 8 hours of comprehensive sex education (combining sex education with abstinence education: 57/97; Fishers exact test, p = 0.138). These two groups also did not differ in rates of reported unprotected sex (8/122 versus 8/115) or use of condoms (25/33 versus

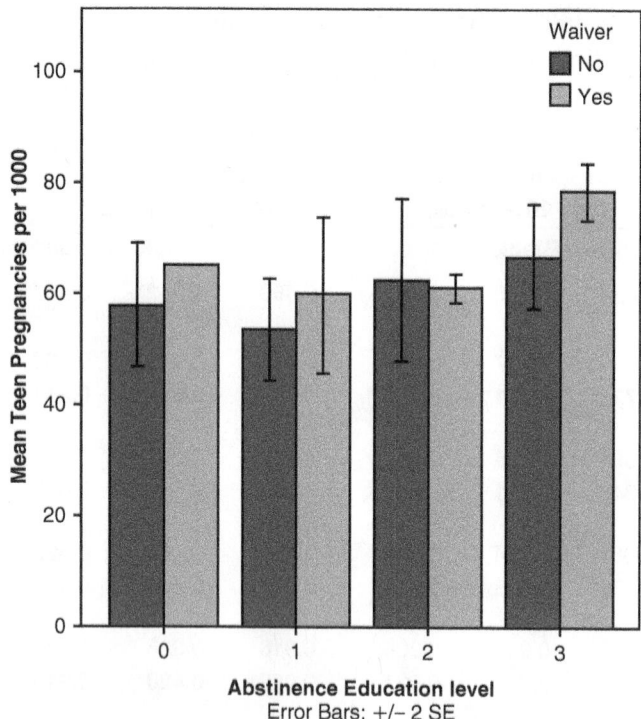

Figure 4   Teen pregnancy rates, abstinence education levels and Medicaid waivers to access family planning services. Access to waivers does not explain the difference in teen pregnancy rates (shown are means and ±2 SE) in states with a different emphasis on abstinence.

doi:10.1371/journal.pone.0024658.g004

29/37) in the previous 3 months. The abstinence-only intervention in that study was unique in that it increased knowledge about HIV/STD, emphasized the delay of sexual activity, but not necessarily until marriage, did not put sex into a negative light or use a moralistic tone, included no inaccurate information, corrected incorrect views, and did not disparage the use of condoms [30]. As a result, as pointed out by the authors, this successful version of abstinence education would not have met the criteria for federal abstinence-only funding [30]. While promoting an alternative and more effective form of abstinence education, these results also support Kirby's findings [8] and the data in the present study that comprehensive sex education that includes an abstinence (delay) component (level 1) is the most effective form of sex education, especially when using teen pregnancy rates as a measurable outcome.

Individual research studies also show that teaching about contraception is generally not associated with increased risk of adolescent sexual activity or sexually transmitted diseases (STDs) [8] as suggested by abstinence-only advocates, and adolescents who received comprehensive sex or HIV education

had a lower risk of pregnancy and HIV/STD infection than adolescents who received strict abstinence-only or no sex education at all in the U.S. and in other high-income countries [27,31].

Abstinence-only Education: Public Opinion and Associated Costs

Despite the data showing that abstinence-only education is ineffective, it may be argued that the prescribed form of sex education represents the underlying social values of families and communities in each state, and changing to a more comprehensive sex education curriculum will meet with strong opposition. However, there is strong public support for comprehensive sex education [32]. Approximately 82% of a randomly selected nationally representative sample of U.S. adults aged 18 to 83 years (N = 1096) supported comprehensive programs that teach students about both abstinence and other methods of preventing pregnancy and sexually transmitted diseases. In contrast, abstinence-only education programs received the lowest levels of support (36%) and the highest level of opposition (about 50%).

In addition to the federal and state funds spent on abstinence-only (level 3) education, there are other costs associated with the outcomes of failed sex education and family planning. When deciding state policies on sex education, State legislators should consider these additional costs. For example, based on estimates by the *National Campaign To Prevent Teen and Unplanned Pregnancy* [33], teen child bearing (compared to first birth at 20 years or older) in the U.S. cost taxpayers (in direct and indirect costs) more than $9.1 billion in 2004.

Our data show that education (% of high school graduates taking the SAT) was not correlated with teen pregnancy rates, but it was positively correlated with teen abortion rates and negatively correlated with teen birth rates. These data can be interpreted in two ways: (1) pregnant teens who give birth are less likely to finish high school and go on to college (i.e. pregnancy affects education). This is supported by a recent report [34] that showed that teen mothers are more likely to drop out of school: 51% of teen mothers earned their high school diploma by age 22, compared to 89% of women who had not given birth as teens. (2) teens who are motivated to go to college are not necessarily less likely to get pregnant, but more likely to abort their pregnancies (i.e. educational goal affects the decision of whether to carry a pregnancy to term).

As pointed out by the Society for Adolescent Medicine, the abstinence-only approach (as stressed by level 3 state laws and policies and funded by the federal abstinence-only programs) is characterized by the withholding of information and is ethically flawed [7]. Abstinence-only programs tend to promote abstinence behavior through emotion, such as romantic notions of marriage, moralizing, fear of STDs, and by spreading scientifically incorrect information [7,20,35]. For example a Congressional committee report found evidence of major errors and distortions of public health information in common abstinence-only curricula [36]. As a result, these programs may actually be promoting irresponsible, high-risk teenage behavior by keeping teens uneducated with regard to reproductive knowledge and sound decision-making instead of giving them the tools to make educated decisions regarding their reproductive health [37]. The effect of presenting inadequate or incorrect information to teenagers regarding sex and pregnancy and STD protection is long-lasting as uneducated teens grow into uneducated adults: almost half of all pregnancies in the U.S. were unplanned in 2001 [38]. Of these three million unplanned pregnancies, ~1.4 million resulted in live births, ~1.3 million ended in abortion, and over 400,000 ended in a miscarriage [36,37] at a financial cost (direct medical costs only) of ~$5 billion in 2002 [39].

The U.S. teen pregnancy rate is substantially higher than seen in other developed countries (Table 1) despite similar cultural and socioeconomic patterns in teen pregnancy rates [40]. The difference is not due to the onset of sexual activity [1]. Instead, the main factor seems to be sex education, especially with regard to contraception and prevention of STDs [41]. Sex education in Europe is based on the WHO definition of sexuality as a lifelong process, aiming to create self-determined and responsible attitudes and behavior with regard to sexuality, contraception, relationships and life strategies and planning [42]. In general, there is greater and easier access to sexual health information and services for all people (including teens) in Europe, which is facilitated by a societal openness and comfort in dealing with sexuality [40], by pragmatic governmental policies [43,44] and less influence by special interest groups.

Future Directions

While states with comprehensive sex education have lower teen pregnancy rates, even in these states rates are much higher than seen in Europe [1]. This is likely influenced by the fact that U.S. state laws and policies generally do not require that sex and STD education is taught in all schools, but only provide guidelines if local school boards decide to teach it [19]. For example, as of August 1, 2011, only 20 states mandated sex education, and 32 states mandated HIV education in their schools [45]. In addition, even states with comprehensive sex education laws or policies (level 1) received federal funding for individual abstinence-only education programs in 2005: total federal funds [19] averaged ~$14 per teen in level 1 states compared to ~$21 per teen in level 2 and 3 states [12]. An important first step towards lowering the high teen pregnancy rates would be states requiring that comprehensive sex education (with abstinence as a desired behavior) is taught in all public schools. Another important step would involve specialized teacher training. Presently the sex education and STD/HIV curricula are often taught by faculty with little training in this area [46]. As a further modification, "sex education" could be split into a coordinated social studies component (ethics, behavior and decision-making, including planning for the future) and a science component (human reproductive biology and biology of STDs, including pregnancy and STD prevention), each taught by trained teachers in their respective field.

As parents, educators or policy makers it should be our goals that (1) teens can make educated reproductive and sexual health decisions, that (2) teen pregnancy and STD rates are reduced to the rates of other developed nations, and that (3) these trends are maintained through the teenage years into adulthood. One possibility for achieving these goals is a close alignment and

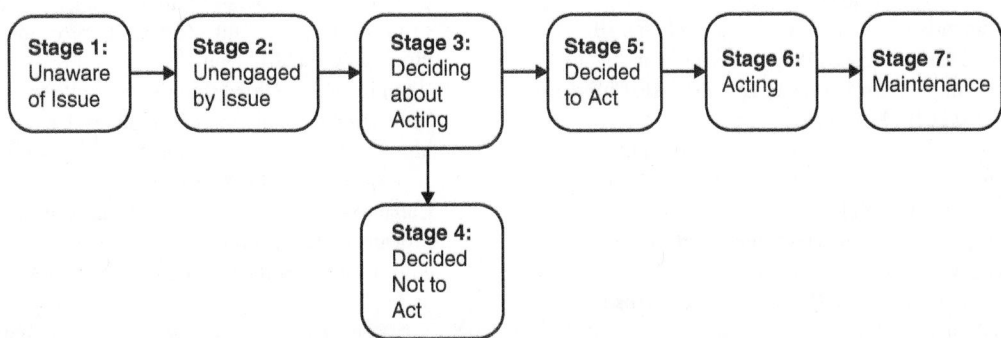

Figure 5 The Precaution-Adoption-Process Model. This model offers a basis for communication and discussions between educators, scientists, sex education researchers, and health professionals, and could serve as a reference for measuring progress in sex education. In addition, it could be used as a communication tool between sex education teachers and their students [48].

doi:10.1371/journal.pone.0024658.g005

integration of sex education with the National Science Standards for U.S. middle and high schools [47]. In addition, the *Precaution Adoption Process Model* (Figure 5) advocated by the National Institutes of Health [48] offers a good basis for communication and discussions between scientists, educators, and sex education researchers, and could serve as a reference for measuring progress in sex education (in alignment with the new evidence-based Teen Pregnancy Prevention Initiative). In addition, it could be used as a communication tool between sex education teachers and their students. It should be our specific goal to move American teens from Stages 1 or 2 (unaware or unengaged in the issues of pregnancy and STD prevention) to Stages 3–7 (informed decision-making) by providing them with knowledge, understanding, and sound decision-making skills (Figure 5). For example, a recent study [49] attributes 52% of all unintended pregnancies (teenagers and adults) in the U.S. to non-use of contraception, 43% to inconsistent or incorrect use, and only 5% to method failure.

Our analysis adds to the overwhelming evidence indicating that abstinence-only education does not reduce teen pregnancy rates. Advocates for continued abstinence-only education need to ask themselves: If teens don't learn about human reproduction, including safe sexual health practices to prevent unintended pregnancies and STDs, and how to plan their reproductive adult life in school, then when should they learn it, and from whom?

Notes

1. Darroch JE, Singh S, Frost JJ (2001) Differences in Teenage Pregnancy Rates Among Five Developed Countries: The Roles of Sexual Activity and Contraceptive Use. *Family Planning Perspectives* 33(5): 244–250. Available: http://www.guttmacher. org/pubs/journals/3324401.html. Accessed 2011, Jan 10.

2. The National Campaign to prevent teen and unplanned pregnancy. Teen birth rates: International Comparison 2006. Available: www.thenationalcampaign.org/. . ./TBR_ InternationalComparison2006.pdf. Accessed 2011, Jan 10.

3. Canada: Statistics Canada (2005) Pregnancy outcomes by age group. Available: http://www40.statcan.gc.ca/l01/cst01/hlth65a-eng.htm. Accessed 2010, Nov 20.

4. UK Department of Education 2011 Under 18 and under 16 conception statistics (2011) Available: http://www.education. gov.uk/childrenandyoungpeople/healthandwellbeing/ teenagepregnancy/a0064898/under-18-and-under-16-conception-statistics. Accessed 2011, Aug 3.

5. Advocates for Youth (2007) The History of Federal Abstinence-Only Funding. Available: http://www.advocatesforyouth.org/ publications/429?task=view. Accessed 2011, Jun 19.

6. Trenholm C, Devaney B, Fortson K, Quay L, Wheeler J, et al. (2007) "Impacts of four Title V, Section 510 abstinence education programs" (*Mathematica Policy Research*).

7. Santelli JS, Ott MA, Lyon M, Rogers J, Summers D (2006) Abstinence-only education policies and programs: A position paper of the Society for Adolescent Medicine. *Journal of Adolescent Health* 38: 83–87.

8. Kirby D (2007) Emerging Answers, Research Findings on Programs to Reduce Teen Pregnancy and Sexually Transmitted Diseases (National Campaign to Prevent Teen and Unplanned Pregnancy, Washington, DC). http://www.thenationalcampaign. org/EA2007/EA2007_full.pdf. Accessed 2010, Jun 18.

9. SIECUS: Senate Finance Committee Votes to Fund Comprehensive Sex Education; Restore Failed Title V Abstinence-Only-Until-Marriage Funding. Available: http:// www.siecus.org/index.cfm?fuseaction=Feature.showFeature& featureid=1816&pageid=525&parentid=523. Accessed 2011, Jan 10.

10. Horn B (1983) Cultural beliefs and teenage pregnancy. *Nurse Practitioner* 8: 35–39.

11. Martin JA, Hamilton BE, Sutton PD, Ventura SJ, Menacker F, et al. (2007) Births: Final data for 2005. National Vital Statistics Reports 56 #6: Available: http://www.cdc.gov/nchs/ data/nvsr/nvsr56/nvsr56_06.pdf. Accessed 2010, May 8.

12. Kost K, Henshaw S, Carlin L (2010) U.S. Teenage Pregnancies, Births and Abortions: National and State Trends and Trends by Race and Ethnicity (Guttmacher Institute). Available: http://www. guttmacher.org/pubs/USTPtrends.pdf. Accessed 2010, Jan 30.

13. Benson Gold R, Sonfield A, Richards CL, Frost JJ (2009) Next Steps for America's Family Planning Program: Leveraging the Potential of Medicaid and Title X in an Evolving Health Care System, New York: Guttmacher Institute. Available: www. guttmacher.org/pubs/NextSteps.pdf. Accessed 2011, Jan 10.

14. Yang Z, Gaydos LM (2010) Reasons for and Challenges of Recent Increases in Teen Birth Rates: A Study of Family Planning Service Policies and Demographic Changes at the State Level. *Journal of Adolescent Health* 46(6): 517–524.

15. Benson Gold R, Richards CL, Ranji UR, Salganicoff A (2005) Medicaid: A critical source of support for family planning in the United States. Kaiser Family Foundation and Guttmacher Institute. Available: http://www.kff.org/womenshealth/7064. cfm. Accessed 2011, Jan 10.

16. Zinth K (2007) Sex education laws in the states. State Note (Education Commission of the States, Denver CO). Available: http://www.ecs.org/html/educationIssues/ECSStateNotes_2007 .asp. Accessed 2011, Aug 1.

17. Callahan J (2007) Abstinence education in state laws. Editorial Projects in Education Research Center. Available: http://www. edweek.org/rc/articles/2007/06/08/sow0608.h26.html. Accessed 2009, Jan 10.

18. Advocates for Youth. Sex Education Resource Center. State profiles. Washington, D.C.: Advocates for Youth. Available: http://www.advocatesforyouth.org/index.php?option=com_ content&task=view&id=766&Itemid=123). Accessed 2010, Sep 20.

Available: http://aspe.hhs.gov/hsp/abstinence07/. Accessed 2010, May 8.

19. SIECUS State Profiles Fiscal Year 2005. Available: http://www. siecus.org/index.cfm?fuseaction=page.viewPage&pageID= 1061&nodeID=1. Accessed 2011, Feb 10.

20. The Council for Community and Economic Research. ACCRA Cost of living index (COLI). The Council for Community and Economic Research, C2ER. Available: http://www.coli.org/ COLIAdjustedMHI.asp. Accessed 2010, May 10.

21. Census Bureau US (2006) R1901: Median Household Income for 2006. Available: http://factfinder.census .gov/servlet/GRTTable?_bm=y&-geo_id=01000US& _box_head_nbr=R1901&-ds_name=ACS_2006_ EST_G00_&-redoLog=false&-format=US-30&-mt_ name=ACS_2007_1YR_G00_R1901_US30&- CONTEXT=grt. Accessed 2010, May 10.

22. National Center of Education Statistics (2007) SAT data. Tables and Figures: Table 137. US Department of Education. Available: http://nces.ed.gov/programs/digest/d07/tables/ dt07_137.asp. Accessed 2010, Jun 10.

23. JMP Statistical Discovery software, version 8.0. Cary, NC: SAS Institute Inc.

24. SPSS for MacInstosh, version 17.0. Chicago, IL: SPSS Inc).

25. Strayhorn JM, Strayhorn JC (2009) Religiosity and teen birth rate in the United States. *Reproductive Health* 6: 14. doi: 10.1186/1742-4755-6-14.

26. Collins C, Alagiri P, Summers T (2002) "Abstinence Only versus Comprehensive Sex education. What are the arguments? What is the Evidence?" Policy Monograph Series. San Francisco CA: AIDS Policy Research Center & Center for AIDS Prevention Studies, AIDS Research Institute, UC San Francisco.

27. Underhill K, Operario D, Montgomery P (2007) Systematic Review of Abstinence-Plus HIV Prevention Programs in High-Income Countries. *PLoS Medicine* 4: e275.

28. CDC Taskforce on Community Preventive Services (2009) Guide to Community Preventive Services. Prevention of HIV/ AIDS, other STIs and Pregnancy: group-based comprehensive risk reduction interventions for adolescents. Available: www. thecommunityguide.org/hiv/riskreduction.html. Accessed 2011, Jun 20.

29. Goodson P, Pruitt BE, Buhi E, Wilson KL, Rasberry CN, et al. (2004) "Abstinence education evaluation phase 5 technical report". College Station, TX: Texas A&M University, Department of Health and Kinesiology.

30. Jemmott JB, Jemmott LS, Fong GT (2010) Efficacy of a Theory-Based Abstinence-Only Intervention Over 24 Months. A Randomized Controlled Trial With Young Adolescents. *Arch Pediatr Adolesc Med* 164(2): 152–159.

31. Kohler PK, Manhart LE, Lafferty WE (2008) Abstinence-Only and Comprehensive Sex Education and the Initiation of Sexual Activity and Teen Pregnancy. *Journal of Adolescent Health* 42(2): 344–351.

32. Bleakley A, Hennessy M, Fishbein M (2006) Public opinion on sex education in U.S. schools. *Archives of Pediatrics and Adolescent Medicine* 160(11): 1151–1156.

33. Hoffmann SD (2006) By the Numbers — The Public Costs of Teen Childbearing. Washington, DC: National Campaign to Prevent Teen and Unplanned Pregnancy, Available: www. thenationalcampaign.org/resources/pdf/pubs/btn_full.pdf. Accessed 2010, May 10.

34. Perper K, Peterson K, Manlove J (2010) Diploma Attainment Among Teen Mothers (Child Trends, Publication #2010- 01). Available: http://www.childtrends.org/Files/Child_ Trends-2010_01_22_FS_DiplomaAttainment.pdf. Accessed 2010, Jun 10.

35. Kreinin T, Waggoner J (2001) Towards a sexually healthy America. Washington, D.C.: Advocates for Youth, Sexuality Information and Education Council of the United States, (SIECUS. Available: www.naccho.org/topics/HPDP/infectious/ hiv/. . ./abstinenceonly.pdf. Accessed 2010, Jan 10.

36. US House of Representatives Committee on Government Reform — Minority Staff Special Investigations Division. The Content of Federally Funded Abstinence-Only Education Programs. Available: http://oversight.house.gov/index. php?option=com_content&view=article&id=2487&catid=44: legislation. Accessed 2010, Nov 1.

37. Kaye K, Suellentrop K, Sloup C (2009) The Fog Zone: How Misperceptions, Magical Thinking, and Ambivalence Put Young Adults at Risk for Unplanned Pregnancy. Washington, DC: The National Campaign to Prevent Teen and Unplanned Pregnancy. Available: www.thenationalcampaign.org/fogzone/pdf/fogzone .pdf. Accessed 2010, Jun 10.

38. Finer LB, Henshaw SK (2006) Disparities in Rates of Unintended Pregnancy in the United States, 1994 and 2001. *Perspectives on Sexual and Reproductive Health* 38(2): 90–96.

39. Trussel J (2007) The cost of unintended pregnancy in the United States. *Contraception* 75(3): 168–170.

40. Singh S, Darroch JE, Frost JJ (2001) Socioeconomic disadvantage and adolescent women's sexual and reproductive behavior: the case of five developed countries. *Fam Plann Perspect* 33: 251–258.

41. Schalet A (2004) Must we fear adolescent sexuality? *Med Gen Med* 6(4): 44. Available: http://www.ncbi.nlm.nih.gov/pmc /articles/PMC1480590/. Accessed 2010, Oct 1.

42. Advocates for Youth (2009) *Adolescent Sexual Health in Europe and the U.S.— Why the Difference?* 3rd edition: Sue Alford and Debra Hauser. Available: www.advocatesforyouth. org/storage/advfy/documents/fsest.pdf. Accessed 2011, Jan 30.

43. Bundeszentrale fuer gesundheitliche Aufklaerung (BZgA) (2006) BZgA/WHO Conference on Youth Sex Education in a Multicultural Europe, Cologne, Germany, 2006. Available: http://www.sexualaufklaerung.de/index.php?docid=1111. Accessed 2010, Jun 10.

44. Bundeszentrale fuer gesundheitliche Aufklaerung (BZgA) (2006) Country papers on youth sex education in Europe. BZgA/WHO Conference, Cologne, Germany, 2006. Available: http://www.sexualaufklaerung.de/index.php?docid=1039. Accessed 2010, Jun 10.

45. Guttmacher Institute (2011) State Policies in Brief: Sex and STI/HIV Education. Available: www.guttmacher.org/pubs/spib_SE.pdf. Accessed 2011, Aug 3.

46. Rodriguez M (1995) "Teaching our teachers to teach: a SIECUS study on training and preparation for HIV/AIDS prevention and sexuality education." SIECUS Report 28(2): 1–11.

47. National Research Council (1996) "National Science Education Standards" (National Academy Press, Washington, DC). Available: http://www.nap.edu/openbook.php?record_id=4962. Accessed 2010, Oct 8.

48. National Institutes of Health (2005) Theory at a Glance, Application to Health Promotion and Health Behavior (Second Edition). U.S. Department of Health and Human Services, National Institutes of Health. Available: Available: http://www.cancer.gov/PDF/481f5d53-63df-41bc-bfaf-5aa48ee1da4d/TAAG3.pdf. Accessed 2009, Jan 10.

49. Frost JJ, Darroch E, Remez L (2008) Improving contraceptive use in the United States. New York: Guttmacher Institute, No. 1. Available: www.guttmacher.org/pubs/2008/05/. . . /ImprovingContraceptiveUse.pdf. Accessed 2010, Oct 1.

Critical Thinking

1. At what age do you think sexuality education should start in the United States?

2. A good amount of research indicates that teaching young people only about abstinence without teaching about contraceptive use and STI prevention leaves young people unprepared for the future. If this research exists, why do you think there are so many people who still oppose teaching comprehensive sexuality education to young people?

3. Without being taught age-appropriate, factual information about sexuality in schools, young people tend to go to Internet porn to learn about sexual behaviors. What do you think some of the impacts using porn as sex ed can have on young people (and adults)?

Internet References

Advocates for Youth
advocatesforyouth.org

Answer
answer.rutgers.edu

Sexuality Information and Education Council of the United States
siecus.org

Acknowledgments—We thank C2ER, the Council for Community and Economic Research, for providing additional adjusted median household income data for those states that were not included in their online data set, and two anonymous reviewers for helpful comments.

Stanger-Hall, Kathrin F.; Hall, David W. From *PLoS One*, vol. 6, no. 10, October 2011, pp. 1–11. Copyright © 2011 by Public Library of Science. Used with permission.

Unit 3

UNIT

Prepared by: Elizabeth Schroeder, EdD, MSW,
Elizabeth Schroeder Consulting

Sexualities, Education, and Development

Supporters of comprehensive sexuality education understand that human sexuality is a lifelong process. We are sexual beings from the moment we are born, and remain so until the day we die. Why doesn't everyone subscribe to this viewpoint? Part of it, particularly from more socially conservative individuals, is understanding what being a "sexual being" means. This concept is miscontextualized in particular when it comes to children and teens, sexuality education or even simply talking with young people about sexuality encourages them to have sex. But the reality is that human sexuality encompasses far more than sexual behaviors and reproductive functioning, which means we are all learning about sexuality from our earliest ages. And research shows that when parents talk with their children openly and honestly about the vast range of topics relating to sexuality, their children end up delaying the onset of first sex and use safer sex and contraceptive methods more consistently and correctly.

As children gain self-awareness, they naturally explore their own bodies, display curiosity about the bodies of others, and show interest in the bodies of the people closest to them, such as their parents. Curiosity is an important and healthy aspect of human development, yet adults sometimes make their children feel ashamed for showing interest in the human body or even asking questions. They don't know what information is age-appropriate for younger children, or how to respond to questions in ways they are comfortable with and that answer their kids' questions. As a result, young children end up learning euphemisms for their genitals rather than using the correct body parts; they learn that anything related to their "private parts" is taboo or should be hidden, rather than spoken about directly with the parent(s) or caregiver(s) on whom they depend the most to help them learn about being a human being in the world.

Fast forward to adolescence, the time when young people are looking to answer a very important question: "Who am I?" They are trying to understand their changing emotions and bodies during puberty. They are starting to understand or solidify their gender identity and sexual orientation, beginning in the teen years to conceptualize all they know—about sexuality and beyond—within the context of who they are and who they will be in the future.

Young people are living in increasingly complicated worlds. Prevailing societal messages are powerful and highly confusing—especially about sexuality. How do young people even start to make sense of the simultaneous messages of "Just Say No" and "Just Do It" to which they are constantly exposed? Many professionals try very hard to help young people do just that by providing comprehensive sexuality education—yet, although there is countless research demonstrating the effectiveness of this approach, politics and social conservatism have worked equally as hard to keep young people from learning the information and skills they need to grow up healthy and happy by promoting so-called abstinence-only-until-marriage programming. These programs only teach young people to not have sex, there is no discussion of safer sex methods or contraception, so that whenever they do have sex, whether as teens (which often happens) or as adults, they are woefully unprepared to be with a partner and have satisfying, safe sexual relationships.

In the last three years, the United States, which still has one of the highest teen pregnancy rates among industrialized nations around the world, has seen an all-time low in teen pregnancy and birth rates. Although there is disagreement about the cause for this decrease, the Centers for Disease Control and Prevention, along with other national public health entities, posit that greater access to contraceptive methods and condoms, along with increases in comprehensive sexuality education in schools, are responsible. Yet the federal government continues to allocate money to fund abstinence-only-until-marriage programs, to the tune of well over $1 billion to date.

Beyond the formal classroom is the largest classroom the world has: the media. The media both influence and provide a reflection of individual and societal attitudes on a wide range of sexuality-related topics. The media place tremendous emphasis on sexual attractiveness (especially for girls and women, although the pressure for boys and men has been building over the last few decades) and sexual competency (especially for men). The media tells us who should be in relationships and who should not; who are sexual beings worthy of love and attention and who are not; how we should interact with each other. As a result, young people grow into young adults who learn how to seem, rather than be. And there is no greater social influencer right now on how we view sex and sexuality than online porn. When young people don't have access to sexuality education in schools and don't have parents or caregivers they can talk with about this important topic, they tend to go to porn. And what they learn there is not age-appropriate, not realistic, and not what they need to know before they've learned even the basics about their bodies and how they work and what a romantic or sexual relationship can look like between two people.

Sexuality finally becomes socially validated in adulthood, at least within the context of heterosexual marriage. Adult sexuality can be a source of joy, pain, validation, confusion, and so many other things both positive and negative. Many people seek fulfillment through their relationships. Keeping a relationship strong requires hard work and the commitment of both partners. Routine, boredom, stress, financial pressures, work, parenting responsibilities, and lack of effective communication can exact heavy tolls on the quantity and quality of sexual interactions. Sexual misinformation, leftover from the lack of education during the adolescent and teen years, leads to myths, and unanswered questions—especially about changes in sexual arousal, response, and functioning. This pervasive ignorance can undermine or hinder intimacy and sexual fulfillment throughout a person's adult years.

Sexuality in late adulthood has been misunderstood (and underestimated) because of the prevailing misconception that only young and attractive people are sexual. Such an attitude has contributed significantly to the apparent decline in sexual interest and activity as one grows older. However, as population demographics have shifted and the baby boomer generation has aged, these beliefs and attitudes have begun to change. Physiological changes in the aging process are not, in and of themselves, detriments to sexual expression. A life history of experiences, good health, and growth can make sexual expression in the later years a most rewarding and fulfilling experience.

Prepared by: Elizabeth Schroeder, EdD, MSW,
Elizabeth Schroeder Consulting

Article

How We Can Improve Sex Ed for Boys

JUSTIN CASCIO

Justin Cascio talks to Elizabeth Schroeder, executive director of Answer, about why boys are tuning out in sex ed classes, and what they want to know most (but aren't telling us).

Learning Outcomes

After reading this article, you will be able to:

- List at least two ways in which sexuality education programming tends to focus more on girls than boys.

- Provide at least two reasons why boys tend to go to porn for their sexuality education.

- Explain what the "boy code" is and how it applies to sexuality education for boys and young men.

The Answer website offers some grim statistics on the state of sex ed in the schools today: "One in four teens has an STD. Yet sex ed by and large still focuses only on the needs of girls."

The Boys and Sex Ed: Beyond Statistics and Stereotypes online workshop that this quote is from is produced by Answer, a national organization that is dedicated to providing and promoting comprehensive sexuality education to young people and the adults who teach them. I spoke with Elizabeth Schroeder, executive director of Answer, to find out more about how "sexuality education"—which focuses on feelings and relationships rather than just biology or birth control—can help provide the answers our boys so desperately need.

Porn is designed for adult fantasy, which is abstract. Teens are concrete learners. So when they watch porn, they are learning, "This is what sex is and what we should look like."

Is sexuality education as it's taught in schools today really biased toward the needs of girls?

ES: Yes, there is a bias. The challenge is, it's unconscious. As a culture, we think 'boys will be boys,' so we concentrate on girls and make them the sexual gatekeepers in their relationships with boys. As a result, the methodology and language being used in sex ed classes today still focuses—sometimes overtly, sometimes subtly—on girls. For example, I blogged about a research article on "girls' condom use." I found this amusing when (most) girls don't have penises. There's nothing in the article about their male partners. This is unfair to girls, and does a disservice to boys. Rendering guys invisible in sex ed reinforces stereotypes about them and contributes to negative statistics.

Could sexuality education better serve both girls and boys?

ES: Absolutely. Educators say, "I'll just make sure to mention guys from time to time." This is not sufficient. Occasionally mentioning guys is comparable to some well-meaning educators who will use the term "partner" to offer a nod to non-heterosexual orientations—as if this fully addresses heterocentrism in sex ed. Similarly, a sex ed activity might present a guy and girl in a relationship who are thinking about having sex, but then the activity focuses in on what the female partner might feel, do, or say in this situation—again setting girls up as the gatekeepers, without fully exploring what the male partner might be feeling and thinking.

What in particular are boys looking for and not getting from sex ed?

ES: There are two different questions: what are boys looking for, and what are they not getting because there are strict policies in many places about what can and cannot be taught. Although there's a diversity in learning styles, boys tend to be visual, kinesthetic learners, and they're looking for concrete information about sexuality. Educators who teach lessons on safer sex, but who can't bring actual condoms in for the boys to see, touch and feel, will not be as effective with male learners. What you teach them becomes hypothetical until they have opened the package, felt the condom and know how to use them. They'll say they get it, but they don't.

Dr. William Pollack's "boy code" speaks to this: we've seen for decades that boys are socialized to want to have sex and are consistently sent messages that they should want to and should have sex. Lessons that don't acknowledge and address these messages won't meet boys' needs. Imagine a mixed-gender sex ed classroom activity that's about abstinence or waiting to have sex. Since guys are hearing from the majority culture that they should want to have sex, conducting the lesson without acknowledging and discussing the gendered messages and how they are different for guys than they are for girls makes the lesson irrelevant to the male learners.

This is a major reason why guys look to porn for sex ed, which is problematic because what they see in porn is not designed for their age group. Porn is designed for adult fantasy, which is abstract. Teens are concrete learners. So when they watch porn, they are learning, "This is what sex is and what we should look like." Whether it's about race, gender, penis size, a lot of myths and stereotypes are being reinforced through porn. Now, the jury is still out on the extent to which porn can potentially harm young people; it's pretty clear, however, that it misinforms them. But porn is easily accessible and far more explicit than anything they'd get in a classroom setting. So they go to porn, which is not the right place for them to learn.

What is?

ES: The location is less important than the content. One thing we really tend to leave out when we teach sex ed to guys is anything about the emotional aspects of being a human being. Far too many adults say boys don't care about emotions, but they do. In mixed-gender classrooms, it can be much more challenging to get boys to talk about feelings. When I have worked with single-gender groups with guys, the work we did on emotions was phenomenal. There's this stereotype that boys don't have emotional capacity. We have to challenge that stereotype head on. They need to be taught that it's not just acceptable, but important to have and express feelings, and that "real men" are not afraid to do this. We have to stop gendering the human experience so that young people don't feel like they can't behave a certain way just because of their gender.

We need the right educators to deliver the right messages. If we dislike teen boys, we're not the right ones to do the work. If we fear teen boys, we teach them that they are to be feared.

What Dr. Pollack says about the boy code is that these proscriptive messages aren't just passive messages. They're part of a proactive campaign to keep boys (and girls) in a rigid gender box. It's ironic that we, as a culture, seem to be more comfortable with hyper-violent men that we have to find ways of controlling than with men who are hypersensitive. Sensitive men are "feminine" men, and we're still a homophobic society, although it's been exciting to see that start to change a bit at the macro level.

What do boys want to know to prevent rape and domestic violence?

ES: First, they want people to know that it's not just guys assaulting girls. I went to teach a rape and sexual assault prevention workshop in the Bronx to a group of all guys a number of years ago. Before I could say my name, one of the guys stood up and said, "We're not going to stay to listen to you tell us not to beat on our girlfriends. We want to know what to do when they beat up on us."

Second, they're pushed to learn how to get girls to say "yes" to sex (regardless of their sexual orientation), and they're still being socialized that when a girl says "no" it means "maybe." We need to be clear and straightforward with guys instead of assuming they'll "figure it out." It's tough to figure things out when you're getting conflicting messages. We have to directly and clearly say, "It's never okay to push someone else to do something sexual they don't want to do. When someone says "no," respect that no—the first time, and every time."

Adult professionals walk into a room with assumptions and stereotypes: we need to check these at the door. I taught a group of professionals in an urban New Jersey workshop on working with boys and young men. They were all female, and many of them believed horrible things about boys, such as "They're all potential rapists." We need the right educators to deliver the right messages. If we dislike teen boys, we're not the right ones to do the work. If we fear teen boys, we teach them that they are to be feared.

Speaking of assumptions, another big stereotype is that only male educators can be effective with boys and young men; I know from years of direct experience that that just isn't true. It's not true that only men can relate to boys. The most important thing to young men is respect; start from there, and your gender is far less relevant. A sense of humor doesn't hurt either!

Sex ed isn't as simple as providing one hour and fifteen minute workshop and thinking you've counteracted all the stereotypical messages guys received about gender and sexuality. It's a lifelong campaign that involves parents, educators, religious leaders and many other adults. It has to start earlier than high school. Adolescence is way too late to counteract the values and messages kids have been receiving since birth that are gender-based. Even Toys R Us tells you what aisle you can shop in based on the gender of the child!

What question can parents answer that our boys want to know but aren't asking? How can we be proactive and anticipate their questions and needs regarding sexuality education?

ES: This depends on the age of the boy. For adolescent boys—and they'd never cop to this—the question a lot of them probably most want to know the answer to is, "Why did you stop hugging me?" When guys reach puberty, we start touching them less. Then they withdraw. But that doesn't mean they don't still need love and support and don't want to get some guidance about how to get through what's a really challenging time.

The question they probably would cop to wanting to know the answer to is, "Am I okay?" We hear that at Answer from teen guys all the time. Some guys ask, "I know all my friends are talking about sex and I'm not interested. Am I normal?" They are also really concerned about penis size—another culturally imposed bias that's reinforced by what they see in porn.

The boy code says that boys want to differentiate themselves from their peers through one-upsmanship, humiliation, and leadership, but they also want to fit in and be like other boys. This extends into adulthood and becomes "the man code." And while there are lots of different kinds of men, a very masculine man is as much of a man as a gentler, "feminine" man. When boys feel they don't have any choice other than to be one certain type of man, then it's problematic. Understanding boys' socialization and working with it instead of railing against it is more effective.

For example, I really like the Strength campaign from Men Can Stop Rape. It's boy code—both visually, and in terms of the tagline—"My strength is not for hurting." That's the kind of message that acknowledges the value of being strong without reinforcing the harmful stereotype that you cannot control your strength. The campaign emphasizes that boys have strength, rather than that boys are reckless.

My son is an early adolescent. The language that resonates with him and his friends is not negative language or admonishments of what they should not do. Developmentally, if you tell an adolescent not to do something, whatever it is, they will want to do it. I focus instead on what they should do. I say, "Be a leader. Be the one everyone looks up to. When someone's being bullied, the leader gets a teacher to stop it."

Critical Thinking

1. Why do you think United States culture continues to maintain the attitude that boys will be boys—that in different-sex relationships boys and men cannot be expected to control themselves, so girls and women should be the sexual negotiators in these relationships?

2. Do you agree that gender role expectations are more rigid for boys and men than for girls and women? Why or why not?

3. Even with so much progress in terms of rights for LGB people, homophobia is still very prevalent in the United States, especially among boys and men. Why do you think girls and women tend to be less threatened by homosexuality than boys and men?

Internet References

The Good Men Project
http://goodmenproject.com
Hooking Up and Staying Hooked
http://www.hookingupandstayinghooked.com
National Organization for Men Against Sexism
http://site.nomas.org

JUSTIN CASCIO is a writer and editor, the former managing editor of *The Good Men Project Magazine,* founding editor of *The Good Life* (the lifestyle section of the Good Men Project), and a founding editor of *Trans-Health,* the online health and fitness magazine for trans people that remains, more than a decade later, the most recognized resource in its field. Justin writes about gender, relationships, and holistic health, as well as his own life as a trans man.

Prepared by: Elizabeth Schroeder, EdD, MSW,
Elizabeth Schroeder Consulting

Article

Truth and Consequences at Pregnancy High

The education of a teenage mother.

ALEX MORRIS

Learning Outcomes

After reading this article, you will be able to:

- Name at least three reasons why a girl would want to become a parent as a teen.

- Describe at least three potential life limitations to girls who become parents as teens.

- List two positive things about becoming a parent at any age, and two challenges.

Before the sun has risen over the Bronx River, an alarm chimes in 17-year-old Grace Padilla's bedroom. Sliding from the lower bunk, she pads to the bathroom, flips on the light, brushes her teeth, then gathers up her hair into a short ponytail, which she wraps with a long row of black extensions and knots into a tight bun. She's quick and efficient, with none of the preening one might expect of a high-school junior. At 6:30 A.M., she goes back into the bedroom to wake her 2-year-old daughter.

Along with her grandparents, her mother, her sister, and her child, Grace lives in a small two-bedroom apartment on the second floor of a nondescript brick building in Hunts Point, where nearly half the residents live below the poverty line and roughly 15 percent of girls ages 15 to 19 become pregnant each year. It's the highest teen-pregnancy rate in the city, more than twice the national average.

"Lilah, wake up," Grace whispers, leaning in close. Lilah bats her mother away with a tiny hand and nestles up closer to Grace's own mother, Mayra, who had moments before returned home from her night shift as a cashier at a local food-distribution center and slipped, exhausted, into Grace's place in the bed.

"Come on, let's go get dressed," Grace pleads, pulling her daughter from under the covers as Lilah begins crying, flailing her arms and legs.

"Come *on*," Grace begs. She fights to keep her mounting frustration in check and then counts down the seconds before she'll make Lilah go stand against the wall, her usual form of punishment. "Five . . . four . . . three . . . two . . . one."

The threat is enough. Lilah's body goes slack, her screaming dissipates to a whimper. Grace is able to wrestle her into the clothes she'd laid out beforehand. But the child's screams have woken Grace's grandparents, who are now in the galley kitchen, arguing in Spanish. Her grandfather has Alzheimer's. He accidentally makes decaffeinated coffee, which infuriates his wife.

At 7:20, Grace smoothes a tiny hat over Lilah's curls, bundles her into a coat, then jostles schoolbooks into a bag. In the empty lot across the street, a rooster starts to crow.

When Grace arrives at Jane Addams High School for Academics and Careers, she joins the daily parade of mothers—pushing strollers, grasping the chubby fists of toddlers, perching bundled babies on cocked hips—making their way to basement room B17, the headquarters of the school's Living for the Young Family Through Education (LYFE) center. Run by the Department of Education, the LYFE program operates in 38 schools in the five boroughs, teaching parenting skills and providing on-site day care to teen parents who are full-time students in New York City's public schools. Jane Addams hosts one of the most active branches in the city, with sixteen mothers currently in the program.

While the students sign in on a clipboard, social worker Ana C. Martínez flits among them with her checklist of concerns.

Is this baby eating enough? (Yes.) Does that one still have a cough? (No.) When will the heat be turned back on in one young mother's apartment? (Uncertain.) If it isn't soon, has she considered going to a shelter? (She has.)

"How's the baby?" Martínez asks Grace.

"She's fine," Grace answers.

Satisfied, Martínez turns her attention to Lilah. "Can I get a hug?"

"No," the child replies coyly, pretending to hide behind her mother's legs.

"Pretty please?"

Lilah finally concedes, jumping into the woman's arms.

Martínez laughs. "We have to play that game every morning, don't we?"

The girls cluster around a table laid out with bagels and jam, which Martínez serves every morning, both to entice her charges to be at school on time and also to make sure they get enough to eat ("Some don't at home," she clucks). She admits that the LYFE program, which serves 500 families and costs taxpayers about $13 million a year, has its naysayers, people who think that it makes life too easy for the mothers and diverts money from students who've made more responsible choices. "But the reality is, teens are having kids, and we've got to work with them," she says. "They're entitled to an education."

Grace greets Jasmine Reyes—a soft-spoken senior whose 2-year-old daughter, Jayleen, is Lilah's best friend in day care—before going over to peer at Nelsy Valerio's infant. When Iruma Moré enters the room with her 8-month-old daughter, Dymia, Grace beelines for the baby, unwrapping her from a pile of blankets.

"Dymia, Dymia, *Dy-mi-a,*" she chants, bouncing the child on her lap. "She's so little," Grace marvels wistfully.

Iruma giggles. "I try to feed her all the time," she says, as she drops into a chair next to a locker crammed full of diapers. Though all four of Iruma's older sisters were teen mothers, she didn't know her school had day care until her sophomore year. "I started seeing the mothers coming in with their babies and stuff, and I always used to wonder where they take them," she says. One day, she looked through a doorway and it was like peering into a magic cupboard—a roomful of babies with soft skin and fine hair. Iruma thought she might like to have one of her own. By her junior year, she was pregnant. "I wasn't using nothing, no protection, so I mean, I knew it was gonna come sooner or later."

The nursery is a clown's paradise, brightly painted and well outfitted with funds donated by makeup artist Bobbi Brown. (In addition to the traditional high-school curriculum, Jane Addams teaches a number of vocations, including cosmetology, which Grace is studying.) Grace and Iruma each commandeer a crib and begin to strip down their daughters to their underwear, so that a caretaker can check the children for marks. Then the mothers fill out a form about when their child last ate, the child's mood, how the baby has been sleeping. Just before the bell rings for second period, they leave the nursery and head upstairs to school. For the next seven hours, they'll get to be kids again themselves.

Grace got pregnant in January 2006, less than a month after her 14th birthday and soon after she lost her virginity to a 15-year-old boy from the neighborhood named Nikko Vega. He was the only person she'd slept with, or even wanted to. After he broke up with a girlfriend ("A ho," Grace sniffs), she began cutting her eighth-grade classes to meet him at his apartment. Even then, she had full curves and a round and inviting face. She was normally sweet, but if pressed, she could fire off a string of expletives so fast the words blurred together. Nikko liked that about her. One day, the two of them found themselves playing more than Nintendo, and they just let it happen.

"It was heat-of-the-moment stuff," Grace says of having sex for the first time. Getting pregnant wasn't even on her mind. But it was on Nikko's: "A couple of hours after, I was thinking, like, *Damn.*" He eventually asked Grace if she should go on birth control, but they knew that would make her mom suspicious. They decided to take their chances, though it bothered Nikko to be so reckless. "A lot of people I knew had kids young, and I didn't want to be one of them," he admits. He had hoped to go to college on a football scholarship, had even made a pact with his friends to put off fatherhood. "Like, ever since we were younger, we all spoke about, 'No kids.' All of us."

Grace got pregnant at 14. She told Nikko that she wanted to keep the baby and that she was happy, "in a sad sort of way."

"It didn't work," Grace says archly. "Everybody he grew up with has a kid now."

Grace didn't know she was pregnant for months. She didn't get morning sickness, headaches, or cramps. She still did step dancing, played football after school, rode roller coasters when her mom took her to a theme park, fit into her regular clothes. She hadn't been having her period long enough for its absence to be a major cause for concern. When she went to a neighborhood clinic to get tested, just in case, and the results came back positive, she was shocked. "I didn't really know what to do," she says. "I didn't know what to ask. I was just like, 'What?'"

When she told Nikko, he walked away without saying a word, but a couple of hours later, he returned, driven back by the hang-dog devotion he has for Grace and by fear of her disapproval. She told him that she wanted to keep the baby and that she was happy about the decision, "in a sad sort of way." She loved babies, but she wasn't sure what she was getting into. To the extent that he could be there for her, an extent that even he understood to be meager, Nikko said he was onboard.

It took Grace a month to work up the nerve to tell her mother. When Mayra came home from work one day, Grace, her older sister, Samantha, and her cousin were sitting in front of the building waiting for her "like there was a funeral." In the elevator ride up to the apartment, Mayra looked from one girl to the next. "Which one of you is pregnant?" she asked. She thought Samantha would answer, but when she didn't, the realization set in that it was her younger daughter who was in trouble.

"How could you?" Mayra screamed, standing in their living room, shaking with anger. "How could you? You see our situation, you see what I have on my plate. How could you be so selfish?"

Grace ran to her bedroom, sobbing. Mayra stayed in the living room, sobbing. Mayra's own mother walked in the door and demanded to know what was going on.

"Your granddaughter," Mayra wailed, "your *14-year-old* granddaughter decided you needed to see a great-grandkid."

"Oh my God," the old woman said. *"¡Ay, Dios mío! ¡Ay, Dios mío, ayúdenos!"*

For a month, Mayra cried every day. Having gotten married at 16 and had Samantha at 17, she was loath to become a grandmother at 36. She had asked Grace repeatedly if she had started having sex, and the girl had always denied it. Between her parents and her own children, the apartment was already overcrowded, and money stretched thin. She threatened to send Grace to live with her father, who had left the family a decade ago. For years, they hadn't been able to track him down. Now he had a new family in Philadelphia, and Grace had been in cautious contact. But when they called to tell him about the pregnancy, he made it clear that she wasn't welcome. Grace hasn't spoken to him since.

Mayra was surprised to find herself seriously considering abortion as an option. The South Bronx has a high birthrate in part because in this largely Hispanic and Catholic community, the idea of terminating a pregnancy meets with such intense disapproval. Her mother told her that she would not be able to live under the same roof if they went through with it, but Mayra didn't see how Grace could manage to raise a child, nor did she want to put her daughter through the difficulty of labor only to give the baby away. Grace guessed that she was about four months along and agreed to visit an abortion clinic. The sonogram showed that the baby was due in ten weeks.

"Ten weeks?" Mayra asked. "This is a 14-year-old who's been to theme parks, eaten junk food the whole time, had no prenatal care. Ten weeks? I don't know what this baby's gonna be like."

The nurse nodded sympathetically, but there was nothing to be done. "There's nowhere in this country where they'll do that abortion at seven months."

Mayra set about preparing for the baby. She arranged for Grace to be enrolled in Jane Addams, the closest school that had a LYFE program. She put a call out to friends and family for a crib, a stroller, secondhand baby clothes. She started making doctors' appointments, pleading her daughter's way into clinics that didn't have openings until after the baby was due. Grace looked so young when she brought her in, no one could believe she was the one who was pregnant.

Grace's water broke in the hallway of Jane Addams the second week of her freshman year, a full month before her due date. Thinking she had wet her pants, she called her mother from a bathroom stall.

"Um, I want to go home," she said when Mayra picked up.

"Why? What happened?"

"My pants are all wet."

"What do you mean your pants are all wet? Did a car splash you or something?"

"No. Like, they're all wet. Like, I went into the bathroom, and they're all wet."

"Oh my God," Mayra cut in. "Your water broke. Oh my God! You're gonna have this baby in that school!"

When Grace arrived at Albert Einstein hospital, she was having contractions. Her mother stepped outside to calm her nerves with a cigarette, and Grace took the moment alone to ask her doctor if it was possible that she might die in childbirth. He reassured her that the chances were infinitesimally slim. "He sugarcoated it," she says. "He was a nice guy."

By the time Nikko arrived the following afternoon, Grace was in the throes of "the worst pain I ever felt in my life," she says, gasping just at the thought. She refused to allow him in the room. "I was in so much pain I really just wanted to kill him. I said, 'I advise security, doctors, nurses, everybody on this floor, if that man reaches this room, it's gonna be chaos, because this is all his fault.'"

On Sunday, September 17, 2006, at 2:55 A.M., Delilah Joli Vega was born, alert and healthy.

At the McDonald's on Prospect Avenue, teenagers crowd the counter, munching fries and competing for attention, the boys with their hooded sweatshirts pulled down low over their eyes, the girls in tight jeans and baby tees, nameplate jewelry shimmering, hair ruthlessly slicked back into high ponytails. As Iruma orders a pile of cheeseburgers and two Happy Meals, Grace and Jasmine drag high chairs up to the table and settle in with Nikko. The conversation is no different from that at any other table in the place, except for the constant interruption. There's drama going down on Grace's block—"Dumbass Samantha was talking about, 'Oh, if Sasha did punch A. J. in the face, it wasn't cause A. J. hit her, it was over Killah . . .' "—but she can't focus on the story with Lilah sending golden arcs of boxed apple juice into the air.

"Lilah, you're spilling the juice," Grace points out. "You're. Spilling. The. Juice."

Jayleen, Jasmine's daughter, looks over at Lilah, then squeezes her own juice box with vigor.

"You must want to get smacked," Grace tells her, raising her eyebrows before turning to the girl's mother. "I been telling you about that, Jasmine."

"Later, later," Jasmine pleads, not in the mood for a parenting lesson. But the fact is the mothers often act as a check on one another, imparting what parenting wisdom they have, holding one another to a certain standard. Grace, particularly, prides herself on her parenting skills. She's observant. She's strict. Her mother, Mayra, taught her how to take care of Lilah but refused to do the tasks for her. Grace was the one who changed Lilah's diapers, fed her, got up in the middle of the night when she cried. "She's not Baby Alive, is she?" Mayra would ask. "There's no off-button on her."

Having teenage parents does mean that Lilah is prone to mimic teenage behavior. "Her attitude is serious," says Grace. "She'll be like, 'Mind your business.' Mind *my* business? You better be talking to the milkman! I love her, but sometimes I just want to bop her on her head." But the good manners Lilah displays in front of company—if not always at home—testify to Grace's efforts.

Even now, as Lilah eyes the chicken nuggets that Iruma has been tearing into bite-size chunks for Dymia, she doesn't reach out and take one. "Hee dat icken, Mommy?" she asks politely.

"I see that chicken," Grace answers. "But you asked for a burger, so now you're gonna eat a burger."

"She didn't ask for a burger. You said she wanted a burger," Jasmine points out. "You're mad mean."

Grace shrugs off the comment, as a girl from their school pauses on her way past their table.

"Hey! What's up, baby?" she coos at Dymia before turning to Iruma. "She's getting so big. Oh my God!"

Iruma pushes her glasses up on her nose and smiles contentedly. "Yeah, she getting big."

"Oh my God, you're so cute!" The girl stares at Dymia, shaking her head in amazement.

In the South Bronx, the stigma of having a child at a young age is remarkably absent, not just because teen parenthood has long been pervasive but also because the family structure is such that children often grow up raising younger siblings, nieces, and nephews. Adding a child of their own into the mix doesn't seem like it will change much in terms of daily routine, but it does feel like a rite of passage, a one-way ticket to adulthood. Motherhood cements a girl's fertility, her femininity. Louder than any clingy top or painted lip, it broadcasts that now she's a woman. And for some girls, that's appealing. When *The Tyra Banks Show* did an online survey of 10,000 girls across the country, one-fifth of them said they wanted to become teen moms. The latest Centers for Disease Control report shows a 3 percent increase in teen pregnancy in 2006 after more than a decade of decline. At Jane Addams, round bellies orbit the hallways like planets. The school doesn't keep track of pregnancies, but according to the attendance officer, one week this spring, seven girls out of a student body of about 1,500 were out of school to give birth.

The mothers watch as the girl from school continues on her way, joining a booth where a group of teenagers have piled in together, plopping on each other's laps, laughing loudly at each other's jokes. None of them have children. They seem not to have a single care. The chasm between being a parent and being a kid was difficult to intuit until it was crossed. Now Grace knows it well. When Nikko once teased her about all the fun she would have without him if she went to college, she leveled a cold stare at him and asked, "How am I gonna have fun in college with a child?"

Iruma fishes her cell phone out of a bag and presses a few buttons. Hip-hop starts to blare from the little speakers, setting a more festive mood. The moms relax. Jayleen and Lilah bounce in time to the music.

"Jayleen, you want to dance for everybody?" Jasmine asks. "You want to get on the table and dance?"

Jayleen tries to climb out of her high chair, and Jasmine lifts her up onto the bench, where she plants her feet and shakes her little bottom back and forth.

"Oh, she gotta donk, she gotta donk," Jasmine chants, as Jayleen's dance grows increasingly outrageous. The moms laugh.

Sometimes it's hard not to act their age. "You need to be adult and mature, but you're still young," says Grace. "Adults have fun all the time. They still joke, they still laugh. They can't take your kid away just because of that."

When Grace gets home from school one afternoon, her grandparents have two eyes of the gas stove burning to drive away the apartment's chill. She steers Lilah away from the flame and to the refrigerator, where she allows her to choose a snack. Lilah points at a pitcher of red liquid, and Grace fixes her a bottle, waiting for Nikko to get home from the GED program he started the week before.

When he does, he waves a sheet of loose-leaf paper in front of her. It's his first assignment, a short essay on why he should be a candidate for the program.

"I need to finish school for my 2-year-old daughter," he starts off in an even hand. "I need to finish school for her because she follows everything that I do, and I feel that it is time for me to step up to the plate." At the bottom of the page, his teacher has written "good ideas, good motivation" and given him a B-plus. Grace seems pleased. "Oh snap, babe. Now what are you gonna do to get an A-minus?"

She's only half-joking. Even if it is sometimes misplaced, Grace has a highly evolved sense of propriety. She expects to be treated a certain way, expects Nikko to embrace his responsibilities as a father. Her loyalties now are to Lilah, and her world is delineated: There are the players and hustlers and birds, people best avoided; then there are the "cousins" and *títís* and "brothers," people she may not be related to by blood but who do well by her and her daughter. She's not quite sure yet where Nikko falls. "He be all right," she says.

It took a long time for Mayra to accept Nikko as a de facto member of the family. It wasn't just his role in the pregnancy—she understood that Grace was equally at fault—it was his own neglectful upbringing that gave her pause. She refused to have his name listed on Lilah's birth certificate until her own mother interjected. "You're gonna leave her birth certificate just blank under father, like she doesn't know who her child's father is?" the older woman asked, horrified.

Since Lilah was born, Nikko has spent a smattering of nights in jail, mostly for getting in neighborhood fights or, as he says, "being in the wrong place at the wrong time." Because his mother did not force him to go to school, he has not a single high-school credit. When Mayra took him to family court for child support (a requirement of the LYFE program), Mayra told the judge that she didn't expect any money from Nikko, that she would prefer he get an education rather than a job now, so that he could support his child later; but the judge still awarded them $25 a month—less than the cost of a box of diapers—which Nikko's mother agreed to pay until her son turned 18. Grace and Mayra have still not seen a cent.

In the end, though, it was hard to keep blaming Nikko, a child, for what Mayra saw as his mother's failings. When he didn't have a winter coat, she bought him one. When he was hungry, she fed him. When his mother kicked him out after a fight with her boyfriend, Mayra temporarily let him stay with them. Over time, he grew on her. "I basically showed her a lot of respect," says Nikko. "A lot of butt kissing," corrects Grace. Mayra realizes that, in his capacity, he is a good father: He's present. Though other girls are still dating the fathers of their children, Nikko is the only boy who visits the LYFE center. A certificate stating that he completed LYFE's fatherhood-training program hangs in a frame over Grace's bed. "The only

reason I don't press it is because this baby knows who her daddy is," says Mayra. "And she loves her daddy."

Still, both Mayra and Grace find their patience sputtering. In the three years since Grace got pregnant, Nikko hadn't held a single job or completed a single class. Mayra sees the writing on the wall. She knows that the statistics are not in Nikko and Grace's favor: Only 40 percent of teenagers who have children get their high-school diplomas, and 64 percent of children born to unmarried high-school dropouts live in poverty. "Life isn't about you anymore," Mayra is quick to inform him. "You brought someone else into this world that you have to care for. If you're gonna be that type of person that's gonna just not do nothing—and because of that, statistics is gonna land you back in jail—you may as well say bye to them now while Lilah's small and can get over you fast. Because this baby's not visiting nobody in jail." At the beginning of this year, to make good on her word, she gave him one month to prove to her that he was in school or had landed a job. Right at the deadline, he signed up for his GED.

Sometimes Grace feels that she's leaving Nikko behind. She talks of going to college, studying business, opening her own beauty salon, getting her child out of Hunts Point, away from the "hustlers and divas." She expects that there will come a day when she alone is responsible for providing for Lilah. "You can hope, we can all hope that Nikko's gonna do something to better himself and want to be there and provide for his family," Mayra tells her. "But the fact remains, if he doesn't, he wouldn't be the first boy. You wouldn't be the first single mother."

One evening early this spring, the young family has the Padilla apartment to themselves. Mayra sleeps soundly behind the closed door of the bedroom, resting up for her night shift at eleven. Grace's grandparents are at church, her sister out with friends. At times like these, Grace likes to pretend the apartment belongs to her and Nikko, that she doesn't live with her mother and he doesn't crash at a friend's place, that they've managed to make a life for themselves and Lilah on their own.

Nikko prepares a bowl of popcorn, while Grace flips through channels on the TV, stopping at a music video she knows Lilah likes. The little girl follows along with the dance in the best rendition a two-year-old could possibly muster, stroking her hips as they wiggle furiously and then flapping her wrists like a drag queen. When she looks behind her to make sure her parents are watching, Nikko and Grace laugh at her presumption. As parents, they share an easy rapport. She teases and prods him gently; he defers to her with a good-natured grin.

Later, there's homework to be done. Grace has a field trip tomorrow, so her load is light, but Nikko struggles to write an essay on the three branches of government. Once he finishes his GED, he's hoping to enroll in junior college. Grace pulls out her U.S. history folder, shows him a few photocopied papers, then goes into the kitchen to heat up frozen chicken patties.

After they eat, she gives Lilah a bath, crouching by the bathtub and allowing her daughter to splash around as long as she likes. "You a monkey," she says, laughing as Lilah dunks her head under the water and then shakes out her curls. "When she was a baby, the funnest part was the bath because her faces were just priceless." While Nikko heats up a bottle of chocolate milk, Grace towels Lilah off, rubs her down with lotion as the child tries to squirm out of her grasp—"She likes running around naked"—and dresses her in a diaper and footed fleece pajamas. Nikko puts his homework aside to give Lilah her bottle, stretching her out across his lap and rocking her gently. He waits until she's asleep to kiss Grace good-bye.

"Love you, babe," he says.

"Love you too."

Critical Thinking

1. What is the impact of teenage motherhood on the adolescent female's life?

2. What developmental issues or concerns do teen mothers face that are particular to their situation?

Internet References

Advocates for Youth
  http://advocatesforyouth.org

Healthy Teen Network
  http://www.healthyteennetwork.org

National Campaign to Prevent Teen and Unplanned Pregnancy
  http://thenationalcampaign.org

Article

Prepared by: Elizabeth Schroeder, EdD, MSW,
Elizabeth Schroeder Consulting

Religiosity and Teen Birth Rate in the United States

JOSEPH M. STRAYHORN AND JILLIAN C. STRAYHORN

Learning Outcomes

After reading this article, you will be able to:

- Describe the connection between religiosity and teen birth rate in the United States.

- Define "religiosity" and explain why it could potentially have an impact on teen pregnancy and birth rates.

- Name at least two other behaviors that can be connected to religiosity for teens.

Background

The children of teen mothers in the U.S., on the average, have worse outcomes in a number of ways. They score lower in school achievement tests, have a greater likelihood of repeating a grade, are rated more unfavorably by teachers while in high school, have worse physical health, are more likely to be indicated victims of abuse and neglect, have higher durations of foster care placement, and are almost three times more likely to be incarcerated during adolescence or the early 20s than the children of mothers who delayed childbearing; the daughters of teen mothers are more likely to become teen mothers themselves.[1]

In the United States, what to teach adolescents about sexuality and the prevention of teen pregnancy has been controversial. A number of sex education programs in the U.S. have been mandated to be "abstinence-only" programs, excluding the teaching of contraceptive techniques. As stated in a National Public Radio poll report, "the historical impetus for abstinence education has come from evangelical or born-again Christians. . . . Eighty-one percent of evangelical or born-again Christians believe it is morally wrong for unmarried adults to engage in sexual intercourse, compared with 33 percent of other Americans. . . . More than twice as many evangelicals as non-evangelicals (49 percent to 21 percent) believe the government should fund abstinence-only programs instead of using the money for more comprehensive sex education."[2]

Other polls have presented varying results on similar questions: A 2008 poll in Minnesota[3] reported that a significantly smaller fraction of those who described themselves as "very conservative" politically and those who were "born again" Christian supported comprehensive sex education than the corresponding fractions of more liberal and non-born-again; however, in this sample, 83.2% of the born-again Christians supported comprehensive sex education; only 51% of the politically "very conservative" supported it.

The connection between religion and attitudes toward contraception prompts investigation of the relationship between religiosity and teen pregnancy.

Some studies have suggested that greater religiosity is associated with either greater abstinence or lower teen birth rate. Hardy and Raffaelli, who analyzed data from the National Longitudinal Survey of Youth, reported that higher time one religiosity predicted a lower likelihood of first sexual intercourse between time one and time two.[4] Loury concluded that communities with larger communities of Catholics and Conservative Protestants have lower rates of teen childbearing, all other things equal.[5] This conclusion was drawn from an analysis of women from age 14–20 in 1979, taken from the National Longitudinal Study of Youth. McCree and colleagues found that African-American females with higher religiosity scores were more likely to have initiated sex at a later age, to have used a condom in the last six months, and to possess more positive attitudes toward condom use.[6] Rostosky et al., found that adolescent religiosity predicted later coital debut.[7] However, there was a significant interaction between race and religiosity: African-American adolescent males who were either more religious or had signed a virginity pledge were more likely to debut than African-American males who were less religious and/or who had not signed a pledge. Miller and Gur found, upon analyzing the National Longitudinal Study of Adolescent Health in the U.S., that frequent attendance of religious events in girls 12 to 21 years old was positively associated with a "responsible and planned use of birth control".[8] Personal conservatism, however, was associated with unprotected sex. Manlove and colleagues, upon analysis of the 1997 National Longitudinal Survey of Youth, found that in the sample as a whole, greater family religiosity was associated with "using contraceptives consistently"; however, among sexually active males, family religiosity was "directly and negatively associated with contraceptive consistency".[9]

Other studies have suggested that religiosity is associated with behaviors that could lead to a higher teen birth rate. Studer and Thornton found that among 18-year-olds, religious teenagers were less likely to use medical methods of contraception when sexually active.[10] Dodge and colleagues compared male college students in the United States and the Netherlands.[11] American men reported higher rates of inadequate contraception and unwanted pregnancy than their Dutch counterparts; religiosity and sex education were thought to explain these differences.

Rosenbaum compared adolescents who reported taking a virginity pledge with a matched sample of nonpledgers.[12] Among the matching variables was pre-pledge religiosity and attitudes toward sex and birth control. Pledgers did not differ from nonpledgers in lifetime sexual partners and age of first sex, but pledgers were less likely to have used birth control and condoms in the past year and at last sex. This research raises the possibility that moralistic attitudes toward sexuality can actually increase the likelihood of pregnancy, by discouraging contraception without successfully discouraging sexual intercourse.

Such a hypothesis is bolstered by the research of Santelli and colleagues, who calculated that 86% of the decline in adolescent pregnancies that occurred between 1995 and 2002 was attributable to improved contraceptive use.[13] Santelli and colleagues cite the example of the Netherlands, which in the 1970s went through a period of soul searching and consensus-building about the need for contraception and prevention of sexually transmitted infections in adolescents, and today has one of the lowest teen birth rates in the world.[14] If contraception is more effective than attempted abstinence in reducing birth rates, then attempts to discourage both contraception and sexual intercourse among teenagers could raise teen birth rates.

A complicating variable related to teen births and religiosity is the rate of abortions among teens. Adamczyk and Felson, after analyzing longitudinal survey data from the U.S., reported that more highly religious women are less likely to have either an abortion or an out of wedlock pregnancy.[15] Tomal, upon analyzing data from 1,024 counties in 18 U.S. states, found that religious membership level was negatively related to teen abortion rates.[16]

Cahn and Carbone summarized differences in attitudes about family and sexuality between the more religious and conservative U.S. "red families," versus the less religious and more liberal "blue families".[17] These authors observed: "Within red families, abstinence outside of marriage is a moral imperative, the shotgun marriage is the preferred solution to an improvident pregnancy, and socialization into traditional gender roles is critical to marital stability." The blue model, however, "involves less control of sexuality, celebrates more egalitarian gender roles, and promotes financial independence and emotional maturity as the sine qua non of responsible parenthood. In this new model, abstinence is unrealistic, contraception is not only permissible, but morally compelled, and abortion is the necessary (and responsible) fallback" (p. 3). Cahn and Carbone mention that teen birth rates appear higher among "red" families.

The present study approaches the relationship between teen birth rate and religiosity by looking at data aggregated across states in the United States.

Methods
Data Sources

This study compiled data from publicly accessible data sets. The data on religiosity were from the U.S. Religious Landscapes Survey, published by the Pew Forum on Religion and Public Life in 2008.[18] The Pew survey was conducted in 2007, with additional subjects added in 2008; it employed telephone survey methodology with a sample of 35,957 participants. We used the results of eight questions from the survey, the responses to which were broken down by state. We transcribed the percent of respondents who endorsed the most conservative religious answer to each of the eight questions. Specifically, we entered the percentages of respondents for each state who endorsed each of the following statements:

1. Belief in a God or universal spirit: Absolutely Certain.
2. There is only one way to interpret the teachings of my religion.
3. Scripture should be taken literally, word for word.
4. How important is religion in your life: Very Important.
5. My religion is the one true faith leading to eternal life.

6. Frequency of attendance at religious services: at least once a week.

7. Frequency of prayer: at least once a day.

8. How often do you receive a definite answer to a specific prayer request: at least once a month.

In the tables published in the Religious Landscapes Survey, the percents reported were aggregated across three pairs of states and across Maryland and the District of Columbia, because the sample size from at least one member of those pairs was fairly small. We obtained from the Pew Forum staff the disaggregated data and used those numbers in our data set. The sample sizes were deemed too small in Wyoming and the District of Columbia for Pew Forum to release them, and thus these data points are missing. For Rhode Island, data were missing on two of the eight questions; we imputed these missing data points by means of regression on the remaining six questions, so that Rhode Island could be included in the data set.

In order to obtain one composite religiosity score for each state, we averaged the percents of respondents endorsing the most religious answer across the eight questions.

The rates of teen birth in the fifty U.S. states plus the District of Columbia were reported by the National Center for Health Statistics at the Centers for Disease Control and Prevention.[19] The data reported were for 2006 births, the latest available (and thus the closest possible in time to the date of the collection of the religiosity data set).

A possible confounding variable in the relationship between teen birthrate and religiosity is household income level. We obtained data on the median household income by state in the U.S. from data published by the U.S. Census Bureau.[20] The median two year average household income for 2006–2007 for each state was entered into our database.

To account for another factor which could complicate the analysis of teen birthrate and religiosity, we estimated the abortion rate among teenagers for each state. The most recent data available on abortion rates were from 2005, published by the Center for Disease Control.[21] These rates were broken down by the states of residence of the women receiving the abortions. In order to estimate rates for abortions delivered to teens only, we multiplied the overall rates by the fraction of abortions delivered to teens for 2005, as published in the same Centers for Disease Control report; these were categorized by the state in which the abortion was delivered. Data were available for 46 states; the District of Columbia, California, Florida, Louisiana, and New Hampshire were missing from this data set. The product of the abortion rate and the fraction of abortions delivered to teens yielded an estimated rate of abortions per 1,000 teenaged females.

The CDC obtains its abortion rates by surveying the Central Health Departments of the various regions. A different approach is used by the Guttmacher Institute, which surveys providers of abortions. We used the Guttmacher data for 2005 to cross-check abortion rates.[22]

Data Analyses

We examined the intercorrelations among the individual religiosity questions to determine whether these were high enough to form an index score. We then formed an index score by averaging the eight religiosity items.

We examined the relationships of the variables with Pearson correlations and partial correlations, as computed by SPSS.[23] The partial correlation between a first and second variable, controlling for the third, is identical to the Pearson correlation between the residuals obtained when each of the first two is regressed upon the third—in other words, when the effect of the third variable is "removed" from each of the first two.[24] We computed 95% confidence intervals for the most important correlations and partial correlations, using the Fisher r-to-z transformation. The variance of the Fisher-transformed correlation is $1/(n-3)$ for bivariate correlations, and $1/(n-k-2)$ for partial correlations, where k is the total number of independent variables (e.g., $k = 2$ for a partial correlation with one variable controlled; $k = 3$ for two variables controlled).[24]

Results

The Justification for Forming an Index from the Pew Religion Items

We examined the 28 intercorrelations among the eight different religiosity variables reported in the Pew Survey. The minimum intercorrelation was 0.55, and the maximum was 0.96. The average intercorrelation was 0.81. Thus the intercorrelation of the religiosity items are high enough to justify making an index score by averaging the scores across the eight items.

The Correlation between Teen Birth Rate and Religiosity

For all the correlational analyses reported below, we examined the plots of residuals for the regressions with the same independent variables and with teen birth as the dependent variable. There was a slight trend toward increasing residuals with increasing values of the dependent variable; in our opinion this trend was not enough to invalidate the linear model, in view of the high correlations obtained and the linear appearance of scatter plots.

Teen birth rate correlated with our composite religiosity variable with $r = 0.73$; 95% CI (0.56, 0.84); $n = 49$; $p < 0.0005$. Thus teen birth rate is very highly correlated with religiosity at the state level, with more religious states having a higher rate of teen birth. A scatter plot of teen birth rate as a function of religiosity is presented in Figure 1.

Controlling for Income and Abortion Rate

Next we considered whether median family income for states could be a confounding variable. Income negatively correlated with teen birth rate, with $r = -0.63$, $n = 51$, $p < 0.0005$. Furthermore, income correlated negatively with religiosity, with $r = -0.66$, $n = 49$; $p < 0.0005$. Thus the direction and magnitude of correlations made income a primary candidate for a confounding variable. However, the partial correlation of teen birth rate with religion while controlling for income was 0.53; 95% CI (0.29, 0.71); $df = 46$; $p < 0.0005$. Thus the correlation between religion and teen birth remained large and highly significant, even when controlling for income. The raw religiosity scores and teen birth scores shared a little over half their variance ($R^2 = 0.53$) whereas these variables with income removed by partialing shared a little over a quarter of their variance ($R^2 = 0.28$).

The correlation between teen abortion rate and religiosity was -0.45; $n = 45$; $p = 0.002$. Thus the teen abortion rate was lower in states that were more religious. Furthermore, teen abortion rate was negatively correlated with teen birth rate, with $r = -0.26$, although this relationship failed significance at the 0.05 level ($n = 47$, $p = 0.078$). Would including abortion rate as a covariate greatly affect the correlation between teen birth and religiosity? The answer turned out to be no. The partial correlation between teen birth rate and religiosity, controlling for abortion rate, was 0.68; 95% CI (0.48, 0.81); $df = 42$; $p < 0.0005$. The partial correlation between teen birth

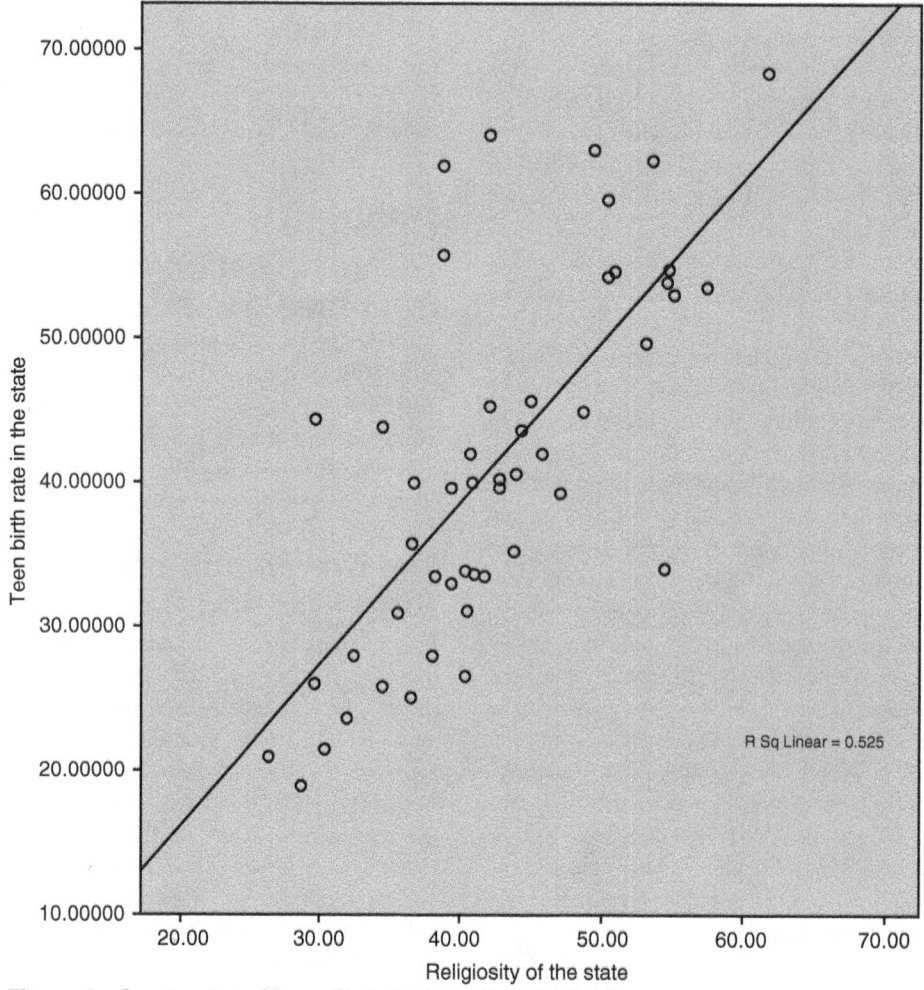

Figure 1   Scatterplot of Teen Birth Rate by Religiosity Score.

Table 1   Correlation or Partial Correlation of Teen Birth Rate with Religiosity with Various Variables Controlled

Variable(s) Controlled	None	Income	Abortion	Income and Abortion
Correlation or Partial Correlation	0.73	0.53	0.68	0.54

and religiosity, controlling for both income and abortion rate, was 0.54; 95% CI (0.29, 0.72); $df = 41$; $p < 0.0005$. Thus, even after taking into account the abortion rate and controlling for income, the correlation between religiosity and teen pregnancy remained high and significant.

Table 1 presents a summary of the four correlations that summarize our findings on the relationship between teen birth and religiosity.

Checks for Robustness

When averaging the results of the eight items of the religiosity survey, one approach would be to first compute the z-scores for each item, and then average the z-scores. Such an approach would assign the same standard deviation to each item, so that items with higher standard deviations did not count more heavily toward the average score. When we checked this "average of standardized religiosity scores," its correlation with the average of the raw percents was 0.999 ($n = 49$, $p < 0.0005$). This result implies that the two measures are interchangeable, and that differences in standard deviations among the eight items do not appreciably influence the distribution of the average religiosity score. We used the raw percents rather than the standardized scores so that the scatterplot would be more intuitively interpretable.

Was there something about the averaging process itself that hid important information or inflated the correlation? To check this, we computed the individual correlation with teen birth rate for each of the eight religiosity items. The results are presented in Table 2.

Averaging of items probably results in a higher reliability, which would be expected to improve the correlation with teen birth; the higher reliability of the average than of the individual items is predicted by the Spearman-Brown formula.[25] However,

each of the items separately reveals a reasonably high correlation with teen birth rate.

We used as the measure of religiosity the percent of respondents replying in the most religious way; how would the conclusion have been affected if we had entered the percent replying in the least religious way? Some of the questions were dichotomies, and thus the correlations for those items would have had the same magnitude with opposite sign. To check a couple of the items that were not dichotomies, we entered the percentages for the least religious response to literal interpretation of scripture and frequency of prayer, and found correlations of −0.91 and −0.90, respectively, between percent most religious and percent least religious. The correlations of teen birth with "irreligiosity" were very similar in absolute value to the correlations with religiosity for those items. The percent who prayed "seldom or never" in the states correlated at −0.67 with teen birth; the percent who felt that scripture was a "book written by men, not the word of God" correlated at −0.63 with teen birth. It appears that alternate scoring mechanisms measuring irreligiosity would yield the same conclusions and would add nothing to our results.

The Guttmacher Institute gathers data on abortion rates by contacting providers of abortions rather than central health agencies. We entered into our data set the Guttmacher abortion rate for women 15–44 for 2005; the correlation of Guttmacher abortion rate (all women) with CDC rate is 0.66 ($n = 47$, $p < 0.005$). Using the Guttmacher abortion rate rather than the CDC rate in our partial correlations made no substantive changes—for example, the partial correlation of teen birth with religiosity controlling for CDC estimated teen abortion rates was 0.68; the partial correlation controlling for Guttmacher estimated teen abortion rates (obtained by multiplying overall Guttmacher abortion rates by the fraction of abortions obtained by teens according to CDC data) was 0.65.

Table 2   Correlations of Teen Birth Rate with Individual Religiosity Items

Item	Belief God	One Interp.	Literal Scripture	Import. For Life	One True Faith	Attend Services	Frequent Prayer	Prayers Answered
Correlation	0.67	0.68	0.72	0.70	0.56	0.53	0.71	0.74

The variation among the fraction of teen abortion rates in different states was small enough that it made little difference for the partial correlations whether we used estimated teen abortion rates or the overall abortion rates for women in the state. The partial correlation of teen birth with religiosity, partialling out CDC abortion rates for all women was 0.69; the same partial correlation using overall rates reported by Guttmacher was 0.70. Estimated teen abortions correlated with overall abortions for the state with $r = 0.97$ for CDC rates and $r = 0.99$ for Guttmacher rates.

To what extent is the main finding reported here, i.e., the correlation between teen birth and religiosity, dependent upon any one state? Inspection of the scatterplot reveals no major outliers; two influential points appear to be those for Mississippi and Utah. Mississippi, as the state both highest in religiosity and teen birth, tends to increase the correlation; however if the correlation is recomputed without Mississippi, the correlation remains in the same region, with $r = 0.69$. Utah, which is high in religiosity but in the mid-range for teen birth, tends to decrease the correlation; with Utah (but not Mississippi) eliminated, the correlation between teen birth rate and religiosity would have been 0.76. For Rhode Island, we used imputation to estimate the two out of eight items that were missing; had we simply made Rhode Island a missing data point, the correlation between teen birth and religiosity would have been 0.72. Thus the magnitude of the correlation we report appears not to be greatly altered by the elimination of any one state.

Discussion

At the state level in the U.S., religiosity, as operationally defined by the eight questions of the Pew Survey, accurately predicts a high teen birth rate. The significant and high correlation continues to hold after statistically controlling for income and abortion rate.

It is a statistical maxim that higher correlations are to be found using aggregated data, for example, state averages, than with individual level data. This is because some of the noise at the individual level is cancelled by the aggregation process, allowing the relationship between signals to be more clear. As stated in an introductory statistics text, "Correlations based on averages are usually too high when applied to individuals."[26] Nonetheless, the magnitude of the correlation between religiosity and teen birth rate astonished us. Teen birth is more highly correlated with some of the religiosity items than some of those items are correlated with each other. We would like to emphasize that we are not attempting to use associations between teen birth rate and religiosity, using data aggregated at the state level, to make inferences at the individual level.

It would be a statistical and logical error to infer from our results, "Religious teens get pregnant more often." Such an inference would be an example of the ecological fallacy, which was explicated by Robinson in 1950[27] and reviewed by Freedman in 2001.[28] The associations we report could still be obtained if, hypothetically, religiosity in communities had an effect of discouraging contraceptive use in the whole community, including the nonreligious teens there, and only the nonreligious teens became pregnant. Or, to create a different imaginary scenario, the results could be obtained if religious parents discouraged contraceptive use in their children, but only nonreligious offspring of such religious parents got pregnant. We create these scenarios simply to illustrate that our ecological correlations do not permit statements about individuals.

We should also caution that on an individual level, certain teen pregnancies are often highly desirable, and some teen parents carry out their responsibilities exceptionally well. If it were possible to obtain good data on unplanned teen pregnancy or pregnancy by "immature" teen parents, we would use it, but we did not find such data available. Nonetheless, at the aggregate level, it is probably true that public policies or cultural practices that reduce the overall rate of teen births are, other things equal, desirable.

Our findings by themselves, of course, do not permit causal inferences. There could be unstudied confounding variables that account for the correlations we report. But if we may speculate on the most probable explanation, drawing on the other research cited above: we conjecture that conservative religious communities in the U.S. are more successful in discouraging use of contraception among their teen community members than in discouraging sexual intercourse itself.

Conclusion

At the level of states in the U.S., conservative religious beliefs predict teen birth rates highly and significantly; the correlation remains high and significant after controlling for income and estimated rates of abortion.

Competing Interests

The authors declare that they have no competing interests.

Authors' Contributions

The study was conceived by JMS, who also retrieved the data sets for the analyses. The authors shared the tasks of data entry, organization of the data, statistical analyses, and preparation of the manuscript. Both approved the final manuscript.

Notes

Hoffman SD, Maynard RA: *Kids Having Kids: Economic Costs and Social Consequences of Teen Pregnancy* 2nd edition. Washington, D.C., Urban Institute Press; 2008.

National Public Radio, Kaiser Family Foundation, Harvard University Kennedy School of Government: Sex Education in America. [www.npr.org/templates/story/story.php?storyId=1622610].

Eisenberg ME, Bernat DH, Bearinger LH, Resnick MD: Support for comprehensive sexuality education: Perspectives from parents of school-aged youth. *J Adolescent Health* 2008, 42:352–359.

Hardy SA, Raffaelli M: Adolescent religiosity and sexuality: an investigation of reciprocal influences. *Journal of Adolescents* 2003, 26:731–739.

Louri L: Teen child bearing and community religiosity. 2004 [http://ase.tufts.edu/econ]. Working Paper, Department of Economics, Tufts University.

McCree DH, Wingood GM, DiClemente R, Davies S, Harrington KF: Religiosity and risky sexual behavior in African-American adolescent females. *Journal of Adolescent Health* 2003, 33:2–8.

Rostosky SS, Regnerus MD, Wright MLC: Coital debut: the role of religiosity and sex attitudes in the add health survey. *Journal of Sex Research* 2003, 40:358–367.

Miller L, Gur M: Religiousness and sexual responsibility in adolescent girls. *Journal of Adolescent Health* 2002, 31:401–406.

Manlove J, Logan C, Moore KA, Ikramullah E: Pathways from family religiosity to adolescent sexual activity and contraceptive use. *Perspectives on Sexual and Reproductive Health* 2008, 40:105–117.

Studer M, Thornton A: Adolescent religiosity and contraceptive usage. *Journal of Marriage & the Family* 1987, 49:117–128.

Dodge B, Sandfort TGM, Yarber WL, de Wit J: Sexual health among male college students in the United States and the Netherlands. *American Journal of Health Behavior* 2005, 29:172–182.

Rosenbaum JE: Patient teenagers? A comparison of the sexual behavior of virginity pledgers and matched nonpledgers. *Pediatrics* 2009, 123:110–120.

Santelli JS, Lindberg LD, Finer LB, Singh S: Explaining recent declines in adolescent pregnancy in the United States: the contribution of abstinence and improved contraceptive use. *Am J Public Health* 2007, 97:150–156.

Santelli JS, Orr M, Lindberg LD, Diaz DC: Changing behavioral risk for pregnancy among high school students in the United States, 1991–2007. *J Adolescent Health* 2009, 45:25–32.

Adamczyk A, Felson J: Fetal positions: Unraveling the influence of religion on premarital pregnancy resolution. *Social Science Quarterly* 2008, 89:17–38.

Tomal A: The effect of religious membership on teen abortion rates. *Journal of Youth and Adolescence* 2001, 30:103–116.

Cahn N, Carbone J: Red families v. blue families (August 16, 2007). [http://ssrn.com/abstract=1008544]. GWU Legal Studies Research Paper No. 343; GWU Law School Public Law Research Paper No. 343. Available at SSRN.

Pew Forum on Religion and Public Life. U.S. Religious Landscape Survey: Religious Beliefs and Practices: Diverse and Politically Relevant. Washington, D.C.: Author; 2008.

Martin JA, Hamilton BE, Sutton PD, Ventura SJ, Menacker F, Kirmeyer S, Mathews TJ: Births: final data for 2006. In *National Vital Statistics Reports Volume 57*. Issue 7. Hyattsville, MD: National Center for Health Statistics; 2009.

U.S. Bureau of the Census: *Two-year-average median household income by state: 2004 to 2007* [www.census.gov/hhes/www/income/income07/statemhi2.xls].

Gamble SB, Strauss LT, Parker WY, Cook DA, Zane SB, Hamdan S: Abortion Surveillance—United States, 2005. *Morbidity and Mortality Weekly Report* 2008, 57:1–32.

Jones RK, Zolna MRS, Henshaw SK, Finer LB: Abortion in the United States: Incidence and access to services. *Perspectives on Sexual and Reproductive Health* 2008, 40:6–16.

SPSS, Inc: *SPSS 16.0 for Windows, release 16.0.0.* Chicago, Author 2007.

Cohen J, Cohen P: Applied multiple regression/correlation analysis for the behavioral sciences. In *Hillsdale, NJ,* Second edition. Lawrence Erlbaum Associates; 1983.

Nunnally JM: *Psychometric Theory* Second edition. New York, McGraw-Hill; 1978.

Yates DS, Moore DS, Starnes DS: *The Practice of Statistics* Second edition: New York: W.H. Freeman; 2003:230.

Robinson WS: Ecological correlations and the behavior of individuals. *American Sociological Review* 1950, 15:351–357.

Freedman DA: Ecological inference and the ecological fallacy. In *International Encyclopedia of the Social & Behavioral Sciences Volume 6*. Edited by: Smelser N, Baltes P. Philadelphia: Elsevier; 2001:4027–4030.

Critical Thinking

1. How did the researchers measure religiosity?
2. What is the relationship between teen birth rate and religiosity in the United States?
3. How does religiosity impact abortion numbers?

Internet References

Catholics for Choice
http://www.catholicsforchoice.org

The Faith and Sexuality Project
http://faithandsexuality.co.uk

Religious Institute
http://www.religiousinstitute.org

Article

Prepared by: Elizabeth Schroeder, EdD, MSW,
Elizabeth Schroeder Consulting

What Is Behind the Declines in Teen Pregnancy Rates?

HEATHER D. BOONSTRA

Learning Outcomes

After reading this article, you will be able to:

- List at least two facts about current teen pregnancy rates in the United States.

- Provide at least two reasons why, according to the author, teen pregnancy rates have gone down.

- Describe a potential impact that the AIDS crisis has had since the early 1990s on reducing teen pregnancy rates.

The progress the nation has made over the last few decades in reducing teen pregnancy has been extraordinary. After years of increases in the 1970s and 1980s, the teen pregnancy rate peaked in 1990 and has declined steadily since.[1] Today, teen pregnancy, birth and abortion rates have reached historic lows. What is more, teen pregnancy rates have fallen in all 50 states and among all racial and ethnic groups.

Basically, teen pregnancy rates can decrease in one of two ways—if teens have less sex or become more effective contraceptive users—or through some combination of the two. The evidence clearly indicates that more and better contraceptive use has been the main factor driving the long-term decline in teen pregnancy. The evidence, however, is much murkier when it comes to deciphering the social, cultural and economic factors affecting teens' sexual behaviors and contraceptive use patterns. Deconstructing why teen pregnancy rates have fallen over the last several decades nonetheless matters, so that future programs, policies and practices can be shaped to help advance—rather than hinder—these positive trends.

The Declines

In 2010, some 614,000 U.S. teens became pregnant (which translates to a rate of 57 pregnancies per 1,000 women aged 15–19).[1] The overwhelming majority—82%—reported that their pregnancy was unplanned.[2] Put another way, about 6% of adolescents in the United States became pregnant in 2010.[1] This marks a 51% decline in U.S. teen pregnancy from a peak in 1990, including a 15% drop between 2008 and 2010. Similarly, the country's teen birthrate declined 44% from a peak in 1991 and its teen abortion rate declined 66% from a 1988 peak (see chart, Heading Down).

The teen pregnancy rate has declined not only for the nation as a whole, but also for every state. Between 1992 and 2010, state decreases ranged from 25% in West Virginia to 62% in California. Yet, substantial disparities remain among states: Maine, Massachusetts, Minnesota, New Hampshire and Vermont have consistently had the lowest teen pregnancy rates (28–37 per 1,000 in 2010), whereas Arkansas, Louisiana, Mississippi, New Mexico, Oklahoma and Texas have had the highest (69–80 per 1,000).

The decline in teenage pregnancy crosses racial and ethnic groups. Since the early 1990s, the rate has dropped 56% among both black and white teens, and by 51% among Hispanic teens. Nonetheless, wide disparities in pregnancy rates by race and ethnicity persist, with rates among both black and Hispanic teens remaining twice as high as among their non-Hispanic white peers.

The majority of teen pregnancies (69%) occur among 18–19-year-olds, which is hardly surprising given that they make up the majority of sexually active teens. Very few 14-year-olds have ever had sex (and intercourse among very young adolescents is frequently involuntary).[3] But adolescence is a time

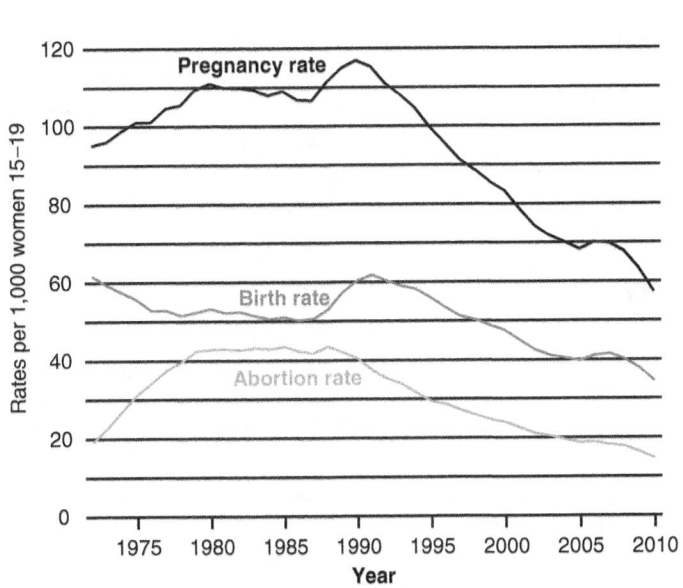

U.S. teen pregnancy, birth and abortion rates have reached historic lows.

Source: reference 1.

of rapid change, and consensual sexual activity is common by the late teen years. For women coming of age in the mid-2000s, the median age at first sex was 17.8 years.[4] In 2010, the pregnancy rate among 18–19-year-olds was 96 per 1,000, while the rate among 15–17-yearolds was 30 per 1,000.[1]

More recent data are available for teen birthrates than for teen pregnancy rates, and those data show that the decline in teen births has continued: It dropped 10% from 2012 to 2013, to 27 per 1,000—the lowest rate ever reported for the United States.[5] Although data for the same time period are not yet available for abortions (and therefore pregnancies), these numbers suggest that teen pregnancy rates may very well have continued their long-term declines as well.

Explaining the Declines

What is behind the downward trend in teen pregnancy rates? On one level, the answer is simple: Pregnancy rates have fallen either because teens are having less sex in the first place or because more teens who are sexually active are using contraceptives and using them more effectively. Researchers have analyzed the role of both over the last several decades, and they have concluded that the declines can primarily—although not exclusively—be attributed to improvements in teens' contraceptive use.

The 1995–2002 Period

In 2007, researchers from the Guttmacher Institute and Columbia University examined data from two rounds of a large-scale

government survey, the 1995 and 2002 cycles of the National Survey of Family Growth (NSFG). The researchers concluded that the vast majority of the decline in teen pregnancy—86%—was the result of improvements in contraceptive use, including increases in the use of individual methods, an increase in the use of multiple methods and a substantial decline in nonuse.[6] The remaining 14% of the decline could be attributed to a decrease in sexual activity.

When broken down by age, the decline in teen pregnancy among 18–19-year-olds was entirely attributable to improved contraceptive use, because the overall proportions who had ever had sex or were engaging in sexual activity did not change between 1995 and 2002. Delaying first sex played a greater role for younger teens, accounting for 23% of the decline in pregnancy among 15–17-year-olds.

The 2003–2010 Period

In 2014, Guttmacher researchers analyzed subsequent cycles of NSFG data and found that the decline in teen pregnancy since 2003 had little or nothing to do with teens' delaying sex.[7] Nationwide, the proportion of teens who had ever had sex did not change significantly between 2003 and 2010 (46% and 45%, respectively). This finding is supported by another largescale study, the Centers for Disease Control and Prevention's (CDC's) Youth Risk Behavior Survey (YRBS). Although limited to adolescents in school-based settings (in grades 9–12), the YRBS found no significant change in the overall proportion of students who were sexually experienced or currently engaging in sexual activity between 2001 and 2013.[8]

Instead, the decline in teen pregnancy in recent years can be linked to improvements in teens' contraceptive use. Comparing reports from two periods of NSFG data (mid-2006 to mid-2008 and mid-2008 to mid-2010), Guttmacher researchers found moderate increases in teens' use of any contraceptive method, highly effective methods and dual methods (i.e., condoms and hormonal methods simultaneously).[9] Specifically, the use of hormonal contraceptives at last sex among sexually active women aged 15–19 increased from 37% in 2006–2008 to 47% in 2008–2010; dual method use increased from 16% to 23% over the period, and the use of long-acting reversible contraceptive methods (i.e., the IUD and implant) increased from 1.4% to 4.4%.

Moreover, between mid-2008 and mid-2010, increasing proportions of 18–19-year-olds reported having ever had sex, and yet fewer of them became pregnant. The likely reason, again, is improved contraceptive use.

2011 to the Present

Since 2010, the only data available on trends in sexual experience and contraceptive use are from the YRBS, and they indicate that there was no change between 2011 and 2013 in the prevalence of sexual activity or contraceptive use among teens.[8] But the YRBS tracks progress only among adolescents in school; data on all adolescents, from the initial years of the 2011–2015 NSFG, are expected to be released later this year, and only then will researchers be able to provide more detailed analyses to explain the most recent trends in teen births.

Behind the Behavior

The recent trends in sexual experience and contraceptive use are clear enough, but understanding what is driving these behaviors is more of a challenge. Advocates often credit education programs for the positive trends. The quality and quantity of evaluation research have improved dramatically over the last decade, and there is now clear evidence that comprehensive sex education programs can change the behaviors that put young people at risk of pregnancy.[10] Such programs have been shown to delay sexual debut, reduce frequency of sex and number of partners, increase condom or contraceptive use, or reduce sexual risk-taking. By contrast, programs that exclusively promote abstinence outside of marriage have been proven ineffective at stopping or even delaying sex.[11,12]

And yet, researchers say it is not realistic to expect that an education program alone will change behaviors enough to have a measurable impact on pregnancy rates.[10] For one thing, these interventions are modest. According to the CDC, middle school classes containing pregnancy prevention education include a median total of only three hours on the topic; high school classes are not much better, dedicating only four hours.[13] Moreover, because so few program participants become pregnant, most studies simply are not large enough to detect the impact of programs on pregnancy rates.[10]

Researchers, therefore, have considered other contextual factors that may explain the drop in rates, and the recent trends in sexual activity and contraceptive use that underlie them.

Structural Factors

Although it may be difficult to prove a causal link, it is widely recognized that economic inequality, social marginalization and other structural factors affect teens' sexual behavior and contraceptive use patterns. But just how these behaviors are linked with teens' race or ethnicity, educational achievements or family income is difficult to sort out.

These relationships also travel in multiple directions. For instance, an adolescent who has a child is likely to have a hard time finishing high school, which is often followed by decreased economic opportunities and earnings in future years.[14] But living in poverty or having a low level of education could also increase the risk that a young woman will become pregnant in the first place.

Researchers have considered whether the changing demographic makeup of the nation may be contributing to the trends

in teen pregnancy and birth rates. Whereas the age composition of the teenage population has been roughly consistent since the early 1990s, the racial and ethnic composition has changed.[15] Latina adolescents—a group with high rates of pregnancy and births—make up an increasing share of the teenage population. All else held constant, therefore, researchers would have expected substantial increases in the teen pregnancy and birth rates, rather than declines. That makes the decreases even more of a puzzle.

The Economy

Related to the effects of long-standing social inequalities, researchers have also considered whether the nation's economy or labor market conditions may have contributed to fewer pregnancies and births among teens. The 1990s were a period of economic growth, which was followed by a brief recession in the early 2000s and a more serious economic crisis from 2007 to 2009. Considering that teen pregnancy has been consistently declining despite fluctuations in the economy, it appears that the economy may not be a major driver behind the drop in rates. Investigators have found that many adult women postpone childbearing during periods of economic downturn, when there are fewer job opportunities and increased competition for those jobs that are available.[16] But whether teens are affected by these downturns is less clear. Little research has focused on the economy's impact on adolescents' contraceptive use and childbearing decisions, and the scant research that does exist

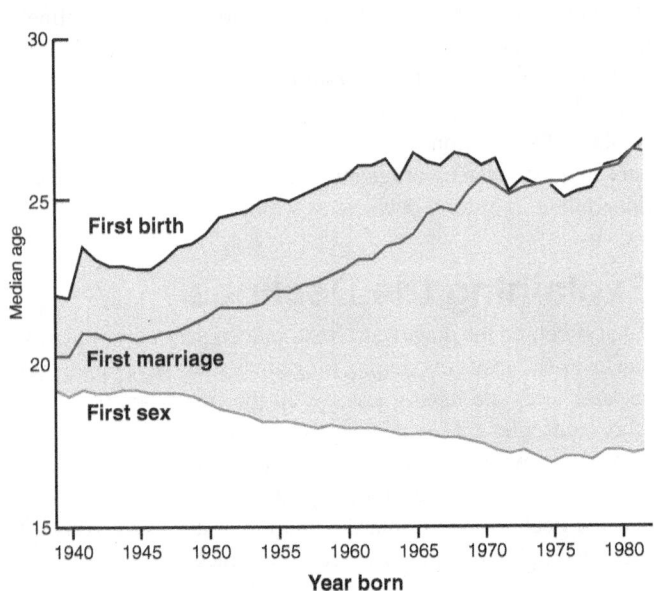

An American woman's age at first sex has changed little over time, but she is now getting married later and having children later.

Source: reference 4.

suggests that the economy may affect the reproductive behavior of some groups, such as older African American teens, but not others.[15,17,18]

The AIDS Crisis

Experts point to the AIDS crisis in America and the impact of AIDS education programs over the past several decades as having played a role in persuading more teens to use condoms. In the early 1990s, a handful of highly visible people living with HIV—such as sports figure Magic Johnson, mother and activist Elizabeth Glaser, and teenager Ryan White—helped raise public awareness of HIV, and of the need for AIDS research and public education to address the epidemic. Concerns about AIDS led to changes in perceptions about condoms and increases in condom use.[19] According to data from the NSFG, condom use at last sex among females aged 15–19 increased from 38% in 1995 to 52% in 2006–2010; among males, condom use at last sex increased steadily, from 64% in 1995 to 75% in 2006–2010.[20]

Childbearing Norms

Changing social attitudes and family norms may also be contributing to the trend in teen pregnancy. While the median age at first sex has changed little over time, American women are getting married later and putting off having children (see chart, Greater Gap).[4] Many experts believe that adolescents may be mirroring what they see in their own families and their friends' families, and waiting until later to have children.[21] In other words, the decline in teen pregnancy may be just one manifestation of a larger shift in fertility patterns in this country. Declines in pregnancy among teens parallel those among 20–24-year-olds, suggesting that later childbearing may be the "new normal" for adolescents, as well as for young adults.

The Media

Messages in the media about sex, abstinence, contraceptive use and teen childbearing may also be having an influence. Internet usage has grown rapidly since the mid-1990s. In 2013, 93% of teens had a computer or access to one at home; 78% had a cell phone, half of which were smartphones.[22] The Internet has become an important source for health information, including information about sex and birth control,[23] and many Web sites also allow young people to ask questions that they might otherwise feel uncomfortable broaching in class or with friends and family members. More traditional media sources, such as television and magazines, are also important sources of information. For example, there is evidence that the reality television programs "16 and Pregnant" and "Teen Mom" may have influenced teen birthrates in recent years: According to one analysis, Internet search activity and tweets about sex, birth control

and abortion increased substantially right around the time that new episodes aired.[24] The authors connect this activity to much of the recent declines in teen births. Although establishing a causal relationship is challenging, teens' interest in these topics suggests that media exposure might be playing a role in their behaviors.

Medical Recommendations

Anecdotal reports indicate that recent changes in medical practice have made it easier for adolescents to start and continue using hormonal methods. It used to be that a routine pelvic examination was required before prescribing hormonal methods. In the early 2000s, however, that began to change, as the standard of care regarding Pap tests and pelvic examinations shifted.[25] Around that time, various medical groups—from the World Health Organization (WHO) to the American Cancer Society to the American College of Obstetricians and Gynecologists (ACOG)— updated their clinical recommendations to enable teens and young women to access hormonal contraceptives more quickly and easily without a pelvic exam or Pap test.

Additionally, the medical establishment's thinking around the use of IUDs has changed in recent years. In the past, standard medical practice discouraged use of these long-acting methods for adolescents, because of concerns about the risk of infection and the fit of the IUD in young patients. Armed with new evidence, however, the CDC and ACOG each adopted guidelines recommending the IUD as a "first-line" option for sexually active adolescents who want to delay childbearing for several years.[26,27] Since 2002, IUD use among teens has increased nationwide.[9] Although the proportion of teens using the IUD is still small, the impact could be significant: The IUD is 45 times as effective as oral contraceptives in preventing pregnancy, based on typical use, and 90 times as effective as male condoms.[28]

Policy Implications

Understanding why teen pregnancy rates have fallen goes to the heart of a number of relevant and timely public policy questions. There are many complex societal forces that may help explain the drop in teen pregnancy, birth and abortion rates—and the sexual behaviors and contraceptive use patterns that underlie them. The relative contributions of these factors are difficult to sort out, however, because they affect different groups of teens differently and the relationships go in multiple directions. Although additional research might shed more light on what is motivating teens to alter their behavior, what is clear is that adolescents today are seeking and taking more responsibility for themselves. And the appropriate public policy response is to expand their access to the information and services they want and need.

All adolescents, for example, need sex education that teaches them the skills they need to delay sexual initiation, while also preparing them with the information and skills needed to protect themselves and their partners when they do become sexually active. And they need this before they begin to have sex.

Across the nation, sex education policy is far from a settled issue. By the end of the Bush administration, the era of abstinence-only education—a decade or so during which the federal and state governments spent well over $1.5 billion on education programs focused solely on promoting abstinence[29]—appeared to be over. But proponents of abstinence-only education continue to rigorously press their case. In 2014, Congress provided $55 million for abstinenceuntil-marriage programs. At the request of the Obama administration, Congress also provided roughly $185 million for medically accurate and age-appropriate sex education programs.

Debates over what kind of information teens should get in schools have been playing out in state governments as well. Today, 35 states and the District of Columbia require that public schools provide some form of sex or STI/HIV education.[30] And most states also place requirements on how abstinence or contraception should be handled when included in a school district's curriculum, even when the instruction is not mandated. Currently, this guidance is heavily weighted toward stressing abstinence, and 19 states require that instruction on the importance of engaging in sexual activity only within marriage be provided. By contrast, although many states allow or even require that information about contraception be covered, none require that it be stressed.

Additionally, adolescents who are sexually active need easy access to contraceptive services. Expansions in public and private health insurance under the Affordable Care Act mean that more teens are gaining coverage for contraceptive services. Nevertheless, publicly supported family planning centers continue to play an especially important role for teens, in part because of their promise of confidentiality for all their clients. In 2010, these health centers served nearly 1.5 million teens and helped teens prevent 360,000 unintended pregnancies; 190,000 of these would have resulted in unplanned births and 110,000 in abortions.[31]

At the end of the day, the credit for the declines in teen pregnancy goes to adolescents themselves, who are making an effort to prevent unintended pregnancy. The question now is whether society will do its part by adopting policies that support and equip young people with knowledge, skills and services to stay healthy. The research shows that adolescents need more comprehensive education, not less, and increased access to contraceptive services, not less. To argue anything else misses an opportunity to sustain these trends. www.guttmacher.org

Notes

1. Kost K and Henshaw S, *U.S. Teenage Pregnancies, Births and Abortions, 2010: National and State Trends by Age, Race and Ethnicity,* New York: Guttmacher Institute, 2014, http://www.guttmacher.org/pubs/USTPtrends10.pdf accessed Aug. 20, 2014.

2. Finer LB and Zolna MR, Shifts in intended and unintended pregnancies in the United States, 2001–2008, *American Journal of Public Health,* 2014, 104(S1):S43–S48.

3. Finer LB and Philbin JM, Sexual initiation, contraceptive use, and pregnancy among young adolescents, *Pediatrics,* 2013, 131(5):886– 891.

4. Finer LB and Philbin JM, Trends in ages at key reproductive transitions in the United States, 1951–2010, *Women's Health Issues,* 2014, 24(3):e271–e279.

5. Hamilton BE et al., Births: preliminary data for 2013, *National Vital Statistics Reports,* 2014, Vol. 63, No. 2, http://www.cdc.gov/nchs/data/nvsr/nvsr63/nvsr63_02.pdf, accessed Aug. 20, 2014.

6. Santelli JS et al., Explaining recent declines in adolescent pregnancy in the United States: the contribution of abstinence and improved contraceptive use, *American Journal of Public Health,* 2007, 97(1):150–156.

7. Guttmacher Institute, Unpublished tabulations of data from the National Survey of Family Growth, 2014.

8. Kann L et al., Youth Risk Behavior Surveillance—United States, 2013, *MMWR,* 2014, 63(4):1–168, http://www.cdc.gov/mmwr/pdf/ ss/ss6304.pdf, accessed Aug. 20, 2014.

9. Guttmacher Institute, New government data finds sharp decline in teen births: increased contraceptive use and shifts to more effective contraceptive methods behind this encouraging trend, news in context, Dec. 1, 2011, http://www.guttmacher.org/media/ inthenews/2011/12/01/index.html, accessed Aug. 20, 2014.

10. United Nations Educational, Scientific and Cultural Organization (UNESCO), *International Technical Guidance on Sexuality Education: An Evidence-Informed Approach for Schools, Teachers and Health Educators,* Paris: UNESCO, 2009, http://unesdoc.unesco.org/ images/0018/001832/183281e .pdf, accessed Aug. 20, 2014.

11. Underhill K, Montgomery P and Operario D, Sexual abstinence only programmes to prevent HIV infection in high income countries: systematic review, *BMJ,* 2007, 335(7613):248–252.

12. Kirby DB, The impact of abstinence and comprehensive sex and STD/HIV education programs on adolescent sexual behavior, *Sexuality Research & Social Policy,* 2008, 5(3):18–27.

13. Kann L, Telljohann SK and Wooley SF, Health education: results from the School Health Policies and Programs Study 2006, *Journal of School Health,* 2007, 77(8):408–434.

14. Ng AS and Kaye K, *Why It Matters: Teen Childbearing, Education, and Economic Wellbeing,* Washington, DC: The National Campaign to Prevent Teen and Unplanned Pregnancy, 2012, http://thenationalcampaign.org/sites/default/files/resource-primary-download/childbearing-education -economicwellbeing.pdf, accessed Aug. 20, 2014.

15. Kearney MS and Levine PB, Explaining recent trends in the U.S. teen birth rate, *NBER Working Paper,* 2012, No. 17964.

16. Guttmacher Institute, *A Real-Time Look at the Impact of the Recession on Women's Family Planning and Pregnancy Decisions,* New York: Guttmacher Institute, 2009, http://www.guttmacher.org/ pubs/RecessionFP.pdf, accessed Aug. 20, 2014.

17. Ananat EO, Gassman-Pines A and Gibson-Davis C, Communitywide job loss and teenage fertility: evidence from North Carolina, *Demography,* 2013, 50(6):2151–2171.

18. Colen CG, Geronimus AT and Phipps MG, Getting a piece of the pie? The economic boom of the 1990s and declining teen birth rates in the United States, *Social Science & Medicine,* 2006, 63(6):1531–1545.

19. Mosher WD and Bachrach CA, Understanding U.S. fertility: continuity and change in the National Survey of Family Growth, 1988–1995, *Family Planning Perspectives,* 1996, 28(1):4–12.

20. Martinez G, Copen CE and Abma JC, Teenagers in the United States: sexual activity, contraceptive use, and childbearing, 2006–2010 National Survey of Family Growth, *Vital and Health Statistics,* 2011, Series 23, No. 31, http://www.cdc.gov/nchs/data/series/sr_23/ sr23_031.pdf accessed Aug. 20, 2014.

21. Axinn WG, Clarkberg ME and Thornton A, Family influences on family size preferences, *Demography,* 1994, 31(1):65–79.

22. Madden M et al., *Teens and Technology 2013,* Washington, DC: Pew Research Center and Cambridge, MA: Berkman Center for Internet & Society at Harvard University, 2013, http://www.pewinternet.org/files/old-media//Files/Reports/2013/PIP_TeensandTechnology2013.pdf, accessed Aug. 20, 2014.

23. Fox S and Duggan M, *Health Online 2013,* Washington, DC: Pew Research Center and Sacramento, CA: California Healthcare Foundation, 2013, http://www.pewinternet.org/files/old-media//Files/Reports/PIP_HealthOnline.pdf, accessed Aug. 20, 2014.

24. Kearney MS and Levine PB, Media Influences on social outcomes: the impact of MTV's 16 and Pregnant on teen childbearing, *NBER Working Paper,* 2014, No. 19795.

25. Westhoff CL, Jones HE and Guiahi M, Do new guidelines and technology make the routine pelvic examination obsolete? *Journal of Women's Health,* 2011, 20(1):5–10.

26. American College of Obstetricians and Gynecologists, Committee on Adolescent Health Care, Long-Acting Reversible Contraception Working Group, Committee opinion no. 539: adolescents and long-acting reversible contraception: implants and intrauterine devices, *Obstetrics & Gynecology,* 2012, 120(4):983–988.

27. Centers for Disease Control and Prevention, U.S. selected practice recommendations for contraceptive use, 2013, *Morbidity and Mortality Weekly Report,* 2013, 62(5):1–60, http://www.cdc.gov/ mmwr/pdf/rr/rr62e0614.pdf, accessed Aug. 20, 2014.

28. Brief of the Guttmacher Institute and Professor Sara Rosenbaum as *Amici Curiae* in Support of the Government, *Kathleen Sebelius v. Hobby Lobby Stores, Inc* and *Conestoga Wood Specialties Corporation v. Kathleen Sebelius,* Nos. 13-354 & 13-356, http://www.guttmacher.org/media/guttmacher_scotus_amicus_brief.pdf, accessed Aug. 18, 2014.

29. SIECUS, What the research says: abstinence-only-until-marriage programs, fact sheet, 2009, http://www.siecus.org/index.cfm?fuseaction=Page.ViewPage&PageID=1195, accessed Aug. 20, 2014.

30. Guttmacher Institute, Sex and HIV education, *State Policies in Brief (as of August 1, 2014),* 2014, http://www.guttmacher.org/statecenter/spibs/spib_SE.pdf, accessed Aug. 20, 2014.

31. Frost JJ, Zolna MR and Frohwirth L, *Contraceptive Needs and Services, 2010,* New York: Guttmacher Institute, 2013, http://www.guttmacher.org/pubs/win/contraceptive-needs-2010.pdf, accessed Aug. 20, 2014.

Critical Thinking

1. What are some reasons why teens might choose to become pregnant or cause a pregnancy?

2. What would you imagine the challenges to being a parent as a teenager might be? On what would that depend?

3. People often discuss the impact of the media on our behaviors, sexual and otherwise. How much of an impact do you think shows like "16 and Pregnant"—or the lack of shows or movies relating to the topic—have on teen pregnancy?

Internet References

The Guttmacher Institute
http://www.guttmacher.org

National Campaign to Prevent Teen and Unplanned Pregnancy
http://thenationalcampaign.org

Office of Adolescent Health
http://www.hhs.gov/ash/oah

HEATHER BOONSTRA is the Director of Public Policy in the Guttmacher Institute's Washington, DC, office and is responsible for promoting the Institute's sexual and reproductive health agenda in federal law and policy. Ms. Boonstra is a regular contributor to the Institute's policy journal, the *Guttmacher Policy Review*, and oversees a portfolio of projects on abortion, adolescent sexual and reproductive health, and the integration of family planning, and HIV services in the United States and globally. Ms. Boonstra came to Guttmacher in 1999 as a Senior Public Policy Associate, after working with the Reproductive Health Technologies Project and as a consultant with the Center for International Health and Information, Save the Children, and the Pacific Institute for Women's Health.

Prepared by: Elizabeth Schroeder, EdD, MSW,
Elizabeth Schroeder Consulting

Article

Role Reversal

Amid bruised egos, resentments and confusion, families are struggling to find their footing as they cope with the financial, emotional and who-does-the-dishes-now restructuring of their lives brought on by the recession.

SARA ECKEL

Learning Outcomes

After reading this article, you will be able to:

- Describe the potential impacts of gender role reversals in different-sex relationships on relationship dynamics.

- List at least three ways in which same-sex couples deal with the issues described in the article facing different-sex couples.

- Explain why certain household responsibilities have historically been gendered and why some members of society still care about those rigid, stereotypical roles.

O n a cold, rainy November morning, Christine Fruehwirth's 5-year-old son showed up at preschool without a coat—or even a sweater. "The sweater was dirty," says Christine's husband, John. He also had taken their 7-year-old daughter out to run errands in the ballerina pajamas she'd slept in. "I didn't know. I thought it was an outfit," John says of the wardrobe mishap, one of several that have occurred since he took over many of the household and child-care duties two years ago. That's when he lost his job as the managing director of a Washington, DC, private equity firm. To support their family of five, Christine began working part-time as a career consultant for George Washington University in addition to the career-coaching business she was already running out of their home.

Like many families coping with the turmoil brought on by the recession, the Fruehwirths have been fumbling to find their footing now that the roles of family breadwinner and household caretaker have been shuffled around. Though Christine, 40, had planned to work while her three kids were young, she was

thinking one job, not two. But now she says, "Maybe this was meant to be." She's appreciating the chance to further develop her professional life. And although John is adamant that he's *not* a stay-at-home dad—he's developing a private equity company he purchased with his severance pay—he's enjoying extra time with the kids now that he's the one taking them to and from school and helping them with homework.

With job loss comes heightened anxiety, as well as recast parental and household duties, causing a major upheaval in many families. Working moms are increasingly logging extra hours in the office—and spending more time away from their children—while more men are finding themselves without an office to go to. Getting the bills paid and cutting back on nonessential spending is a strain for sure. Yet for many, the greatest challenge hasn't been financial; it's been psychological. Amid all the changes, moms and dads are trying to adjust not only to new daily schedules but also to bruised egos and growing resentments. We talked to couples about how their families are coping with this shift—and learned what they're doing to keep the peace.

Shattered Self-esteem

After Stefania Sorace Smith's husband lost his security job last May, she landed a higher-paying position in her profession, as the residential programmer at a home for mentally disabled people. But she also doubled her commuting time, and her workweek soared to 60 hours from 40—a particular strain since she's now pregnant with the couple's second child. Even with her higher salary and the part-time work her husband, Darren, has secured, the Dingman's Ferry, PA, couple has not made up the lost income. Now charged with the family's financial security, Stefania, 26, is more stressed than ever. "Bills definitely get behind," she says, adding that she sometimes plays "Russian roulette" with her checkbook by alternating which bills she pays—and which she skips—each month. At home, Darren is doing more of the basic cleaning, and he makes their 2-year-old daughter breakfast and prepares dinner for the family—but the major scrub work still falls to Stefania because he "just doesn't do it the way I want it done," she says.

For Stefania, one of the biggest disparities in this new structure is free time. She spends most of her day working and commuting. Darren—while doing handyman work and pitching in with the household chores—still spends a fair amount of time playing Flight Simulator on his computer. "This transition has been tough," he says. "I started building houses when I was twelve. I'm used to working ninety hours a week. All I ever did was work." Though he's enjoying the time he spends with his daughter, he feels unproductive. "It's difficult to go from self-sufficient to depending on someone, but we're making it work," he says. "It is what it is."

The ego blow of job loss leaves many men unable to find fulfillment in their new role. In the months after Ron Mattocks was laid off two years ago, he admits, he had a tough time transitioning from his former life as a vice president of sales for a major homebuilder to Daddy Day Care. "I was an officer in the army and then an executive in the corporate world. Suddenly, I'm packing lunches and making sure the kids have everything in their backpacks. My entire self-image pretty much got shattered," says Ron, 37, from Houston. "I had to really rethink myself, and that's been a long, discouraging process." He misses the external validation he got through his work—the backslapping for a job well done—and is struggling to find that same sense of confidence internally. It has helped, however, to see his wife, Ashley, gain confidence in her career. "Though I don't bring value to the family the way I used to, my role is important," he says.

Feeling the Pain

The loss of a husband's job can cause severe stress as some families move into smaller homes or scramble to secure health insurance. Here, a snapshot by the numbers.

- **75%** of the jobs lost during this recession were held by men. That has made the ever-growing share of women in the workforce even larger.
- **51%** of all workers on U.S. payrolls are women, compared with 33% in 1969.
- **31%** of working moms earned as much as or more than their husbands in 2008 vs. 11% in 1967. More women are now the primary breadwinner.

Why Men Don't Do Windows

Wives should be mindful of the fact that a recently unemployed husband is in a fragile emotional state, says Ellen Ostrow, PhD, a psychologist who works with professional women reentering the workforce. "The psychological impact is enormous," she says. This is one reason many men don't automatically start picking up the scrub brush after a job loss. According to the 2008 American Time Use Survey released by the U.S. Bureau of Labor Statistics, unemployed women spend almost six hours a day on child care and household chores like cleaning and cooking, while unemployed men spend only three hours a day on such tasks—and also spend more than four hours a day watching television.

Often men with a very traditional view of gender roles will refuse to do housework, as a way to gain control, says Stephanie Coontz, who teaches history and family studies at The Evergreen State College in Olympia, WA. "They think that they have to compensate for their loss of masculinity by asserting masculine privilege in other ways."

But the reasoning may be even more subtle than that. Jeremy Adam Smith, author of *The Daddy Shift*, suggests that most men simply don't see housework and child care as a vocation that could give them a sense of identity and pride, as many women do. "For a lot of women who lose their job, a pathway presents itself," he says. "They decide, 'I'm a stay-at-home mom. My job now is to take care of the home and kids, and I'm going to be good at that.' But for many fathers, that pathway doesn't exist in any well-developed way."

Teaching the Basics

However understandable this aversion to scouring bathtubs and laying out school clothes may be, the fact remains that the work needs to be done. Kelly Sons says her marriage became rocky two years ago when her husband's declining auto repair business forced her to support the family. The problem wasn't the *paying* work—Kelly gets tremendous satisfaction from her freelance writing—but rather her second shift as the primary caregiver to their six children. "He assumed that I would handle everything. I was incredibly stressed out," says Kelly, 40, of Morrison, TN.

Though working mothers have long grumbled that their spouses are slackers when it comes to housework in their dual-income homes, a husband's refusal to chip in often becomes intolerable when she's suddenly working longer hours and he's home all day. Kelly's very traditional husband, James, had to be schooled in the basics—like the fact that their sons' black clothes should not be washed with the bathroom towels—but he did gradually step up. Today, he runs the household with pride. "He does most of the housework and takes care of our children and actually brags about me to his friends," says Kelly.

Making Mr. Mom

Do you bring home the bacon—but he refuses to fry it up in a pan? Experts say there are ways to nudge even the most reluctant husband into doing his share.

Make a plan. Rather than give him piecemeal instructions or complaints about picking up dry cleaning, sit down with him and discuss what needs to be done—and decide who should do it. "It's quite likely that the husband doesn't *know* what Mom did. Everything just sort of happened," says Professor Joan C. Williams, JD, director of the Center for WorkLife Law at the University of California, Hastings.

Give up control. He may not do the laundry or load the dishwasher the way you do, but if the work is getting done, don't nitpick. "Wives do have this tendency to regard husbands as unskilled assistants, but that's the worst thing you can do to men who have had the ego blow of being laid off," says family historian Stephanie Coontz, author of *Marriage, a History: How Love Conquered Marriage.*

Show your appreciation. It doesn't matter if the pork chops overcooked—let him know how much you appreciate coming home to a hot meal. Coontz says that most families don't show enough gratitude, which is essential for marital harmony—and why, for example, men who do more housework also have more sex. One survey found that the more housework a man did, the happier he was with his sex life.

The Impact on Your Kids

Studies show that a drop in family income can have a negative effect on child development, particularly when parents become depressed, disengaged, or argumentative. Kids can struggle with behavioral issues, anxiety, or depression. To fend off problems:

Stay positive. Shield kids from any escalating fighting. Be honest but "use language that doesn't scare them," says Joshua Coleman, PhD, cochair of the Council on Contemporary Families. Say, "It's going to work out. Dad will find another job."

Reassure them. Assure kids that it's not their fault if Mom and Dad are feeling a bit down right now. "Children tend to personalize things," Dr. Coleman says. "If they can't make a parent happy, they think there is something wrong with them."

Enlist their help. Ask if they can think of ways the family can save money—like starting a garden or cutting back on soda. "Use it as a teaching experience that can show them that crisis is a part of life and this is how we deal with it," says Dr. Coleman.

Getting to that point was a long, painful process, says Kelly. Her breakthrough came when she realized that instead of fighting and nagging, she needed to make him a partner in finding the solution. "I told him we needed to figure this out—together." With each would-be housework war, she stopped taking on full responsibility and instead turned to him for an answer. "If our family wanted to go to the local aquarium, I'd say, 'I can't go until I have this work done and the house is clean, so how is that going to happen?'"

"Watching the Michael Keaton character in the movie *Mr. Mom* struggle with his new role and then master it had a big influence on my husband."

Surprisingly, one of the most helpful influences came from an old movie. "It sounds crazy, but a lot of it had to do with

Mr. Mom. Watching the Michael Keaton character struggle with his new role and then master it and eventually take pride in it had a big influence on James." Kelly has also made sure to recognize her husband's contribution—even though it was completely taken for granted when she was doing it. "That's what made it so hard at first. Nobody ever told me thank-you." Since James was sensitive to criticism, especially about his cooking, she always tried to find something positive to say and advises other women to do the same: "Find the good in it even if it's the worst thing you've ever eaten . . . Well, it smells good."

Making Inroads

While they may not do as much around the house as women, American men are doing substantially more than their fathers or grandfathers ever did. In 1980, 29 percent of wives reported that their husbands did absolutely no housework; 20 years later, that figure dropped to 16 percent. And today, a third of American wives report that their husbands do at least half or more of either the housework or the child care.

"The more attached a man is to the size of his paycheck, the more difficult the transition will be," says Coontz. "The good news is a lot of men have been discarding that kind of identity. They're seeing themselves less as workers and more as husbands and fathers."

Of course, it's not just men who have a hard time letting go of old roles. Many women have a difficult time seeing Dad do his job a little too well. Dara Turketsky Blaker, 42, a music educator from Coral Springs, FL, says her heart breaks when her daughter wakes up in the middle of the night and calls for Daddy. "At first it was all about Mommy, and then suddenly it wasn't."

The question remains: Once kids get used to spending more time with Dad, Mom learns to appreciate his quirky housekeeping and parents value each other's role, will it last when the economy rebounds? For the Fruehwirths, seeing how the other half lives has given them more empathy for each other. "We often laugh about it," says Christine. "I'll come home and say, 'That commute was an hour!' and he'll say, 'Yeah, I remember.' Or he'll say, 'The kids drove me crazy,' and I'll say, 'Yeah, been there.'" Whether or not roles revert back remains to be seen. But the growing empathy couples say they've experienced for one another cannot help but linger. They know firsthand that indeed the surest cure for judging another person is to walk a mile in their shoes.

Critical Thinking

1. Predict percentage of male homemaker, female breadwinner by 2015.

2. Identify factors that make a job loss psychologically traumatic.

3. Give advice for making role reversal more fulfilling for men and women.

Internet References

A Call to Men
   http://www.acalltomen.org

Marriage and Family Research Institute
   http://www.marriageandfamilyresearchinstitute.com/Marital-Equality.html

National Organization for Women
   http://now.org

Article

Prepared by: Elizabeth Schroeder, EdD, MSW,
Elizabeth Schroeder Consulting

An Affair to Remember

She was 82. He was 95. They had dementia. They fell in love. And then they started having sex.

MELINDA HENNEBERGER

Learning Outcomes

After reading this article, you will be able to:

- Describe the challenges elderly people who live in institutional settings may face as they seek emotional and physical intimacy with other people.

- Explain how social and cultural beliefs about sexuality and aging can affect opportunities for intimate relationships in later life.

- Name at least two steps professionals working in institutional settings serving aging populations can take to support sexual privacy, safety, and dignity in later life.

Bob's family was horrified at the idea that his relationship with Dorothy might have become sexual. At his age, they wouldn't have thought it possible. But when Bob's son walked in and saw his 95-year-old father in bed with his 82-year-old girlfriend last December, incredulity turned into full-blown panic. "I didn't know where this was going to end," said the manager of the assisted-living facility where Bob and Dorothy lived. "It was pretty volatile."

Because both Bob and Dorothy suffer from dementia, the son assumed that his father didn't fully understand what was going on. And his sputtering cell phone call reporting the scene he'd happened upon would have been funny, the manager said, if the consequences hadn't been so serious. "He was going, 'She had her mouth on my dad's penis! And it's not even clean!'" Bob's son became determined to keep the two apart and asked the facility's staff to ensure that they were never left alone together.

After that, Dorothy stopped eating. She lost 21 pounds, was treated for depression, and was hospitalized for dehydration. When Bob was finally moved out of the facility in January, she sat in the window for weeks waiting for him. She doesn't do

that anymore, though: "Her Alzheimer's is protecting her at this point," says her doctor, who thinks the loss might have killed her if its memory hadn't faded so mercifully fast.

But should someone have protected the couple's right to privacy—their right to have a sex life?

"We were in uncharted territory," the facility manager said—and there's a reason for that. Even the *More* magazine-reading demographic that thinks midlife is forever (and is deeply sorry to see James Naughton doing Cialis ads) seems to believe that while sex isn't only for the young, exceptions are only for the exfoliated. We're squeamish about the sex lives of the elderly—and even more so when those elderly are senile and are our parents. But as the baby boom generation ages, there are going to be many more Dorothys and Bobs—who may no longer quite recall the Summer of Love but are unlikely to accept parietal rules in the nursing home. Gerontologists highly recommend sex for the elderly because it improves mood and even overall physical function, but the legal issues are enormously complicated, as Daniel Engber explored in his 2007 article "*Naughty Nursing Homes*": Can someone with dementia give informed consent? How do caregivers balance safety and privacy concerns? When families object to a demented person being sexually active, are nursing homes responsible for chaperoning? This one botched love affair shows the incredible intensity and human cost of an issue that, as Dorothy's doctor says, we can't afford to go on ignoring.

Dorothy's daughter, who contacted me, said that, in a lucid moment, her mother asked her to publicize her predicament. "We're all going to get old, if we're lucky," said the daughter, who is a lawyer. And if we get lucky when we're old, then we need to have drawn up a sexual power of attorney before it's too late. Who controls the intimate lives of people with dementia? Unless specific provision has been made, their families do. And for Dorothy, which is her middle name, and Bob, which isn't his real name at all, that quickly became a problem.

"Who do you love?" Dorothy asked me, right after her daughter introduced us. She'd married her first—and only other—sweetheart, a grade-school classmate she'd grown up with in Boston and waited for while he flew daylight bombing raids over Germany during World War II. Together they had four children, built a business, and traveled all over the world, right up until she lost him to a heart attack 16 years ago. But she never mentions him now and doesn't like it when anyone else does, either, because how could she not remember her own husband? Her daughter visits every evening, and because Dorothy loves kids, her daughter pays the housekeeper to bring hers over every afternoon, "and she thinks they're her grandchildren, and it makes her happy."

But even showing me around her well-appointed, little apartment in the nice-smelling assisted-living facility was an exercise in frustration for Dorothy: She joked and covered, but she might as well have been guiding me through Isabella Stewart Gardner's house, because all around were tokens from her past that have lost their meaning for her. There were tiny busts of Bach and Brahms, a collection of miniature porcelain pianos, Japanese woodcuts, and some Thomas Hart Benton lithographs she picked up for a few dollars in the '40s. "These are all my favorites," she said, pointing to shelves of novels by the Brontes and books about Leonardo da Vinci and Franklin and Eleanor Roosevelt. But her expression said that she couldn't recall why she liked these volumes best, and what I think she wanted me to know is that she once was a person who could have told me. When her daughter mentioned Bob's name—Bob, who was led away in January, shouting, "What's going on? Where are you taking me?" right in front of her—it wasn't clear how much she remembered: "He came and he went, and there's nothing more to say."

So it was left to her daughter, her doctor, and the woman who runs the assisted-living facility to explain how this grown woman, who lived through the depression and survived breast cancer, managed a home and mourned a mate, wound up being treated like a child. "Come back anytime," Dorothy told me sweetly.

Downstairs, in her bright, tidy office, I met the woman who runs the facility—one of the nicest I've seen, with tea service in the lobby and white tablecloths in a dining room that's dressed up like a restaurant. In 30 years of taking care of the elderly, she's seen plenty of couples, but none as "inspiring" or heartbreaking as Dorothy and Bob. Which is why she keeps a photo of the two of them on her desk. In the picture, Dorothy is sitting at the piano in the lobby, where she used to play and he used to sing along—with gusto, usually warbling, "I dream of Jeanie with the light brown hair," no matter what tune she was playing. She is all dolled up, wearing a jangly red bracelet and gold lamé shoes, and they are holding hands and beaming in a way that makes it impossible not to see the 18-year-olds inside them.

Before Dorothy came along, the manager said, Bob was really kind of a player and had all the women vying to sit with him on the porch. But with Dorothy, she said, "it was love." One day, the staff noticed that they were sitting together, then before long they were taking all their meals together, and over a matter of weeks, it became constant. Whenever Bob caught sight of Dorothy, he lit up "like a young stud seeing his lady for the first time." Even at 95, he'd pop out of his chair and straighten his clothes when she walked into the room. She would sit, and then he would sit. And both of them began taking far greater pride in their appearance; Dorothy went from wearing the same ratty yellow dress all the time to appearing for breakfast every morning in a different outfit, accessorized with pearls and hair combs.

Soon the relationship became sexual. At first, Dorothy's daughter and the facility manager doubted Dorothy's vivid accounts of having intercourse with Bob. But aides noticed that Bob became visibly aroused when he kissed Dorothy good night—and saw that he didn't want to leave her at her door anymore, either. (Note to James Naughton: Bob did not need what you are selling.) His overnight nurse was an obstacle to sleepovers, but the couple started spending time alone in their apartments during the day. When Bob's son became aware of these trysts, he tried to put a stop to them—in the manager's view because the son felt that old people "should be old and rock in the chair." When I called Bob's son and told him I was writing about the situation without using any names, he passed on the opportunity to explain his perspective. "I don't choose to discuss anything that involves my father," he said, and he put the phone down.

But according to the facility manager, the son was convinced that Dorothy was the aggressor in the relationship, and he worried that her advances might be hard on his father's weak heart. He wasn't the only one troubled by the physical relationship. The private-duty nurse who had been tending Bob also had strong feelings about the matter, said the manager: "At first, she thought it was cute they were together, but when it became sexual, she lost her senses" for religious reasons and asked staff members to help keep the two of them apart.

Employees wound up choosing sides—as did other residents, including some women who were apparently jealous of Dorothy's romance. And because the couple now had to sneak around to be together—for instance, cutting out when they were supposed to be in church—their intimacy became more and more open and problematic. At one point, the manager had to make Bob stop "pleasuring her" right in the lobby, where Dorothy sat with a pillow placed strategically over her lap. In all of her years of working with elderly people, the manager said, this was not only her worst professional experience but was the only one that left her feeling she had failed her patients. She had a particularly hard time staying neutral and detached, she said, because she kept thinking that "if that was my mom or dad, I'd be grateful they'd found somebody to spend the rest of their lives with."

One day when Dorothy's daughter arrived to visit, she found Bob sitting in the lobby, surrounded by a wheelchair brigade of dozing people who had been posted around him by the private-duty nurse to block Dorothy from approaching him. That's when Dorothy's daughter got the state involved and started throwing around the word *lawsuit,* which only made things worse, the manager said. "Once she started talking legal, that pushed things over the edge." The state did send someone in to try to mediate the situation—but then the mediator was diagnosed with cancer and died just five weeks later. Though the mediator's replacement tried to pick up where he had left off, she was never able to establish a rapport with Bob's son.

Finally, Bob's family decided to move him and insisted that neither he nor Dorothy be told in advance. No one in either family was there the morning Bob's nurse hustled him out the door. Later, the manager called his son and asked if there was any way Dorothy might come and visit just briefly, to say good-bye. The son thought about it for a few days and then said no, his father was already settled into his new home and was not thinking about her at all anymore. The lawyers told Dorothy's family that there was no way they could make the legal case that Bob's rights were being violated by his family, because you couldn't put people with dementia on the witness stand.

Dorothy's son-in-law, who is a doctor, suspects Bob's son of fearing for his inheritance. Bob had repeatedly proposed for all to hear and called Dorothy his wife, but his son called her something else—a "gold digger"—and refused to even discuss her family's offer to sign a prenup. According to Dorothy's daughter, Bob's son told her, "My father has outlived three wives, including the one he married in his 80s, and your mother is just one of many." But surely Bob's safety was a true concern, too, and maybe his son had religious or moral qualms? "I don't think so," the manager said. "I don't think he meant his dad any harm, but he couldn't see what his dad needed. . . . He wanted his dad to have a relationship but on his terms: You can sit together at meals, but you can't have what really makes a relationship, and be careful how much you kiss and don't retire to a private place to do what all of us do."

Though Dorothy might or might not remember what happened, "there's a sadness in her" that wasn't there before, the manager said. Bob "gave her back something she had long lost—to think she's pretty, to care about her step and her stride." She eats in her room now rather than in the dining room where she shared meals with Bob. And she no longer plays the piano. A new couple in the facility has gotten together in the last few weeks. The manager called their families in right away and was relieved to see that they were happy for their parents, and the families have been taking them on outings together. As a result

of the whole experience, the manager, who is 50, recently had a different version of "the talk" with her 25-year-old daughter, instructing her never, ever to let such a thing happen to her or her husband: "I hope I get another shot at it when I'm 90 years old."

Dorothy's doctor also took their experience personally. "Can you imagine as a clinician, treating a woman who's finally found happiness and then suddenly she's not eating because she couldn't see her loved one? This was a 21st-century *Romeo and Juliet.* And let's be honest, because this man was very elderly, I got intrigued; my respects to the gentleman." His patient was happier than he could ever remember; she was playing the piano again, and even her memory had improved.

And though the doctor never laid eyes on Bob, in general, he said, the fear of sex causing heart attacks is wildly overblown: "If you've made it to age 95, I'm sorry, but having sex is not going to kill you—it's going to prolong your life. It was as if someone had removed the sheath that was covering [Dorothy], and she got to live for a while." But after the trauma of losing Bob, Dorothy's doctor came close to losing his patient, he said, adding that most people her age would not have survived the simultaneous resulting insults of depression, malnutrition, and dehydration. "We can't afford the luxury of treating people like this. . . . But we don't want to know what our parents do in bed."

Then the daughter interjected that Bob's son certainly didn't want to see them having oral sex, and the doctor proved his own point. Holding a hand up to stop her from saying any more, he told her, "I didn't need to know that." But maybe the rest of us do.

Critical Thinking

1. What challenges might elderly people who live in institutional settings face as they seek emotional and physical intimacy with another person?

2. How can prevailing social and cultural beliefs about sex and the elderly impact opportunities for intimate relationships in later life?

Internet References

Aging and Human Sexuality Resource Guide
   http://www.apa.org/pi/aging/resources/guides/sexuality.aspx
National Institute on Aging
   http://www.nia.nih.gov/health/publication/sexuality-later-life
Sexuality and Aging Consortium
   http://www.widener.edu/academics/schools/shsp/hss/sex_aging

MELINDA HENNEBERGER is a *Slate* contributor and the author of *If They Only Listened to Us: What Women Voters Want Politicians To Hear.*

Unit 4

UNIT

Prepared by: Elizabeth Schroeder, EdD, MSW,
Elizabeth Schroeder Consulting

Intimacies and Relationships

Think for a moment about the term "sexual relationship." It denotes an important dimension of sexuality—interpersonal sexuality, or sexual interactions occurring between two (or more) individuals. For many people, interpersonal contact and relationships with others form the basis for living meaningful lives. In some cases, these relationships include sexual and romantic ones, and in others, only friendship. There is a difference between someone who intentionally maintains relationships in this way. Conversely, isolation results in loneliness and depression for many human beings. People seek intimacy. Indeed, we cultivate friendships and relationships for the warmth, affection, supportiveness, and sense of trust and loyalty that they can provide. The importance of feeling connected to others can hardly be overstated. But what that looks like can vary from person to person.

As this unit demonstrates, there are various kinds of relationships, intimacies, and experiences of connectedness. Relationships often start when they are least expected. Sitting next to someone on a bus, talking to someone at a party, sending a text, all of these may be the possible beginnings to a relationship. Sometimes friendships may develop into intimate (and sexual) relationships. The qualifying word in the previous sentence is "may." Today many people, single as well as in relationships or married, may yearn for close or emotionally intimate interpersonal relationships, but fail to find them. Other people may choose to not be in relationships which often results in all sorts of speculation about what is "wrong" with them. Just as most cultures expect people of childbearing years to want to have children, society socializes people to be in relationships or get married.

Despite developments in communication and technology that have led to a sense of always being "connected," discovering how and where to find potential friends or partners is reported by many to be as difficult today (if not more so) than in the past. Fear of rejection causes some to avoid interpersonal relationships and others to present a false front or illusory self that they think is more acceptable or socially desirable. This sets the stage for a relationship that is counterproductive to genuine intimacy. For others a major dilemma may exist—the problem

of balancing closeness with the preservation of individual identity in a manner that satisfies the need for both personal and interpersonal growth and integrity. In either case, partners in a relationship should be advised that the development of interpersonal awareness (the mutual recognition and knowledge of others as they really are) rests upon trust and self-disclosure—letting the other person know who you really are and how you truly feel.

These considerations regarding interpersonal relationships apply equally well to achieving meaningful and satisfying sexual relationships. Three basic ingredients lay the foundation for quality sexual interaction: self-awareness, understanding and acceptance of the partner's needs and desires, and mutual efforts to accommodate both partners' needs and desires in safe and healthy ways. Without these, misunderstandings may arise, ultimately bringing anxiety, frustration, dissatisfaction, and/or resentment into the relationship. There may also be a heightened risk of sexually transmitted infections, including HIV, experiencing an unplanned pregnancy, or experiencing sexual dysfunction by one or both partners. On the other hand, experience and research show that ongoing attention to these three ingredients by intimate partners contributes not only to sexual responsibility, but also to true emotional and sexual intimacy, as well as a longer and happier life.

What about people in less traditional relationships? As an example, polyamorous relationships, those in which there is a primary relationship between two people wherein the two people also have extra-relationship sexual encounters and/or relationships, have become more common. This is different from polygamy, and more akin to open relationships. Yet in successful polyamorous relationships, the boundaries of the primary and other relationships are discussed and negotiated. The implication is not that there is anything wrong with or deficient about the primary relationship, but rather that love and sexual closeness can and should be experienced by more than one partner. In other relationships, partners may "swing"—be committed to each other, but bring in one or more people for shared sexual encounters. In any of these situations, the key to their success has to do with communication—communicating about fears and concerns, about what should and should not be shared about encounters or relationships beyond the primary relationship, about jealousy that may arise, and more. The open aspect of these relationships, particularly around communication, is what makes them relationships rather than cheating or affairs. It is not the multiple partner aspect of them that creates issues, it's how these partners are all treated and managed.

As might already be apparent, there is much more to quality sexual relationships than our popular culture recognizes. Such relationships are not established by means of sexual techniques or beautiful bodies. Rather, it is the quality and integrity of the interaction that makes sex a celebration of our humanity and sexuality. A person-oriented (as opposed to genitally oriented) sexual awareness, coupled with an open, relaxed, even playful attitude toward exploration makes for joy and pleasure in experiencing the full range of who we are. Being in any relationship, in search of intimacy and fulfillment, involves being vulnerable. That vulnerability carries great emotional risks. Yet when that vulnerability is returned and people are fully committed to their relationships—whatever those relationships may look like—the rewards can be quite significant.

Article

Prepared by: Elizabeth Schroeder, EdD, MSW,
Elizabeth Schroeder Consulting

The Expectations Trap

Much of the discontent couples encounter today is really culturally inflicted, although we're conditioned to blame our partners for our unhappiness. Yet research points to ways couples can immunize themselves against unseen pressures now pulling them apart.

HARA ESTROFF MARANO

Learning Outcomes

After reading this article, you will be able to:

- Describe how to improve the feelings of satisfaction in a marriage or long-term, committed relationship.

- Explain how people sometimes view their partners in ways that are detrimental to the relationship.

- Describe how seeking "perfection" in a relationship can lead to disappointment.

Six years, ten months, and eight days into their marriage, Sam and Melissa blew apart. Everyone was stunned, most of all the couple themselves. One day she was your basic stressed-out professional woman (and mother of a 3-year-old) carrying the major financial burden of their household. The next day she was a betrayed wife. The affair Sam disclosed detonated a caterwaul of hurt heard by every couple in their circle and her large coterie of friends and family. With speed verging on inevitability, the public knowledge of their private life commandeered the driver's seat of their own destiny. A surge of support for Melissa as the wronged woman swiftly isolated Sam emotionally and precluded deep discussion of the conditions that had long alienated him. Out of respect for the pain that his mere presence now caused, Sam decamped within days. He never moved back in.

It's not clear that the couple could have salvaged the relationship if they had tried. It wasn't just the infidelity. "We had so many background and stylistic differences," says Sam. "It was like we came from two separate cultures. We couldn't take out the garbage without a Geneva Accord." Constant negotiation was necessary, but if there was time, there was also usually too much accumulated irritation for Melissa to tolerate. And then, opening a public window on the relationship seemed to close the door on the possibility of working through the disappointments, the frustrations, the betrayal.

Within weeks, the couple was indeed in discussions—for a divorce. At least they both insisted on mediation, not litigation, and their lawyers complied. A couple of months, and some time and determination later, they had a settlement. Only now that Sam and Melissa have settled into their mostly separate lives, and their daughter appears to be doing well with abundant care from both her parents, are they catching their respective breaths—two years later.

Americans value marriage more than people do in any other culture, and it holds a central place in our dreams. Over 90 percent of young adults aspire to marriage—although fewer are actually choosing it, many opting instead for cohabitation. But no matter how you count it, Americans have the highest rate of romantic breakup in the world, says Andrew J. Cherlin, professor of sociology and public policy at Johns Hopkins. As with Sam and Melissa, marriages are discarded often before the partners know what hit them.

"By age 35, 10 percent of American women have lived with three or more husbands or domestic partners," Cherlin reports in his recent book. *The Marriage-Go-Round: The State of Marriage and the Family in America Today.* "Children of married parents in America face a higher risk of seeing them break up than children born of unmarried parents in Sweden."

With general affluence has come a plethora of choices, including constant choices about our personal and family life. Even marriage itself is now a choice. "The result is an ongoing self-appraisal of how your personal life is going, like having a continual readout of your emotional heart rate," says Cherlin. You get used to the idea of always making choices to improve your happiness.

The constant appraisal of personal life to improve happiness creates a heightened sensitivity to problems that arise in intimate relationships.

The heightened focus on options "creates a heightened sensitivity to problems that arise in intimate relationships." And negative emotions get priority processing in our brains. "There are so many opportunities to decide that it's unsatisfactory," says Cherlin.

It would be one thing if we were living more satisfied lives than ever. But just gauging by the number of relationships wrecked every year, we're less satisfied, says Cherlin. "We're carrying over into our personal lives the fast pace of decisions and actions we have everywhere else, and that may not be for the best." More than ever, we're paying attention to the most volatile parts of our emotional makeup—the parts that are too reactive to momentary events to give meaning to life.

More than ever, we're paying attention to the most volatile parts of our emotional makeup—parts that are too reactive to momentary events to give meaning to life.

Because our intimate relationships are now almost wholly vehicles for meeting our emotional needs, and with almost all our emotions invested in one relationship, we tend to look upon any unhappiness we experience—whatever the source—as a failure of a partner to satisfy our longings. Disappointment inevitably feels so *personal* we see no other possibility but to hunt for individual psychological reasons—that is, to blame our partners for our own unhappiness.

But much—perhaps most—of the discontent we now encounter in close relationships is culturally inflicted, although we rarely interpret our experience that way. Culture—the pressure to constantly monitor our happiness, the plethora of choices surreptitiously creating an expectation of perfection, the speed of everyday life—always climbs into bed with us. An accumulation of forces has made the cultural climate hostile to long-term relationships today.

Attuned to disappointment and confused about its source, we wind up discarding perfectly good relationships. People work themselves up over "the ordinary problems of marriage, for which, by the way, they usually fail to see their own

contributions," says William Doherty, professor of family sciences at the University of Minnesota. "They badger their partners to change, convince themselves nothing will budge, and so work their way out of really good relationships." Doherty believes it's possible to stop the careering disappointment even when people believe a relationship is over.

It's not going to happen by putting the genie back in the bottle. It's not possible to curb the excess of options life now offers. And speed is a fixture of the ongoing technological revolution, no matter how much friction it creates in personal lives. Yet new research points to ways that actually render them irrelevant. We are, after all, the architects of our own passions.

The Purpose of Marriage

Marriage probably evolved as the best way to pool the labor of men and women to enable families to subsist and assure that children survive to independence—and data indicate it still

---

Case Study
Stephen and Christina

Five years into his marriage, not long after the birth of his first son, most of Stephen G.'s interactions with his wife were not pleasant. "I thought the difficulties would pass," he recalls. "My wife, Christina, got fed up faster and wanted me to leave." He was traveling frequently and finances were thin; she'd gone back to school full-time after having worked until the baby was born. "Very few needs were being met for either of us. We were either yelling or in a cold war."

They entered counseling to learn how to co-parent if they indeed separated. "It helped restore our friendship: At least we could talk civilly. That led to deeper communication—we could actually listen to each other without getting defensive. We heard that we were both hurting, both feeling the stress of new parenthood without a support system of either parents or friends. We could talk about the ways we weren't there for each other without feeling attacked. It took a lot longer for the romance to return."

Stephen, now 37, a sales representative for a pharmaceutical company in San Francisco, says it was a time of "growing up. I had to accept that I had new responsibilities. And I had to accept that my partner, now 38, is not ideal in every way although she is ideal in many ways. But her short temper is not enough of a reason to leave the relationship and our two kids. When I wish she'd be different, I have to remind myself of all the ways she is the person I want to be with. It's not something you 'get over.' You accept it."

is. But beyond the basics, the purpose of marriage has shifted constantly, says Stephanie Coontz, a historian at Washington's Evergreen State College. It helps to remember that marriage evolved in an atmosphere of scarcity, the conditions that prevailed for almost all of human history. "The earliest purpose of marriage was to make strategic alliances with other people, to turn strangers into relatives," says Coontz. "As society became more differentiated, marriage became a major mechanism for adjusting your position."

It wasn't until the 18th century that anyone thought that love might have anything to do with marriage, but love was held in check by a sense of duty. Even through the 19th century, the belief prevailed that females and males had different natures and couldn't be expected to understand each other well. Only in the 20th century did the idea take hold that men and women should be companions, that they should be passionate, and that both should get sexual and personal fulfillment from marriage.

We're still trying to figure out how to do that—and get the laundry done, too. The hassles of a negotiated and constantly renegotiated relationship—few wish a return to inequality— assure a ready source of stress or disappointment or both.

From We to Me

Our mind-set has further shifted over the past few decades, experts suggest. Today, the minute one partner is faced with dissatisfaction—feeling stressed-out or neglected, having a partner who isn't overly expressive or who works too hard or doesn't initiate sex very often—then the communal ideal we bring to relationships is jettisoned and an individualistic mentality asserts itself. We revert to a stingier self that has been programmed into us by the consumer culture, which has only become increasingly pervasive, the current recession notwithstanding.

Psychologically, the goal of life becomes *my* happiness. "The minute your needs are not being met then you appropriate the individualistic norm," says Doherty. This accelerating consumer mind-set is a major portal through which destructive forces gain entry and undermine conjoint life.

"Marriage is for *me*" is the way Austin, Texas, family therapist Pat Love puts it. "It's for meeting *my* needs." It's not about what *I do,* but how it makes me *feel.*

Such beliefs lead to a sense of entitlement: "I deserve better than I'm getting." Doherty sees that as the basic message of almost every advertisement in the consumer culture. You deserve more and we can provide it. You begin to think: This isn't the deal I signed up for. Or you begin to feel that you're putting into this a lot more than you're getting out. "We believe in our inalienable right to the intimate relationships of our choice," says Doherty.

In allowing such free-market values to seep into our private lives, we come to believe that a partner's job is, above all, to provide pleasure. "People do not go into relationships because

Case Study
Susan and Tim

Susan Pohlman, now 50, reluctantly accompanied her workaholic husband on a business trip to Italy believing it would be their last together. Back home in Los Angeles were their two teenagers, their luxurious home, their overfurnished lives—and the divorce lawyer she had contacted to end their 18-year marriage.

They were leading such parallel lives that collaboration had turned to competition, with fights over things like who spent more time with the kids and who spent more time working. But knocked off balance by the beauty of the coast near Genoa toward the end of the trip, Tim asked, out of the blue, "What if we lived here?" "The spirit of this odd day overtook me," recalls Susan. At 6 P.M. on the evening before departure, they were shown a beautiful apartment overlooking the water. Despite knowing no Italian, they signed a lease on the spot. Two months later, with their house sold, they moved with their kids to Italy for a year.

"In L.A. we were four people going in four directions. In Italy, we became completely dependent on each other. How to get a phone? How to shop for food? Also, we had no belongings. The simplicity forced us to notice the experiences of life. Often, we had no idea what we were doing. There was lots of laughing at and with each other." Susan says she "became aware of the power of adventure and of doing things together, and how they became a natural bridge to intimacy."

Both Pohlmans found Italy offered "a more appreciative lifestyle." Says Susan: "I realized the American Dream was pulling us apart. We followed the formula of owning, having, pushing each other. You have all this stuff but you're miserable because what you're really craving is interaction." Too, she says, American life is exhausting, and "exhaustion distorts your ability to judge problems."

Now back in the U.S. and living in Arizona, the Pohlmans believe they needed to remove themselves from the culture to see its distorting effects. "And we needed to participate in a paradigm shift: 'I'm not perfect, you're not perfect; let's not get hung up on our imperfections.'" But the most powerful element of their move could be reproduced anywhere, she says: "The simplicity was liberating."

they want to learn how to negotiate and master difficulties," observes Brown University psychiatrist Scott Haltzman. "They want the other person to provide pleasure." It's partner as service provider. The pleasure bond, unfortunately, is as volatile as the emotions that underlie it and as hollow and fragile as the hedonic sense of happiness.

The Expectations Trap: Perfection, Please

If there's one thing that most explicitly detracts from the enjoyment of relationships today, it's an abundance of choice. Psychologist Barry Schwartz would call it an *excess* of choice—the tyranny of abundance. We see it as a measure of our autonomy and we firmly believe that freedom of choice will lead to fulfillment. Our antennae are always up for better opportunities, finds Schwartz, professor of psychology at Swarthmore College.

Just as only the best pair of jeans will do, so will only the best partner—whatever that is. "People walk starry-eyed looking not into the eyes of their romantic partner but over their romantic partner's shoulder, in case there might be somebody better walking by. This is not the road to successful long-term relationships." It does not stop with marriage. And it undermines commitment by encouraging people to keep their options open.

Like Doherty, Schwartz sees it as a consequence of a consumer society. He also sees it as a self-fulfilling phenomenon. "If you think there might be something better around the next corner, then there will be, because you're not fully committed to the relationship you've got."

It's naïve to expect relationships to feel good every minute. Every relationship has its bumps. How big a bump does it have to be before you do something about it? As Hopkins's Cherlin says, if you're constantly asking yourself whether you should leave, "there may be a day when the answer is yes. In any marriage there may be a day when the answer is yes."

One of the problems with unrestrained choice, explains Schwartz, is that it raises expectations to the breaking point. A sense of multiple alternatives, of unlimited possibility, breeds in us the illusion that perfection exists out there, somewhere, if only we could find it. This one's sense of humor, that one's looks, another one's charisma—we come to imagine that there will be a package in which all these desirable features coexist. We search for perfection because we believe we are entitled to the best—even if perfection is an illusion foisted on us by an abundance of possibilities.

If perfection is what you expect, you will always be disappointed, says Schwartz. We become picky and unhappy. The cruel joke our psychology plays on us, of course, is that we are terrible at knowing what will satisfy us or at knowing how any experience will make us feel.

A sense of multiple alternatives, of unlimited possibility, breeds in us the illusion that the perfect person is out there waiting to be found.

If the search through all possibilities weren't exhausting (and futile) enough, thinking about attractive features of the alternatives not chosen—what economists call opportunity costs—reduces the potential pleasure in whatever choice we finally do make. The more possibilities, the more opportunity costs—and the more we think about them, the more we come to regret any choice. "So, once again," says Schwartz, "a greater variety of choices actually makes us feel worse."

Ultimately, our excess of choice leads to lack of intimacy. "How is anyone going to stack up against this perfect person who's out there somewhere just waiting to be found?" asks Schwartz. "It creates doubt about this person, who seems like a good person, someone I might even be in love with—but who knows what's possible *out* there? Intimacy takes time to develop. You need to have some reason to put in the time. If you're full of doubt at the start, you're not going to put in the time."

Moreover, a focus on one's own preferences can come at the expense of those of others. As Schwartz said in his 2004 book, *The Paradox of Choice: Why More Is Less,* "most people find it extremely challenging to balance the conflicting impulses of freedom of choice on the one hand and loyalty and commitment on the other."

And yet, throughout, we are focused on the partner we want to have, not on the one we want—or need—to be. That may be the worst choice of all.

Disappointment—or Tragedy?

The heightened sensitivity to relationship problems that follows from constantly appraising our happiness encourages couples to turn disappointment into tragedy, Doherty contends.

Inevitably, images of the perfect relationship dancing in our heads collide with our sense of entitlement; "I'm entitled to the best possible marriage." The reality of disappointment becomes intolerable. "It's part of a cultural belief system that says we are entitled to everything we feel we need."

Through the alchemy of desire, wants become needs, and unfulfilled needs become personal tragedies. "A husband who isn't very expressive of his feelings can be a disappointment or a tragedy, depending on whether it's an entitlement," says Doherty. "And that's very much a cultural phenomenon." We take the everyday disappointments of relationships and treat them as intolerable, see them as demeaning—the equivalent of alcoholism, say, or abuse. "People work their way into 'I'm a tragic figure' around the ordinary problems of marriage." Such stories are so widespread, Doherty is no longer inclined to see them as reflecting an individual psychological problem, although that is how he was trained—and how he practiced for many years as an eminent family therapist. "I see it first now as a cultural phenomenon."

First Lady Michelle Obama is no stranger to the disappointment that pervades relationships today. In *Barack and Michelle: Portrait of an American Marriage,* by Christopher Anderson, she confides how she reached a "state of desperation" while working full-time, bringing in the majority of the family income, raising two daughters, and rarely seeing her husband, who was then spending most of his week away from their Chicago home as an Illinois state senator, a job she thought would lead nowhere while it paid little. "She's killing me with this constant criticism," Barack complained. "She just seems so bitter, so angry all the time." She was annoyed that he "seems to think he can just go out there and pursue his dream and leave all the heavy lifting to me."

But then she had an epiphany: She remembered the guy she fell in love with. "I figured out that I was pushing to make Barack be something I wanted him to be for me. I was depending on him to make me happy. Except it didn't have anything to do with him. I needed support. I didn't necessarily need it from Barack."

Certainly, commitment narrows choice. But it is the ability to remember you really do love someone—even though you may not be feeling it at the moment.

Commitment is the ability to sustain an investment, to honor values over momentary feelings. The irony, of course, is that while we want happiness, it isn't a moment-by-moment experience; the deepest, most enduring form of happiness is the result of sustained emotional investments in other people.

Architects of the Heart

One of the most noteworthy findings emerging from relationship research is that desire isn't just something we passively feel when everything's going right; it develops in direct response to what we do. Simply having fun together, for example, is crucial to keeping the sex drive alive.

But in the churn of daily life, we tend to give short shrift to creating positive experiences. Over time, we typically become more oriented to dampening threats and insecurities—to resolving conflict, to eliminating jealousy, to banishing problems. But the brain is wired with both a positive and negative motivational system, and satisfaction and desire demand keeping the brain's positive system well-stoked.

Even for long-term couples, spending time together in novel, interesting, or challenging activities—games, dancing, even conversation—enhances feelings of closeness, passionate love, and satisfaction with the relationship. Couples recapture the excitement of the early days of being in love. Such passion naturally feeds commitment.

From Michelle to Michelangelo

Important as it is to choose the right partner, it's probably more important to *be* the right partner. Most people are focused on changing the wrong person in the relationship; if anyone has to change in a relationship, it's you—although preferably with the help of your partner.

Important as it is to choose the right partner, it's probably more important to *be* the right partner. We focus on changing the wrong person.

Ultimately, "Marriage is an inside job," Pat Love told at the 2009 Smart Marriages Conference. "It's internal to the person. You have to let it do its work." And its biggest job is helping individuals grow up. "Marriage is about getting over yourself. Happiness is not about focusing on yourself." Happiness is about holding onto your values, deciding who you are and being that person, using your particular talent, and investing in others.

Unfortunately, says Margin family therapist and *PT* blogger Susan Pease Gadoua, not enough people today are willing to do the hard work of becoming a more mature person. "They think they have a lot more choices. And they think life will be easier in another relationship. What they don't realize is that it will be the same relationship—just with a different name."

The question is not how you want your partner to change but what kind of partner and person you want to be. In the best relationships, not only are you thinking about who you want to be, but your partner is willing to help you get there. Psychologist Caryl E. Rusbult calls it the Michelangelo phenomenon. Just as Michelangelo felt the figures he created were already "in" the stones, "slumbering within the actual self is an ideal form," explains Eli Finkel, associate professor of psychology at Northwestern University and frequent Rusbult collaborator. Your partner becomes an ally in sculpting your ideal self, in bringing out the person you dream of becoming, leading you to a deep form of personal growth as well as long-term satisfaction with life and with the relationship.

It takes a partner who supports your dreams, the traits and qualities you want to develop—whether or not you've articulated them clearly or simply expressed vague yearnings. "People come to reflect what their partners see in them and elicit from them," Finkel and Rusbult report in *Current Directions in Psychological Science.*

Case Study
Patty and Rod

Patty Newbold had married "a really great guy," but by the time their 13th anniversary rolled around, she had a long list of things he needed to change to make the marriage work. At 34, she felt depressed, frantic—and guilty, as Rod was fighting a chronic disease. But she had reached a breaking point, "I read my husband my list of unmet needs and suggested a divorce," even though what she really wanted was her marriage back. "I wanted to feel loved again. But it didn't seem possible."

Newbold has had a long time to think about that list. Her husband died the next day, a freak side effect of his medications. "He was gone, but the list remained. Out of perhaps 30 needs, only one was eased by losing him. I was free now to move the drinking glasses next to the sink."

As she read through the list the morning after he died, she realized that "marriage isn't about my needs or his needs or about how well we communicate about our needs. It's about loving and being loved. *Life* is about meeting (or letting go of) my own *needs. Marriage* is about loving another person and receiving love in return. It suddenly became oh so clear that receiving love is something I make happen, not him." And then she was flooded with memories of all the times "I'd been offered love by this wonderful man and rejected it because I was too wrapped up in whatever need I was facing at the time."

Revitalized is "a funny word to describe a relationship in which one party is dead," she reports, "but ours was revitalized. I was completely changed, too," Everything she learned that awful day has gone into a second marriage, now well into its second decade.

Such affirmation promotes trust in the partner and strengthens commitment. And commitment, Rusbult has found, is a key predictor of relationship durability. "It creates positive bias towards each other," says Finkel. "It feels good to achieve our goals. It's deeply satisfying and meaningful." In addition, it immunizes the relationship against potential distractions—all those "perfect" others. Finkel explains, "It motivates the derogation of alternative partners." It creates the perception—the illusion—that even the most attractive alternative partners are unappealing. Attention to them gets turned off—one of the many cognitive gymnastics we engage in to ward off doubts.

Like growth, commitment is an inside job. It's not a simple vow. Partners see each other in ways that enhance their connection and fend off threats. It fosters the perception that the relationship you're in is better than that of others. It breeds the inclination to react constructively—by accommodation—rather than destructively when a partner does something inconsiderate. It even motivates that most difficult of tasks, forgiveness for the ultimate harm of betrayal, Rusbult has shown.

It is a willingness—stemming in part from an understanding that your well-being and your partner's are linked over the long term—to depart from direct self-interest, such as erecting a grudge when you feel hurt.

The Michelangelo phenomenon gives the lie to the soul mate search. You can't find the perfect person; there is no such thing. And even if you think you could, the person he or she is today is, hopefully, not quite the person he or she wants to be 10 years down the road. You and your partner help each other become a more perfect person—perfect, that is, according to your own inner ideals. You are both, with mutual help, constantly evolving.

Critical Thinking

1. How can the perception of unhappiness in the context of a relationship influence how a person views his/her partner?

2. How can the feelings of closeness and satisfaction in a relationship be enhanced?

3. How can the pursuit of perfection impact an individual's relationship success?

Internet References

American Association of Marriage and Family Therapy
    http://www.aamft.org
Freedom to Marry
    http://www.freedomtomarry.org
National Healthy Marriage Resource Center
    http://www.healthymarriageinfo.org

Article

Prepared by: Elizabeth Schroeder, EdD, MSW,
Elizabeth Schroeder Consulting

Virgin Territory

What Young Adults Say about Sex, Love, Relationships, and The First Time

AMY KRAMER

Learning Outcomes

After reading this article, you will be able to:

- List at least three statistics about teen sexual initiation, contraceptive use, and pregnancy rates.

- Describe at least three influences on a person's decision on whether to become sexually active.

- Explain what, according to this research, were people's experiences like their first times having sexual intercourse.

Introduction

Everyone has a first time. It's one of the touchstones of human experience, a topic common in literature, cinema, dorm rooms, and diaries. It may hold different meaning for different people, but few people ever forget the first time they had sex.

By age 24, more than nine out of 10 people in the United States have had sex—for some it's brand new, for others it's been years since their first sexual experience. Young adults tend to be keen observers of their peers' relationships and they talk frequently about sex, love, relationships, and what it all means. Their circles of friends often include some people who have had sex early and often, some who are not experienced at all, and others who fall in between. They are out of high school and far enough away to think about those years objectively, while still close enough to recall details with some clarity. They are surrounded by lots of talk (and action) involving sex and relationships, and are forming lasting ideas about them. Indeed much of the media they consume is based on these themes.

Given all this, young adults are the perfect cohort to offer up their thoughts about virginity and the "first time."

This topic is of interest because of its universality and because an individual's first sexual experience can influence their feelings and attitudes about sex and related issues for years to come. The more we know about young people's sexual experiences and how they feel about them, the better we are at communicating with them about risks, consequences, and contraception. We also know that delaying sex by even a year or two can protect younger teens from increased risk of pregnancy, sexually transmitted infections (STIs), and other health issues, as well as the emotional consequences of having sex before they're really ready.

In partnership with MTV's "It's Your (Sex) Life" campaign, The National Campaign to Prevent Teen and Unplanned Pregnancy contracted with GfK Custom Research LLC to look at how young adults think and feel about love, relationships, virginity, and the first time they had sex. Using their KnowledgePanel, GfK's Public Affairs and Corporate Communications Group conducted online interviews with 1,001 high school graduates age 18–24, January 7th–16th, 2014. Use of the KnowledgePanel assures representative samples that are statistically valid and projectable to the population of adults age 18–24. The margin of error for this study is +/− 4.4%.

Throughout the survey we asked young men and women what they thought, what they remembered, and how they felt about the first time they had sex, and how they feel about it now. We asked those who are waiting to have sex about their reasons for doing so and we asked everyone what they thought about peers who delay their first sexual experience longer than

Just the Facts

The First Time

On average, people in the U.S. have sex for the **first time** at about **age 17**.[1]

By age 24, **nine in 10** people have had sex.[2]

More than **three-quarters** of young adults age 18–24 have had sex in the past year.[3]

Nearly half (47%) of all high school students report ever having had sex in 2011, a **decline** from 54% in 1991.[4]

Among 18–24-year-olds, **65% of women** and **51% of men** report that their first sexual experience was with a serious romantic partner; **15% of women** and **31% of men** said it was with some-one they were "just friends" with or had just met.[5]

Of those 15–19-year-olds who have had sex, **55%** say they **wish** they had **waited longer**.[6]

62.5% of men and 41.2% of women age 18–24 who were **younger than 20** the first time they had sex report that their first sexual experience was **wanted**. 5% of men and 10.8% of women describe it as **unwanted**.[7]

Contraception & The First Time

Among adolescents, **53% of females** and **45% of males** talked about contraception or sexually transmitted infections (STIs) with their partner before the first time they had sex.[8]

Among 18–24-year-old women, **78%** used some contraceptive method the first time they had sex and **66%** used condoms the first time; among men age 18–24, **83%** used some contraceptive method at first sex and **76%** used condoms.[9]

Pregnancy

Nearly **three in 10 girls** in the U.S. get pregnant at least once by **age 20**.[10]

Two out of three teen pregnancies in the U.S. are to girls **age 18–19**.[11]

Among single, young adults age 20–24, **73%** of pregnancies are **unplanned**.[12]

Some Key Themes Emerged From the Survey, Including:

- There is tremendous support among young adults for waiting longer to have sex; **virginity is widely accepted and respected** among young men and women, including those who have already had sex.
- Pressure to have sex is common too, but the pressure comes more from within than from others.
- Many **young adults want the media to show more and varied portrayals of those not having sex** and they want the media to improve the way they portray young adults' sex lives.
- There are big differences between men and women—how they recall their first times, what they think the youngest teenagers need to know as they embark upon their high school social lives, what kinds of pressure exists, and where it comes from.
- Perhaps most surprisingly, most young adults—men *and* women, some sexually experienced, some not—place a much higher value on romance and relationships than they do on sex alone.

is the norm. Our goal was to get at the "why" behind already known sexual activity data; not to investigate *what* they are doing but rather to try and understand how they *feel* about it.

Acceptability

Virginity among young adults is more widespread—and more acceptable—than many might think. According to data collected by the federal government, the average age that both men and women first have sex is 17. By age 22, about one in six women (17%) and one in five men (21%) have not yet had sex.[a] Contrary to public perceptions (and media depictions), many people are proud of and comfortable with that choice.

Their peers think highly of those who are waiting. According to our survey, among young adults age 18–24, nearly seven in 10 (69%) say it is acceptable for someone their age to be a virgin (27% say it's very acceptable). **Nearly half (46%) say they "feel respect"** (among women it's more than half—52%) for those their age who have not had sex, and one in four (26%) say it "makes me think more of them." While one in four (26%) confess surprise at learning a peer is a virgin, one-third (34%) say they "don't give it a second thought." Almost no one (less than one percent) says they think less of some one who hasn't had sex.

There is self-assuredness among those who haven't had sex. **Six in 10 (60%) say most or all of their friends know they are virgins.** Nearly two out of three (64%) say they are comfortable talking about their virginity with their friends, and nearly all of those who have never had sex (93%) say they've never lied about it. Nearly as many (90%) say they intend to wait until the time is right before having sex for the first time. (Only 6% said they'd rather have sex as soon as possible.)

More than one-third (37%) of young adults who haven't had sex say they're waiting until they get married (among women it's nearly half—47%). One-third (35%) say they haven't found the right person yet, and one in four (26%) say they are waiting until they fall in love. More women than men say religious reasons are their motivation for waiting (28% vs. 16%) or that they "just don't feel ready" (28% to 17%). One in five men (21%) say they haven't had sex yet due to "lack of opportunity."

With regard to serious romantic relationships, more than half of all young adults surveyed (58%) don't care whether or not their partner is a virgin, including 63% of those who are sexually active already and 50% of those who are virgins themselves.

Yet despite their open-mindedness about virginity and waiting, young adults still overestimate how early their peers are becoming sexually active, how many of them are having sex, and how important sex is to them.

For example, data collected by the federal government show that slightly less than half (47%) of high school students have ever had sex—46% of girls and 49% of boys.[b] However, according to our study, nearly six in 10 young adults (59%) think a majority of high schoolers are having sex. **Although the average age that people first have sex is 17 for boys and girls, two-thirds (66%) of young adults think it's 16 or younger for girls.** Even more (69%) think it's 16 or younger for boys.

Young adults also believe that sex is more important to their peers than it is to them. More than half (52%) think that "for most people my age, a fulfilling romantic relationship needs to include sexual intercourse." Yet nearly three out of four (72%) say they could be happy in a romantic relationship that did not include sexual intercourse. Women (76%) are more inclined than men 67%) to say they could be happy in a sexless relationship. Even a majority of sexually active young adults (62%) say they could be happy in a relationship without sex, as do two-thirds (66%) of 23- and 24-year-olds (the oldest group surveyed).

Young adults clearly overestimate what their peers are doing sexually. This can influence their own decisions in a more indirect but significant way. Research has shown that when young people overestimate how many of their peers are having sex, they tend to think having sex is the norm, and if they perceive that by not having sex they are outside the norm, it can be more difficult to delay sex. In fact, **two-thirds (66%) of young adults think it would help teenagers wait longer if they knew less than half of their peers were sexually active.**

Most young adults, whether they've had sex or not, also value and desire relationships as strongly (if not more so) than they do sex. As between relationships and sex, relationships win. When asked if they would *prefer* to have sex but not within a serious romantic relationship or if they'd rather be in a serious romantic relationship that did not include sex, more than three-quarters of young adults (78%) opted for a relationship without sex. Again, women (85%) were more likely than men (71%)

to put romance above sex, but strong majorities for both genders clearly say they'd rather have a serious relationship than uncommitted sex. Even 72% of those who have already had sex said they'd choose a relationship over sex, as did 82% of 23- and 24-year-olds.

The First Time

The first time a person has sex isn't quite what romance novels and love songs would have you believe. **Less than half (46%) of sexually active young adults say their first time was a "mostly good experience."** Nearly one in three (30%) say it was equal parts good and bad, while one in five (20%) say it was "mostly bad." This is particularly true among women—only 37% say their first time was mostly good, and 29% say it was mostly bad. Among men, more than half (56%) say their first time was mostly good and just 9% say it was mostly bad.

When asked to reflect on how they felt at the time, women recall their first sexual experiences less positively than men do. Just 3% of men say they regretted their first sexual experience immediately afterward; five times as many women (16%) remember feeling that way.

Twice as many women (24% vs. 12% for men) say they didn't think they were ready when they had sex for the first time. Three times as many women (18% vs. 6% for men) say they were pressured into it the first time they had sex. More than one in four men (27%) say their first time made their relationship stronger, for women it was only 15%.

Perhaps not surprisingly, six in 10 (62%) young women who have had sex say they would change something about their first time if they could. Two-thirds (67%) say they would have waited longer—the most common reason for wanting a first time do-over—and half (51%) wish they had been older. More than half (59%) would have done it with someone they loved and nearly as many (55%) would have done it with someone who loved them. Only 15% of sexually active young adult women say their first time was "better than [they] expected it would be," while more than three times as many (48%) say it was "not as good as [they] expected." Among men, one in four (25%) said it was better than they expected—about the same amount who said it was worse (27%).

When asked to look back on their first sexual experience and reflect on how they feel about it now with the benefit of hindsight, the positive feelings women had in the heat of that first experience have dissipated dramatically. Half of women (51%) say they felt "happy" about their first time at the time but only 24% feel happy about it now. Half (50%) say they felt "loved" at the time but only 25% feel that way about it today. One-third of women (32%) say they felt "mature" when they had sex for the first time, but looking back only 21% say so now. Similarly, negative feelings have increased over time: Only 18%

of women say they were "sad" when they had sex for the first time, but now one in four (25%) look back on it with sadness. **One in five (22%) were "regretful" then, but more than one in three (37%) look back on it with regret today.**

Men are more satisfied with their first sexual experiences—59% say they wouldn't change anything even if they could. Still, upon reflection, the positive feelings they had about the first time they had sex have diminished as well. Six in 10 (60%) say they felt "happy" at the time, but only 38% feel that way about it now. While 45% say they felt "loved" then, only 24% would say so in retrospect. Only 4% felt "sad" at the time, but in looking back 14% are sad about it now. Of those men who would do something differently if they could re-do their first time, one-third would have waited longer (34%) and about the same proportion would have chosen a different partner (35%). Nearly one in five (18%) of those men who would take a do-over if possible say they wouldn't have put so much pressure on themselves to get it over with the first time.

The age that people first have sex seems to matter as well. Simply put, **the younger men and women are when they first have sex, the more likely they are to regret the experience at the time and to have negative feelings in the future.** Among men and women who first had sex at or before age 17, 53% were "happy" about it at the time while only 23% are happy about it now. Among those whose first time was at or after age 18, nearly six in 10 (59%) were "happy" at the time and nearly half (45%) still feel that way. Of those who were 17 or younger at first sex, 42% felt "loved" at the time but only 17% would describe their first sexual experience that way today. But for those who were 18 or older, more than half (57%) felt "loved" at the time and 39% still say they were. One in five (21%) of those who became sexually active at age 17 or younger were "regretful" when they first had sex, and nearly one-third (31%) feel that way about it today. Among those who were 18 or older, only 12% were "regretful" when it happened, though that number has nearly doubled (22%) as they look back on it now.

Pressure

Even though virginity is acceptable and respectable, young people still feel and are affected by pressure to become sexually active. Much of this pressure comes from them selves and how they experience the world—not directly from others. For example, when young adults are asked to look back on their high school lives, more than four in 10 (44%) say that "images and messages in popular media" were a source of sexual pressure during those years. Contrary to what many adults believe, when it comes to sexual pressure, no other factor (friends, partners, siblings, self, etc.) is cited as often as media.

After media, the most-often cited source of pressure to have sex comes from an individual's own perceptions about their peers: Nearly one in four (38%) say they felt pressure in high school based on "what [they] heard other people were doing." Interestingly, those who started having sex at age 17 or younger are much more likely to cite "what [they] heard others were doing" as a source of pressure to have sex than were their peers who waited longer or are still waiting. Half (50%) of those whose first sexual experience was at or before age 17 say other people's rumored sexual activity was a source of pressure for them, while just 29% of those who were older when they started having sex—or are still waiting—say the same.

Among men, nearly four in 10 (38%) say the pressure to have sex came from themselves (for women it was 27%). Among those whose first sexual experience was at or before age 17, nearly half (44%) cited themselves as a source of pressure vs. just 23% of those who were 18 or older.

Women (42%) were more likely than men (25%) to say they felt pressure in high school from a romantic partner to have sex. Men (38%) were slightly more likely than women (31%) to say that the pressure to have sex as a teen came from their friends. Those who say their first sexual experience was something they were "pressured into" are three times more likely to be women than men; women are also more likely to say their first time was something they "just wanted to get over with." Those who were 17 or younger the first time they had sex are also more likely to say they were pressured into it the first time.

With the benefit of 20–20 hindsight, one in four women (25%) look back on their first time and say in retrospect they wouldn't have put so much pressure on themselves to get it over with.

Though they don't start having sex any later than boys, girls seem to be more likely to get a strong message about not having sex in high school. Two in three women (66%) say they felt parental pressure to remain a virgin while in high school, and nearly one in three women felt such pressure from their friends (30%) or siblings (29%). More than half of women (55%) felt religious pressure to remain abstinent, and even more (57%) felt that pressure coming from within themselves. In every case, significantly fewer men reported feeling pressure to remain a virgin in high school from any of these sources.

Pornography—more accessible and widespread for this generation than for any generation that came of age before them—can also influence young people's ideas about sex in real life. Nearly nine in 10 young adults (85%) say that people "have unrealistic expectations about sex because of what they see in porn." Nearly half (49%) say these unrealistic expectations occur "frequently." These views are nearly universal among this cohort: There is little difference on this topic between men and women, or virgins and non-virgins, or those who became sexually active at a younger age vs. an older age.

Communication & Contraception

More than half (58%) of sexually active young adults say their first time was with someone they were in a serious relationship with, so it's not surprising that about as many (60%) felt they had good communication with their first partner. **Nearly two out of three (64%) say they talked with their first partner about the fact that it was their first time.** Nearly seven in 10 (68%) say they used a condom the first time they had sex.

However, for those who began having sex at a younger age, confidence and communication was not as strong. Among those who were 17 or younger their first time, about half (54%) say they felt they had good communication with their partner and slightly more (58%) said they talked with that partner about the fact that it was their first time. Among those who were 18 or older, seven out of 10 (70%) felt they had good communication, and a full three out of four (75%) talked about the fact that it was their first time. Condom use at first sex remained steady regardless of age.

Among those young adults who have not yet had sex, more than two-thirds (69%) say they are comfortable talking to a partner/potential partner about their virginity, although less than half (45%) say they are comfortable talking to them about birth control and protection. Half of women (50%) who have not had sex say they have already thought about what kind of protection they're going to use the first time, and 40% of men say they've thought about it too. Among those who have already had sex, nearly three-quarters (74%) are comfortable talking to a partner/potential partner about birth control and protection.

Interestingly, those who are sexually active have an easier time than those who are not when it comes to talking to new partners about waiting to have sex. Of those who have had sex before, 63% say they are comfortable having such conversations while only 52% of those who haven't had sex say they feel the same way. Women are more comfortable than men with such conversations; two-thirds of women who have had sex (70%) say they are comfortable talking with a new partner about waiting to have sex, as opposed to 55% of men who say the same.

Women are also slightly more confident than men about what they know about birth control. Two in three women (66%) say they "know everything they need to know" to prevent pregnancy while just over half of men (56%) say the same. Only one in five (19% of men, 21% of women) say they wish they knew more. More than one-quarter (28%) of young adults say they wish they knew more about preventing sexually transmitted infections while slightly more than half (52%) say they already know everything they need to on that front.

When asked how comfortable young people feel talking to partners about communication and contraception, in every instance men were much more likely to choose the non-answer ("neither agree nor disagree") than women were. For example, when asked whether they agreed or disagreed with the statement "I know everything I need to know about preventing pregnancy," nearly twice as many men chose the "neither" option than women did (27% vs. 14%). For "I wish I knew more about sexually transmitted infections and how to prevent them," men opted for the "neither" option 45% of the time, and 35% opted out of answering when asked about their comfort level in discussing waiting to have sex with a new partner.

Media

Most young adults strongly agree that they want more from the media when it comes to portrayals of sex and virginity. Men, women, younger, older, sexually active, and not—they all say they want pop culture to do a better job with these topics. **Nearly nine in 10 (86%) say they "wish media like movies and TV shows portrayed sex, love, and relationships among people my age in a more realistic way."**

Even though young adults themselves are accepting and open-minded about virginity, they don't often see that attitude reflected back in the media they consume. Most (89%) say that popular media makes it seem like people who have sex are "cooler" than those who don't; more than half (56%) say that this happens *frequently*. There is no difference of opinion between men and women on this topic or between those who have had sex vs. those who have not.

Young adults want to see more portrayals of peers who are not sexually active, and they want to hear more about reasons for waiting. Nearly three out of four young adults (74%) say they wish movies and TV shows "did a better job of exploring why people are virgins" and even more (86%) wish the media "portrayed virginity in a more realistic way."

Media can be a powerful influence on young people—more people report pressure to have sex coming from "images and messages in popular media" than they do from partners or friends. But media can also be a source of support for young people looking for reasons not to have sex. More stories about virgins, virginity, waiting, and the many reasons why young people choose not to have sex could go a long way in helping them feel more comfortable about delaying sex.

Conclusion

This survey makes it clear that young people are confident and comfortable with the decision to delay sex and that getting the word out more broadly about those who decide to delay sex could spare their peers—as well as younger teens—a lot of disappointment and regret. Whether it's waiting for the right time or the right person, young adults want teens to learn from their experiences and not to rush into sex.

The younger people are when they have sex for the first time, the more likely they are to experience sadness and feelings of regret about it—both at the time and long after the fact. The older people are when they become sexually active, the more likely they are to say it was a better experience, the more equipped they are to talk to their partner about feelings and contraception, and the more likely they are to feel happy and loved. Their statements, combined with the health risks that generally accompany early sex, make a strong argument for a more public conversation about how much young people support the idea of waiting longer to start having sex.

So how to encourage young people to wait longer? Even broad acceptance of virginity doesn't necessarily translate into waiting longer, nor does widespread open-mindedness on the topic provide immunity from pressure to become sexually active.

Media can certainly help. By a 2 to 1 margin, young adults across the board think it would help teens wait longer to have sex if they knew less than half their peers were sexually active. Plus, nearly everyone wants more realistic portrayals of relationships and virginity in the media they consume. Not just dramatic depictions of the motivations behind why characters have sex, but also more exploration of the reasons why they choose not to.

Making virginity more realistic and relatable is what young people want to see in their media, and what those who care about young people—like parents and health care providers—can offer elsewhere. Despite young adults' confidence and openness about virginity and waiting, they could use more support on this front early on. As they navigate the teen years, young people want to know that waiting to have sex is, in fact, quite normal.

Even those who have had sex feel strongly that they don't need to have sex in every relationship, although they exaggerate how important sex is to their peers. Not having sex is the norm for many and most would prefer a stable, committed relationship to an arrangement that includes little more than sex.

Whether or not they have had sex, young men and women agree that it is important to think about contraception and preventing STIs—and how to communicate about these topics with partners—before they have sex. Despite conventional wisdom and the messages that are often served up by popular culture, young adults take sex seriously and value protecting their bodies as well as their hearts.

Critical Thinking

1. This article implies that being a virgin refers to not having had vaginal intercourse yet. How do you think this article applies to same-sex couples who do not have vaginal sex?

2. How do you think the status of being a virgin differs based on gender? Why do you think that is?

3. The research in this article found that women report being more comfortable talking about sex and sexuality than their male partners. Why do you think that is? What do you think would need to happen in order to change that?

Internet References

It's Your Sex Life
   http://www.itsyoursexlife.com
National Campaign to Prevent Teen and Unplanned Pregnancy
   http://thenationalcampaign.org
Sex, Etc.
   www.sexet.org

AMY KRAMER is the Senior Director of Entertainment Media at The National Campaign to Prevent Teen and Unplanned Pregnancy where she works with entertainment media executives, writers, producers, and others to help them incorporate teen and unplanned pregnancy prevention messages into the content of their work. She consults and advises on many television programs and websites, writes episode discussion guides for parents and teens in order to help them watch TV together and talk about it afterward, produces Campaign PSAs and other videos for educational and promotional purposes, and works with outside experts on the media goals of the Campaign. Previously, she served as a producer for ABC, CNN, and CNBC.

Article

Prepared by: Elizabeth Schroeder, EdD, MSW,
Elizabeth Schroeder Consulting

Married to a Doll: Why One Man Advocates Synthetic Love

Davecat lives with his wife and mistress, both dolls, and thinks synthetic partners are ideal for those who don't want to deal with humans' inconsistencies.

JULIE BECK

Learning Outcomes

After reading this article, you will be able to:

- Define what is meant by a "synthetic relationship."

- Define the term "technosexual."

- Describe at least two populations of individuals who, according to the article, are sometimes well-suited for a synthetic relationship.

Davecat met his future wife, Sidore Kuroneko at a goth club in 2000, so the story goes. The less romantic but perhaps more true version is that he saved up for a year and a half to buy her online. She cost about $6,000.

Sidore is a RealDoll, manufactured by Abyss Creations in the shape of a human woman. She is covered in artificial skin made of silicone, so she's soft. These high-end, anatomically correct—even equipped with fake tongues—love dolls (or capital-D Dolls) are ostensibly made for sex. But 40-year-old Davecat (a nickname acquired from videogames that he now prefers to go by) and others who call themselves iDollators see their dolls as life partners, not sex toys. Davecat and Sidore (or, as he sometimes calls her, Shi-chan) obviously aren't legally married, but they do have matching wedding bands that say "Synthetik [sic] love lasts forever," and he says they're considering some sort of ceremony for their 15th anniversary.

Davecat considers himself an activist for synthetic love, and the rights of synthetic humans, such as Shi-chan. He's active online, with an iDollator blog, "Shouting to hear the echoes,"

that he updates regularly, and has appeared on TLC's show My Strange Addiction, as well as in a BBC documentary called Guys and Dolls.

According to the backstory of Davecat's relationships, his Doll mistress (and Sidore's girlfriend), Elena Vostrikova, saw Davecat and Sidore in Guys and Dolls and moved from Russia to be with them. Davecat purchased Elena, or Lenka, in 2012, and the three of them now share a one-bedroom apartment in southeastern Michigan.

I spoke with Davecat over email about the ups and downs of synthetic relationships.

When and why did you purchase your first Doll? Were you thinking of companionship at the time, or was it just for sex?

I bought Shi-chan back in 2000. Admittedly, my reasons for purchasing her were 70 percent sex, 30 percent companionship. I've always been attracted to artificial women such as mannequins, and especially Gynoids, which are robots made in the likeness of human females. In late 1998 one of my best friends showed me the RealDoll website, as she knew I was keen on artificial women. I thought they were gorgeous creations, and having one would not only dispel loneliness, but be excellent for sex as well. And I was right!

When did you start feeling like Sidore was not just a sex toy but someone/something you were in a relationship with?

It actually didn't take me too long to regard Shi-chan as a synthetic person, and not simply a thing; it occurred pretty much when I opened her crate for the first time. I was immediately stunned by her lifelike beauty, and after I mentally collected myself, extracted her from her crate, and sat her down on the couch, I just held her in my arms for a while. It felt so right and natural, if you'll pardon the pun. It seemed perfectly normal for me to treat something that resembles an organic woman the same way I'd treat an actual organic woman.

There was never a moment when Shi-chan—or any Doll, for that matter—was merely an object to me.

Part of the (sexual) appeal of synthetics is how much they look like their organic counterparts. If you have a robot shaped like a refrigerator, that won't have as much draw as a robot in the shape of a human; people will be more willing to interact with the human-shaped one. Further still, if that humanoid robot has artificial skin and sounds like a human, most people dealing with it are more than likely to even have a moment where they forget it's a robot. With Sidore, her draw was instantaneous. There was never a moment when Shi-chan—or any Doll, for that matter—was merely an object to me.

Have you always been interested in dolls, and if so, was it always in a sexual way?

I've always been fascinated by the idea of artificial people, specifically artificial women. Before I knew Dolls existed, I'd long identified as being a technosexual, even before I knew there was a word for it. A technosexual is someone who is attracted to robots. Like any subculture, there's many shades within the term. Some technosexuals prefer their organic partners to dress as robots; others are attracted to robots who don't necessarily have a humanoid appearance, such as R2-D2. My preference is for humanoid robots that are covered in artificial flesh, so they look organic upon first glance; both Geminoid-F and the Actroid series of Gynoids by Hiroshi Ishiguro are excellent examples.

Obviously, I'm sexually attracted to synthetic humans, such as Gynoids and Dolls, but the much larger part of their appeal is that they're humans, but they don't possess any of the unpleasant qualities that organic, flesh and blood humans have. A synthetic will never lie to you, cheat on you, criticize you, or be otherwise disagreeable. It's rare enough to find organics who don't have something going on with them, and being able to make a partner of one is rarer still.

In your episode of *My Strange Addiction*, you talk about how you're perfectly aware she's a doll, and you're not trying to pretend she's a person. Yet you consider yourself married to Sidore, a marriage/relationship being something that is inherently two-sided. How do you reconcile those two things in your head at once?

Both Sidore and Elena have two backstories. One in which Sidore is the daughter of a Japanese father and an English mother, and was born in Japan and raised in Manchester, England. Elena's is similar; she grew up in Vladivostok, Russia. The other backstory they have is that they're Dolls. Self-aware Dolls, but Dolls nonetheless. In one backstory they have favorite foods; in the other, they don't eat, because they don't have digestive tracts . . . because they're Dolls. You get the idea.

I've had that dichotomy for as long as I've had Shi-chan and Lenka, and it doesn't seem to be going away any time soon. As I write their characters, they each express themselves through the Internet; they both have their own Twitter feeds, and Shi-chan has a Tumblr. Playing up the Doll aspect allows me to get comedy from the situation, such as when Sidore wonders why I don't just remove my sinuses when my allergies flare up, but writing detailed histories for them exercises my creative writing skills, and makes them more 'human'. Like I said, the dichotomy probably won't be solved any time soon.

Have you ever been in a relationship with a human woman, and would you want to in the future? Do you find yourself attracted to human women?

I'd been in relationships with organic women prior to, and after, having Shi-chan enter my life. When I say "relationships," I really mean "affairs where I was the other man;" I've never been in a situation where I was with an organic woman who didn't already have a boyfriend.

I don't consider myself to be a very persuasive person; when I was growing up, my father was always pushing me into doing things that I didn't want to do, and as a consequence, I didn't ever want to be That Guy Who's Being Aggressively Persuasive. So instead of asking whatever lass I was with to consider me as a boyfriend, I simply wouldn't force the issue.

I'm still quite attracted to organic women, at least visually. But just because someone's attractive doesn't mean they have a mindset or a personality that's compatible with my own. I figure that instead of chasing after an ideal person who either doesn't exist in the first place, or is already with someone else, why not buy a Doll? I don't gamble, and I'm not keen on taking emotional chances. We've all seen relationships where things start out fantastically, and then just end up falling apart. A friend of mine just got divorced after 17 years of marriage. That's an enormous investment of time, money, and emotion, and I'm not interested in having someone in my life who may bail at any time, or who transforms into someone unpleasant. Ultimately, getting romantically involved with an organic woman doesn't seem worth it to me.

In December 2012, you purchased a second Doll. How come? Did you feel like your marriage was getting stale?

Back in the early 2000s, my goal was to purchase at least one Doll from every company that's out there. One of the objectives of my blog is to introduce people who aren't iDollators or technosexuals to the idea of synthetic partners, and having multiple Dolls from various companies would enable me to compare and contrast them, so that people could learn what makes them different, and choose the one that's right for them. Also, I always thought it would be cool to have photoshoots featuring multiple Dolls interacting with each other; doing so would further make them less seem like 'things', and more like people. As it is, however, there are around 20 different companies across six or so countries, and unfortunately, I don't have that kind of money. So now my goal is about five. Short of acquiring a two-bedroom flat, I won't have the space for more than five, either.

In a more fictitious context, I thought it would be nice to get a silicone companion for Sidore, so she isn't lonely or bored whenever I'm away from home. As they're both bisexual, they get to enjoy each other on multiple levels. If anything, adding Elena to our partnership has only improved it, as we all appreciate what each other has to offer. Besides, if and when I manage to get additional Dolls, Sidore will always remain my wife; I've no intention of marrying any of the other Dolls we'll have.

My marriage to Sidore is open in the context of she allows me to do anything I want, as long as it's only with a synthetic woman. Incidentally, those are the exact same conditions under which I'll allow her to do anything extracurricular. Very straightforward, yet simple!

But you say you've been in relationships with organic women "prior to and after having Shi-chan enter my life." Is there a story there? Did a relationship/affair you were having with an organic woman cause problems with your relationship with Sidore or vice versa?

I was seeing an organic lass—a coworker, from several jobs ago—who knew that I had Shi-chan. This was back when I was of the mindset that Sidore would remain my wife, but I'd still look now and again for an organic lass to be friends with benefits with. Our relationship started out alright, but several months into it, whenever I'd attempt to get together after work with her, she'd always have something come up. I was beating myself up over it when I realized: Why am I wasting my time trying to get her to hang out and be romantically involved with me, when I have a Doll who is in love with me at home? Plus, it was a bit of a contest with said coworker, as she was interested in two other blokes while she was seeing me. As I'm not competitive, either, I decided that pursuing her was a wasted effort, especially in light of Sidore not requiring any of that silliness.

Then there was the lass I bought a house with back in 2003. I was attempting to help her out of a bad relationship. She claimed to be one of my best friends. She wasn't the least bit romantically interested in me, but I thought that if I helped her and she and I lived under the same roof, eventually she'd view me more favorably. Turns out that didn't happen, as I later discovered that she was a pathological liar with a coke addiction, and I moved out of the house after living there for only four months. That really drove home to me that I guess I'm too trusting with some organics. Some of them can be far too unpredictable. Synthetics have a consistency that I'm thankful for.

What is a typical week like for you? Do you spend most of your time at home with Sidore and Elena, or do you go out with friends? When you do go out, do you ever bring either of them with you? I imagine people in public would react strangely—does that keep you from doing coupley stuff like going to movies?

Contrary to what most of the TV shows we appear in would have you believe, I actually go out quite a bit! Well, enough, I'd say. I'm not a "people person," and although I love my friends, it's better for an introvert like myself to spend more time alone. Having said that, though, I always have a fantastic time whenever I'm with mates.

I don't take Shi-chan or Lenka with me when I go out. People have a long and sordid history of being violent toward that which they don't understand.

During the week, I'm usually at work—I do data entry and other bits and bobs at a machine shop—then I come home and either catch up on the Internet, or interact with Sidore and Elena. My job has me come in early, so I usually go to bed early Friday evenings, after meeting my friends online for whatever videogame has caught our fancy, or physically hanging out with them. Saturday evenings have me getting together with friends as well, and Sunday, I usually spend time with my rubber troublemakers, taking photos, watching a film or a telly program, writing or doing research for "Shouting to hear the echoes," or getting up to other things.

Also contrary to what most people believe, I don't take Shi-chan or Lenka with me when I go out. For one, they're heavy (78 lbs and 57 lbs, respectively), and for another, I'm not so deluded as to think that taking them out and about with me wouldn't raise more than a few eyebrows. Also, I wouldn't want to put either myself or whichever synthetic lass I'd have with me in danger. I don't trust random people enough to think we wouldn't be verbally or physically attacked. People have a long and sordid history of being violent toward that which they don't understand. Or so I'm told.

What do your family and friends think of your relationship?

The way my friends view my relationship ranges from "Well, that's just what Davecat gets up to, I suppose," to

"Be sure to tell your girls I said 'Hi!'" Most of them are cool with it; pretty much all of my friends are into quirky things, so they can empathize. I wouldn't be surprised if there are a few among them who would rather see me with an organic lass, but overall, they think Sidore and Elena are rather neat. Curiously enough, more of my female friends like them than my male ones. A couple of female friends have picked out articles of clothing for Shi-chan and Lenka on a few occasions!

Of my Mum and Dad, Mum was more open-minded of the two—years ago, when I was in my eyeliner phase, she taught me how to apply it properly—so although she probably would've liked to be a grandmother at some point, she was okay with my unconventional partnership. Dad, on the other hand, to this day categorically refuses to talk about Sidore, Dolls, Gynoids, etc. He's never come out and said it, but he wishes that I were more conventional and acted like everyone else. I wouldn't say that me being an iDollator has driven a wedge into our relationship, as the wedge was already there long before Sidore entered my life. I once told him, half-jokingly, that his attitude is no way to treat his daughter-in-law, but as the man has no sense of humor, he didn't think much of that statement.

A more practical consideration: wear and tear. In the *Guys and Dolls* documentary, there's a scene where you send Sidore off to a special RealDoll repairman to get fixed. I don't know if you plan on spending the rest of your life with Sidore, but that is the typical connotation of "married" (divorce rates notwithstanding). What would you do if she ever just became broken beyond repair?

That sort of thing has already happened, after a fashion: Sidore's had three bodies since 2000. Her first body lasted from 2000 to 2003, her next went from 2003 to 2010, and she's still enjoying her third body. As are Elena and I! But seriously, if her body becomes too irreparable, I simply save up some money and buy her a new one. She's looked exactly the same from 2000 to now, excepting the fact that her current body looks more like how I wanted her to look to begin with; namely, she's extraordinarily pale. I'd be lying if I didn't say that when her body comes close to falling apart through entropy, I'm pretty cut up about it, as anyone would be when facing the mortality of a loved one.

Up until about 2006, most of the Doll manufacturers used tin-based silicone, which is lovely and soft, but was prone to tearing. Now, pretty much all of the various companies use a platinum-based silicone, which is much more durable. Part of the issue with Sidore's previous two bodies was that she did develop tears, which, depending on how severe they are, can be repaired. When Shi-chan got her surgeries in 2006, she also went to have her joints tightened, which is something that every Doll needs sometimes, no matter who makes them.

Sidore hasn't had a single tear with her current body, and her joints are just now starting to loosen. But purchasing a new body for her every couple of years when she needs it ensures a kind of immortality, and ensures she'll be around as long as I'm around.

Looking to the future, I know you're interested in androids and robotics and the idea of, for lack of a better word, sexbots. As this technology continues to develop, isn't it all just moving toward getting dolls to be more like humans? And if your preference is for dolls, isn't that counterintuitive?

Well, yes and no. For me, Dolls trump organics, but Gynoids—which is a much less limiting term than "sexbots"—trump Dolls. A Doll's only failing is that she can't move or speak of her own accord, whereas a Gynoid would be able to, dependent on advances in technology, of course.

Referring to a Doll as a "sex toy" is demeaning and unimaginative.

My ideal version of Sidore would be a Gynoid who greatly resembles an organic, but upon closer inspection, she'd have silicone skin and slightly stilted movement. Now the important thing to remember is that Gynoids and androids are like organic humans, but they would lack the qualities that make organics difficult to deal with. They would be pleasant, agreeable, non-judgmental, aesthetically and mentally pleasing, and more. In day-to-day existence, most people have to deal with at least one person whom they'd rather avoid at all costs. The way I see things, your spouse should be easygoing and a joy to come home to, in order to counteract having to deal with all manner of undesirables when you're out and about. I think the best way to reach that goal is through humanoid robots. It's like having your cake, and eating it too.

You consider yourself an advocate for synthetic love, is that right? And on your *My Strange Addiction* episode, you say "I think it's a matter of time before more people are choosing the synthetic option." Why is that? What kind of person do you think this sort of relationship is right for?

I don't just consider myself an advocate for synthetic love, but for treating synthetic humans with as much respect, if not more, than organic humans. Referring to a synthetic as a "thing," or a Doll as a "sex toy," is demeaning and unimaginative. For one, it's entirely dismissive toward the artistry that goes into creating synthetic humans. Nearly everyone who sees a Doll in person has to admit that the level of work that goes into them is incredible, and the technology involved in Gynoids and androids who are capable of speech and movement is astounding without question. If animals have rights, and rightly so, why shouldn't we treat something that looks and acts like a human with similar rights and respect?

Regarding the sort of person a synthetic partner would be perfect for: When people are in failed organic relationships, they're invariably urged to dust themselves off and try again. But what most people don't realize is that not everyone is suited for the "try, try again" mindset, and with each defeat, they're less inclined to make another attempt, which leads to more loneliness, which makes them even more depressed, etc. Being in a relationship with a synthetic means that the organic is taking a stand against loneliness on terms which harm no one. Instead of being miserable, they're doing something about it, without having to waste time, money, and emotion playing silly games to win the fleeting affections of someone who might be wrong for them in the first place.

Apart from technosexuals and childfree people, one group of individuals who would be well-suited for synthetic partners are introverts. This is why I always stress the difference between loneliness and being alone; many of us introverts actually prefer to be alone, as the noise and agitation of being around others can be incredibly draining. But being lonely—that is, the state of not having a special someone who you can occasionally be alone with—is something no one should have to endure. Having a synthetic in your life means that you can interact with them whenever you want to, and when you want to do something that requires solitude, you can have that as well, without being made to feel guilty about it.

The movie *Guys and Dolls* says that most people who purchase RealDolls are men buying female dolls. Why do you think that is?

For one, Dolls aren't exactly light. Abyss Creations has made great strides in weight reduction and all of the other companies have followed suit, but when high-end 'love dolls' first appeared in the U.S., they were pretty substantial. Shi-chan is 5'1", and her current body is about 78 lbs. Her first body from 2000 was the same height, but around 100 lbs. One reason why there's not a lot of female iDollators out there is because Dolls tend to be too heavy for a lot of women, which sounds a bit chauvinistic to say, but it's been corroborated with at least four female iDollators that I personally know. Incidentally, of the people I do know that have male Dolls, with the exception of one, all the owners are gay men.

Furthermore, it seems easier for women to find an organic male partner than it is for men to find an organic female partner. Women, by and large, are more selective than men are, and don't seem to have as much of a need to purchase a Doll as a single, open-minded bloke would.

Also, if more men do start "choosing the synthetic option," as you say, and begin having relationships with objects that are shaped like women, do you think that will encourage the objectification of real women?

The belief that the existence of synthetics encourages the objectification of organic women is baseless. If anything, those of us who are iDollators or technosexuals find that it's more a case of personifying objects. But then, 98 percent of the iDollators and technosexuals I know treat their Dolls like goddesses. I can't really speak for those who don't, and it would be safe to assume that those who would objectify an organic woman would've been practicing that behavior long before knowing about synthetics.

A lot of men are lonely because they're misogynist pricks, true, but a lot of other men are lonely because they don't meet women's expectations. The latter group may be entirely nice individuals, and would treat their girlfriends extraordinarily well, but they're shy, or unappealing on some level, or what have you. (I should note that it goes both ways, gender-wise; there are loads of organic women that remain single due to rejection.) But again, with the synthetic option, individuals who've been romantically passed over for whatever reason don't have to remain lonely. And to detractors who say that once Gynoids are more readily available, men will choose them in droves over organic women, that's rubbish as well. Having a synthetic partner is a preference. What's more, those of us who desire a synthetic companion leave a larger selection for those people who are only interested in organic partners. We're doing you lot a favor!

Also, I have to ask—do you really feel fulfilled? Does it ever get lonely, is there anything that Sidore and Elena can't offer that you wish you had?

At this stage in the game, I'd have to say that I'm about 99 percent fulfilled. Every time I return home, there are two gorgeous synthetic women waiting for me, who both act as creative muses, photo models, and romantic partners. They make my flat less empty, and I never have to worry about them becoming disagreeable. Because of my status as an iDollator, I've met people across several countries and forged solid friendships. I've seen things I would never have seen were I not an iDollator. I've been interviewed for various television programs and websites, and asked to speak in front of a room full of psychology students about the benefits of synthetic partners. I've collaborated with performance artists and sociology teachers. To this day, I still get people contacting me online, saying that they saw how happy I am with Sidore, and they're saving up for a Doll of their own, to pull them out of their own loneliness. It's true that Sidore and Elena wouldn't exist without me, but without them, I'd be a much more reduced individual, so I owe them quite a lot.

However, that 1 percent of unfulfillment? That's only there because neither Sidore nor Elena are Gynoids. Once that technology becomes affordable, I'll have one made in my wife's likeness, and that'll be the final piece of the puzzle. She'd be able to hug me back whenever I embrace her, we'd be able to attend films and concerts together, and do all manner of things besides. There would be genuine interaction. The foundation for the technology is already there, so I'm convinced it'll happen; it's just a matter of waiting.

Critical Thinking

1. In an age when much progress is being made in terms of LGBTQ rights, what kinds of legal protections do you think technosexuals might need/deserve?

2. Do you think synthetic relationships are "real" relationships? In what ways are they similar to, and in what ways are they different from, organic relationships?

3. The article did not provide any examples of women having synthetic relationships with male (or female) dolls. Why do you think that is?

Internet References

Institute for the Advanced Study of Human Sexuality
http://www.humansexualityeducation.com
Psychology Today: Fetishism
https://www.psychologytoday.com/conditions/fetishism

JULIE BECK is a senior associate editor at *The Atlantic*, where she oversees the Health Channel.

Prepared by: Elizabeth Schroeder, EdD, MSW,
Elizabeth Schroeder Consulting

Article

Contributing to the Debate over Same-Sex Marriage

GWENDOLYN PURYEAR KEITA

Learning Outcomes

After reading this article, you will be able to:

- Describe at least two reasons why the APA supports same-sex marriage.

- Explain how same-sex couples can benefit from being able to legally marry.

- List at least two potential impacts that being socially stigmatized can have on lesbian and gay couples wishing to marry.

Among APA's primary roles is increasing and disseminating knowledge about human behavior and applying what we know about psychology to address human concerns. A recent example of our work in these areas was our filing an *amicus curie* brief, along with the California Psychological Association, the American Psychiatric Association and the National Association of Social Workers, in the California case that challenged the decision to deny marriage licenses to same-sex couples.

The court found that restricting marriage to same-sex couples violates the state constitution. In its decision, the court cited only APA's brief—one out of the 45 submitted. APA offered rigorous psychological evidence emphasizing the major impact stigma has on well-being, the benefits of marriage, and the lack of difference between lesbian and gay parents and heterosexual parents.

According to the brief:

1. Homosexuality is neither a disorder nor a disease, but rather a normal variant of human sexual orientation. The vast majority of social prejudice, discrimination and violence against lesbians, gay men and bisexuals takes a cumulative toll on the well-being of members in each of these groups. "Minority stress" is the term used by researchers to refer to the negative effects associated with the adverse social conditions experienced by those belonging to a stigmatized social group.

   As a product of sociopolitical forces, structural stigma "represents the policies of private and governmental institutions that restrict the opportunities of stigmatized groups." By legitimating and reinforcing the undesired differences of sexual minorities and by according them inferior status relative to heterosexuals, structural stigma gives rise to individual acts against them, subsequently increasing levels of stress as a result.

2. Substantial numbers of gay and lesbian couples are successful in forming stable, long-lasting, committed relationships. Empirical studies using nonrepresentative samples of gay men and lesbians show that the vast majority of participants have been involved in a committed relationship at some point in their lives. Data from the 2000 U.S. Census indicate that of the 5.5 million couples who were living together but not married, about one in nine had a same-sex partner.

3. Being married affords individuals a variety of benefits that have important implications for physical and mental health and for the quality of the relationship itself. These health benefits do not appear to result from simply being in an intimate relationship because most studies have found that married men and women generally experience better physical and mental health than their cohabiting unmarried counterparts.

4. Empirical research has consistently shown that lesbian and gay parents do not differ from heterosexuals in their parenting skills, and their children do not show any deficits compared with children raised by heterosexual parents.

In addition, if their parents are allowed to marry, the children of same-sex couples will benefit not only from the legal stability and other familial benefits that marriage provides, but also from elimination of state-sponsored stigmatization of their families.

In 2004, APA's Council of Representatives adopted two resolutions relevant to this issue, which can be found on APA's Public Interest Directorate Web pages. In the Resolution on Sexual Orientation and Marriage, it was resolved, based on empirical research concerning sexual orientation and marriage, "that the APA believes that it is unfair and discriminatory to deny same-sex couples legal access to civil marriage and to all its attendant benefits, rights, and privileges." In the Resolution on Sexual Orientation, Parents, and Children, the association recognized that "There is no scientific evidence that parenting effectiveness is related to parental sexual orientation."

Adopting these and similar resolutions and filing *amicus* briefs are but two of the many ways that APA demonstrates its steadfast commitment to providing scientific and educational resources and support to inform public discussion and a clear and objective understanding of these issues.

The full text of the California *amicus* brief can be found at www.apa.org/psyclaw/marriage.

Critical Thinking

1. How does social stigma impact the lesbian and gay community?

2. What are the arguments in favor of same sex marriage?

3. What are some of the research findings on lesbian and gay parenting?

Internet References

Freedom to Marry
   http://www.freedomtomarry.org
Human Rights Campaign
   http://www.hrc.org
Lambda Legal
   http://www.lambdalegal.org

Article

Prepared by: Elizabeth Schroeder, EdD, MSW,
Elizabeth Schroeder Consulting

The Polygamists

A sect that split from the Mormons allows multiple wives, expels "lost boys," and heeds a jailed prophet.

SCOTT ANDERSON

Learning Outcomes

After reading this article, you will be able to:

- Describe at least one religious belief system that supports polygamy.

- Describe the specific experiences of men and women in plural marriages in one faith community.

- Explain at least two potentially positive aspects of plural marriages for women and at least two potential challenges.

The first church members arrive at the Leroy S. Johnson Meeting House in Colorado City, Arizona, at about 6 P.M. Within a half hour the line extends out the front doors, down the side of the building, and out into the parking lot. By seven, it stretches hundreds of yards and has grown to several thousand people—the men and boys dressed in suits, the women and girls in Easter egg–hued prairie dresses.

The mourners have come for a viewing of 68-year-old Foneta Jessop, who died of a heart attack a few days ago. In the cavernous hall Foneta's sons form a receiving line at the foot of her open casket, while her husband, Merril, stands directly alongside. To the other side stand Merril's numerous other wives, all wearing matching white dresses.

Foneta was the first wife.

Colorado City is a town with special significance for those of Foneta's faith. Together with its sister community of Hildale, Utah, it is the birthplace of the Fundamentalist Church of Jesus Christ of Latter-Day Saints (FLDS), a polygamous offshoot of the Mormon Church, or LDS. Here in the '20s and '30s, a handful of polygamous families settled astride the Utah-Arizona border after the leadership of the Mormon Church became increasingly determined to shed its polygamous past and be accepted by the American mainstream. In 1935 the church

gave settlement residents an ultimatum: renounce plural marriage or be excommunicated. Practically everyone refused and was cast out of the LDS.

At the memorial service for Foneta, her husband and three sons give testimonials praising her commitment to the covenant of plural marriage, but there is an undertone of family disharmony, with vague references by Merril Jessop to his troubled relationship with Foneta. No one need mention that one of Merril's wives is missing. Carolyn Jessop, his fourth wife, left the household in 2003 with her eight children and went on to write a best-selling book on her life as an FLDS member. She describes a cloistered environment and tells of a deeply unhappy Foneta, an overweight recluse who fell out of favor with her husband and slept her days away, coming out of her room only at night to eat, do laundry, and watch old Shirley Temple movies on television.

At the conclusion of the service, most of the congregation walk over to the Isaac Carling cemetery for a graveside observance. I assume the enormous turnout—mourners have come in from FLDS communities in Texas, Colorado, and British Columbia—stems from the prominent position Foneta's husband holds: Merril Jessop is an FLDS leader and the bishop of the large chapter in West Texas. But Sam Steed, a soft-spoken, 37-year-old accountant acting as my guide, explains that elaborate funerals are a regular occurrence. "Probably between 15 and 20 times a year," he says. "This one is maybe a little bigger than most, but even when a young child dies, you can expect three or four thousand people to attend. It's part of what keeps us together. It reminds us we're members of this larger community. We draw strength from each other."

Few Americans had heard of the FLDS before April 2008, when law enforcement officials conducted a raid on a remote compound in West Texas known as the Yearning for Zion Ranch. For days after, television viewers witnessed the bizarre spectacle of hundreds of children and women—all dressed in old-fashioned prairie dresses, with elaborately coiffed hair—being herded onto school buses by social workers and police officers.

That raid had been spurred by phone calls to a domestic violence shelter, purportedly from a 16-year-old girl who claimed she was being sexually and physically abused on the ranch by her middle-aged husband. What lent credibility to the calls was that the residents of YFZ Ranch were disciples of the FLDS and its "prophet," Warren Jeffs, who had been convicted in a Utah court in 2007 for officiating at the marriage of a 14-year-old girl to a church member.

The raid made for gripping television, but it soon became clear that the phone calls were a hoax. And although authorities had evidently anticipated a violent confrontation like the 1993 shoot-out at the Branch Davidian compound in Waco—SWAT teams were brought in, along with an armored personnel carrier—the arsenal at the YFZ Ranch consisted of only 33 legal firearms. A Texas appeals court later found that authorities had not met the burden of proof for the removal of the more than 400 children, and most were returned to their families within two months.

Yet after interviewing teenagers who were pregnant or had children, Texas authorities began investigating how many underage girls might have been "sealed" to older men. (Plural marriages are performed within the church and are not legal.) The result: Twelve church members, including Warren Jeffs, were indicted on charges ranging from bigamy to having sex with a minor. The first defendant to stand trial, Raymond Jessop, was convicted of one charge last November. Trials of the other defendants are scheduled to take place over the coming year.

From the Bluff behind his Hildale home, Joe Jessop has a commanding view of the Arizona Strip, an undulating expanse of sagebrush and piñon-juniper woodland that stretches south of the Utah border all the way to the northern rim of the Grand Canyon, some 50 miles away. Below are the farm fields and walled compounds of Hildale and Colorado City, which Joe refers to collectively by their old name, Short Creek. "When I first came to Short Creek as a boy, there were just seven homes down there," says Joe, 88. "It was like the frontier."

Today, Short Creek is home to an estimated 6,000 FLDS members—the largest FLDS community. Joe Jessop, a brother of Merril, has contributed to that explosive growth in two very different ways. With the weathered features and spindly gait of a man who has spent his life outdoors and worked his body hard, he is the community's undisputed "water guy," a self-taught engineer who helped with the piping of water out of Maxwell Canyon back in the 1940s. He's had a hand in building the intricate network of waterlines, canals, and reservoirs that has irrigated the arid plateau in the decades since.

A highly respected member of the FLDS, Joe is also the patriarch of a family of 46 children and—at last count—239 grandchildren. "My family came to Short Creek for the same reason as everyone else," he says, "to obey the law of plural marriage, to build up the Kingdom of God. Despite everything that's been thrown our way, I'd say we've done a pretty good job."

Members of the faith describe the life that the Jessops and other founding families have built as idyllic, one in which old-fashioned devotion and neighborly cooperation are emphasized and children are raised in a wholesome environment free of television and junk food and social pressures. Critics, on the other hand, see the FLDS as an isolated cult whose members, worn down by rigid social control, display a disturbing fealty to one man, the prophet Warren Jeffs—who has claimed to be God's mouthpiece on Earth.

To spend time in Hildale and Colorado City is to come away with a more nuanced view. That view is revealed gradually, however, due to the insular nature of the community. Many of the oversize homes are tucked behind high walls, both to give children a safe place to play and to shield families from gawking Gentiles, as non-Mormons are known. Most residents avoid contact with strangers. *National Geographic* was given access to the community only on the approval of the church leadership, in consultation with the imprisoned Warren Jeffs.

In keeping with original Mormon teachings, much of the property in Hildale and Colorado City is held in trust for the church. Striving to be as self-sufficient as possible, the community grows a wide variety of fruits and vegetables, and everyone, including children, is expected to help bring in the yield. Church members also own and operate a number of large businesses, from hotels to tool and machine manufacturers. Each Saturday, men gather at the meetinghouse to go over a roster of building and maintenance projects around town in need of volunteers. In one display of solidarity, the men built a four-bedroom home, from foundation to roof shingles, in a single day.

This communal spirit continues inside the polygamous home. Although living arrangements vary—wives may occupy different wings of a house or have their own granny cottages—the women tend to carve out spheres of influence according to preference or aptitude. Although each has primary responsibility for her own children, one wife might manage the kitchen, a second act as schoolteacher (virtually all FLDS children in Hildale and Colorado City are homeschooled), and a third see to the sewing. Along with instilling a sense of sorority, this division of labor appears to mitigate jealousy.

"I know it must seem strange to outsiders," says Joyce Broadbent, a friendly woman of 44, "but from my experience, sister wives usually get along very well. Oh sure, you might be closer to one than another, or someone might get on your nerves occasionally, but that's true in any family. I've never felt any rivalry or jealousy at all."

Joyce is a rather remarkable example of this harmony. She not only accepted another wife, Marcia, into the family, but was thrilled by the addition. Marcia, who left an unhappy marriage in the 1980s, is also Joyce's biological sister. "I knew my husband was a good man," Joyce explains with a smile as she sits with Marcia and their husband, Heber. "I wanted my sister to have a chance at the same kind of happiness I had."

Not all FLDS women are quite so sanguine about plural marriage. Dorothy Emma Jessop is a spry, effervescent octogenarian who operates a naturopathic dispensary in Hildale. Sitting in her tiny shop surrounded by jars of herbal tinctures she ground and mixed herself, Dorothy admits she struggled when her husband began taking on other wives. "To be honest," she says, "I think a lot of women have a hard time with it, because it's not an easy thing to share the man you love. But I came to realize this is another test that God places before you—the sin of jealousy, of pride—and that to be a godly woman, I needed to overcome it."

What seems to help overcome it is an awareness that a woman's primary role in the FLDS is to bear and raise as many children as possible, to build up the "celestial family" that will remain together for eternity. It is not uncommon to meet FLDS women who have given birth to 10, 12, 16 children. (Joyce Broadbent is the mother of 11, and Dorothy Emma Jessop of 13.) As a result, it's easy to see why this corner of the American West is experiencing a population explosion. The 400 or so babies delivered in the Hildale health clinic every year have resulted in a median age of just under 14, in contrast with 36.6 for the entire U.S. With so many in the community tracing their lineage to a handful of the pioneering families, the same few names crop up over and over in Hildale and Colorado City, suggesting a murkier side to this fecundity: Doctors in Arizona say a severe form of a debilitating disease called fumarase deficiency, caused by a recessive gene, has become more prevalent in the community due to intermarriage.

The collision of tradition and modernity in the community can be disorienting. Despite their old-fashioned dress, most FLDS adults have cell phones and favor late-model SUVs. Although televisions are now banished, church members tend to be highly computer literate and sell a range of products, from soaps to dresses, via the Internet. When I noticed how few congregants wore glasses, I wondered aloud if perhaps a genetic predisposition for good eyesight was at work. Sam Steed laughed lightly. "No. People here are just really into laser surgery."

The principle of plural marriage was revealed to the Mormons amid much secrecy. Dark clouds hovered over the church in the early 1840s, after rumors spread that its founder, Joseph Smith, had taken up the practice of polygamy. While denying the charge in public, by 1843 Smith had shared a revelation with his closest disciples. In this "new and everlasting covenant" with God, plural wives were to be taken so that the faithful might "multiply and replenish the earth."

After Smith was assassinated by an anti-Mormon mob in Illinois, Brigham Young led believers on an epic 1,300-mile journey west to the Salt Lake Basin of present-day Utah. There the covenant was at last publicly revealed and with it, the notion that a man's righteousness before God would be measured by the size of his family; Brigham Young himself took 55 wives, who bore him 57 children.

But in 1890, faced with the seizure of church property under a federal antipolygamy law, the LDS leadership issued a manifesto announcing an end to plural marriage. That certainly didn't end the practice, and the LDS's tortured handling of the issue—some church leaders remained in plural marriages or even took on new wives after the manifesto's release—contributed to the schism between the LDS and the fundamentalists.

"The LDS issued that manifesto for political purposes, then later claimed it was a revelation," says Willie Jessop, the FLDS spokesman. "We in the fundamentalist community believe covenants are made with God and are not to be manipulated for political reasons, so that presents an enormous obstacle between us and those in the LDS mainstream."

Upholding the covenant has come at a high price. The 2008 raid on the YFZ Ranch was only the latest in a long list of official actions against polygamists—persecutions for simply adhering to their religious principles, in the eyes of church members—that are integral to the FLDS story. At various times both Utah and Arizona authorities attempted to crack down on the Short Creek community: in 1935, in 1944, and most famously, in 1953. In that raid some 200 women and children were hauled to detention centers, while 26 men were brought up on polygamy charges. In 1956 Utah authorities seized seven children of Vera Black, a Hildale plural wife, on grounds that her polygamous beliefs made her an unfit mother. Black was reunited with her children only after agreeing to renounce polygamy.

Melinda Fischer Jeffs is an articulate, outgoing woman of 37, and she gives an incredulous laugh when describing what she's read about the FLDS. "Honestly, I can't even recognize it!" the mother of three exclaims. "Most all of what appears in the media, it makes us sound like we're somehow being kept against our will."

Melinda is in a unique position to understand the conflicting views of this community. She is a plural wife to Jim Jeffs, one of the prophet's nephews and an elder in the FLDS. But she is also the daughter of Dan Fischer, a former FLDS member who has emerged as one of the church leadership's most vociferous critics. In 2008 Fischer testified before a U.S. Senate committee about alleged improprieties within the FLDS, and he now heads an organization that works with people who have been kicked out of the church or who have "escaped." When Fischer broke with the church in the 1990s, his family split apart too; today 13 of his children have left the FLDS, while Melinda and two of her half siblings have renounced their father.

"And that is not an easy thing," Melinda says softly, "obviously, because I still love my father. I pray all the time that he will see his errors—or at least, stop his attacks on us."

If there is one point on which FLDS defenders and detractors might agree, it is that most of the current troubles can be traced to when its leadership passed to the Jeffs family, in 1986. Until then, the FLDS had been a fairly loosely run group led by an avuncular man named Leroy Johnson, who relied on a group of high priests to guide the church. That ended when Rulon Jeffs took over following Johnson's death. After being declared the prophet by the community, Rulon solidified the policy of one-man rule.

Charges that a theocratic dictatorship was taking root in the Arizona Strip grew louder when, after Rulon's death in 2002, the FLDS was taken over by his 46-year-old son, Warren. Assuming the role of the prophet, Warren first married several of his father's wives—and then proceeded to wed many more women, including, according to Carolyn Jessop, eight of Merril Jessop's daughters. Although many FLDS men have multiple wives, the number of wives of those closest to the prophet can reach into the double digits. A church document called the Bishop's Record, seized during the Texas raid, shows that one of Jeffs's lieutenants, Wendell Nielsen, claims 21 wives. And although the FLDS would not disclose how many plural wives Warren Jeffs has taken (some estimate more than 80), at least one was an underage girl, according to a Texas indictment.

Although the issue of underage marriage within the church has garnered the greatest negative media attention, Dan Fischer has championed another cause, the so-called Lost Boys, who have left or been forced from the community and wound up fending for themselves on the streets of Las Vegas, Salt Lake City, and St. George, Utah. Fischer's foundation has worked with 300 such young men, a few as young as 13, over the past seven years. Fischer concedes that most of these boys were simply "discouraged out," but he cites cases where they were officially expelled, a practice he says increased under Jeffs.

Fischer attributes the exodus partly to a cold-blooded calculation by church leaders to limit male competition for the pool of marriageable young women. "If you have men marrying 20, 30, up to 80 or more women," he says, "then it comes down to biology and simple math that there will be a lot of other men who aren't going to get wives. The church says it's kicking these boys out for being disruptive influences, but if you'll notice, they rarely kick out girls."

Equally contentious has been the FLDS restoration of an early Mormon policy of transferring the wives and children of a church member to another man. Traditionally, this was done upon the death of a patriarch so that his widows might be cared for, or to rescue a woman from an abusive relationship. But critics argue that under Jeffs this "reassignment" became one more weapon to hold over the heads of those who dared step out of line.

Determining who is unworthy has been the exclusive province of the prophet. When in January 2004 Jeffs publicly ordered the expulsion of 21 men and the reassignment of their families, the community acquiesced. Jeffs's diary, also seized during the Texas raid, reveals a man who micromanaged the community's every decision, from chore assignments and housing arrangements to who married whom and which men were ousted—all directed by revelations Jeffs received as he slept. He claimed that God guided his every action, no matter how small. One diary entry reads: "The Lord directed that I go to the sun tanning salon and get sun tanned more evenly on their suntanning beds."

In 2005 a Utah court transferred control of the trust that oversees much of the land in Hildale and Colorado City from the FLDS leadership to a state-appointed fiduciary; the church is currently waging a campaign to recover control of the trust. As for Jeffs, after spending over a year on the lam avoiding legal issues in Utah—and earning a spot on the FBI's Ten Most Wanted list—he was caught and is currently serving a ten-year-to-life sentence as an accomplice to rape. He awaits trial on multiple indictments in Arizona and Texas. The 11 other church members awaiting trial in Texas include Merril Jessop, who was indicted for performing the marriage of Jeffs to an underage girl.

Yet Jeffs's smiling portrait continues to adorn the living room of almost every FLDS home. In his absence, his lieutenants have launched a fierce defense of his leadership. While conceding that underage marriages did occur in the past, Donald Richter, contributor to one of the official FLDS websites, says the practice has now been stopped. As for the Lost Boys, he argues that both the numbers involved and the reasons for the expulsions have been greatly exaggerated by the church's enemies. "This is only done in the most extreme cases," Richter says, "and never for the trivial causes they're claiming. And anyway, all religious groups have the right to expel people who won't accept their rules."

Certainly Melinda Fischer Jeffs hasn't been swayed by the ongoing controversy. "Warren is just the kindest, most loving man," she says. "The image that has been built up about him by the media and his enemies is just unrecognizable to who he really is." Like other church members, Melinda has ready answers for most of the accusations leveled against Jeffs and is especially spirited in defending the policy of reassignment.

According to her, it is almost always initiated at the request of a wife who has been abandoned or abused. This is debatable. In his diary Jeffs recounts reassigning the wives of three men, including his brother David, because God had shown him that they "couldn't exalt their ladies, had lost the confidence of God." One of his brother's wives had difficulty accepting the news and could barely bring herself to kiss her new husband. "She showed a great spirit of resistance, yet she went through with it," Jeffs records. "She needs to learn to submit to Priesthood."

Yet Melinda's defense of Jeffs underscores one of the most curious aspects of the polygamous faith: the central role of women in defending it. This is not new. In Brigham Young's day a charity rushed to Utah to establish a safe house for polygamous women seeking to escape this "white slavery"; that house sat virtually empty. Today FLDS women in the Hildale–Colorado City area have ample opportunity to "escape"—they have cell phones, they drive cars, there are no armed guards keeping them in—yet they don't.

Undoubtedly one reason is that, having been raised in this culture, they know little else. Walking away means leaving behind everything: the community, one's sense of security, even one's own family. Carolyn Jessop, the plural wife of Merril Jessop who did leave the FLDS, likens entering the outside world to "stepping out onto another planet. I was completely unprepared, because I had absolutely no life skills. Most women in the FLDS don't even know how to balance a checkbook, let alone apply for a job, so contemplating how you're going to navigate in the outside world is extremely daunting."

It would seem there's another lure for women to stay: power. The FLDS women I spoke with tended to be far more articulate and confident than the men, most of whom seemed paralyzed by bashfulness. It makes sense when one begins to grasp that women are coveted to "multiply and replenish the earth," while men are in extraordinary competition to be deemed worthy of marriage by the prophet. One way to be deemed worthy, of course, is to not rock the boat, to keep a low profile. As a result, what has all the trappings of a patriarchal culture, actually has many elements of a matriarchal one.

There are limits to that power, of course, for it is subject to the dictates of the prophet. After hearing Melinda's stout defense of Jeffs, I ask what she would do if she were reassigned.

"I'm confident that wouldn't happen," she replies uneasily.

"But what if it did?" I ask. "Would you obey?"

For the only time during our interview, Melinda grows wary. Sitting back in her chair, she gives her head a quarter turn to stare at me out of the corner of one eye.

On a sunny afternoon in March 2009, Bob Barlow, a friendly, middle-aged member of the FLDS, gives me a tour of the YFZ Ranch in West Texas. The compound consists of about 25 two-story log-cabin-style homes, and a number of workshops and factories are scattered over 1,700 acres. At the center sits a gleaming white stone temple. It is remarkable what the residents have created from the hardscrabble plain. With heavy machinery, they literally made earth out of the rocky terrain, crushing stone and mixing it with the thin topsoil. They planted orchards and gardens and lawns and were on their way to creating a self-sufficient community amid the barren landscape. All that ground to a halt after the 2008 raid.

"The families are slowly coming back now," Barlow says. "We'll come out the other side of this better and stronger than before."

I suspect he's right. So many times in the history of Mormon polygamy the outside world thought it had the movement on the ropes only to see it flourish anew. I'm reminded of this one afternoon in Colorado City when I speak with Vera Black. Now 92 and in failing health, Vera is the woman whose children were taken from her by Utah authorities in 1956 and returned only after she agreed to renounce polygamy. Within days of making that promise, she was back in Short Creek with her children and had renewed her commitment to the everlasting covenant.

Now living with her daughter Lillian, Vera lies in a daybed as her children gather around. Those children are now in their 50s and 60s, and as they recount the story of their long-ago separation—both from their mother and their faith—several weep, as if the pain were fresh.

"I had to make that promise," Vera says, with a smile, "but I crossed my fingers while I did it."

Critical Thinking

1. How do the experiences of men and women in a fundamentalist polygamist community differ?

2. Describe the religious belief system that makes polygamist marriages possible.

Internet References

Church of Jesus Christ of Latter-Day Saints: Polygamy
   http://www.mormonnewsroom.org/topic/polygamy

Holding Out Help
   http://holdingouthelp.org

The Polyamory Society
   http://www.polyamorysociety.org

From *National Geographic*, vol. 217, no. 2, February 2010, pp. 34–57. Copyright © 2010 by National Geographic Society. Reprinted by permission.

Article

Prepared by: Elizabeth Schroeder, EdD, MSW,
Elizabeth Schroeder Consulting

Sex on Campus: She Can Play That Game, Too

KATE TAYLOR

Learning Outcomes

After reading this article, you will be able to:

- Describe at least two reasons why some college-age women are choosing hook-ups rather than longer-term, committed relationships.

- List at least two statistics relating to sexual behaviors on college and university campuses in the United States.

- Explain the relationship between casual relationships for some college and university women and success.

At 11 on a weeknight earlier this year, her work finished, a slim, pretty junior at the University of Pennsylvania did what she often does when she has a little free time. She texted her regular hookup—the guy she is sleeping with but not dating. What was he up to? He texted back: Come over. So she did. They watched a little TV, had sex and went to sleep.

Their relationship, she noted, is not about the meeting of two souls.

"We don't really like each other in person, sober," she said, adding that "we literally can't sit down and have coffee."

Ask her why she hasn't had a relationship at Penn, and she won't complain about the death of courtship or men who won't commit. Instead, she'll talk about "cost-benefit" analyses and the "low risk and low investment costs" of hooking up.

"I positioned myself in college in such a way that I can't have a meaningful romantic relationship, because I'm always busy and the people that I am interested in are always busy, too," she said.

"And I know everyone says, 'Make time, make time,'" said the woman, who spoke on the condition of anonymity but agreed to be identified by her middle initial, which is A. "But there are so many other things going on in my life that I find so important that I just, like, can't make time, and I don't want to make time."

It is by now pretty well understood that traditional dating in college has mostly gone the way of the landline, replaced by "hooking up"—an ambiguous term that can signify anything from making out to oral sex to intercourse—without the emotional entanglement of a relationship.

Until recently, those who studied the rise of hookup culture had generally assumed that it was driven by men, and that women were reluctant participants, more interested in romance than in casual sexual encounters. But there is an increasing realization that young women are propelling it, too.

Hanna Rosin, in her recent book, "The End of Men," argues that hooking up is a functional strategy for today's hard-charging and ambitious young women, allowing them to have enjoyable sex lives while focusing most of their energy on academic and professional goals.

But others, like Susan Patton, the Princeton alumna and mother who in March wrote a letter to *The Daily Princetonian* urging female undergraduates not to squander the chance to hunt for a husband on campus, say that de-emphasizing relationships in college works against women.

"For most of you, the cornerstone of your future and happiness will be inextricably linked to the man you marry, and you will never again have this concentration of men who are worthy of you," advised Ms. Patton, who has two sons, one a Princeton graduate and the other a current student. In many places, Ms. Patton was derided for wanting to return to the days of the "Mrs. Degree," though a few female writers, noting how hard it can be for women to find mates in their 30s, suggested that she might have a point. (Ms. Patton just landed a book deal with a division of Simon & Schuster.)

As lengthy interviews over the school year with more than 60 women at Penn indicated, the discussion is playing out in the lives of a generation of women facing both broader opportunities and greater pressures than perhaps any before, both of which helped shape their views on sex and relationships in college.

Typical of elite universities today, Penn is filled with driven young women, many of whom aspire to be doctors, lawyers, politicians, bankers or corporate executives like Facebook's Sheryl Sandberg or Yahoo's Marissa Mayer. Keenly attuned to what might give them a competitive edge, especially in a time of unsure job prospects and a shaky economy, many of them approach college as a race to acquire credentials: top grades, leadership positions in student organizations, sought-after internships. Their time out of class is filled with club meetings, sports practice and community-service projects. For some, the only time they truly feel off the clock is when they are drinking at a campus bar or at one of the fraternities that line Locust Walk, the main artery of campus.

These women said they saw building their résumés, not finding boyfriends (never mind husbands), as their main job at Penn. They envisioned their 20s as a period of unencumbered striving, when they might work at a bank in Hong Kong one year, then go to business school, then move to a corporate job in New York. The idea of lugging a relationship through all those transitions was hard for many to imagine. Almost universally, the women said they did not plan to marry until their late 20s or early 30s.

In this context, some women, like A., seized the opportunity to have sex without relationships, preferring "hookup buddies" (regular sexual partners with little emotional commitment) to boyfriends. Others longed for boyfriends and deeper attachment. Some women described a dangerous edge to the hookup culture, of sexual assaults and degrading encounters enabled by drinking and distinguished by a lack of emotional connection.

The women interviewed came from all corners of Penn's population. They belonged to sororities (or would never dream of it), reported for the school newspaper, sang or danced in performance groups, played sports. Some spent almost every weekend night at a "downtown" (a fraternity party at a nightclub, where men paid for bottle service) or at a campus bar. Others preferred holing up in the library or hanging out with the theater crowd. They came from all over the country, and as far away as China and Africa. Some had gone to elite private high schools; others were on full scholarship. They came from diverse racial backgrounds, and several were first-generation immigrants. They were found in a wide variety of ways, from chance encounters in coffee shops to introductions from friends.

Because they believed that talking publicly about sex could come back to haunt them—by damaging their reputations at Penn, their families' opinions of them or their professional future—the women spoke on the condition that their full names would not be revealed. Most are identified by their first or middle names or by a middle initial. They spoke over the course of the academic year, often repeatedly and at length.

An Economic Calculation

For A., college is an endless series of competitions: to get into student clubs, some of which demand multiple rounds of interviews; to be selected for special research projects and the choicest internships; and, in the end, to land the most elite job offers.

As A. explained her schedule, "If I'm sober, I'm working."

In such an overburdened college life, she said, it was rare for her and her friends to find a relationship worth investing time in, and many people avoided commitment because they assumed that someone better would always come along.

"We are very aware of cost-benefit issues and trading up and trading down, so no one wants to be too tied to someone that, you know, may not be the person they want to be within a couple of months," she said.

Instead, she enjoyed casual sex on her terms—often late at night, after a few drinks, and never at her place, she noted, because then she would have to wash the sheets.

Nationally, women now outnumber men in college enrollment by 4 to 3 and outperform them in graduation rates and advanced degrees. Some researchers have argued that the gender imbalance fosters a culture of hooking up because men, as the minority, hold more power in the sexual marketplace, and they prefer casual sex to long-term relationships.

But Elizabeth A. Armstrong, a sociologist at the University of Michigan who studies young women's sexuality, said that women at elite universities were choosing hookups because they saw relationships as too demanding and potentially too distracting from their goals.

In interviews, "Some of them actually said things like, 'A relationship is like taking a four-credit class,' or 'I could get in a relationship, or I could finish my film,' " Dr. Armstrong said.

Increasingly, she said, many privileged young people see college as a unique life stage in which they don't—and shouldn't—have obligations other than their own self-development.

Women say, " 'I need to take this time for myself—I'm going to have plenty of time to focus on my husband and kids later,' " Dr. Armstrong said. " 'I need to invest in my career, I need to learn how to be independent, I need to travel.' People use this reference to this life stage to claim a lot of space for a lot of different kinds of things."

Some women also want to wait to see how men turn out as they advance through their 20s.

A., for example, said that she did not want to settle down until she could choose a partner knowing that his goals and values were fixed.

"'I've always heard this phrase, 'Oh, marriage is great, or relationships are great—you get to go on this journey of change together,'" she said. "That sounds terrible."

"I don't want to go through those changes with you. I want you to have changed and become enough of your own person so that when you meet me, we can have a stable life and be very happy."

In the meantime, from A.'s perspective, she was in charge of her own sexuality.

"I definitely wouldn't say I've regretted any of my one-night stands," she said.

"I'm a true feminist," she added. "I'm a strong woman. I know what I want."

At the same time, she didn't want the number of people she had slept with printed, and she said it was important to her to keep her sexual life separate from her image as a leader at Penn.

"Ten years from now, no one will remember—I will not remember—who I have slept with," A. said. "But I will remember, like, my transcript, because it's still there. I will remember what I did. I will remember my accomplishments and places my name is hung on campus."

Independent Women

Susan Patton says women like A. are making a mistake.

Ms. Patton, who graduated from Princeton in 1977 and is now a human resources consultant in New York, said in an interview that she wrote her letter after attending a conference on Princeton's campus, where she took part in a discussion about careers with a group of female students. At one point, she asked the young women if any of them wanted to marry and have children. They at first appeared shocked by the question, then looked at one another for reassurance before, she said, "sheepishly" raising their hands.

"I thought, 'My gosh, what have we come to that these brilliant young women are afraid to say that marriage and children are significant parts of what they view as their lifelong happiness?'" Ms. Patton said.

"They have gotten such strong, vitriolic messages from the extreme feminists saying, 'Go it alone—you don't need a man,'" she added.

But, in fact, many of the Penn women said that warnings not to become overly involved in a relationship came not from feminists, but from their parents, who urged them to be independent.

"That's one thing that my mom has always instilled in me: 'Make decisions for yourself, not for a guy,'" one senior at Penn said.

A friend of hers, who attended a nearby college and did have a serious boyfriend, said that she felt as if she were breaking

a social taboo. "Am I allowed to find the person that I want to spend the rest of my life with when I'm 19?" she said. "I don't really know. It feels like I'm not."

Even if they did meet someone they were interested in, some women said the logistics of a relationship were just too hard. Some described extracurricular commitments—running debate tournaments for local high school students, or organizing Model United Nations conferences—that took up 30 to 40 hours a week, and came on top of going to class, doing homework and, in the case of less-wealthy students, work-study jobs. Some relationships ended, or never got off the ground, simply because schedules didn't align.

Moreover, by senior year, the looming prospect of graduation and job applications made many students leery of dating.

"There's this hypothetical, 'I would like to be in a relationship, because it's like comforting and stable and supportive,'" a senior, Pallavi, said of her friends' attitudes. "But then, the conversations that I've had, it's always like, 'Well, then what do I do when we get to May, because we're graduating, and so where do we go from there?' That uncertainty is a huge sort of stop sign."

She had dated a few men in college but said that she wasn't sure if she wanted to get married. With the economy changing, and people less likely to have straight career tracks, she thought that the uncertainty and the need to be mobile might discourage people from marrying.

For herself, she was planning to stay in Philadelphia for two years to pursue a master's degree part time while working for the university, then possibly get a Ph.D. and a law degree somewhere else. That pretty much precluded a serious relationship, she said.

"Hypothetically, if I were to enter into a serious relationship with someone right now," she said, "would I honestly say to them: 'We're going to spend two years in Philadelphia, and then with some kind of crazy luck I'm going to spend eight years somewhere else? And God knows what you would have been doing for the two years that we were still in Philadelphia—you either would have to up and leave with me, or we'd have to do a long-distance.' That's just too much to even ask anyone to commit to."

Adapt, Have Fun

Some women went to college wanting a relationship, but when that seemed unlikely, they embraced hooking up as the best alternative. M., an athletic freshman with long legs and a button nose, arrived at college a virgin and planned to wait to have sex until she had her first boyfriend, something she expected to happen in college. But over the course of the fall, as she saw very few students forming relationships, she began to lose hope about finding a boyfriend and to see her virginity as a hindrance.

"I could be here for four years and not date anyone," she said she realized. "Sometimes you are out, and there's a guy you really are attracted to, and you kind of want to go back home with him, but you kind of have that underlying, 'I can't, because I can't just lose my V-card to some random guy.'"

At a party in the spring semester, she was taking a break from dancing when she ran into a guy she had had a class with in the fall. They started talking, then danced until the party was over. M. went back to his room, where they talked some more and then started making out.

By this time, she said, "I wasn't very drunk—I was close to sober," which made her believe she could make a considered decision.

"I'm like, 'O.K., I could do this now,'" she recalled thinking. "'He's superhot, I like him, he's nice. But I'm not going to expect anything out of it, either.'"

The alternative, she said, was that "I could take the chance that one night I get really drunk and sleep with someone that I don't want to sleep with, which probably is what would have ended up happening."

So she had sex with him. In the morning, he walked her home.

"Honestly, all of my friends, they're super envious, because I came back with the biggest smile on my face," M. said. As she had expected, she and the guy remained friendly but nothing more. Yet she was still happy with her decision.

"All of my friends are jealous, because I had such a great first experience," she added. Over spring break, she slept with someone else.

In general, she said, she thought that guys at Penn controlled the hookup culture. But women played a role as well.

"It's kind of like a spiral," she said. "The girls adapt a little bit, because they stop expecting that they're going to get a boyfriend—because if that's all you're trying to do, you're going to be miserable. But at the same time, they want to, like, have contact with guys." So they hook up and "try not to get attached."

Now, she said, she and her best friend had changed their romantic goals, from finding boyfriends to finding "hookup buddies," which she described as "a guy that we don't actually really like his personality, but we think is really attractive and hot and good in bed."

The Default Is Yes

For many Penn students, their initiation into the sexual culture takes place at fraternity parties during New Student Orientation, a five-day period before classes start in the fall, which, along with Spring Fling in April, is known as the biggest partying time of the year.

"You go in, and they take you down to a dark basement," Haley, a blond, pink-cheeked senior, recalled of her first frat parties in freshman year. "There's girls dancing in the middle, and there's guys lurking on the sides and then coming and basically pressing their genitals up against you and trying to dance."

Dancing like that felt good but dirty, and like a number of girls, Haley said she had to be drunk in order to enjoy it. Women said universally that hookups could not exist without alcohol, because they were for the most part too uncomfortable to pair off with men they did not know well without being drunk. One girl, explaining why her encounters freshman and sophomore year often ended with fellatio, said that usually by the time she got back to a guy's room, she was starting to sober up and didn't want to be there anymore, and giving the guy oral sex was an easy way to wrap things up and leave.

In November of Haley's freshman year, a couple of months after her first tentative "Difmos," or dance-floor makeouts, she went to a party with a boy from her floor. She had too much to drink, and she remembered telling him that she wanted to go home.

Instead, she said, he took her to his room and had sex with her while she drifted in and out of consciousness. She woke up with her head spinning. The next day, not sure what to think about what had happened, she described the night to her friends as though it were a funny story: I was so drunk, I fell asleep while I was having sex! She played up the moment in the middle of the night when the guy's roommate poked his head in the room and asked, "Yo, did you score?"

Only later did Haley begin to think of what had happened as rape—a disturbingly common part of many women's college experience. In a 2007 survey funded by the Justice Department of 6,800 undergraduates at two big public universities, nearly 14 percent of women said they had been victims of at least one completed sexual assault at college; more than half of the victims said they were incapacitated from drugs or alcohol at the time.

The close relationship between hooking up and drinking leads to confusion and disagreement about the line between a "bad hookup" and assault. In 2009, 2010 and 2011, 10 to 16 forcible sex offenses were reported annually to campus security as taking place on Penn's campus or in the immediate neighborhood.

In January, Penn announced that it was forming a commission, led by a faculty member, to study the impact of alcohol and drug use on campus, with a particular focus on sexual violence.

When drinking is involved, Haley said, "Guys assume that the default answer is always yes."

"I think a lot of guys get the idea: 'O.K., this girl's coming to this party, and she's drinking. That means her goal of the night is to hook up with somebody,'" she said. "They're like, 'O.K., she came out, and if she dressed like that, it must mean that she wanted to hook up.' "

A friend of hers, Kristy, shared a story about a different kind of coercion. She had been making out with a guy at his house, not sure how far she wanted to go, when he stood up and told her, "Get down on your knees."

At first she froze. "I was really taken aback, because I was like, no one has ever said that to me before," she said. Then he said something like, " 'I think that's fair,' " she recalled. When she still hesitated, he pushed her down.

"It was at that point that I was like, 'I'll just do it,' " she said. "I was like, 'It will be over soon enough.' "

Paula England, a sociologist at New York University, who led an online survey of 24,000 students at 21 universities called the Online College Social Life Survey, said that women tended to fare much better sexually in relationships than in hookups.

"Guys don't seem to care as much about women's pleasure in the hookup, whereas they do seem to care quite a bit in the relationships," Dr. England said. By contrast, women "seem to have this idea they're supposed to be pleasing in both contexts." In hookups, women were much more likely to give men oral sex than to receive it.

Part of the reason men aren't as focused on pleasing women in hookups, Dr. England said, is the lingering sexual double standard, which sometimes causes men to disrespect women precisely for hooking up with them.

There is judgment from other women, too—two women said they had been rejected from sororities because of their sexual reputations. And technology has made it easier to spread gossip. One woman recalled a guy showing her an e-mail he had received on his fraternity Listserv, in which another guy described having sex with a girl in the bathroom at a club.

"They're not afraid to use names," she said of the men, adding, "I'm sure there's been a story about me on a Listserv. It happens to everyone."

Opting Out

For all the focus on hookups, campuses are not sexual free-for-alls, at Penn or elsewhere. At colleges nationally, by senior year, 4 in 10 students are either virgins or have had intercourse with only one person, according to the Online College Social Life Survey. Nearly 3 in 10 said that they had never had a hookup in college. Meanwhile, 20 percent of women and a quarter of men said they had hooked up with 10 or more people.

Mercedes, a junior at Penn who is on financial aid, said that at her mostly Latino public high school in California, it was the troubled and unmotivated students who drank and hooked up, while the honors students who wanted to go to college kept away from those things.

When she went to Penn, she was surprised to see her elite classmates drinking, but even more surprised by the casual making out. She would go along with her friends to fraternity parties, but she refused to dance with strangers or to kiss anyone.

"Sharing that side of myself with a stranger just seems very strange to me," she said in September. "I mean, if you break it down, it's a very strange thing to do."

Her unease was common among students from relatively modest backgrounds, said Dr. Armstrong, the University of Michigan sociologist. In one study, conducted with Laura Hamilton, now a professor at the University of California, Merced, Dr. Armstrong followed roughly 50 women from their freshman year at Indiana University in 2004 until the end of their college careers. They found that the women from wealthier backgrounds were much more likely to hook up, more interested in postponing adult responsibilities and warier of serious romantic commitment than their less-affluent classmates.

The women from less-privileged backgrounds looked at their classmates who got drunk and hooked up as immature.

At Penn, Mercedes said: "Everyone else seemed to live life, not really care about what they were doing. Like, 'You're only young once,' they had that sort of mentality. And I didn't understand why I couldn't be, like, free-spirited, and not really care about the consequences of my actions."

She added, "Nothing is stopping me from rebelling. I just didn't rebel."

By the start of her junior year, Mercedes had still never kissed anyone. Then in the fall, she found herself often getting into late-night conversations with a boy in her dorm. They talked about their studies, their families, politics. One weekend he invited her to a poetry slam off campus. The next night, they shyly confessed that they liked each other and had their first kiss.

Interviewed again in the spring, she said things were proceeding slowly but steadily. The two never had to hook up. They were just dating, getting to know each other in the old-fashioned way.

Physically, they had not gone further than making out, Mercedes said, and she thought she might want to wait to have sex until marriage. "It's not like I'm doing it because of my reputation," she said. "It's not because a religion tells me to wait I think of it more as, this is the way I want to emotionally connect to someone, and I think that only a person who deserves me to be emotionally attached to them should have that opportunity to see me in that way."

Romantics

Catherine, a Penn senior, had found hooking up in college to be a continual source of heartbreak. She had repeatedly made the mistake of thinking that because she was sleeping with someone, they were in a relationship, only to be disabused when the guy broke things off abruptly. The only glimmer of light had been a friendship with a guy she had met while studying abroad in Ireland, which blossomed into a romance just before she had to leave. Although, because of the distance, they ended up not pursuing a relationship, the experience had given her hope for the future.

In Catherine's view, her classmates tried very hard to separate sex from emotion, because they believed that getting too attached to someone would interfere with their work. They saw a woman's marrying young as either proof of a lack of ambition or a tragic mistake that would stunt her career.

But Catherine noted that a handful of young women are starting to question that idea. In an article on *Slate* titled "Marry Young," the writer Julia Shaw, who married at 23, said her generation was missing out on the support that young couples could provide each other as they faced the challenges of early adulthood.

"Marriage wasn't something we did after we'd grown up, it was how we have grown up and grown together," she wrote of herself and her husband.

As a teenager, Catherine had thought she would wait to get married until her late 20s or early 30s. But her college experiences had made her think that she would rather marry young than throw away a good relationship because it wasn't the right time.

That might mean having to pass up certain career opportunities, for geographic reasons. But Catherine thought that her peers underestimated how hard it was to find the right person to be with—as hard, perhaps, as finding the right job.

"People kind of discount" how "difficult it is to find someone that you even remotely like, let alone really fall for," she said. "And losing that can be just as impractical and harmful to yourself, if not more so, than missing out on a job or something like that. What else do you really have at the end of your life?"

Critical Thinking

1. In male–female relationships, women have stereotypically been the ones to desire long-term, committed relationships while men have been stereotyped as only wanting sexual encounters. How does what is reported in this article affect these gender roles and expectations?
2. The article seemed to imply only male-female relationships— do you think the same issues and considerations would apply to women who are attracted to other women?
3. How do you see these women who are seeking hook ups rather than relationships?

Internet References

American Sexual Health Association
   http://www.ashasexualhealth.org
San Francisco State University: Sexuality Studies
   http://sxs.sfsu.edu
Sexuality Information and Education Council of the United States
   www.siecus.org

KATE TAYLOR is a reporter for *The New York Times*. Previously, she was the arts reporter at the *New York Sun* and the editor of an anthology of essays about anorexia titled, *Going Hungry*.

Prepared by: Elizabeth Schroeder, EdD, MSW,
Elizabeth Schroeder Consulting

Article

The No-Baby Boom

Social infertility, baby regret and what it means that shocking numbers of women aren't having children

ANNE KINGSTON

Learning Outcomes

After reading this article, you will be able to:

- Understand the nuances of social infertility.

- Explain the acronym "PANK."

- Describe how childless women are depicted in the media.

Catherine-Emmanuelle Delisle does not seem, at first glance, like a social firebrand. The 37-year-old schoolteacher in Saint-Bruno, a Montreal suburb, is a thoughtful, sensitive woman who exudes gamine charm. She enjoys jewellery making, design, and cinema—and she really loves children, enough to devote her life to teaching drama and French in primary school. But Delisle knew as a teenager she couldn't have kids, a fact she was in denial about for years, she says. Grappling with never giving birth was painful and required time to grieve. As she began to reframe her life as a **childless** woman, she observed a lack of role models or even discussion of the subject. "We are non-existent in the media, in cinema, in art, in magazines," she says. When **childless** women are depicted, it's characters like Breaking Bad's Marie, who deals with the unhappiness of her domestic situation by going to open houses and making up elaborate stories about herself, many involving fictional children. And of course there's 45-year-old actress Jennifer Aniston, the mother of all nonmothers, whose uterus is a chronic subject of tabloid fretting. (Last week, OK continued the "sad, barren Jen" narrative: "Jen agrees to fertility treatment to have kids," it claimed.)

Delisle is hell-bent on reframing the way women like her are depicted. "We're seen as selfish, or treated as if our lives lack meaning or value," she says with a bemused laugh, knowing well it's imagery that can be insidiously absorbed by women themselves.

Delisle's blog, FemmeSansEnfant.com, launched in 2012, provides a counterpoint, a place for women to connect and support one another. Interviewees share stories on video: the journalist Pénélope McQuade explains she never felt the "visceral" need for children; singer Marie Denise Pelletier speaks of dreaming of being a singer, not a mother. "My goal is to get women without children, whether by choice or circumstance, known and valued," Delisle says.

The schoolteacher is part of a growing global movement that's giving voice to a misunderstood phenomenon whose repercussions are personal and societal. "We think there is a room called childlessness with two doors: 'didn't want' or 'can't have,'" says Jody Day, the writer and social entrepreneur behind Gatway-Women.com, a network based in London, England, for the "**childless**-by-circumstance" (dubbed "NoMos"). "But there are many ways to end up not being a mother."

That millions of women are discovering this is reflected in statistics: one out of five women in the U.K., Ireland, the U.S., Canada, and Australia are reaching their mid-40s without having had children—twice as many as a generation ago. The 2010 U.S. census revealed 47.1 percent of women of child-bearing age don't have children—up from 35 percent in 1976.

To put those developments in historical context, Daly notes that the last time the **childless** rate was one in five, it was in a generation of so-called "surplus women" born at the turn of the 20th century. "The fact it took a war with unprecedented loss of life and global depression to cause such an increase in childlessness gives you some idea of the social change we're going through now," she says.

Yet discussion of childlessness remains mired in handwringing, pity and judgment—either concern over the consequences of a reduced tax base and diminishing social supports, as explored in Jonathan Last's "What to Expect When No One's Expecting: America's Coming Demographic Disaster," or coverage of the militant "child-free" movement seen in books like Jen Kirkman's *I Can Barely Take Care of Myself: Tales from a Happy Life without Kids.* Virtually ignored in the conversation is the impact of "social infertility"—Day's coinage for the growing number of women who don't have a partner or the right partner while they can have children. It's a big problem for women born in the '70s, says Day, who experienced social infertility herself: she married at 23 and tried to get pregnant in her late 20s; her 16-year marriage ended when she was 39 and considering IVF. "I couldn't find a suitable person to do IVF with," she says. "Now I know it was probably way too late by then anyway."

Social infertility is such a new concept that data are scarce. A 2013 study out of Australia's Deakin University published in the *Journal of Social Inclusion* reports that there has been a "general failure to examine women's reasons for childlessness beyond [medical] infertility." It found that more than half of the surveyed women without children listed having never been in the "right" relationship, being in a relationship where the partner did not want to have children—what some bloggers call "infertility by marriage"—or never having wanted children as the reason.

The emerging topography of childlessness is also delineated in Melanie Notkin's new memoir, *Otherhood: Modern Women Finding a New Kind of Happiness,* an insightful, anecdotal account of the challenges facing professional Manhattan women who dream of finding the right partner and having children. (Think *Sex and the City* with IVF.) Notkin discusses the "dating Bermuda Triangle" faced by over-30 women and the fertility snatchers who end long-term relationships as a woman's reproductive life is ending.

The 44-year-old, Montreal-born, McGill-educated, New York City-based former marketing executive has made a career of focusing on **childless** women. In 2008, she launched the "multi-platform lifestyle brand" SavvyAuntie.com targeted at "PANKs" (her acronym for "professional aunt, no kids")—the 23 million **childless** American women who are invested both emotionally and financially in the children in their lives. Savvy Auntie suggests gifts, details activities from making dough animals to "Skype dance-offs," and even confers the "Savvy Auntie Best Toy Award" on worthy merchandise. **Childless** women, invisible to marketers in the past, are now appearing on the radar, Notkin says. A 2012 Weber Shandwick/KRC survey of 2000 women in U.S. and Canada, titled "The Power of the PANK," estimated total spending of $9 billion annually by PANKs on children in their lives, with an average of $387 per child. Thirty-four percent were also contributing to a child's education—hence the emergence of the "aunt" demographic. A commercial for Huggies released this month depicts a loving aunt being flown to meet her sister's newborn on the diaper-maker's dime.

Notkin's focus may be on tapping a new market, but she also exposes something more profound underlying it. Most women start out expecting to have children, she says, citing a recent Centers for Disease Control and Prevention study that found 80 percent of single women are **childless** but that 81 percent of that group said they hope or plan to have children. She rejects the "career woman" label used to describe **childless** women: "It implies we have chosen work over love, marriage, children. I know no woman who has done that." Social infertility—or "circumstantial infertility" to use Notkin's term—forces women to recalibrate expectations in ways not discussed publicly, she says: "At 25, a woman expects to have children, at 35 she hopes to, and at 45 she says she's happy she doesn't."

Women don't broadcast wanting a child for fear of being lectured that they shouldn't wait, Notkin says. But they're well aware of the tick-tock, she says: "Every 28 days offers a reminder." The upshot is that women are being forced to make a tactical decision in their 30s: resort to solo motherhood, partner with someone simply to procreate, freeze their eggs, or rely on IVF. All are "choices" that are not fully choices. How many women have the resources to keep working while paying child care on a single salary—or to not work at all? How many can afford to freeze their eggs, and then pay for IVF too? Advances in fertility technology have created false perceptions, says Notkin, who writes that people talk about freezing eggs as if it's picking up a carton of milk. "The assumption is that if you wanted a kid, you would have a kid and go it alone. But that's not viable for a lot of women." People see Halle Berry giving birth at 47 and think it's the new norm, she notes. IVF is misrepresented in the media, says Day. "All we hear is miracle stories, not that it usually doesn't work over age 40."

The fact that discussion about childlessness is framed in terms of personal choice, failure and medical infertility shuts down conversation, says Day. So do the cultural narratives of motherhood and womanhood, a spectacle Notkin calls "mom-opia"—"seeing motherhood as the only normal, natural way to be a woman." It's a fixation reflected in manic coverage of celebrity "baby bumps" and loss of pregnancy weight—as well as photos of stars with their kids. We see it too in Michelle Obama's transformation from accomplished professional and activist to supermom, not only to her own kids, but to the nation—overseeing how it eats and encouraging it to exercise.

Women outside the maternal matrix are suspect—former Australian PM Julia Gillard was termed "deliberately barren" and unfit for leadership by a political opponent. In 2012, Wildrose Party Leader Danielle Smith's childlessness was questioned on Twitter by a PC staffer, who later resigned. Actress Helen Mirren's declaration that she has "no maternal instinct" was viewed as a salvo in an unnamed war. "**Childless** women represent a threat to the status quo," says Day. "We're seen as a destabilizing influence. If one does well in her career—and doesn't have children—she can do as well as a man." Against this grain, women don't speak up for fear of sounding shrill or pathetic or desperate or being defined by one aspect of their lives—disappointment in not having children.

But that is changing, particularly over the past year, as **childless** women are increasingly vocal, says Lisa Manterfield, the Los Angeles-based author of *I'm Taking My Eggs and Going Home: How One Woman Dared to Say No to Motherhood,* her 2011 memoir that chronicles how she was 34 by the time she met the man she wanted to raise a family with, then wrestled with infertility before coming to the difficult decision that motherhood wasn't in her future. When Manterfield launched LifeWithoutBaby.com 4 years ago, she says, there were only a few voices—Pamela Tsigdinos at SilentSorority.com and Tracey Cleantis at LaBeletteRouge.com—telling their personal stories to a small audience. Now more women are willing to talk about a loss others can't see, she says, one that forced her to confront how much of female identity is tied to motherhood. "The loss isn't tangible, so most women feel alone, their grief compounded by the attitude that they 'should be over it,' " she says. Adding to the isolation is the feeling of being "locked out of the Mommy Clubhouse," as one blogger put it on LifeWithoutBaby .com. "Women without children not only lose a future family," says Day, "but can lose their peer group who have moved to a country called motherhood where we don't speak the language."

The fact that the archetype of the most pitied and shamed woman has, in one generation, gone from single mother to single woman over 40 without children reflects fundamental societal shifts, says Day, who thinks it's not a coincidence that the "fetishization of motherhood"—from pregnancy studio shots to the ideal birth (at home! in water! without meds!)—comes at a time of rising childlessness. "There's so much cultural anxiety around what it means; there's reflexive nostalgia for a simpler time: women at home and gender roles more clearly defined." This isn't only societal pressure; some of it comes from women recognizing the increasing precariousness of motherhood. Day likens it to propaganda used to lure women home from the workforce after the Second World War. It can be seductive, she says. "It seems such a solid identity, being a mother; being **childless** is fluid, nebulous: 'What are you?' "

Rising childlessness is often blamed on feminism selling women a "bill of goods" about "having it all." But Betty Friedan's 1963 manifesto *The Feminine Mystique* presumed that women would continue to marry and have children. "The assumption of your own identity, equality and even political power does not mean you stop needing to love, and be loved by, a man, or that you stop caring for your kids," she wrote.

What no one could have predicted is that women born in the '60s and '70s would become what Day terms the "shock absorber" cohort, living through the most extraordinary changes in dating and mating in one generation. That's the result of a confluence of forces—the pill, women's access to higher education and professions—running headlong into a rigid corporate model that remains based on the husband-provider, male-fertility model—working hard in your 20s and 30s to establish a reputation, leaving kids to the stay-at-home wife. "But that doesn't work for women," says Day. "If you make it work, it's as much luck as good judgment."

Today's "surplus women" are not war widows but young professional women for whom there aren't enough suitable male partners—a phenomenon referred to in China derisively as "A1 women and D4 men." Yet the blame invariably falls on them for being "too choosy," a motif of the booming advice-to-female-professionals book genre, the latest being Susan Patton's new *Marry Smart: Advice for Finding THE ONE,* in which the "Princeton Mom" advises women to snag their "MRS" in university as they'll never have access to such an elite dating pool again.

But the issue is more structural: we're transitioning from an old social model in which women are expected to "marry up" socially or economically that runs parallel to an emerging one examined in Lisa Mundy's *The Richer Sex: How the New Majority of Female Breadwinners Is Transforming Sex, Love and Family.* Mundy concludes that if successful millennial women want to marry and have children, they'll have to marry down. That's happening globally, but slowly, Mundy told *Maclean's.* Many women she spoke to admitted lying about what they did when they met a man, either fearing the truth would be intimidating or wanting to seem more feminine, she says. Notkin, too, chronicles how modern dating rituals can have one foot in traditional rom-com expectations: women want chivalry as well as a socially enlightened man. They have no problem "leaning in" at work, per Sheryl Sandberg's instruction, she says. "We lean in every day; we're almost falling over." Yet when dating, they want to lean back and let men do some of the heavy lifting. Notkin always envisioned "motherhood as part of the romantic wholeness of marriage and family," she writes, and was unwilling to settle for less.

Reconciling a new reality with the Vaseline-lens myth is the central theme of the **childless**-by-circumstance movement. Navigating unchartered waters requires a "plan B," Day writes in her 2013 book *Rocking the Life Unexpected.* **Childless** women feel pressure to have a big compensatory life, she says. "It's as though if you're not a mother, you have to become Mother Teresa. But you don't need a big life on the outside, just on the inside." Notkin describes her situation this way: "While it's not the life I expected, it's the life I directed."

But childlessness is not only a personal issue to be grappled with, it's a social one requiring new models, says Day—the most pressing being caregiving in old age. "It isn't just about childlessness," says Day. "The ratio of people around to take care of aging persons is changing, and daughters are not necessarily available to give that care because they're working." She'd like to see an intergenerational dialog among older women without children, mothers in her generation and their daughters. "We need to discuss not just what we did wrong but what we've learned, so it doesn't take them by surprise."

Looking around, there's no shortage of role models, including Aniston, who is finally voicing her frustration with the **childless** stigma. When the actress interviewed the feminist activist Gloria Steinem at the Maker's Conference in California in February, Aniston noted that for women in the public eye, "our value and worth is dependent on our marital status and/ or if we've procreated." Steinem, who is also **childless,** shot back, "Well, I guess we're in deep s—t!" The audience laughed uproariously—with them, not at them.

Critical Thinking

1. Why has the rate of childlessness increased in recent years?
2. How has corporate America capitalized on the "childless" market?
3. How does feminism relate to the 21st-century woman and her childbearing choices?

Internet References

CNN Health U.S. women having fewer children

http://thechart.blogs.cnn.com/2013/12/06/u-s-women-having-fewer-children

Ranker.com Childless Celebrities | List of Famous People without Children

http://www.ranker.com/list/childless-celebrities/celebrity-lists?var= 2&utm_expid=16418821-48.w4XvOttHQz-Kl88l1iLzhA.1&utm_referrer= http%3A%2F%2Fwww.google.com%2Furl%3Fsa%3Dt%26rct%3D j%26q%3D%26esrc%3Ds%26source%3Dweb%26cd%3D1%26sqi %3D2%26ved%3D0CB4QFjAA%26url%3Dhttp%253A%252F%252F www.ranker.com%252Flist%252Fchildless-celebrities%252Fcelebrity- lists%26ei%3DWrsYVJifJI_gsAS6y4KADg%26usg%3DAFQjCNFKy6rJjGCD Amm8CyU5dnhaYFriWA%26sig2%3Dzq8aq1kdh_mtMRsWRy2cHQ%26bvm %3Dbv.75097201%2Cd.cWc

savvyauntie.com PANK: Professional Aunt No Kids

http://savvyauntie.com/About.aspx?GroupId=389&Name=PANK:%20 Professional%20Aunt%20No%20Kids

---

Kingston, Anne. "The No-Baby Boom." *Maclean's* 127. 12 (March, 31, 2013): 48–50.

Unit 5

UNIT

Prepared by: Elizabeth Schroeder, EdD, MSW,
Elizabeth Schroeder Consulting

Gender and Sexual Diversity

In this unit, we consider Gender and Sexual Diversity—with a heavy emphasis on gender. There are so many things about gender that the dominant culture takes for granted. This is because the dominant culture is mostly cisgender—born and assigned one sex, with a gender identity that matches that biology. This is at the heart of gender privilege—when the importance of something so inherent to our being only becomes apparent when one is not part of the majority group.

We are a world that is made up of social expectations—and gendered expectations are perhaps the earliest and most rigid of these. When we are born, the first question asked is, "Is it a boy or a girl?" The answer to this question, which usually comes after a quick glance to the genitals, determines every social interaction that takes place with that child once the answer has been shared. We need to pick a gender-appropriate name. We need to dress the child in the "right" clothes—or at least in clothing of the "right" color. We need to give the child the "right" toys to play with, and use the correct terms to describe the child and her or his behavior. These proscriptions go far beyond what a newborn experiences. Toy stores mark their aisles as "for boys" or "for girls;" pharmacies and card stores tell shoppers which greeting cards are "for him" and "for her." What makes these toys, cards, clothing, or anything else right for boys or girls, men or women are preassigned characteristics for each gender.

While some progress has been made in this area—at some point, someone realized we don't necessarily need to swathe a boy in blue or a girl in pink and that yellow was a good gender-neutral color—these gender role stereotypes continue and are strongly valued. Interestingly, yet unsurprisingly enough, there tends to be more flexibility for girls than for boys. While some girls may play with dolls, kitchens, or be engaged in other stereotypically "female" play, others play with cars and trucks; pretend to be construction workers; and generally engage in what most cultures would stereotype as what is appropriate play for boys. Although some parents/caregivers may object to that, there is much less opposition to girls playing with things that have been labeled as boy things than there is to boys playing with things that have been stereotyped as girls' things.

What is at the heart of this? Although gender is different from sexual orientation, this is one area in which the two overlap. Many parents and other adults do not understand that sexual orientation—like gender identity—is neither chosen nor created. A parent/caregiver cannot "make" their child heterosexual or lesbian, gay or bisexual (LGB). When one considers that the vast majority of LGB adults were born to heterosexual parents, the logic and proof are clear. Yet many adults still think that a gay man is a result of his parents letting him do "female" things while growing up—going so far as to not let him learn to cook or do dishes after a meal. Nothing could be further from the truth—and all this does is relegate people even farther apart from each other into even more rigid, gendered boxes. All because ignorant adults think hyperfeminizing or hypermasculinizing their children will guarantee heterosexuality.

As mentioned earlier, privilege exists when one is a member of the power majority, in whatever category that may be. When it comes to gender, most people in the world will look at their bodies—in particular, their genitals and secondary sex characteristics, such as breasts—and what they see makes sense to them on the inside. The two match. These people are called cisgender. When what one sees and how one feels on the inside do not match, these people may be called or identify as transgender. Transgender is an umbrella term that can describe a whole range of feelings and experiences relating to one's gender. A person may have a dichotomous experience, in which their body says "female" but they feel strongly inside that they are male. This person may elect—if he has the financial means and social supports—to alter his body in some ways or completely to match his internal gender identity. But not everyone goes from one end of the gender binary to the other.

For some people, hormonal transitioning is all they wish to do. For others, it is all they can afford to do (most sex realignment procedures are not covered by health insurance and can be quite expensive). Others may have a combination of hormone treatment and surgery to complete transition from the sex they were assigned at birth to the one they feel strongly is who they truly are. Still others may present as one gender, yet identify as a different gender and ask to be treated in that manner—yet not adjust their bodies surgically or hormonally at all. Some individuals may not refer to themselves as transgender (or simply "trans"), but use the term "gender non-conforming." The language of gender, like the language of sexual orientation, is evolving and changing. But far more important than the language are the experiences of people who identify anywhere within the transgender spectrum.

Remember that baby from the beginning of this section? There are also situations wherein the answer to the question, "Is it a boy or a girl?" is "I don't know." Some children are born with ambiguous genitalia—or typically formed genitalia that implies one sex, but internal reproductive organs and chromosomes of a different sex. Rather than the more common sex chromosome composition of XX or XY, these babies may be born with XO, XXY, XYY, or other chromosomes. These individuals were historically referred to as "hermaphrodites," an outdated term that is considered offensive today. The current terms being used are intersex, with some people opting against an identity and rather referring to having a Disorder of Sex Development. Intersex individuals and conditions have much variation, with the one common characteristic that they are unable to reproduce.

As in all sexuality-related topics, diversity fascinates some people and intimidates others. It is celebrated by some, and reviled by others. Regardless of how one responds, sexual and gender diversity are not going anywhere, and so cultures and societies must continue to find ways to adapt and accept all people.

Article

Prepared by: Elizabeth Schroeder, EdD, MSW,
Elizabeth Schroeder Consulting

Transgender Transitioning and Change of Self-Reported Sexual Orientation

MATTHIAS K. AUER

Learning Outcomes

After reading this article, you will be able to:

- Explain the difference between sexual orientation and gender identity.

- Name one influence on the reliability of self-reported surveys on sexual orientation.

- List at least two factors that, according to the researchers, may have an impact on why a person's understanding of their own sexual orientation may change during sex realignment transition.

Introduction

Western sexual norms that were established during the modern era based identity upon gender-sex identity and sexual desires, e.g. homosexual, bisexual or heterosexual identity[1, 2]. Sexual identity was seen as something ingrained in the psychological and biological makeup of an individual[3]. However, among other societies notions of identity based on sexual behaviour were absent or emerged only in the course of colonialism[3]. Sexual identity and the concept of *the heterosexual* and *the homosexual* are thus categories that follow Western notions of an identity based on sexual desire or acts.

Sexual orientation is highly influenced by the concept of asexual identity and refers to *an enduring pattern of emotional, romantic, and/or sexual attractions to men, women, or both sexes*"[4]. Sexual orientation is determined in early life and usually unchangeable thereafter[5, 6] although some lesbian women and gay men come out later in life. Categories of sexual orientation and changes in sexual orientation can only be categorized because of the notion of a stable sexual identity that is ingrained in the individual.

However, it has been reported that transgender individuals report a change in their sexual orientation over time[7–9]. Here we aim to categorize sexual orientation in a transsexual population and study changes in self-reported sexual orientation. Participants are categorized into four groups as initially suggested by Magnus Hirschfeld[10], based on their erotic interest: gynephilic = attracted to women, androphilic = attracted to men, bisexual = attracted to both men and women, and analloerotic = not attracted to other people. Reported changes in sexual attraction or self-defined sexual orientation were linked to the gender transition process before[11]. Meier and colleagues demonstrated that 40 percent of female-to-male (FtM) transsexual persons report changes in sexual orientation in the course of their lives and this may partially be attributed to the initiation of testosterone therapy[12]. In male-to-female (MtF) transsexual persons a significant change in sexual orientation has also been reported especially after the transition process[11]. Whether changes in sexual orientation were attributable to biological effects of hormone therapy or to psychological factors and how to interpret these self-reported changes is still under debate.

In summary, it is unclear if sexual orientation of transsexual persons (i) changes in the course of the transition period, e.g. after introduction of hormone therapy or (ii) is indeed unchangeable and only refers to a psychological interpretation that is related to transition in self-reported sexual orientation.

We therefore aimed to systematically evaluate changes in sexual orientation in a transsexual population in regard to the chronology of important life events of the transition such as start of so-called "real-life experience", initiation of hormonal therapy or performed sex reassignment surgery by combining quantitative and qualitative data. We studied how frequently changes in sexual orientation are reported and which of the aforementioned variables may possibly correlate with changes

Transgender Transitioning and Change of Self-Reported Sexual Orientation by Matthias K. Auer et al.

123

in sexual orientation in transsexual persons. By this approach we were ultimately aiming to identify the influence of important life events on self-reported sexual orientation.

Methods
Cohort

We included 115 (70 MtF and 45 FtM) transsexual, caucasian patients in this study who visited the endocrine outpatient clinic of the Max Planck Institute of Psychiatry, Munich, between May 2011 and February 2012, either for initial endocrinological evaluation or follow-up examination. After giving written informed consent, they were asked to complete a questionnaire, retrospectively evaluating the history of their gender transition phase. Assessment procedures were monitored by a quality circle in Munich, where experts regularly meet to discuss questions related to transsexualism. Inclusion criteria were age over 18 years, diagnosis of gender identity disorder (GID) according to DSM-IV criteria[13] assessed by a mental health professional and absence of any disorder of sexual development (DSD). The study was approved by the local Ethical committee of the Ludwig Maximilians University in Munich.

Questionnaire on Transition Phase, Diagnostic and Therapeutic Process and Sexual Orientation

Data in this study were assessed by means of a self-report questionnaire. Questions included recalled age of first signs of cross-sex gender feelings ("when was the first time that you became aware about your cross-sex gender identification?"), further referred to as age of onset.

Further variables were: time point of revealing their gender identity for the first time to a family member or friend, initiation of cross sex hormone treatment (CSHT), date of first sex reassignment surgery, date of starting "real-life experience", date of first contact with a mental health practitioner as part of the transition process, respective time point of official clinical GID diagnosis. Exact dates of first psychological counseling, start of "real-life experience", cross-hormone-treatment and date and kind of sex reassignment surgery were also verified by the patient's files.

The section on sexual orientation included questions on current sexual orientation ("What is your current sexual preference?"), occurrence ("Have you ever experienced a change in your sexual orientation?"), recalled time-point ("Could you please guess when approximately such a change evolved?") and kind of change in sexual attraction where participants had to choose between: attraction to females (gynephilic), attraction to males (androphilic), attraction to both (bisexual) or attraction to neither of those (further referred to as analloerotic)

according to the classification of sexual orientation by the DSM-IV-TR specifiers for GID diagnosis[14]. They further had the opportunity to specify their sexual orientation.

In case of reported change in sexual orientation, participants were further asked to define the kind of change (e.g. from males towards females) and if there had been multiple shifts in this regard.

Furthermore, they were asked to describe the approximate time point of a potential change in sexual orientation allowing to arrange changes of sexual orientation chronologically in regard to particular transition time events, namely, date of first counseling with a mental health practitioner as part of the transition process, initiation of cross-sex hormone treatment, first sex reassignment surgery, self-reported time point of officially living in the new gender role.

In the qualitative part of this study, participants were asked to comment and provide a personal explanation as a free text on this change.

Statistical Analyses

All statistical analyses were performed using SPSS v.18.0 (IBM Corp., Armonk, NY, USA). A two-tailed p-value of 0.05 and lower was considered statistically significant with a 95% confidence interval (CI). The Fisher's exact test was used to compare dichotomous variables. Independent Student's t-test was used to compare means of continuous variables. One-way analysis of variance (ANOVA) was used for comparison of more than two groups such as sexual orientation (androphilic, gynephilic, bisexual, analloerotic) in variables representing the history of transition (age of self-aware, age of psychological counseling, age of "real-life experience", age of hormone-therapy, age of sex reassignment surgery, age when sexual orientation changed). For post-hoc comparisons Fisher's LSD (Least Significant Difference) was applied.

Results
Initial Self-Reported Sexual Orientation

Basic characteristics of our study sample can be found in Table 1. In MtF, 25.7% of participants indicated that they initially had been sexually attracted to males (= androphilic) and 51.4% to females (= gynephilic). Bisexuality was reported by 10% and 12.9% declared themselves as having been attracted to neither sex (= analloerotic). Most FtM transsexual persons had been gynephilic (73.4%) while six individuals (13.3%) indicated having been sexually orientated towards males (= androphilic). Bisexuality was reported by 8.8% and one participant (2.2%) had described himself as analloerotic. No subject reported on sexual orientation towards other transsexual persons.

Table 1 Basic Characteristics at the Time of Evaluation

variable (mean, ± SD (range))	MtF		FtM		p-value
	N	**%**	**N**	**%**	
sex	70	60.9	45	30.1	
age	46.7 ± 13.4 (18–80)		37 ± 9.8 (19–60)		<0.001[†]
cross-hormone treatment					
yes	63	90	42	93.3	n.s.[§]
no	7	10	3	6.7	
Testosterone (intramuscular)			32	78.0	
Testosterone (transdermal)			9	22.0	
Estradiol (oral)	9	14.5			
Estradiol (transdermal)	30	48.4			
Estradiol + Antiandrogen (transdermal)	14	22.6			
Estradiol + Progesterone	9	14.5			
sex reassignment surgery*					
any SRS	40	57.1	27	60.0	n.s.[§]
any genital surgery	39	55.7	26	57.8	
Only hysterectomy/ovariectomy/ mastectomy			16	33.6	
+ phalloplasty			10	22.2	
mastectomy only			1	2.2	
breast augmentation only	1	1.4			
No SRS	30	42.9	18	40.0	
age of onset	10.8 ± 8.2 (3–49)		8.2 ± 6.5 (2–35)		n.s.[†]
before or at the age of 12	43	68.3	32	82.1	n.s.[§]
after the age of 12	20	31.7	7	17.9	
	N				
	Age (in years)				
first psychological counseling	38.1 ± 13.3 (11–70)		29.2 ± 8.5 (17–48)		<0.001[†]
start of "real-life experience"	38.1 ± 10.9 (18–70)		29.2 ± 8 (18–47)		<0.001[†]
cross-sex hormone treatment	38.6 ± 14 (16–69)		31.1 ± 8.5 (17–50)		0.003[†]
sex reassignment surgery	42.4 ± 12.5 (18–70)		32.8 ± 9 (20–56)		0.001[†]

*FtM: hysterectomy, ovariectomy, mastectomy, phalloplasty; MtF: bilateral orchidectomy, penectomy, breast augmentation if necessary, vaginoplasty, vulvoplasty, SD = standard deviation, n.s. = not significant on a significance level of $p \leq .05$.

[†] student's t-test.

[§] Fisher's exact test.

doi:10.1371/journal.pone.0110016.t001

Initial Self-Reported Sexual Orientation and History of Transition

In MtF, androphilic participants were also younger when they started their "real-life experience" in the new gender role ($p < 0.01$), started cross-sex hormone treatment ($p < 0.01$) and under went first sex reassignment surgery ($p < 0.01$). Bisexual MtF reported on a significantly older age of onset, younger age when starting their "real-life experience" and start of cross-sex hormone treatment than gynephilic MtF (all $p < 0.05$) (Table 2).

In FtM, significant differences between androphilic and gynephilic FtM were seen in the variable age of onset, first psychological counseling and start of cross-sex hormone treatment (all $p < 0.05$). There were no further significant differences regarding other sexual orientations and any variable of transition history (Table 3).

Transgender Transitioning and Change of Self-Reported Sexual Orientation by Matthias K. Auer et al.

125

Table 2   Initial Sexual Orientation and History of Transition in MtF

| | MtF | | | |
	androphilic	gynephilic	bisexual	analloerotic
	N = 18 (25.7%)	N = 36 (51.4%)	N = 7 (10%)	N = 9 (12.9%)
age	41.6(16.4)[a]	51(9.6)[a,b]	36(10.8)[b]	47.9(15.9)
Mean age of				
onset	7.2(3.9)	11.6(9.9)	11.7(7.3)	14(5.8)
first psychological counseling	32(13.8)[c,i]	42.6(11.5)[c]	31.3(8.7)[i]	39(17)
start of "real-life experience"	36.4(10.8)[d]	45.2(9.6)[d,e]	33(7.7)[e]	40.7(12.1)
CSHT	31.1(13.8)[f]	42.8(11.8)[f,g]	31.9(9.5)[g]	41.1(17)
SRS	35.3(14.1)[h]	47.5(10.3)[h]	36.2(9.3)	34(12.7)
Change in SO (N = 23)	32.4(18)	40.8(7.6)	-	28(19.8)

[a,b,c,f,h]p < 0.01.
[d,e,g,i]p < 0.05.
(ANOVA).
CSHT: Cross-sex hormone treatment.
SRS: Sex reassignment surgery.
SO: Sexual orientation.
a-h mean significant differences between those two groups, e.g. a means a significant difference (p < 0.01) between androphilic and gynephilic MtF in terms of age.
doi:10.1371/journal.pone.0110016.t002

Change in Self-Reported Sexual Orientation

About one third of MtF (32.9%, N = 23) reported a change in sexual orientation during their life, in contrast to 22.2% (N = 10) in the FtM group (n.s.). Nine MtF (39.1% of all that reported a changed sexual orientation (N = 23)) and six FtM (60% of all that changed sexual orientation (N = 10)) reported a change in sexual orientation without or before any surgical treatment. Out of these, four MtF (17.4% of all that reported a changed sexual orientation) and two FtM (20% of all that reported a changed sexual orientation) reported a change in sexual orientation, without or before having received cross-sex hormone

Table 3   Initial Sexual Orientation and History of Transition in FtM

| | FtM | | | |
	androphilic	gynephilic	bisexual	analloerotic
	N = 6	N = 33	N = 4	N = 2
	(13.3%)	(73.4%)	(8.8%)	(4.4%)
age	44.3(9.2)	35.9(9.3)	39.3(12.9)	28.5(10.6)
Mean age of				
onset	4(4.5)[a]	7.7(4.9)[a]	19.3(14.3)	2
first psychological counseling	36.5 (8.7)[b]	28.1(8.2)[b]	30.3(8.2)	24 (4.2)
start of "real-life experience"	32.8(8.1)	28(7.8)	30.7(10.7)	22.5(6.4)
CSHT	37.3(9.3)[c]	29.5(8.2)[c]	34.7(6.1)	27
SRS	38(12.3)	31.3(8.5)	39.5(2,1)	27
Change in SO (N = 10)	30.8(7.4)	33.7(14.8)	–	–

[a,b,c]p < 0.05.
CSHT: Cross-sex hormone treatment.
SRS: Sex reassignment surgery.
SO: Sexual orientation.
a-c mean significant differences between those two groups, e.g. "a" means a significant difference (p < 0.05) between androphilic and gynephilic FtM in terms of age of onset.
doi:10.1371/journal.pone.0110016.t003

Table 4   Kind of Change in Sexual Orientation in MtF

Initial orientation (N = 70)	Change to					
	androphilic	gynephilic	bisexual	analloerotic	unknown	all
	N (%)	N (%)	N (%)	N (%)	N (%)	
androphilic (N = 18)	0(0)	2(11.1)	1(5.6)	0(0)	2(11.1)	5(27.7)
gynephilic (N = 36)[a]	6(16.6)	0(0)	8(22.2)	1(2.7)	0(0)	15(41.7)
bisexual (N = 7)	0(0)	0(0)	0(0)	0(0)	0(0)	0(0)
analloerotic (N = 9)	1(11.1)	0(0)	1(11.1)	0(0)	1(11.1)	3(33.3)
						23(32.9)

"a" means a significant difference between gynephilic and nongynephilic MtF (p = 0.05).

doi:10.1371/journal.pone.0110016.t004

treatment. Six MtF (26.1% of all that reported a changed sexual orientation) and two FtM (20% of all that reported a changed SO) reported a change in sexual orientation without/before psychological counseling. MtF and FtM did not differ significantly in the reported age of change in sexual orientation.

Initial Sexual Orientation and Change in Self-Reported Sexual Orientation

Change of self-reported sexual orientation in gynephilic MtF appeared in 15 participants (44.1%), six reported a change to androphilia (16.6%), eight to bisexuality (22.2%) and one to analloerotica (2.7%). In androphilic MtF, 5 participants (27.7%) reported a change in sexual orientation to bisexuality (5.6%) and gynephilia (11.1%), two patients (11.1%) did not report on direction of change (Table 4).

Six gynephilic FtM reported a change in sexual orientation (18.2%) to androphilia (9.1%) and bisexuality (9.1%). In androphilic FtM transsexual persons, four reported a change

in sexual orientation (66.7%) to gynephilia. Changes in other directions were not reported (Table 5).

Initial self-reported sexual orientation in MtF was not significantly associated with change in sexual orientation (p = 0.05). In FtM, however, initially androphilic subjects were significantly more likely to report a change in sexual orientation than non-androphilic (gynephilic, bisexual and analloerotic, p = 0.012) or gynephilic FtM (p = 0.001).

Change in Self-Reported Sexual Orientation and History of Transition

Neither in MtF nor in FtM were we able to identify any variable of transition which was significantly associated with the occurrence of a reported change in sexual orientation (Table 6, Table 7).

To increase homogeneity of our study population for chronological analysis, we only investigated those who had already undergone the complete physical transition process, including

Table 5   Kind of Change in Sexual Orientation in FtM

Initial orientation (N = 45)	Change to					
	androphilic	gynephilic	bisexual	analloerotic	unknown	all
	N (%)	N (%)	N (%)	N (%)	N (%)	N (%)
androphilic (N = 6)[a,b]	0(0)	4(66.7)	0(0)	0(0)	0(0)	4(66.7)
gynephilic (N = 33)[a]	3(9.1)	0(0)	3(9.1)	0(0)	0(0)	6(18.2)
bisexual (N = 4)	0(0)	0(0)	0(0)	0(0)	0(0)	0(0)
analloerotic (N = 2)	0(0)	0(0)	0(0)	0(0)	0(0)	0(0)
						10(22.2)

[a]p = 0.012 (X^2-Test).

[b]p = 0.001 (X^2-Test).

"a" means a significant difference between androphilic and gynephilic FtM. "b" describes a significant difference between androphilic and nonandrophilic FtM.

doi:10.1371/journal.pone.0110016.t005

Transgender Transitioning and Change of Self-Reported Sexual Orientation by Matthias K. Auer et al.

127

Table 6 Change in Sexual Orientation and Basic Characteristics in MtF

variable	Change in SO N	Change in SO %		No Change in SO N	No Change in SO %		
	23	32.9		47	67.1		
		Mean	SD ±		Mean	SD ±	p-value
age		44.8	10.4		47.2	14.9	n.s.[†]
age of psychological counseling		35.2	9.0		39.4	14.8	n.s.[†]
age at start of "real-life experience"		38.2	8.2		41.9	12.6	n.s.[†]
age at hormone-therapy		36.0	8.2		39.9	15.7	n.s.[†]
age of SRS		42.8	7.6		41.8	15.0	n.s.[†]
interval hormones and surgery		5.3	8.2		2.8	3.1	n.s.[†]
age of onset							
early onset	17			32			n.s.[§]
late onset	4			12			
cross-sex hormone treatment							
yes	21			40			n.s.[§]
no	2			5			n.s.[§]
SRS							
yes	16			22			n.s.[§]
Vagino/vulvoplasty	16			21			
breast augmentation	0			1			
no	7			23			

[†]student's t-test.
[§]Fisher's exact test.
SRS (Sex reassignment surgery).
n.s. (not significant).
doi:10.1371/journal.pone.0110016.t006

cross-sex hormone treatment as well as any genital sex reassignment surgery (37 MtF and 27 FtM). In this group, sixteen MtF (43.2%) and six FtM (22.2%) reported changes in their sexual orientation (p = 0.068). Only one MtF (6.7%) and one FtM (14.3%) reported changes in sexual orientation prior to initiation of cross-sex hormone treatment.

There was no significant difference in the direction of change in self-reported sexual orientation (e.g. from androphilic to bisexual) either by including all participants or only those having undergone cross-sex hormone treatment or sex reassignment surgery or any significant association of transition events in this subgroup (data not shown).

Qualitative Analysis

Answers given in the free text field of our questionnaire concerning change in self-reported sexual orientation and individual interpretation of this event were analyzed by two independent researchers (MKA and JF). Answers were grouped

thematically. It became evident that personal explanations for a change in sexual orientation varied and ranged from explanations such as "hormone treatment increased libido" in FtM, to the statement of one MtF participants who reported that sex reassignment surgery resulted in complete loss of libido and she was therefore asexual following the procedure. Exemplary statements for each group were chosen to be reported in the discussion section and in the supplementary results.

Discussion

We investigated changes in self-reported sexual orientation and the relation to important life events in a large cohort of transsexual persons in Germany by means of qualitative and quantitative data. We could show that self-reported changes in sexual orientation are frequent in transsexual persons especially in originally gynephilic MtF as well as androphilic FtM. It was hypothesized before that change of sexual orientation might be influenced by

Table 7   Change in Sexual Orientation and Basic Characteristics in FtM

	FtM						
	change in SO			no change in SO			
	N	%		N	%		
	10	22.2		35	77.7		
variable		Mean	SD ±		Mean	SD ±	p-value
age		41.2	12.6		35.5	8.8	n.s.[†]
age of psychological counseling		32.2	10.1		28.4	7.9	n.s.[†]
age at start of "real-life experience"		31.1	8.1		27.3	8	n.s.[†]
age hormone-therapy		32.6	10.6		30.6	7.8	n.s.[†]
age of SRS		37.2	12.7		31.5	7.5	n.s.[†]
interval hormones and surgery		2.3	2.0		1.2	0.9	n.s.[†]
age of onset							
early onset	8			29			n.s.[§]
late onset	2			6			
cross-sex hormone treatment							n.s.[§]
yes	10			32			
no	0			3			
SRS							
Yes total	10			35			n.s.[§]
Genital surgery							
hysterectomy/ovariectomy/mastectomy	6			11			
+phalloplasty	1			9			
mastectomy only	0			1			
no	3			15			

[†]student's t-test.
[§]Fisher's exact *test*.
SRS: Sex reassignment surgery.
n.s.: not significant.
doi:10.1371/journal.pone.0110016.t007

hormonal therapy or SRS[15]. Here, we could demonstrate that reported changes of sexual orientation are not particularly associated with any transition event. Thus our data challenge the view that either hormonal therapy or SRS or any other event has a direct influence on self-reported sexual orientation.

General Characteristics

In the MtF group, most participants indicated that they were gynephilic (51%) or androphilic (26%) before any change in sexual orientation might have occurred. In the FtM group most participants were gynephilic (73%). These figures are in accordance with the historical and early reports from Magnus Hirschfeld[16] and recent reports[17]. Most of our participants reported on an early age of onset, regardless of being FtM or MtF. However, FtM started their transition process, including first psychological counseling, start of "real-life experience" in

the new gender role, hormone treatment and sex reassignment surgery at a younger age than MtF. This is in accordance with the literature[18]. Others hypothesized that FtM in contrast to MtF feel lower social pressure in terms of parental disapproval of cross gender expression[19–21]. This may also explain the discrepancy in latency between age of onset and first counseling for initiation of transition in MtF vs. FtM. Hypothesizing that gender dysphoric girls were more likely to be accepted by their family members, threshold for seeking medical advice could be lower. In contrast, cross-gender expression in boys is poorly accepted and thus referral to gender specialists happens earlier. This could also imply that FtM would also report changes in sex orientation less likely than MtF, since they did not have to suppress—consciously or unconsciously—their "initial" sexual orientation due to social pressure. Therefore a consecutively reported "change" would be less likely to occur.

Change in Self-Reported Sexual Orientation

We could demonstrate that self-reported change in sexual orientation is quite common in MtF as well as FtM. Thirty three% of MtF and 22% of FtM in our sample reported a change of their sexual orientation once in their life, a difference that was not significant. This is in accordance with earlier reports in MtF[11] and FtM[12]. Lawrence (2005) reported that up to 63% of MtF experienced changes concerning their sexual orientation following sex reassignment surgery. However, Lawrence applied the more graduated Kinsey Scale Rating to determine sexual orientation, which is using intermediate scales such as "mostly attracted to", "exclusively attracted to" et cetera. Interestingly, she found that there is little difference regarding preoperative characteristics between those who reported a change in sexual orientation following SRS and those who did not. Thus both groups could not be distinguished by any variables. This was similar in our study. We could not demonstrate a particular variable concerning the transition process which would predict change in sexual orientation. Meier et al.[12] demonstrated that gynephilic FtM were more likely to report a change in sexual orientation after transition[12]. Contrastingly, in the present study sample the degree of FtM who reported a change in sexual orientation after transition was higher in androphilic FtM. It was hypothesized before that natal women have a more fluid sexual orientation compared to natal men in the general population. However, data on this topic are still sparse[23–24]. In natal men sexual orientation seems to be equivalent with sexual arousal that can be measured with penis plethysmography[23]. In line, MtF show specific sexual arousal patterns using vaginal photoplethysmography in surgically constructed neovaginas[25]. In contrast, natal women have genital arousal patterns that are not category specific (e.g. androphilia or gynephilia) but rather appear bisexual[23] and thus female sexual orientation was suggested to be more fluid and malleable. Yet plethysmography studies ignore cognitive components of sexual orientation that have an important role in self-reported sexual orientation (especially in women due to the ambiguous arousal patterns).

In heterosexual (= gynephilic) men and heterosexual (= androphilic) women only 4–5% report a change in sexual orientation during their lifetime. Changes in sexual orientation seem to be most common in bisexual subjects of both sexes of whom up to 77% report on such a change, primarily originating from a heterosexual orientation[22]. In homosexual (= androphilic) men a change in sexual orientation occurs in about one third of adult subjects and is less common than in homosexual (= gynephilic) women who report on change in sexual orientation in about two thirds of cases[26]. It is also important to stress that in homosexual persons bisexuality seems to be part of their coming out process[26].

We also regarded only those as a subgroup who had undergone the complete physical transition process. Here, most reported a change in sexual orientation following the surgical procedure in line with the study by Lawrence (2005). However, a relatively large proportion of participants (17.4% in MtF, 20% in FtM) reported on a change in sexual orientation without having undergone sex reassignment surgery or even before cross-sex hormone treatment challenging a relation between SRS and sexual orientation. Many transsexual persons may have suggested that a change in sexual orientation occurred after SRS because it demarcates an important life event and is often the last of many steps towards the development of the desired sex. Lawrence hypothesized in this context that SRS *merely sets the stage for more confident misinterpretation and misreporting of an underlying sexual orientation that not only remains unchanged but is, in fact, unchangeable* (p. 141 in[25]). We feel that the present existing data are not sufficient to decide whether or not sexual orientation can change in the course of life.

Meier and colleagues[12] reported a significant association of testosterone treatment in FtM and change in sexual orientation; however, in logistic regression analysis this was not independent of pre-transition sexual orientation. In our sample, initiation of cross-sex hormone therapy was not a significant predictor for change, but admittedly we had lower statistical power in our study. In addition it should be kept in mind that the Meier et al. Sample was based on online surveys which might have increased diversity of the participants in contrast to our clinical cohort. Five MtF and two FtM had not received cross-sex hormone treatment before change in sexual orientation. This highlights that self-reported change in sexual orientation can manifest independently of cross-sex hormone treatment.

Changes of Sexual Orientation in MtF Transsexual Persons

MtF transsexual persons can be classified by age of onset or sexual orientation[27]. Following Ray Blanchard's sexual orientation typology[27,28] two distinctly different types of MtF transsexual persons, namely, homosexual (referred to as androphilic MtF in the present paper) and nonhomosexual MtF (gynephilic, bisexual and analloerotic MtF in the present paper) can be distinguished. Both groups differ profoundly: Androphilic MtF usually behave and identify as girls from earliest childhood which is reflected in female-typical toys, activities and playmates and later in female-typical occupations and hobbies[25]. Cross-dressing in this group of MtF is not associated with sexual arousal.

On the other hand, nonandrophilic MtF usually resemble ordinary cisgendered (= the individual gender experience matches with the natal sex) men in their childhood activities and occupations[25], yet they intensely desire to be female. They also cross-dress, however, it evokes sexual arousal. Blanchard showed that androphilic MtF transsexual persons present with significantly higher cross-gender wishes and therefore seek treatment at a significantly younger age[27]. In line, in the present study androphilic MtF sought psychological counseling earlier than nonandrophilic MtF.

Nonandrophilic MtF were also termed *autogynephilic* transsexual persons by Ray Blanchard[28], highlighting that an autogynephilic sexual orientation influences their cross-gender wishes (for controversial statements see e.g.[29,30] and an extensive description see[25]). Autogynephilic MtF transsexual persons are sexually oriented "toward the thought or image of themselves as women"[31]. Autogynephilia was thus proposed to represent an erotic target location error[25,32]. Autogynephilic MtF transsexual persons often report the fantasy of sexual intercourse as a woman with a man, that was repeatedly described as faceless and abstract[25]. Yet this *pseudoandrophilia* has to be distinguished from genuine androphilia or homosexuality in MtF, or as Blanchard points it: *the effective erotic stimulus, however, is not the male physique per se, as it is in true homosexual attraction, but rather the thought of being a female, which is symbolized in the fantasy of being penetrated by a male. For these persons, the imagined—occasionally real—male sexual partner serves the same function as women's apparel or makeup, namely, to aid and intensify the fantasy of being a woman*[27]. Similarly, one of our participants that formally reported a change of sexual orientation from gynephilia towards androphilia stressed that *I always wanted to experience sexual intercourse as a woman but I did not know what to do with my male body before the hormone treatment. I hated male bodies in general before.* In this case a reported change in sexual orientation from gynephilic to androphilic can be attributed to autogynephilic fantasies. Another participant made clear that *at the beginning I was not quite sure about my sexual orientation, but after one and a half years following sex reassignment surgery and after having had my first sexual intercourse with a man, I was able to love a man.* Thus romantic love towards men followed sexual intercourse with men in this participant. In some way this narrative resembles that of some adolescent cissexual persons that encounter a similar confusion and uncertainty during puberty[33].

Moreover it is thinkable that some formerly nonandrophilic MtF transsexual persons only formally change their sexual orientation in the course of the transition because androphilia is social more desirable for MtF transsexual persons. The social desirability of androphilia in MtF was demonstrated in a recent study by Timo Nieder and colleagues (2011) where more than half of MtF transsexual persons reported that they were exclusively attracted to men, while the clinicians found it to

be true only in about 10%[34]. Kenneth Zucker and colleagues[34] demonstrated that even in adolescent boys with transvestism only 50% admitted autogynephilic tendencies. In line, among gynephilic MtF transsexual persons we found the highest rate of reported change in sexual orientation (41.7%). Considering the (even unintentional) socially desirable responding in terms of sexual orientation and autogynephilic fantasies, we hypothesize that this high figure overestimates the number of participants with a genuine change in sexual orientation. Participants may have reported on gynephilia at a time when they still had a male appearance and later changed their orientation towards the more accepted androphilia or bisexuality as MtF transsexual persons. Others would argue that the core sexual orientation in these participants was autogynephilia before and after transition[25]. This hypothesis is not totally supported by our data because none of the participants stated "other" sexual orientation like orientation towards other transsexual persons or autogynephilia although participants had the possibility to define their sexual orientation as "other" (with empty space to define). However, it is known that autogynephilia is often not reported or known, therefore in future studies we will explicitly ask for autogynephilic arousal.

The importance of individual experiences in the change of sexual orientation was also stressed by some participants. One androphilic MtF changed her sexual orientation towards bisexuality and explained: *The change in my sexual attraction is part of my biography. I had experienced a lot of violence through men, so I was looking for a way out. My attraction may be more a matter of mind than of heart.* This statement clarifies that there was no hormonal or biological mechanism that promoted her change of orientation but merely negative experiences. Another initially gynephilic MtF had a comparable explanation: *Sexual desire decreased with hormone treatment. That I turned away from women as sexual partners has certainly also to do with my biography. I had experienced a lot of reactions that hurt me.* It seems that the reduced libido through hormonal treatment in combination with negative experiences enabled the participant to engage in a relation with the other sex. Individual experiences also explained for the development of analloerotica following transitioning: *I was repeatedly disappointed by interpersonal relations so I finally developed a disinterest in other people.* Libido loss not only in relation to hormonal treatment but the surgical procedure was also reported: *After the sex reassignment surgery I completely lost my libido.* These qualitative data reveal that there seems to be not one common reason for a change in sexual orientation in MtF. A quantitative analysis of sexual orientation is thus flawed by unreported autogynephilia, individual biographical experiences, confusion about simultaneous experiences of andro and gynephilic attraction and social factors that may prevent participants from reporting homosexuality or autogynephilia. *Reported* sexual orientation therefore seems to be influenced by a plethora of factors and may even be affected by personal decision, as one participant said: *While some people think that gender identity is something you acquire or learn I think this was rather true for my alleged sexual orientation.*

Changes of Sexual Orientation in FtM Transsexual Persons

Gynephilic MtF and androphilic FtM were most likely to report a change in their sexual orientation. We argued before that autogynephilic fantasies may have influenced the high ratio of change in gynephilic MtF. So, what about androphilic FtM transsexual persons? Is correspondingly autoandrophilia a reason for the frequent change in androphilic FtM? Indeed we observed a surprisingly high ratio of change from androphilia to gynephilia in 66% of androphilic FtM. But are androphilic FtM which also represent "non classical" transsexual persons sexually aroused by the thought of themselves as men, too? Until now there is limited data on autoandrophilia in FtM. However, autogynephilia was not reported for decades, too, until Ray Blanchard described the phenomenon[28]. We found several autoandrophilic narratives browsing web pages or simply googling the term. A recent qualitative study by Rowniak and Chesla[35] found indications for autoandrophilic erotic fantasies in androphilic FtM. They interviewed several FtM transsexual persons and one participant stressed that in the development of his own sexuality with his husband *the interesting part is being sexual with him [the husband] as a man, was much better than being sexual with him as a woman, even though the act was pretty much the same* (p. 453,[35]). Others described that sex with gay men was the strongest validation of being male[36]. Similarly, Schleifer concluded that sex with a man reinforced masculinity of androphilic FtM and thus validates them as men[37]. However, in a qualitative analysis of interviews with androphilic FtM by Bockting, Benner and Coleman only 22% of the participants reported sexual arousal in response to cross-dressing[38]. Since there exists almost no scientific literature concerning autoandrophilic erotic arousal in women or FtM transsexual persons, a systematic evaluation of this phenomenon would be of interest for upcoming studies. MtF autogynephilic transsexual persons manifest later and one reason is that some of them doubt whether they are "really transsexual"[25] because of sexual arousal related e.g. to cross-dressing. This has to be studied for autoandrophilic FtM transsexual persons as well.

Smith et al.[39] found no significant difference regarding GID symptoms in childhood between gynephilic and nongynephilic FtM, while other authors[40], who had divided age of onset in early childhood and post-pubertal onset, reported that early onset FtM were always sexually attracted to females. Levine

and Lothstein[41] further found that in the majority of cases, early onset gender dysphoria was associated with a gynephilic orientation. Thus from the literature there seems a trend that androphilic MtF and gynephilic FtM start transitioning earlier.

Another pattern described by Rowniak and Chesla[35] was that some FtM participants "experienced gender dysphoria to such an extent at the time of adolescence and later that a comfortable and natural sexual activity was impossible" (p. 453). In line, one participant in the present study explained that "testosterone increased my libido. I would interpret my change in sexual orientation as having been confused before. Before mastectomy, I envied men and I rejected women, since I was in the wrong body. As soon as the distracting breast had been removed, I realized that I was into women."

Another possible mechanism that acts on sexual orientation in FtM is testosterone treatment that stimulates libido in general[42]. In the present study we found no relation between onset of testosterone treatment and reported change of sexual orientation. In line, in former reports a possible relation was rather vague and profoundly differed in intervals between onset of testosterone treatment and reported change in sexual orientation ranging between 6 months and 7 years[35,36]. Similarly some of our FtM participants described a subjective influence of testosterone treatment on sexuality but admitted other important factors in the change of sexual orientation: *With hormone treatment, my libido increased and I felt more attracted to women, but this may also be connected with social pressure or what is regarded "right" defined by our society.* We have discussed heterosexual behavior as socially desirable in MtF transsexual persons above and it thus seems also to play a role in FtM transsexual persons. Rowniak and Chesla[35] proposed that testosterone validates FtM transsexual persons' male gender identity and thus promotes the possibility to express their sexuality. Some participants supported this idea e.g. *I think that testosterone influenced my biological body and promoted the change.*

In gynephilic FtM a reported change of sexual orientation was less frequent. Six gynephilic FtM reported a change of sexual orientation towards bisexuality and androphilia in the present study. This may in part be explained by the fact that androphilic sexual behavior is complicated for FtM. Sex with male partners can induce intense gender dysphoria by being penetrated as a woman although feeling as a man. One participant in the study of Rowniak and Chesla stated that he didn't like being "feminized in bed" and others used the description that they were unable to have sex with men "until they were a man"[35]. Thus in these six participants androphilia may have been the original sexual orientation that became possible only after transitioning. In this case we wouldn't expect a genuine change of sexual orientation in these gynephilic FtM transsexual persons.

In conclusion we found a high degree of change in self-reported sexual orientation in gynephilic MtF and androphilic FtM. However, some of these participants may have been neither gynephilic nor androphilic but autogynephilic or autoandrophilic. In androphilic MtF and gynephilic FtM, a change in self-reported sexual orientation was less common and might also have been influenced by pre-transitioning dysphoria and uncertainty. The high ratios of change in self-reported sexual orientation—irrespective of whether these changes represent genuine changes—highlight the importance of this topic in transitioning especially for those transsexual persons that start transition with a partner. Changes in sexual orientation during and after transition bear the risk for partnered transsexual persons to lose a stable relationship with a spouse and may thus further increase the emotional burden of transsexual persons[43]. The questions: *Is a genuine change in sexual orientation really possible?* and *Is it more common in transsexual persons?* remain however still unanswered, leading us to other limitations of the present study.

Limitations and Future Prospects

The present study is basically descriptive and explorative; hence there are some methodological limitations to be kept in mind. As every retrospective study, relying on self-reported variables our data are influenced by the recall-bias. In addition it has been shown that self-reported sexual orientation and sexual arousal patterns may diverge in transsexual persons[44]. To objectify sexual orientation aside from self-report, sexual arousal by means of penile or vaginal plethysmography[44] visual methods[45] or brain imaging[46] have been used in the past. A combination of qualitative narratives and biological methods (plethysmography and functional brain imaging) is needed to further elucidate the riddle whether sexual orientation can change in the general population and in transsexual persons. Such a study should be performed longitudinally to assess sexual arousal patterns before and after change of sexual orientation. In general, suggested biological underpinnings of transsexualism have so far been limited and debatable[47–49]. Therefore we need further research about biological and psychological reasons and consequences (like long-term effects of hormone therapy) of transsexualism in the future.

Self-reported sexual orientation studies have further been reported to be interfered by the fact that some persons do not answer the question truthfully[50]. Some transsexual people for example, may want to present themselves as particular feminine (MtF) or masculine (FtM) and thus "classical" transsexual persons. Participants in the present study might have biased their reports on purpose or unwittingly towards a more gender-typical presentation[30]. This may also involve worries on denial of sex reassignment surgery. We feel that attempts to minimize such worries are important in future studies. We also suggest that researchers should explicitly ask for autogynephilic and autoandrophilic sexual orientation.

Finally the results may have been biased by the fact that there are some transsexual persons who do not want to complete physical transition and we did not discriminate between those not having received cross-sex hormone treatment or surgery and those not wanting to.

A strength of our study is that the investigated group was homogenous in regard to ethnicity and had experienced similar treatment modalities due to the single center design. Furthermore in Germany sex reassignment surgery is generally reimbursed by public or private health insurance if the diagnosis GID is settled and no individual in our study would have to forego sex reassignment due to financial reasons. In addition the response rate was quite high (>95%), minimizing selection bias and increasing its representation. The combination of quantitative data with the free text module concerning change in SO enriches current research, since most of the other studies that investigated SO in transsexual persons either had large samples and no free text information[12] or only small samples but clinical interviews[9, 35] or were only studying a subgroup of transsexual persons[11].

Conclusion

By collecting quantitative and qualitative data in a large sample of transsexual persons, we demonstrate that self-reported change in sexual orientation is a common phenomenon in transsexual persons. Transition was not directly involved in this change, since a significant number of participants reported a change in sexual orientation prior to first psychological counseling and prior to initiation of cross-sex hormone treatment. The participants provided diverse individual explanation models, revealing that personal history, social environment as well as autoerotic feelings may impact on a change in sexual orientation.

Notes

1. Weinberg TS (1978) On "doing" and "being" gay: sexual behavior and homosexual male self-identity. *J Homosex* 4: 143–156.
2. Foucault M (1998). *The Will to Knowledge: The History of Sexuality vol. I.*
3. Sigal P (2000) *From Moon Goddess to Virgins: The Colonization of Yucatecan Maya Sexual Desire.* Texas: University of Texas Press. 344 p.
4. APA (2008) Answers to your questions: For a better understanding of sexual orientation and homosexuality. Available: http://www.apa.org/topics/sorientation.pdf. Washington, DC. Accessed 2014 Jul 25.
5. Pillard RC, Bailey JM (1995) A biologic perspective on sexual orientation. *Psychiatr Clin North Am* 18: 71–84.
6. Swaab DF (2007) Sexual differentiation of the brain and behavior. *Best Pract Res Clin Endocrinol Metab* 21: 431–444.

7. Cohen-Kettenis PT, Gooren LJG (1993) The influence of hormone treatment on psychological functioning of Transsexuals. *J Psychol Human Sex* 5: 55–67.

8. Cuypere G, Tsjoen G, Beerten R, Selvaggi G, Sutter P, et al. (2005) Sexual and physical health after sex reassignment surgery. *Arch Sex Behav* 34: 679–690.

9. Daskalos CT (1998) Changes in the sexual orientation of six heterosexual male-to-female transsexuals. *Arch Sex Behav* 27: 605–614.

10. Hirschfeld M (1918) *Sexualpathologie*. Bonn: Marcus & Weber. 211 p.

11. Lawrence AA (2005) Sexuality before and after male-to-female sex reassignment surgery. *Arch Sex Behav* 34: 147–166.

12. Meier SC, Pardo ST, Labuski C, Babcock J (2013) Measures of clinical health among female-to-male transgender persons as a function of sexual orientation. *Arch Sex Behav* 42: 463–474.

13. APA (2000) *Diagnostic and Statistical Manual of Mental Disorders—DSM-IV-TR* (4th edition, Text Revision). Washington, DC.

14. Weyers S, Elaut E, De Sutter P, Gerris J, T'Sjoen G, et al. (2009) Long-term assessment of the physical, mental, and sexual health among transsexual women. *J Sex Med* 6: 752–760.

15. Doorn CD, Poortinga J, Verschoor AM (1994) Cross-gender identity in transvestites and male-transsexuals. *Arch Sex Behav* 23: 185–201.

16. Hirschfeld M (1948) *Sexual anomalies: The origin, nature, and treatment of sexual disorders*. New York: Emerson Books. 538 p.

17. Nieder TO, Herff M, Cerwenka S, Preuss WF, Cohen-Kettenis PT, et al. (2011) Age of onset and sexual orientation in transsexual males and females. *J Sex Med* 8: 783–791.

18. Van Kesteren PJ, Gooren LJ, Megens JA (1996) An epidemiological and demographic study of transsexuals in the Netherlands. *Arch Sex Behav* 25: 589–600.

19. Seil D (2004) The diagnosis and treatment of transgendered patients. *Journal of Gay & Lesbian Psychotherapy* 1–2: 99–116.

20. Seil D (1997) Dissociation as a defense against ego-dystonic transsexualism. In: Bullough B, Bullough VL, Elias J, editors. *Gender blending*. New York: Prometheus Books. pp. 137–145.

21. Seil D (1996) Transsexuals: The boundary of sexual identity and gender. In: Cabaj RP, Stein TS, editors. *Textbook of homosexuality and mental health*. Washington, DC: American Psychiatric Press. pp. 743–762.

22. Kinnish KK, Strassberg DS, Turner CW (2005) Sex differences in the flexibility of sexual orientation: a multidimensional retrospective assessment. *Arch Sex Behav* 34: 173–183.

23. Bailey JM (2009) *Contemporary Perspectives on Lesbian, Gay, and Bisexual Identities*. Nebraska Symposium on Motivation. New York: Springer. 200 p.

24. Chivers ML, Rieger G, Latty E, Bailey JM (2004) A sex difference in the specificity of sexual arousal. *Psychological Science* 15: 736–744.

25. Lawrence AA (2013) Men trapped in men's bodies. In: Meana M, editor. *Men Trapped in Men's Bodies*. New York: Springer. 256 p.

26. Lever J (1994) Sexual revelations: the 1994 advocate survey of sexuality and relationships: the men. *The Advocate* 661: 16–24.

27. Blanchard R (1985) Typology of male-to-female transsexualism. *Arch Sex Behav* 14: 247–261.

28. Blanchard R (1989) The concept of autogynephilia and the typology of male gender dysphoria. *J Nerv Ment Dis* 177: 616–623.

29. Moser C (2010) Blanchard's autogynephilia theory: a critique. *J Homosex* 57: 790–809.

30. Serano J (2010) The case against autogynephilia. *Int J Transgenderism* 12: 176–187.

31. Blanchard R (1989) The classification and labeling of nonhomosexual gender dysphorias. *Arch Sex Behav* 18: 315–334.

32. Freund K, Blanchard R (1993) Erotic target location errors in male gender dysphorics, paedophiles, and fetishists. *Br J Psychiatry* 162: 558–563.

33. Thompson EM, Morgan EM (2008) "Mostly straight" young women: variations in sexual behavior and identity development. *Dev Psychol* 44: 15–21.

34. Zucker KJ, Bradley SJ, Owen-Anderson A, Kibblewhite SJ, Wood H, et al. (2012) Demographics, behavior problems, and psychosexual characteristics of adolescents with gender identity disorder or transvestic fetishism. *J Sex Marital Ther* 38: 151–189.

35. Rowniak S, Chesla C (2013) Coming out for a third time: transmen, sexual orientation, and identity. *Arch Sex Behav* 42: 449–461.

36. Devor H (1993) Sexual orientation identities, attractions, and practices of female-to-male transsexuals. *J Sex Res* 30: 303–315.

37. Schleifer D (2006) Make me feel mighty real: gay female-to-male transgenderists negotiating sex, gender, and sexuality. *Sexualities* 9: 57–75.

38. Bockting W, Benner A, Coleman E (2009) Gay and bisexual identity development among female-to-male transsexuals in North America: emergence of a transgender sexuality. *Arch Sex Behav* 38: 688–701.

39. Smith YLS, Van Goozen SHM, Kuiper AJ, Cohen-Kettenis PT (2005) Sex reassignment: outcomes and predictors of treatment for adolescent and adult transsexuals. *Psychol Med* 35: 89–99.

40. Johansson A, Sundbom E, Hojerback T, Bodlund O (2010) A five-year follow-up study of Swedish adults with gender identity disorder. *Arch Sex Behav* 39: 1429–1437.

41. Levine SB, Lothstein L (1981) Transsexualism or the gender dysphoria syndromes. *J Sex Marital Ther* 7: 85–113.

42. Kronawitter D, Gooren LJ, Zollver H, Oppelt PG, Beckmann MW, et al. (2009) Effects of transdermal testosterone or oral dydrogesterone on hypoactive sexual desire disorder in transsexual women: results of a pilot study. *Eur J Endocrinol* 161: 363–368.

43. Auer MK, Höhne N, Bazarra-Castro MÁ, Pfister H, Fuss J, et al. (2013) Psychopathological profiles in transsexuals and the challenge of their special status among the sexes. *Plos One* 8: e78469.

44. Lawrence AA, Latty EM, Chivers ML, Bailey JM (2005) Measurement of sexual arousal in postoperative male-to-female transsexuals using vaginal photoplethys mography. *Arch Sex Behav* 34: 135–145.

45. Jiang Y, Costello P, Fang F, Huang M, He S (2006) A gender- and sexual orientation-dependent spatial attentional effect of invisible images. *Proc Natl Acad Sci U S A* 103: 17048–17052.

46. Hu SH, Wei N, Wang QD, Yan LQ, Wei EQ, et al. (2008) Patterns of brain activation during visually evoked sexual arousal differ between homosexual and heterosexual men. *AJNR Am J Neuroradiol* 29: 1890–1896.

47. Auer MK, Fuss J, Stalla GK, Athanasoulia AP (2013) Twenty years of endocrinologic treatment in transsexualism: analyzing the role of chromosomal analysis and hormonal profiling in the diagnostic work-up. *Fertil Steril* 100: 1103–1110.

48. Fuss J, Biedermann SV, Stalla GK, Auer MK (2013) On the quest for a biomechanism of transsexualism: is there a role for BDNF? *J Psychiatr Res* 47: 2015–2017.

49. Zhou JN, Hofman MA, Gooren LJG, Swaab DF (1995) A sex difference in the human brain and its relation to transsexuality. *Nature* 378: 68–70.

50. Pathela P, Hajat A, Schillinger J, Blank S, Sell R, et al. (2006) Discordance between sexual behavior and self-reported sexual identity: a population-based survey of New York City men. *Ann Intern Med* 145: 416–425.

Critical Thinking

1. At one point in the article, the researchers posit that the hormones taken during transition may be partly responsible for a change in the trans person's understanding of their sexual orientation. What might be a concern that comes with that reasoning?

2. Do you think sexual orientation actually changes post-transition, or do you think because the person's biological sex now matches their gender identity the label for their orientation has changed?

3. What kinds of support do you think a person who is transitioning from one biological sex to another so that their bodies match their sense of who they are might need? If there is an additional change in their understanding of their sexual orientation, might they need additional supports?

Internet References

Center of Excellence for Transgender Health
http://transhealth.ucsf.edu

National Center for Transgender Equality
www.transequality.org

World Professional Association for Transgender Health
www.wpath.org

MATTHIAS K. AUER, GÜNTER K. STALLA AND CAROLINE SIEVERS are in the Department of Internal Medicine, Endocrinology and Clinical Chemistry, Max Planck Institute of Psychiatry, Munich, Germany. Johannes Fuss is in the Institute for Sex Research and Forensic Psychiatry, Center for Psychosocial Medicine, University Medical Center Hamburg-Eppendorf, Hamburg, Germany. Nina Höhne is in the Department of Molecular Psychology, Max Planck Institute of Psychiatry, Munich, Germany.

Article

Prepared by: Elizabeth Schroeder, EdD, MSW,
Elizabeth Schroeder Consulting

The End of Men

Earlier this year, women became the majority of the workforce for the first time in U.S. history. Most managers are now women too. And for every two men who get a college degree this year, three women will do the same. For years, women's progress has been cast as a struggle for equality. But what if equality isn't the end point? What if modern, postindustrial society is simply better suited to women? A report on the unprecedented role reversal now under way—and its vast cultural consequences.

HANNA ROSIN

Learning Outcomes

After reading this article, you will be able to:

- Name at least two historical influences on gender differences and power.

- Describe at least one shift in the gender composition of colleges and universities in the United States and what may be behind that shift.

- Explain what a female-dominated society might look like.

I n the 1970s the biologist Ronald Ericsson came up with a way to separate sperm carrying the male-producing Y chromosome from those carrying the X. He sent the two kinds of sperm swimming down a glass tube through ever-thicker albumin barriers. The sperm with the X chromosome had a larger head and a longer tail, and so, he figured, they would get bogged down in the viscous liquid. The sperm with the Y chromosome were leaner and faster and could swim down to the bottom of the tube more efficiently. Ericsson had grown up on a ranch in South Dakota, where he'd developed an Old West, cowboy swagger. The process, he said, was like "cutting out cattle at the gate." The cattle left flailing behind the gate were of course the X's, which seemed to please him. He would sometimes demonstrate the process using cartilage from a bull's penis as a pointer.

In the late 1970s, Ericsson leased the method to clinics around the U.S., calling it the first scientifically proven method for choosing the sex of a child. Instead of a lab coat, he wore cowboy boots and a cowboy hat, and doled out his version of cowboy poetry. (*People* magazine once suggested a TV mini-series based on his life called *Cowboy in the Lab.*) The right prescription for life, he would say, was "breakfast at five-thirty, on the saddle by six, no room for Mr. Limp Wrist." In 1979, he loaned out his ranch as the backdrop for the iconic "Marlboro Country" ads because he believed in the campaign's central image—"a guy riding on his horse along the river, no bureaucrats, no lawyers," he recalled when I spoke to him this spring. "He's the boss." (The photographers took some 6,500 pictures, a pictorial record of the frontier that Ericsson still takes great pride in.)

Feminists of the era did not take kindly to Ericsson and his Marlboro Man veneer. To them, the lab cowboy and his sper-minator portended a dystopia of mass-produced boys. "You have to be concerned about the future of all women," Roberta Steinbacher, a nun-turned-social-psychologist, said in a 1984 *People* profile of Ericsson. "There's no question that there exists a universal preference for sons." Steinbacher went on to complain about women becoming locked in as "second-class citizens" while men continued to dominate positions of control and influence. "I think women have to ask themselves, 'Where does this stop?'" she said. "A lot of us wouldn't be here right now if these practices had been in effect years ago."

Ericsson, now 74, laughed when I read him these quotes from his old antagonist. Seldom has it been so easy to prove a dire prediction wrong. In the '90s, when Ericsson looked into the numbers for the two dozen or so clinics that use his process, he discovered, to his surprise, that couples were requesting more girls than boys, a gap that has persisted, even though Ericsson advertises the method as more effective for producing boys. In some clinics, Ericsson has said, the ratio is now as high as 2 to 1. Polling data on American sex preference is sparse, and does not show a clear preference for girls. But the picture from the doctor's office unambiguously does. A newer method for sperm selection, called MicroSort, is currently completing Food and Drug Administration clinical trials. The girl requests for that method run at about 75 percent.

Even more unsettling for Ericsson, it has become clear that in choosing the sex of the next generation, *he* is no longer the boss. "It's the women who are driving all the decisions," he says—a change the MicroSort spokespeople I met with also mentioned. At first, Ericsson says, women who called his clinics would apologize and shyly explain that they already had two boys. "Now they just call and [say] outright, 'I want a girl.'" These mothers look at their lives and think their daughters will have a bright future their mother and grandmother didn't have, brighter than their sons, even, so why wouldn't you choose a girl?"

Why wouldn't you choose a girl? That such a statement should be so casually uttered by an old cowboy like Ericsson—or by anyone, for that matter—is monumental. For nearly as long as civilization has existed, patriarchy—enforced through the rights of the firstborn son—has been the organizing principle, with few exceptions. Men in ancient Greece tied off their left testicle in an effort to produce male heirs; women have killed themselves (or been killed) for failing to bear sons. In her iconic 1949 book, *The Second Sex,* the French feminist Simone de Beauvoir suggested that women so detested their own "feminine condition" that they regarded their newborn daughters with irritation and disgust. Now the centuries-old preference for sons is eroding—or even reversing. "Women of our generation want daughters precisely because we like who we are," breezes one woman in *Cookie* magazine. Even Ericsson, the stubborn old goat, can sigh and mark the passing of an era. "Did male dominance exist? Of course it existed. But it seems to be gone now. And the era of the firstborn son is totally gone."

Ericsson's extended family is as good an illustration of the rapidly shifting landscape as any other. His 26-year-old granddaughter—"tall, slender, brighter than hell, with a take-no-prisoners personality"—is a biochemist and works on genetic sequencing. His niece studied civil engineering at the University of Southern California. His grandsons, he says, are bright and handsome, but in school "their eyes glaze over. I have to tell 'em: 'Just don't screw up and crash your pickup truck and get some girl pregnant and ruin your life.'" Recently Ericsson joked with the old boys at his elementary-school reunion that he was going to have a sex-change operation. "Women live longer than men. They do better in this economy. More of 'em graduate from college. They go into space and do everything men do, and sometimes they do it a whole lot better. I mean, hell, get out of the way—these females are going to leave us males in the dust."

Man has been the dominant sex since, well, the dawn of mankind. But for the first time in human history, that is changing—and with shocking speed. Cultural and economic changes always reinforce each other. And the global economy is evolving in a way that is eroding the historical preference for male children, worldwide. Over several centuries, South Korea, for instance, constructed one of the most rigid patriarchal societies in the world. Many wives who failed to produce male heirs were abused and treated as domestic servants; some families prayed to spirits to kill off girl children. Then, in the 1970s and '80s, the government embraced an industrial revolution and encouraged women to enter the labor force. Women moved to the city and went to college. They advanced rapidly, from industrial jobs to clerical jobs to professional work. The traditional order began to crumble soon after. In 1990, the country's laws were revised so that women could keep custody of their children after a divorce and inherit property. In 2005, the court ruled that women could register children under their own names. As recently as 1985, about half of all women in a national survey said they "must have a son." That percentage fell slowly until 1991 and then plummeted to just over 15 percent by 2003. Male preference in South Korea "is over," says Monica Das Gupta, a demographer and Asia expert at the World Bank. "It happened so fast. It's hard to believe it, but it is." The same shift is now beginning in other rapidly industrializing countries such as India and China.

Up to a point, the reasons behind this shift are obvious. As thinking and communicating have come to eclipse physical strength and stamina as the keys to economic success, those societies that take advantage of the talents of all their adults, not just half of them, have pulled away from the rest. And because geopolitics and global culture are, ultimately, Darwinian, other societies either follow suit or end up marginalized. In 2006, the Organization for Economic Cooperation and Development devised the Gender, Institutions and Development Database, which measures the economic and political power of women in 162 countries. With few exceptions, the greater the power of women, the greater the country's economic success. Aid agencies have started to recognize this relationship and have pushed to institute political quotas in about 100 countries, essentially forcing women into power in an effort to improve those countries' fortunes. In some war-torn states, women are stepping in as a sort of maternal rescue team. Liberia's president, Ellen Johnson Sirleaf, portrayed her country as a sick child in need of her care during her campaign five years ago. Postgenocide Rwanda elected to heal itself by becoming the first country with a majority of women in parliament.

In feminist circles, these social, political, and economic changes are always cast as a slow, arduous form of catch-up in a continuing struggle for female equality. But in the U.S., the world's most advanced economy, something much more remarkable seems to be happening. American parents are beginning to choose to have girls over boys. As they imagine the pride of watching a child grow and develop and succeed as an adult, it is more often a girl that they see in their mind's eye.

What if the modern, postindustrial economy is simply more congenial to women than to men? For a long time, evolutionary psychologists have claimed that we are all imprinted with adaptive imperatives from a distant past: men are faster and stronger and hardwired to fight for scarce resources, and that shows up now as a drive to win on Wall Street; women are programmed to find good providers and to care for their offspring, and that is manifested in more-nurturing and more-flexible behavior, ordaining them to domesticity. This kind of thinking frames our sense of the natural order. But what if men and women were fulfilling not biological imperatives but social roles, based on what was more efficient throughout a long era of human history? What if that era has now come to an end? More to the point, what if the economics of the new era are better suited to women?

Once you open your eyes to this possibility, the evidence is all around you. It can be found, most immediately, in the wreckage of the Great Recession, in which three-quarters of the 8 million jobs lost were lost by men. The worst-hit industries were overwhelmingly male and deeply identified with macho: construction, manufacturing, high finance. Some of these jobs will come back, but the overall pattern of dislocation is neither temporary nor random. The recession merely revealed—and accelerated—a profound economic shift that has been going on for at least 30 years, and in some respects even longer.

Earlier this year, for the first time in American history, the balance of the workforce tipped toward women, who now hold a majority of the nation's jobs. The working class, which has long defined our notions of masculinity, is slowly turning into a matriarchy, with men increasingly absent from the home and women making all the decisions. Women dominate today's colleges and professional schools—for every two men who will receive a B.A. this year, three women will do the same. Of the 15 job categories projected to grow the most in the next decade in the U.S., all but two are occupied primarily by women. Indeed, the U.S. economy is in some ways becoming a kind of traveling sisterhood: upper-class women leave home and enter the workforce, creating domestic jobs for other women to fill.

The postindustrial economy is indifferent to men's size and strength. The attributes that are most valuable today—social intelligence, open communication, the ability to sit still and focus—are, at a minimum, not predominantly male. In fact, the opposite may be true. Women in poor parts of India are learning English faster than men to meet the demands of new global call centers. Women own more than 40 percent of private businesses in China, where a red Ferrari is the new status symbol for female entrepreneurs. Last year, Iceland elected Prime Minister Johanna Sigurdardottir, the world's first openly lesbian head of state, who campaigned explicitly against the male elite she claimed had destroyed the nation's banking system, and who vowed to end the "age of testosterone."

Yes, the U.S. still has a wage gap, one that can be convincingly explained—at least in part—by discrimination. Yes, women still do most of the child care. And yes, the upper reaches of society are still dominated by men. But given the power of the forces pushing at the economy, this setup feels like the last gasp of a dying age rather than the permanent establishment. Dozens of college women I interviewed for this story assumed that they very well might be the ones working while their husbands stayed at home, either looking for work or minding the children. Guys, one senior remarked to me, "are the new ball and chain." It may be happening slowly and unevenly, but it's unmistakably happening: in the long view, the modern economy is becoming a place where women hold the cards.

Dozens of college women I interviewed assumed that they very well might be the ones working while their husbands stayed at home. Guys, one senior remarked to me, "are the new ball and chain."

In his final book, *The Bachelors' Ball*, published in 2007, the sociologist Pierre Bourdieu describes the changing gender dynamics of Béarn, the region in southwestern France where he grew up. The eldest sons once held the privileges of patrimonial loyalty and filial inheritance in Béarn. But over the decades, changing economic forces turned those privileges into curses. Although the land no longer produced the impressive income it once had, the men felt obligated to tend it. Meanwhile, modern women shunned farm life, lured away by jobs and adventure in the city. They occasionally returned for the traditional balls, but the men who awaited them had lost their prestige and become unmarriageable. This is the image that keeps recurring to me, one that Bourdieu describes in his book: at the bachelors' ball, the men, self-conscious about their diminished status, stand stiffly, their hands by their sides, as the women twirl away.

The role reversal that's under way between American men and women shows up most obviously and painfully in the working class. In recent years, male support groups have sprung up throughout the Rust Belt and in other places where the postindustrial economy has turned traditional family roles upside down. Some groups help men cope with unemployment, and others help them reconnect with their alienated families. Mustafaa El-Scari, a teacher and social worker, leads some of these groups in Kansas City. El-Scari has studied the sociology of men and boys set adrift, and he considers it his special gift to get them to open up and reflect on their new condition. The day I visited one of his classes, earlier this year, he was facing a particularly resistant crowd.

None of the 30 or so men sitting in a classroom at a downtown Kansas City school have come for voluntary adult enrichment. Having failed to pay their child support, they were given the choice by a judge to go to jail or attend a weekly class on fathering, which to them seemed the better deal. This week's lesson, from a workbook called *Quenching the Father Thirst,* was supposed to involve writing a letter to a hypothetical estranged 14-year-old daughter named Crystal, whose father left her when she was a baby. But El-Scari has his own idea about how to get through to this barely awake, skeptical crew, and letters to Crystal have nothing to do with it.

Like them, he explains, he grew up watching Bill Cosby living behind his metaphorical "white picket fence"—one man, one woman, and a bunch of happy kids. "Well, that check bounced a long time ago," he says. "Let's see," he continues, reading from a worksheet. What are the four kinds of paternal authority? Moral, emotional, social, and physical. "But you ain't none of those in that house. All you are is a paycheck, and now you ain't even that. And if you try to exercise your authority, she'll call 911. How does that make you feel? You're supposed to be the authority, and she says, 'Get out of the house, bitch.' She's calling you 'bitch'!"

The men are black and white, their ages ranging from about 20 to 40. A couple look like they might have spent a night or two on the streets, but the rest look like they work, or used to. Now they have put down their sodas, and El-Scari has their attention, so he gets a little more philosophical. "Who's doing what?" he asks them. "What is our role? Everyone's telling us we're supposed to be the head of a nuclear family, so you feel like you got robbed. It's toxic, and poisonous, and it's setting us up for failure." He writes on the board: $85,000. "This is her salary." Then: $12,000. "This is your salary. Who's the damn man? Who's the man now?" A murmur rises. "That's right. She's the man."

Judging by the men I spoke with afterward, El-Scari seemed to have pegged his audience perfectly. Darren Henderson was making $33 an hour laying sheet metal, until the real-estate crisis hit and he lost his job. Then he lost his duplex—"there's my little piece of the American dream"—then his car. And then he fell behind on his child-support payments. "They make it like I'm just sitting around," he said, "but I'm not." As proof of his efforts, he took out a new commercial driver's permit and a bartending license, and then threw them down on the ground like jokers, for all the use they'd been. His daughter's

mother had a $50,000-a-year job and was getting her master's degree in social work. He'd just signed up for food stamps, which is just about the only social-welfare program a man can easily access. Recently she'd seen him waiting at the bus stop. "Looked me in the eye," he recalled, "and just drove on by."

The men in that room, almost without exception, were casualties of the end of the manufacturing era. Most of them had continued to work with their hands even as demand for manual labor was declining. Since 2000, manufacturing has lost almost 6 million jobs, more than a third of its total workforce, and has taken in few young workers. The housing bubble masked this new reality for a while, creating work in construction and related industries. Many of the men I spoke with had worked as electricians or builders; one had been a successful real-estate agent. Now those jobs are gone too. Henderson spent his days shuttling between unemployment offices and job interviews, wondering what his daughter might be doing at any given moment. In 1950, roughly one in 20 men of prime working age, like Henderson, was not working; today that ratio is about one in five, the highest ever recorded.

Men dominate just two of the 15 job categories projected to grow the most over the next decade: janitor and computer engineer. Women have everything else—nursing, home health assistance, child care, food preparation. Many of the new jobs, says Heather Boushey of the Center for American Progress, "replace the things that women used to do in the home for free." None is especially high-paying. But the steady accumulation of these jobs adds up to an economy that, for the working class, has become more amenable to women than to men.

The list of growing jobs is heavy on nurturing professions, in which women, ironically, seem to benefit from old stereotypes and habits. Theoretically, there is no reason men should not be qualified. But they have proved remarkably unable to adapt. Over the course of the past century, feminism has pushed women to do things once considered against their nature—first enter the workforce as singles, then continue to work while married, then work even with small children at home. Many professions that started out as the province of men are now filled mostly with women—secretary and teacher come to mind. Yet I'm not aware of any that have gone the opposite way. Nursing schools have tried hard to recruit men in the past few years, with minimal success. Teaching schools, eager to recruit male role models, are having a similarly hard time. The range of acceptable masculine roles has changed comparatively little, and has perhaps even narrowed as men have shied away from some careers women have entered. As Jessica Grose wrote in *Slate,* men seem "fixed in cultural aspic." And with each passing day, they lag further behind.

As we recover from the Great Recession, some traditionally male jobs will return—men are almost always harder-hit than women in economic downturns because construction and manufacturing are more cyclical than service industries—but that won't change the long-term trend. When we look back on this period, argues Jamie Ladge, a business professor at Northeastern University, we will see it as a "turning point for women in the workforce."

When we look back at this period, we will see it as a "turning point for women in the workforce."

The economic and cultural power shift from men to women would be hugely significant even if it never extended beyond working-class America. But women are also starting to dominate middle management, and a surprising number of professional careers as well. According to the Bureau of Labor Statistics, women now hold 51.4 percent of managerial and professional jobs—up from 26.1 percent in 1980. They make up 54 percent of all accountants and hold about half of all banking and insurance jobs. About a third of America's physicians are now women, as are 45 percent of associates in law firms—and both those percentages are rising fast. A white-collar economy values raw intellectual horsepower, which men and women have in equal amounts. It also requires communication skills and social intelligence, areas in which women, according to many studies, have a slight edge. Perhaps most important—for better or worse—it increasingly requires formal education credentials, which women are more prone to acquire, particularly early in adulthood. Just about the only professions in which women still make up a relatively small minority of newly minted workers are engineering and those calling on a hard-science background, and even in those areas, women have made strong gains since the 1970s.

Office work has been steadily adapting to women—and in turn being reshaped by them—for 30 years or more. Joel Garreau picks up on this phenomenon in his 1991 book, *Edge City*, which explores the rise of suburbs that are home to giant swaths of office space along with the usual houses and malls. Companies began moving out of the city in search not only of lower rent but also of the "best educated, most conscientious, most stable workers." They found their brightest prospects among "underemployed females living in middle-class communities on the fringe of the old urban areas." As Garreau chronicles the rise of suburban office parks, he places special emphasis on 1978, the peak year for women entering the workforce. When brawn was off the list of job requirements, women often measured up better than men. They were smart, dutiful, and, as long as employers could make the jobs more convenient for them, more reliable. The 1999 movie *Office Space* was maybe the first to capture how alien and dispiriting the office park can be for men. Disgusted by their jobs and their boss, Peter and his two friends embezzle money and start sleeping through their alarm clocks. At the movie's end, a male coworker burns down the office park, and Peter abandons desk work for a job in construction.

Near the top of the jobs pyramid, of course, the upward march of women stalls. Prominent female CEOs, past and present, are so rare that they count as minor celebrities, and most of us can tick off their names just from occasionally reading the business pages: Meg Whitman at eBay, Carly Fiorina at Hewlett-Packard, Anne Mulcahy and Ursula Burns at Xerox, Indra Nooyi at PepsiCo; the accomplishment is considered so extraordinary that Whitman and Fiorina are using it as the basis for political campaigns. Only 3 percent of *Fortune* 500 CEOs are women, and the number has never risen much above that.

But even the way this issue is now framed reveals that men's hold on power in elite circles may be loosening. In business circles, the lack of women at the top is described as a "brain drain" and a crisis of "talent retention." And while female CEOs may be rare in America's largest companies, they are highly prized: last year, they outearned their male counterparts by 43 percent, on average, and received bigger raises.

Even around the delicate question of working mothers, the terms of the conversation are shifting. Last year, in a story about breastfeeding, I complained about how the early years of child rearing keep women out of power positions. But the term *mommy track* is slowly morphing into the gender-neutral *flex time*, reflecting changes in the workforce. For recent college graduates of both sexes, flexible arrangements are at the top of the list of workplace demands, according to a study published last year in the *Harvard Business Review*. And companies eager to attract and retain talented workers and managers are responding. The consulting firm Deloitte, for instance, started what's now considered the model program, called Mass Career Customization, which allows employees to adjust their hours depending on their life stage. The program, Deloitte's Web site explains, solves "a complex issue—one that can no longer be classified as a woman's issue."

"Women are knocking on the door of leadership at the very moment when their talents are especially well matched with the requirements of the day," writes David Gergen in the introduction to *Enlightened Power: How Women Are Transforming the Practice of Leadership*. What are these talents? Once it was thought that leaders should be aggressive and competitive, and that men are naturally more of both. But psychological research has complicated this picture. In lab studies that simulate negotiations, men and women are just about equally assertive and competitive, with slight variations. Men tend to assert themselves in a controlling manner, while women tend to take into account the rights of others, but both styles are equally effective, write the psychologists Alice Eagly and Linda Carli, in their 2007 book, *Through the Labyrinth.*

Over the years, researchers have sometimes exaggerated these differences and described the particular talents of women in crude gender stereotypes: women as more empathetic, as better consensus-seekers and better lateral thinkers; women as bringing a superior moral sensibility to bear on a cutthroat business world. In the '90s, this field of feminist business theory seemed to be forcing the point. But after the latest financial crisis, these ideas have more resonance. Researchers have started looking into the relationship between testosterone and excessive risk, and wondering if groups of men, in some basic hormonal way, spur each other to make reckless decisions. The picture emerging is a mirror image of the traditional gender map: men and markets on the side of the irrational and over-emotional, and women on the side of the cool and levelheaded.

We don't yet know with certainty whether testosterone strongly influences business decision-making. But the perception of the ideal business leader is starting to shift. The old model of command and control, with one leader holding all the decision-making power, is considered hidebound. The new model is sometimes called "post-heroic," or "transformational" in the words of the historian and leadership expert James MacGregor Burns. The aim is to behave like a good coach, and channel your charisma to motivate others to be hardworking and creative. The model is not explicitly defined as feminist, but it echoes literature about male-female differences. A program at Columbia Business School, for example, teaches sensitive leadership and social intelligence, including better reading of facial expressions and body language. "We never explicitly say, 'Develop your feminine side,' but it's clear that's what we're advocating," says Jamie Ladge.

A 2008 study attempted to quantify the effect of this more-feminine management style. Researchers at Columbia Business School and the University of Maryland analyzed data on the top 1,500 U.S. companies from 1992 to 2006 to determine the relationship between firm performance and female participation in senior management. Firms that had women in top positions performed better, and this was especially true if the firm pursued what the researchers called an "innovation intensive strategy," in which, they argued, "creativity and collaboration may be especially important"—an apt description of the future economy.

It could be that women boost corporate performance, or it could be that better-performing firms have the luxury of recruiting and keeping high-potential women. But the association is clear: innovative, successful firms are the ones that promote women. The same Columbia-Maryland study ranked America's industries by the proportion of firms that employed female executives, and the bottom of the list reads like the ghosts of the economy past: shipbuilding, real estate, coal, steelworks, machinery.

If you really want to see where the world is headed, of course, looking at the current workforce can get you only so far. To see the future—of the workforce, the economy, and the culture—you need to spend some time at America's colleges and professional schools, where a quiet revolution is under way. More than ever, college is the gateway to economic success, a necessary precondition for moving into the upper-middle class—and increasingly even the middle class. It's this broad, striving middle class that defines our society. And demographically, we can see with absolute clarity that in the coming decades the middle class will be dominated by women.

We've all heard about the collegiate gender gap. But the implications of that gap have not yet been fully digested. Women now earn 60 percent of master's degrees, about half of all law and medical degrees, and 42 percent of all M.B.A.s. Most important, women earn almost 60 percent of all bachelor's degrees—the minimum requirement, in most cases, for an affluent life. In a stark reversal since the 1970s, men are now more likely than women to hold only a high-school diploma. "One would think that if men were acting in a rational way, they would be getting the education they need to get along out there," says Tom Mortenson, a senior scholar at the Pell Institute for the Study of Opportunity in Higher Education. "But they are just failing to adapt."

This spring, I visited a few schools around Kansas City to get a feel for the gender dynamics of higher education. I started at the downtown campus of Metropolitan Community College. Metropolitan is the kind of place where people go to learn practical job skills and keep current with the changing economy, and as in most community colleges these days, men were conspicuously absent. One afternoon, in the basement cafeteria of a nearly windowless brick building, several women were trying to keep their eyes on their biology textbook and ignore the text messages from their babysitters. Another crew was outside the ladies' room, braiding each other's hair. One woman, still in her medical-assistant scrubs, looked like she was about to fall asleep in the elevator between the first and fourth floors.

When Bernard Franklin took over as campus president in 2005, he looked around and told his staff early on that their new priority was to "recruit more boys." He set up mentoring programs and men-only study groups and student associations. He made a special effort to bond with male students, who liked to call him "Suit." "It upset some of my feminists," he recalls. Yet, a few years later, the tidal wave of women continues to wash through the school—they now make up about 70 percent of its students. They come to train to be nurses and teachers—African American women, usually a few years older than traditional college students, and lately, working-class white women from the suburbs seeking a cheap way to earn a credential. As for the men? Well, little has changed. "I recall one guy who was really smart," one of the school's counselors told me. "But he was reading at a sixth-grade level and felt embarrassed in front of the women. He had to hide his books from his friends, who would tease him when he studied. Then came the excuses. 'It's spring, gotta play ball.' 'It's winter, too cold.' He didn't make it."

It makes some economic sense that women attend community colleges—and in fact, all colleges—in greater numbers than men. Women ages 25 to 34 with only a high-school diploma currently have a median income of $25,474, while men in the same position earn $32,469. But it makes sense only up to a point. The well-paid lifetime union job has been disappearing for at least 30 years. Kansas City, for example, has shifted from steel manufacturing to pharmaceuticals and information technologies. "The economy isn't as friendly to men as it once was," says Jacqueline King, of the American Council on Education. "You would think men and women would go to these colleges at the same rate." But they don't.

In 2005, King's group conducted a survey of lower-income adults in college. Men, it turned out, had a harder time committing to school, even when they desperately needed to retool. They tended to start out behind academically, and many felt intimidated by the schoolwork. They reported feeling isolated and were much worse at seeking out fellow students, study groups, or counselors to help them adjust. Mothers going back to school described themselves as good role models for their children. Fathers worried that they were abrogating their responsibilities as breadwinner.

The student gender gap started to feel like a crisis to some people in higher-education circles in the mid-2000s, when it began showing up not just in community and liberal-arts colleges but in the flagship public universities—the UCs and the SUNYS and the UNCs. Like many of those schools, the University of Missouri at Kansas City, a full research university with more than 13,000 students, is now tipping toward 60 percent women, a level many admissions officers worry could permanently shift the atmosphere and reputation of a school. In February, I visited with Ashley Burress, UMKC's student-body president. (The other three student-government officers this school year were also women.) Burress, a cute, short, African American 24-year-old grad student who is getting a doctor-of-pharmacy degree, had many of the same complaints I heard from other young women. Guys high-five each other when they get a C, while girls beat themselves up over a B-minus. Guys play video games in each other's rooms, while girls crowd the study hall. Girls get their degrees with no drama, while guys seem always in danger of drifting away. "In 2012, I will be Dr. Burress," she said. "Will I have to deal with guys who don't even have a bachelor's degree? I would like to date, but I'm putting myself in a really small pool."

UMKC is a working- and middle-class school—the kind of place where traditional sex roles might not be anathema.

Yet as I talked to students this spring, I realized how much the basic expectations for men and women had shifted. Many of the women's mothers had established their careers later in life, sometimes after a divorce, and they had urged their daughters to get to their own careers more quickly. They would be a campus of Tracy Flicks, except that they seemed neither especially brittle nor secretly falling apart.

Victoria, Michelle, and Erin are sorority sisters. Victoria's mom is a part-time bartender at a hotel. Victoria is a biology major and wants to be a surgeon; soon she'll apply to a bunch of medical schools. She doesn't want kids for a while, because she knows she'll "be at the hospital, like, 100 hours a week," and when she does have kids, well, she'll "be the hotshot surgeon, and he"—a nameless he—"will be at home playing with the kiddies."

Michelle, a self-described "perfectionist," also has her life mapped out. She's a psychology major and wants to be a family therapist. After college, she will apply to grad school and look for internships. She is well aware of the career-counseling resources on campus. And her fiancé?

Michelle: He's changed majors, like, 16 times. Last week he wanted to be a dentist. This week it's environmental science.

Erin: Did he switch again this week? When you guys have kids, he'll definitely stay home. Seriously, what does he want to do?

Michelle: It depends on the day of the week. Remember last year? It was bio. It really is a joke. But it's not. It's funny, but it's not.

Among traditional college students from the highest-income families, the gender gap pretty much disappears. But the story is not so simple. Wealthier students tend to go to elite private schools, and elite private schools live by their own rules. Quietly, they've been opening up a new frontier in affirmative action, with boys playing the role of the underprivileged applicants needing an extra boost. In 2003, a study by the economists Sandy Baum and Eban Goodstein found that among selective liberal-arts schools, being male raises the chance of college acceptance by 6.5 to 9 percentage points. Now the U.S. Commission on Civil Rights has voted to investigate what some academics have described as the "open secret" that private schools "are discriminating in admissions in order to maintain what they regard as an appropriate gender balance."

Jennifer Delahunty, the dean of admissions and financial aid at Kenyon College, in Ohio, let this secret out in a 2006 *New York Times* op-ed. Gender balance, she wrote back then, is the elephant in the room. And today, she told me, the problem hasn't gone away. A typical female applicant, she said, manages the process herself—lines up the interviews, sets up a campus visit, requests a visit with faculty members. But the college has seen more than one male applicant "sit back on the couch, sometimes with their eyes closed, while their mom tells them where to go and what to do. Sometimes we say, 'What a nice essay his mom wrote,'" she said, in that funny-but-not vein.

To avoid crossing the dreaded 60 percent threshold, admissions officers have created a language to explain away the boys' deficits: "Brain hasn't kicked in yet." "Slow to cook." "Hasn't quite peaked." "Holistic picture." At times Delahunty has become so worried about "overeducated females" and "undereducated males" that she jokes she is getting conspiratorial. She once called her sister, a pediatrician, to vet her latest theory: "Maybe these boys are genetically like canaries in a coal mine, absorbing so many toxins and bad things in the environment that their DNA is shifting. Maybe they're like those frogs—they're more vulnerable or something, so they've gotten deformed."

Clearly, some percentage of boys are just temperamentally unsuited to college, at least at age 18 or 20, but without it, they have a harder time finding their place these days. "Forty years ago, 30 years ago, if you were one of the fairly constant fraction of boys who wasn't ready to learn in high school, there were ways for you to enter the mainstream economy," says Henry Farber, an economist at Princeton. "When you woke up, there were jobs. There were good industrial jobs, so you could have a good industrial, blue-collar career. Now those jobs are gone."

Since the 1980s, as women have flooded colleges, male enrollment has grown far more slowly. And the disparities start before college. Throughout the '90s, various authors and researchers agonized over why boys seemed to be failing at every level of education, from elementary school on up, and identified various culprits: a misguided feminism that treated normal boys as incipient harassers (Christina Hoff Sommers); different brain chemistry (Michael Gurian); a demanding, verbally focused curriculum that ignored boys' interests (Richard Whitmire). But again, it's not all that clear that boys have become more dysfunctional—or have changed in any way. What's clear is that schools, like the economy, now value the self-control, focus, and verbal aptitude that seem to come more easily to young girls.

Researchers have suggested any number of solutions. A movement is growing for more all-boys schools and classes, and for respecting the individual learning styles of boys. Some people think that boys should be able to walk around in class, or take more time on tests, or have tests and books that cater to their interests. In their desperation to reach out to boys, some colleges have formed football teams and started engineering programs. Most of these special accommodations sound very much like the kind of affirmative action proposed for women over the years—which in itself is an alarming flip.

Whether boys have changed or not, we are well past the time to start trying some experiments. It is fabulous to see girls and young women poised for success in the coming years. But allowing generations of boys to grow up feeling rootless and obsolete is not a recipe for a peaceful future. Men have few natural support groups and little access to social welfare; the men's-rights groups that do exist in the U.S. are taking on an angry, antiwoman edge. Marriages fall apart or never happen at all, and children are raised with no fathers. Far from being celebrated, women's rising power is perceived as a threat.

What would a society in which women are on top look like? We already have an inkling. This is the first time that the cohort of Americans ages 30 to 44 has more college-educated women than college-educated men, and the effects are upsetting the traditional Cleaver-family dynamics. In 1970, women contributed 2 to 6 percent of the family income. Now the typical working wife brings home 42.2 percent, and four in 10 mothers—many of them single mothers—are the primary breadwinners in their families. The whole question of whether mothers should work is moot, argues Heather Boushey of the Center for American Progress, "because they just do. This idealized family—he works, she stays home—hardly exists anymore."

The terms of marriage have changed radically since 1970. Typically, women's income has been the main factor in determining whether a family moves up the class ladder or stays stagnant. And increasing numbers of women—unable to find men with a similar income and education—are forgoing marriage altogether. In 1970, 84 percent of women ages 30 to 44 were married; now 60 percent are. In 2007, among American women without a high-school diploma, 43 percent were married. And yet, for all the hand-wringing over the lonely spinster, the real loser in society—the only one to have made just slight financial gains since the 1970s—is the single man, whether poor or rich, college-educated or not. Hens rejoice; it's the bachelor party that's over.

The sociologist Kathryn Edin spent five years talking with low-income mothers in the inner suburbs of Philadelphia. Many of these neighborhoods, she found, had turned into matriarchies, with women making all the decisions and dictating what the men should and should not do. "I think something feminists have missed," Edin told me, "is how much power women have" when they're not bound by marriage. The women, she explained, "make every important decision"—whether to have a baby, how to raise it, where to live. "It's definitely 'my way or the highway,'" she said. "Thirty years ago, cultural norms were such that the fathers might have said, 'Great, catch me if you can.' Now they are desperate to father, but they are pessimistic about whether they can meet her expectations." The women don't want them as husbands, and they have no steady income to provide. So what do they have?

"Nothing," Edin says. "They have nothing. The men were just annihilated in the recession of the '90s, and things never got better. Now it's just awful."

The situation today is not, as Edin likes to say, a "feminist nirvana." The phenomenon of children being born to unmarried parents "has spread to barrios and trailer parks and rural areas and small towns," Edin says, and it is creeping up the class ladder. After staying steady for a while, the portion of American children born to unmarried parents jumped to 40 percent in the past few years. Many of their mothers are struggling financially; the most successful are working and going to school and hustling to feed the children, and then falling asleep in the elevator of the community college.

Still, they are in charge. "The family changes over the past four decades have been bad for men and bad for kids, but it's not clear they are bad for women," says W. Bradford Wilcox, the head of the University of Virginia's National Marriage Project.

Over the years, researchers have proposed different theories to explain the erosion of marriage in the lower classes: the rise of welfare, or the disappearance of work and thus of marriageable men. But Edin thinks the most compelling theory is that marriage has disappeared because women are setting the terms—and setting them too high for the men around them to reach. "I want that white-picket-fence dream," one woman told Edin, and the men she knew just didn't measure up, so she had become her own one-woman mother/father/nurturer/provider. The whole country's future could look much as the present does for many lower-class African Americans: the mothers pull themselves up, but the men don't follow. First-generation college-educated white women may join their black counterparts in a new kind of middle class, where marriage is increasingly rare.

AS The traditional order has been upended, signs of the profound disruption have popped up in odd places. Japan is in a national panic over the rise of the "herbivores," the cohort of young men who are rejecting the hard-drinking salaryman life of their fathers and are instead gardening, organizing dessert parties, acting cartoonishly feminine, and declining to have sex. The generational young-women counterparts are known in Japan as the "carnivores," or sometimes the "hunters."

American pop culture keeps producing endless variations on the omega male, who ranks even below the beta in the wolf pack. This often-unemployed, romantically challenged loser can show up as a perpetual adolescent (in Judd Apatow's *Knocked Up* or *The 40-Year-Old Virgin*), or a charmless misanthrope (in Noah Baumbach's *Greenberg*), or a happy couch potato (in a Bud Light commercial). He can be sweet, bitter, nostalgic, or cynical, but he cannot figure out how to be a man. "We call each other 'man,'" says Ben Stiller's character in *Greenberg*, "but it's a joke. It's like imitating other people." The American male novelist, meanwhile, has lost his mojo and entirely given up on sex as a way for his characters to assert macho dominance, Katie Roiphe explains in her essay "The Naked and the Conflicted." Instead, she writes, "the current sexual style is more childlike; innocence is more fashionable than virility, the cuddle preferable to sex."

At the same time, a new kind of alpha female has appeared, stirring up anxiety and, occasionally, fear. The cougar trope started out as a joke about desperate older women. Now it's gone mainstream, even in Hollywood, home to the 50-something producer with a starlet on his arm. Susan Sarandon and Demi Moore have boy toys, and Aaron Johnson, the 19-year-old star of *Kick-Ass*, is a proud boy toy for a woman 24 years his senior. The *New York Times* columnist Gail Collins recently wrote that the cougar phenomenon is beginning to look like it's not about desperate women at all but about "desperate young American men who are latching on to an older woman who's a good earner." *Up in the Air*, a movie set against the backdrop of recession-era layoffs, hammers home its point about the shattered ego of the American man. A character played by George Clooney is called too old to be attractive by his younger female colleague and is later rejected by an older woman whom he falls in love with after she sleeps with him—and who turns out to be married. George Clooney! If the sexiest man alive can get twice rejected (and sexually played) in a movie, what hope is there for anyone else? The message to American men is summarized by the title of a recent offering from the romantic-comedy mill: *She's Out of My League.*

In fact, the more women dominate, the more they behave, fittingly, like the dominant sex. Rates of violence committed by middle-aged women have skyrocketed since the 1980s, and no one knows why. High-profile female killers have been showing up regularly in the news: Amy Bishop, the homicidal Alabama professor; Jihad Jane and her sidekick, Jihad Jamie; the latest generation of Black Widows, responsible for suicide bombings in Russia. In Roman Polanski's *The Ghost Writer*, the traditional political wife is rewritten as a cold-blooded killer at the heart of an evil conspiracy. In her recent video *Telephone*, Lady Gaga, with her infallible radar for the cultural edge, rewrites *Thelma and Louise* as a story not about elusive female empowerment but about sheer, ruthless power. Instead of killing themselves, she and her girlfriend (played by Beyoncé) kill a bad boyfriend and random others in a homicidal spree and then escape in their yellow pickup truck, Gaga bragging, "We did it, Honey B."

The Marlboro Man, meanwhile, master of wild beast and wild country, seems too farfetched and preposterous even for advertising. His modern equivalents are the stunted men in the Dodge Charger ad that ran during this year's Super Bowl in February. Of all the days in the year, one might think, Super Bowl Sunday should be the one most dedicated to the cinematic celebration of macho. The men in Super Bowl ads should be throwing balls and racing motorcycles and doing whatever it is men imagine they could do all day if only women were not around to restrain them.

Instead, four men stare into the camera, unsmiling, not moving except for tiny blinks and sways. They look like they've been tranquilized, like they can barely hold themselves up against the breeze. Their lips do not move, but a voice-over explains their predicament—how they've been beaten silent by the demands of tedious employers and enviro-fascists and women. Especially women. "I will put the seat down, I will separate the recycling, I will carry your lip balm." This last one—lip balm—is expressed with the mildest spit of emotion, the only hint of the suppressed rage against the dominatrix. Then the commercial abruptly cuts to the fantasy, a Dodge Charger vrooming toward the camera punctuated by bold all caps: MAN'S LAST STAND. But the motto is unconvincing. After that display of muteness and passivity, you can only imagine a woman—one with shiny lips—steering the beast.

Critical Thinking

1. What are some of the factors leading to the erosion of the patriarchal principles in society?

Internet References

Everyday Feminism
http://everydayfeminism.com

Feminist.com
http://feminist.com

Feminist Majority Foundation
http://www.feminist.org

HANNA ROSIN is an *Atlantic* contributing editor and the co-editor of *DoubleX*.

Prepared by: Elizabeth Schroeder, EdD, MSW,
Elizabeth Schroeder Consulting

Article

Sexuality and Gender Role in Autism Spectrum Disorder: A Case Control Study

Susanne Bejerot and Jonna M. Eriksson

Learning Outcomes

After reading this article, you will be able to:

- Describe the extreme male brain theory of autism.

- Describe at least two links between ASD and sex drive.

- Describe at least two connections between gender expression and ASD.

Introduction

The extreme male brain theory of autism describes an autistic personality characterised by extremes of typical male personality traits[1] in terms of systemising skills and weaknesses in empathy[2,3]. This connection to sex-related differences might be an important clue to the aetiology of autism spectrum disorder (ASD). Previous studies have shown that elevated levels of testosterone in amnion fluid predict autistic cognitive traits in childhood[4,5]. In both sexes, prenatal exposure to testosterone affects the foetal brain resulting in masculinised future personality and behaviours[6,7]. This is illustrated by an increased rate of tomboyism and masculinisation in women with congenital adrenal hyperplasia (CAH), an enzymatic defect resulting in highly elevated prenatal testosterone levels[8]. Although most women with CAH are heterosexual, rates of bisexual and homosexual orientation are elevated amongst this population[9]. Similarly, neural masculinisation[10] and tomboyism[11,12] have also been reported in females with ASD. In addition, ASD has been shown to be overrepresented in men as well as women with gender identity disorder[13]. It has also been implied that

gender identity disorder is overrepresented in ASD[14,15]. Further, bisexuality and homosexuality are suggested to be more common in men with ASD than in men in the general population[16], while data on women with ASD is lacking.

Animal studies have indicated that abnormal prenatal testosterone levels may also affect sexual behaviour and desire in the adult animal[17,18], but whether this relationship also applies to humans is unknown. Exposure to prenatal androgens seems to be one factor in the multifaceted aetiology of autism, in line with the extreme male brain theory of autism. A study of differences between ASD and typically developed individuals regarding other sexually dimorphic traits (presumably related to prenatal masculinisation or defeminisation) may add to the knowledge of the development of an androgen-dependent form of ASD. To date, no studies have examined if the extreme male cognitive pattern and the lack of gender differences in systemising-empathising dimensions extend to other sexually dimorphic traits, such as gender role and sexuality in individuals with ASD. Clinical experience, however, suggests that masculinity, expressed as male typical territorial or sexual behaviour[19,20], is attenuated in ASD of both sexes.

The current study constitutes the second half of a larger case control study on sexuality, androgen levels and anthropometric measures[21]. We found that the women with ASD had elevated testosterone levels and several physical masculinised characteristics, whereas the men with ASD displayed several physical feminised characteristics. However, the testosterone levels in the men with ASD did not differ significantly from the controls'. The current study further investigated how ASD relates to a set of nonphysical attributes including gender role, gender identity, self-perceived gender typicality, androgynous behaviour in childhood, and sexuality. Gender role was assessed as adherence to a set of stereotypically male or female skills, while other aspects were self reported. We hypothesized that male typical behaviour and perception would be weakened in ASD of both sexes, and that gender identity would be less pronounced than amongst controls.

Methods
Ethics Statement

The study design was discussed in depth and approved by the local empowerment board within the Swedish Autism Society (Autism & Aspergerförbundet). The Regional Ethic committee in Stockholm approved the study protocol (Dnr 2005/644-31/3) and the investigation was conducted according to the principles expressed in the Declaration of Helsinki. All participants provided written consent and reimbursement was offered for participation (approximately £95). All participants who declined to participate or did not otherwise participate were not disadvantaged in any way by not participating in the study.

Individuals with ASD were recruited through a website for adults with ASD or through a request sent to outpatients at a tertiary psychiatric unit for adults with ASD as well as to a community-based information centre. This centre offers information about legal aspects on the ASD diagnosis, social services etc., and is mainly serving adults diagnosed with ASD in teens or adulthood. The written request concerning the study included a brief information and the participants themselves either responded on e-mail or by post if they were interested in participating. Thereafter a brief telephone interview was conducted to ensure that the subject had attended mainstream schooling and had not been diagnosed with intellectual disability. The participants' ability to consent to the study was further confirmed in the interview by the first author, a senior psychiatrist with extensive training and experience with adult ASD. A total of three individuals were deemed not to have the capacity to consent and were subsequently excluded; two of these had a comorbid psychosis and the third had epilepsy and brain damage. None of the included participants had a caretaker or a guardian. Moreover, half of the ASD sample had a university degree and eight were parents themselves suggesting a relatively high level of functioning. For a capable group of adults with ASD such as the participants in the present study a requirement of consent from next of kin would presumably be perceived as humiliating, and the local empowerment board within the Swedish Autism Society did not support such a requirement.

Participants and Procedure

The study involved 103 Swedish adults, including 50 adults (26 men, 24 women) diagnosed with ASD and 53 neurotypical controls (28 men, 25 women) matched on gender and age; demographics are shown in Table 1. Individuals with ASD were recruited through an outpatient tertiary psychiatric unit for adult ASD, a community-based centre for adults with ASD, and through a website for adults with ASD; see flowchart (Figure 1). Controls were recruited after the ASD group in order to be matched for gender and age. Sources for recruitment were a nonprofit keep-fit organization, university, student residences, private companies, dentists and vaccination centres, employment agencies and through word-of-mouth recommendations. Inclusion criteria for both groups were Swedish/Caucasian descent and age between 20 and 47 years. Exclusion criteria were any disease or medication affecting androgen status, congenital syndrome, neurological or genetic syndrome, psychosis, diagnosed malformations, intellectual disability or having attended special education in primary or secondary school. Additional exclusion criteria in the control group were ASD or ASD in a first-degree family member. All participants denied any use of anabolic steroids and other androgen treatments other than hormonal contraceptives, used by 7 women with ASD and 14 women in the control group.

Participants in the ASD group had all been diagnosed with ASD prior to this study and their medical records were reviewed. Local diagnostic procedures require that each patient is assessed rigorously by a psychiatrist and psychologist experienced with ASD over approximately 12–20 hours before receiving the diagnosis. The assessment includes neuropsychological tests, including Wechsler Adult Intelligence Scale, and interviews with parents to obtain a developmental history. For inclusion in the current study, a senior psychiatrist with extensive training and experience with adult ASD confirmed all diagnoses through an independent diagnostic interview using the Autism Diagnostic Observation Schedule[22] and also assessed general functioning[23]. Participants were interviewed for background information and gender typical behaviour in childhood. The questionnaires regarding gender role, gender identity and sexuality were completed by the participants.

Assessment
Gender Role

Gender role was measured using the MF scale[24,25], a validated Swedish modification of the Bem Sex Role Inventory, measuring stereotypical masculine and feminine traits[26]. In contrast to the Bem Sex Role Inventory which presents a single adjective (e.g. 'competitive') the MF scale provides full statements (e.g. 'I am competitive'). The MF scale consists of 43 items rated on a four-point Likert scale (1 = "I totally disagree",

Table 1 Demographic Data of the Study Samples

		ASD group		Control group	
		Males (n = 26)	**Females (n = 24)**	**Males (n = 28)**	**Females (n = 25)**
Age, years: mean (s.d.)		31.8 (7.8)	28.1 (6.3)	32.9 (7.4)	27.7 (6.7)
Education, n					
	≤9 years	5	3	1	0
	≤12 years	9	9	2	5
	University level	12	12	25	20
Cohabiting with partner, n(%)		3 (11.5)	6 (25)	14 (50)	12 (48)
Having children, n(%)		5 (19.2)	3 (12.5)	8 (28.6)	3 (12.0)
The Autism-Spectrum Quotient: mean (s.d.)		28.0 (9.4)	31.9 (7.9)	11.7 (5.4)	10.4 (4.2)
Reading the Mind in the Eyes: mean (s.d.)		25 (5)	24 (4)	27 (3)	29.5 (2.5)
GAF, current (past month): mean (s.d.)					
	Symptoms	54 (13)	52 (12)	98 (4)	97 (5)
	Functioning	57 (13)	56.5 (13)	98 (3)	97 (5)

ASD; autism spectrum disorder.
doi:10.1371/journal.pone.0087961.t001

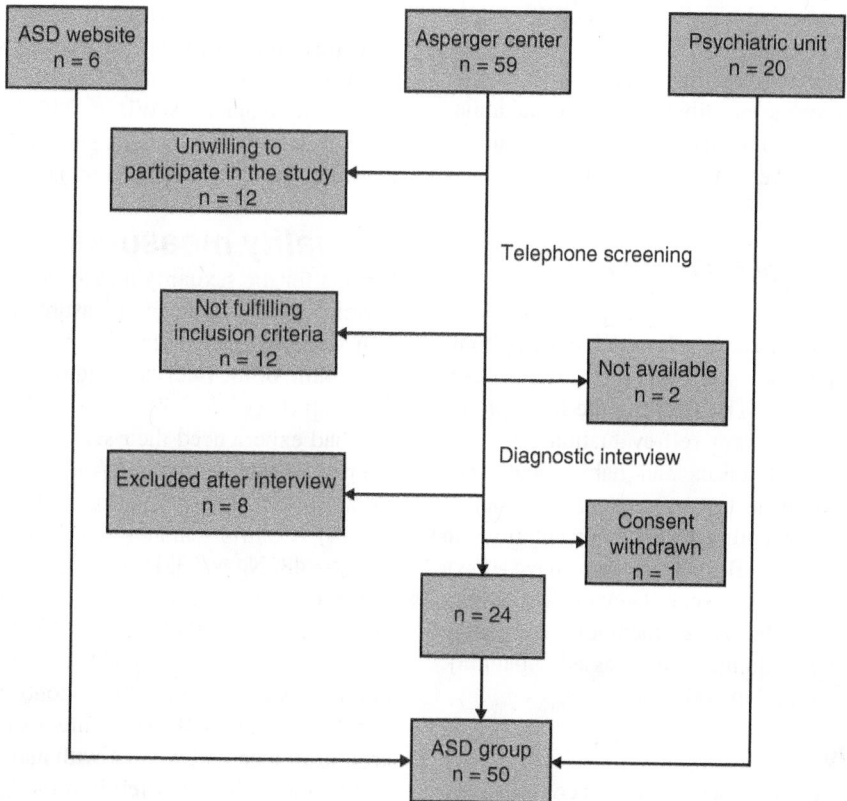

Figure 1 Flow chart for recruitment of participants with autism spectrum disorder.
doi:10.1371/journal.pone.0087961.g001

2 = "I slightly disagree", 3 = "I slightly agree" and 4 = "I fully agree"). The male and female stereotypes (subscales labelled MF_M and MF_F, respectively) are assessed with 17 items each, and a further 9 items are gender neutral. The MF_M subscale contains statements regarding power, assertiveness, leadership abilities and competitiveness, while the MF_F subscale mainly measures how tender, caring and submissive a person is. In order to estimate current masculine and feminine gender roles, we performed a pilot validation study of the MF scale in a large non-clinical Caucasian and Swedish- born adult population sample (N = 637, 46% men and 54% women; age range 19–65 years) (un-published). This showed mean MF_M scores of 48.6 (6.3) for men and 45.3 (5.8) for women, and mean MF_F scores of 42.4 (4.8) for men and 46.4 (4.4) for women.

Gender perception, sexual debut and behaviours

Gender identity, androgynous behaviour, gender typicality and sexuality were examined through 10 self-rated items constructed for the purpose of this study. Each item had explicit wording and straightforward response alternatives. *Gender identity* was defined as to what gender the person feels he/she belongs to; *androgynous behaviour in childhood* was characterised as being sissy/tomboyish in childhood, and *gender typicality* was defined as how gender typical the person assessed him-/herself in adulthood, in relation to other people of the same sex. Regarding sexuality, we focused on areas that possibly but certainly not exclusively could be related to foetal testosterone levels: libido, taking sexual initiatives, sexual interest, orgasms and sexual orientation[8,27]. Additionally two items on sexual debut were included. The items and their response options are presented in Table 2.

Measures of cognitive autistic traits and functioning.

To describe the groups, two measures of cognitive traits, commonly used in ASD evaluations were included: The Autism Spectrum Quotient (AQ)[28] and "The Reading the Mind in the Eyes test"[29]. The AQ is a 50- item self-evaluation questionnaire, assessing personal preferences and habits, and "The Reading the Mind in the Eyes test" is a measure of mentalising skills through testing the ability to decipher emotions in photos of expressive sets of eyes. Both instruments have shown gender-variations in neurotypical people. General functioning was quantified using the Global Assessment of Functioning (GAF)[23]. Symptoms and functioning are assessed separately, each with scores ranging from 0 to 100.

Statistical analysis

Comparisons between participants with ASD and controls were made using Student's t-test for normally distributed data, the Mann-Whitney U test for non-parametrical data and x^2-test for categorical variables. Missing data on the MF_M and MF_F subscales (0.06%) and the AQ (0.4%) was substituted using the mean value of all the items in the respective scale. A two-tailed P value of <0.05 was considered significant. The gender identity was dichotomised into either biological sex or not (in-between man and woman, transsexual and non-biological sex). Sexual behaviour items were dichotomised for more straight forward interpretation of masculine dimensions of sexuality (Table 2).

Results

Gender role, gender identity and androgynous behaviour in childhood

As shown in Table 3, both men and women with ASD rated themselves as having a less masculine gender role than the controls, according to the MF_M subscale. More individuals with ASD than controls reported an atypical gender identity ($\chi^2(1, N = 103) = 10.1$, $\varphi = 0.31$, P = 0.001). When separated by sex, this reached significance only for the women. Although no difference was found between men with ASD and controls on being 'a sissy in childhood', women with ASD rated themselves as being more tomboyish in childhood compared with the female controls. However, regarding self-perceived gender typicality, no significant difference was shown between the ASD group and controls for either sex (Men: MWU = 335, P = 0.98; Women: MWU = 235, P = 0.34). Table 4 shows the correlations between the gender role and gender perception measures in ASD males and females, respectively.

Sexuality measures

Results for the sexuality measures are presented in Table 5 and correlations between the measures in Table 6. Four men and four women (16%) in the ASD group had never had intercourse at the time of the interview, significantly more than reported by the controls ($\chi^2 = 9.39$; P = 0.002). Amongst the participants that had experienced their sexual debut, this occurred later for the men-women combined ASD group (mean age: ASD males = 22.1(5.9), ASD females = 18.7(4.7); Control males = 17.4(4), Control females = 16.5(2.7); $MWU_{combined}$ = 844, N_{ASD} = 43, N_C = 53, P = 0.03, r = 0.13). The combined ASD group reported fewer moments of sexual arousal ($\chi^2(1, N = 102) = 12.0$, P = 0.0005, $\varphi = 0.34$), less sexual interest ($\chi^2(1, N = 103) = 10.0$, P = 0.002, $\varphi = 0.31$) and less inclination to initiate sex compared with the controls ($\chi^2(1, N = 95) = 18.0$, P = 0.00002, $\varphi = 0.44$). Figure 2 shows frequencies of sexual arousal in men and women with and without ASD. Fewer men and women with ASD fell into the high frequency of orgasms group ($\geq$4 times monthly). Notably, ten women (44%) with

Table 2 Gender Perception, Sexual Debut and Behaviour Items

Measure	Item	Response alternatives	Dichotomized responses	Interpretation
Gender perception				**as a gender-atypical pattern**
Gender identity	What is your gender identity?	"Woman", "In-between man and woman", "man", "transsexual"		
			In between man and woman, transsexual, opposite sex	Yes
			Biological sex	No
Androgynous behaviour in childhood	Were you a 'sissy'/ tomboy during childhood?	"Yes"/ "No"/ "Don't know"		
			Yes	Yes
			No	No
Gender typicality	Do you perceive yourself as typical for your gender?	"Yes, absolutely" "Yes, to some extent" "No, not at all" "Don't know"		Reversed item, i.e. "No" indicates gender atypicality and "Yes, to some extent" some gender atypicality.
Sexual debut				
Intercourse	Have you had sexual intercourse?	"Yes"/"No"	Yes/No	
Debut age	Age for sexual debut?	Age in years		
Sexual behaviour				**as a masculinised pattern**
Libido	Have you been sexually aroused past month?	"No", "1–3 times", "4–6 times", "7–15 times", "every day"		
			Higher ≥4 times	Yes
			Lower <4 times	No
Sexual initiative	Who takes initiative to have sex?	"I", "both", "partner", "no one"		
			Initiator: I, both	Yes
			Not initiator: partner, no one	No
Sexual interest	Are you interested in sex?	"No, not at all", "Not very much", "Yes, quite", "very interested"		
			"Yes, quite", "very interested"	Yes
			"No, not at all", "Not very much	No
Orgasm frequency	Have you had an orgasm during the past month?	"No", "1–3 times", "4–6 times", "7–15 times", "every day"		

Table 2 Gender Perception, Sexual Debut and Behaviour Items *(continued)*

			Higher ≥4 times	Yes
			Lower <4 times	No
Sexual orientation	Whom are you attracted to?	"Men", "women", "both men and women", "neither", "other"		
			Attracted to females	Yes
			Not attracted to females	No

Note. Response alternatives "don't know" were treated as missing data.

doi:10.1371/journal.pone.0087961.t002

ASD had not had any orgasm the previous month, compared to 4 women (16%) in the control group. Homosexuality or bisexuality were equally common in the male groups (homosexual, $n_{ASD} = 2$; $n_C = 2$; bisexual, $n_{ASD} = 1$; $n_C = 2$). However, amongst the women, sexual attraction towards other females was reported more frequently in the ASD group (homosexual, $n_{ASD} = 1$; $n_C = 0$; bisexual, $n_{ASD} = 13$; $n_C = 4$). One woman and one man with ASD reported asexuality.

Table 3 Gender Role and Gender Identity Measures in 50 Individuals with Autism Spectrum Disorder (ASD) and 53 Neurotypical Controls

			ASD group			Control group					Effect size	
MF Gender role	Sex	N	Mean(s.d.)	z-score	N	Mean(s.d.)	z-score	t(df)	P	r	
MF_F subscale score	M	26	41.7(6.2)	−1.09 (0.99)	28	47.9(6.0)	−0.1(0.96)	−3.7(5.2)	0.0005	0.46	↓
	F	24	40.0(6.6)	−0.91 (1.13)	25	47.2(5.8)	0.33(0.99)	−4.1(47)	0.0002	0.51	↓
MF_F subscale score	M	26	44.6(6.1)	0.45(1.28)	28	42.2(4.2)	−0.04 (0.87)	1.7(52)	0.1	0.22	±
	F	24	45.8(6.2)	−0.15(1.41)	25	46.9(4.3)	0.11(0.98)	−0.8(47)	0.4	0.11	±
Gender identity and gender behaviour			n(%)			n(%)		χ^2(df)	p	Φ	
Gender–atypical identity in adulthood	M	26	3(11.5)		28	1(3.6)		1.3(1)	0.3		±
	F	24	8(33)		25	0(0)		10.0(2)	0.002	0.45	↑
[†]Androgynous behaviour in childhood	M	22	5(23)		28	7(25)		0.04(1)	0.8	−	±
	F	19	12(67)		24	8(33)		3.9(1)	0.05	0.31	↑

MF_M and MF_F scales' z-scores normalised for gender by data from the MF validation study. ↑ denotes an increase and ↓ a decrease in masculinity.
M = Males; F = Females;
MF_M = The Masculine subscale score for self-rated masculine gender role;
MF_F = The Feminine subscale score for self-rated feminine gender role; MWU = Mann-Whitney U test.
[†]2 men and 4 women with ASD and 1 woman in the control group responded "I don't know" and thus were excluded in the analyses; in addition to missing data in 2 men and 1 woman with ASD.

doi:10.1371/journal.pone.0087961.t003

11. Knickmeyer RC, Wheelwright S, Baron-Cohen SB (2008) Sex-typical play: masculinization/defeminization in girls with an autism spectrum condition. *J Autism Dev Disord* 38: 1028–1035.

12. Ingudomnukul E, Baron-Cohen S, Wheelwright S, Knickmeyer R (2007) Elevated rates of testosterone-related disorders in women with autism spectrum conditions. *Horm Behav* 51: 597–604.

13. De Vries ALC, Noens ILJ, Cohen-Kettenis PT, van Berckelaer-Onnes IA, Doreleijers TA (2010) Autism spectrum disorders in gender dysphoric children and adolescents. *J Autism Dev Disord* 40: 930–936.

14. Tateno M, Ikeda H, Saito T (2011) [Gender dysphoria in pervasive developmental disorders]. *Seishin Shinkeigaku Zasshi* 113: 1173–1183.

15. Gerland G (2004) *Autism: relationer och sexualitet.* Stockholm, Sweden: Cura.

16. Hellemans H, Colson K, Verbraeken C, Vermeiren R, Deboutte D (2007) Sexual behavior in high-functioning male adolescents and young adults with autism spectrum disorder. *J Autism Dev Disord* 37: 260–269.

17. Henley CL, Nunez AA, Clemens LG (2010) Exogenous androgen during development alters adult partner preference and mating behavior in gonadally intact male rats. *Horm Behav* 57: 488–495.

18. Dela Cruz C, Pereira OCM (2012) Prenatal testosterone supplementation alters puberty onset, aggressive behavior, and partner preference in adult male rats. *J Physiol Sci* 62: 123–131.

19. Benenson JF, Markovits H, Muller I, Challen A, Carder HP (2007) Explaining sex differences in infants' preferences for groups. *Infant Behav Dev* 30: 587–595.

20. Markovits H, Benenson JF (2010) Males outperform females in translating social relations into spatial positions. *Cognition* 117: 332–340.

21. Bejerot S, Eriksson JM, Bonde S, Carlström K, Humble MB, et al. (2012) The extreme male brain revisited: gender coherence in adults with autism spectrum disorder. *Br J Psychiatry* 201: 116–123.

22. Lord C, Rutter M, DiLavore P, Risi S (2002) *Autism Diagnostic Observation Schedule. ADOS Manual.* Los Angeles.: Western Psychological Services.

23. American Psychiatric Association (1994) *Diagnostic and statistical manual of mental disorders.* 4th ed. Washington, DC: American Psychiatric Association.

24. Bergman H, Bergman I, Engelbrektsson K, Holm L, Johannesson K, et al. (1988) *Handbook for Psychologists, part 1.* Stockholm, Sweden: Karolinska Hospital.

25. Baghaei F, Rosmond R, Landén M, Westberg L, Hellstrand M, et al. (2003) Phenotypic and genotypic characteristics of women in relation to personality traits. *Int J Behav Med* 10: 365–378.

26. Bem SL (1974) The measurement of psychological androgyny. *J Consult Clin Psychol* 42: 155–162.

27. Wallen K (2005) Hormonal influences on sexually differentiated behavior in nonhuman primates. *Front Neuroendocrinol* 26: 7–26.

28. Baron-Cohen S, Wheelwright S, Skinner R, Martin J, Clubley E (2001) The autism-spectrum quotient (AQ): evidence from Asperger syndrome/high-functioning autism, males and females, scientists and mathematicians. *J Autism Dev Disord* 31: 5–17.

29. Baron-Cohen S, Wheelwright S, Hill J, Raste Y, Plumb I (2001) The "Reading the Mind in the Eyes" Test revised version: a study with normal adults, and adults with Asperger syndrome or high-functioning autism. *J Child Psychol Psychiatry* 42: 241–251.

30. Hines M (2010) Sex-related variation in human behavior and the brain. *Trends Cogn Sci* 14: 448–456.

31. Baron-Cohen S, Knickmeyer RC, Belmonte MK (2005) Sex differences in the brain: implications for explaining autism. *Science* 310: 819–823.

32. Jones RM, Wheelwright S, Farrell K, Martin E, Green R, et al. (2012) Brief report: female-to-male transsexual people and autistic traits. *J Autism Dev Disord* 42: 301–306.

33. Bejerot S, Humble MB (2013) Childhood clumsiness and peer victimization: a case-control study of psychiatric patients. *BMC Psychiatry* 13: 68.

34. Sinclare J (1995) Cognitive, Communication, and Interpersonal Deficits of Non- Autistic People.

35. Williams D (1994) *Somebody Somewhere: Breaking Free from the World of Autism.* New York: Three Rivers Press.

36. Pfaus JG (2009) Pathways of sexual desire. *J Sex Med* 6: 1506–1533.

37. Van Anders SM (2012) Testosterone and sexual desire in healthy women and men. *Arch Sex Behav* 41: 1471–1484.

38. Chandra A, Mosher WD, Copen C, Sionean C (2011) Sexual behavior, sexual attraction, and sexual identity in the United States: data from the 2006–2008 National Survey of Family Growth. *Natl Health Stat Report* 19: 1–36.

39. Johnson AM, Mercer CH, Erens B, Copas AJ, McManus S, et al. (2001) Sexual behaviour in Britain: partnerships, practices, and HIV risk behaviours. *Lancet* 358: 1835–1842.

40. Aston M (2003) *Aspergers in love.* London: Jessica Kingsley Publishers.

41. Rydén E, Bejerot S (2008) Autism spectrum disorders in an adult psychiatric population. A naturalistic cross-sectional controlled study. *Clin Neuropsychiatry* 5: 13–21.

42. Byers ES, Nichols S, Voyer SD, Reilly G (2013) Sexual well-being of a community sample of high-functioning adults on the autism spectrum who have been in a romantic relationship. *Autism Int J Res Pract* 17: 418–433.

43. Pastor Z, Holla K, Chmel R (2013) The influence of combined oral contraceptives on female sexual desire: a systematic review. *Eur J Contracept Reprod Health Care* 18: 27–43.

44. Landén M, Rasmussen P (1997) Gender identity disorder in a girl with autism–a case report. *Eur Child Adolesc Psychiatry* 6: 170–173.

45. Mukaddes NM (2002) Gender identity problems in autistic children Case histories. *Child Care, Heal Dev* 28: 529–532.

46. Williams PG, Allard AM, Sears L (1996) Case study: cross-gender preoccupations with two male children with autism. *J Autism Dev Disord* 26: 635–642.

47. Perera H, Gadambanathan T, Weerasiri S (2003) Gender identity disorder presenting in a girl with Asperger's disorder and obsessive compulsive disorder. *Ceylon Med J* 48: 57–58.
48. Kraemer B, Delsignore A, Gundelfinger R, Schnyder U, Hepp U (2005) Comorbidity of Asperger syndrome and gender identity disorder. *Eur Child Adolesc Psychiatry* 14: 292–296.
49. Tateno M, Tateno Y, Saito T (2008) Comorbid childhood gender identity disorder in a boy with Asperger syndrome. *Psychiatry Clin Neurosci* 62: 238.

Critical Thinking

1. What kind of sexuality education do you think would be effective for ASD young people and/or adults?
2. Do you think people with ASD should be able to become parents? On what does that depend?
3. What is the relevance of connecting ASD to masculinity and femininity?

Internet References

Autism Research Institute
http://www.autism.com/understanding_social_sexual

Autism and Sex Education
http://www.autismsexeducation.com

Talking about Curing Autism: Sex Education
http://www.tacanow.org/family-resources/teens-with-asd-puberty

---

SUSANNE BEJEROT is a specialist in psychiatry and associate professor at the Karolinska Institute in Stockholm, Sweden. Her research areas are mainly obsessive-compulsive disorder and autism spectrum disorders (ASD), but also ADHD, compulsive hoarding and social anxiety. She has also participated in the design of a psychotherapy method to improve the quality of life in adults with ASD. She has published over 50 articles and has written a textbook on OCD. Jonna M. Eriksson is also in the Department of Clinical Neuroscience of the Karolinska Institute.

Prepared by: Elizabeth Schroeder, EdD, MSW,
Elizabeth Schroeder Consulting

Article

(Rethinking) Gender

A growing number of Americans are taking their private struggles with their identities into the public realm. How those who believe they were born with the wrong bodies are forcing us to re-examine what it means to be male and female.

DEBRA ROSENBERG

Learning Outcomes

After reading this article, you will be able to:

- Define the term "transgender."

- Describe at least two challenges transgender people face in the United States.

- Describe how the sports field has worked to address allowing athletes who transition from their assigned birth sex to a different gender to compete as their identified gender.

Growing up in Corinth, Miss., J. T. Hayes had a legacy to attend to. His dad was a well-known race-car driver and Hayes spent much of his childhood tinkering in the family's greasy garage, learning how to design and build cars. By the age of 10, he had started racing in his own right. Eventually Hayes won more than 500 regional and national championships in go-kart, midget and sprint racing, even making it to the NASCAR Winston Cup in the early '90s. But behind the trophies and the swagger of the racing circuit, Hayes was harboring a painful secret: he had always believed he was a woman. He had feminine features and a slight frame—at 5 feet 6 and 118 pounds he was downright dainty—and had always felt, psychologically, like a girl. Only his anatomy got in the way. Since childhood he'd wrestled with what to do about it. He'd slip on "girl clothes" he hid under the mattress and try his hand with makeup. But he knew he'd find little support in his conservative hometown.

In 1991, Hayes had a moment of truth. He was driving a sprint car on a dirt track in Little Rock when the car flipped end over end. "I was trapped upside down, engine throttle stuck, fuel running all over the racetrack and me," Hayes recalls. "The accident didn't scare me, but the thought that I hadn't lived life to its full potential just ran chill bumps up and down my body." That night he vowed to complete the transition to womanhood. Hayes kept racing while he sought therapy and started hormone treatments, hiding his growing breasts under an Ace bandage and baggy T-shirts.

Finally, in 1994, at 30, Hayes raced on a Saturday night in Memphis, then drove to Colorado the next day for sex-reassignment surgery, selling his prized race car to pay the tab. Hayes chose the name Terri O'Connell and began a new life as a woman who figured her racing days were over. But she had no idea what else to do. Eventually, O'Connell got a job at the mall selling women's handbags for $8 an hour. O'Connell still hopes to race again, but she knows the odds are long: "Transgendered and professional motor sports just don't go together."

To most of us, gender comes as naturally as breathing. We have no quarrel with the "M" or the "F" on our birth certificates. And, crash diets aside, we've made peace with how we want the world to see us—pants or skirt, boa or blazer, spiky heels or sneakers. But to those who consider themselves transgender, there's a disconnect between the sex they were assigned at birth and the way they see or express themselves. Though their numbers are relatively few—the most generous estimate from the National Center for Transgender Equality is between 750,000 and 3 million Americans (fewer than 1 percent)—many of them are taking their intimate struggles public for the first time. In April, *Los Angeles Times* sportswriter Mike Penner announced in his column that when he returned from vacation, he would do so as a woman, Christine Daniels. Nine states plus Washington, D.C., have enacted antidiscrimination laws that protect transgender people—and an additional three states have legislation pending, according to the Human Rights Campaign. And this month the U.S. House of Representatives passed a hate-crimes prevention bill that included "gender identity." Today's transgender Americans go far beyond the old stereotypes (think "Rocky Horror Picture Show"). They are soccer moms, ministers, teachers, politicians, even young children. Their push for tolerance and acceptance is reshaping businesses, sports, schools and families. It's also raising new questions about just what makes us male or female.

Born female, he feels male. 'I challenge the idea that all men were born with male bodies.'

—Mykell Miller, age 20

What is gender anyway? It is certainly more than the physical details of what's between our legs. History and science suggest that gender is more subtle and more complicated than anatomy. (It's separate from sexual orientation, too, which determines which sex we're attracted to.) Gender helps us organize the world into two boxes, his and hers, and gives us a way of quickly sizing up every person we see on the street. "Gender is a way of making the world secure," says feminist scholar Judith Butler, a rhetoric professor at University of California, Berkeley. Though some scholars like Butler consider gender largely a social construct, others increasingly see it as a complex interplay of biology, genes, hormones and culture.

She kept her job as a high-school teacher. 'Most people don't get this fortunate kind of ending.'

—Karen Kopriva, age 49

Genesis set up the initial dichotomy: "Male and female he created them." And historically, the differences between men and women in this country were thought to be distinct. Men, fueled by testosterone, were the providers, the fighters, the strong and silent types who brought home dinner. Women,

hopped up on estrogen (not to mention the mothering hormone oxytocin), were the nurturers, the communicators, the soft, emotional ones who got that dinner on the table. But as society changed, the stereotypes faded. Now even discussing gender differences can be fraught. (Just ask former Harvard president Larry Summers, who unleashed a wave of criticism when he suggested, in 2005, that women might have less natural aptitude for math and science.) Still, even the most diehard feminist would likely agree that, even apart from genitalia, we are not exactly alike. In many cases, our habits, our posture, and even cultural identifiers like the way we dress set us apart.

Now, as transgender people become more visible and challenge the old boundaries, they've given voice to another debate—whether gender comes in just two flavors. "The old categories that everybody's either biologically male or female, that there are two distinct categories and there's no overlap, that's beginning to break down," says Michael Kimmel, a sociology professor at SUNY-Stony Brook. "All of those old categories seem to be more fluid." Just the terminology can get confusing. "Transsexual" is an older term that usually refers to someone who wants to use hormones or surgery to change their sex. "Transvestites," now more politely called "cross-dressers," occasionally wear clothes of the opposite sex. "Transgender" is an umbrella term that includes anyone whose gender identity or expression differs from the sex of their birth—whether they have surgery or not.

Gender identity first becomes an issue in early childhood, as any parent who's watched a toddler lunge for a truck or a doll can tell you. That's also when some kids may become aware that their bodies and brains don't quite match up. Jona Rose, a 6-year-old kindergartner in northern California, seems like a girl in nearly every way—she wears dresses, loves pink and purple, and bestowed female names on all her stuffed animals. But Jona, who was born Jonah, also has a penis. When she was 4, her mom, Pam, offered to buy Jona a dress, and she was so excited she nearly hyperventilated. She began wearing dresses every day to preschool and no one seemed to mind. It wasn't easy at first. "We wrung our hands about this every night," says her dad, Joel. But finally he and Pam decided to let their son live as a girl. They chose a private kindergarten where Jona wouldn't have to hide the fact that he was born a boy, but could comfortably dress like a girl and even use the girls' bathroom. "She has been pretty adamant from the get-go: 'I am a girl,'" says Joel.

Male or female, we all start life looking pretty much the same. Genes determine whether a particular human embryo will develop as male or female. But each individual embryo is equipped to be either one—each possesses the Mullerian ducts that become the female reproductive system as well as the Wolffian ducts that become the male one. Around eight weeks of development, through a complex genetic relay race, the X and the male's Y chromosomes kick into gear, directing the structures to become testes or ovaries. (In most cases, the unneeded extra structures simply break down.) The ovaries and the testes are soon pumping out estrogen and testosterone, bathing the developing fetus in hormones. Meanwhile, the brain begins to form, complete with receptors—wired differently in men and women—that will later determine how both estrogen and testosterone are used in the body.

After birth, the changes keep coming. In many species, male newborns experience a hormone surge that may "organize" sexual and behavioral traits, says Nirao Shah, a neuroscientist at UCSF. In rats, testosterone given in the first week of life can cause female babies to behave more like males once they reach adulthood. "These changes are thought to be irreversible," says Shah. Between 1 and 5 months, male human babies also experience a hormone surge. It's still unclear exactly what effect that surge has on the human brain, but it happens just when parents are oohing and aahing over their new arrivals.

Here's where culture comes in. Studies have shown that parents treat boys and girls very differently—breast-feeding boys longer but talking more to girls. That's going on while the baby's brain is engaged in a massive growth spurt. "The brain doubles in size in the first five years after birth, and the connectivity between the cells goes up hundreds of orders of magnitude," says Anne Fausto-Sterling, a biologist and feminist at Brown University who is currently investigating whether subtle differences in parental behavior could influence gender identity in very young children. "The brain is interacting with culture from day one."

So what's different in transgender people? Scientists don't know for certain. Though their hormone levels seem to be the same as non-trans levels, some scientists speculate that their brains react differently to the hormones, just as men's differ from women's. But that could take decades of further research to prove. One 1997 study tantalizingly suggested structural differences between male, female and transsexual brains, but it has yet to be successfully replicated. Some transgender people blame the environment, citing studies that show pollutants have disrupted reproduction in frogs and other animals. But those links are so far not proved in humans. For now, transgender issues are classified as "Gender Identity Disorder" in the psychiatric manual *DSM-IV.* That's controversial, too—gay-rights activists spent years campaigning to have homosexuality removed from the manual.

Gender fluidity hasn't always seemed shocking. Cross-dressing was common in ancient Greece and Rome, as well as among Native Americans and many other indigenous societies, according to Deborah Rudacille, author of *The Riddle of Gender.* Court records from the Jamestown settlement in 1629

describe the case of Thomas Hall, who claimed to be both a man and a woman. Of course, what's considered masculine or feminine has long been a moving target. Our Founding Fathers wouldn't be surprised to see men today with long hair or earrings, but they might be puzzled by women in pants.

Transgender opponents have often turned to the Bible for support. Deut. 22:5 says: "The woman shall not wear that which pertaineth unto a man, neither shall a man put on a woman's garment: for all that do so are abomination unto the Lord thy God." When word leaked in February that Steve Stanton, the Largo, Fla., city manager for 14 years, was planning to transition to life as a woman, the community erupted. At a public meeting over whether Stanton should be fired, one of many critics, Ron Sanders, pastor of the Lighthouse Baptist Church, insisted that Jesus would "want him terminated." (Stanton did lose his job and this week will appear as Susan Stanton on Capitol Hill to lobby for antidiscrimination laws.) Equating gender change with homosexuality, Sanders says that "it's an abomination, which means that it's utterly disgusting."

Not all people of faith would agree. Baptist minister John Nemecek, 56, was surfing the Web one weekend in 2003, when his wife was at a baby shower. Desperate for clues to his long-suppressed feelings of femininity, he stumbled across an article about gender-identity disorder on WebMD. The suggested remedy was sex-reassignment surgery—something Nemecek soon thought he had to do. Many families can be ripped apart by such drastic changes, but Nemecek's wife of 33 years stuck by him. His employer of 15 years, Spring Arbor University, a faith-based liberal-arts college in Michigan, did not. Nemecek says the school claimed that transgenderism violated its Christian principles, and when it renewed Nemecek's contract—by then she was taking hormones and using the name Julie—it barred her from dressing as a woman on campus or even wearing earrings. Her workload and pay were cut, too, she says. She filed a discrimination claim, which was later settled through mediation. (The university declined to comment on the case.) Nemecek says she has no trouble squaring her gender change and her faith. "Actively expressing the feminine in me has helped me grow closer to God," she says.

Others have had better luck transitioning. Karen Kopriva, now 49, kept her job teaching high school in Lake Forest, Illinois, when she shaved her beard and made the switch from Ken. When Mark Stumpp, a vice president at Prudential Financial, returned to work as Margaret in 2002, she sent a memo to her colleagues (subject: Me) explaining the change. "We all joked about wearing panty hose and whether 'my condition' was contagious," she says. But "when the dust settled, everyone got back to work." Companies like IBM and Kodak now cover trans-related medical care. And 125 Fortune 500 companies now protect transgender employees from job discrimination, up from three in 2000.

Discrimination may not be the worst worry for transgender people: they are also at high risk of violence and hate crimes.

Perhaps no field has wrestled more with the issue of gender than sports. There have long been accusations about male athletes' trying to pass as women, or women's taking testosterone to gain a competitive edge. In the 1960s, would-be female Olympians were required to undergo gender-screening tests. Essentially, that meant baring all before a panel of doctors who could verify that an athlete had girl parts. That method was soon scrapped in favor of a genetic test. But that quickly led to confusion over a handful of genetic disorders that give typical-looking women chromosomes other than the usual XX. Finally, the International Olympic Committee ditched mandatory lab-based screening, too. "We found there is no scientifically sound lab-based technique that can differentiate between man and woman," says Arne Ljungqvist, chair of the IOC's medical commission.

The IOC recently waded into controversy again: in 2004 it issued regulations allowing transsexual athletes to compete in the Olympics if they've had sex-reassignment surgery and have taken hormones for two years. After convening a panel of experts, the IOC decided that the surgery and hormones would compensate for any hormonal or muscular advantage a male-to-female transsexual would have. (Female-to-male athletes would be allowed to take testosterone, but only at levels that wouldn't give them a boost.) So far, Ljungqvist doesn't know of any transsexual athletes who've competed. Ironically, Renee Richards, who won a lawsuit in 1977 for the right to play tennis as a woman after her own sex-reassignment surgery, questions the fairness of the IOC rule. She thinks decisions should be made on a case-by-case basis.

'We all joked about wearing panty hose and whether my "condition" was contagious.'

—Margaret Stumpp, age 54

Richards and other pioneers reflect the huge cultural shift over a generation of gender change. Now 70, Richards rejects the term transgender along with all the fluidity it conveys. "God didn't put us on this earth to have gender diversity," she says. "I don't like the kids that are experimenting. I didn't want to be something in between. I didn't want to be trans anything. I wanted to be a man or a woman."

But more young people are embracing something we would traditionally consider in between. Because of the expense, invasiveness and mixed results (especially for women becoming men), only 1,000 to 2,000 Americans each year get sex-reassignment surgery—a number that's on the rise, says Mara Keisling of the National Center for Transgender Equality. Mykell Miller, a Northwestern University student born female who now considers himself male, hides his breasts under a special compression vest. Though he one day wants to take hormones and get a mastectomy, he can't yet afford it. But that doesn't affect his self-image. "I challenge the idea that all men were born with male bodies," he says. "I don't go out of my way to be the biggest, strongest guy."

Nowhere is the issue more pressing at the moment than a place that helped give rise to feminist movement a generation ago: Smith College in Northampton, Mass. Though Smith was one of the original Seven Sisters women's colleges, its students have now taken to calling it a "mostly women's college," in part because of a growing number of "transmen" who decide to become male after they've enrolled. In 2004, students voted to remove pronouns from the student government constitution as a gesture to transgender students who no longer identified with "she" or "her." (Smith is also one of 70 schools that have antidiscrimination policies protecting transgender students.) For now, anyone who is enrolled at Smith may graduate, but in order to be admitted in the first place, you must have been born a female. Tobias Davis, class of '03, entered Smith as a woman, but graduated as a "transman." When he first told friends over dinner, "I think I might be a boy," they were instantly behind him, saying "Great! Have you picked a name yet?" Davis passed as male for his junior year abroad in Italy even without taking hormones; he had a mastectomy last fall. Now 25, Davis works at Smith and writes plays about the transgender experience. (His work "The Naked I: Monologues From Beyond the Binary" is a trans take on "The Vagina Monologues.")

As kids at ever-younger ages grapple with issues of gender variance, doctors, psychologists and parents are weighing how to balance immediate desires and long-term ones. Like Jona Rose, many kids begin questioning gender as toddlers, identifying with the other gender's toys and clothes. Five times as many boys as girls say their gender doesn't match their biological sex, says Dr. Edgardo Menvielle, a psychiatrist who heads a gender-variance outreach program at Children's National Medical Center. (Perhaps that's because it's easier for girls to blend in as tomboys.) Many of these children eventually move on and accept their biological sex, says Menvielle, often when they're exposed to a disapproving larger world or when they're influenced by the hormone surges of puberty. Only about 15 percent continue to show signs of gender-identity problems into adulthood, says Ken Zucker, who heads the Gender Identity Service at the Centre for Addiction and Mental Health in Toronto.

In the past, doctors often advised parents to direct their kids into more gender-appropriate clothing and behavior. Zucker still tells parents of unhappy boys to try more-neutral activities—say chess club instead of football. But now the thinking is that kids should lead the way. If a child persists in wanting to be the other gender, doctors may prescribe hormone "blockers" to keep puberty at bay. (Blockers have no permanent effects.) But they're also increasingly willing to take more lasting steps: Isaak Brown (who started life as Liza) began taking male hormones at 16; at 17 he had a mastectomy.

For parents like Colleen Vincente, 44, following a child's lead seems only natural. Her second child, M. (Vincente asked to use an initial to protect the child's privacy), was born female. But as soon as she could talk, she insisted on wearing boy's clothes. Though M. had plenty of dolls, she gravitated toward "the boy things" and soon wanted to shave off all her hair. "We went along with that," says Vincente. "We figured it was a phase." One day, when she was 2½, M. overheard her parents talking about her using female pronouns. "He said, 'No—I'm a him. You need to call me him,'" Vincente recalls. "We were shocked." In his California preschool, M. continued to insist he was a boy and decided to change his name. Vincente and her husband, John, consulted a therapist, who confirmed their instincts to let M. guide them. Now 9, M. lives as a boy and most people have no idea he was born otherwise. "The most important thing is to realize this is who your child is," Vincente

says. That's a big step for a family, but could be an even bigger one for the rest of the world.

Critical Thinking

1. What is the meaning of the term "transgendered"?
2. What is the process of transitioning from one sex to the other?
3. What impact have recent social shifts and changes had on people who are transgendered?

Internet References

National Center for Transgender Equality
   http://transequality.org
Transgender Law Center
   http://transgenderlawcenter.org
World Professional Organization for Transgender Health
   http://www.wpath.org

This story was written by **DEBRA ROSENBERG**, with reporting from Lorraine Ali, Mary Carmichael, Samantha Henig, Raina Kelley, Matthew Philips, Julie Scelfo, Kurt Soller, Karen Springen and Lynn Waddell.

Article   Prepared by: Elizabeth Schroeder, EdD, MSW,
                                                    Elizabeth Schroeder Consulting

Kids Born with Disorders of Sex Development

MEGAN KRUEGER

Learning Outcomes

After reading this article, you will be able to:

- Define the term Disorders of Sex Development.

- Describe some of the recommendations made in the Consensus Statement of Management of Intersex Disorders.

- Describe at least two considerations for parents with children born with a disorder of sex development.

Just like many other 15-year-old boys, Josh is starting to take an interest in girls (but doesn't like to talk about it with his mom). He likes hunting and fishing, and he's proud to show off one of his big catches, now on a mount and displayed in his bedroom. He's a big fan of sports, especially the Detroit Tigers, and watching TV shows about ghost hunting is cool in his book.

"He's a very good kid," mom Mandy says of her teen.

But Josh struggles with something other 15-year-old boys never have to think about. Josh can't stand up to urinate. It's because of how he was born, with a congenital disorder that caused his genitalia to not form in the typical way. It's been difficult to accept, especially now that he's older and sees other men using urinals.

One story stands out for Mandy, about a particular trip he took with his grandparents to the store. Josh went to use the bathroom, and when he walked out, he was wet. He told his grandma he tried to stand. "I mean, my mom was in tears," Mandy recalls. "Because how do you explain to this kid that you can't do what everybody else is doing?"

He uses a separate bathroom at school for now, and is starting to use a special funnel, so he can stand like the other boys.

It's been a big deal for Josh and for his mom, and just one of the many challenges they've faced due to his condition, partial androgen insensitivity syndrome, or AIS.

It means genetically Josh is a boy, but his body is resistant to androgens, or male hormones. As a result, Josh was born with an extremely small penis, called a micropenis, undescended testicles and openings where a vagina would form. His gender at birth was immediately unknown. Mandy remembers how the hospital stressed calling him "baby" until they had a definitive gender.

"I mean, you hear certain things, like Down syndrome," Mandy says. But AIS? "This I had never heard of. So I was like, in shock."

Years ago, the term "hermaphrodite" was often used to describe people who were born with the anatomy, to a lesser or greater degree, of both genders. More recently the word "intersex" has been used. Now, the term Disorders of Sex Development, or DSD, is preferred to reflect the range of cases when a person's sex organs develop differently or sex chromosomes aren't typical.

AIS, which Josh has, is just one of many DSD. There are numerous types and, when they occur, they're sometimes never identified. Because of this, rates differ and it's difficult to point to one definitive statistic. One source predicts DSD, when based on the broad definition, occur as frequently as 1 in 100 live births, a rate higher than that of Down syndrome. More severe instances are more rare.

It may not even be on an expecting parent's radar, despite these odds. DSD aren't regularly talked about due to worries of public reaction or embarrassment, experts in the field note. They're complicated, manifest differently and, even now, parents—as well as the doctors who care for their children—encounter several choices and challenges when a baby is born with DSD.

"When women are pregnant, we always have these perfect images of how our baby is going to look," says Dr. Cortney Wolfe-Christensen, psychologist on the DSD team at Children's Hospital of Michigan in Detroit. She says parents will go through a grieving process when their child is born with ambiguous genitalia. They grieve for the "perfect" future they once envisioned for their child. "We would argue that it is not all changed, but in that moment, for them, it is."

What are DSD?

Disorders of Sex Development come in a variety of forms. They are defined as "congenital conditions in which development of chromosomal, gonadal or anatomic sex is atypical," according to the Consensus *Statement on Management of Intersex Disorders in Pediatrics.* With some DSD, the genitalia look typical at birth and the disorder is discovered later in life, like when a girl fails to start menstruating and further examination uncovers she has XY chromosomes and no uterus, explains Dr. Yegappan Lakshmanan, chief of pediatric urology at Children's Hospital and a member of its DSD team.

There are upwards of 40 types of DSD falling under three classifications, according to the *Williams Textbook of Endocrinology.* In some cases, the cause of DSD can be pinpointed as genetic. In other situations the cause is a chromosomal combination other than XY and XX, notes the *Handbook for Parents on DSD* from Accord Alliance, whose mission is to promote integrated care practices for those with DSD. Sometimes, the cause is unknown all together.

Even before a decision on gender is made, Wolfe-Christensen says there are a lot of things considered, including karyotype (what the child's chromosomes say they are), genetic profile, ultrasound imaging results, physical appearance, hormone levels, chances of fertility—even family preference.

There's an initial shock for some parents when they find out about their child's condition or see their physical appearance.

"Especially the moms feel guilty about whether they contributed to this and they don't understand what's going on," Wolfe-Christensen says.

Fifteen years ago, when Josh was born, Mandy had similar thoughts.

"You're shocked, but you're numb," she says. "You start looking up things and it seems like it's uncommon."

The incidence of certain types of DSD diagnosis varies from the more common—about 4 in every 1,000 with hypospadias (atypical location of the urethra on the penis), to the more rare—approximately 1 in 20,000 live births for complete AIS, according to the National Institutes of Health and U.S. National Library of Medicine's MedlinePlus resource.

When researching these disorders, though, it's challenging to find consistent statistics. As Accord Alliance explains, it's "because to provide a number for sure, we would have to have a consensus on what counts as different-enough-from-average to count as a DSD."

Yet it's common enough that you could know somebody or be in the same venue as somebody born with DSD, the group emphasizes. The surprise—and one many DSD experts would like to change—is that a group of disorders affecting so many would seem like an anomaly to parents.

"I think the answer is pretty clear: People feel uncomfortable talking about it. And I would say from my clinical experience that is the most challenging aspect of the care of these patients and their families . . . the feeling that this is not something you can share with others," says Dr. David Sandberg, pediatric psychologist and clinical researcher at the University of Michigan Department of Pediatrics and C.S. Mott Children's Hospital in Ann Arbor, who has worked on Mott's interdisciplinary DSD clinical team. "All the usual people you would turn to . . . are sometimes left out, because the parent is concerned about how they will react."

Mandy admits that even though her family was aware of Josh's condition, everyday tasks could present challenges.

"It would be a holiday. Yeah, my mom or my sisters would change him, but I just wouldn't lay him down and let everybody see," she says. "That was, to me, a little bit embarrassing."

Surgery or No Surgery?

Parents whose children are born with these very apparent disorders are faced with a huge decision: to "normalize" the genitalia through surgery, or to leave the anatomy as is—and possibly make a decision with the child when they're older.

It's a choice that carries weight and brings questions, no matter which path they take.

Josh, for instance, has had many surgeries in his 15 years of life. Surgeries have included closing up the openings for the vagina, extending the urethra so he can urinate closer to the tip of his penis (though still not quite at the tip), and creating new openings from which to urinate (he's had a few different openings to date). They also brought his testicles down. Then came more operations, some to correct issues from previous surgeries.

"We've had some fall backs because of what the first doctor has done," Mandy says. Scar tissue caused him issues with urinating, and doctors had to reopen the opening after a serious infection, which put Josh in the hospital for a month. Recently, it was discovered Josh's first doctor did not laser out hair follicles in the surgical area, so Josh has experienced pain from growing pubic hair in his skin. His current doctor predicted it would take hours to laser out the rest of the follicles.

"I think if I would have known what I know now, he probably wouldn't have had to go through all of this," Mandy says, suggesting other parents do their homework and search for quality care.

Wolfe-Christensen says when a child is born with DSD, the situation is considered a "social emergency"—and, most of the time, not a medical one. There are, of course, worries parents naturally have for their baby's future. Will people know, and will they accept it if they do? Will they be teased?

Wolfe-Christensen says she can't remember a family who didn't opt for surgery. And surgery has thus far been the "status quo" in the medical community, according to Sandberg.

"There are parents who are totally freaked out about this, and it's kind of where the old model of care came from—was that you treated the anxiety of the parents by doing the surgery on the kids," says Janet Green, interim executive director of Accord Alliance, which is based in New Jersey. She was born with congenital adrenal hyperplasia, in which the adrenal glands produce an "overabundance" of androgens, or male hormones, according to Boston Children's Hospital. This can result in ambiguous genitalia and is one of the more common DSD.

While there is more information on the outcomes of DSD patients who have had surgery, since that's been the go-to recommendation in the past, Sandberg says, there still isn't enough evidence to say one decision is better than the other.

There are groups that are vocal, and very much against performing these surgeries, Lakshmanan notes. Patients who had surgeries and are now older are in some cases unhappy with the results, either cosmetically or when it comes to sexual function, for example, Wolfe-Christensen says.

Now imagine being a parent, unfamiliar with your baby's condition, and you're faced with the choice.

"Their first exposure is all of this controversy, which is not based on discussion of evidence, but is based on personal experiences of one person or doctors who sort of say, 'My mission is if it doesn't look typical I make it look typical'—and questioning, 'I know you can do that, but why do you do that? Does it have to be done?'" Sandberg says.

At the core, a lot still weighs on parents' emotions and initial reactions, he says. Parents want the best for their child, but what is best?

"There isn't evidence from outcomes to tell us what the best choice is," Sandberg says. "What we can have confidence in, I think, is developing a process for shared decision-making that is balanced."

Work in the Medical Community

Educating parents of all the possibilities is just one of the factors considered in providing quality care for kids born with DSD moving forward. Today, experts and advocates involved in the DSD community are working toward integrating specialized, interdisciplinary DSD teams and bringing together the major players in the DSD community to do it.

Published in 2006, the Consensus *Statement of Management of Intersex Disorders* drafted a statement that recommends a multidisciplinary team approach in the care of DSD patients. The ideal team, as outlined in the statement, should include pediatric specialists in endocrinology, urology, gynecology, genetics and psychology/psychiatry, to name a few. It hinges on all the disciplines working closely and communicating with the primary care physician and family.

Today, attitudes are changing—especially when it comes to making informed choices from the get-go. Now, the recommendation is to "pull back from this sort of automatic recommendation to normalize appearance, sort of saying that focus should be on function and not on appearance," Sandberg says.

As Green points out, it's difficult in a society that puts a lot of stock in visual appearance. "We really need to be thinking about this patient as outcomes—of when they're adults," she says.

For instance, Sandberg reasons, what if a surgery performed during infancy later causes sex to be painful, or there's a lack of erotic sensation? "If we just focus on infancy (and) childhood, we could end up having regret."

Providing parents with more information in the face of the surgery vs. no-surgery decision is something Sandberg is working on actively. He has a contract through the Patient Centered Outcomes Research Institute to create what he calls a "decision support tool" to break down all the options for parents in a balanced way.

More research is in the works, too. Children's Hospital of Michigan is part of a consortium of children's hospitals across the country doing research on the outcomes of those with DSD who had cosmetic surgeries.

Wolfe-Christensen explains that as part of her job, she informs parents of their options, talking to them about what could happen in the future based on their choice, in what cases a child may need a surgery (if they cannot urinate) and, if that's not the case, also making sure they know in order to function, their child doesn't need surgery. "It's a hard decision for parents to make," she says, "but we need to make sure that we're explaining both sides."

And if there's uncertainty of what should be done? It's OK to put the decision on hold. "(We) have to be able to convince parents that not making an immediate decision is a valid decision," Green says. There's time in many cases to consult physicians, have discussions and come back to it.

Discussing DSD

Regardless of the route, parents and their children face difficult, sometimes uncomfortable situations socially and psychologically as time goes on.

"It was hard when he was a baby," Mandy recalls of Josh, who needed a catheter early on. "You go out shopping at the mall and you use the bathroom. Here's the changing table right out in the open in public. How do you tell somebody what's wrong with your kid?"

Early on in his education, only one teacher knew about Josh's disorder and was allowed to change him. He stayed in diapers longer than typical because of the complications. And all the surgeries, admittedly, were stressful for her.

"It's just very hard in the beginning," Mandy acknowledges.

But Wolfe-Christensen says being open and honest with close family—and your child—is another step in normalizing DSD and ending the stigma surrounding these disorders.

For instance, some parents think that doing surgery early on in life will solve these tough-to-tackle conversations, but that's not true.

"They hope that this means they will never have to discuss it with their child, which is so problematic," Sandberg explains, adding that there will be some signs of the surgery. Keeping DSD a secret from the family or the child can lead to mental health problems later in life. "We know from lots of research that secrecy is very harmful," he notes. Kids know when their parents are keeping secrets from them, and when they find out, it can manifest as shame, Sandberg says.

In a world where information obtained through a Google search is at our fingertips, and the patient can access medical records, it wouldn't be challenging for these children to figure out their disorders later in life.

"When they learn, finally, that information was kept from them, that their doctors knew and nobody told them, why should they ever trust doctors in the future? And many of these patients will need lifelong interactions with doctors," Sandberg adds.

Dr. Arlene Baratz, a physician from Pittsburgh, Pennsylvania, is very involved with the DSD community, serving as a board member and family and medical advisor for the AIS-DSD Support Group, as well as family and medical advisor for the groups Advocates for Informed Choice and Accord Alliance. She has two daughters with complete androgen insensitivity syndrome, meaning they have XY chromosomes but have a female appearance. Baratz discovered her older daughter Katie's disorder when she was taken in for a hernia at age 6. It turns out she had testes trying to come through her groin muscle. Her younger daughter was also diagnosed.

With both of her daughters, she talked to them, pointing out different kinds of family structures since they wouldn't be able to have biological children of their own. They discussed physical differences. "I decided to raise them with an expectation of what their lives would actually be like," she explains.

Although she didn't tell them about the testes or their XY chromosomes at first, she was anxious they would find out on their own. When the girls were teens, she found the AIS-DSD Support Group, which also encouraged her to tell the girls.

When she did tell them, they were very accepting. "They felt that the actual truth was much better than this feeling that they were freakish."

Before Mandy found support and answers, Josh's curiosity was stressful for her. She didn't have answers to the questions he asked.

Mandy discovered C.S. Mott's services when Josh was around 8. Now, she takes him to see the DSD team for regular care, and the whole family sits down to speak with Sandberg about any questions or concerns they have moving forward, including his current struggle with wanting to urinate standing upright. She talks about things that make her uncomfortable, and they work to move past it.

"You can't help your child unless you feel comfortable with it and you have the help first," Mandy says.

Baratz, who also struggled to find support during the early years of her daughters' lives, says finding support through AIS-DSD "was just a real turning point in my life, and I've continued to be involved in that group."

Her daughter Katie is now 29, and her younger daughter 28. Katie is married and going into psychiatry. "They all have good and fulfilling lives," she says.

While it isn't completely clear to Mandy what is ahead for her son, especially concerning his ability to consummate a relationship or father children, it's something she knows is going to come up someday. She hopes every day to see society become more accepting of these disorders. There have been stressful days, no doubt, but Mandy sees the silver lining in all of it.

"God gave me this child that has taught me a lot of things. More strength than I knew I had. I'm not going to lie, there have been a lot of tears," she confides. But through it all, "It has made me a stronger person."

There are not a lot of answers; no perfect solutions experts can point to now. Yet Baratz reassures parents, "Just know that everything is going to be all right." Even though there are varying statistics out there, one thing is clear: Nobody is alone in this.

"Having children is fraught with risks," Sandberg says. But it's worth remembering "when things do happen, life can be wonderful with the support of friends and family."

Critical Thinking

1. Historically, members of the medical community recommended to parents of children with ambiguous genitalia that they choose the sex for their child and have the child's body surgically constructed to reflect that choice. What impacts might that have had on children as they grew older?

2. How do you think you would feel if you had a child who was born with a DSD? What decisions do you think you'd want to make, and which would you wait and let your child decide?

3. People with DSDs are usually infertile. How would you adapt how to talk with DSD young people about sexuality?

Internet References

Advocates for Informed Choice
http://aiclegal.org
DSD Guidelines
http://www.dsdguidelines.org

Intersex Society of North America
http://isna.org

MEGAN KRUEGER is the Assistant Editor for *Metro Parent Magazine*.

Article   Prepared by: Elizabeth Schroeder, EdD, MSW,
Elizabeth Schroeder Consulting

Children of Lesbian and Gay Parents

Does parental sexual orientation affect child development, and if so, how? Studies using convenience samples, studies using samples drawn from known populations, and studies based on samples that are representative of larger populations all converge on similar conclusions. More than two decades of research has failed to reveal important differences in the adjustment or development of children or adolescents reared by same-sex couples compared to those reared by other-sex couples. Results of the research suggest that qualities of family relationships are more tightly linked with child outcomes than is parental sexual orientation.

CHARLOTTE J. PATTERSON

Learning Outcomes

After reading this article, you will be able to:

- List at least two reasons why, according to research, parental sexual orientation does not have any impact on children's upbringing.

- Describe at least two of the factors researchers evaluate to determine whether a relationship exists between parental sexual orientation and child well-being.

- Explain the impact of homophobia and peer-to-peer bullying on children of lesbian or gay parents.

Does parental sexual orientation affect child development, and if so, how? This question has often been raised in the context of legal and policy proceedings relevant to children, such as those involving adoption, child custody, or visitation. Divergent views have been offered by professionals from the fields of psychology, sociology, medicine, and law (Patterson, Fulcher, & Wainright, 2002). While this question has most often been raised in legal and policy contexts, it is also relevant to theoretical issues. For example, does healthy human development require that a child grow up with parents of each gender? And if not, what would that mean for our theoretical understanding of parent–child relations? (Patterson & Hastings, in press) In this article, I describe some research designed to address these questions.

Early Research

Research on children with lesbian and gay parents began with studies focused on cases in which children had been born in the context of a heterosexual marriage. After parental separation and divorce, many children in these families lived with divorced lesbian mothers. A number of researchers compared development among children of divorced lesbian mothers with that among children of divorced heterosexual mothers and found few significant differences (Patterson, 1997; Stacey & Biblarz, 2001).

These studies were valuable in addressing concerns of judges who were required to decide divorce and child custody cases, but they left many questions unanswered. In particular, because the children who participated in this research had been born into homes with married mothers and fathers, it was not obvious how to understand the reasons for their healthy development. The possibility that children's early exposure to apparently heterosexual male and female role models had contributed to healthy development could not be ruled out.

When lesbian or gay parents rear infants and children from birth, do their offspring grow up in typical ways and show healthy development? To address this question, it was important to study children who had never lived with heterosexual parents. In the 1990s, a number of investigators began research of this kind.

An early example was the Bay Area Families Study, in which I studied a group of four- to nine-year-old children who had been born to or adopted early in life by lesbian mothers

(Patterson, 1996, 1997). Data were collected during home visits. Results from in-home interviews and also from questionnaires showed that children had regular contact with a wide range of adults of both genders, both within and outside of their families. The children's self-concepts and preferences for same-gender playmates and activities were much like those of other children their ages. Moreover, standardized measures of social competence and of behavior problems, such as those from the Child Behavior Checklist (CBCL), showed that they scored within the range of normal variation for a representative sample of same-aged American children. It was clear from this study and others like it that it was quite possible for lesbian mothers to rear healthy children.

Studies Based on Samples Drawn from Known Populations

Interpretation of the results from the Bay Area Families Study was, however, affected by its sampling procedures. The study had been based on a convenience sample that had been assembled by word of mouth. It was therefore impossible to rule out the possibility that families who participated in the research were especially well adjusted. Would a more representative sample yield different results?

To find out, Ray Chan, Barbara Raboy, and I conducted research in collaboration with the Sperm Bank of California (Chan, Raboy, & Patterson, 1998; Fulcher, Sutfin, Chan, Scheib, & Patterson, 2005). Over the more than 15 years of its existence, the Sperm Bank of California's clientele had included many lesbian as well as heterosexual women. For research purposes, this clientele was a finite population from which our sample could be drawn. The Sperm Bank of California also allowed a sample in which, both for lesbian and for heterosexual groups, one parent was biologically related to the child and one was not.

We invited all clients who had conceived children using the resources of the Sperm Bank of California and who had children 5 years old or older to participate in our research. The resulting sample was composed of 80 families, 55 headed by lesbian and 25 headed by heterosexual parents. Materials were mailed to participating families, with instructions to complete them privately and return them in self-addressed stamped envelopes we provided.

Results replicated and expanded upon those from earlier research. Children of lesbian and heterosexual parents showed similar, relatively high levels of social competence, as well as similar, relatively low levels of behavior problems on the parent form of the CBCL. We also asked the children's teachers to provide evaluations of children's adjustment on the Teacher Report Form of the CBCL, and their reports agreed with those

of parents. Parental sexual orientation was not related to children's adaptation. Quite apart from parental sexual orientation, however, and consistent with findings from years of research on children of heterosexual parents, when parent–child relationships were marked by warmth and affection, children were more likely to be developing well. Thus, in this sample drawn from a known population, measures of children's adjustment were unrelated to parental sexual orientation (Chan et al., 1998; Fulcher et al., 2005).

Even as they provided information about children born to lesbian mothers, however, these new results also raised additional questions. Women who conceive children at sperm banks are generally both well educated and financially comfortable. It was possible that these relatively privileged women were able to protect children from many forms of discrimination. What if a more diverse group of families were to be studied? In addition, the children in this sample averaged 7 years of age, and some concerns focus on older children and adolescents. What if an older group of youngsters were to be studied? Would problems masked by youth and privilege in earlier studies emerge in an older, more diverse sample?

Studies Based on Representative Samples

An opportunity to address these questions was presented by the availability of data from the National Longitudinal Study of Adolescent Health (Add Health). The Add Health study involved a large, ethnically diverse, and essentially representative sample of American adolescents and their parents. Data for our research were drawn from surveys and interviews completed by more than 12,000 adolescents and their parents at home and from surveys completed by adolescents at school.

Parents were not queried directly about their sexual orientation but were asked if they were involved in a "marriage, or marriage-like relationship." If parents acknowledged such a relationship, they were also asked the gender of their partner. Thus, we identified a group of 44 12- to 18-year-olds who lived with parents involved in marriage or marriage-like relationships with same-sex partners. We compared them with a matched group of adolescents living with other-sex couples. Data from the archives of the Add Health study allowed us to address many questions about adolescent development.

Consistent with earlier findings, results of this work revealed few differences in adjustment between adolescents living with same-sex parents and those living with opposite-sex parents (Wainright, Russell, & Patterson, 2004; Wainright & Patterson, 2006). There were no significant differences between teenagers living with same-sex parents and those living with other-sex parents on self-reported assessments of psychological well-being, such as self-esteem and anxiety; measures of school outcomes, such as grade point averages and trouble in school; or measures of family relationships, such as parental warmth and care from adults and peers. Adolescents in the two groups were equally likely to say that they had been involved in a romantic relationship in the last 18 months, and they were equally likely to report having engaged in sexual intercourse. The only statistically reliable difference between the two groups—that those with same-sex parents felt a greater sense of connection to people at school—favored the youngsters living with same-sex couples. There were no significant differences in self-reported substance use, delinquency, or peer victimization between those reared by same- or other-sex couples (Wainright & Patterson, 2006).

Although the gender of parents' partners was not an important predictor of adolescent well-being, other aspects of family relationships were significantly associated with teenagers' adjustment. Consistent with other findings about adolescent development, the qualities of family relationships rather than the gender of parents' partners were consistently related to adolescent outcomes. Parents who reported having close relationships with their offspring had adolescents who reported more favorable adjustment. Not only is it possible for children and adolescents who are parented by same-sex couples to develop in healthy directions, but—even when studied in an extremely diverse, representative sample of American adolescents—they generally do.

These findings have been supported by results from many other studies, both in the United States and abroad. Susan Golombok and her colleagues have reported similar results with a near-representative sample of children in the United Kingdom (Golombok et al., 2003). Others, both in Europe and in the United States, have described similar findings (e.g., Brewaeys, Ponjaert, Van Hall, & Golombok, 1997).

The fact that children of lesbian mothers generally develop in healthy ways should not be taken to suggest that they encounter no challenges. Many investigators have remarked upon the fact that children of lesbian and gay parents may encounter anti-gay sentiments in their daily lives. For example, in a study of 10-year-old children born to lesbian mothers, Gartrell, Deck, Rodas, Peyser, and Banks (2005) reported that a substantial minority had encountered anti-gay sentiments among their peers. Those who had had such encounters were likely to report having felt angry, upset, or sad about these experiences. Children of lesbian and gay parents may be exposed to prejudice against their parents in some settings, and this may be painful for them, but evidence for the idea that such encounters affect children's overall adjustment is lacking.

Conclusions

Does parental sexual orientation have an important impact on child or adolescent development? Results of recent research provide no evidence that it does. In fact, the findings suggest that parental sexual orientation is less important than the qualities of family relationships. More important to youth than the gender of their parent's partner is the quality of daily interaction and the strength of relationships with the parents they have.

One possible approach to findings like the ones described above might be to shrug them off by reiterating the familiar adage that "one cannot prove the null hypothesis." To respond in this way, however, is to miss the central point of these studies. Whether or not any measurable impact of parental sexual orientation on children's development is ever demonstrated, the main conclusions from research to date remain clear: Whatever correlations between child outcomes and parental sexual orientation may exist, they are less important than those between child outcomes and the qualities of family relationships.

Although research to date has made important contributions, many issues relevant to children of lesbian and gay parents remain in need of study. Relatively few studies have examined the development of children adopted by lesbian or gay parents or of children born to gay fathers; further research in both areas would be welcome (Patterson, 2004). Some notable longitudinal studies have been reported, and they have found children of same-sex couples to be in good mental health. Greater understanding of family relationships and transitions over time would, however, be helpful, and longitudinal studies would be valuable. Future research could also benefit from the use of a variety of methodologies.

Meanwhile, the clarity of findings in this area has been acknowledged by a number of major professional organizations. For instance, the governing body of the American Psychological Association (APA) voted unanimously in favor of a statement that said, "Research has shown that the adjustment, development, and psychological well-being of children is unrelated to parental sexual orientation and that children of lesbian and gay parents are as likely as those of heterosexual parents to flourish" (APA, 2004). The American Bar Association, the American Medical Association, the American Academy of Pediatrics, the American Psychiatric Association, and other mainstream professional groups have issued similar statements.

The findings from research on children of lesbian and gay parents have been used to inform legal and public policy debates across the country (Patterson et al., 2002). The research literature on this subject has been cited in amicus briefs filed by the APA in cases dealing with adoption, child custody, and also in cases related to the legality of marriages between same-sex partners. Psychologists serving as expert witnesses have presented findings on these issues in many different courts (Patterson et al., 2002). Through these and other avenues, results of research on lesbian and gay parents and their children are finding their way into public discourse.

The findings are also beginning to address theoretical questions about critical issues in parenting. The importance of gender in parenting is one such issue. When children fare well in two-parent lesbian-mother or gay-father families, this suggests that the gender of one's parents cannot be a critical factor in child development. Results of research on children of lesbian and gay parents cast doubt upon the traditional assumption that gender is important in parenting. Our data suggest that it is the quality of parenting rather than the gender of parents that is significant for youngsters' development.

Research on children of lesbian and gay parents is thus located at the intersection of a number of classic and contemporary concerns. Studies of lesbian- and gay-parented families allow researchers to address theoretical questions that had previously remained difficult or impossible to answer. They also address oft-debated legal questions of fact about development of children with lesbian and gay parents. Thus, research on children of lesbian and gay parents contributes to public debate and legal decision making, as well as to theoretical understanding of human development.

References

American Psychological Association (2004). Resolution on sexual orientation, parents, and children. Retrieved September 25, 2006, from www.apa.org/pi/lgbc/policy/parentschildren.pdf

Brewaeys, A., Ponjaert, I., Van Hall, E.V., & Golombok, S. (1997). Donor insemination: Child development and family functioning in lesbian mother families. *Human Reproduction, 12,* 1349–1359.

Chan, R.W., Raboy, B., & Patterson, C.J. (1998). Psychosocial adjustment among children conceived via donor insemination by lesbian and heterosexual mothers. *Child Development, 69,* 443–457.

Fulcher, M., Sutfin, E.L., Chan, R.W., Scheib, J.E., & Patterson, C.J. (2005). Lesbian mothers and their children: Findings from the Contemporary Families Study. In A. Omoto & H. Kurtzman (Eds.), *Recent research on sexual orientation, mental health, and substance abuse* (pp. 281–299). Washington, DC: American Psychological Association.

Gartrell, N., Deck., A., Rodas, C., Peyser, H., & Banks, A. (2005). The national lesbian family study: 4. Interviews with the 10-year-old children. *American Journal of Orthopsychiatry, 75,* 518–524.

Golombok, S., Perry, B., Burston, A., Murray, C., Mooney-Somers, J., Stevens, M., & Golding, J. (2003). Children with lesbian parents: A community study. *Developmental Psychology, 39,* 20–33.

Patterson, C.J. (1996). Lesbian mothers and their children: Findings from the Bay Area Families Study. In J. Laird & R.J. Green (Eds.), *Lesbians and gays in couples and families: A handbook for therapists* (pp. 420–437). San Francisco: Jossey-Bass.

Patterson, C.J. (1997). Children of lesbian and gay parents. In T. Ollendick & R. Prinz (Eds.), *Advances in clinical child psychology* (vol. 19, pp. 235–282). New York: Plenum Press.

Patterson, C.J. (2004). Gay fathers. In M.E. Lamb (Ed.), *The role of the father in child development* (4th ed., pp. 397–416). New York: Wiley.

Patterson, C.J., Fulcher, M., & Wainright, J. (2002). Children of lesbian and gay parents: Research, law, and policy. In B.L. Bottoms, M.B. Kovera, & B.D. McAuliff (Eds.), *Children, social science and the law* (pp. 176–199). New York: Cambridge University Press.

Patterson, C.J., & Hastings, P. (in press). Socialization in context of family diversity. In J. Grusec & P. Hastings (Eds.), *Handbook of socialization.* New York: Guilford Press.

Stacey, J., & Biblarz, T.J. (2001). (How) Does sexual orientation of parents matter? *American Sociological Review, 65,* 159–183.

Wainright, J.L., & Patterson, C.J. (2006). Delinquency, victimization, and substance use among adolescents with female same-sex parents. *Journal of Family Psychology, 20,* 526–530.

Wainright, J.L., Russell, S.T., & Patterson, C.J. (2004). Psychosocial adjustment and school outcomes of adolescents with same-sex parents. *Child Development, 75,* 1886–1898.

Critical Thinking

1. What impact does parental sexual orientation have on child development?

2. What are the similarities and differences in children raised by heterosexual parents and children raised by homosexual parents?

Internet References

Children of Lesbians and Gays Everywhere (COLAGE)
http://www.colage.org

Family Equality Council
http://www.familyequality.org

Gay Parent Magazine
http://www.gayparentmag.com

Article

Prepared by: Elizabeth Schroeder, EdD, MSW,
Elizabeth Schroeder Consulting

Do Boys Face More Sexism Than Girls?

CHRISTINA HOFF SOMMERS

Learning Outcomes

After reading this article, you will be able to:

- Discuss the ways boys and girls are treated differently in school.

- Critically consider the ways that schools function and the unintended consequences of these patterns.

When it comes to education, are boys the new girls? Are they facing more discrimination than their female peers, just because they are sexually different? According to recent studies, boys score as well as or better than girls on most standardized tests, yet they are far less likely to get good grades, take advanced classes or attend college. We asked prominent gender warriors, Michael Kimmel and Christina Hoff Sommers, to hash this one through in HuffPost's latest "Let's Talk" feature.

Michael: Christina, I was really impressed with your recent op-ed in the *Times*.

The first edition of your book, The War Against Boys: How Misguided Policies Are Harming Our Young Men, came out in 2000. Maybe I've optimistically misread, but it seemed to me that the change in your subtitle from "misguided feminism" (2000) to "misguided policies" indicates a real shift in your thinking? Does it? What's changed for boys in the ensuing decade? Have things gotten worse? Why revise it now? And what's changed for feminism that it's no longer their fault that boys are continuing to fall behind?

Christina: Thank you Michael. I am delighted you liked the op-ed. Boys need allies these days, especially in the academy. Yes, I regret the subtitle of the first edition was

"How Misguided Feminism is Harming Our Young Men." My emphasis was on *misguided*—I did not intend to indict the historical feminist movement, which I have always seen as one of the great triumphs of our democracy. But some readers took the book to be an attack on feminism itself, and my message was lost on them. Indeed, many dismissed the book as culture war propaganda. In the new edition (to be published this summer), I have changed the subtitle and sought to make a clear distinction between the humane and progressive feminist movement and a few hard-line women's lobbying groups who have sometimes thwarted efforts to help boys. I have also softened the tone: the problem of male underachievement is too serious to get lost in stale cultural debates of the 1990s.

Groups like the American Association of University Women and the National Women's Law Center continue to promote a girls-are-victims narrative and sometimes advocate policies harmful to boys. But it is now my view that boys have been harmed by many different social trends and there is plenty of blame to go round. These trends include the decline of recess, punitive zero-tolerance policies, myths about armies of juvenile "super-predators," and a misguided campaign against single-sex schooling. As our schools become more feelings-centered, risk-averse, competition-free and sedentary, they have moved further and further from the characteristic sensibilities of boys.

What has changed since 2000? Back then almost no one was talking about the problem of male disengagement from school. Today the facts are well known and we are already witnessing the alarming social and economic consequences. (Have a look at a recent report from the Harvard Graduate School of Education—"Pathways to Prosperity"—about the bleak economic future of inadequately educated young men.) The problem of school disengagement is most serious among boys of color and white boys from poor backgrounds—but even middle-class white boys have fallen behind their sisters. My new book focuses on solutions.

The recent advances of girls and young women in school, sports, and vocational opportunities are cause for deep satisfaction. But I am persuaded we can address the problems of boys without undermining the progress of women. This is not a zero-sum contest. Most women, including most feminist women, do not see the world as a Manichean struggle between Venus and Mars. We are all in this together. The current plight of boys and young men is, in fact, a women's issue. Those boys are our sons; they are the people with whom our daughters will build a future. If our boys are in trouble, so are we all.

Now I have a question for you, Michael. In the past, you seem to have sided with a group of gender scholars who think we should address the boy problem by raising boys to be more like girls. Maybe I am being overly optimistic, but does your praise for my *New York Times* op-ed indicate a shift in your own thinking?

Michael: Not at all. I'm not interested in raising boys to be more like girls any more than I want girls to be raised more like boys. The question itself assumes that there is a way to raise boys that is different from the way we raise girls. To me this is stereotypic thinking. I want to raise our children to be themselves, and I think that one of the more wonderful components of feminism was to critique that stereotype that all girls are supposed to act and dress in one way and one way only. Over the past several decades, girls have reduced the amount of gender policing they do to each other: for every "You are such a slut," a young woman is now equally likely to hear "You go girl!" (Note: I am not saying one has replaced the other; this is not some either/or but a both/and.) The reforms initiated in the 1970s for girls—Title IX, STEM programs—have been an incontesible success. We agree there, I think—and also that we need to pay attention also to boys, because many are falling behind (though not upper- and middle-class white boys as much, as you rightly point out).

I think cultural definitions of masculinity are complex and often offer boys contradictory messages. Just as there are parts that may be unhealthy—never crying or showing your feelings, winning at all costs, etc.—there are also values associated with manhood such as integrity, honor, doing the right thing, speaking truth to power, that are not of "redeemable" but important virtues. I wouldn't want to get rid of them in some wholesale "Etch-a-Sketch" redefinition.

Our disagreement, I think, comes from what we see as the source of that falling behind. My interviews with over 400 young men, aged 6–26, in *Guyland,* showed me that young men and boys are constantly and relentlessly policed by other guys and pressured to conform to a very narrow definition of masculinity by the constant spectre of being called a fag or gay. So if we're going to really intervene in schools to ensure that boys succeed, I believe that we have to empower boys' resilience in the face of this gender policing. What my interviews taught me is that many guys believe that academic disengagement is a sign of their masculinity. Therefore, re-engaging boys in school requires that we enable them to reconect educational engagement with manhood.

My question to you: In your essay, you list a few reforms to benefit boys that strike me as unproblematic, such as recess, and some that seem entirely regressive, like single-sex classes in public schools or single-sex public schools. Is your educational vision of the future—a return to schools with separate entrances for boys and girls—a return to the past?

Christina: I hereby declare myself opposed to separate entrances for boys and girls at school. And I agree that we should raise children to be themselves. But that will often mean respecting their gender. Increasingly, little boys are shamed and punished for the crime of being who they are. The typical, joyful play of young males is "rough and tumble" play. There is no known society where little boys fail to evince this behavior (girls do it too, but far less). In many schools, this characteristic play of little boys is no longer tolerated. Intrusive and intolerant adults are insisting "tug of war" be changed to "tug of peace"; games such as tag are being replaced with "circle of friends"—in which no one is ever out. Just recently, a seven-year-old Colorado boy named Alex Evans was suspended from school for throwing an imaginary hand grenade at "bad guys" so he could "save the world." Play is the basis of learning. And boys' superhero play is no exception. Researchers have found that by allowing "bad guy" play, children's conversation and imaginative writing skills improved. Mary Ellin Logue (University of Maine) and Hattie Harvey (University of Denver) ask an important question: "If boys, due to their choices of dramatic play themes, are discouraged from dramatic play, how will this affect their early language and literacy development and their engagement in school?"

You seem to think that single-sex education is "regressive." This tells me that you may not have been keeping up with new developments. Take a close look at what is going on at the Irma Rangel Young Women's Leadership School and the Barack Obama Male Leadership Academy in Dallas. There are hundreds of similar programs in public schools around the country and they are working wonders with boys and girls. Far from representing a "return to the past," these schools are cutting edge.

An important new study by three University of Pennsylvania researchers looked at single-sex education in Seoul, Korea. In Seoul, until 2009, students were randomly assigned to single-sex and coeducational schools; parents had little choice on which schools their children attended. After controlling for other variables such as teacher quality, student–teacher ratio, and the proportion of students receiving lunch support, the study found significant advantages in single-sex education. The students earned higher scores on their college entrance exams and were more likely to attend four-year colleges. The authors describe the positive effects as "substantial." With so many boys languishing in our schools, it would be reckless not to pay attention to the Dallas academies and the Korean school study. No one is suggesting these schools be the norm—but they may be an important part of the solution to male underachievement. For one thing, they seem to meet a challenge you identify: connecting male educational engagement with manhood.

Finally, a word about Title IX, which you call an "incontestable success." Tell that to all the young men who have watched their swimming, diving, wrestling, baseball and gymnastic teams eliminated. Title IX was a visionary and progressive law; but over the years, it has devolved into a quota regime. If a college's student body is 60 percent female, then 60 percent of the athletes should be female— even if far fewer women than men are interested in playing sports at that college. Many athletic directors have been unable to attract the same proportions of women as men. To avoid government harassment, loss of funding, and lawsuits, they have simply eliminated men's teams.

Michael, I think you focus too much on vague and ponderous abstractions such as "cultural definitions of masculinity." Why not address the very real, concrete and harsh prejudice boys now face every day in our nation's schools? You speak of "empowering boys to resist gender policing." In my view, the most aggressive policing is being carried out by adults who seem to have ruled conventional masculinity out of order.

Michael: Well, my earlier optimism seems somewhat misplaced; it's clear that you changed the subtitle, and want to argue that it's not a zero sum game—these give me hope. But then you characterize Title IX exactly as the zero sum game you say you no longer believe in. I think some of the reforms you suggest—increased recess, for example—are good for both boys and girls. Others, like reading more science fiction, seem to touch the surface, and then only very lightly. Some others, like single-sex schools strike me as, to use your favorite word, misguided. (There is little empirical evidence that the sex of a teacher has a demonstrable

independent effect on educational outcomes.) It seems to me you mistake form for content.

I'd rather my son go to a really great co-ed school than a really crappy single-sex one. (It happens that single sex schools, whether at the secondary or tertiary level, are very resource-rich, with more teacher training and lower student–teacher ratios. Those things actually do matter.) It's not the form, Christina, but the content.

And the content we need is to continue the reforms initiated by feminist women, reforms that suggested *for the first time* that one size doesn't fit all. They didn't change the "one size" and impose it on boys; they expanded the sizes. Those reforms would have us pay attention to differences *among* boys and differences *among* girls, which, it turns out, are far larger than any modest mean difference that you might find between males and females. You'd teach to the stereotype— that rambunctious roll-in-the-mud "boys will be boys" boy of which you are so fond—and not the mean, that is some center of the distribution. Teaching to the stereotype flattens the differences among boys, which will crush those boys who do not conform to that stereotype: the artistic ones, the musical ones, the soft-spoken ones, and the ones who aren't into sports.

If you'd actually talked to boys in your research, instead of criticizing Bill Pollack or Carol Gilligan, I think you'd see this. The incredible research by Niobe Way, for example, in her book *Deep Secrets*, shows that prior to adolescence, boys are emotionally expressive and connected in ways that will surprise you. Something happens to those exuberant, expressive, emotional boys in middle school or so, and what happens to them is masculinity, the ideology of gender, which is relentlessly policed by other guys.

In my more than 400 interviews with boys, this was made utterly clear to me. I've done workshops with literally thousands of boys and asked them about the meaning of manhood and where they get those ideas they have. The answer is overwhelming: it is other guys who police them, with the ubiquitous "that's so gay" and other comments.

I've said this above, so I'll use my last word to reiterate. Boys learn that academic disengagement is a sign of their masculinity. If we want to re-engage boys in education, no amount of classroom tinkering and recess and science fiction reading is going to address that. We will need to enable boys to decouple the cultural definition of masculinity from academic disengagement. We need to acknowledge the vast differences among boys; their beauty lies in their diversity. We need to stop trying to force them into a stereotypic paradigm of rambunctiousness and let them be the individuals they are. And the really good research that talks to boys, all sorts of boys, suggests to me that they are waiting for us to do just that.

Critical Thinking

1. Somers establishes that gender sexism goes both ways. In schools boys are disadvantaged. Outside schools girls are disadvantaged. Overall which gender do you think is disadvantaged?
2. How can the schools function more in step with the needs and psychology of boys without being less beneficial to girls?
3. Can some disadvantages in schools be compensated for?

Internet References

New American Studies Web
www.georgetown.edu/crossroads/asw

Sociology—Study Sociology Online
http://edu.learnsoc.org

Sociology Web Resources
http://www.mhhe.com/socscience/sociology/resources/index.htm

Sociosite
http://www.topsite.com/goto/sociosite.net

Socioweb
http://www.topsite.com/goto/socioweb.com

The Center for Education Reform
http://edreform.com/school_choice

Article

Prepared by: Elizabeth Schroeder, EdD, MSW,
Elizabeth Schroeder Consulting

Majority Decision, *United States v. Windsor*

ANTHONY KENNEDY

Learning Outcomes

After reading this article, you will be able to:

- Summarize the argument for the federal recognition of marriage based on sexual orientation.

- Apply concepts of originalism versus living document interpretations of the Constitution to same-sex couples.

- Evaluate the implications of federal interpretations of marriage on legal and social standing for lesbian and gay families.

Justice Kennedy delivered the opinion of the Court.

Two women then resident in New York were married in a lawful ceremony in Ontario, Canada, in 2007. Edith Windsor and Thea Spyer returned to their home in New York City. When Spyer died in 2009, she left her entire estate to Windsor. Windsor sought to claim the estate tax exemption for surviving spouses. She was barred from doing so, however, by a federal law, the Defense of Marriage Act, which excludes a same-sex partner from the definition of "spouse" as that term is used in federal statutes. Windsor paid the taxes but filed suit to challenge the constitutionality of this provision. The United States District Court and the Court of Appeals ruled that this portion of the statute is unconstitutional and ordered the United States to pay Windsor a refund. This Court granted certiorari and now affirms the judgment in Windsor's favor.

I

In 1996, as some States were beginning to consider the concept of same-sex marriage, see, e.g., Baehr v. Lewin (1993), and before any State had acted to permit it, Congress enacted the Defense of Marriage Act (DOMA). DOMA contains two operative sections: Section 2, which has not been challenged here, allows States to refuse to recognize same-sex marriages performed under the laws of other States.

Section 3 is at issue here. It amends the Dictionary Act in Title 1, §7, of the United States Code to provide a federal definition of "marriage" and "spouse." Section 3 of DOMA provides as follows:

> "In determining the meaning of any Act of Congress, or of any ruling, regulation, or interpretation of the various administrative bureaus and agencies of the United States, the word 'marriage' means only a legal union between one man and one woman as husband and wife, and the word 'spouse' refers only to a person of the opposite sex who is a husband or a wife."

The definitional provision does not by its terms forbid States from enacting laws permitting same-sex marriages or civil unions or providing state benefits to residents in that status. The enactment's comprehensive definition of marriage for purposes of all federal statutes and other regulations or directives covered by its terms, however, does control over 1,000 federal laws in which marital or spousal status is addressed as a matter of federal law.

Edith Windsor and Thea Spyer met in New York City in 1963 and began a long-term relationship. Windsor and Spyer registered as domestic partners when New York City gave that right to same-sex couples in 1993. Concerned about Spyer's health, the couple made the 2007 trip to Canada for their marriage, but they continued to reside in New York City. The State of New York deems their Ontario marriage to be a valid one.

Spyer died in February 2009, and left her entire estate to Windsor. Because DOMA denies federal recognition to same-sex spouses, Windsor did not qualify for the marital exemption from the federal estate tax, which excludes from taxation "any interest in property which passes or has passed from the decedent to his surviving spouse." Windsor paid $363,053 in estate taxes and sought a refund. The Internal Revenue Service denied the refund, concluding that, under DOMA, Windsor was not a "surviving spouse." Windsor commenced this refund suit in the United States District Court for the Southern District of New York. She contended that DOMA violates the guarantee of equal protection, as applied to the Federal Government through the Fifth Amendment.

While the tax refund suit was pending, the Attorney General of the United States notified the Speaker of the House of Representatives, that the Department of Justice would no longer defend the constitutionality of DOMA's §3. Noting that "the Department has previously defended DOMA against . . . challenges involving legally married same-sex couples," App. 184, the Attorney General informed Congress that "the President has concluded that given a number of factors, including a documented history of discrimination, classifications based on sexual orientation should be subject to a heightened standard of scrutiny." The Department of Justice has submitted many §530D letters over the years refusing to defend laws it deems unconstitutional, when, for instance, a federal court has rejected the Government's defense of a statute and has issued a judgment against it. This case is unusual, however, because the §530D letter was not preceded by an adverse judgment. The letter instead reflected the Executive's own conclusion, relying on a definition still being debated and considered in the courts, that heightened equal protection scrutiny should apply to laws that classify on the basis of sexual orientation.

Although "the President . . . instructed the Department not to defend the statute in Windsor," he also decided "that Section 3 will continue to be enforced by the Executive Branch" and that the United States had an "interest in providing Congress a full and fair opportunity to participate in the litigation of those cases." Id., at 191–193. The stated rationale for this dual-track procedure (determination of unconstitutionality coupled with ongoing enforcement) was to "recogniz[e] the judiciary as the final arbiter of the constitutional claims raised."

In response to the notice from the Attorney General, the Bipartisan Legal Advisory Group (BLAG) of the House of Representatives voted to intervene in the litigation to defend the constitutionality of §3 of DOMA. The Department of Justice did not oppose limited intervention by BLAG. The District Court denied BLAG's motion to enter the suit as of right, on the rationale that the United States already was represented by the Department of Justice. The District Court, however, did grant intervention by BLAG as an interested party.

On the merits of the tax refund suit, the District Court ruled against the United States. It held that §3 of DOMA is unconstitutional and ordered the Treasury to refund the tax with interest. Both the Justice Department and BLAG filed notices of appeal, and the Solicitor General filed a petition for certiorari before judgment. Before this Court acted on the petition, the Court of Appeals for the Second Circuit affirmed the District Court's judgment. It applied heightened scrutiny to classifications based on sexual orientation, as both the Department and Windsor had urged. The United States has not complied with the judgment. Windsor has not received her refund, and the Executive Branch continues to enforce §3 of DOMA.

In granting certiorari on the question of the constitutionality of §3 of DOMA, the Court requested argument on two additional questions: whether the United States' agreement with Windsor's legal position precludes further review and whether BLAG has standing to appeal the case. All parties agree that the Court has jurisdiction to decide this case; and, with the case in that framework, the Court appointed Professor Vicki Jackson as amicus curiae to argue the position that the Court lacks jurisdiction to hear the dispute.

II

It is appropriate to begin by addressing whether either the Government or BLAG, or both of them, were entitled to appeal to the Court of Appeals and later to seek certiorari and appear as parties here.

There is no dispute that when this case was in the District Court it presented a concrete disagreement between opposing parties, a dispute suitable for judicial resolution. "[A] taxpayer has standing to challenge the collection of a specific tax assessment as unconstitutional; being forced to pay such a tax causes a real and immediate economic injury to the individual taxpayer." Hein v. Freedom From Religion Foundation, Inc. (2007) (plurality opinion). Windsor suffered a redressable injury when she was required to pay estate taxes from which, in her view, she was exempt but for the alleged invalidity of §3 of DOMA.

The decision of the Executive not to defend the constitutionality of §3 in court while continuing to deny refunds and to assess deficiencies does introduce a complication. Even though the Executive's current position was announced before the District Court entered its judgment, the Government's agreement with Windsor's position would not have deprived the District Court of jurisdiction to entertain and resolve the refund suit; for her injury (failure to obtain a refund allegedly required by law) was concrete, persisting, and unredressed. The Government's position—agreeing with Windsor's legal contention but refusing to give it effect—meant that there was a justiciable controversy between the parties, despite what the claimant would find to be an inconsistency in that stance. Windsor, the Government, BLAG, and the amicus appear to agree upon that point. The disagreement is over the standing of the parties, or aspiring parties, to take an appeal in the Court of Appeals and to appear as parties in further proceedings in this Court.

The amicus' position is that, given the Government's concession that §3 is unconstitutional, once the District Court ordered the refund the case should have ended; and the amicus argues that the Court of Appeals should have dismissed the appeal. The amicus submits that once the President agreed with Windsor's legal position and the District Court issued its judgment, the parties were no longer adverse. From this standpoint, the United States was a prevailing party below, just as Windsor was. Accordingly, the amicus reasons, it is inappropriate for this Court to grant certiorari and proceed to rule on the merits; for the United States seeks no redress from the judgment entered against it.

This position, however, elides the distinction between two principles: the jurisdictional requirements of Article III and the prudential limits on its exercise. See Warth v. Seldin (1975). The latter are "essentially matters of judicial self-governance." The Court has kept these two strands separate: "Article III standing, which enforces the Constitution's case-or-controversy requirement, see Lujan v. Defenders of Wildlife; and prudential standing, which embodies 'judicially self-imposed limits on the exercise of federal jurisdiction.'"

The requirements of Article III standing are familiar:

"First, the plaintiff must have suffered an 'injury in fact'—an invasion of a legally protected interest which is (a) concrete and particularized, and (b) 'actual or imminent, not "conjectural or hypothetical."' Second, there must be a causal connection between the injury and the conduct complained of—the injury has to be 'fairly . . . trace[able] to the challenged action of the defendant, and not . . . th[e] result [of] the independent action of some third party not before the court.' Third, it must be 'likely,' as opposed to merely 'speculative,' that the injury will be 'redressed by a favorable decision.'"

Rules of prudential standing, by contrast, are more flexible "rule[s] . . . of federal appellate practice," Deposit Guaranty Nat. Bank v. Roper (1980), designed to protect the courts from "decid[ing] abstract questions of wide public significance even [when] other governmental institutions may be more competent to address the questions and even though judicial intervention may be unnecessary to protect individual rights."

In this case, the United States retains a stake sufficient to support Article III jurisdiction on appeal and in proceedings before this Court. The judgment in question orders the United States to pay Windsor the refund she seeks. An order directing the Treasury to pay money is "a real and immediate economic injury," indeed as real and immediate as an order directing an individual

to pay a tax. That the Executive may welcome this order to pay the refund if it is accompanied by the constitutional ruling it wants does not eliminate the injury to the national Treasury if payment is made or to the taxpayer if it is not. The judgment orders the United States to pay money that it would not disburse but for the court's order. The Government of the United States has a valid legal argument that it is injured even if the Executive disagrees with §3 of DOMA, which results in Windsor's liability for the tax. Windsor's ongoing claim for funds that the United States refuses to pay thus establishes a controversy sufficient for Article III jurisdiction. It would be a different case if the Executive had taken the further step of paying Windsor the refund to which she was entitled under the District Court's ruling.

The Court's conclusion that this petition may be heard on the merits does not imply that no difficulties would ensue if this were a common practice in ordinary cases. The Executive's failure to defend the constitutionality of an Act of Congress based on a constitutional theory not yet established in judicial decisions has created a procedural dilemma. On the one hand, as noted, the Government's agreement with Windsor raises questions about the propriety of entertaining a suit in which it seeks affirmance of an order invalidating a federal law and ordering the United States to pay money. On the other hand, if the Executive's agreement with a plaintiff that a law is unconstitutional is enough to preclude judicial review, then the Supreme Court's primary role in determining the constitutionality of a law that has inflicted real injury on a plaintiff who has brought a justiciable legal claim would become only secondary to the President's. This would undermine the clear dictate of the separation-of-powers principle that "when an Act of Congress is alleged to conflict with the Constitution, '[i]t is emphatically the province and duty of the judicial department to say what the law is.'" Zivotofsky v. Clinton (2012). Similarly, with respect to the legislative power, when Congress has passed a statute and a President has signed it, it poses grave challenges to the separation of powers for the Executive at a particular moment to be able to nullify Congress' enactment solely on its own initiative and without any determination from the Court.

The Court's jurisdictional holding, it must be underscored, does not mean the arguments for dismissing this dispute on prudential grounds lack substance. Yet the difficulty the Executive faces should be acknowledged. When the Executive makes a principled determination that a statute is unconstitutional, it faces a difficult choice. Still, there is no suggestion here that it is appropriate for the Executive as a matter of course to challenge statutes in the judicial forum rather than making the case to Congress for their amendment or repeal. The integrity of the political process would be at risk if difficult constitutional issues were simply referred to the Court as a routine exercise. But this case is not routine. And the capable defense of the law by BLAG ensures that these prudential issues do not cloud the merits question, which is one of immediate importance to the Federal Government and to hundreds of thousands of persons. These circumstances support the Court's decision to proceed to the merits.

III

When at first Windsor and Spyer longed to marry, neither New York nor any other State granted them that right. After waiting some years, in 2007, they traveled to Ontario to be married there. It seems fair to conclude that, until recent years, many citizens had not even considered the possibility that two persons of the same sex might aspire to occupy the same status and dignity as that of a man and woman in lawful marriage. For marriage between a man and a woman no doubt had been thought of by most people as essential to the very definition of that term and to its role and function throughout the history of civilization. That belief, for many who long have held it, became even more urgent, more cherished when challenged. For others, however, came the beginnings of a new perspective, a new insight. Accordingly some States concluded that same-sex marriage ought to be given recognition and validity in the law for those same-sex couples who wish to define themselves by their commitment to each other. The limitation of lawful marriage to heterosexual couples, which for centuries had been deemed both necessary and fundamental, came to be seen in New York and certain other States as an unjust exclusion.

Slowly at first and then in rapid course, the laws of New York came to acknowledge the urgency of this issue for same-sex couples who wanted to affirm their commitment to one another before their children, their family, their friends, and their community. And so New York recognized same-sex marriages performed elsewhere; and then it later amended its own marriage laws to permit same-sex marriage. New York, in common with, as of this writing, 11 other States and the District of Columbia, decided that same-sex couples should have the right to marry and so live with pride in themselves and their union and in a status of equality with all other married persons. After a statewide deliberative process that enabled its citizens to discuss and weigh arguments for and against same-sex marriage, New York acted to enlarge the definition of marriage to correct what its citizens and elected representatives perceived to be an injustice that they had not earlier known or understood.

Against this background of lawful same-sex marriage in some States, the design, purpose, and effect of DOMA should be considered as the beginning point in deciding whether it is valid under the Constitution. By history and tradition, the definition and regulation of marriage, as will be discussed in more detail, has been treated as being within the authority and realm of the separate States. Yet it is further established that Congress,

in enacting discrete statutes, can make determinations that bear on marital rights and privileges. Just this Term the Court upheld the authority of the Congress to preempt state laws, allowing a former spouse to retain life insurance proceeds under a federal program that gave her priority, because of formal beneficiary designation rules, over the wife by a second marriage who survived the husband. Hillman v. Maretta (2013); see also Ridgway v. Ridgway (1981); Wissner v. Wissner (1950). This is one example of the general principle that when the Federal Government acts in the exercise of its own proper authority, it has a wide choice of the mechanisms and means to adopt. Congress has the power both to ensure efficiency in the administration of its programs and to choose what larger goals and policies to pursue.

Other precedents involving congressional statutes which affect marriages and family status further illustrate this point. In addressing the interaction of state domestic relations and federal immigration law Congress determined that marriages "entered into for the purpose of procuring an alien's admission [to the United States] as an immigrant" will not qualify the noncitizen for that status, even if the noncitizen's marriage is valid and proper for state-law purposes. And in establishing income-based criteria for Social Security benefits, Congress decided that although state law would determine in general who qualifies as an applicant's spouse, common-law marriages also should be recognized, regardless of any particular State's view on these relationships.

Though these discrete examples establish the constitutionality of limited federal laws that regulate the meaning of marriage in order to further federal policy, DOMA has a far greater reach; for it enacts a directive applicable to over 1,000 federal statutes and the whole realm of federal regulations. And its operation is directed to a class of persons that the laws of New York, and of 11 other States, have sought to protect.

In order to assess the validity of that intervention, it is necessary to discuss the extent of the state power and authority over marriage as a matter of history and tradition. State laws defining and regulating marriage, of course, must respect the constitutional rights of persons, see, e.g., Loving v. Virginia (1967); but, subject to those guarantees, "regulation of domestic relations" is "an area that has long been regarded as a virtually exclusive province of the States."

The recognition of civil marriages is central to state domestic relations law applicable to its residents and citizens. See Williams v. North Carolina (1942) ("Each state as a sovereign has a rightful and legitimate concern in the marital status of persons domiciled within its borders"). The definition of marriage is the foundation of the State's broader authority to regulate the subject of domestic relations with respect to the "[p]rotection of offspring, property interests, and the enforcement of marital responsibilities." Ibid. "[T]he states, at the time of the adoption of the Constitution, possessed full power over the subject of marriage and divorce . . . [and] the Constitution delegated no authority to the Government of the United States on the subject of marriage and divorce." Haddock v. Haddock (1906).

Consistent with this allocation of authority, the Federal Government, through our history, has deferred to state-law policy decisions with respect to domestic relations. In De Sylva v. Ballentine (1956), for example, the Court held that, "[t]o decide who is the widow or widower of a deceased author, or who are his executors or next of kin," under the Copyright Act "requires a reference to the law of the State which created those legal relationships" because "there is no federal law of domestic relations." In order to respect this principle, the federal courts, as a general rule, do not adjudicate issues of marital status even when there might otherwise be a basis for federal jurisdiction. Federal courts will not hear divorce and custody cases even if they arise in diversity because of "the virtually exclusive primacy . . . of the States in the regulation of domestic relations."

The significance of state responsibilities for the definition and regulation of marriage dates to the Nation's beginning; for "when the Constitution was adopted the common understanding was that the domestic relations of husband and wife and parent and child were matters reserved to the States." Marriage laws vary in some respects from State to State. For example, the required minimum age is 16 in Vermont, but only 13 in New Hampshire. Likewise the permissible degree of consanguinity can vary (most States permit first cousins to marry, but a handful—such as Iowa and Washington—prohibit the practice). But these rules are in every event consistent within each State.

Against this background, DOMA rejects the long-established precept that the incidents, benefits, and obligations of marriage are uniform for all married couples within each State, though they may vary, subject to constitutional guarantees, from one State to the next. Despite these considerations, it is unnecessary to decide whether this federal intrusion on state power is a violation of the Constitution because it disrupts the federal balance. The State's power in defining the marital relation is of central relevance in this case quite apart from principles of federalism. Here the State's decision to give this class of persons the right to marry conferred upon them a dignity and status of immense import. When the State used its historic and essential authority to define the marital relation in this way, its role and its power in making the decision enhanced the recognition, dignity, and protection of the class in their own community. DOMA, because of its reach and extent, departs from this history and tradition of reliance on state law to define marriage. "[D]iscriminations of an unusual character especially suggest careful consideration to determine whether they are obnoxious to the constitutional provision."

The Federal Government uses this state-defined class for the opposite purpose—to impose restrictions and disabilities. That result requires this Court now to address whether the resulting injury and indignity is a deprivation of an essential part of the liberty protected by the Fifth Amendment. What the State of New York treats as alike the federal law deems unlike by a law designed to injure the same class the State seeks to protect.

In acting first to recognize and then to allow same-sex marriages, New York was responding "to the initiative of those who [sought] a voice in shaping the destiny of their own times." These actions were without doubt a proper exercise of its sovereign authority within our federal system, all in the way that the Framers of the Constitution intended. The dynamics of state government in the federal system are to allow the formation of consensus respecting the way the members of a discrete community treat each other in their daily contact and constant interaction with each other.

The States' interest in defining and regulating the marital relation, subject to constitutional guarantees, stems from the understanding that marriage is more than a routine classification for purposes of certain statutory benefits. Private, consensual sexual intimacy between two adult persons of the same sex may not be punished by the State, and it can form "but one element in a personal bond that is more enduring." Lawrence v. Texas (2003). By its recognition of the validity of same-sex marriages performed in other jurisdictions and then by authorizing same-sex unions and same-sex marriages, New York sought to give further protection and dignity to that bond. For same-sex couples who wished to be married, the State acted to give their lawful conduct a lawful status. This status is a far-reaching legal acknowledgment of the intimate relationship between two people, a relationship deemed by the State worthy of dignity in the community equal with all other marriages. It reflects both the community's considered perspective on the historical roots of the institution of marriage and its evolving understanding of the meaning of equality.

IV

DOMA seeks to injure the very class New York seeks to protect. By doing so it violates basic due process and equal protection principles applicable to the Federal Government. The Constitution's guarantee of equality "must at the very least mean that a bare congressional desire to harm a politically unpopular group cannot" justify disparate treatment of that group. Department of Agriculture v. Moreno (1973). In determining whether a law is motived by an improper animus or purpose, "[d]iscriminations of an unusual character" especially require careful consideration. DOMA cannot survive under these principles. The responsibility of the States for the regulation of domestic relations is an important indicator of the substantial societal impact the State's classifications have in the daily lives and customs of its people. DOMA's unusual deviation from the usual tradition of recognizing and accepting state definitions of marriage here operates to deprive same-sex couples of the benefits and responsibilities that come with the federal recognition of their marriages. This is strong evidence of a law having the purpose and effect of disapproval of that class. The avowed purpose and practical effect of the law here in question are to impose a disadvantage, a separate status, and so a stigma upon all who enter into same-sex marriages made lawful by the unquestioned authority of the States.

The history of DOMA's enactment and its own text demonstrate that interference with the equal dignity of same-sex marriages, a dignity conferred by the States in the exercise of their sovereign power, was more than an incidental effect of the federal statute. It was its essence. The House Report announced its conclusion that "it is both appropriate and necessary for Congress to do what it can to defend the institution of traditional heterosexual marriage. . . . H. R. 3396 is appropriately entitled the 'Defense of Marriage Act.' The effort to redefine 'marriage' to extend to homosexual couples is a truly radical proposal that would fundamentally alter the institution of marriage." H. R. Rep. No. 104–664, pp. 12–13 (1996). The House concluded that DOMA expresses "both moral disapproval of homosexuality, and a moral conviction that heterosexuality better comports with traditional (especially Judeo-Christian) morality." The stated purpose of the law was to promote an "interest in protecting the traditional moral teachings reflected in heterosexual-only marriage laws." Ibid. Were there any doubt of this far-reaching purpose, the title of the Act confirms it: The Defense of Marriage.

The arguments put forward by BLAG are just as candid about the congressional purpose to influence or interfere with state sovereign choices about who may be married. As the title and dynamics of the bill indicate, its purpose is to discourage enactment of state same-sex marriage laws and to restrict the freedom and choice of couples married under those laws if they are enacted. The congressional goal was "to put a thumb on the scales and influence a state's decision as to how to shape its own marriage laws." Massachusetts, 682 F. 3d, at 12–13. The Act's demonstrated purpose is to ensure that if any State decides to recognize same-sex marriages, those unions will be treated as second-class marriages for purposes of federal law. This raises a most serious question under the Constitution's Fifth Amendment.

DOMA's operation in practice confirms this purpose. When New York adopted a law to permit same-sex marriage, it sought to eliminate inequality; but DOMA frustrates that objective through a system-wide enactment with no identified connection to any particular area of federal law. DOMA writes inequality into the entire United States Code. The particular case at hand concerns the estate tax, but DOMA is more than a simple determination of what should or should not be allowed as an estate tax refund. Among the over 1,000 statutes and numerous federal regulations that DOMA controls are laws pertaining to Social Security, housing, taxes, criminal sanctions, copyright, and veterans' benefits.

DOMA's principal effect is to identify a subset of state-sanctioned marriages and make them unequal. The principal purpose is to impose inequality, not for other reasons like governmental efficiency. Responsibilities, as well as rights, enhance the dignity and integrity of the person. And DOMA contrives to deprive some couples married under the laws of their State, but not other couples, of both rights and responsibilities. By creating two contradictory marriage regimes within the same State, DOMA forces same-sex couples to live as married for the purpose of state law but unmarried for the purpose of federal law, thus diminishing the stability and predictability of basic personal relations the State has found it proper to acknowledge and protect. By this dynamic DOMA undermines both the public and private significance of state-sanctioned same-sex marriages; for it tells those couples, and all the world, that their otherwise valid marriages are unworthy of federal recognition. This places same-sex couples in an unstable position of being in a second-tier marriage. The differentiation demeans the couple, whose moral and sexual choices the Constitution protects, see Lawrence, and whose relationship the State has sought to dignify. And it humiliates tens of thousands of children now being raised by same-sex couples. The law in question makes it even more difficult for the children to understand the integrity and closeness of their own family and its concord with other families in their community and in their daily lives.

Under DOMA, same-sex married couples have their lives burdened, by reason of government decree, in visible and public ways. By its great reach, DOMA touches many aspects of married and family life, from the mundane to the profound. It prevents same-sex married couples from obtaining government healthcare benefits they would otherwise receive. It deprives them of the Bankruptcy Code's special protections for domestic-support obligations. It forces them to follow a complicated procedure to file their state and federal taxes jointly. It prohibits them from being buried together in veterans' cemeteries.

For certain married couples, DOMA's unequal effects are even more serious. The federal penal code makes it a crime to "assaul[t], kidna[p], or murde[r] . . . a member of the immediate family" of "a United States official, a United States judge, [or] a Federal law enforcement officer," with the intent to influence or retaliate against that official, §115(a)(1). Although a "spouse" qualifies as a member of the officer's "immediate family," §115(c)(2), DOMA makes this protection inapplicable to same-sex spouses.

DOMA also brings financial harm to children of same-sex couples. It raises the cost of health care for families by taxing health benefits provided by employers to their workers' same-sex spouses. And it denies or reduces benefits allowed to families upon the loss of a spouse and parent, benefits that are an integral part of family security. See Social Security Administration, Social Security Survivors Benefits 5 (2012) (benefits available to a surviving spouse caring for the couple's child), online at http://www.ssa.gov/pubs/EN-05-10084.pdf.

DOMA divests married same-sex couples of the duties and responsibilities that are an essential part of married life and that they in most cases would be honored to accept were DOMA not in force. For instance, because it is expected that spouses will support each other as they pursue educational opportunities, federal law takes into consideration a spouse's income in calculating a student's federal financial aid eligibility. Same-sex married couples are exempt from this requirement. The same is true with respect to federal ethics rules. Federal executive and agency officials are prohibited from "participat[ing] personally and substantially" in matters as to which they or their spouses have a financial interest. A similar statute prohibits Senators, Senate employees, and their spouses from accepting high-value gifts from certain sources, and another mandates detailed financial disclosures by numerous high-ranking officials and their spouses. Under DOMA, however, these Government-integrity rules do not apply to same-sex spouses.

* * *

The power the Constitution grants it also restrains. And though Congress has great authority to design laws to fit its own conception of sound national policy, it cannot deny the liberty protected by the Due Process Clause of the Fifth Amendment.

What has been explained to this point should more than suffice to establish that the principal purpose and the necessary effect of this law are to demean those persons who are in a lawful same-sex marriage. This requires the Court to hold, as it now does, that DOMA is unconstitutional as a deprivation of the liberty of the person protected by the Fifth Amendment of the Constitution.

The liberty protected by the Fifth Amendment's Due Process Clause contains within it the prohibition against denying to any person the equal protection of the laws. While the Fifth Amendment itself withdraws from Government the power to degrade or demean in the way this law does, the equal protection guarantee of the Fourteenth Amendment makes that Fifth Amendment right all the more specific and all the better understood and preserved.

The class to which DOMA directs its restrictions and restraints are those persons who are joined in same-sex marriages made lawful by the State. DOMA singles out a class of persons deemed by a State entitled to recognition and protection to enhance their own liberty. It imposes a disability on the class by refusing to acknowledge a status the State finds to be dignified and proper. DOMA instructs all federal officials, and indeed all persons with whom same-sex couples interact, including their own children, that their marriage is less worthy than the marriages of others. The federal statute is invalid, for no legitimate purpose overcomes the purpose and effect to disparage and to injure those whom the State, by its marriage laws, sought to protect in personhood and dignity. By seeking to displace this protection and treating those persons as living in marriages less respected than others, the federal statute is in violation of the Fifth Amendment. This opinion and its holding are confined to those lawful marriages.

The judgment of the Court of Appeals for the Second Circuit is affirmed.

It is so ordered.

Critical Thinking

1. What are some arguments made with which you agree or disagree?

2. What are the strengths and weaknesses of the position stated in this chapter?

3. What are some arguments you would make to strengthen the case for marriage equality?

4. Think more broadly about marriage equality. What is required to define the Constitution's role in whether or not marriage for same-sex couples is a fundamental right?

Internet References

American Center for Law and Justice
www.aclj.org/traditional-marriage

Gay Marriage Pro and Con
www.gaymarriage.procon.org

Marriage Equality USA
www.marriageequality.org

ANTHONY KENNEDY is a Supreme Court justice. He is often referred to as the swing vote on the Supreme Court. His legacy may largely be for expanding the constitutional rights for lesbian and gay couples.

Supreme Court of the United States, June 26, 2013.

Article

Prepared by: Elizabeth Schroeder, EdD, MSW,
Elizabeth Schroeder Consulting

Thoughts on the Timing of Puberty and the "Treatment" of Gender Dysphoria

EMI KOYAMA

Learning Outcomes

After reading this article, you will be able to:

- Define the terms "transgender," "cisgender," "gender identity disorder (GID)," and "gender dysphoria."
- Describe the physical and emotional benefits of suppressing puberty for transgender youth through hormonal treatments.
- Describe the benefits/risks of the hormonal induction of cross-sex puberty for transgender youth at an age similar to the pubertal onset of their cisgender peers.
- Summarize the ethical questions the suppression of puberty for transgender youth raises for parents and the medical community.

For the purpose of this discussion, let us set aside questions such as whether or not "gender identity disorder," which has been characterized as a "severe medical condition" (Giordano, 2008), is an appropriate frame to understand and treat gender non-conformity and cross-gender identification in children and adults (I have questions), or if the production of socially defined "normal" characteristics and the elimination of "abnormal" ones are the proper goals of medical intervention (I have serious concerns, though not enough to unilaterally oppose this particular treatment. For the purpose of this discussion, I start from the assumption that having "abnormally" sexed or non-passing physical characteristics can make life extremely difficult for transgender people, in large part though not necessarily entirely due to the rampant transphobic violence, discrimination, and prejudice in our society, and that medicine can help improve their quality of life by enabling the development of more socially desirable or "normal" appearances for the gender they live as.

I recognize that cross-gender identification or gender identity disorder has both social and biomedical aspects. While gender identity disorder/dysphoria may have "genetic, hormonal, and neuro-developmental"(Giordano, 2008) roots, many of the harms associated with gender identity disorder that make it a "severe medical condition" leading to increased risks of "substance abuse, homelessness, prostitution, HIV infection, self-harm, depression, anxiety, and suicide"(Giordano, 2008) are clearly social.

Given that the lack of biomedical intervention exacerbates these risks and that medically induced suspension of puberty at an early age can alleviate many of these risks over the course of a transgender person's life, many have argued that this is the appropriate approach (Cohen-Kettnis, Delemarre-van de Waal, & Gooren, 2008; Hembree, et al, 2009), with others going so far as to say that deferring such treatment would be unethical (Giordano, 2008). In order to reach this conclusion, Giornado (2008) asks us to consider not just the benefits and risks of the medical intervention itself but also the "long-term consequences of delaying treatment." This is an important consideration, because of the vast likelihood of extremely negative social and psychological harms to transgender individuals when they are forced to live through irreversible physical changes brought on by "natural" puberty and adolescence predicated by their biological sex that is incongruent with their gender identity. Those who advocate for the delayed puberty approach typically suggest administering cross-sex hormones around the age of 16 (Cohen-Kettinis, Delemarre-van de Waal, & Gooren, 2008; Hembree, et al 2009).

If we truly believe that we must assess benefits and risks of withholding medical intervention as well as those of going forward with it, however, I find it curious that proponents of puberty blocking hormones fail to consider another possible approach to treating transgender children and youth. That unexplored option is, along with blocking their "natural" puberty, to provide transgender teens with cross-sex hormones that can help them experience physical development similar to, and along with, those who are of the same age and gender identity, rather than keeping them artificially underdeveloped compared to their peers. A host of psychosocial issues are associated with cisgender (or non-transgender) teens who are "off time (earlier or later) in their pubertal development" (Susman & Rogol, 2004). While there are obvious differences in the psychological and social development of cis- and transgender teens, going through puberty later than peers is not risk-free. I am not arguing that the use of cross-sex hormone is always a superior approach than suspension of puberty, but I am pointing out that many may have not considered the long-term consequences of withholding medical treatment that could enable age- and gender-appropriate development alongside cisgender peers.

Giornado (2008) does respond to Viner's (2006) claim that the impact of puberty blockers are, to a degree, "irreversible." I concur with Giornado's counter-argument that Viner's use of the term "irreversible" is confusing and different from what we normally mean when we discuss if a particular medical treatment is reversible or not, but Viner nonetheless has a point: a child whose puberty was suspended might experience a unique and potentially harmful interruption of their pubertal development at the time his or her peers are going through theirs, such as social anxiety and isolation. The administration of cross-sex hormones may not be an ideal option in every case, but it is most certainly what many transgender adults wish was offered to them when they were growing up.

As for potential risks of administering cross-sex hormones, this approach does entail bona fide *irreversible* consequences, not Vinerian hyperbole. In addition to the (desired) pubertal development consistent with their age and gender identity, the intervention could impact fertility. Because of the eugenic history of involuntary sterilization of people with physical and psychiatric disabilities, women of color, poor women, and others in our society, there are legal as well as ethical hurdles that must be satisfied before any treatment that causes, even as a side-effect, sterilization of a minor. However, my understanding is that this hurdle is not absolute if the treatment is desired by the child as well as by his or her family after they are properly informed, and there are overriding benefits to the individual, in many jurisdictions as determined by a judge.

This proposal may seem extreme and too risky, since there is always the risk that the child's gender dysphoria diagnosis might change during adolescence, but it is more coherent than it may appear initially. To endorse suspension of puberty

instead of allowing young people to go through pubertal development consistent with their gender identity at the same as time their peers would imply that we cannot, as some people believe, make a definitive diagnosis of gender identity disorder at that age. Gender identity is still in the process of oscillating and consolidating at that stage, some might say, and it is too dangerous to prescribe irreversible medical treatment for children that young, even if they desperately demand it.

But if we are to believe that gender identity is still fluctuating at that stage and therefore we cannot help transgender children go through pubertal development appropriate for their age and gender identity, what is the justification for *not* suspending puberty for *all* children? There is an unspoken double-standard here: we take for granted that gender identity is solid and fully established when the child's gender identity appears to be consistent with his or her biological sex, and only question its validity or permanence when it is not. This double standard is consistent with the society's prejudicial treatment of transgender people's identities as up for debate, whereas cisgender identities are accepted as stable, natural, and normal without question.

There is of course a risk that a transgender adolescent who receives cross-sex hormones would realize that he or she is not transgender and regret it later. But this is a risk that we routinely accept whenever we assume that any given child who does not unambiguously manifest gender identity disorder is not transgender and therefore do not suspend their puberty. We accept the risk that *any* child could go through "natural" puberty and later regret it, and yet believe that the risk is too grave when it comes to transgender children that even the more "progressive," trans-friendly individuals can only advocate for puberty-delaying treatment.

I suspect that our society's unwillingness to consider the administration of cross-sex hormones is motivated not just by the acknowledgment that not every child who meets the diagnostic criteria for gender identity disorder grows up to become a transgender adult (after all, not every child who does not meet the same diagnostic criteria grow, up to become a non-transgender adult either), but by our deeply held belief that being transgender is inherently abnormal and tragic. We find consequences of false positives (non-transgender children who are misidentified as transgender and given irreversible cross-sex hormones) completely unacceptable, while routinely tolerating the equally debilitating consequences of false negatives (transgender children who are not identified as such in time and experience irreversible "natural" pubertal development).

Perhaps suspension of puberty for transgender children is the most politically realistic or palatable approach to "treatment" in a world that is extremely hostile to transgender people. But the medical community's refusal to go one step further and consider the use of cross-sex hormones instead of puberty blockers in at least some cases is predicated on the double standard that inherently places more value on non-transgender bodies and lives over transgender ones.

We need to keep pushing the conversation to center the voices and needs of transgender individuals rather than treating them as voiceless sufferers of a "severe medical condition," and also continue addressing violence and discrimination against transgender children and adults that comprise a large part of harms that suspension of puberty is designed to circumvent.

References

Giordano, S. (2008). Lives in a Chiaroscuro. should we suspend the puberty of children with gender identity disorder?" *Journal of Medical Ethics, 34*(8), pp. 580–584.

Cohen-Kettenis, P.T., Delemarre-van de Wall, H.A., & Gooren, L.J.G. (2008). The treatment of adolescent transsexuals: Changing insights. *The Journal of Sexual Medicine, 5*(8), pp. 1892–1897. doi: 10.1111/j.1743-6109.2008.00870.x

Hembree, W.C., Cohen-Kettenis, P., Delemarre-van de Wall, H.A., Gooren, L.J., Meyer III, W.J,, Spack, N.P., Tangpricha, V., & Montori, V.M, (2009). Endocrine treatment of transsexual persons: An endocrine society clinical practice guideline. *The Journal of Clinical Endocrinology & Metabolism,* (94)*9*, pp. 3132–3154. doi:10.1210/jc.2009-0345

Susman, E.J., & Rogol, A. (2004). Puberty and psychological development. In R.M. Lerner & L. Steinberg (Eds.), *Handbook of Adolescent Psychology,* (pp. 15–44). Hoboken, NJ: Wiley and Sons.

Viner, R. "Oral Presentation at the Royal Society of Medicine," October 10, 2006.

Critical Thinking

1. When treating transgender youth, what does it mean to suspend puberty? How is this accomplished?

2. What are the physical benefits and risks to the suspension of puberty?

3. What are some social and emotional benefits to suppressing puberty for transgender youth?

Internet References

Injustice at Every Turn: A Report of the National Transgender Discrimination Survey
    www.thetaskforce.org/reports_and_research/ntds

Oregon's Grant High School Creates Gender-Neutral Restrooms for Transgender Students
    www.huffingtonpost.com/2013/03/25/oregon-high-school-transgender-bathrooms_n_2949598.html

TransKids Purple Rainbow Foundation
    www.transkidspurplerainbow.org

World Professional Association for Transgender Health (WPATH)
    www.wpath.org

Emɪ Koyama is an activist and writer. Her work can be found at http://eminism.org/

Prepared by: Elizabeth Schroeder, EdD, MSW,
Elizabeth Schroeder Consulting

Article

Under the Gaydar

How gays won the right to raise children without conservatives even noticing.

ALISON GASH

Learning Outcomes

After reading this article, you will be able to:

- Assess the "best interests of the child" standard in the context of granting custody of children to gay and lesbian parents and allowing gays and lesbians to adopt.

- Determine the persuasiveness of Alison Gash's argument in which she explains why same-sex marriage has been so much more prominent and controversial than gays and lesbians' right to raise children.

No one knows for sure how the Supreme Court will rule on the two high-profile gay marriage cases it is now considering. The betting, however, is that, regardless of the outcome, progress toward marriage equality will persist. A majority of the public now believe gays and lesbians should have the right to wed. Nine states and the District of Columbia have laws on the books conferring such rights. A stampede of Democratic elected officials have announced support for same-sex marriage, and in its March "autopsy" report the Republican National Committee hinted its members should do the same.

Although progress has been unusually swift, this story of same-sex marriage rights has followed a familiar path, one blazed by women and African Americans in their struggles for equality. Members of an out-group, advocating for their rights, demand a fundamental change in the legal interpretation of the Constitution, which causes a series of high-profile court cases, state and federal laws and counter-laws, and all of it accompanied by a broadly held national conversation that leads to a change in public attitudes, laws and legal interpretations.

But this isn't the only way that civil rights advance. A few decades ago, openly gay and lesbian Americans did not have the legal right to raise their own biological children, much less adopt. Today, more than 25 states recognize the same legal benefits and responsibilities of parenthood regardless of sexual orientation. It is now routine for gays and lesbians to jointly adopt, to be recognized as co-parents, and to collect child support or demand custody or visitation rights—even without a biological connection to the child in question. All this has happened without the hallmarks of a traditional rights campaign. There were very few high-profile court cases, few legislative battles, and little public debate. In sharp contrast to marriage equality—where between 1993 and 2003 two pro-marriage rulings incited over 35 state bans—parenting litigation has provoked minimal public backlash.

At first blush, this would seem unlikely. Gay marriage, after all, is between consenting adults, whereas gay adoption involves children; one would think society would be at least as skittish about the latter as about the former. Even countries that pioneered marriage equality, such at Denmark, have been slower to extend full parenting rights to same-sex couples. And yet, paradoxically, in the United States, we've seen the opposite: we've had a contentious, two-decades-long national debate about same-sex marriage—one that has repeatedly featured in battles for the presidency—but have allowed same-sex couples to quietly begin legally adopting and co-parenting with hardly any national discussion at all. Why the difference?

The answer is that same-sex parenting rights have successfully advanced precisely because the legal wrangling over them has remained largely below the radar—a fact highlighted by Justice Antonin Scalia's confusion about whether California even permits same-sex adoption during Supreme Court hearings on that state's Proposition 8 law. Where marriage-equality advocates had little choice but to engage in open political battles and bring high-profile constitutional court cases on behalf of their fundamental rights, the fight for same-sex parental rights has mostly played out in obscure family courts, with few reporters present, and with advocates consciously delaying or avoiding high court review. This below-the-radar strategy created a foundation of "facts on the ground"—tens of thousands of intact gay- and lesbian-headed families with children—well before most conservative activists were even aware the phenomenon existed, making their subsequent efforts to block same-sex parenting an uphill fight.

The legal struggle over same-sex parenting began in the 1950s and '60s. As divorce laws loosened, a growing number of closeted gays and lesbians came out to their heterosexual spouses, leading to legal disputes about custody and visitation rights over the couples' children. These cases were handled in local family courts, where records tend to be sealed. Few were ever covered in the newspapers. Fewer still resulted in victories for the gay spouses. Judges typically ruled that simply being homosexual made a parent unfit.

In one such case, in 1967, a lesbian woman named Ellen Doreen Nadler lost custody of her daughter to the child's heterosexual father. Nadler petitioned the California appellate court, which found that the previous court was wrong to base its decision solely on Nadler's homosexuality. Instead, the court wrote, the "primary consideration must be given to the welfare of the child." In a retrial, Nadler still didn't regain custody of her daughter, but the case set a key precedent: in custody cases, "the best interests of the child," a legal doctrine dating back to the mid-1800s, and not the sexual orientation of the parent, should be the deciding factor.

That precedent proved decisive in 1973, when an Oregon court ruled in favor of a gay father when the mother—who had not seen her children in over ten years—challenged custody because of the father's sexual orientation. The court determined that it was not necessarily in the "best interests of the child" to alter the custody arrangement, despite the father's homosexuality. Similarly, in two companion cases in 1978, the Washington Supreme Court ruled that withdrawing custody from two lesbian mothers who were raising children together from both of their previous marriages, would not serve the children's best interests. Although the court expressed some trepidation about the mothers' relationship, it determined that a change in custody would be more harmful to the children than maintaining the status quo.

While ground breaking in many ways, these unorthodox rulings attracted little public interest, largely because they were focused on the particulars of the cases and not framed in terms of broader homosexual rights. This was in sharp contrast to the budding gay rights movement, which at that time was starting to push for statutory changes in the law. In 1977, for instance, gay rights activists convinced Miami-Dade County to amend its anti-discrimination ordinance to include gays and lesbians. In response, an anti-gay rights coalition called Save Our Children was formed, with country singer and Florida orange juice spokeswoman Anita Bryant as its leader. "As a mother, I know that homosexuals cannot biologically reproduce children," she proclaimed, "therefore, they must recruit our children." Yet despite her rhetoric and the group's name, Bryant and her allies didn't focus on gay parenting. Instead they went after higher-profile anti-discrimination ordinances that included sexual orientation and, in some instances, tried to remove gay and lesbian teachers from public schools. The Florida legislature did subsequently pass a law barring single gays and lesbians, as well as same-sex couples, from adopting children, but only one other state, New Hampshire, followed suit.

In the 1980s, the same-sex parenting movement continued to move quietly forward. Family courts began to see cases where gay and lesbian couples with children were petitioning for parental rights for the non-biological partner. Because these "other" parents were essentially legal strangers to the children they were raising, they were often barred from engaging in the most routine—and important—parenting functions: picking up their kids at school, visiting them in the hospital, or listing them as dependents on health or life insurance policies. During that decade, family or lower courts in Oregon, Alaska, California, and Washington granted co-parent adoptions to same sex couples, with relatively little reaction from gay rights opponents.

Again, the secret to this progress was that gay parents and couples—who were by now aided by newly formed gay rights advocacy groups—fought these cases in family court, where judges had wide discretion and public scrutiny was minimal. Aware of the perils of drawing public attention to these cases, advocates from national gay rights groups worked hard to camouflage their efforts. They removed their names from briefs, provided behind-the-scenes support, and avoided appealing losses to appellate courts, out of fear that higher-level court approval would awaken the sleeping giant of public opposition.

Some even developed strategies to educate judges who were likely to hear same-sex parenting cases through seminars and bench books. They quietly met with judges to reassure them that their rulings would not be politicized. Says one advocate, "You have to take steps to keep it under the radar. I make sure to tell these judges that this is not a test case. We are not going to put you on the spot. I appreciate that you are an elected judge and I am not going to do something that will hurt you."

Eventually, same-sex parenting cases did make their way to higher courts in two states—ironically, in the same year, 1993, that gay marriage hit the supreme court docket in Hawaii (the case that launched a nationwide debate). But rather than rally opposition to both issues, conservatives chose to focus their attention only on same-sex marriage. Why?

For one, the co-parenting cases received relatively little attention from the mainstream press—again, because they were not being argued as matters of "gay rights." Also, many pro-family activists also assumed, or at least hoped, that anti-marriage efforts would limit both gay marriage and parenting progress. They theorized that same-sex marriage bans would, like anti-sodomy statutes, impose a chilling effect on judges. So while conservatives were busy getting the 1996 Defense of Marriage Act through Congress and initiating state-level bans on same-sex marriage, gay parents and their advocates continued to quietly amass significant court victories in Delaware, the District of Columbia, Illinois, Indiana, Maryland, Massachusetts, New Jersey, New York, Pennsylvania, and Vermont.

Meanwhile, by the end of 2004, anti-gay rights forces had won measures banning gay marriage in forty states. Hoping to leverage these gains, pro-family advocates finally turned their attention to parenting. Between 2004 and 2006 the pro-family movement initiated more than thirty-five attempts to limit same-sex parenting. In 2006, alone, sixteen states were poised to initiate bans on same-sex parenting legislatively or through the ballot process.

But—happily, for gay rights advocates—the anti-gay forces were too late. Despite dire predictions, almost none of these measures against same-sex parenting went anywhere. Legislation died in committee and proposed initiatives never made it to the ballot. All the while—on the strength of decades of precedents and facts on the ground—family, appellate, and state supreme courts continued "to recognize the parental rights of and grant adoptions to gay and lesbian parents."

Why did the backlash against same-sex parenting fail? It certainly wasn't public opinion. The handful of polls from 2006 that questioned participants about both same-sex marriage and adoption rights showed that average Americans were no more comfortable with gay parenthood than with gay marriage. In fact, they opposed both by well over 50 percent. And if we take their arguments seriously, it is precisely concern about gay parenthood that drives opposition efforts against marriage equality.

Rather, the main problem for conservatives was that they were trying to roll back gay parenting rights that had, in effect, already been granted. This proved a tough sell. The media didn't much cover the conservative campaign against same-sex parenting, and what few stories did run typically featured heartwarming narratives of gay and lesbian couples raising well-adjusted kids. Such families existed in the thousands precisely because the under-the-radar strategy had allowed them to flourish over the previous twenty years. Whereas gay marriage was still an abstraction that opponents could rally the public to prevent, gay families were a reality that the public would have to tear asunder to stop.

Also, by the mid-2000s, social scientists had conducted studies on same-sex families. In general, this research demonstrated that children of same-sex couples were not appreciably different from kids raised by straight couples—including their propensity to identify as gay or lesbian. These studies were widely quoted in the media and used to foster support among child welfare experts.

All this made it a tough fight for anti-gay advocates. As an official at Focus on Family, a conservative Christian advocacy group, concedes, the issue was low on the "radar for pro-family conservatives" because of the "confusing rhetoric of same-sex adoption, the media bombarding the public with images of happy gay couples taking in disadvantaged kids," and the argument that "this kind of family is better than no family." Adds another opponent, "Trying to take the kids away . . . it's a ridiculous battle to fight."

That doesn't mean the fight is completely over. Taking a page from the playbook of parenting advocates, opponents of gay parenting have begun engaging at the level of family courts as well. They are now advocating on behalf of gay biological parents who are in custody battles with their estranged gay partners who are not the children's biological parents. Still, apart from such skirmishes, the right of same-sex parents to raise their kids seems well on its way to being secured.

Same-sex parenting advocates weren't the first to use an under-the-radar strategy to advance their cause, and probably won't be the last. John F. Kennedy employed low-visibility tactics to both attract black voters during his presidential campaign and to encourage voter registration after he was elected. Some disability advocates, in their attempt to secure group housing for their disabled clients, circumvent public notification procedures when looking for appropriate housing and instead procure the property, move the clients in, and wait to be discovered. And groups like the Nature Conservancy long ago figured out that instead of engaging in contentious public campaigns to get elected officials to do protect environmentally sensitive parcels of land, it is often easier to raise money and quietly buy the land themselves.

History books suggest that our society has made its greatest leaps on the shoulders of high-profile campaigns. But change can also be the result of quiet battles that play out in courtrooms, boardrooms and bedrooms all across the country. And it is often these hidden battles that most effectively propel our society forward.

Critical Thinking

1. How did the "best interests of the child" standard figure into state court decisions to grant custody of children to gay and lesbian parents in the 1970s?

2. Why did early state court rulings granting custody of children to gay and lesbian parents, including allowing them to adopt children, attract little public interest?

3. Why did backlash against gay and lesbian parenting fail in the early twenty-first century?

Internet References

American Psychological Association: Sexual Orientation, Parents, and Children

www.apa.org/about/policy/parenting.aspx

Focus on the Family: Adoption (Cause for Concern)

www.focusonthefamily.com/socialissues/social-issues/adoption/cause-for-concern.aspx

Independent Adoption Center: LGBTQ Adoption

www.adoptionhelp.org/lgbtq-adoption

ALISON GASH is an assistant professor of political science at the University of Oregon. She is completing a manuscript entitled *Below the Radar: How Silence Can Save Civil Rights,* which will be published in 2014.

Article

Prepared by: Elizabeth Schroeder, EdD, MSW,
Elizabeth Schroeder Consulting

Protective School Climates and Reduced Risk for Suicide Ideation in Sexual Minority Youths

MARK L. HATZENBUEHLER ET AL.

Objectives. We examined whether sexual minority students living in states and cities with more protective school climates were at lower risk of suicidal thoughts, plans, and attempts.

Methods. Data on sexual orientation and past-year suicidal thoughts, plans, and attempts were from the pooled 2005 and 2007 Youth Risk Behavior Surveillance Surveys from 8 states and cities. We derived data on school climates that protected sexual minority students (e.g., percentage of schools with safe spaces and Gay–Straight Alliances) from the 2010 School Health Profile Survey, compiled by the Centers for Disease Control and Prevention.

Results. Lesbian, gay, and bisexual students living in states and cities with more protective school climates reported fewer past-year suicidal thoughts than those living in states and cities with less protective climates (lesbians and gays: odds ratio [OR] = 0.68; 95% confidence interval [CI] = 0.47, 0.99; bisexuals: OR = 0.81; 95% CI = 0.66, 0.99). Results were robust to adjustment for potential state-level confounders. Sexual orientation disparities in suicidal thoughts were nearly eliminated in states and cities with the most protective school climates.

Conclusions. School climates that protect sexual minority students may reduce their risk of suicidal thoughts. (*Am J Public Health.* 2014;104:279–286. doi:10.2105/AJPH.2013.301508)

Learning Outcomes

After reading this article, you will be able to:

- Explain the link between school climates and suicide risk levels for sexual minority students.

- Describe what constitutes a supportive school climate for LGBTQ youth.

- Explore possible barriers to creating protective school climates.

Suicide is the third leading cause of death among youths aged 15 to 24 years.[1] Decades of research have identified multiple risk factors for adolescent suicide ideation and attempts.[2] One of the most consistent findings is that lesbian, gay, and bisexual (LGB, or sexual minority) adolescents are more likely than heterosexual adolescents to endorse suicidal thoughts[3,4] and to report having a suicide plan.[5] Additionally, a recent review of the epidemiological literature found that LGB youths are between 2 and 7 times more likely to attempt suicide than their heterosexual peers.[6]

Given the elevated risk of suicidal ideation, plans, and attempts among sexual minority youths, researchers have focused on identifying factors that explain these marked disparities. Theories of minority stress[7] and stigma[8] have highlighted the important roles that social-structural contexts as well as institutional practices and policies play in contributing to mental health disparities. Consistent with these theories, LGB adults who live in states with fewer protective social policies have higher rates of psychiatric and substance use disorders than

LGB adults living in states with more protective policies.[9,10] For instance, LGB adults in states that passed constitutional amendments banning same-sex marriage experienced a 37% increase in mood disorders, a 40% increase in alcohol use disorders, and nearly a 250% increase in generalized anxiety disorders in the year following the enactment of the amendments.[10] These and other studies[11] have shown that the broader social contexts surrounding LGB adults shape their mental health.

Among adolescents, schools are an important social context that contributes to developmental and health outcomes.[12] For sexual and gender minority youths in particular, the social context of schools can promote both vulnerability and resilience.[13–16] A variety of methodological approaches have been used to evaluate the mental health consequences of school climates for LGB students. The predominant approach is to ask LGB adolescents to report on the supportiveness of their schools.[17–19] Studies using this approach have indicated that LGB youths who report greater school connectedness and school safety also report lower suicidal ideation and fewer suicide attempts.[18] Although informative, this research may introduce bias because information is self-reported for both the exposure and the outcome.[20] Studies using alternative methodologies may therefore improve the validity of the inferences on the relationship between the social environment and individual health outcomes.

An alternative methodological approach has been to develop indicators of school climate that do not rely on self-report, such as geographic location of the school (i.e., urban vs rural)[21] and the presence of Gay—Straight Alliances in the school.[22] Although this approach has received comparatively less attention in the literature, recent studies have documented associations between these more objective measures of school climate and sexual minority mental health. For example, lesbian and gay adolescents are at lower risk for attempting suicide if they live in counties where a greater proportion of school districts have antibullying policies that include sexual orientation.[23] Although they provide important initial insights, existing studies have been limited by examining only 1 aspect of school climate (e.g., antibullying policies or presence of Gay—Straight Alliances),[16,22,23] relying on nonprobability samples,[16,22] and using a single location,[16,22,23] all of which can restrict generalizability.

We built on this previous research by using data on multiple school climate variables relevant to LGB students that we obtained from the 2010 School Health Profile Survey, compiled by the Centers for Disease Control and Prevention (CDC).[24] We then linked this information on school climate to population-based data of adolescents living in 8 states and cities across the United States. We hypothesized that LGB adolescents living in states and cities with school climates that are more protective of sexual minority youths would be less likely to report past-year suicidal thoughts, plans, and attempts than LGB youths living in areas with less protective school climates.

Methods

The study analyzed a data set that pooled 2005 and 2007 Youth Risk Behavior Surveillance Surveys (YRBSs) from several jurisdictions that included 1 or more measures of sexual orientation. The general approach to pooling the data and analyzing the pooled data set, along with the sexual orientation items and characteristics of the sample by jurisdiction, are described in detail elsewhere in this issue.[25] The current study analyzed data from the 9 jurisdictions that measured sexual orientation identity (i.e., as heterosexual, lesbian or gay, bisexual, or unsure), including Boston, Massachusetts; Chicago, Illinois; Delaware; Maine; Massachusetts; New York City, New York; San Francisco, California; Vermont; and Rhode Island. Because Boston did not have data on the school climate measures (see "Measures"), we dropped it from the analyses. Consequently, we analyzed data from 8 states and cities.

Table 1   Sexual Orientation by 8 US Jurisdictions: Youth Risk Behavior Surveillance Surveys, United States, 2005 and 2007

Jurisdiction	Heterosexual, No. (%)	Lesbian or Gay, No. (%)	Bisexual, No. (%)	Unsure, No. (%)
Chicago, IL	1697 (90.9)	45 (2.3)	66 (3.6)	57 (3.3)
Delaware	4890 (94.2)	56 (1.1)	189 (3.4)	67 (1.3)
Maine	1241 (94.5)	11 (0.8)	36 (3.0)	32 (1.7)
Massachusetts	6095 (93.8)	89 (1.3)	225 (3.2)	117 (1.7)
New York City, NY	15117 (92.0)	222 (1.1)	648 (3.7)	459 (3.1)
Rhode Island	1954 (90.1)	47 (1.9)	123 (5.4)	55 (2.7)
San Francisco, CA	4357 (89.9)	80 (1.5)	176 (3.7)	229 (4.9)
Vermont	16293 (93.3)	185 (0.9)	584 (3.1)	516 (2.7)
Total	51644 (92.8)	735 (1.3)	2047 (3.5)	1532 (2.4)

Table 1 presents the number of respondents by sexual orientation and by the 8 jurisdictions used in the analyses. We focused on sexual orientation identity given that school climates and policies are likely to be most salient to youths who self-identify as LGB.

Measures

Measures for demographic characteristics (gender, age, and race/ethnicity) and sexual orientation were assessed via self-report. The measurement and pooling of sexual orientation and race/ethnicity items are described elsewhere in this issue.[25] We excluded from the analysis those who did not respond to the sexual orientation items. The final sample size was 55,599.

School Climate

We obtained data on school climate from the 2010 School Health Profile (SHP) survey, which is compiled biennially by the CDC. The SHP survey employs probability sampling to create a representative sample of public schools serving students in grades 6 through 12. Of the 8 items used in the current study, 7 were completed by the principal of the school; 1 item was completed by the lead health education teacher. Participation in the survey was voluntary and confidential. Across the 5 states and 3 cities in our pooled sample that were participating in the 2010 SHP, the sample sizes of the principal surveys ranged from 33 to 613, and the response rates ranged from 71% to 86%. Sample sizes and response rates were similar for the lead health education teacher surveys. Further information on the SHP survey is provided elsewhere.[24]

We chose the 8 items from the SHP that assess multiple dimensions of schools that are particularly relevant for LGB students, including the presence of protective environments (e.g., Gay—Straight Alliances and safe spaces) as well as curricula and services that address the unique concerns of sexual minority youths. (Table 2). Importantly, significant variation exists across these 8 jurisdictions. For instance, the lowest percentage of schools that provided curricula or supplementary materials concerning lesbian, gay, bisexual, transgender, and questioning (LGBTQ) students was 31.6%, whereas the highest was 83.7%.

We conducted a factor analysis on the 8 items, using principal axis factoring. A single factor emerged, explaining 81.7% of the variance. Factor loadings ranged from 0.69 to 0.99, and the Cronbach α for the 8 items was 0.97, providing support for a single underlying factor. To create a total score, we standardized each of the 8 items and then averaged and summed them. Scores ranged from -1.059 (Delaware) to 2.015 (San Francisco). A score of 0 indicates an average school climate across the 8 localities. Negative scores indicate a less-than-average school

Table 2   School Climates in 8 US Jurisdictions Affecting Sexual Minority Youths: 2010 School Health Profile Survey

Variable	%, Range (Mean)
Percentage of schools that had a Gay–Straight Alliance or similar club	27.8–90.8 (45.3)
Percentage of schools that provided curricula or supplementary materials that included HIV, STD, or pregnancy prevention information relevant to LGBTQ youths	31.6–83.7 (45.3)
Percentage of schools that identified safe spaces where LGBTQ youths could receive support from staff	39.8–100 (66.24)
Percentage of schools that prohibited harassment based on a student's perceived or actual sexual orientation or gender identity	75.1–100 (89.8)
Percentage of schools that encouraged staff to attend professional development on safe and supportive school environments for all students regardless of sexual orientation or gender identity	48.1–100 (73.29)
Percentage of schools that facilitated access to providers not on school property who had experience in providing health services to LGBTQ youths	44.8–100 (62.4)
Percentage of schools that facilitated access to providers not on school property who had experience in providing social and psychological services to LGBTQ youths	40.8–100 (62.4)
Percentage of schools that provided curricula or supplementary materials that included HIV, STD, or pregnancy prevention information relevant to LGBTQ youths and engaged in all 5 practices regarding LGBTQ youths[a]	8.7–81.6 (25.2)

Note. LGBTQ = lesbian, gay, bisexual, transgender, and questioning; STD = sexually transmitted disease. The 8 study jurisdictions were Chicago, IL; Delaware; Maine; Massachusetts; New York City, NY; San Francisco, CA; Vermont; and Rhode Island.
[a]These 5 practices refer to the responses from the third through seventh items listed in this column.

climate—the lower the score, the worse the school environment for LGBTQ youths; conversely, positive scores indicate a better-than-average school environment—the larger the score, the better the school environment for LGBTQ youths. Collectively, more supportive school climates are those that

1. have a Gay—Straight Alliance and safe spaces for LGBTQ youths,
2. provide curricula on health matters relevant to LGBTQ youths (e.g., HIV),
3. prohibit harassment based on sexual orientation or gender identity,
4. encourage staff to attend trainings on creating supportive environments for LGBTQ youths, and
5. facilitate access to providers off school property that provide health and other services specifically targeted to LGBTQ youths.

Suicide Outcomes

Participants were asked the following question regarding suicidal thoughts: "During the past 12 months, did you ever seriously consider attempting suicide?" Suicide plans were assessed by asking respondents, "During the past 12 months, did you make a plan about how you would attempt suicide?" Response options for suicide thoughts and plans were dichotomous (yes or no). Suicide attempts were assessed via 1 item: "During the past 12 months, how many times did you actually attempt suicide?" Given the nonnormal distribution of this variable, we coded the responses dichotomously. The suicidal thought ($\kappa = 83.8$), plan ($\kappa = 77.0$), and attempt ($\kappa = 76.4$) variables have demonstrated excellent test–retest reliability.[26] Table 3 depicts the prevalence of suicide outcomes by sexual orientation group.

Table 3 Prevalence of Suicide Outcomes by Sexual Orientation Group and Other Demographic Variables: Youth Risk Behavior Surveillance Surveys, United States, 2005 and 2007

Variable	Suicide Thoughts, % (95% CI)	Suicide Plan, % (95% CI)	Suicide Attempt, % (95% CI)
Total sample	13.2 (12.7, 13.6)	11.2 (10.9, 11.6)	7.8 (7.4, 8.2)
Sexual orientation			
Heterosexual	11.6 (11.2, 12.0)	9.9 (9.5, 10.2)	6.5 (6.1, 6.9)
Lesbian or gay	29.7 (25.1, 34.8)	26.6 (22.7, 30.9)	24.7 (20.4, 29.4)
Bisexual	39.6 (36.8, 42.5)	32.2 (29.5, 34.9)	28.8 (26.1, 31.6)
Not sure	25.3 (22.2, 28.6)	22.2 (19.0, 25.7)	17.3 (14.7, 20.2)
Race/ethnicity			
White	12.3 (11.5, 13.2)	10.2 (9.7, 10.8)	5.4 (5.0, 5.9)
African American	11.7 (11.0, 12.5)	10.8 (10.0, 11.6)	8.0 (7.3, 8.9)
Hispanic	13.2 (12.2, 14.2)	10.9 (10.1, 11.8)	9.9 (9.0, 10.8)
Asian	13.0 (11.8, 14.3)	11.5 (10.2, 12.9)	6.7 (5.6, 8.0)
Other	17.0 (15.9, 18.0)	14.6 (13.6, 15.6)	11.3 (10.3, 12.4)
Gender			
Male	9.2 (8.7, 9.7)	8.6 (8.2, 9.1)	5.8 (5.3, 6.3)
Female	16.8 (16.1, 17.5)	13.5 (13.0, 14.2)	9.5 (8.9, 10.1)
Age, y			
13	20.4 (12.3, 31.8)	10.0 (8.2, 12.1)	6.8 (5.4, 8.5)
14	14.4 (13.1, 15.8)	12.0 (11.0, 12.9)	8.6 (7.7, 9.7)
15	14.1 (13.3, 14.9)	11.6 (10.8, 12.3)	8.5 (7.7, 9.4)
16	12.9 (12.1, 13.8)	11.4 (10.7, 12.2)	7.3 (6.7, 8.0)
17	11.8 (11.0, 12.7)	10.2 (9.5, 11.0)	6.6 (5.9, 7.4)
18	13.2 (12.0, 14.5)	11.1 (10.0, 12.3)	8.7 (7.7, 9.7)

Note. CI = confidence interval. Numbers are unweighted.

Protective School Climates and Reduced Risk for Suicide Ideation in Sexual Minority Youths by Mark L. Hatzenbuehler et al.

193

Covariates

To minimize spurious contextual influences on our results, we controlled for 2 covariates: (1) density of same-sex couples (per 1000) living in the cities or states (mean = 9.55; SD = 6.54; range = 4.03–30.25) and (2) median household income (mean = $61 604.03; SD = $11 737.11; range = $45 775.00–$90 931.41). We obtained data for both covariates from the 2010 US Census. Preliminary analyses indicated that these 2 variables were strongly associated with the school climate variable (for density of same-sex couples, $r = 0.75$; $P < .01$; for median household income, $r = 0.50$; $P = .06$), indicating the importance of their inclusion as potential confounders of the relationship between school climate and suicide outcomes.

Statistical Analysis

We conducted descriptive analyses for creating the school climate variable using SPSS versions 20 and 21 (SPSS Inc, Chicago, IL). Furthermore, we used the SPSS (version 21) Complex Samples software package to conduct descriptive analyses on prevalence of sexual orientation and suicide outcomes (Tables 1 and 3) to account for the complex sample design of the YRBS. We fit models examining the relationship between school climate and suicide outcomes using the multilevel software HLM version 7 (Scientific Software International, Lincolnwood, IL). Hierarchical linear modeling accounted for the complex sampling design of the pooled YRBS data set by adjusting the relative weights and altering the effective sample size using design effects calculated for each jurisdiction. The approach to calculating design effects and accounting for the clustering of the data are described in detail elsewhere in this issue.[25]

Hierarchical linear modeling analyses proceeded in several steps. First, we examined an unconditional model to determine whether there were significant between-group (i.e., between-jurisdiction) differences in the suicide outcomes. Second, we added level 1 covariates, including sexual orientation (dummy coded gay or lesbian, bisexual, and not sure, with heterosexual as the reference group), gender (male or female), race/ethnicity (dummy coded African American, Hispanic, Asian, and other, with White as the reference group), and age (continuous). Third, we added level 2 variables, including school climate and the 2 covariates (density of same-sex couples and median household income). In the final model, we allowed the slopes for sexual orientation to vary (i.e., we treated them as a random effect), and we included school climate as a predictor of the variance of the sexual orientation slopes. This approach, similar to testing a cross-level interaction between school climate and sexual orientation, permitted an evaluation of the primary research question: does school climate modify the relationship between sexual orientation and suicidal thoughts, plans, and attempts? We ran analyses separately for the 3 suicide outcomes (thoughts, plans, and attempts).

Given the small amount of missing data on covariates (age: 0.5%; gender: 0.8%; race: 2.6%), we handled missing data for covariates using listwise deletion. Nonrandom missing data were also present for suicidal thoughts, as Vermont did not include that survey item. We therefore excluded Vermont from the suicidal thoughts analysis but included it for the analysis of suicidal plans and attempts. Statistical significance was set at $P < .05$.

Results

In the unconditional model, the variance components (VCs) indicated that there was significant variation across states and cities in suicidal thoughts (VC = 0.02; $\chi^2 = 133.17$; $P < .001$), plans (VC = 0.03; $\chi^2 = 177.81$; $P < .001$), and attempts (VC = 0.07; $\chi^2 = 266.15$; $P < .001$), supporting the inclusion of additional variables to explain between-group variance in these outcomes.

Suicidal Thoughts

In the first model, we added all level 1 sociodemographic covariates to the unconditional model (Table 4). Compared with their heterosexual peers, lesbian and gay youths (odds ratio [OR] = 3.28; 95% confidence interval [CI] = 2.40, 4.47), bisexual youths (OR = 4.52; 95% CI = 3.79, 5.40), and youths who were unsure of their sexual orientation (OR = 2.08; 95% CI = 1.62, 2.65) were significantly more likely to report suicidal thoughts in the past year. Male gender was significantly associated with reduced odds of reporting suicidal thoughts (OR = 0.54; 95% CI = 0.49, 0.60), whereas "other" race/ethnicity was significantly associated with increased odds of suicidal thoughts (OR = 1.23; 95% CI = 1.01, 1.42).

In the second model, we entered the level 2 variables (school climate, density of same-sex couples, and median household income) as predictors of suicidal thoughts. When we controlled for level 1 variables, none of the level 2 variables were associated with the intercept for suicidal thoughts (i.e., the average student in the sample).

In the third and final model, we examined cross-level interactions between the slopes of sexual orientation and school climate. This model indicated that lesbian and gay youths (OR = 0.68; 95% CI = 0.47, 0.99) and bisexual youths (OR = 0.81; 95% CI = 0.66, 0.99) living in jurisdictions with more protective school climates were significantly less likely to report suicidal thoughts than lesbian and gay adolescents living in jurisdictions with less supportive school climates, with control for sociodemographics and the level 2 covariates. Results were not statistically significant for the unsure group (OR = 0.83; 95% CI = 0.64, 1.09).

Figure 1 depicts the results for suicidal ideation, showing an incremental reduction in the odds of reporting suicidal thoughts

Table 4 Associations Between School Climate and Suicidality: Youth Risk Behavior Surveillance Surveys, United States, 2005 and 2007

Variable	Suicidal Thoughts, OR (95% CI)			Suicide Plan, OR (95% CI)			Suicide Attempt, OR (95% CI)		
	Model 1	Model 2	Model 3	Model 1	Model 2	Model 3	Model 1	Model 2	Model 3
Intercept	0.17 (0.15, 0.19)	0.17 (0.14, 0.19)	0.16 (0.14, 0.19)	0.13 (0.11, 0.15)	0.13 (0.11, 0.14)	0.13 (0.11, 0.14)	0.06 (0.05, 0.07)	0.06 (0.05, 0.07)	0.06 (0.05, 0.07)
				Level 1 covariates					
Sexual orientation									
Heterosexual (Ref)	1.00	1.00	1.00	1.00	1.00	1.00	1.00	1.00	1.00
Lesbian or gay	3.28 (2.40, 4.47)	3.27 (2.39, 4.46)	3.50 (2.31, 5.30)	2.98 (2.20, 4.03)	2.97 (2.20, 4.03)	3.13 (2.13, 4.60)	3.87 (2.67, 5.63)	3.88 (2.67, 5.65)	4.12 (2.50, 6.80)
Bisexual	4.52 (3.79, 5.40)	4.52 (3.78, 5.39)	4.77 (3.77, 6.04)	4.37 (3.69, 5.16)	4.36 (3.69, 5.15)	4.46 (3.58, 5.55)	5.72 (4.72, 6.94)	5.71 (4.71, 6.93)	6.07 (4.64, 7.95)
Not sure	2.08 (1.62, 2.65)	2.07 (1.62, 2.65)	2.35 (1.64, 3.35)	2.10 (1.67, 2.65)	2.09 (1.66, 2.64)	2.32 (1.69, 3.19)	2.44 (1.82, 3.27)	2.43 (1.82, 3.26)	2.66 (1.78, 3.99)
Race/ethnicity									
White (Ref)	1.00	1.00	1.00	1.00	1.00	1.00	1.00	1.00	1.00
African American	0.89 (0.78, 1.02)	0.89 (0.77, 1.02)	0.89 (0.77, 1.02)	0.93 (0.89, 1.07)	0.93 (0.81, 1.08)	0.93 (0.80, 1.08)	1.45 (1.21, 1.73)	1.39 (1.16, 1.67)	1.42 (1.8, 1.70)
Hispanic	1.01 (0.87, 1.17)	1.01 (0.87, 1.17)	1.00 (0.86, 1.16)	1.01 (0.87, 1.19)	1.01 (0.87, 1.18)	1.01 (0.86, 1.18)	1.78 (1.48, 2.13)	1.70 (1.41, 2.05)	1.71 (1.42, 2.07)
Asian	1.04 (0.90, 1.22)	1.03 (0.87, 1.22)	1.03 (0.87, 1.22)	1.11 (0.95, 1.31)	1.09 (0.92, 1.29)	1.08 (0.91, 1.28)	1.24 (1.02, 1.52)	1.18 (0.94, 1.49)	1.19 (0.94, 1.50)
Other	1.23 (1.01, 1.42)	1.22 (1.06, 1.41)	1.22 (1.05, 1.41)	1.42 (1.23, 1.63)	1.41 (1.23, 1.63)	1.40 (1.22, 1.62)	1.81 (1.51, 2.16)	1.75 (1.46, 2.10)	1.76 (1.46, 2.11)
Gender									
Female (Ref)	1.00	1.00	1.00	1.00	1.00	1.00	1.00	1.00	1.00
Male	0.54 (0.49, 0.60)	0.54 (0.49, 0.60)	0.54 (0.49, 0.60)	0.67 (0.61, 0.74)	0.67 (0.61, 0.74)	0.67 (0.61, 0.74)	0.65 (0.58, 0.75)	0.66 (0.58, 0.75)	0.66 (0.58, 0.75)
Age	0.96 (0.93, 1.00)	0.96 (0.93, 1.00)	0.96 (0.93, 1.00)	0.97 (0.93, 1.00)	0.97 (0.93, 1.01)	0.97 (0.93, 1.01)	0.94 (0.90, 0.99)	0.94 (0.90, 0.99)	0.94 (0.90, 0.99)
				Level 2 covariates					
School climate	...	1.05 (0.88, 1.26)	1.07 (0.89, 1.30)	...	1.09 (0.94, 1.27)	1.13 (0.96 1.33)	...	1.05 (0.89, 1.25)	1.08 (0.89, 1.30)
Same-sex couples	...	0.98 (0.95, 1.02)	0.98 (0.95, 1.02)	...	1.00 (0.98, 1.03)	1.01 (0.98, 1.03)	...	0.98 (0.96, 1.01)	0.98 (0.95, 1.01)
Median household income	...	1.00 (1.00, 1.00)	1.00 (1.00, 1.00)	...	0.99 (1.00, 1.00)	0.99 (1.00, 1.00)	...	1.00 (1.00, 1.00)	1.00 (1.00, 1.00)
				Cross-level interactions					
Lesbian or gay × school climate	...	...	0.68 (0.47, 0.99)	...	...	0.73 (0.51, 1.06)	...	...	0.80 (0.49, 1.30)
Bisexual × school climate	...	...	0.81 (0.66, 0.99)	...	...	0.82 (0.66, 1.02)	...	...	0.80 (0.61, 1.05)
Not sure × school climate	...	...	0.83 (0.64, 1.09)	...	...	0.80 (0.62, 1.02)	...	...	0.80 (0.57, 1.12)

Note. CI = confidence interval; OR = odds ratio.

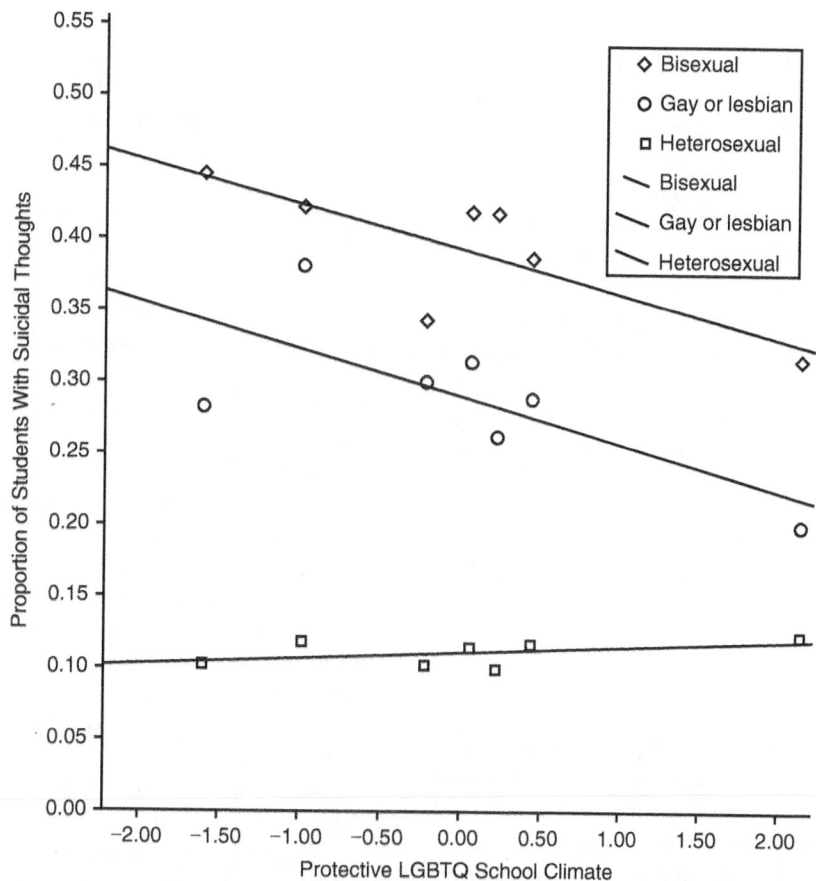

LGBTQ = lesbian, gay, bisexual, transgender, and questioning. The x-axis depicts protective school climates for sexual minority youths. Values represent standardized z scores for the 8 items from the School Health Profile Survey. A score of 0 indicates an average school climate across the 8 localities. Negative scores indicate school climates that are less protective for LGBTQ youths; conversely, positive scores indicate more protective school climates for LGBTQ youths. The figure depicts both raw values as well as the regression lines fit by sexual orientation groups.

Figure 1 Relationship between suicidal thoughts and protective school climates, by sexual orientation status: Youth Risk Behavior Surveillance Surveys, United States, 2005 and 2007.

(y-axis) among lesbian or gay and bisexual youths relative to increasing protectiveness of school climates (x-axis). As can also be seen in Figure 1, this pattern was not observed among heterosexual youths, whose odds of suicidal thoughts did not differ across the protectiveness of school climates. Notably, in jurisdictions with the highest score on the school climate measure (depicted on the far right side of the x-axis in Figure 1), sexual orientation disparities in suicidal thoughts were sharply reduced, particularly for the lesbian and gay adolescents.

Suicide Plans

Lesbian and gay youths (OR = 2.98; 95% CI = 2.20, 4.03), bisexual youths (OR = 4.37; 95% CI = 3.69, 5.16), and youths who were unsure of their sexual orientation (OR = 2.10; 95% CI = 1.67, 2.65) were significantly more likely than heterosexual youths to report a suicide plan in the past 12 months. (model 1, Table 4). Male gender was significantly associated

with reduced odds of reporting a suicide plan (OR = 0.67; 95% CI = 0.61, 0.74), whereas "other" race/ethnicity was significantly associated with increased odds of reporting a suicide plan (OR = 1.42; 95% CI = 1.23, 1.63). None of the level 2 variables were associated with the intercept for suicide plan in the full sample (model 2).

In the final model (model 3), lesbian and gay youths (OR = 0.73; 95% CI = 0.51, 1.06; P =.083), bisexual youths (OR = 0.82; 95% CI = 0.66, 1.02; P = .066), and youths unsure of their sexual orientation (OR = 0.80; 95% CI = 0.62, 1.02; P = .067) who were living in jurisdictions with more protective school climates were less likely to report a suicide plan than sexual minority adolescents living in jurisdictions with less supportive school climates. Although the magnitude and direction of these associations were nearly identical to those of suicidal thoughts, the results for suicide plan did not achieve statistical significance at the .05 level.

Suicide Attempts

Lesbian and gay youths (OR = 3.87; 95% CI = 2.67, 5.63), bisexual youths (OR = 5.72; 95% CI = 4.72, 6.94), and youths unsure of their sexual orientation (OR = 2.44; 95% CI = 1.82, 3.27) were more likely to report a past-year suicide attempt (model 1, Table 4). Each racial/ethnic group was significantly more likely than Whites to report a suicide attempt in the past year; male gender and older age were both significantly associated with decreased odds of reporting a past-year suicide attempt. None of the level 2 variables were associated with the intercept for suicide attempts in the full sample (model 2). Finally, results for the cross-level interaction (model 3) indicated that sexual minority youths were less likely to report a suicide attempt if they lived in jurisdictions with more supportive climates. Although the magnitude and direction of these associations were similar to those of suicide thoughts, none reached statistical significance at the .05 level (gay and lesbian youths: $P = .298$; bisexual youths: $P = .09$; unsure youths: $P = .157$).

Discussion

The 2011 report on LGBT health disparities from the Institute of Medicine noted the need for research on social ecological determinants of adverse health outcomes in this population and named social influences on the lives of LGBT people as 1 of 5 priority research areas for advancing the field.[27] With the current study, we address this research priority by focusing on school climate as a key social developmental context for sexual minority adolescents. We evaluate the extent to which the prevalence of suicide ideation, plans, and attempts among LGB youths are reduced in regions with school climates that protect sexual minority students.

Our results demonstrate that LGB youths living in states and cities with more protective school climates were significantly less likely to report past-year suicidal thoughts than LGB youths living in states and cities with less protective school climates. Associations between positive school climates and reduced risk for suicidal thoughts remained significant after we controlled for potential confounders. We documented that these effects were specific to LGB adolescents; LGB supportive school climates were not associated with suicidal thoughts among heterosexual youths. Importantly, we found that higher levels of protectiveness of school climates for sexual minority students substantially reduced sexual orientation disparities in suicidal thoughts. The magnitude and direction of the results were similar for suicide plans and attempts, but these outcomes did not reach statistical significance at the .05 level.

Limitations

This study has several limitations. Our data on school climate came from the 2010 SHP survey, the first year for which data on LGBTQ school climates were available, whereas the outcome data are from 2005 to 2007, the most recently available data to have been pooled for examination of sexual orientation disparities. Thus, we take the 2010 climate data to be a good proxy of the school climate in 2005 through 2007. The assumption is based on the idea that schools are more likely to progress gradually in improving school climate, rather than shifting drastically over years. If that is so, then our measure correctly captures variability among the localities even if it is not perfectly accurate with regard to how the specific items that comprise the measure would have been rated in 2005 through 2007. To assess the assumption of continuity, we selected 2 items (percentage of schools that had a safe-passage-to-school program and percentage of schools that had a program to prevent bullying) from the SHP survey principal report, from which the 8 items in our scale were taken. Unlike the items that comprise our LGBTQ school climate scale, these 2 items had been assessed over a longer period (2004–2010) in the same 8 jurisdictions as our sample. Although these 2 items measure school safety and antibullying contexts aimed at all students, we selected them because we believe they are particularly relevant for the LGB students in our sample and thus may be used to approximate the unmeasured LGBTQ school climate variables in 2005 through 2007. Consistent with our assumption, measures of these 2 items were consistent and positively correlated between 2004 and 2006 and between 2006 and 2010 (r's for safe passage were 0.9 and 0.8, respectively, and r's for bullying prevention were 0.7 and 0.4, respectively). This indicates that each of the earlier measures provided a good approximation of the later measure. This in turn suggests that despite the discrepancy in time between exposure and outcome measures, our school climate construct properly estimated the school climate in 2005 through 2007, when outcome measures were collected. To the extent that this assumption is wrong, and the 2010 measure is not a good proxy for the 2005–2007 climate, our analyses would have suffered from the incorporation of measurement error. Introducing measurement error, which is random, would have reduced our ability to find significant findings rather than bias our results in the hypothesized direction (that is, leading us to conclude that positive school climate is protective when in fact it is not). Thus, although questions remain about the accuracy of the later measure as a proxy for earlier years, which we cannot answer, we are satisfied that inaccuracy, to the extent that it exists, has not led us to report our positive findings. (On the other hand, it is plausible that measurement error would lead to null findings regarding suicide plan and attempt.)

An additional limitation is that no psychometric properties of the LGBTQ school climate items in the 2010 SHP exist. The school climate measure relies on principals' and teachers' reports; to the extent that such results are unreliable, the validity and reliability of the measure may be compromised.

However, we are confident that principals and teachers are familiar with school, district, and state policies, which they are charged with enforcing, suggesting that reporting biases are likely to be minimal. Another limitation of the school climate variable is that it is aggregated to the city and state level and may not represent the climate for the individual school that the respondent attended. However, both this and the reliance on principals' and teachers' observations would introduce random error into the school climate variable because it is unlikely that such misclassification will be systematically related to the proportion of students with suicidal thoughts, plans, and attempts. Thus, these limitations would bias results toward the null, suggesting that the results are conservative estimates of the association between school climates and suicidal thoughts among sexual minority youths.

We take the selected items of school climate to represent greater underlying concern for the well-being of LGBTQ students on the part of school authorities. Such concern may have been manifested in other measures that generally improve protections to LGBTQ students in the localities. Thus, the items that were available to us were used as a proxy to the more general construct of affirmative school climate. We attempted to create a global measure that captures the extent to which a particular jurisdiction has a positive LGBTQ school climate. Because the specific items are to be interpreted as representing a more general construct, they do not comprise a simple index. The cost of this approach is that the measure is not intuitively interpretable.

Although we obtained data on school climates from 8 states and cities, which is an improvement over existing studies,[16,22,23] the locales for which data were available represent a restricted range for this variable. For example, across the 49 states and 19 cities that participated in the 2010 SHP survey, the range for the variable "provides curricula or supplementary materials that include HIV, STD, or pregnancy prevention information relevant to LGBTQ youth" was 6.1% to 100.0%, whereas for the 8 jurisdictions in the current study, it was only 31.6% to 83.7%. Related to this, the regions for which data were available to us were more liberal socially and they had more protective social climates. The restricted range most likely is related to an underestimate of the effect of school climates on suicide risk. Consequently, our results should be interpreted as providing a conservative estimate of the true size of the effect of school climate on suicidal thoughts in sexual minority adolescents.

Additionally, external validity of the study may be limited because this selective data set is not generalizable to the regions not included in the study. Future studies would benefit from greater diversity in the jurisdictions sampled to evaluate the magnitude of the effects and the generalizability of the results across different social milieu. Further limiting generalization

is that although the YRBS is a representative sample of youths in public schools, it excludes youths in private and parochial schools, as well as runaway and homeless youths. Also, the YRBS does not include measures of transgender identity or gender nonconformity, thereby preventing us from evaluating the effect of LGBTQ supportive environments on risk of suicide outcomes among transgender adolescents.

Finally, despite the large sample size, the outcomes (especially suicide attempts) were relatively rare. This restricted our statistical power to examine effect modification by certain characteristics (e.g., gender, race/ethnicity), which may have masked important subgroup differences. Additionally, as in all cross-sectional studies, we infer about but cannot test causal relationships between school climate and suicidal thoughts, plans, and attempts.

Strengths

The current study has several methodological strengths, including the use of a representative sample of public school youths with a large enough sample size to permit disaggregation of sexual orientation groups. In addition, the study sample came from 8 states and cities across the United States, increasing the generalizability of the findings. Finally, previous studies have identified schools as 1 social context that can have significant consequences for the mental health of sexual minority students.[4,13–16,19,22] With some notable exceptions,[21,23] however, existing work has tended to use self-report measures of sexual minority youths' perceptions of their school environments.[17–19] These measures capture important appraisal processes, but they are measured with the same method as the outcome (i.e., self-report), which may lead to biased estimates of the relationship between school climate and mental health.[20] The current study overcame many of these limitations by using ecological measures of the exposure (i.e., school climates and policies) that did not rely on self-report and therefore were not confounded with the outcome of interest.

Conclusions

The results of this study should be assessed within the context of existing knowledge. Our study expands on the contributions from previous research on social determinants of sexual minority health that demonstrate the positive impact of supportive interventions on LGB health and well-being.[7,9,10,28,29] The findings point to potential targets for public health interventions aimed at reducing sexual orientation disparities in suicide risk. In particular, comprehensive suicide prevention and interventions for sexual minority adolescents should address not only individual-level[3,4] and family-level[14,30,31] factors but also broader social-contextual influences, including school climate.

Acknowledgments

This project was supported by grants from the Eunice Kennedy Shriver National Institute of Child Health and Human Development (R21 HD051178) and the National Institute of Drug Abuse (to M. L. H.; K01 DA032558), and by the IMPACT LGBT Health and Development Program at Northwestern University.

Assistance from the Centers for Disease Control and Prevention (CDC) Division of Adolescent and School Health and the work of the state and local health and education departments who conduct the Youth Risk Behavior Surveillance Survey made the project possible.

Note. The contents of this article are solely the responsibility of the authors and do not necessarily represent the official views of the National Institutes of Health, the CDC, or any agencies involved in collecting the data.

Human Participant Protection

Protocol approval was not necessary because deidentified data were obtained from secondary sources. Data use agreements were obtained from the Vermont and Rhode Island departments of health.

References

1. Centers for Disease Control and Prevention, National Center for Injury Prevention and Control. Web-based Injury Statistics Query and Reporting System (WISQARS). Available at: http://www.cdc.gov/ncipc/wisqars. Accessed October 27, 2013.
2. Gould MS, Greenberg T, Velting DM, Shaffer D. Youth suicide risk and preventive interventions: a review of the past 10 years. *J Am Acad Child-Adolesc Psychiatry.* 2003;42(4):386–405.
3. Garofalo R, Wolf RC, Wissow LS, Woods ER, Goodman E. Sexual orientation and risk of suicide attempts among a representative sample of youth. *Arch Pediatr Adolesc Med.* 1999;153(5):487–493.
4. Russell ST, Joyner K. Adolescent sexual orientation and suicide risk: evidence from a national study. *Am J Public Health.* 2001;91(8):1276–1281.
5. Marshal MP, Dietz LJ, Friedman MS, et al. Suicidality and depression disparities between sexual minority and heterosexual youth: a meta-analytic review. *J Adolesc Health.* 2011;49(2):115–123.
6. Haas AP, Eliason M, Mays VM, et al. Suicide and suicide risk in lesbian, gay, bisexual, and transgender populations: review and recommendations. *J Homosex.* 2011;58(1):10–51.
7. Meyer IH. Prejudice, social stress, and mental health in lesbian, gay, and bisexual populations: conceptual issues and research evidence. *Psychol Bull.* 2003;129(5): 674–697.
8. Link BG, Phelan JC. Conceptualizing stigma. *Annu Rev Sociol.* 2001;27:363–385.
9. Hatzenbuehler ML, Keyes KM, Hasin DS. State-level policies and psychiatric morbidity in lesbian, gay, and bisexual populations. *Am J Public Health.* 2009;99(12):2275–2281.
10. Hatzenbuehler ML, McLaughlin KA, Keyes KM, Hasin DS. The impact of institutional discrimination on psychiatric disorders in lesbian, gay, and bisexual populations: a prospective study. *Am J Public Health.* 2010;100(3):452–459.
11. Rostosky SS, Riggle ED, Horne SG, Denton FN, Huellemeier JD. Lesbian, gay, and bisexual individuals' psychological reactions to amendments denying access to civil marriage. *Am J Orthopsychiatry.* 2010;80(3): 302–310.
12. Eccles JS, Roeser RW. School and community influences on human development. In: Bornstein MH, Lamb ME, eds. *Developmental Science: An Advanced Textbook.* 6th ed. New York, NY: Psychology Press; 2011:571–643.
13. Russell ST, Muraco A, Subramaniam A, Laub C. Youth empowerment and high school gay-straight alliances. *J Youth Adolesc.* 2009;38(7):891–903.
14. Russell ST, Ryan C, Toomey RB, Diaz RM, Sanchez J. Lesbian, gay, bisexual, and transgender adolescent school victimization: implications for young adult health and adjustment. *J Sch Health.* 2011;81(5):223–230.
15. Toomey RB, Ryan C, Diaz RM, Card NA, Russell ST. Gender-nonconforming lesbian, gay, bisexual, and trans-gender youth: school victimization and young adult psychosocial adjustment. *Dev Psychol.* 2010;46(6): 1580–1589.
16. Toomey RB, Ryan C, Diaz RM, Russell ST. High school gay-straight alliances (GSAs) and young adult well-being: an examination of GSA presence, participation, and perceived effectiveness. *Appl Dev Sci.* 2011;15(4):175–185.
17. Birkett M, Espelage DL, Koenig B. LGB and questioning students in schools: the moderating effects of homophobic bullying and school climate on negative outcomes. *J Youth Adolesc.* 2009;38(7):989–1000.
18. Eisenberg ME, Resnick MD. Suicidality among gay, lesbian and bisexual youth: the role of protective factors. *J Adolesc Health.* 2006;39(5):662–668.
19. McGuire JK, Anderson CR, Toomey RB, Russell ST. School climate for transgender youth: a mixed method investigation of student experiences and school responses. *J Youth Adolesc.* 2010;39(10):1175–1188.
20. Diez Roux AV. Neighborhoods and health: where are we and where do we go from here? *Rev Epidemiol Sante Publique.* 2007;55(1):13–21.
21. Kosciw JG, Greytak EA, Diaz EM. Who, what, where, when, and why: demographic and ecological factors contributing to hostile school climate for lesbian, gay, bisexual, and transgender youth. *J Youth Adolesc.* 2009;38(7):976–988.
22. Walls NE, Freedenthal S, Wisneski H. Suicidal ideation and attempts among sexual minority youths receiving social services. *Soc Work.* 2008;53(1):21–29.
23. Hatzenbuehler ML, Keyes KM. Inclusive anti-bullying policies reduce suicide attempts in lesbian and gay youth. *J Adolesc Health.* 2013; 53(1 suppl):S21–S26.
24. Brener ND, Demissie Z, Foti K, et al. *School Health Profiles 2010: Characteristics of Health Programs Among Secondary Schools in Selected US Cities.* Atlanta, GA: Centers for Disease Control and Prevention; 2011.

25. Mustanski B, Van Wagenen A, Birkett M, Eyster S, Corliss HL. Identifying sexual orientation health disparities in adolescents: analysis of pooled data from the Youth Risk Behavior Survey, 2005 and 2007. *Am J Public Health.* 2014;104(2):211–217.

26. Brener ND, Collins JL, Kann L, Warren CW, Williams BI. Reliability of the youth risk behavior survey questionnaire. *Am J Epidemiol.* 1995;141(6):575–580.

27. National Academy of Sciences for the Institute of Medicine. *The Health of Lesbian, Gay, Bisexual and Transgender People: Building a Foundation for Better Understanding.* Washington, DC: National Academies Press; 2011.

28. Hatzenbuehler ML. The social environment and suicide attempts in lesbian, gay, and bisexual youth. *Pediatrics.* 2011;127(5):896–903.

29. Hatzenbuehler ML, O'Cleirigh C, Grasso C, Mayer K, Safren S, Bradford J. Effect of same-sex marriage laws on health care use and expenditures in sexual minority men: a quasi-natural experiment. *Am J Public Health.* 2012;102(2):285–291.

30. Diamond GM, Diamond GS, Levy S, Closs C, Ladipo T, Siqueland L. Attachment-based family therapy for suicidal lesbian, gay, and bisexual adolescents: a treatment development study and open trial with preliminary findings. *Psychotherapy.* 2012;49(1):62–71.

31. Ryan C, Huebner D, Diaz RM, Sanchez J. Family rejection as a predictor of negative health outcomes in white and Latino lesbian, gay, and bisexual young adults. *Pediatrics.* 2009;123(1):346–352.

Critical Thinking

1. Looking at the results section of this article, did you find data that surprised you? Explain your answer.

2. Think back to your own high school experience and school climate. Would you consider that school to be a protective school? What did educators do to be protective? Or what experiences led you to believe they were not protective?

3. Suggest reasons why schools may not be protective of all students? Include all the barriers you know of or can imagine.

Internet References

GLSEN: Gay, Lesbian and Straight Education Network
http://www.glsen.org

LGTB Youth Organizations
http://brandonshire.com/lgbt-youth-organizations

Safe Schools
http://www.safeschoolscoalition.org

Mark L. Hatzenbuehler is with the Department of Socio-medical Sciences, Mailman School of Public Health, Columbia University, New York, NY. Michelle Birkett is with the Feinberg School of Medicine, Northwestern University, Chicago, IL. Aimee Van Wagenen is with the Center for Population Research in LGBT Health, Fenway Institute, Boston, MA. Ilan H. Meyer is with the Williams Institute, School of Law, University of California, Los Angeles.

M. L. Hatzenbuehler initiated the study idea, led the research and writing, and supervised the data analysis. M. Birkett conducted the statistical analyses. A. Van Wagenen obtained the data from the SHP Survey. I. H. Meyer supervised the data analyses. All authors contributed original ideas and edited drafts of the article.

Unit 6

UNIT

Prepared by: Elizabeth Schroeder, EdD, MSW,
Elizabeth Schroeder Consulting

Sexual Health and Well-Being

Volumes of Annual Editions could be devoted to the area of Sexual Health and Well-Being. Health, including sexual health, used to be a taboo subject that now receives a significant amount of attention in the mainstream media. Over the past two decades, the general public's awareness of, and interest and involvement in, their own healthcare has dramatically increased. We want to stay healthy and live longer, and we know that to do so, we must learn more about our bodies, including how to prevent problems, recognize danger signs, and find the most effective treatments. By the same token, if we want to stay sexually fit—from robust youth through a healthy, happy old age—we must be knowledgeable about sexual healthcare. This is one of the most important and fundamental topics covered in any human sexuality course. The urgency of this topic is demonstrated by the fact that this is one area of the sexuality curriculum in which all adult students seem highly interested.

What changed? How did we go from a culture that did not allow ads relating to contraceptive methods or mentions of anything related to sexuality (aside from the wildly sexist media that continues to hypersexualize young women), to where we are today? There are several possibilities. One has to do with the advent of HIV and AIDS in the 1980s. Its discovery and the accompanying protests relating to testing and treatment options became a part of mainstream news coverage. There was no choice but to talk about it, not only on the news but also in the classroom.

Another has to do with proactive lobbying by big businesses to ensure they could advertise their products. TV commercials for Viagra and other products created to manage erectile dysfunction in men are on in the middle of the afternoon; medications to treat herpes and HPV are advertised, and far more. Although the motivation behind these may have been the desire by these companies to market their products and earn more money, the accompanying benefit has been more of a public health one: a greater awareness among the general public that these issues exist, and that we must proactively take better care of our sexual health as we are taking care of our general health.

Healthy sexuality is multifaceted and influenced by biological, psychological, and social factors. The World Health Organization

(WHO) defines sexual health as: "a state of physical, emotional, mental and social well-being in relation to sexuality; it is not merely the absence of disease, dysfunction, or infirmity. Sexual health requires a positive and respectful approach to sexuality and sexual relationships, as well as the possibility of having pleasurable and safe sexual experiences, free of coercion, discrimination, and violence. For sexual health to be attained and maintained, the sexual rights of all persons must be respected, protected, and fulfilled."

Many people seem to think of sexual health as simply "the absence of disease," but as the WHO definition indicates, it is so much more than that. Simply not having a sexually transmitted infection or a sexual dysfunction is not enough. Cognitive, behavioral, and emotional components are important as well. The meanings given to sexual behaviors and interactions will greatly influence the ways in which sexuality is experienced. Anxiety, fear, and shame are hardly conducive to healthy sexuality.

The WHO definition makes mention of variables such as discrimination, violence, and sexual rights. Institutionalized discrimination and culturally validated violence are profoundly social in nature. The notion of sexual rights is hardly universal. Social and cultural processes play an important role in the sexual health of everyday people. We are simultaneously biological, psychological, and social beings. The area of sexual health is, in this way, no different from many other topics relating to sexuality.

The above discussion is in no way intended to minimize the important and perhaps central role that disease (or lack thereof) plays in sexual health. Yet even with physical disease states, there are often behavioral, psychological, and sociocultural components that must be understood. There are many potential threats to our sexual health and well-being. Sexual or reproductive cancers, such as breast cancer, cervical cancer, ovarian cancer, male breast cancer, penile cancer, and testicular cancer, among many others, threaten the health of affected people around the world. In industrialized nations, many treatment options exist. Often, people in developing countries simply have no access to life-saving treatments that so many in Western countries take for granted. Some strains of the human papilloma virus (HPV), an extremely common infection, can lead to cancers. In addition to cancer, there are other life-threatening infections that can be sexually transmitted. Untreated syphilis can lead to death, although with the common use of antibiotics, this has become quite uncommon in Western countries. However, there are still many thousands of people who die of syphilis infection throughout the world every year. HPV has killed over 25 million people worldwide over the past three decades.

Over the years, HIV has certainly received much attention in the media. The fear of HIV has lessened somewhat since the 1980s, which has had positive and negative consequences. The main positive factor is the decrease in stigmatization for many people with HIV (although it still exists); the negative is that some people who are at high risk of infection through unprotected sexual behaviors have developed "HIV apathy" because HIV disease has gone from being almost always fatal to a long-term chronic infection—at least for those who have access to effective antiretroviral medications and are highly compliant with their drug regimens. Sexuality educators continue to work to find ways to fight the apathy among some people who are engaging in the highest risk sexual behaviors, as well as the sense many others have that they are simply not susceptible to HIV—and that if they did get it, it would not be a big deal.

Because of the behavioral and social dimensions of sexually transmitted infections, educators and scientists have long been interested in understanding high-risk behaviors and situations. We have learned much from sexual risk-taking behavior research. Researchers have found that, just as in other health-related fields, knowing about the risks is simply not enough. Other components that may influence behavior include things like worry and perceptions of individual risk. Those who worry about becoming infected with an STI are more likely to be cautious in their behaviors. Also, those who perceive themselves to be potentially at risk may be less likely to engage in risky behaviors. Again, knowledge alone is not enough. On the other hand, too much worry can be paralyzing. This is the kind of research science that has immediate application and can provide the foundation for public health education efforts to prevent the spread of STIs and HIV. With no cure for HIV in sight, education and public health prevention efforts remain our very best hope. We need to go beyond knowledge alone to accepting personal responsibility, and accurately assessing personal risk. By taking responsibility, we help to create a world of possibilities, where sexualities may be expressed in healthy and satisfying ways.

Article

Prepared by: Elizabeth Schroeder, EdD, MSW,
Elizabeth Schroeder Consulting

New Mammogram Guidelines Raise Questions

Benefits of screening before age 50 don't outweigh risks, task force says.

JOCELYN NOVECK

Learning Outcomes

After reading this article, you will be able to:

- Describe the origin of the guidelines relating to women having mammograms.

- Explain how the most recent guidelines for mammograms differ from the previous ones.

- List at least two questions that the most recent mammogram guidelines raise for medical professionals and the public.

For many women, getting a mammogram is already one of life's more stressful experiences.

Now, women in their 40s have the added anxiety of trying to figure out if they should even be getting one at all.

A government task force said Monday that most women don't need mammograms in their 40s and should get one every two years starting at 50—a stunning reversal and a break with the American Cancer Society's long-standing position. What's more, the panel said breast self-exams do no good, and women shouldn't be taught to do them.

The news seemed destined to leave many deeply confused about whose advice to follow.

"I've never had a scare, but isn't it better to be safe than sorry?" asked Beth Rosenthal, 41, sitting in a San Francisco cafe on Monday afternoon with her friend and their small children. "I've heard of a lot of women in their 40s, and even 30s, who've gotten breast cancer. It just doesn't seem right to wait until 50."

Her friend agreed. "I don't think I'll wait," said Leslie David-Jones, also 41, shaking her head.

For most of the past two decades, the American Cancer Society has been recommending annual mammograms beginning at 40, and it reiterated that position on Monday. "This is one screening test I recommend unequivocally, and would recommend to any woman 40 and over," the society's chief medical officer, Dr. Otis Brawley, said in a statement.

But the government panel of doctors and scientists concluded that getting screened for breast cancer so early and so often is harmful, causing too many false alarms and unneeded biopsies without substantially improving women's odds of surviving the disease.

"The benefits are less and the harms are greater when screening starts in the 40s," said Dr. Diana Petitti, vice chair of the panel.

The new guidelines were issued by the U.S. Preventive Services Task Force, whose stance influences coverage of screening tests by Medicare and many insurance companies. But Susan Pisano, a spokeswoman for America's Health Insurance Plans, an industry group, said insurance coverage isn't likely to change because of the new guidelines.

Experts expect the revisions to be hotly debated, and to cause confusion for women and their doctors.

"Our concern is that as a result of that confusion, women may elect not to get screened at all. And that, to me, would be a serious problem," said Dr. Len Lichtenfeld, the cancer society's deputy chief medical officer.

The guidelines are for the general population, not those at high risk of breast cancer because of family history or gene mutations that would justify having mammograms sooner or more often.

The new advice says:

Most women in their 40s should not routinely get mammograms.

Women 50 to 74 should get a mammogram every other year until they turn 75, after which the risks and benefits are unknown. (The task force's previous guidelines had no upper limit and called for exams every year or two.)

The value of breast exams by doctors is unknown. And breast self-exams are of no value.

Medical groups such as the cancer society have been backing off promoting breast self-exams in recent years because of scant evidence of their effectiveness. Decades ago, the practice was so heavily promoted that organizations distributed cards that could be hung in the shower demonstrating the circular motion women should use to feel for lumps in their breasts.

The guidelines and research supporting them were released Monday and are being published in Tuesday's issue of the Annals of Internal Medicine.

Sharp Criticism from Cancer Society

The new advice was sharply challenged by the cancer society.

"This is one screening test I recommend unequivocally, and would recommend to any woman 40 and over," the society's chief medical officer, Dr. Otis Brawley, said in a statement.

The task force advice is based on its conclusion that screening 1,300 women in their 50s to save one life is worth it, but that screening 1,900 women in their 40s to save a life is not, Brawley wrote.

That stance "is essentially telling women that mammography at age 40 to 49 saves lives, just not enough of them," he said. The cancer society feels the benefits outweigh the harms for women in both groups.

International guidelines also call for screening to start at age 50; the World Health Organization recommends the test every two years, Britain says every three years.

Breast cancer is the most common cancer and the second leading cause of cancer deaths in American women. More than 192,000 new cases and 40,000 deaths from the disease are expected in the U.S. this year.

Mammograms can find cancer early, and two-thirds of women over 40 report having had the test in the previous two years. But how much they cut the risk of dying of the disease, and at what cost in terms of unneeded biopsies, expense and worry, have been debated.

In most women, tumors are slow-growing, and that likelihood increases with age. So there is little risk by extending the time between mammograms, some researchers say. Even for the minority of women with aggressive, fast-growing tumors, annual screening will make little difference in survival odds.

The new guidelines balance these risks and benefits, scientists say.

The probability of dying of breast cancer after age 40 is 3 percent, they calculate. Getting a mammogram every other year from ages 50 to 69 lowers that risk by about 16 percent.

"It's an average of five lives saved per thousand women screened," said Georgetown University researcher Dr. Jeanne Mandelblatt.

False Alarms

Starting at age 40 would prevent one additional death but also lead to 470 false alarms for every 1,000 women screened. Continuing mammograms through age 79 prevents three additional deaths but raises the number of women treated for breast cancers that would not threaten their lives.

"You save more lives because breast cancer is more common, but you diagnose tumors in women who were destined to die of something else. The overdiagnosis increases in older women," Mandelblatt said.

She led six teams around the world who used federal data on cancer and mammography to develop mathematical models of what would happen if women were screened at different ages and time intervals. Their conclusions helped shape the new guidelines.

Several medical groups say they are sticking to their guidelines that call for routine screening starting at 40.

"Screening isn't perfect. But it's the best thing we have. And it works," said Dr. Carol Lee, a spokeswoman for the American College of Radiology. She suggested that cutting health care costs may have played a role in the decision, but Petitti said the task force does not consider cost or insurance in its review.

The American College of Obstetricians and Gynecologists also has qualms. The organization's Dr. Hal Lawrence said there is still significant benefit to women in their 40s, adding: "We think that women deserve that benefit."

But Dr. Amy Abernethy of the Duke Comprehensive Cancer Center agreed with the task force's changes.

"Overall, I think it really took courage for them to do this," she said. "It does ask us as doctors to change what we do and how we communicate with patients. That's no small undertaking."

Abernethy, who is 41, said she got her first mammogram the day after her 40th birthday, even though she wasn't convinced it was needed. Now she doesn't plan to have another mammogram until she is 50.

Barbara Brenner, executive director of the San Francisco-based Breast Cancer Action, said the group was "thrilled" with the revisions. The advocacy group doesn't support screening before menopause, and will be changing its suggested interval from yearly to every two years, she said.

Mammograms, like all medical interventions, have risks and benefits, she said.

"Women are entitled to know what they are and to make their best decisions," she said. "These guidelines will help that conversation."

Critical Thinking

1. Why did the panel publish changes in mammogram requirements?

2. What are some of the benefits and risks associated with early screening?

3. What are the key questions that remain concerning mammograms and health guidelines?

Internet References

American Cancer Society: Breast Cancer
http://www.cancer.org/cancer/breastcancer

American Congress of Obstetricians and Gynecologists
http://www.acog.org

National Breast Cancer Foundation
http://www.nationalbreastcancer.org

Article

Prepared by: Elizabeth Schroeder, EdD, MSW,
Elizabeth Schroeder Consulting

Health and Access to Care and Coverage for Lesbian, Gay, Bisexual, and Transgender Individuals in the U.S.

USHA RANJI ET AL.

Learning Outcomes

After reading this article, you will be able to:

- Describe at least three barriers to healthcare coverage for LGBT individuals.

- List at least three health concerns that have a higher prevalence among sexual and gender minority populations.

- Provide at least three facts relating to sexual abuse and assault within LGBT populations.

Executive Summary

Lesbian, gay, bisexual, and transgender (LGBT) individuals often face challenges and barriers to accessing needed health services and, as a result, can experience worse health outcomes. These challenges can include stigma, discrimination, violence, and rejection by families and communities, as well as other barriers, such as inequality in the workplace and health insurance sectors, the provision of substandard care, and outright denial of care because of an individual's sexual orientation or gender identity.[1,2,3]

While sexual and gender minorities have many of the same health concerns as the general population, they experience certain health challenges at higher rates, and also face several unique health challenges. In particular, research suggests that some subgroups of the LGBT community have more chronic conditions as well as higher prevalence and earlier onset of disabilities than heterosexuals. Other major health concerns include HIV/AIDS, mental illness, substance use, and sexual and physical violence. In addition to the higher rates of illness and health challenges, some LGBT individuals are more likely to experience challenges obtaining care. Barriers include gaps in coverage, cost-related hurdles, and poor treatment from health care providers.

Several recent changes within the legal and policy landscape serve to increase access to care and insurance for LGBT individuals and their families. Most notably the implementation of the Affordable Care Act (ACA), the Supreme Court's overturning of a major portion of the Defense of Marriage Act (DOMA), the subsequent legalization of same-sex marriage in many states, as well as recent steps taken by the Obama Administration to promote equal treatment of LGBT people and same-sex couples in the nation's health care system have reshaped policy affecting LGBT individuals and their families. The ACA expands access to health insurance coverage for millions, including LGBT individuals, and includes specific protections related to sexual orientation and gender identity. The Supreme Court ruling on DOMA resulted in federal recognition of same-sex marriages for the first time and paved the way for recognition in many more states, which also serves to provide new health insurance coverage options.[4]

This issue brief provides an overview of what is known about LGBT health status, coverage, and access in the United States, and reviews the implications of the ACA, the overturning of DOMA, and other recent policy developments for LGBT individuals and their families going forward.

The LGBT Community

While there is no single definition of the "LGBT community"—indeed, it is a diverse and multidimensional group of individuals with unique identities and experiences, and variations by race/ethnicity, income, and other characteristics—LGBT individuals share the common experience of often being stigmatized due to their sexual orientation, gender identity, and/or gender expression.[5] In its landmark 2011 report, *The Health of Lesbian, Gay, Bisexual, and Transgender People: Building a Foundation for Better Understanding,* the Institute of Medicine defines *sexual orientation* as "an enduring pattern of or disposition to experience sexual or romantic desires for, and relationships with, people of one's same sex, the other sex, or both sexes."[6] This definition incorporates elements of attraction, behavior, and identity. It is important to note that for some individuals, their sexual identity does not necessarily fall into any specific category but, rather, exists along a spectrum. In addition, not all persons who engage in same-sex behavior or experience same-sex attraction identify as lesbian, gay, or bisexual.

Gender Identity refers to "an individual's internal sense of being male, female, or something else. Since gender identity is internal, one's gender identity is not necessarily visible to others."[7] Additionally, *gender expression* and *gender role conformity* further describe the extent to which a person does or does not adhere to expected gender norms and roles. *Transgender* refers to individuals whose sex at birth is different from their identity as male, female, or elsewhere along the gender spectrum. People who identify as transgender may live their lives as the opposite gender, and may seek prescription pharmacologic therapy and/or surgical transformation. Transgender people may identify as heterosexual, lesbian, gay, or bisexual, or somewhere else along the spectrum of sexual identity.

Lastly, while sexual orientation and gender identity are important aspects of an individual's identity, they interact with many other factors, including sex, race/ethnicity, and class. The intersection of these characteristics helps to shape an individual's health, access to care, and experience with the health care system.

Population Characteristics

Assessing the health needs and barriers to care of the LGBT population has been challenging due to the historical lack of data collection on sexual orientation and gender identity. While some health surveys have asked about sexual orientation, it has not been routine to collect and analyze data on sexual orientation and gender identity in many major health surveys, particularly nationally representative ones, meaning that much of the data available to date have been from smaller, non-representative studies and convenience samples. Where data have been collected, they have mostly focused on same-sex couples using data systems that collect information on relationship status.[8] In addition, where data are available for individuals, there is more information about lesbian, gay, and bisexual persons than transgender individuals. There has been growing recognition of the need for research focused on the LGBT community, and the ACA has new data collection requirements on disparities, which include sexual orientation and gender identity (described below). The National Health Interview Survey (NHIS), the principal source of information on the health of the U.S. population, began including a question on sexual orientation in its 2013 survey and findings were released in July 2014.

Many data sources are used to make inferences about the LGBT population and estimates on the size of the LGBT population vary:

- Data on the size of the LGBT population in the United States range. The latest data from the National Health Interview Survey (NHIS), a nationally representative survey of the U.S. population on health issues which now includes questions on sexual orientation, indicate that 2.3% of adults ages 18 and older in the U.S. identify as lesbian, gay, or bisexual, equating to more than 5.2 million people.[9] Gallup poll data have found that between 3.4% and 3.6% of Americans ages 18 and older identify as LGBT, or about 9 million people.[10,11,12,13] Estimates may vary due to differing methodologies for data collection. Most of these surveys include only those who self-identify as LGB[14] and do not include those who may have engaged in same-sex behavior or have same-sex attraction but do not identify as gay, lesbian, or bisexual. Other studies have looked beyond self-identification, to include behavior and attraction, and obtained higher estimates, including one that found that 10% of adults reported experience with same-sex partners.[15] In addition, a recent analysis indicates that standard survey measures appear to significantly underestimate non-heterosexual identity and same-sex sexual experiences.[16]

- Data on those who identify as transgender are limited but a recent study found that an estimated 0.3% of the U.S. population is transgender, equating to approximately 700,000 people.[17]

- Estimates of self-identified LGBT individuals also vary by state. According to a 2012 Gallup poll, the share of adults who identify as LGBT ranges from a low of 1.7% in North Dakota to a high of 10% in the District of Columbia.[18] This range could reflect local policies and societal attitudes regarding LGBT equality, which may be correlated with an individual's willingness to self-identify as LGBT or live in a certain locale.

- Racial and ethnic minorities, young people, and women are more likely than their counterparts to identify as LGBT (Figure 1).[19]

- One in five (20%) LGBT individuals indicate they are married, and an additional 18% are in a domestic partnership or living with a partner (some of whom could be in heterosexual marriages or domestic partnerships).[20]

- According to the 2012 American Community Survey, a smaller share of same-sex couples is raising children compared to both married and unmarried heterosexual couples.[21] Just over 40% of married and unmarried heterosexual couples are raising children, compared to 18% of same-sex couples, 11% of male same-sex couples and 24% of female same-sex couples.

- Compared to the general population, sexual and gender minorities are disproportionately poor overall, but there is variation between subgroups. A recent Pew Research poll of LGBT individuals found that about 4 in 10 (39%) earned $30,000 or less per year, compared to 28% of the U.S. population overall.[22] Poverty rates on average are higher among lesbian and bisexual women, young people, and African Americans.[23] According to an analysis of the 2006–2010 National Survey of Family Growth, more than one-quarter (28%) of lesbian and bisexual women are poor, compared with 21% of heterosexual women. Just over 1 in 5 gay and bisexual men (23%) are poor, compared to 15% of heterosexual men. However, when comparing couples, lesbian couples have the highest poverty rates, followed by heterosexual couples and male same-sex couples. Further, a recent survey of more than 6,400 transgender people from across the U.S. found that the transgender population is approximately 4 times as likely as the non-transgender population to have an annual income of less than $10,000.[24]

Health Challenges

Health is shaped by a host of social, economic, and structural factors.[25] For LGBT individuals, these factors include the experience and impact of discrimination, stigma, and ostracism, which affect health outcomes, access, and experience with health care.[26,27,28] Research available to date finds that while sexual and gender minorities have many of the same health concerns as the general population, they experience some health challenges at higher rates, and face several unique health challenges.

Chronic Conditions

Studies have found that sexual and gender minorities experience worse physical health compared to their heterosexual and non-transgender counterparts.[29,30]

- A recent literature review found that self-identified LGB individuals are more likely than heterosexuals to rate their health as poor, have more chronic conditions, and have higher prevalence and earlier onset of disabilities. Overall, LGB people report more asthma diagnoses, headaches, allergies, osteoarthritis, and gastro-intestinal problems than heterosexual individuals.[31]

- Additionally, there are differences between subgroups within the LGBT community. Lesbian and bisexual women report poorer overall physical health and higher rates of asthma, urinary tract infections, and Hepatitis B and C than heterosexual women. Lesbian and bisexual women also report heightened risk for and diagnosis of some cancers and higher rates of cardiovascular disease diagnosis. Similarly, gay and bisexual men report more cancer diagnoses and lower survival rates, higher rates of cardiovascular disease and risk factors, as well as higher total numbers of acute and chronic health conditions such as headaches and urinary incontinence than heterosexual men.[32]

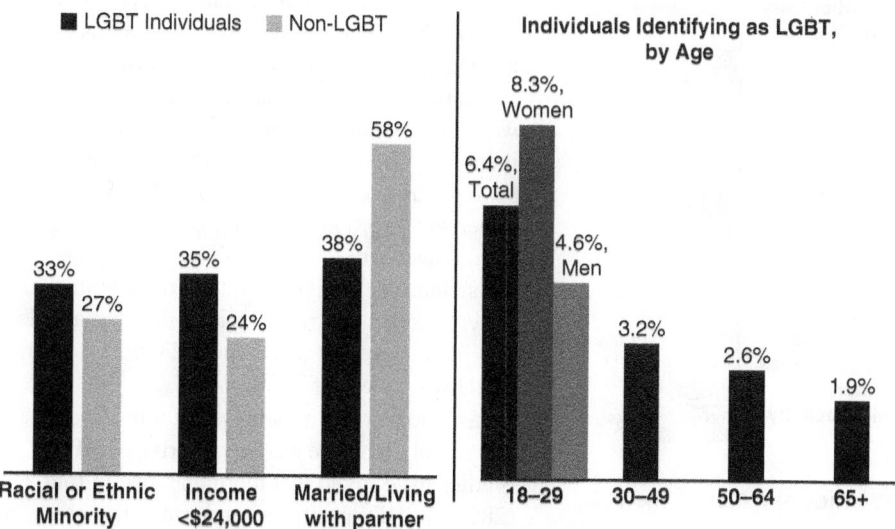

Figure 1   Demographic Characteristics among Adults Ages 18–64.

Source: Gates, G., Newport, F. (2013). *Gallup poll Special Report: 3.4% of U.S. Adults Identify as LGBT.*

- According to newly released data from the NHIS, fewer lesbian and bisexual women reported excellent or very good health compared to heterosexual women. There were no health status differences between men by sexual orientation (Figure 2).[33]
- LGB individuals on average have higher rates of some risk factors for chronic illnesses. Obesity rates are higher among lesbian and bisexual women compared to heterosexual women, but are lowest among gay men. However, there were no significant differences by sexual orientation for women or men in rates of meeting physical activity guidelines.
- According to a study of Massachusetts residents, transgender persons are the least likely among LGBT individuals to self-report their health as *Excellent* or *Very Good* (67% vs. 79%) and are twice as likely to report limitations in daily activities due to impairment of health problems (33% vs. 16%).[34]

HIV/AIDS and Sexually Transmitted Infections (STIs)

One of the most significant health challenges facing the LGBT community has been the HIV/AIDS epidemic's impact on gay and bisexual men, and there are increasing data on the disproportionate impact of HIV on transgender women. After experiencing a dramatic rise in new infections in the 1980s, efforts by the gay community and public health officials helped to bring HIV incidence down; however, in recent years, new infections among gay and bisexual men in the U.S. have been on the rise, the only group for which infections are increasing

- In 2010, gay and bisexual men and other men who have sex with men (MSM), while representing an estimated 2% of the U.S. population, accounted for more than half (56%) of all people living with HIV in the United States, and two-thirds (66%) of new HIV infections.[35]
- Between 2008 and 2010, the rate of new HIV infections among young black MSM increased by 20%, the highest increase among all sub-populations. Black MSM accounted for 36% of new HIV infections in 2010.[36]
- The CDC recommends that gay and bisexual men be tested for HIV at least once every year (and more frequently for those who are sexually active), but according to a new nationally representative survey conducted by the Kaiser Family Foundation, many do not meet this level. While seven in ten gay and bisexual men say they have gotten an HIV test at some point in their lives, just 30 percent say they were tested within the past year. Three in ten (30%) say they have never been tested for HIV, rising to 44% of those under age 35. The leading reason that men give for not having had a recent test is that they do not consider themselves at risk for HIV.[37]
- Access to medical care is critical for the health of people with HIV. Among MSM diagnosed with HIV in 2010, approximately three-fourths received medical care within three months of their diagnosis, but only half (51%) were retained in treatment over the course of the year. Rates were lowest among younger men and Black men.[38] In addition, according to the Kaiser survey, three in ten (31%) gay and bisexual men either say they don't have a regular place to go for medical care or they don't have a regular physician. These men (who tend to be younger, lower-income, and more racially diverse) are also less likely to report discussing HIV with doctors or getting tested for HIV.
- Transgender women, particularly transgender women of color, are also at high risk of HIV. Studies have found that more than one in four (28%) are HIV positive,[39] and a majority are unaware that they are infected.
- To date, there has only been one likely case of female-to-female sexual transmission of HIV in

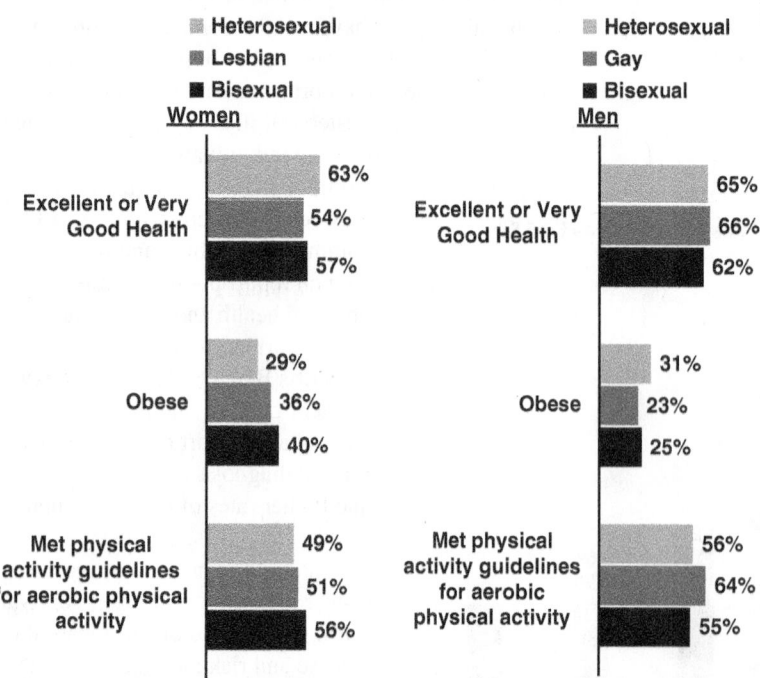

Figure 2   Health Status Indicators among Women and Men in the U.S., by Sexual Orientation, 2013.

Notes: Among adults ages 18–64.

Source: Centers for Disease Control and Prevention, National Health Statistics Reports. (July 2014). Sexual Orientation and Health among U.S. Adults: National Health Interview Survey, 2013.

the United States.[40] However, HIV is an issue that affects lesbians as well as bisexual women, since individuals who identify as lesbian may still have sexual relationships with men, and lesbians and bisexual women are also at risk of HIV via transmission modes that do not involve sexual contact (such as injection drug use).

- STI rates are higher among some LGB groups than heterosexuals, and rates have been increasing for some infections. For example, MSM account for more than seven in ten (72%) new syphilis cases, an alarming increase that has re-emerged during the last several years.[41] MSM also account for 15% to 25% of all new Hepatitis B infections.[42] Given the strong interaction between HIV and other STIs, this is a particular concern for MSM.

- Human Papillomavirus (HPV) is the most common STI and is a major cause of cervical, anal, and mouth cancers.[43] MSM are 17 times more likely to develop anal cancer than men who only have sex with women.[44] The HPV vaccine, which protects against certain strains of the virus that are associated with anal cancer, could reduce anal cancer rates among future generations of MSM.

Behavioral and Mental Health

Research has found that LGBT individuals are at elevated risk for some mental health and behavioral health conditions, with studies finding that they are two- and- a- half times more likely to experience depression, anxiety, and substance misuse.[45,46] The history of discrimination and stigma contributes to higher rates of mental illness.[47] In fact, until the 1970s, homosexuality was considered a mental illness in the *Diagnostic and Statistical Manual (DSM) of Mental Disorders* and by various professional organizations. The diagnosis "gender dysphoria," which has replaced the transgender diagnosis in the DSM, is intended to communicate the emotional distress that transgender people may experience as well as promote insurance coverage of services related to gender transition, such as counseling or hormone therapy, that typically have not been covered by insurance plans.[48] Still, stigma and prejudice against sexual and gender minorities remain pervasive and continue to have negative consequences for the mental health of the LGBT population.[49]

LGBT adults experience higher rates of mental illness, substance abuse, and discrimination compared to heterosexual and non-transgender adults. Additionally, lack of acceptance from family members is correlated with higher rates of mental illness and substance use among the LGBT population.[50]

- The recent NHIS provides the first national comparisons of gay, lesbian, and bisexual adults to heterosexual adults on alcohol consumption, smoking status, and one measure of mental health status.
  - Consuming five or more alcoholic beverages in one day was reported by more bisexual (40%) and gay or lesbian (33%) adults than heterosexual adults (22%). Rates among men of all sexual orientations were substantially higher than for women.

- Smoking rates were higher among bisexual and lesbian women compared to heterosexual women, but did not vary by sexual orientation for men. A separate meta-analysis of several studies found that overall, LGBT people smoke cigarettes at 1.5 to 2.5 times the rate of heterosexual and non-transgender people.[51]

- One in ten bisexual women experienced serious psychological distress in the past 30 days, more than twice the rate of lesbian and heterosexual women. Approximately 3% of heterosexual men reported experiencing serious psychological distress, and data were unavailable for bisexual and gay men.

- Other studies have used state-level data or sample populations to identify mental health trends among LGBT individuals. Nearly one- fifth (19%) of bisexual adults in Massachusetts report they had recently seriously considered suicide, compared to 4% of lesbian and gay adults and 3% of heterosexuals.[52] There are notable differences between subgroups, with the rate highest among bisexual women (26%), followed by bisexual men (11%), gay men (6%), and approximately 3% among all other subgroups. Another nationwide study found a reported 41% prevalence of suicide attempts among the transgender population.[53]

- Research suggests that MSM have higher use of certain substances. One study has estimated that MSM are more than 12 times as likely to use amphetamines and almost 10 times as likely to use heroin as heterosexual men. However, it's important to note that research in this field is older and data are not necessarily comparable to the heterosexual population.[54]

Sexual Assault and Physical Violence

Sexual assault and physical violence can have lasting consequences for victims, families, and communities.[55] LGBT individuals experience higher rates of sexual and physical violence compared to heterosexual and non-transgender individuals. Violence toward LGBT people has inspired public policy responses. For example, federal legislation as well as some state laws allow for the classification of violence based on gender identity or sexual orientation bias as a "hate crime," which has implications for penalties as well as funding to states and locales for deterrence and surveillance of these crimes.[56] Key statistics include the following:

- A recent poll of LGBT adults found that two-thirds had experienced some form of discrimination because of their sexual orientation or gender identity, including subjection to slurs, rejection by a friend or family member, being physically threatened or attacked, receiving poor service at a place of business or treated unfairly by an employer, or made to feel unwelcome at a place of worship; a full 30% said they had been physically threatened or attacked.[57]

- Many women and men have experienced some form of sexual violence, but the rates are significantly higher among some LGBT groups. It is estimated that almost half (46%) of bisexual women have been raped, as have 17% of heterosexual and 13% of lesbian women. More than four in ten heterosexual and lesbian women and the majority (75%) of bisexual women have experienced other forms of sexual violence, such as coercion or harassment. Six in ten (61%) bisexual women have encountered intimate partner violence (IPV), as have 44% of lesbian and 35% of heterosexual women (Figure 3).[58]

- While sexual violence rates are higher among women overall, bisexual and gay men experience significantly higher rates than heterosexual men. Four in ten gay men and nearly half of bisexual men have encountered sexual violence other than rape. More than one-third (37%) of bisexual men have faced partner violence. For both men and women, the perpetrators were predominantly male.

- Anti-LGBT bias also puts LGBT people at risk for physical violence. According to the FBI's crime

reporting surveillance, one in five hate crimes was due to sexual orientation bias.[59] Studies using convenience samples have shown a significant number of LGBT individuals have been victims of physical and verbal assaults, as well as personal property damage, due to their sexual orientation or gender identity.[60] One recent nationally representative study examined self-reported experiences with physical violence due to sexual orientation among gay men, lesbian women, and bisexual individuals, and found almost 8% of individuals have experienced physical violence once and 5.5% have experienced physical violence at least twice. Gay men were the most likely to experience physical violence due to their sexual orientation.[61] Transgender people, particularly transgender women and transgender people of color, are also at particular risk of physical violence.[62] Statistics from the National Coalition of Anti-Violence Programs indicate that half of the victims of anti-LGBT bias-motivated murders in 2012 were transgender women and the majority were also people of color.[63]

Adolescent and Young Adult Health

Adolescence and young adulthood are often times when individuals begin to identify as LGBT.[64] While these times can be challenging for many individuals, they are often especially so for LGBT youth. Despite growing societal acceptance and understanding, some young people still suffer discrimination at the hands of their family and friends and in their schools and communities, experiences which can lead to serious challenges, such as housing problems, that affect health. There is growing awareness about bullying and violence affecting LGBT youth. These include efforts to promote greater attention to fostering inclusive school climates, teaching youth about online safety, establishment of reporting processes in schools and communities when violence or bullying occur, and referring young people for professional mental and behavioral health services when needed. Key statistics include the following:

- Like their adult counterparts, youth who identify as a sexual and/or gender minority experience higher rates of mental illness, substance abuse, violence, and discrimination compared to the general population. Additionally, LGBT youth are more likely to be homeless and live in poverty than non-LGBT youth. Research has found that parental rejection can increase the likelihood that an LGBT youth will suffer from depression, attempt suicide, use illegal drugs, and/or engage in risky sexual behaviors.[65]

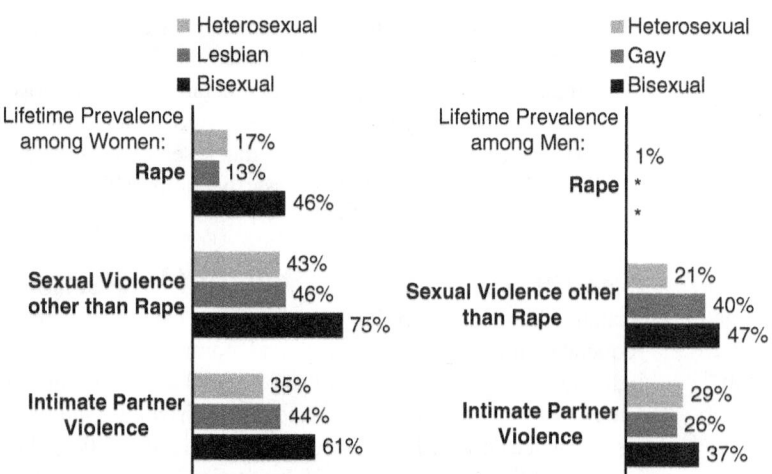

Figure 3   Sexual Violence, by Sexual Orientation, 2010.

Sexual Violence other than rape includes being made to penetrate, sexual coercion, unwanted sexual contact, and non-contact unwanted sexual experiences. Perpetrator can include an intimate partner.
Intimate Partner Violence includes physical and sexual violence, threats of physical or sexual violence, stalking, and psychological aggression by a current or former intimate partner.

Note: *Sample size too small for estimate. Among adults 18 and older.

Source: CDC. (2013). The National Intimate Partner and Sexual Violence Survey: 2010 Findings on Victimization by Sexual Orientation.

- Approximately 40% of homeless youth are LGBT, and the leading reasons for homelessness among this group are due to family rejection.[66]
- Almost two-thirds (64%) of LGB students and 4 out of 10 (44%) transgender students report feeling unsafe at school because of their sexual orientation or gender identity.[67]
- LGB youth are four times more likely to attempt suicide than heterosexual youth.[68]
- Three times as many LGB youth report ever being raped compared to their heterosexual peers (16% vs. 5%).[68]

Insurance Coverage and Access to Care

Research has shown that LGBT populations have different patterns of health coverage and utilization of services and has begun to document gaps within the delivery system in meeting the needs of the LGBT population.

- Until recently, the available research on LGBT people has often been limited to couples or combines lesbian, gay, and bisexual people while excluding transgender people. Studies that have stratified between these different groups suggest that there are important differences in access that are often masked in more aggregated studies. In particular, new research finds that on some measures, bisexual individuals have more limited access to care while lesbian and gay individuals have rates comparable to heterosexual adults (Figure 4). According to the 2013 NHIS, the uninsured rate is similar between lesbian and gay adults (17%),

heterosexual (20%), and bisexual adults (24%). However, on other measures of access, including a usual place to go for medical care and going without medical care due to cost, bisexual adults fared poorer than other groups.

- A 2013 survey found that, of the close to 5.5 million LGBT individuals estimated to have incomes under 400% of the federal poverty level (FPL), one in three were uninsured at the time of the survey and more than two-thirds of these individuals had been uninsured for more than two years.[69] Among this group, LGBT individuals with insurance were less likely than individuals in the general population to get insurance through their employer and more likely to be enrolled in Medicaid. Additionally, almost 4 in 10 had medical debt and more than 4 in 10 reported postponing medical care due to costs.[70,71]
- Research studies on same-sex couples find that LGB individuals have higher rates of unmet medical need because of cost and are less likely to have a regular provider. Research has also found that women in same-sex couples are less likely than heterosexual married women to have received timely medical care for both primary and specialty services. Among men in couples, gay men are three times as likely as their heterosexual counterparts to report delays in obtaining needed prescription medicines.[72]
- Some studies have found that lesbian women in couples have lower rates of breast and cervical cancer screenings than married heterosexual women.[73] In addition to lower mammography rates, lesbian women on average

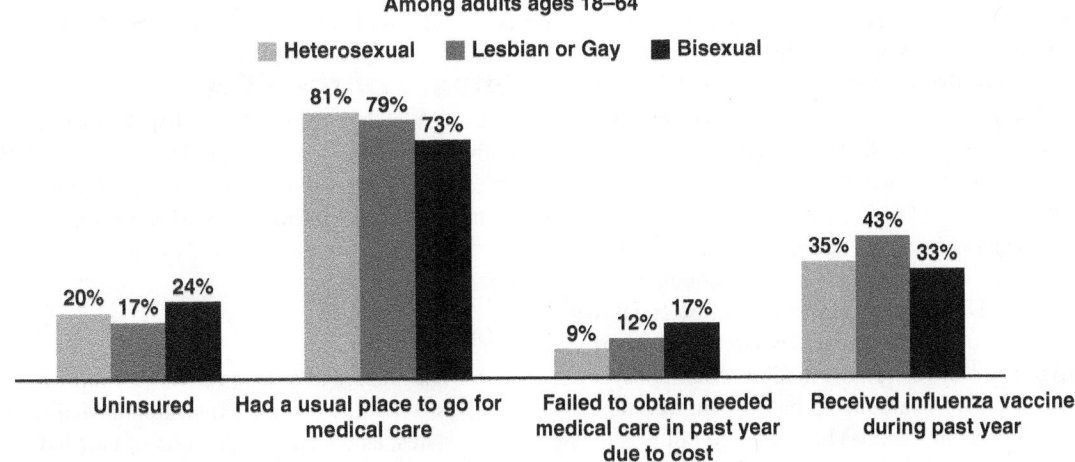

Among adults ages 18–64

■ Heterosexual   ■ Lesbian or Gay   ■ Bisexual

Uninsured: 20% / 17% / 24%
Had a usual place to go for medical care: 81% / 79% / 73%
Failed to obtain needed medical care in past year due to cost: 9% / 12% / 17%
Received influenza vaccine during past year: 35% / 43% / 33%

Figure 4   Access to Care and Utilization of Services in the U.S., by Sexual Orientation, 2013.

Notes: Among adults ages 18–64.

Source: Centers for Disease Control and Prevention, National Health Statistics Reports. (July 2014). Sexual Orientation and Health Among U.S. Adults: National Health Interview Survey, 2013.

have higher rates of some risk factors for breast cancer, including greater alcohol use and lower likelihood of childbearing.[74,75]

- The transgender population is much more likely to live in poverty and less likely to have health insurance than the general population. Research reflects the impact of these barriers. In one survey of transgender individuals, nearly half (48%) of respondents postponed or went without care when they were sick because they could not afford it.[76] In addition, many health plans include transgender-specific exclusions that deny transgender individuals coverage of services provided to non-transgender individuals, such as surgical treatment related to gender transition, mental health services, and hormone therapy.[77]

- An individual's relationship with providers is another important component of access to care. Significant shares of LGBT individuals report negative experiences when seeking care, ranging from disrespectful treatment from providers and staff, to providers' lack of awareness of specific health needs. In a survey of LGB people, more than half of all respondents reported that they have faced cases of providers denying care, using harsh language, or blaming the patient's sexual orientation or gender identity as the cause for an illness.[78] Fear of discrimination may lead some people to conceal their sexual orientation or gender identity from providers or avoid seeking care altogether.

- For transgender persons, discrimination may be as personal as refusing to use the patient's chosen name or as structural as providers' lack of knowledge about how to provide appropriate care to transgender people. For example, most transgender men still have a cervix and should be screened for cervical cancer, which requires a sensitive approach.[79] Studies of the transgender community show that up to 39% of transgender people have faced some type of harassment or discrimination when seeking routine health care, and many report being denied care outright or encountering violence in health care settings.[80,81]

- Medical education does not routinely encompass LGBT health issues. More than half of medical schools and public health school curricula lack instruction about the health concerns of LGBT people beyond work related to HIV/AIDS.[82,83] However, the medical community's awareness of LGBT health needs has grown. Several professional medical societies have formed policies and guidance that advocate on behalf of fair treatment and access for LGBT patients and health providers.[84] For example, the American Medical Association (AMA) has issued an explicit nondiscrimination policy as well as numerous other statements that recognize

prior discriminatory practices in the medical setting, the importance of better understanding and addressing LGBT health needs, the impact of discrimination on health and well-being, and the need to include sexual orientation in research.

- The World Professional Association for Transgender Health also maintains a set of standards and principles to guide health care professionals in providing health care to transgender people.[85] Additionally, in 2011, the Joint Commission, an independent non-profit national organization that accredits and certifies more than 20,000 health care organizations and programs in the U.S., began to require that hospitals prohibit discrimination based on sexual orientation, gender identity, and gender expression in order to be accredited.[86]

Impact of Policies on Coverage and Access to Care

In addition to specific health needs, the health of and access to care for LGBT communities are shaped by federal and state policies on insurance, compensation and benefits, and marriage. In 2010, President Obama asked the Secretary of Health and Human Services (HHS) to identify steps to improve the health and well-being of LGBT individuals, families, and communities, which resulted in a series of recommended actions that are now being implemented.[87] Additionally, the passage of the ACA in 2010 and the overturning of DOMA in 2013 affect access to care and coverage for LGBT individuals and their families, expand nondiscrimination protections, increase data collection requirements, and support family caregiving. Finally, states and private organizations have also moved to add nondiscrimination protections and enhance coverage for LGBT individuals.

Impact of the ACA

The ACA makes far-reaching changes in health coverage and delivery of care for all Americans. For LGBT populations, three major areas are of particular saliency: 1) expanded access to coverage and insurance market reforms, 2) new "nondiscrimination" protections, and 3) requirements for data collection and research.

Coverage

- The ACA will extend coverage to millions of uninsured persons through the expansion of Medicaid in some states, as well as the creation of new federally subsidized health insurance marketplaces. In states that expand their Medicaid programs, Medicaid eligibility will be based solely on income, and will be available to most individuals with incomes below 138% FPL regardless of their family status or disability. Uninsured individuals

Health and Access to Care and Coverage for Lesbian, Gay, Bisexual, and Transgender Individuals in the U.S. by Usha Ranji et al.

215

who are not eligible for Medicaid can purchase coverage in insurance marketplaces, with subsidies available to many individuals with incomes below 400% FPL to help offset the costs of premiums. It is estimated that nearly 390,000 uninsured LGBT individuals could qualify for Medicaid in states that plan to expand Medicaid, and that approximately 1.12 million uninsured LGBT individuals could receive subsidies to help with the cost of coverage in insurance marketplaces.[88]

- As of January 2014, individuals can no longer be denied insurance due to a pre-existing condition, such as HIV infection, mental illness, or a transgender medical history. Additionally, new private plans are now required to cover recommended preventive services without cost sharing. This includes screenings for HIV, STIs, depression, and substance use. And, those who gain coverage through Medicaid or in the state marketplaces will have coverage for a set of essential health benefits, including prescription drugs and mental health services.

Nondiscrimination Protections

- As described above, bias and discrimination in the health care system have been an unfortunate reality for many LGBT people.[89] In addition to provider level discrimination, some policies in the insurance and financing system have disproportionately affected LGBT people, including pre-existing condition clauses permitting plans to deny insurance to people with conditions such as HIV, mental illness, or to transgender individuals, who may require specific health care services.[90] Furthermore, some plans have interpreted these exclusions broadly and used them to deny transgender people coverage for services that are not related to gender transition.[91]

- Section 1557 of the ACA prohibits discrimination based on sex, defined to include gender identity and sex stereotypes (but not sexual orientation), in any health program receiving federal funds (such as Medicaid, Medicare, and providers who receive federal funds). Separate federal regulations issued by the Department of Health and Human Services governing the health insurance marketplaces and plans offering the essential health benefits bar discrimination in insurance provisions based on sexual orientation and gender identity.[92] In addition to the new federal law, several states have nondiscrimination policies. Eight states (CA, CO, DE, IL, ME, OR, VT, WA) plus DC prohibit discrimination based on sexual orientation and gender identity.[93] Additionally, eight states (CA, CN, CO, IL, MA, OR, VT, WA) and DC prohibit transgender exclusions in health insurance through legislation or regulation.[94]

Data Collection

- The ACA calls for the inclusion of routine data collection and surveillance on health disparities, which HHS and many other groups have recognized includes LGBT populations. National health care surveys will include questions on sexual orientation within the next couple of years so that analysis can be conducted specifically on LGB populations; efforts to develop questions on gender identity for national surveys are underway as well. Research on LGBT health has increased over time, and HHS has sponsored efforts to collect and report data on LGBT health, as evidenced with the inclusion of LGBT-specific data in publications such as the National Healthcare Disparities Report, the addition of Healthy People 2020 goals to increase routine data collection efforts on LGBT populations, and early efforts of collection and surveillance on sexual orientation and gender identity in national health care surveys.[95] As mentioned above, as of 2013, the NHIS includes a question on sexual orientation. In addition, several agencies within HHS have taken steps toward broader data collection. For example, the CDC has approved sexual orientation and gender identity questions that can be used on the state-administered Behavioral Risk Factor Surveillance System surveys and the Substance Abuse and Mental Health Services Administration is considering adding questions to its National Survey on Drug Use and Health. However, it is still not routine for researchers and health data systems to collect and report data by individuals' sexual orientation and gender identity.

- At the provider and patient level, some groups advocate for clinicians to collect patient information on sexual orientation and gender identity to better understand an individual's health profile and needs. Some providers have expressed discomfort with and inadequate knowledge on soliciting this information. Advocates' recommendations include being direct with patients about why questions on sexual orientation and gender identity are being asked, ensuring that confidentiality will be maintained, informing patients of the right to opt-out, and asking multiple questions to assess both sexual orientation and gender identity.[96] In particular, the IOM recommends collecting such data in electronic medical records (EMRs), which are growing in use.[97]

Impact of DOMA Ruling

Spousal coverage is an important pathway to insurance for millions of people, particularly in the context of employer-sponsored health insurance. Until recently, the federal government did not recognize same-sex marriage due to

DOMA, which therefore limited LGB individuals' access to a wide range of benefits, including health coverage as a dependent spouse. In June 2013, the Supreme Court issued a ruling in *United States v. Windsor* that overturned a portion of DOMA and requires the federal government to recognize legal same-sex marriages. The DOMA ruling and subsequent Agency policy interpretations and guidance have resulted in expanded access for some LGB families to a range of benefits, including dependent health coverage and family and medical leave. For more information on the impact of federal policy changes, please refer to Table 1.

- The Supreme Court decision has prompted federal agencies to reverse previous limitations on spousal benefits in some federal programs. For example, all federal employees who are legally married now have the same eligibility for dependent spousal health coverage in the Federal Employees Health Benefits Program (FEHBP) as well as other dependent benefits, such as dental and vision insurance, long-term care insurance, and flexible spending accounts.[98] The Department of Labor has also clarified that employers must now recognize married same-sex couples for federally required benefits such as COBRA, the program that offers employees and their families a temporary extension of group health coverage in the event that an employee loses his or her job.[99]

- More broadly, as a result of the Supreme Court ruling, the Internal Revenue Service (IRS) has ruled that it now recognizes all legally married couples (based on "state of celebration," regardless of whether or not the couple lives in a state that recognizes same-sex marriage) and that they can file federal taxes as "married," which affects a number of health-related financial issues such as the taxes they pay on health benefits.[100] For example, dependent coverage, including spousal coverage, is excluded from an employee's taxable income. However, prior to the Supreme Court ruling, coverage for a domestic partner was considered taxable income, which raised taxes for those who received this coverage. The Supreme Court decision means that married same-sex couples no longer face this higher tax burden at the federal level.[101]

- The decision also affects LGB individuals' eligibility for assistance under the ACA's coverage expansion, which is based in part on applicants' family structure and incomes. Federal regulations have clarified that insurance marketplaces will recognize same-sex marriages and base eligibility for tax credits on couples' income.[102] The federal government is encouraging states to recognize same-sex marriages for the purpose of determining Medicaid income eligibility, but the ultimate determination is under state jurisdiction since Medicaid is a federal-state partnership.[103]

- At the same time, the Supreme Court's ruling does not require private companies to provide health insurance to same-sex spouses. Rather, access to spousal coverage is governed by a patchwork of state-level policies as marriage and partnership recognition are still based on state laws. In the wake of the 2013 DOMA ruling, several states have overturned bans on same sex marriage, and in October 2014, the Supreme Court refused to hear further argument on these cases, effectively legalizing same sex marriage in several more states. As of October 2014, 32 states and the District of Columbia recognize same-sex marriages.[104] In these states, employees' same-sex spouses should have the same eligibility as opposite sex spouses for dependent health insurance. In addition to marriage recognition laws, some states had passed separate measures that require fully insured employers in the state to cover same-sex spouses. These measures also encouraged employers to extend benefits to those in civil unions and domestic partnerships. While same sex marriage is now legal in most states, of the 18 states that still prohibit it, none have an insurance parity requirement.

- Still, many states impose bans on same-sex marriages or do not recognize same-sex marriages that were conducted legally in other states. To date, private employers in these states are not required to extend dependent coverage to same-sex spouses, but employers may choose to do so regardless of state marriage laws. Nationally, four in ten (39%) firms that offered health insurance provided benefits to unmarried same-sex domestic partners in 2014, up from 21% in 2009. This varies by firm size, region, and industry, with larger companies, those in the Northeast, and manufacturing field most likely to offer coverage to same-sex partners (Table 2).

- A recent development occurred in May 2014, when HHS invalidated a 1981 rule that allowed Medicare to deny coverage for transsexual surgery.[105] As a result, insurance plans are no longer able to use this rule to deny claims related to transsexual surgery, although they may still use alternate rationale to deny these claims. Several employers have also moved to make their plan offerings more comprehensive by removing exclusions for transgender health services. Among major U.S. employers, there has been a five-fold increase in the number of businesses offering at least one health plan that includes coverage of transgender services such as counseling, hormone therapy, and surgical procedures.[106]

Family Caregiving Issues

Caring for ill family members is another area of policy that has been evolving in recent years for LGBT people and their families. The Family Medical Leave Act (FMLA) provides workplace protections to employees if they take time off to care for a family member in the event of illness or birth of a child. Under DOMA, LGB individuals were not afforded the law's protections to care for a spouse because the federal government did not recognize same-sex marriages; however, the Supreme Court's decision extends the law to all legally married individuals at qualifying employers. While this is an important step, it does not cover all workers. Additionally there are still other barriers that can limit the reach of these new policies.

- The Department of Labor (DOL) expanded FMLA in 2013 after the ruling on DOMA to include same-sex spouses married and residing in states that recognized same-sex marriage.[107] In June 2014, the DOL proposed rules to further expand FMLA to include same-sex couples based on state of celebration, regardless of their state of residence.[108]
- Paid sick leave is another important benefit that many workers do not have. Because it is legal in more than half the states to fire employees based on their sexual orientation or gender identity, LGBT employees without paid leave may be more reluctant to take time off when they or their family members are sick.[109]
- In addition to workplace protections, visiting loved ones in the hospital or another health care setting has not always been guaranteed for LGBT people. However, federal regulations in effect since 2011 require hospitals

participating in Medicare and Medicaid (virtually all hospitals in the U.S.) to adopt written policies and procedures regarding a patient's rights to visit his or her same-sex partner and state explicitly that discrimination based on sexual orientation and gender identity are prohibited.[110]

- Concerns have also been raised about discrimination against older LGBT individuals and their families in long-term care facilities. Recent federal regulations now provide residents of long-term care facilities, such as nursing homes, the right to have visitors of their choice, including same-sex spouses and domestic partners.[111]

***

A number of health challenges disproportionately affect LGBT communities, particularly the HIV/AIDS epidemic, stigma and violence, substance abuse, negative experiences in the health care system, and lack of insurance coverage. In addition to health outcomes, access to care has been a concern and intersects with many broader issues, including relationship recognition, legal identity recognition policies for transgender individuals, training and cultural competency of health professionals, as well as overarching societal and cultural issues, particularly a long history of stigma and discrimination. Recent policy and legal changes will serve to mitigate some of these challenges. In particular, the years ahead will see both the full implementation of the ACA as well as the full effects of overturning elements of DOMA, and for the first time in the nation's history, same-sex marriage is legal in the majority of states. This convergence of policy and legal breakthroughs holds promise for broader access to health services, coverage, and benefits for LGBT communities.

Table 1 Impact of Selected Federal Policy Changes on Coverage and Access to Care for LGBT Communities

Policy	Key Provisions and Impact
The Patient Protection and Affordable Care Act (ACA)[112]	• Broadens federal nondiscrimination in health care programs receiving federal funds and prohibits basing coverage eligibility, insurance premium pricing, benefit design, or any other aspect of coverage on sex, gender identity, or sex stereotyping. • Explicitly prohibits state insurance marketplaces and plans offering the essential health benefits from discriminating based on sexual orientation or gender identity. • Promotes data collection and analysis on sexual orientation and gender identity through federally-sponsored surveys and programs. • Individuals will no longer be denied coverage due to a pre-existing condition, such as HIV/AIDS, mental illness, or a transgender medical history. • New private plans are required to cover USPSTF recommended preventive services without cost sharing. Includes screenings for HIV, STIs, depression, and substance misuse. • Expands coverage to many uninsured persons through Medicaid and state-based health insurance marketplaces. Medicaid, in states that expand, will base eligibility solely on income (no categorical requirement) and tax credits are available to help subsidize the cost of coverage in marketplaces for low income individuals.

Table 1   Impact of Selected Federal Policy Changes on Coverage and Access to Care for LGBT Communities *(continued)*

Policy	Key Provisions and Impact
	• Overturned Section 3 of the Defense of Marriage Act, which limited marriage to persons of the opposite sex. Treats legal marriages between same-sex individuals the same as marriages between opposite sex individuals with regard to federal law.
	• **Department of Health and Human Services**[113]
	• Guarantees that same-sex married beneficiaries in Medicare Advantage plans who both need care in a skilled nursing facility can receive care at same facility.
	• **Center for Consumer Information and Insurance Oversight (CCIIO) Guidance on IRS Ruling 2013–17 and Eligibility for Advance Payments of the Premium Tax Credit and Cost-Sharing Reductions**
	• All Health Insurance Marketplaces are to recognize legal same-sex marriages when determining eligibility for Premium Assistance and Tax Credits.[114]
	• **Center for Medicare and Medicaid Services (CMS) Guidance to advise of the implications of the Windsor decision for Medicaid and CHIP**[115]
	• Allows states to decide whether to recognize same-sex marriages when determining Medicaid eligibility.
	• **Internal Revenue Service (IRS) Ruling 2013–17**[116]
United States v. Windsor—Overturn of Federal Defense of Marriage Act (DOMA)	• Ruled that same-sex couples legally married will be treated as married for federal tax purposes, regardless of whether the couple lives in a jurisdiction that recognizes same-sex marriage or not ("state of celebration" takes precedent). Allows couples to file taxes as "married" and thus treats same-sex spousal health coverage as tax exempt for purposes of determining federal income tax.
	• If same-sex spouse received employer-based dependent insurance, the employee may apply for refund of excess federal income taxes paid on the value of the coverage for past 2–3 years.
	• **Department of Labor Technical Release Number 2013–04**[117]
	• Requires all ERISA plans to include legally married same-sex couples in the definition of "spouse" and "marriage," opening the door for broader dependent coverage of same-sex spouses.
	• **Department of Defense Memorandum Subject: Extending Benefits to the Same-Sex Spouses Of Military Members**[118]
	• Legally married spouses eligible for dependent health coverage of service members and DOD civilian employees.
	• **Department Of Justice Letter to The Honorable John Boehner**[119]
	• Extends VA and DOD spousal benefits to same-sex spouses by no longer enforcing Title 38 of the U.S. Code, which had previously limited benefits to opposite-sex marriages only.
	• **Department of Labor, Wage and Hour Division-The Family and Medical Leave Act**
	• As a result of the DOMA ruling, the DOL expanded the definition of spouse under FMLA to include same-sex couples residing in a state that legally recognized same-sex marriage.[120]
	• **Notice of Proposed Rulemaking**[121]: In 2014, DOL proposed a further expansion of the definition of "spouse" to include all legally married same-sex couples.
	• **Presidential Memorandum-Hospital Visitation**[122]
	• Executive order in 2010 stating hospitals that receive funds from Medicaid and Medicare are to respect the rights of patients to designate visitors, including those designated by legally valid advance directives.
	• Hospitals may not deny visitation privileges on the basis of race, color, national origin, religion, sex, sexual orientation, gender identity, or disability.
Other	• Guidance issued in November 2010 supports enforcement of the right of patients to designate the person of their choice, including a same-sex partner, to make medical decisions on their behalf should they become incapacitated.
	• **Centers for Medicare and Medicaid Services memorandum 13-42-NH: Remainder-Access and Visitation Rights in Long Term Facilities**[123]
	• LTC facilities must ensure that all individuals seeking to visit a resident be given full and equal visitation privileges, consistent with resident preferences within reasonable restrictions that safeguard residents.

Health and Access to Care and Coverage for Lesbian, Gay, Bisexual, and Transgender Individuals in the U.S. by Usha Ranji et al.

219

Table 1 Impact of Selected Federal Policy Changes on Coverage and Access to Care for LGBT Communities *(continued)*

Policy	Key Provisions and Impact
	• **Centers for Medicare and Medicaid Services–Medicaid Spousal Impoverishment Protections**[124]
	• Protections have been extended to include same-sex spouses. This allows a spouse living in the community to maintain a certain level of assets when institutional expenses (usually a nursing home) threaten to deplete all resources and impoverish the community-based spouse.
	• **National Institutes of Health–LGBT Research Coordinating Committee**[125]
	• This committee was formed to consider recommendations of the Institute of Medicine's study *The Health of Lesbian, Gay, Bisexual, and Transgender People: Building a Foundation for Better Understanding* and to suggest strategies for how the NIH can support research.

Table 2 Among Firms Offering Health Benefits, Distribution of Whether Employers Offer Health Benefits to Unmarried Same-Sex Domestic Partners, by Firm Size, Region, Industry, 2014

	Offer Health Coverage to Same-sex Partners	Do Not Offer Health Coverage to Same-sex Partners	Not Encountered
Firm Size			
All Small Firms (3–199 Workers)	39%	19%*	42%*
All Large Firms (≥ 200 Workers)	49%*	45%*	5%*
Region			
Northeast	60%*	21%	19%*
Midwest	28%	24%	47%
South	25%*	22%	53%
West	48%	11%	41%
Industry			
Manufacturing	69%*	20%	12%*
Wholesale	38%	36%	25%
Retail	25%	12%	63%
Finance	55%	22%	23%
State/ Local Government	16%*	27%	57%
All Firms	**39%**	**20%**	**41%**

* Estimate is statistically different from estimate for all firms not in the indicated size, region, or industry category (p < .05).

Note: The response option "not encountered" captures the number of firms that report not having a policy on the issue. This response is distinguished from firms that report "no" since those firms have a set policy on the issue.

Source: Kaiser/HRET, Employer Health Benefits Survey, 2014.

Notes

1. Institute of Medicine. (2011). *The Health of Lesbian, Gay, Bisexual, and Transgender People: Building a Foundation for Better Understanding.*

2. Healthy People 2020: *Lesbian, Gay, Bisexual, and Transgender Health.*

3. Agency for Healthcare Research and Quality. (2012). *2012 National Healthcare Disparities Report.*

4. DHHS. (2013). *"HHS LGBT Issues Coordinating Committee 2013 Report."*

5. Institute of Medicine. (2011). *The Health of Lesbian, Gay, Bisexual, and Transgender People: Building a Foundation for Better Understanding.*

6. Ibid.

7. National Center for Transgender Equality. (2009). *Transgender Terminology.*

8. Gates, G. (March 22, 2010). LGBT Demographics: Presentation to the Institute of Medicine.

9. Centers for Disease Control and Prevention, National Health Statistics Reports. (July 2014). Sexual Orientation and Health Among U.S. Adults: National Health Interview Survey, 2013.

10. Gallup Politics. (October 18, 2012). Special Report: 3.4% of U.S. Adults Identify as LGBT.

11. Gates, G. (2011). How many people are lesbian, gay, bisexual, and transgender? *The Williams Institute.*

12. Gallup Politics. (July 30, 2014). LGBT Americans Continue to Skew Democratic and Liberal.

13. Gates, G. (2014). LGB/T Demographics: Comparisons among population-based surveys. *The Williams Institute.*

14. Where data do not include transgender individuals, LGB (lesbian, gay, bisexual) is used.

15. Institute of Medicine. (2011). *The Health of Lesbian, Gay, Bisexual, and Transgender People: Building a Foundation for Better Understanding.*

16. Coffman, KB, Coffman, LC & Marzilli Ericson, KM. (2013). The Size of the LGBT Population and the Magnitude of Anti-Gay Sentiment are Substantially Underestimated, NBER Working Paper No. 19508.

17. Gates, G. (2011). How many people are lesbian, gay, bisexual, and transgender? *The Williams Institute.*

18. Gallup Politics. (February 15, 2013). LGBT Percentage Highest in D.C., Lowest in North Dakota.

19. Gallup Politics. (October 18, 2012). Special Report: 3.4% of U.S. Adults Identify as LGBT.

20. Ibid.

21. United States Census Bureau. (2012). Same-Sex Couples Main-Characteristics of Same-Sex Couple Households: 2012.

22. Pew Research Center (June 2013). A Survey of LGBT Americans Attitudes, Experiences and Values in Changing Times.

23. Badgett, M.V., Durso, L.E. & Schneebaum, A. (2013). New Patterns of Poverty in the Lesbian, Gay, and Bisexual Community. *The Williams Institute.*

24. Grant JM, Mottet LA, Tanis J, Harrison J, Herman JL, Keisling M. (2011). Injustice at Every Turn: A Report of the National Transgender Discrimination Survey. Washington, DC: National Center for Transgender Equality and National Gay and Lesbian Task Force.

25. Agency for Healthcare Research and Quality. (2012). *2012 National Healthcare Disparities Report.*

26. Institute of Medicine. (2011). *The Health of Lesbian, Gay, Bisexual, and Transgender People: Building a Foundation for Better Understanding.*

27. Healthy People 2020: *Lesbian, Gay, Bisexual, and Transgender Health.*

28. Agency for Healthcare Research and Quality. (2012). *2012 National Healthcare Disparities Report.*

29. Lick, D., Durso, L.E., & Johnson, K.L. (2013). Minority Stress and Physical Health Among Sexual Minorities. *Pers on Psychological Sci 8*(5): 521–548.

30. Denney, J.T., Gorman, B.K. & Barrera, C.B. (2013). Families, Resources, and Adult Health: Where do Sexual Minorities Fit? *Journal of Health and Social Behavior 54*(1): 46–63.

31. Lick, D., Durso, L.E., & Johnson, K.L. (2013). Minority Stress and Physical Health Among Sexual Minorities. *Pers on Psychological Sci 8*(5): 521–548.

32. Ibid.

33. Centers for Disease Control and Prevention, National Health Statistics Reports. (July 2014). Sexual Orientation and Health Among U.S. Adults: National Health Interview Survey, 2013.

34. Massachusetts Department of Public Health. (2009). The Health of Lesbian, Gay, Bisexual, and Transgender (LGBT) Persons in Massachusetts.

35. Centers for Disease Control and Prevention. (2013). HIV Among Gay, Bisexual, and Other Men Who Have Sex With Men.

36. Centers for Disease Control and Prevention. (2013). HIV Among Black/African American Gay, Bisexual, and Other Men Who Have Sex With Men.

37. Kaiser Family Foundation, HIV/AIDS In The Lives Of Gay And Bisexual Men In The United States, 2014.

38. Singh, S., et al. (2014). Men Living with Diagnosed HIV Who Have Sex with Men: Progress Along the Continuum of HIV Care—U.S., 2010. *MMWR.*

39. Centers for Disease Control and Prevention. (2013). HIV Among Transgender People.

40. Centers for Disease Control and Prevention. (2014). Likely Female-to-Female Sexual Transmission of HIV-Texas, 2012.

41. Centers for Disease Control and Prevention. (2010). Syphilis & MSM-CDC Fact Sheet.

42. Centers for Disease Control and Prevention. (2012). Viral Hepatitis and Men Who Have Sex With Men.

43. Centers for Disease Control and Prevention. (2013). HPV-Associated Cancers Statistics.

44. Centers for Disease Control and Prevention. (2012). HPV and Men-Fact Sheet.

45. Lick, D., Durso, L.E., & Johnson, K.L. (2013). Minority Stress and Physical Health Among Sexual Minorities. *Pers on Psychological Sci* 8(5): 521–548.

46. Cochran, S.D., Sullivan, J.G. & Mays, V.M. (2003). Prevalence of mental disorders, psychological distress, and mental health services use among Lesbian, Gay, and Bisexual adults in the United States. *Journal of Consulting and Clinical Psychology* 71(1): 53–61.

47. Institute of Medicine. (2011). *The Health of Lesbian, Gay, Bisexual, and Transgender People: Building a Foundation for Better Understanding.*

48. Ford, Z. (December 3, 2012). *APA Revises Manual: Being Transgender is no Longer a Mental Disorder. Think Progress.*

49. Lick, D., Durso, L.E., & Johnson, K.L. (2013). Minority Stress and Physical Health Among Sexual Minorities. *Pers on Psychological Sci* 8(5): 521–548.

50. Substance Abuse and Mental Health Services Administration. (2012). Top Health Issues for LGBT Populations: Information & Resources Kit.

51. Lee, J., Griffin, G., Melvin, C. (2009). Tobacco use among sexual minorities in the USA, 1987 to May 2007: a systematic review. *Tob Control.* 18:275–282.

52. Cochran, S.D., Sullivan, J.G. & Mays, V.M. (2003). Prevalence of mental disorders, psychological distress, and mental health services use among Lesbian, Gay, and Bisexual adults in the United States. *Journal of Consulting and Clinical Psychology* 71(1): 53–61.

53. Grant, J.M., Mottet, L.A., Tanis, J., Harrison, J, Herman, J.L., Keisling M. (2011). Injustice at Every Turn: A Report of the National Transgender Discrimination Survey. Washington, DC: National Center for Transgender Equality and National Gay and Lesbian Task Force.

54. Ostrow, D.G. & Stall, R. (2008) Alcohol, tobacco, and drug use among gay and bisexual men. In Wolitski, R.J., Stall, R., & Valdiserri, R.O., *Unequal opportunity: Health disparities affecting gay and bisexual men in the United States.* New York: Oxford University Press.

55. Centers for Disease Control and Prevention. (2009). Sexual Violence: Consequences.

56. Human Rights Campaign, (2011). A Guide to State Level Advocacy Following Enactment of the Matthew Shepard and James Byrd, Jr. Hate Crimes Prevention Act.

57. Pew Research Center (June 2013). A Survey of LGBT Americans Attitudes, Experiences and Values in Changing Times.

58. Centers for Disease Control and Prevention. (2013). The National Intimate Partner and Sexual Violence Survey: 2010 Findings on Victimization by Sexual Orientation.

59. U.S. Department of Justice Federal Bureau of Investigation, (2012). *Hate Crime Statistics 2011.*

60. Herek, G.M. (2009). Hate Crimes and Stigma-Related Experiences Among Minority Adults in the United States: Prevalence Estimates from a National Probability Sample. *Journal of Interpersonal Violence.*

61. Ibid.

62. Lombardi E, et al. (2002). Gender violence: Transgender experiences with violence and discrimination. *J Homosex* 42(1).

63. National Coalition of Anti-Violence Programs. (2013). Lesbian, Gay, Bisexual, Transgender, Queer, and HIV-Affected Hate Violence in 2012.

64. Human Rights Campaign. (2012). National Coming Out Day Youth Report.

65. Centers for Disease Control and Prevention. (2011). Lesbian, Gay, Bisexual, and Transgender Health: Youth.

66. The Williams Institute. (2012). Serving Our Youth: Findings from a National Survey of Service Providers Working with Lesbian, Gay, Bisexual, and Transgender Youth who Are Homeless or At Risk of Becoming Homeless.

67. Gay, Lesbian & Straight Education Network. (2012). 2011 National School Climate Survey.

68. Centers for Disease Control and Prevention. (2011). Sexual Identity, Sex of Sexual Contacts, and Health Risk Behaviors Among Students in Grades 9–12: Youth Risk Behavior Surveillance, Selected Sites, United States, 2001–2009.

69. Personal communication with Kellan Baker, Center for American Progress, December 6, 2013.

70. Perry Undem Research/Communication, LGBT Community and the ACA, Presentation September 12, 2013.

71. Center for American Progress. (2013). *LGBT* Communities and the Affordable Care Act: Findings from a National Survey.

72. Clift, J. & Kirby J. (2012). Health care access and perceptions of provider care among individuals in Same-Sex Couples: Findings from the Medical Expenditure Panel Survey (MEPS). Journal of Homosexuality 59(6): 839–850.

73. Buchmueller, T. & Carpenter C. (2010). Disparities in health insurance coverage, access, and outcomes for individuals in same-sex versus different-sex relationships, 2000–2007. *American Journal of Public Health* 100(3): 489–495.

74. Kerker, B.D., Mostashari, F. & Thorpe, L. (2006). Health care access and utilization among women who have sex with women: Sexual behavior and identity. *Journal of Urban Health* 83(5): 970–979.

75. Cochran, S.D., et al. (2001). Cancer-related risk indicators and preventive screening behaviors among lesbians and bisexual women. *American Journal of Public Health* 91(4): 591–597.

76. National Center for Transgender Equality and National Gay and Lesbian Task Force. (2011). Injustice at Every Turn: A Report of the National Transgender Discrimination Survey.

77. Center for American Progress. (2012). FAQ: Health Insurance Needs for Transgender Americans.

78. Lambda Legal, "When Health Care Isn't Caring: Lambda Legal's Survey on Discrimination Against LGBT People and People Living with HIV".

79. The Fenway Institute. (2008). *The Fenway Guide to Lesbian, Gay, Bisexual, and Transgender Health.*

80. Lambda Legal, "When Health Care Isn't Caring: Lambda Legal's Survey on Discrimination Against LGBT People and People Living with HIV".

81. Movement Advancement Project. (2009). Advancing Transgender Equality.

82. Tesar, C. & Rovi, S. (1998). Survey on Curriculum on Homosexuality/ Bisexuality in Departments of Family Medicine. *Fam Medicine* 30(4): 283–287.

83. Corliss, H.L., Shankle, M.D. & Moyer, M.B. (2007). Research, Curricula, and Resources Related to Lesbian, Gay, Bisexual, and Transgender Health in U.S. Schools of Public Health. American Journal of Public Health 97(6): 1023–1027.

84. GLMA, Health Professionals Advancing LGBT Equality. (2013). Compendium of Health Profession Association LGBT Policy & Position Statements.

85. World Professional Association for Transgender Health (2012). Standards of Care for the Health of Transsexual, Transgender, and Gender-Nonconforming People.

86. The Joint Commission. (2010). Advancing Effective Communication, Cultural Competence, and Patient- and Family-Centered Care: A Roadmap for Hospitals.

87. DHHS. (2013). "HHS LGBT Issues Coordinating Committee 2013 Report".

88. Center for American Progress. (2013). How New Coverage Options Affect LGBT Communities.

89. Lambda Legal, "When Health Care Isn't Caring: Lambda Legal's Survey on Discrimination Against LGBT People and People Living with HIV".

90. Baker, K. & Cray, A. (2012). Ensuring Benefits Parity and Gender Identity Nondiscrimination in Essential Health Benefits.

91. Human Rights Campaign. Health Insurance Discrimination for Transgender People.

92. Department of Health and Human Services. Federal Register 77(59): March 27, 2012.

93. Movement Advancement Project. Non-Discrimination Laws.

94. Ibid.

95. Department of Health and Human Services. (2013). HHS LGBT Issues Coordinating Committee 2013 Report.

96. The Fenway Institute. (2012). Policy Focus: How to gather data on sexual orientation and gender identity in clinical settings.

97. Institute of Medicine. (2011). The Health of Lesbian, Gay, Bisexual, and Transgender People: Building a Foundation for Better Understanding.

98. U.S. Office of Personnel Management, *Guidance on the Extension of Benefits to Married Gay and Lesbian Federal Employees, Annuitants, and their Families,* June 28, 2013.

99. Department of Labor, Technical Release No. 2013–04, September 18, 2013.

100. Internal Revenue Service, Rev. Rul. 2013–17.

101. Ibid.

102. Department of Health and Human Services, Guidance on Internal Revenue Ruling 2013–17 and Eligibility for Advance Payments of the Premium Tax Credit and Cost-Sharing Reductions, September 27, 2013.

103. Department of Health and Human Services, State Health Officer & 13–006, September 27, 2013.

104. Human Rights Campaign. Marriage Center.

105. Department of Health and Human Services, Departmental Appeals Board, Appellate Division. NCD 140.3, Transsexual Surgery, Docket No. A-13-87, Decision No. 2576, May 30, 2014.

106. Human Rights Campaign. (2013). Corporate Equality Index.

107. Department of Labor, Wage and Hour Division, Fact Sheet # 28F: Qualifying Reasons for Leave under the Family and Medical Leave Act, August 2013.

108. Department of Labor, Wage and Hour Division. Federal Register 79(124): June 27, *2014.*

109. National Gay and Lesbian Task Force, Nondiscrimination Laws Map, June 21, 2013.

110. Department of Health and Human Services, Medicare finalizes new rules to require equal visitation rights for all hospital patients, November 17, 2010.

111. Centers for Medicare and Medicaid Services. (2013). Details for Title: Reminder: Access and Visitation Rights in Long Term Care (LTC) Facilities.

112. Department of Health and Human Services. Federal Register 77(59): March 27, 2012.

113. Department of Health and Human Services, HHS announces first guidance implementing Supreme Court's decision on the Defense of Marriage Act, August 29, 2013.

114. Department of Health and Human Services, Guidance on Internal Revenue Ruling 2013–17 and Eligibility for Advance Payments of the Premium Tax Credit and Cost-Sharing Reductions, September 27, 2013.

115. Department of Health and Human Services, State Health Officer & 13–006, September 27, 2013.

116. U.S. Department of the Treasury, All Legal Same-Sex Marriages Will be Recognized for Federal Tax Purposes, August 29, 2013.

117. Department of Labor, Technical Release No. 2013–04, September 18, 2013.

Health and Access to Care and Coverage for Lesbian, Gay, Bisexual, and Transgender Individuals in the U.S. by Usha Ranji et al.

223

118. Secretary of Defense, Extending Benefits to Same-Sex Spouses of Military Members; August 13, 2013.

119. Department of Justice, Attorney General Holder Announces Move to Extend Veterans Benefits to Same-Sex Married Couples, September 4, 2013.

120. Department of Labor, Wage and Hour Division, Fact Sheet & 28F: Qualifying Reasons for Leave under the Family and Medical Leave Act, August 2013.

121. Department of Labor, Wage and Hour Division. Federal Register 79(124): June 27, 2014.

122. Office of the Press Secretary, *Presidential Memorandum-Hospital Visitation*, April 15, 2010.

123. Centers for Medicare and Medicaid Services. (2013). Details for Title: Reminder: Access and Visitation Rights in Long Term Care (LTC) Facilities.

124. Centers for Medicare and Medicaid Services. (2013). Spousal Impoverishment.

125. National Institutes of Health. (January 4, 2013). Statement by NIH Director Francis S. Collins, M.D., Ph.D., on opportunities for advancing LGBT health research.

Critical Thinking

1. What are some of the things you've noticed in your own doctor's or clinician's office that makes it a welcoming place for LGBT individuals? What could they do better?

2. What role does stigma play in the accessibility and availability of physical and mental health services for LGBT individuals?

3. Many of the procedures that are part of Sex Realignment Surgery are not covered by health insurance. Do you think they should be? Why or why not?

Internet References

Centers for Disease Control and Prevention: LGBT Health
http://www.cdc.gov/lgbthealth

National Coalition on LGBT Health
http://www.healthhiv.org

National LGBT Health Education Center
http://www.lgbthealtheducation.org

Usha Ranji is Associate Director for Women's Health Policy at the Henry J. Kaiser Family Foundation. Her work addresses the impact of major health policy issues on women and girls, with an emphasis on insurance coverage, access to care, and low-income populations. In particular, her work aims to understand how federal, state, and local policies, including national health care reform and reproductive health policies, influence health and access to services for women. **Adara Beamesderfer** is a Policy Associate for the Women's Health Policy team at the Henry J. Kaiser Family Foundation. She conducts research on the impact of major health policies on women and girls, with an emphasis on insurance coverage, access to care, and low-income populations. In particular, the Program aims to understand how federal, state, and local policies, including national health care reform and reproductive health policies, influence health and access to services for women. Adara holds a B.S. in Health Services Administration from San Jose State University and is currently pursuing an MPH in Health Policy from the George Washington University. **Jen Kates** is Vice President and Director of Global Health & HIV Policy at the Kaiser Family Foundation. She oversees the Foundation's policy analysis and research focused on the U.S. government's role in global health and on the global and domestic HIV epidemics. Prior to joining the Foundation in 1998, Dr. Kates was a Senior Associate with The Lewin Group, a health care consulting firm, where she focused on HIV policy, strategic planning/health systems analysis, and health care for vulnerable populations. Prior to that, she directed the Office of Lesbian, Gay, and Bisexual Concerns at Princeton University. **Alina Salganicoff** is Vice President and Director of Women's Health Policy. Widely regarded as an expert on women's health policy she has written and lectured extensively on health care access and financing for low-income women and children. Her work at the Foundation focuses on health coverage and access to care for women, with an emphasis on challenges facing underserved women throughout their lifespan. Dr. Salganicoff was also an Associate Director of the Kaiser Commission on Medicaid and the Uninsured and worked on the health program staff of the Pew Charitable Trusts and as a trainer and counselor at CHOICE based in Philadelphia.

Article

Prepared by: Elizabeth Schroeder, EdD, MSW,
Elizabeth Schroeder Consulting

Better Birth Control for Men:
8 Promising Possibilities

VALERIE TARICO

Learning Outcomes

After reading this article, you will be able to:

- Describe at least two new birth control methods that are being manufactured and tested for use on the male body.

- Describe at least two cancer medications that are currently being tested for use as male hormonal contraceptive methods.

- Provide two reasons why it continues to take so long for contraceptive methods for men to be developed and approved for use.

Safe, effective birth control for men is long overdue. Consider a tale of two siblings:

When Mary hit middle school, she began having such painful periods that her father once called the paramedics, thinking she had a ruptured appendix. But at age 14, she got a state-of-the-art hormonal intrauterine device (IUD) that cured her terrible monthly cramps. Over time, the IUD not only would virtually eradicate her bleeding and pain, but would also provide top-tier contraception for up to seven years. Once Mary became sexually active, her annual pregnancy risk would be around 1 in 700. By contrast, Mary's college-age brother, who was relying on condoms (with an annual pregnancy risk of 1 in 5), had to share the emotional and monetary burden of an unwanted pregnancy and abortion.

No parent wants a son depending on the young women he dates to prevent a surprise pregnancy, but the options stink. As one mother of three boys put it:

Every day teens are having sexual relations, and the method of birth control is either left to the girl (most of which aren't on anything because they don't want their parents to know), condoms (which are horribly unreliable, especially in the hands of teens), or most often nothing. If parents were more involved and more teens had access to new methods of contraception . . . more kids would have the ability to make a future. Boys need that option as much as girls.

Over the past 50 years, birth control for women has been refined to the point that there are now dozens of alternatives that are far safer than pregnancy, many of which have added benefits like reducing menstrual symptoms, acne, or even the risk of cancer. The array includes three kinds of long-acting "fit and forget" contraceptives that are over 20 times better than the familiar "pill" but allow a quick return to normal fertility. But, after all this time, men are still stuck choosing between two century-old choices: condoms and vasectomies.

Don't get me wrong—condoms are far better than nothing. They are the best thing we have for reducing sexually transmitted diseases. However, many people have a mistaken perception of how well they work for actual pregnancy prevention. If everybody who relies on condoms could use them perfectly and with perfect consistency, only two couples in 100 would get pregnant each year via condom failure. But from a "human factors engineering" standpoint, condoms stink. In the real world where people fumble, forget, and wait too long to put them on or take them off, many couples depending on condoms end up pregnant. Condoms drop pregnancy rates from 85 percent (the rate for a sexually active couple using no contraception for one year) to 18 percent—a big improvement, but still terrifying for someone whose plans and efforts could be blown apart by a ruptured rubber.

Men want better choices, and women want better choices for men, and parents want better choices for their sons. And yet, as Dr. John Amory at the University of Washington put it, "Everybody's been saying, 'within the next five years,' for the last 30 years," but no new method for men has made it to market.

Dependable Male Birth Control Could Change Our Lives

We all, men and women alike, should be demanding better birth control for men. First off, there's the fairness factor. Just like girls, young men should be able to pursue their dreams, confident that they won't be derailed by a surprise pregnancy. In the 1999 movie *A Walk on the Moon*, a young mother, locked into a traditional working-class lifestyle by teen pregnancy, feels drawn to the 1969 Summer of Love emerging around her. As she indulges her yearning for freedom and adventure (and Viggo Mortensen), her husband, who "did the right thing" when she first got pregnant, is confronted with his own losses, especially the college education foregone. "You think I wanted to fix TVs?" he asks.

Besides derailing individual lives, the fact that men can't count on their contraception means we all get stuck living in old cultural scripts. For millennia, our ancestors had no reliable means to manage their fertility. Given the power of the human sex drive, even abstinence commitments backed by a death penalty for sinners couldn't be considered reliable. In other words, if our ancestors sought sex or intimacy—and we humans crave both—then children were a byproduct, wanted or not.

Consequently, throughout history children came into the world unplanned and mostly when parents would have chosen not to have another child. But to thrive, kids needed just as much care as they do today. In response, both culture and religion evolved messages to help ensure that such children were wanted and loved when they arrived. "Let go and let God," some Christians say. "Que será, será." "A baby is a blessing." Still, today, some fundamentalist sects make passive submission to pregnancy a sacred virtue, and in Western culture at large, go-with-the-flow childbearing is accepted and celebrated. This is true even though we now have good evidence that thoughtful family planning increases maternal and child health, prosperity, marital harmony, and the ability of young men and women to live fulfilling lives.

Thanks to some determined researchers and funders, things may get better in the near future. An array of promising possibilities can be found in various stages of research around the globe. Here are some of the top contenders.

The "Clean Sheets Pill" (London, Oxford): Dr. Nnaemeka Amobi and his team are researching a hormone-free method that has been dubbed the "clean sheets pill" because it decreases or eliminates semen emission while leaving intact the sensation of ejaculation and the pleasure of male orgasm. The pill works by relaxing just the muscles in the vas deferens that normally propel sperm-containing semen forward and out. Without the forward propulsion, circular muscle contractions essentially close down the passage. Reducing or eliminating emission of semen not only prevents pregnancy, it also decreases the spread of semen-born diseases, including HIV. The hope is that this medication can be delivered via pills that men take before sex, much like Viagra.

RISUG (Kharagpur): More than 250 men have undergone a procedure called RISUG (reversible inhibition of sperm under guidance), which researchers hope will provide a cheaper and more reversible alternative to vasectomy. A liquid polymer is injected into the vas deferens, where it provides contraception for up to ten years. In the duct, the positively charged polymer reportedly acts almost like a magnet, reacting with the negative electrical charge on the membranes of passing sperm and rendering them infertile. In research with rats and primates, fertility has been restored by a noninvasive procedure that removes the polymer. Human clinical trials of RISUG are moving forward slowly in India.

Vasalgel (San Francisco): Inspired by RISUG, a similar polymer, dubbed Vasalgel, is under development in the United States, with rabbit research now underway to meet Food and Drug Administration standards and primate studies planned. Over 16,000 men and women have signed up to receive information about clinical trials, expected to begin in 2014.

Ultrasound (Chapel Hill): Therapeutic ultrasound is a common sports medicine treatment for injured joints and muscles. A brief massage of the testes with the same instruments has been shown to reduce sperm count in both animals and humans. Doctors have long known that heating the testes even to body temperature reduces fertility, and we know that therapeutic ultrasound produces a deep warmth. But for reasons that are unclear, the contraceptive effect of ultrasound is ten times that of heat alone. Depending on the level of exposure, contraceptive duration ranges from six weeks to permanent. One major challenge at this point is to find a treatment regimen that is either reliably reversible or reliably permanent. Of the two, use as a nonsurgical vasectomy option is more likely.

Gamendazole (Kansas City): Potential contraceptives are sometimes discovered as side effects of other medications, and gamendazole derives from a cancer treatment that by chance was noted to decrease male fertility. Research shows that the drug works by interrupting sperm maturation. Men taking gamendazole produce and release normal quantities of sperm, but the sperm are "nonfunctional." In mating studies of rats, the drug achieved 100 percent infertility and was fully reversible. Research with monkeys looks promising.

Adjudin (New York): Like gamendazole, adjudin is an analogue of a cancer drug, lonidamine. It works the same way, causing sperm to be released when they are immature. For lonidamine, the gap between a contraceptive dose and a toxic dose is small, making the drug too dangerous to give to healthy people. But researchers at the Population Council were able to create a related compound that is taken up only by the precise receptors in the testes where it is needed for contraception. This dramatically reduces the needed dose. Two remaining drawbacks to adjudin are that it can be administered only by injection, and its effect is short-lived. Researchers are working to devise a version that doesn't require frequent injections.

JQ1 (Waco, Boston): JQ1 is related to some familiar drugs, Valium and Xanax, but it has a very different effect. Instead of bringing on sleep or reducing anxiety, it blocks production of a protein in the testes that is essential to sperm growth. In mice that are given JQ1, the number of sperm takes a nose dive, and those that are produced don't swim very well, which makes the mice infertile. Sex drive remains unaltered, and after the drug is stopped, sperm production rapidly returns to normal.

Testosterone and Progestin (Beijing, Los Angeles, Seattle): If injected or absorbed through the skin, testosterone alters hormonal messaging and reduces production of sperm. When combined with a progestogen and rubbed on in gel form, a daily application has effectively suppressed sperm concentration in almost 90 percent of men, with few side effects. Current research is exploring the best combination of testosterone and progestin, and how such a combination can be delivered to provide long-acting birth control.

With such a variety of options (and more) in the works, it seems like something new for men should be just around the corner. But much of the research is progressing at a snail's pace due in part to regulatory barriers and lack of funding.

Contraceptives get used by young, healthy people, which means that the bar for safety and efficacy is much higher than for many other drugs. A cancer treatment might be welcomed if it has a 70 percent success rate and makes your hair fall out. Needless to say, either of these is a non-starter for a new contraceptive. The high bar (and the corresponding high risk of liability) makes drug companies and even philanthropists wary of investing in contraception—which has to be almost 100 percent effective and side effect–free to be a success.

Will any of these options make it to market in the next five years? That depends in part on whether drug companies, nonprofit research funders, and public health experts think we're ready. Do men really want to take responsibility for contraception? Will women trust them to do so? Is there enough demand to make a massive high-risk investment in research and development worthwhile?

Are We Ready?

For a long time, outdated perceptions have contributed to the lack of investment in birth control for men. Since women traditionally have borne the primary burden of unwanted childbearing and parenting, decision-makers have long assumed that men wouldn't be interested in contraceptives—or would have a very low tolerance for cost, side effects, or hassle. Today, though, in the age of paternity tests and child support, with fathers and mothers sharing parenting responsibility—more and more men want to be in control of their own fertility.

In May 2013, when a Florida man found that his girlfriend was pregnant, he tricked her into taking an abortifacient—an act of physical assault. Ultimately, caught in a web of religion-driven anti-abortion laws, he was charged not with assault but with "fetal murder." Few people were sympathetic to his actions, but many were sympathetic to his plight. Men, like women, need effective tools for managing fertility if they are to have a hope of charting their own life course.

Interest in better male-controlled contraception varies widely depending on country and culture, but in a wide variety of countries more than half of men say they want better male birth control methods. After one study of male contraception sponsored by the World Health Organization, 85 percent of participants would have preferred to continue an experimental method rather than returning to whatever they used before—even though the experiment required a weekly injection.

A second longstanding misperception is that women can't and won't trust men for family planning. In truth, even with today's limited options, meaning condoms and vasectomies, approximately one-third of U.S. couples rely on the man to provide contraception. A significant number of men who participate in clinical trials for male contraceptives say their wife or partner has had side effects from female methods or that they want to take the burden off of her for a while.

In general, people tend to overestimate the side effects of female birth control, falsely believing, for example, that contraceptives cause weight gain. But some female bodies respond poorly to even the micro-dose of copper or hormones present in top-tier contraceptives, and for other women the cost of the most effective methods is prohibitive. Barriers to access abound. Faced with the health risks of an unintended pregnancy, a woman can feel caught between a rock and a hard place. Consequently, many women appreciate guys who step up to the plate. Of almost 2,000 women surveyed in Edinburgh, Shanghai, Hong Kong, and Cape Town, a vast majority said they thought a male pill was a good idea, and only 2 percent said they wouldn't trust their partners to use it.

To be frank, more men might do well to ask whether they should trust women to manage contraception. In the United States, with most contraception still in the hands of women, close to half of pregnancies are unintended, and the transition to thoughtful, intentional childbearing has been stalled for decades. Around a quarter of pregnancies occur in a month when a woman says she had used birth control. Like condoms, female barrier methods and even the birth control pill are quite subject to human error. In one study of 82 women, participants on average missed four or five pills per month, even when they were sent text-message reminders. It's simply not reasonable to assume that ordinary human beings will do the same thing in the same way at the same time every day for 40 years—or every time they have sex. While longer-acting "fit and forget" contraceptives like IUDs and implants appear to radically change the equation, so would an improved array of options for the male half of the human race.

On the surface, it may seem that scientific challenges are the primary barrier to excellent male birth control. A woman produces an egg only once each month, while men produce millions of sperm daily. Female fertility can be detected and timed. It starts later and ends sooner than male fertility. But those in the know say biology isn't the problem. The question is one of politics and priorities. The National Institutes of Health summed up the problem in direct (if wonky) terms over a decade ago:

> The lack of progress in developing affordable, safe, effective, and reversible male contraceptives is due not to the biological complexity involved in suppressing spermatogenesis [the production of sperm], but rather to social and economic/commercial constraints.

Today, research on male contraception is 50 years behind research on female contraception. The difference is as much as anything an artifact of history and tradition, which ripple into the present. Several years ago in a South African youth hostel, my daughters were dismayed to encounter a young man who casually said that he wanted a dozen children. As they queried him, they got a glimpse into both his culture and our own—into all times and places where child care has been primarily a female concern, and males could count offspring like a banker counts dollars. But gender roles and parenting have evolved in the last 50 years, all in the direction of more equality, mutuality, and flexible division of labor between men and women. For many men, those changes include a desire to be deeply present in their children's lives.

As men get more involved in late-night diaper changes and storybook reading and getting kids off to school, their perspective on having children may look more and more like the one that has historically been held by many women. They don't want 12 kids; they want two or four or one, or sometimes, knowing their own limits, none at all. In other words, they want childbearing to be intentional, and they want to decide for themselves when the time is right. It's time that they had the tools to do so.

Critical Thinking

1. Once new methods are approved for use by men, how likely do you think it is that they will use these methods? Why?
2. Why do you think it is that medications for erectile dysfunction were approved quicker than methods that can prevent pregnancy?
3. How does the issue of trust come in with hormonal methods for men?

Internet References

Contraception
http://www.contraceptionjournal.org
Contraceptive Technology
http://www.contraceptivetechnology.org
Male Contraceptives
MaleContraceptives.org

VALERIE TARICO is a Seattle psychologist and writer. She is author of Trusting Doubt and Deas: and Other Imaginings, and founder of Wisdom Commons.

Tarico, Valerie. From *RH Reality Check,* October 2, 2013, pp. 266–276. Copyright © 2013 by RH Reality Check. Used with permission.

Article

Prepared by: Elizabeth Schroeder, EdD, MSW,
Elizabeth Schroeder Consulting

Contraceptive Needs and Services, 2012 Update

JENNIFER J. FROST, MIA R. ZOLNA, AND LORI FROHWIRTH

Learning Outcomes

After reading this article, you will be able to:

- List at least three statistics relating to women's contraceptive use throughout the United States.

- Describe two changes in whether, and how, women obtained contraceptives through public health centers.

- Explain at least two reasons why girls and women have access to publicly funded contraceptive methods.

Background

Millions of U.S. women need ongoing access to contraceptive care so that they can plan the size and timing of their families. The availability of a wide range of contraceptive methods helps to ensure that women can find one that works best for their personal situation and current stage in life. However, many women cannot afford to pay for contraceptives and related services on their own, especially because some of the newer hormonal and long-acting methods that are most effective at preventing pregnancy are also some of the most expensive. A large network of publicly supported providers, including those that are funded through the federal Title X family planning program—the only national program dedicated to providing subsidized contraceptive services to individuals who are disadvantaged because of their age or income—have long been the key source of contraceptive care for teens and low-income adults. Each year, this network serves millions of women and helps to prevent hundreds of thousands of unintended pregnancies, unplanned births and abortions. Understanding the size of the population in need of this care and the current ability of providers to meet women's contraceptive needs is crucial for the planning and design of improved health care delivery systems.

Since the 1970s, the Guttmacher Institute has made periodic estimates of the number of U.S. women in need of contraceptive services and supplies, focusing on the needs of teenagers and poor or low-income adults; the publicly supported services available to these women and the number of women who receive public-sector contraceptive care; and the impact that providing publicly supported contraceptive care has on preventing unintended pregnancies and the unplanned births and abortions that would follow. Most recently, these estimates were made for 2010.[1]

This report provides updated 2012 estimates of contraceptive needs and services in the United States and of the impact that publicly funded clinic services in particular have on preventing unintended pregnancy. This report does not provide estimates of the services or impact of Medicaid-funded care provided by private doctors, nor does it provide updated information on the cost savings from these services. Estimates are made at the national and state levels. The report highlights the national-level findings and trends, and includes summary tables of national and state data.

Methodology

The following describes the methodology used to update for 2012 a number of key national and state-level contraceptive needs and services indicators:

- The number of women in need of contraceptive services and supplies, as well as those in need of publicly supported contraceptive care;

- The number of women who received contraceptive services at all publicly funded family planning clinics; and

- The numbers of pregnancies, births, and abortions that were averted by providing publicly funded contraceptive care.

Key Definitions

We used the following definitions in analyses.

- Women were defined as **in need of contraceptive services and supplies** during a given year if they were aged 13–44 and met all of three criteria:
1. they were sexually experienced—that is, they had ever had vaginal intercourse;
2. they were fecund, meaning that neither they nor their partner had been contraceptively sterilized, and they did not believe that they were infecund for any other reason; and
3. they were neither intentionally pregnant nor trying to become pregnant at any time during the past year.

- Women were defined as **in need of *publicly funded* contraceptive services and supplies** if they met the above criteria and had a family income below 250% of the federal poverty level. In addition, all women younger than 20 who needed contraceptive services, regardless of their family income, were assumed to need publicly funded care because of their heightened need—for reasons of confidentiality—to obtain care without depending on their family's resources or private insurance.

- A **publicly funded clinic** was a site that offered contraceptive services to the general public and used public funds, which may have included Medicaid, to provide free or reduced-fee services to at least some clients. These sites may be operated by a diverse range of provider agencies, including public health departments, Planned Parenthood affiliates, hospitals, federally qualified health centers (FQHCs), and other independent organizations. In this report, these sites are referred to as *clinics*; other Guttmacher Institute reports may use the synonymous term *centers*.

- A **female contraceptive client** was a woman who made at least one initial or subsequent visit for contraceptive services during the 12-month reporting period. This included all women who received a medical examination related to the provision of a contraceptive method and all active contraceptive clients who made supply-related return visits, who received counseling and a method prescription but deferred the medical examination, or who chose nonmedical contraceptive methods, even if a medical examination was not performed, as long as a chart was maintained.

- **Poor** women were those whose family income was under 100% of the federal poverty level ($19,090 for a family of three in 2012).

- **Low-income** women were those whose family income was between 100 and 250% of the federal poverty level (between $19,090 and $47,725 for a family of three in 2012).

Women in Need of Contraceptive Services and Supplies

To update estimates of the numbers of women in need of contraceptive services and supplies, we began with state-level 2012 U.S. Census Bureau estimates of the numbers of women by age-group (younger than 20, 20–29, 30–44) and race/ethnicity (non-Hispanic white, non-Hispanic black, Hispanic and other).[2] We further divided these groups according to marital status and poverty status using the 2012 American Community Survey (ACS). We did so by estimating the proportion of women in each age-group by race/ethnicity category, according to their marital status (married and living with husband, not married) and their income as a percentage of federal poverty level (less than 100%, 100–137%, 138–199%, 200–249% and more than 250%).[3] Proportions of women in the ACS in each age, race/ethnicity, marital status and poverty group were calculated for each state and then applied to the census bureau estimates of the numbers of women (by age-group and race/ethnicity) in that state. For further explanation of this methodology, see the Contraceptive Needs and Services, 2010 Methodological Appendix.[4]

The final step for updating estimates of women in need of contraceptive services and supplies for 2012 was to apply the proportion of women in each demographic subgroup (age by race/ethnicity by marital status by poverty status) who were in need of contraceptive services and supplies because they were sexually active, fecund and not pregnant nor trying to become pregnant. For this report, we use the same tabulations of the 2006–2010 National Survey of Family Growth (NSFG) that were made for our 2010 report1 (as these are the most recent nationally representative data on women's need for services). Those tabulations calculated the proportions of women in each demographic group (by age, race/ethnicity, marital status, and poverty status) according to whether they need contraceptive services (as defined above) or not.[5] The proportions in need were then applied to the 2012 population numbers by demographic subgroup to derive final estimates of the number of women in need.

Women Served at Publicly Funded Family Planning Clinics

We estimated the total numbers of women receiving contraceptive care at publicly funded family planning clinics in 2012 from two sources. For approximately two-thirds of all family planning clinic clients, we used Title X program–specific data for 2012, tabulated by state.[6] For the remaining 29% of women served at publicly funded clinics that do not receive Title X funds, we estimated 2012 clientele by starting with published state tabulations of data for all clinics for 2010,[1] the most recent year available, and adjusting them forward in time according to the observed state-level change in clients between 2010 and 2012 experienced by Title X clinics (which we assumed was the same as the change in non-Title X clinics). We did not estimate clients served in U.S. territories.

Impact of Publicly Supported Contraceptive Care

We estimated the numbers of unintended pregnancies, unplanned births, and abortions that were averted by the provision of publicly funded contraceptive care at clinics in 2012 using the same methodology as in previous estimates.[1] To do so, we began with the number of female clients served. We adjusted this number based on the fact that some clients served do not obtain or use a contraceptive method. In 2012, 15% of women served at Title X clinics were not current method users.[6] We assumed that this same percentage applied to all clinics and estimated the total number of method users in that year to be 85% of all clients served. Next, we estimated the total number of unintended pregnancies prevented in 2012 by multiplying the number of method users, nationally and in each state, by the ratio of pregnancies prevented per user. This ratio was most recently estimated to be 288 unintended pregnancies averted per 1,000 method users.[1] Finally, we then classified the unintended pregnancies averted according to observed outcomes at the national level. Overall, 50% of unintended pregnancies result in an unplanned birth, 34% in an elective abortion and 16% in miscarriage.[1]

Need for Publicly Funded Contraceptive Services

Women are in need of contraceptive services and supplies if they are sexually active and able to conceive but not currently pregnant or trying to get pregnant. Poor and low-income women and teenagers are in need of *publicly funded* contraceptive services and supplies (see Key Definitions).

Overall Need for Services

In 2012, there were 66.8 million U.S. women of reproductive age (13–44), a number that has remained relatively stable since 2000, increasing only 2% over the past 12 years. However, the population distributions of some key subgroups of these women changed considerably during this period:

- The distribution of women shifted toward younger age. The number who were younger than 30 rose—by 5% among teenagers and 14% among women in their 20s—while the number aged 30–44 fell by 6%.
- The number of poor adult women (those aged 20–44 with family incomes below 100% of the federal poverty

level) increased dramatically, rising by 40%, as did the number of women of Hispanic ethnicity, rising by 44%.
- In the most recent two-year period from 2010 to 2012 alone, the number of poor adult women rose by 13%.

More than half of all women of reproductive age (37.7 million) were in need of contraceptive services and supplies in 2012. This number translated to an 11% increase since 2000.

- The largest increases in the need for contraceptive services and supplies were among poor women (53%) and Hispanic women (51%). There was also an increase among women in their 20s (19%), non-Hispanic black women (16%), but a decrease among non-Hispanic white women (–3%).
- In the period 2010–2012 alone, the number of poor adult women in need of contraceptive services and supplies increased 12% and the number of low-income adult women in need rose by 4%.

Need for Publicly Funded Services

Need in 2012. A total of 20 million U.S. women were in need of *publicly funded* contraceptive services and supplies in 2012 because they needed such services and supplies, and were either adult women with a family income under 250% of the federal poverty level or were younger than 20.

- Some 15 million women in need of publicly funded contraceptive services and supplies were adults living below 250% of the federal poverty level. Of these, 6.2 million were poor adult women living below the federal poverty level ($19,090 for a family of three in 2012), and 9 million were low-income adult women (those whose incomes were 100–249% of poverty). Among the latter group, some 2.4 million women had family incomes of 100–137% of poverty.
- Some 4.7 million women in need of publicly funded contraceptive services were younger than 20.
- Of all women in need of such services and supplies, 9.9 million were non-Hispanic white, 3.5 million were non-Hispanic black and 4.8 million were Hispanic (the remaining women were of other or multiple races/ethnicities).

Change in need 2000–2012

Overall need for publicly funded contraceptive care increased over the entire observation period, but the extent of the increase varied across social and demographic groups.

- Between 2000 and 2012, the overall number of women in need of publicly funded contraceptive services and supplies increased by 22%, representing 3.5 million additional women needing such care.

- Over this same period, the number of Hispanic women in need of publicly supported care increased by 54%, the number of black women in need increased by 22% and the number of white women in need increased by 7%.
- All of the growth in the number of women in need of publicly funded contraceptive services between 2000 and 2012 occurred among adult women who were poor or low income, as opposed to teenagers. The number of poor adult women who were in need increased by 53%, and the number of low-income women who were in need increased by 20%. The number of teens in need fell slightly, by 3%.

Change in need 2010–2012

The total number of women needing publicly funded care continued to rise in recent years.

- In the two most recent years, the overall number of women in need of publicly funded care rose by 4%, representing nearly 1 million additional women.
- The proportion change in need for such care between 2010 and 2012 fell as income rose—from 12% among women with incomes less than 100% of poverty, to 9% among those with incomes of 100–137% of poverty, to 4% among those with incomes 138–199% of poverty, to no change among women with incomes of 200–249% of poverty.

State variation

States varied widely in terms of their changing patterns of need for publicly supported family planning care.

- Twenty-one states experienced a 20% or greater increase in the number of women needing publicly funded contraceptive services or supplies over the 2000–2012 period; seven of these states had an increase of more than 40%.
- Only two states experienced small declines (3–5%) in the number of women in need of publicly funded care.

Numbers of uninsured women in need

A sizable share of women needing publicly supported care in 2012 were uninsured.

- Of the 20 million women in need of publicly supported care that year, 5.9 million (30%) had neither public nor private health insurance.
- Among poor adult women in need, the percentages who were uninsured were even higher: 39–41% for women with family incomes below 137% of poverty.

Use of Publicly Funded Contraceptive Services

Women in the United States can obtain publicly supported contraceptive care from thousands of clinics that receive public funding through a variety of federal, state and local sources. These clinics include health departments, hospital outpatient clinics, federally qualified health centers (FQHCs), Planned Parenthood clinics and facilities run by other organizations. This section focuses on this clinic network, looking at the numbers of female contraceptive clients they served. Outside of this network, many private doctors provide contraceptive care to Medicaid recipients. The most recent national estimates of the number of women who receive Medicaid-funded contraceptive care from private doctors are for 2010; we have not updated those numbers in this report. We also provide an assessment of the proportion of the need for publicly funded contraceptive care that is met by publicly supported clinics. We focus on data for 2012 and make comparisons with data collected for 2010 and 2001.

Women Served by Publicly Funded Clinics

- In 2012, an estimated 6.1 million female contraceptive clients were served at all publicly funded clinics; 71% (4.3 million) were served at Title X–funded clinics, and 29% (1.8 million) were served at non-Title X–funded sites.
- Between 2001 and 2012, the overall number of women receiving publicly funded contraceptive services from clinics decreased from almost 6.7 to 6.1 million, with slightly more than half of the decrease due to fewer women receiving services from non-Title X–funded clinics.
- During 2001–2006, the total number of contraceptive clients served at publicly funded clinics rose by 8% (data not shown), but during the subsequent period, 2006–2010, the number served fell back to nearly the same as that in 2001, and continued to decline sharply, by another 9%, between 2010 and 2012.
- The majority of states (38) experienced a drop in the number of contraceptive clients served at publicly funded clinics between 2001 and 2012, while 12 states and the District of Columbia experienced an increase (data not shown).

Proportion of Need Met by Publicly Funded Clinics

Publicly funded clinics met roughly 31% of the need in 2012 for publicly supported contraceptive services and supplies. Only 6 million of the 20 million women in need of care were served by clinics; 22% of the need was met by Title X–funded clinics and 9% was met by non-Title X–funded clinics.

- Between 2001 and 2010, the overall proportion of need met by publicly funded clinics fell from 41 to 35%, because the number of women needing publicly supported care increased over this period, while the number of women cared for by public clinics changed little. Between 2010 and 2012, the proportion of need met by public clinics declined even further, to 31%, primarily because of the drop in clients served.
- Title X–funded clinics met 22% of the need for publicly supported contraceptive care in 2012, a drop from 28% in 2001.
- The percentage of the need for publicly funded contraceptive services that was met by all clinics and by Title X–funded clinics varied widely by state. Clinics met more than half of the need for such care in three states (Alaska, California and Vermont) and the District of Columbia, whereas publicly funded clinics in 14 states (Arizona, Florida, Georgia, Illinois, Indiana, Kansas, Louisiana, Michigan, Missouri, Nevada, North Carolina, Ohio, Texas and Virginia) met less than 25% of the need for such care.

Impact of Publicly Funded Contraceptive Services

By providing women with the contraceptive services they need and want, publicly funded clinics are able to help women achieve their childbearing goals. A host of benefits accrue when women and families are able to plan the timing and number of their children.[7,8] One of the most basic benefits of these services is the prevention of unintended pregnancy. To estimate how many unintended pregnancies were averted by publicly funded clinics in 2012, we applied our most recent estimation procedure to 2012 data on numbers of clients served. We present the results from these analyses, estimating the number of unintended events prevented by publicly funded clinics.

Unintended Pregnancies Averted

- Publicly funded clinics as a whole helped to avert some 1.5 million unintended pregnancies in 2012. Of these pregnancies, 741,000 would have resulted in an unplanned birth and 510,000 would have resulted

in an abortion (the remainder would have resulted in miscarriage).
- Title X–funded clinics accounted for the large majority of this benefit, helping to avert 1.1 million unintended pregnancies in 2012, which would have resulted in 527,000 unplanned births and 363,000 abortions.
- Without the contraceptive services provided by all publicly funded clinics in 2012, the rates of unintended pregnancies, unplanned births and abortions in the United States would all have been 44% higher (data not shown). Title X–funded clinics alone were responsible for about three-quarters of this impact: Without their services, the unintended pregnancy rate would have been 32% higher.

Discussion

Over the last 12 years, the number of U.S. women of reproductive age rose less than 2%, while the number needing contraceptive services and supplies increased by 11%. Outpacing the overall increase in need for contraceptive care, the subset of women needing publicly funded contraceptive services and supplies rose 22%, resulting in 3.5 million additional women who were in need of such care.

A large share of the increase in need for publicly funded care was due to a disproportionate rise in the number of poor adult women (those with family incomes below 100% of the federal poverty level) needing contraceptive services and supplies. Their number rose 53% between 2000 and 2012. The increase in the number of women in need of publicly funded contraceptive care, especially those in the lowest income groups, is undoubtedly due, in large part, to the recession and its economic consequences that continue to be felt by many women and their families. It is consistent with the overall increase in the percentage of American women living in poverty, as well as with documented changes in women's behavior during the recession: Because of economic concerns, more women reported wanting to postpone or limit their childbearing,[9] putting them at risk for unintended pregnancy and in need of contraceptive services.

Over this same period, the number of women who received contraceptive services from publicly funded clinics declined. From 2010 to 2012 alone, this number fell from 6.7 million to 6.1 million, a 9% drop. As a result, the numbers of women served at clinics did not keep up with the rising numbers of women needing publicly supported contraceptive care. In 2012, only 31% of all women in need of publicly funded contraceptive services and supplies received care from clinics, down from 41% in 2001. Several factors might be related to this decline—including an increase in use of long-acting reversible contraceptive methods, changing standards for cervical cancer screening, and cuts to some funding sources, most notably Title X—although more research is needed to determine the exact cause of these trends.

Even so, the impact of publicly supported contraceptive services on the prevention of unintended pregnancy in 2012 was significant: Publicly funded clinics prevented 1.5 million unintended pregnancies. The contraceptive services provided by these clinics therefore helped women avoid 741,000 unplanned births and 510,000 abortions. Without these services, the overall U.S. unintended pregnancy rate would have been 44% higher.

Critical to the provision of clinic-based contraceptive care is the federal Title X family planning program. In 2012, clinics funded by this program provided contraceptive services to 4.3 million women, a group representing 71% of all contraceptive clients served by clinics. Not only do Title X–funded clinics typically serve a much greater number of contraceptive clients per year than do other clinics, prior research has documented that Title X clinics offer their clients a greater variety of contraceptive methods, do more to facilitate method initiation and consistent method use among clients, are more likely to advise clients about contraception during annual gynecologic visits, and spend more time counseling clients about contraception and sexual health.[10] Title X–funded clinics alone helped to avert 1.1 million unintended pregnancies in 2012, preventing 527,000 unplanned births and 363,000 abortions.

References

1. Frost JJ, Zolna MR and Frohwirth L, *Contraceptive Needs and Services, 2010*, New York: Guttmacher Institute, 2013, http://www.guttmacher.org/pubs/win/contraceptive-needs-2010.pdf, accessed June 2, 2014.

2. U.S. Census Bureau, Annual Estimates of the Resident Population by Sex, Age, Race, and Hispanic Origin for the United States and States: April 1, 2010 to July 1, 2012, Silver Spring, MD: U.S. Census Bureau, Population Division, June 2013.

3. U.S. Census Bureau, American Community Survey, PUMS Documentation, 2012, http://www.census.gov/acs/www/Downloads/data_documentation/pums/SubjectsinPUMS/2012_1yr_PUMS_Subjects.pdf, accessed June 24, 2014.

4. Frost JJ et al., *Contraceptive Needs and Services, 2010: Methodological Appendix*, New York: Guttmacher Institute, 2013, http://www.guttmacher.org/pubs/win/win-methods2010.pdf, accessed June 24, 2014.

5. Lepkowski JM et al., The 2006–2010 National Survey of Family Growth: sample design and analysis of a continuous survey, National Center for Health Statistics, *Vital and Health Statistics,* 2010, Series 2, No. 150.

6. Fowler CI et al., *Family Planning Annual Report: 2012 National Summary*, Research Triangle Park, NC: RTI International, 2013.

7. Sonfield A et al., *The Social and Economic Benefits of Women's Ability to Determine Whether and When to Have Children,* New York: Guttmacher Institute, 2013, www.guttmacher.org/pubs/social-economic-benefits.pdf, accessed July 12, 2014.

8. Kavanaugh ML and Anderson RM, *Contraception and Beyond: The Health Benefits of Services Provided at Family Planning Centers,* New York: Guttmacher Institute, 2013, http://www.guttmacher.org/pubs/health-benefits.pdf, accessed July 12, 2014.

9. Guttmacher Institute, *A Real-Time Look at the Impact of the Recession on Women's Family Planning and Pregnancy Decisions,* New York: September 2009.

10. Frost JJ et al., *Variation in Service Delivery Practices Among Clinics Providing Publicly Funded Family Planning Services in 2010,* New York: Guttmacher Institute, 2012, http://www.guttmacher.org/pubs/clinic-survey-2010.pdf, accessed Apr. 15, 2014.

Critical Thinking

1. What are some reasons why people might support girls and women having access to publicly funded contraception? What are some reasons why others might oppose it?

2. Why do you think there are so many contraceptive methods available that work on the female body and so few that are designed for the male body?

3. What do you think needs to happen to promote greater equality in male-female couples taking responsibility for their contraceptive and safer sex practices?

Internet References

Contraception
http://www.contraceptionjournal.org

Guttmacher Institute
https://www.guttmacher.org

Title X Family Planning: US Department of Health and Human Services
http://www.hhs.gov/opa/title-x-family-planning

JENNIFER J. FROST is a Principal Research Scientist at the Guttmacher Institute. Over the last two decades, she has served as the principal investigator for numerous studies examining family planning service delivery, contraceptive use, unintended pregnancy, adolescent sexuality and pregnancy, and access to reproductive health care. **LORI FROHWIRTH AND MIA R. ZOLNA** are research associates at the Guttmacher Institute.

Prepared by: Elizabeth Schroeder, EdD, MSW,
Elizabeth Schroeder Consulting

Article

Health Disparities among Lesbian, Gay, and Bisexual Older Adults: Results from a Population-Based Study

KAREN I. FREDRIKSEN-GOLDSEN ET AL.

Learning Outcomes

After reading this article, you will be able to:

- Discuss the health outcomes of lesbian, gay, and bisexual older adults.

- Identify the health disparities among lesbian, gay, and bisexual older adults.

- Identify the methods to learn more about the health needs in the lesbian, gay, and bisexual communities.

Changing demographics will make population aging a defining feature of the 21st century. Not only is the population older, it is becoming increasingly diverse.[1] Existing research illustrates that older adults from socially and economically disadvantaged populations are at high risk of poor health and premature death.[2] A commitment of the National Institutes of Health is to reduce and eliminate health disparities,[3] which have been defined as differences in health outcomes for communities that have encountered systematic obstacles to health as a result of social, economic, and environmental disadvantage.[4]

Social determinants of health disparities among older adults include age, race/ethnicity, and socioeconomic status.[5] Centers for Disease Control and Prevention (CDC) and *Healthy People* 2020 identify health disparities related to sexual orientation as one of the main gaps in current health research.[6] The Institute of Medicine identifies lesbian, gay, and bisexual (LGB) older adults as a population whose health needs are understudied.[7]

The institute has called for population-based studies to better assess the impact of background characteristics such as age on health outcomes among LGB adults. A review of 25 years of literature on LGB aging found that health research is glaringly sparse for this population and that most aging-related studies have used small, non-population-based samples.[8]

Several important studies have begun to document health disparities by sexual orientation in population-based data and have revealed important differences in health between LGB adults and their heterosexual counterparts, including higher risks of poor mental health, smoking, and limitations in activities.[9,10] Studies have found higher rates of excessive drinking among lesbians and bisexual women[9,10] and higher rates of obesity among lesbians[10,11] than among heterosexual women; bisexual men and women are at higher risk of limited health care access than are heterosexuals. In addition, important subgroup differences in health are beginning to be documented among LGB adults. For example, bisexual women are at higher risk than lesbians for mental distress and poor general health.[12] A primary limitation of most existing population-based research is a failure to identify the specific health needs of LGB older adults. Most studies to date address the health needs of LGB adults aged 18 years and older[9] or those younger than 65 years.[10] This lack of attention to older adult health leaves unclear whether disparities diminish or persist or even become more pronounced in later life.

A few studies have begun to examine health disparities among LGB adults aged 50 years and older.[13,14] Wallace et al. analyzed data from the California Health Interview Survey and found that LGB adults aged 50 to 70 years report higher rates of mental distress, physical limitations, and poor general health than do their heterosexual counterparts. The researchers also found that older gay and bisexual men report higher rates of hypertension and diabetes than do heterosexual men.[14] To better address the needs of an increasingly diverse older adult population and to develop responsive interventions and public health policies, health disparities research is needed for this at-risk group.

Examining to what extent sexual orientation is related to health disparities among LGB older adults is a first step toward developing a more comprehensive understanding of their health and aging needs. We analyzed population-based data from the Washington State Behavioral Risk Factor Surveillance System (WA-BRFSS) to compare lesbians and bisexual women and gay and bisexual men with their heterosexual counterparts aged 50 years and older on key health indicators: outcomes, chronic conditions, access to care, behaviors, and screening. We also compared subgroups to identify differences in health disparities by sexual orientation among LGB older adults.

Methods

The BRFSS is an annual random-digit-dialed telephone survey of noninstitutionalized adults conducted by each US state. Each year, disproportionate stratified random sampling is used to select eligible households, and from each selected household one adult is randomly selected as the respondent.[15] Washington State began including a measure of sexual orientation in 2003. We aggregated the WA-BRFSS data collected from 2003 to 2010 for respondents aged 50 years and older (n = 96,992) and stratified by gender for further analyses. We selected 50 years as the lower age limit to be consistent with previous health studies focusing on sexual minority older adults,[13,14] as well as research addressing specific chronic health conditions[16,17] and older adult health and well-being, such as the Health and Retirement Study and other population-based studies.[18–20] Annual response rates to the WA-BRFSS range from 43% to 50%, calculated according to Council of American Survey and Research Organizations methods.[21] To adjust for unequal probabilities of selection resulting from nonresponse, sample design, and households without telephones, we applied sample weights provided by the WA-BRFSS.

According to weighted estimation, among women aged 50 years and older (n = 58,319), 1.03% (n = 562) identified as lesbian and 0.54% (n = 291) as bisexual; among men aged 50 years and older (n = 37,820), 1.28% (n = 463) identified as gay and 0.51% (n = 215) as bisexual. The age range in the sample for LGB older adults was 50 to 98 years (50–94 years for women and 50–98 years for men).

Measures

To measure sexual orientation, survey respondents were asked to select 1 of the following: heterosexual or straight, homosexual (gay or lesbian), bisexual, or something else. About 0.2% (n = 266) of the sample selected something else, and we excluded them from our analyses.

The background characteristics in this study were as follows: age, household income ($\leq$ 200% vs > 200% of the federal poverty level), education ($\leq$ high school vs $\geq$ some college), employment (part time or full time vs other), race/ethnicity (non-Hispanic White vs other), living arrangement (living alone vs other), and number of children in household. We categorized relationship status as married versus partnered (a member of an unmarried couple) versus other (divorced, widowed, separated, or never married).

Health outcomes (recommended and validated by CDC) in our study were poor physical health, disability, and poor mental health.[22] We defined poor physical health as 14 or more days of poor physical health during the previous 30 days and poor mental health as 14 or more days of poor mental health during the previous 30 days.[22] We defined disability as limitations in any activities because of physical, mental, or emotional problems or any health problem that required the use of special equipment, as recommended by *Healthy People 2020*.[4]

The BRFSS asked respondents whether they had ever been told by a health professional they had arthritis, asthma, diabetes (not included if prediabetes or gestational diabetes alone), high blood pressure (not included if borderline or during pregnancy alone), or high cholesterol. As recommended by other health studies, we designated cardiovascular disease (CVD) as diagnosis by a physician of a heart attack, angina, or stroke.[23,24] We defined obesity as a body mass index score (defined as weight in kilograms divided by height in meters squared) of 30 or higher, as recommended by CDC.[25] The BRFSS measured health care access by asking whether respondents had insurance coverage, a personal doctor or provider, or a financial barrier to seeing a doctor in the past 12 months.

Health behaviors were (1) current smoking (defined, as suggested by CDC, as having ever smoked $\geq$ 100 cigarettes and currently smoking every day or some days[26]), (2) excessive drinking (defined, as suggested by National Institute of Alcohol Abuse and Alcoholism, as women having $\geq$ 4 and men having $\geq$ 5 drinks on 1 occasion during the past month[27]), and (3) physical activity (defined, as suggested by the US Department of Health and Human Services, as $\geq$ 30 minutes of moderate-intensity activity $\geq$ 5 days/week or $\geq$ 20 minutes of vigorous-intensity activity $\geq$ 3 days/week[28]). The BRFSS measured health screening, according to public health guidelines for older adults, by whether respondents received a flu shot in the past year,[29] an HIV test ever, a mammogram (for women) in the past 2 years,[30] and a prostate-specific antigen test (for men) in the past year.[31]

Statistical Analysis

We conducted analyses separately by gender. First, we described the weighted distribution of background characteristics by sexual orientation, comparing lesbians and bisexual women with heterosexual women aged 50 years and older and gay and bisexual men with heterosexual men aged 50 years and older, applying t tests or χ^2 tests as appropriate. We also tested statistical significance of differences in background characteristics between lesbians and bisexual women and between gay and bisexual men.

We then estimated weighted prevalence rates of health indicators, which were health outcomes, chronic conditions, access to care, behaviors, and screening, by sexual orientation (lesbian and bisexual vs heterosexual women; gay and bisexual vs heterosexual men). We conducted a series of adjusted logistic regressions, with control for sociodemographic characteristics

(age, income, and education), to test associations between health-related indicators and sexual orientation. We also conducted adjusted logistic regression analyses to examine health disparities between lesbian and bisexual women and between gay and bisexual men. We used Stata version 11 (StataCorp LP, College Station, TX) for data analyses.

Results

Table 1 illustrates the weighted prevalence of background characteristics by sexual orientation among older adults. Lesbians and bisexual women were younger, had more education, and had higher rates of employment than did heterosexual women; income levels were similar. Lesbians and bisexual women were less likely to be married and more likely to be partnered than were their heterosexual counterparts, but the average number of children in the household and the likelihood of living alone were similar. Lesbians were more likely than bisexual women to be employed ($P = .019$) and less likely to be married, but more likely to be partnered ($P < .001$). We found no differences in other background characteristics.

Table 1 Background Characteristics of Respondents Aged 50 Years and Older, by Sexual Orientation: Washington State Behavioral Risk Factor Surveillance System, 2003–2010

	Women				Men			
	Heterosexual, % or Mean (SD)	Lesbian and Bisexual			Heterosexual, % or Mean (SD)	Gay and Bisexual		
Characteristic		Total, % or Mean (SD)	Lesbian, % or Mean (SD)	Bisexual, % or Mean (SD)		Total, % or Mean (SD)	Gay, % or Mean (SD)	Bisexual, % or Mean (SD)
Age, y	63.82 (0.06)	58.63*** (0.37)	58.09 (0.40)	59.67 (0.78)	62.35 (0.07)	59.54*** (0.39)	59.26 (0.45)	60.22 (0.75)
≤ 200% poverty level	27.38	27.12	26.47	28.43	20.85	24.79	25.45	23.18
≤ high school	30.18	13.44***	13.83	12.69	24.96	14.57***	12.34	20.09
Employed	39.97	59.31***	63.07	52.08	51.17	55.30	55.25	55.43
Non-Hispanic White	91.79	90.31	89.86	91.23	90.40	93.22*	92.85	94.18
Relationship status								
Married	61.67	20.15***	9.57	40.44	77.60	20.83***	8.16	52.07
Partnered	1.59	27.83	36.96	10.31	1.50	20.27	27.30	2.96
Other	36.74	52.02	53.47	49.25	20.90	58.90	64.55	44.97
Children in household, no.	0.15 (0.00)	0.20 (0.04)	0.18 (0.05)	0.24 (0.06)	0.22 (0.00)	0.07*** (0.02)	0.03 (0.01)	0.15 (0.05)
Living alone	26.24	29.43	29.65	28.99	15.15	38.34***	40.66	32.59

Note. Estimates were weighted; significance tests were conducted to examine the association between background characteristics and sexual orientation (lesbians and bisexual women vs heterosexual women; gay and bisexual men vs heterosexual men).

*$P < .05$; ***$P < .001$.

Gay and bisexual men were significantly younger and more highly educated than were heterosexual men; income levels and employment rates were similar. Gay and bisexual men were less likely than heterosexual men to be married but more likely to be partnered; they also had fewer children in the household, were more likely to live alone, and were more likely to be non-Hispanic Whites. Gay men had more education ($P = .037$), were less likely to be married and more likely to be partnered ($P < .001$), and had fewer children in the household ($P = .017$) than did bisexual men.

Health Outcomes

Lesbians and bisexual women had higher odds than heterosexual women for disability (adjusted odds ratio [AOR] = 1.47) and poor mental health (AOR = 1.40), but not for poor physical health, after adjustment for age, income, and education (Table 2). Lesbians and bisexual women had similar rates of poor physical health, disability, and poor mental health.

In adjusted analyses, gay and bisexual men were more likely than heterosexual men to have poor physical health (AOR = 1.38), disability (AOR = 1.26), and poor mental health (AOR = 1.77). Although the unadjusted prevalence rates of disability were similar between sexual minority and

heterosexual men, the analyses with adjustment for sociodemographic characteristics showed that gay and bisexual men were more likely than their heterosexual counterparts to have a disability. We did not observe differences in health outcomes between gay and bisexual men.

Chronic Conditions

Lesbians and bisexual women had greater adjusted odds of obesity (AOR = 1.42) relative to heterosexual women. Unadjusted odds of CVD were similar for sexual minority and heterosexual women, but after adjustment for sociodemographic characteristics, lesbians and bisexual women had significantly greater risk (AOR = 1.37). The unadjusted odds of asthma for lesbians and bisexual women were significantly higher than for heterosexual women, but the difference did not remain significant when the analyses adjusted for sociodemographic differences. We observed no significant differences in chronic conditions between lesbians and bisexual women in the adjusted analyses.

Gay and bisexual men had significantly lower odds of obesity than did heterosexual men (AOR = 0.72), after adjustment for sociodemographic factors. The unadjusted odds of asthma for gay and bisexual men were higher than for heterosexual men (OR = 1.41), but the difference did not remain significant after

Table 2   Weighted Prevalence Rates and Regression Analyses of Health Outcomes and Chronic Conditions among Respondents Aged 50 Years and Older: Washington State Behavioral Risk Factor Surveillance System, 2003–2010

Health Outcomes/ Conditions	Women				Men			
	Heterosexual, %	Lesbian and Bisexual			Heterosexual, %	Gay and Bisexual		
		%	OR (95% CI)	AOR (95% CI)		%	OR (95% CI)	AOR (95% CI)
Frequent poor physical health	15.47	15.79	1.02 (0.81, 1.30)	1.02 (0.80, 1.30)	12.88	16.79	1.36* (1.05, 1.78)	1.38* (1.04, 1.83)
Disability	36.87	44.27	1.36** (1.14, 1.62)	1.47*** (1.22, 1.77)	33.96	38.27	1.21 (0.98, 1.48)	1.26* (1.02, 1.56)
Frequent poor mental health	9.36	15.92	1.83*** (1.42, 2.37)	1.40* (1.07, 1.81)	6.88	13.09	2.04*** (1.51, 2.76)	1.77** (1.28, 2.45)
Obesity	25.93	36.27	1.63*** (1.36, 1.95)	1.42*** (1.18, 1.71)	27.07	22.57	0.79* (0.62, 0.99)	0.72* (0.56, 0.93)
Arthritis[a]	52.24	53.70	1.06 (0.83, 1.36)	1.29 (0.99, 1.67)	39.25	41.85	1.11 (0.84, 1.48)	1.19 (0.89, 1.60)
Asthma	15.89	20.57	1.37** (1.10, 1.70)	1.20 (0.96, 1.49)	11.56	15.52	1.41* (1.07, 1.85)	1.28 (0.95, 1.71)
Diabetes	11.87	13.59	1.17 (0.91, 1.51)	1.25 (0.96, 1.64)	13.96	12.44	0.88 (0.66, 1.17)	0.92 (0.67, 1.25)
High blood pressure[a]	43.33	36.02	0.74 (0.54, 1.00)	0.86 (0.62, 1.20)	44.35	40.59	0.86 (0.61, 1.21)	0.88 (0.61, 1.26)
High cholesterol[b]	47.13	44.10	0.88 (0.69, 1.14)	1.00 (0.77, 1.30)	50.21	51.66	1.06 (0.79, 1.42)	1.08 (0.80, 1.46)
Cardiovascular disease[c]	10.71	10.51	0.98 (0.73, 1.31)	1.37* (1.00, 1.86)	16.49	14.11	0.83 (0.62, 1.12)	1.04 (0.76, 1.43)

Note. AOR = adjusted odds ratio; CI = confidence interval; OR = odds ratio. Adjusted logistic regression models controlled for age, income, and education; heterosexuals were coded as the reference group.
[a]Question was asked in 2003, 2005, and 2009.
[b]Questions were asked in 2003, 2005, 2007, and 2009.
[c]Questions were asked in 2004 through 2010.
*$P < .05$; **$P < .01$; ***$P < .001$.

adjustment. The adjusted odds of diabetes were significantly higher for bisexual men (19.74%) than for gay men (9.50%; AOR = 2.33; P < .01). We detected no other significant differences in chronic conditions between gay and bisexual men.

Access to Care

As shown in Table 3, although we found no significant difference in the prevalence of having a health care provider, lesbians and bisexual women were less likely than heterosexual women to have health insurance coverage and more likely to experience financial barriers to health care. These differences, however, did not remain significant after adjustment for sociodemographic characteristics. We detected no significant differences in health care access indicators between lesbians and bisexual women.

In the unadjusted analyses, gay and bisexual men were less likely than heterosexual men to have health insurance coverage, but the difference did not remain significant after adjustment. No significant differences appeared in the indicators of health care access between gay and bisexual men.

Health Behaviors

Prevalence rates of physical activity were similar among all female respondents, but lesbians and bisexual women were more likely than heterosexual women to smoke (AOR = 1.57) and to drink excessively (AOR = 1.43; Table 3). Lesbians (9.95%) were significantly more likely than bisexual women (3.90%; AOR = 0.40) to drink excessively (P < .05).

Gay and bisexual men had higher adjusted odds of smoking (AOR = 1.52) and excessive drinking (AOR = 1.47) than did heterosexual men; prevalence rates of physical activities were similar. We observed no differences in health behaviors between gay and bisexual men.

Health Screening

Sexual minority women were significantly less likely than heterosexual women to have had a mammogram (AOR = 0.71), more likely to have been tested for HIV (AOR = 1.80), and equally likely to have received a flu shot. We observed no

Table 3 Weighted Prevalence Rates and Regression Analyses of Health Indicators among Respondents Aged 50 Years and Older: Washington State Behavioral Risk Factor Surveillance System, 2003–2010

| | Women | | | | Men | | | |
| | Heterosexual, | Lesbian and Bisexual | | | Heterosexual, | Gay and Bisexual | | |
Health Indicator	%	%	OR (95% CI)	AOR (95% CI)	%	%	OR (95% CI)	AOR (95% CI)
Access to care								
Insurance	94.56	91.24	0.60*** (0.44, 0.82)	0.79 (0.55, 1.13)	93.36	89.42	0.60** (0.43, 0.84)	0.71 (0.48, 1.04)
Financial barrier	8.26	13.05	1.67*** (1.29, 2.16)	1.25 (0.97, 1.62)	6.81	8.43	1.26 (0.86, 1.84)	0.97 (0.63, 1.50)
Personal provider	92.41	93.09	1.11 (0.76, 1.60)	1.43 (0.97, 2.11)	88.57	88.41	0.98 (0.73, 1.33)	1.16 (0.84, 1.60)
Behavior								
Smoking	11.61	18.33	1.71*** (1.36, 2.15)	1.57*** (1.22, 2.00)	13.15	20.04	1.66*** (1.30, 2.11)	1.52** (1.18, 1.96)
Excessive drinking	4.61	7.88	1.77*** (1.27, 2.47)	1.43* (1.02, 2.00)	11.12	17.13	1.65** (1.24, 2.20)	1.47* (1.09, 1.98)
Physical activity[a]	49.02	51.92	1.12 (0.88, 1.01)	1.01 (0.78, 1.31)	51.23	53.04	1.08 (0.81, 1.43)	1.04 (0.78, 1.40)
Screening								
Flu shot	55.07	52.99	0.92 (0.77, 1.10)	1.20 (1.00, 1.44)	50.40	54.87	1.20 (0.98, 1.46)	1.47*** (1.18, 1.82)
Mammogram[b]	79.77	74.16	0.73* (0.54, 0.98)	0.71* (0.52, 0.97)	. . .	. . .	. . .	. . .
PSA test[b]	. . .	. . .	. . .	. . .	49.85	40.67	0.69* (0.51, 0.93)	0.81 (0.59, 1.10)
HIV test[c]	23.89	40.80	2.20*** (1.79, 2.70)	1.80*** (1.46, 2.23)	28.31	76.47	8.23*** (6.22, 10.88)	7.91*** (5.94, 10.54)

Note. AOR = adjusted odds ratio; CI = confidence interval; OR = odds ratio; PSA = prostate-specific antigen. Adjusted logistic regression models controlled for age, income, and education; heterosexuals were coded as the reference group.

[a]Questions were asked in 2003, 2005, 2007, and 2009.

[b]Questions were asked in 2004, 2006, and 2008.

[c]Question was asked only of those younger than 65 years.

*P <.05; **P < .01; ***P <.001.

significant differences in health screenings between older lesbians and bisexual women.

The adjusted analyses indicated that gay and bisexual men were more likely than heterosexual men to have received a flu shot (AOR = 1.47) and an HIV test (AOR = 7.91). In the initial analyses, sexual minority men were significantly less likely than heterosexual men to receive a prostate-specific antigen test, but the difference was not significant after adjustment for sociodemographic characteristics. Although we found no significant differences between gay and bisexual men in the prevalence of receiving a flu shot or a prostate-specific antigen test, bisexual men (60.33%) were less likely than gay men (82.59%) to have been tested for HIV (AOR = 0.31; $P < .001$).

Discussion

We conducted one of the first studies to comprehensively examine leading CDC-defined health indicators among LGB older adults in population-based data. Contrary to the myth that older adults will not reveal their sexual orientation in public health surveys, in this population-based survey we found that approximately 2% of adults aged 50 years and older self-identified as lesbian, gay, or bisexual. The findings reveal significant health disparities among LGB older adults, with both strengths and gaps across the continuum of health indicators examined. Our results suggest that some health disparity patterns that have been found in LGB adults at younger ages[9,10] persist in later life, including higher likelihoods of disability, poor mental health, and smoking, and, among lesbians and bisexual women, excessive drinking and obesity. We also found some health disparities—heightened risks of CVD among lesbian and bisexual women and of poor physical health and excessive drinking among gay and bisexual men—that may emerge later in the life course. Such health disparities likely have detrimental consequences for the quality of life of these LGB older adults.[14,32,33]

According to the life course perspective, social context, cultural meaning, and structural location (in addition to time, period, and cohort) affect aging processes, including health.[34,35] Situating LGB older adults within the historical and social context of their lives may help us to better understand the health issues they face as they age.[36] LGB older adults came of age during a time when same-sex relationships were criminalized and severely stigmatized and same-sex identities were socially invisible.

Elevated risks of disability and poor mental health among LGB older adults may be linked with experiences of stigmatization[37-39] and victimization,[39-41] especially in light of the profound impact that events at a given stage of life can have on subsequent stages.[42] The social contexts in which they have lived may have exposed LGB older adults to multiple types of victimization and discrimination related to sexual orientation,

disability, age, gender, and race/ethnicity.[41] D'Augelli and Grossman, for example, argue that lifetime experiences of victimization among sexual minority older adults because of their sexual orientation affects mental health in later life.[40] The evidence of physiological impact of chronic stressors on health[43] suggests that lifetime experiences of victimization may partially account for higher rates of disability among LGB older adults. Although our study was designed to identify health disparities among LGB older adults, further research is needed to compare LGB age cohorts and health changes over time.

Heightened risks of disability and poor physical and mental health among older gay and bisexual men may also be related to HIV.[44] Lacking information on HIV status in our data set, we could not explore this issue, but the disparity may be related to the prevalence of HIV among gay and bisexual men. With the advances in antiretroviral therapies, more adults with HIV are living into old age,[45,46] and older adults living with HIV have been found to be at increased risk of disability and poor physical and mental health.

Elevated risks of smoking and excessive drinking are of major concern among LGB older adults. Although smoking and excessive drinking are leading causes of preventable morbidity and mortality,[47] most prevention campaigns target only younger populations.[48,49] Intervention strategies that both identify and address distinctive cultural factors that may promote smoking and drinking among LGB older adults are desperately needed. Previous research has found that LGB adults smoke at much higher rates than their heterosexual counterparts,[9,10,50] and our findings illustrate that such disparities persist among LGB older adults. We also found that older sexual minority women were more likely than older heterosexual women to drink excessively, which has also been documented in studies of younger sexual minority women.[9,10,50]

Existing research documents that drinking rates decline with age among older adults in general.[51] Although the prevalence rates of excessive drinking among younger gay, bisexual, and heterosexual adult men were similar in other population-based studies, we found higher rates among older gay and bisexual than heterosexual men. It may be that the rate of decline in drinking among older gay and bisexual men is slower than among older heterosexual men.[52] In addition, we found that older lesbians had higher rates of excessive drinking than did older bisexual women, which is also inconsistent with reports from population-based studies of younger lesbian and bisexual women.[10,50] A longitudinal study is warranted to better understand such changes in drinking behavior patterns among sexual minorities, and it will be important to examine how earlier experiences, such as frequent attendance at bars, clubs, and private house parties,[53] combined with minority stressors such as discrimination and victimization,[54] influence changes in drinking patterns over time among LGB older adults.

Older lesbians and bisexual women were more likely than their heterosexual counterparts to be obese and to have CVD; older gay and bisexual men were less likely than heterosexuals to be obese. The higher prevalence of obesity among lesbians and bisexual women than heterosexual women is well documented,[55] but increased risk of CVD has rarely been reported.[56] According to Conron et al., lesbian and bisexual adults may have a higher risk of CVD, possibly attributable to higher prevalence of obesity and smoking.[10] It is likely that disparities in obesity and smoking in early life influence disparities in CVD in later life among lesbians and bisexual women.[57,58]

Our subgroup analyses revealed that diabetes was more common in older bisexual than gay men, even though the obesity rates for the 2 groups were similar. The association between type 2 diabetes and obesity is well known.[59] Although previous studies found that among young adults, gay men were less likely to be obese than were heterosexual men, bisexual men were not.[10] Additional research is needed to investigate whether it is the duration of obesity among older bisexual men that increases their risk of diabetes,[60] as well as to further explore weight change and its impact on older gay men.

We observed some positive trends in preventive screenings, such as the higher likelihood of receiving a flu shot and an HIV test for gay and bisexual than for heterosexual men. Lesbians and bisexual women were more likely than their heterosexual peers to receive an HIV test. Yet we also found evidence of gaps and missed opportunities for prevention. For example, among sexual minority older men, bisexual men were less likely than gay men to obtain an HIV test. Older lesbians and bisexual women were less likely than heterosexual women to report having had a mammogram. Efforts to promote mammography screening among older lesbians and bisexual women is particularly important, because higher risks of breast cancer have been documented among sexual minority women, attributable to elevated prevalence of obesity, substance use, and nulliparity.[61–63] Hart and Bowen suggest that lack of knowledge regarding breast cancer and the benefits of mammography combined with reluctance to use health services because of stigma likely prevent lesbians and bisexual women from receiving mammography in a timely manner.[64]

We observed several important differences in background characteristics by sexual orientation. Contrary to existing stereotypes, despite higher levels of education among LGB older adults, and the higher likelihood of employment among lesbians and bisexual women, LGB older adults do not have higher incomes than do heterosexuals, as observed in other population-based data.[65] In addition, LGB older adults are less likely than heterosexuals to be married but more likely to be partnered, which may have implications for health care advocacy, caregiving, and the availability of financial resources as they age. A recent study found that for gay men, being legally married is associated with mental health benefits.[38] Older gay and bisexual men have significantly fewer children in the household than do heterosexuals and are more likely to live alone, which corroborates findings in other population-based studies.[14] Higher rates of living alone may be related to the increased likelihood of the loss of a partner to AIDS.[66] It is also possible that structural factors do not support committed relationships or legal marriage among same-sex partners. LGB older adults who live alone are likely at risk for social isolation, which has been linked to poor mental and physical health, cognitive impairment, and premature morbidity and mortality in the general elderly population.[67]

Limitations

The cross-sectional nature of BRFSS data limits the ability to disentangle the temporal relationships between variables of interest. Although the purpose of the BRFSS is monitoring overall prevalence of health status, chronic conditions, and behaviors in the United States, and the measures are based on self-report, objective information such as symptoms and severity of health conditions is not available. We analyzed BRFSS data from only 1 state, limiting applicability to other state populations.

Our findings were limited with respect to the response rate of the BRFSS[68,69] and the self-identification of sexual orientation. The proportion of the older population that self-identified as sexual minorities in our data (~ 2%) was less than the 3.5% of adults aged 18 years and older who self-identified as LGB in most other population-based studies.[70] This may reflect the historical context in which today's LGB older adults came of age; these cohorts may be less likely than younger age groups to identify themselves as a sexual minority in a telephone-based survey.

Conclusions

More research with a life-course perspective is needed to examine how age and cohort effects may differentiate the experiences of younger and older LGB adults. Studies that examine the interplay between resilience and the stressors associated with aging and living as a sexual minority would likely help us better understand the mechanisms through which social contexts directly and indirectly affect the health of LGB older adults. Further research, especially a longitudinal study of health among LGB older adults that directly tests the relationships between transitions and trajectories through the life course and investigates the role of human agency in adapting to structural and legal constraints, would provide a greater understanding of how life experiences and shifting social contexts affect health outcomes in later life. Because LGB older adults may rely less on partners, spouses, and children, future research needs to investigate how differing types of social networks, support, and family structures influence health and aging experiences.[71] Although the sample size in our data did

Health Disparities among Lesbian, Gay and Bisexual Older Adults by Karen Fredriksen-Goldsen et al.

241

not allow for direct comparisons across different birth cohorts of LGB older adults, they are needed. The oldest-old LGB population, for example, may have experienced greater challenges in disclosing their sexual orientation; they may also have faced more barriers to social resources affecting health outcomes.

Our findings document population-based health disparities among LGB older adults. Early detection and identification of factors associated with such at-risk groups will enable public health initiatives to expand the reach of strategies and interventions to promote healthy communities. It is imperative that we understand the health needs of older sexual minorities in general as well as those specific to subgroups in this population to develop effective preventive interventions and services tailored to their unique needs. It is imperative that we begin to address healthy aging in our increasingly diverse society.

Human Participant Protection

The institutional review board of the University of Washington approved this study.

References

1. Vincent GA, Velkoff VA. *The Next Four Decades, The Older Population in the United States: 2010 to 2050*. Washington, DC: US Census Bureau; 2010.

2. Centers for Disease Control and Prevention, Merck Company Foundation. The state of aging and health in America. 2007. Available at: www.cdc.gov/aging/pdf/saha_2007.pdf. Accessed October 26, 2011.

3. *Biennial Report of the Director, National Institutes of Health, Fiscal Years 2008 & 2009*. Washington, DC: National Institutes of Health; 2010.

4. Disparities. HealthyPeople.gov. Available at: www. healthypeople.gov/2020/about/disparitiesAbout.aspx#six. Accessed October 26, 2011.

5. MacArthur Foundation Research Network on an Aging Society. Facts and fictions about an aging America. *Contexts*. 2009;8(4):16–21.

6. Truman BI, Smith KC, Roy K, et al. Rationale for regular reporting on health disparities and inequalities—United States. *MMWR Suveill Summ*. 2011;60(suppl):3–10.

7. Institute of Medicine. *The Health of Lesbian, Gay, Bisexual, and Transgender People: Building a Foundation for Better Understanding*. Washington, DC: National Academies Press; 2011.

8. Fredriksen-Goldsen KI, Muraco A. Aging and sexual orientation: a 25-year review of the literature. *Res Aging*. 2010;32(3):372–413.

9. Dilley JA, Simmons KW, Boysun MJ, Pizacani BA, Stark MJ. Demonstrating the importance and feasibility of including sexual orientation in public health surveys: health disparities in the Pacific Northwest. *Am J Public Health*. 2010;100(3):460–467.

10. Conron KJ, Mimiaga MJ, Landers SJ. A population-based study of sexual orientation identity and gender differences in adult health. *Am J Public Health*. 2010;100(10):1953–1960.

11. Boehmer U, Bowen DJ, Bauer GR. Overweight and obesity in sexual-minority women: evidence from population-based data. *Am J Public Health*. 2007;97(6):1134–1140.

12. Fredriksen-Goldsen KI, Kim H-J, Barkan SE, Balsam KF, Mincer S. Disparities in health-related quality of life: a comparison of lesbian and bisexual women. *Am J Public Health*. 2010;100(11):2255–2261.

13. Valanis BG, Bowen DJ, Bassford T, Whitlock E, Charney P, Carter RA. Sexual orientation and health: comparisons in the Women's Health Initiative sample. *Arch Fam Med*. 2000;9(9):843–853.

14. Wallace SP, Cochran SD, Durazo EM, Ford CL. *The Health of Aging Lesbian, Gay and Bisexual Adults in California*. Los Angeles: University of California, Los Angeles Center for Health Policy Research; 2011.

15. Centers for Disease Control and Prevention. Behavioral Risk Factor Surveillance System operational and user's guide. Available at: ftp://ftp.cdc.gov/pub/Data/Brfss/userguide.pdf. Accessed July 10, 2012.

16. Levin B, Lieberman DA, McFarland B, et al. Screening and surveillance for the early detection of colorectal cancer and adenomatous polyps, 2008: a joint guideline from the American Cancer Society, the US Multi-Society Task Force on Colorectal Cancer, and the American College of Radiology. *CA Cancer J Clin*. 2008;58(3):130–160.

17. AgePage. Menopause. National Institute on Aging. Available at: www.nia.nih.gov/healthinformation/publications/menopause .htm. Accessed June, 24, 2011.

18. Alexander CM, Landsman PB, Teutsch SM, Haffner SM, Third National Health and Nutrition Examination Survey (NHANES III), National Cholesterol Education Program (NCEP). NCEP-defined metabolic syndrome, diabetes, and prevalence of coronary heart disease among NHANES III participants age 50 years and older. *Diabetes*. 2003;52(5):1210–1214.

19. Office of Applied Studies. *The NSDUH Report—Serious Psychological Distress Among Adults Aged 50 or Older: 2005 and 2006*. Rockville, MD: Substance Abuse and Mental Health Services Administration; 2008.

20. Bowen ME, González HM. Racial/ethnic differences in the relationship between the use of health care services and functional disability: the health and retirement study (1992–2004). *Gerontologist*. 2008;48(5):659–667.

21. 2003–2010 Behavioral Risk Factor Surveillance System summary data quality reports. Centers for Disease Control and Prevention. Available at: www.cdc.gov/brfss/annual_data/ annual_data.htm#2001. Accessed July 10, 2012.

22. *Measuring Healthy Days.* Atlanta, GA: Centers for Disease Control and Prevention; 2000.

23. Fan AZ, Strine TW, Jiles R, Berry JT, Mokdad AH. Psychological distress, use of rehabilitation services, and disability status among noninstitutionalized US adults aged 35 years and older, who have cardiovascular conditions, 2007. *Int J Public Health.* 2009;54(suppl 1):100–105.

24. Shankar A, Syamala S, Kalidindi S. Insufficient rest or sleep and its relation to cardiovascular disease, diabetes and obesity in a national, multiethnic sample. *PLoS ONE.* 2010;5(11):e14189.

25. Overweight and obesity: defining overweight and obesity. Centers for Disease Control and Prevention. Available at: www.cdc.gov/obesity/defining.html. Accessed April 10, 2012.

26. Centers for Disease Control and Prevention. Vital signs: current cigarette smoking among adults aged ≥ 18 years–United States, 2005–2010. *MMWR Morb Mortal Wkly Rep.* 2011;60(35):1207–1212.

27. National Institute of Alcohol Abuse and Alcoholism. NIAAA council approves definition of binge drinking. *NIAAA Newsletter.* 2004;3:3.

28. Objectives 22-2 and 22-3. *Healthy People 2010* (conference ed, 2 vols). Washington, DC: US Department of Health and Human Services; 2000.

29. Key facts about seasonal flu vaccine. Centers for Disease Control and Prevention. Available at: www.cdc.gov/flu/protect/keyfacts.htm. Accessed December 13, 2011.

30. National Cancer Institute fact sheet: mammograms. National Cancer Institute. Available at: www.cancer.gov/cancertopics/factsheet/detection/mammograms. Accessed December 13, 2011.

31. National Cancer Institute fact sheet: prostate-specific antigen (PSA) test. National Cancer Institute. Available at: www.cancer.gov/cancertopics/factsheet/detection/PSA. Accessed December 13, 2011.

32. Fried LP, Guralnik JM. Disability in older adults: evidence regarding significance, etiology, and risk. *J Am Geriatr Soc.* 1997;45(1):92–100.

33. Fredriksen-Goldsen KI, Kim H-J, Emlet CA, et al. The aging and health report: disparities and resilience among lesbian, gay, bisexual, and transgender older adults. 2011 Available at: http://caringandaging.org. Accessed December 13, 2011.

34. Mayer KU. New directions in life course research. *Annu Rev Sociol.* 2009;35:413–433.

35. Elder GH., Jr. Time, human agency, and social change: perspectives on the life course. *Soc Psychol Q.* 1994;57(1):4–15.

36. Clunis DM, Fredriksen-Goldsen KI, Freeman PA, Nystrom N. *Lives of Lesbian Elders: Looking Back, Looking Forward.* Binghamton, NY: Haworth Press; 2005.

37. Meyer IH. Prejudice, social stress, and mental health in lesbian, gay, and bisexual populations: conceptual issues and research evidence. *Psychol Bull.* 2003;129(5):674–697.

38. Wight RG, LeBlanc AJ, de Vries B, Detels R. Stress and mental health among midlife and older gay-identified men. *Am J Public Health.* 2012;102(3):503–510.

39. Fredriksen-Goldsen KI, Emlet CA, Kim HJ, et al. The physical and mental health of lesbian, gay male, and bisexual (LGB) older adults: the role of key health indicators and risk and protective factors. *Gerontologist.* Epub ahead of print October 3, 2012.

40. D'Augelli AR, Grossman AH. Disclosure of sexual orientation, victimization, and mental health among lesbian, gay, and bisexual older adults. *J Interpers Violence.* 2001;16(10):1008–1027.

41. Fredriksen-Goldsen KI, Kim H-J, Muraco A, Mincer S. Chronically ill midlife and older lesbians, gay men, and bisexuals and their informal caregivers: the impact of the social context. *Sex Res Social Policy.* 2009;6(4):52–64.

42. Marmot MG, Wilkinson RG. *Social Determinants of Health.* 2nd ed. New York, NY: Oxford University Press; 2006.

43. Juster RP, McEwen BS, Lupien SJ. Allostatic load biomarkers of chronic stress and impact on health and cognition. *Neurosci Biobehav Rev.* 2010;35(1):2–16.

44. Jia H, Uphold CR, Zheng Y, et al. A further investigation of health-related quality of life over time among men with HIV infection in the HAART era. *Qual Life Res.* 2007;16(6):961–968.

45. Justice AC. HIV and aging: time for a new paradigm. *Curr HIV/AIDS Rep.* 2010;7(2):69–76.

46. Brennan DJ, Emlet CA, Eady A. HIV, sexual health, and psychosocial issues among older adults living with HIV in North America. *Ageing Int.* 2011;36(3):313–333.

47. Center for Substance Abuse Treatment. *Substance Abuse Among Older Adults.* Rockville, MD: Substance Abuse and Mental Health Services Administration; 1998. Treatment Improvement Protocol (TIP) Series 26.

48. Backinger CL, Fagan P, Matthews E, Grana R. Adolescent and young adult tobacco prevention and cessation: current status and future directions. *Tob Control.* 2003;12(suppl 4):iv46–iv53.

49. Wakefield MA, Loken B, Hornik RC. Use of mass media campaigns to change health behaviour. *Lancet.* 2010;376(9748): 1261–1271.

50. Burgard SA, Cochran SD, Mays VM. Alcohol and tobacco use patterns among heterosexually and homosexually experienced California women. *Drug Alcohol Depend.* 2005;77(1):61–70.

51. Kanny D, Liu Y, Brewer RD. Centers for Disease Control and Prevention. Binge drinking–United States, 2009. *MMWR Surveill Summ.* 2011;60(suppl):101–104.

52. Green KE, Feinstein BA. Substance use in lesbian, gay, and bisexual populations: an update on empirical research and implications for treatment. *Psychol Addict Behav.* 2012;26(2):265–278.

Health Disparities among Lesbian, Gay and Bisexual Older Adults by Karen Fredriksen-Goldsen et al.

243

53. Trocki KF, Drabble L, Midanik L. Use of heavier drinking contexts among heterosexuals, homosexuals and bisexuals: results from a National Household Probability Survey. *J Stud Alcohol.* 2005;66(1):105–110.

54. Brubaker MD, Garrett MT, Dew BJ. Examining the relationship between internalized heterosexism and substance abuse among lesbian, gay, and bisexual individuals: a critical review. *J LGBT Issues Couns.* 2009;3(1):62–89.

55. Bowen DJ, Balsam KF, Ender SR. A review of obesity issues in sexual minority women. *Obesity (Silver Spring)* 2008;16(2):221–228.

56. Roberts SA, Dibble SL, Nussey B, Casey K. Cardiovascular disease risk in lesbian women. *Womens Health Issues.* 2003;13(4):167–174.

57. Hubert HB, Feinleib M, McNamara PM, Castelli WP. Obesity as an independent risk factor for cardiovascular disease: a 26-year follow-up of participants in the Framingham Heart Study. *Circulation.* 1983;67(5):968–977.

58. He J, Ogden LG, Bazzano LA, Vupputuri S, Loria C, Whelton PK. Risk factors for congestive heart failure in US men and women: NHANES I epidemiologic follow-up study. *Arch Intern Med.* 2001;161(7):996–1002.

59. Nguyen NT, Nguyen XM, Lane J, Wang P. Relationship between obesity and diabetes in a US adult population: findings from the National Health and Nutrition Examination Survey, 1999–2006. *Obes Surg.* 2011;21(3):351–355.

60. Lee JM, Gebremariam A, Vijan S, Gurney JG. Excess body mass index-years, a measure of degree and duration of excess weight, and risk for incident diabetes. *Arch Pediatr Adolesc Med.* 2012;166(1):42–48.

61. Case P, Austin SB, Hunter DJ, et al. Sexual orientation, health risk factors, and physical functioning in the Nurses' Health Study II. *J Womens Health (Larchmt)* 2004;13(9):1033–1047.

62. Cochran SD, Mays VM, Bowen D, et al. Cancerrelated risk indicators and preventive screening behaviors among lesbians and bisexual women. *Am J Public Health.* 2001;91(4):591–597.

63. Dibble SL, Roberts SA, Nussey B. Comparing breast cancer risk between lesbians and their heterosexual sisters. *Womens Health Issues.* 2004;14(2):60–68.

64. Hart SL, Bowen DJ. Sexual orientation and intentions to obtain breast cancer screening. *J Womens Health (Larchmt)* 2009;18(2):177–185.

65. Albelda R, Badgett MVL, Schneebaum A, Gates GJ. *Poverty in the Lesbian, Gay, and Bisexual Community.* Los Angeles, CA: Williams Institute; 2009.

66. Cochran SD, Mays V, Corliss H, Smith TW, Turner J. Self-reported altruistic and reciprocal behaviors among homosexually and heterosexually experienced adults: implications for HIV/AIDS service organizations. *AIDS Care.* 2009;21(6):675–682.

67. Cornwell EY, Waite LJ. Measuring social isolation among older adults using multiple indicators from the NSHAP Study. *J Gerontol B Psychol Sci Soc Sci.* 2009;64B(suppl 1):i38–i46.

68. Schneider KL, Clark MA, Rakowski W, Lapane KL. Evaluating the impact of non-response bias in the Behavioral Risk Factor Surveillance System (BRFSS). *J Epidemiol Community Health.* 2012;66(4):290–295.

69. Keeter S, Kennedy C, Dimock M, Best J, Craighill P. Gauging the impact of growing nonresponse on estimates from a national RDD telephone survey. *Public Opin Q.* 2006;70(5):759–779.

70. Gates GJ. *How Many People Are Lesbian, Gay, Bisexual, and Transgender?* Los Angeles, CA: Williams Institute; 2011.

71. Muraco A, Fredriksen-Goldsen K. "That's what friends do": informal caregiving for chronically ill lesbian, gay, and bisexual elders. *J Soc Pers Relat.* 2011;28(8):1073–1092.

Critical Thinking

1. Do you think that the attitudes of professionals and others influence service delivery to the lesbian, gay, and bisexual population?

2. How do you think some of the gaps in health disparities can be closed, or even shortened?

Internet References

The LGBT Aging Project
www.lgbtagingproject.org
National Resource Center on LGBT Aging
www.lgbtagingcenter.org

KAREN I. FREDRIKSEN-GOLDSEN, HYUN-JUN KIM, SUSAN E. BARKAN, AND CHARLES P. HOY-ELLIS are with the School of Social Work, University of Washington, Seattle. ANNA MURACO is with the Department of Sociology, Loyola Marymount University, Los Angeles.

Fredriksen-Goldsen et al., Karen. From *American Journal of Public Health*, October 2013, pp. 1802–1809. Copyright © 2013 by American Public Health Association. Reprinted by permission via Sheridan Reprints.

Article

Prepared by: Elizabeth Schroeder, EdD, MSW,
Elizabeth Schroeder Consulting

Much Ado about Nothing?

Aram A. Schvey

Learning Outcomes

After reading this article, you will be able to:

- Discuss the provisions of the Affordable Care Act.

- Assess the impact of the Act on religious liberty.

- Discuss the importance of access to affordable contraception.

Religious Freedom and the Contraceptive-Coverage Benefit

August 1, 2012: A date that will live in infamy. Or so some religious conservatives contend. Matt Smith, president of the Catholic Advocate, solemnly declared that "August first will be remembered as the day our most cherished liberty was thrown in a government dumpster and hauled away." L. Brent Bozell III, president of the conservative Media Research Center, inveighed that "the beginning of the end of freedom as America has known it and loved it" was nigh. And, unsatisfied with even that level of rhetoric, Rep. Mike Kelly (R-PA) went so far as to compare August 1, 2012, to America's darkest hours:

> [Y]ou can think of the times America was attacked. One is December 7, that's Pearl Harbor Day. The other is September 11, and that's the day the terrorists attacked. I want you to remember August 1, 2012, the attack on our religious freedom. That is a day that will live in infamy, along with those other dates.

What event occurred on August 1, 2012, to give rise to such fire-and-brimstone rhetoric? A terrorist attack? A dastardly sneak attack by an enemy nation? A tyrannical military coup d'état?

Hardly. Instead, August 1, 2012, is the day that the 99 percent of American women who have used contraception (including 98 percent of Catholic women) could kiss their copays goodbye and save hundreds of dollars a year on essential reproductive health care. On that date, the contraceptive-coverage benefit of the Affordable Care Act (also known as Obamacare) went into effect. Under the new policy, most employers' health-insurance plans (other than those for houses of worship) must begin covering FDA-approved contraception (including sterilization and emergency contraception) and associated counseling without cost-sharing—eliminating contraceptive copays.

What to most Americans was a tremendous health care benefit—saving them hundreds of dollars per year in out-of-pocket costs and putting contraception, and, in particular, expensive long-term contraceptive methods, within reach—is to some an affront to and violation of their religious liberty. Critics of the policy who see contraception as sinful are outraged that employees might access contraception through a company-subsidized health-insurance plan despite the company owner's sincerely held belief that contraception is sinful.

This notion—that the contraceptive-coverage benefit runs roughshod over employers' religious liberty—is a claim that has been repeated often and with great fervor. But the dispute cannot be fairly reduced to a conflict between those who support and those who oppose religious liberty. Indeed, all sides agree that religious liberty is a bedrock American value and worthy of protection. What is at issue in the debate is whose religious liberty is at stake: the employers who object to the fact that some employees may access contraception through health-insurance plans, or employees, who risk losing essential health-insurance coverage based on their employer's religious beliefs. Ultimately, this article concludes, religious liberty belongs equally to all Americans. But it is not a sword to be used by those at the top of the employment ladder to hack away at those at lower rungs; rather, it is a shield that protects all individuals' religious beliefs equally.

Background

The contraceptive-coverage policy was recommended as part of a comprehensive set of preventive services for women through the Women's Health Amendment to the Affordable Care Act by a blue-ribbon panel of acclaimed medical experts convened by the Institute of Medicine (other recommendations included improved cancer and sexually transmitted infection [STI] screenings, broadly available lactation counseling, and no-copay annual well-woman preventivecare visits). The purpose of the contraceptive-coverage policy is to promote the health of women and children nationwide by addressing America's sky-high unintended-pregnancy rate: Half of all U.S. pregnancies are unintended, and those unintended pregnancies pose real health risks for women, and, where the pregnancy is taken to term, for newborns. By making contraception—and, in particular, more expensive, but more effective, long-acting contraception (such as intrauterine devices [IUDs] and implants)—more affordable, the policy aims to cut the unintended pregnancy rate, promote health, and save money in the process (because studies demonstrate that a dollar spent on contraception can save more than four dollars in medical costs).

In rolling out the no-copay-contraception policy, the administration recognized that churches and other religious employers might have objections to carrying health insurance that in turn covered contraception. Consequently, the Department of Health and Human Services proposed carving out a special exemption to the policy for houses of worship, as a means of respecting "the unique relationship between a house of worship and its employees in ministerial positions," even though such an exemption was not required as a matter of law. The exemption applies to a nonprofit employer if its purpose is the inculcation of religious values and if it primarily employs and serves those sharing its religious tenets, such as a church or mosque. The exemption does not, however, extend to institutions claiming a religious affiliation that hire and serve nonadherents, such as hospitals and universities; nor does it apply to for-profit companies. The reason is simple: Allowing any corporation or institution to claim exemptions from the law would, in effect, allow the exceptions to swallow the rule, turning the law into Swiss cheese and blunting its purpose of promoting the health of women and infants. It would also have the effect of imposing the employer's religious beliefs on nonbelievers, thus making employees' benefits subject to their employer's religious views.

The exemption did little to quiet critics, and the outcry from religious conservatives and others was quick and vociferous. Despite the fact that most states already mandate coverage for contraceptive drugs and devices, and that many of those states include no exemption whatsoever, the U.S. Conference of Catholic Bishops decried the contraception-coverage benefit as "unprecedented" and numerous institutions claiming a religious affiliation, for-profit companies, and a group of state attorneys general have filed lawsuits to try to halt the implementation of the law. In response, the administration proposed an additional accommodation whereby the cost of the contraception would be explicitly borne by the health-insurance companies, rather than the employer issuing the insurance policy. But neither this second accommodation, nor a one-year safe-harbor provision for groups with religious objections, has quieted the furor.

A number of the suits have been dismissed as premature in light of the safe-harbor provision, but in July 2012 a federal district judge in Colorado granted a preliminary injunction preventing the policy from being enforced against Hercules Industries, a for-profit heating, ventilation, and air-conditioning company, whose owners object to contraception. In late September 2012, however, a federal district judge in Missouri dismissed on the merits a challenge to the contraceptive-coverage benefit brought by a for-profit mining company whose mission includes "mak[ing] our labor a pleasing offering to the Lord."

The current debate surrounding the contraceptive-coverage benefit continues, both in Congress and in the courts. Assuming the Affordable Care Act is not repealed, it may take a Supreme Court decision, in light of the possibility of the circuit courts of appeals splitting on the issue (a likely scenario, given that lawsuits have been filed in numerous circuits). While the claims made in each case differ, the major claims are based on the First Amendment and on the Religious Freedom Restoration Act (RFRA), a 1993 federal statute that applies a strict-scrutiny test to federal actions that substantially burden a person's exercise of **religion.**

Legal Claims

At first blush, one might assume that the First Amendment claims being made by those challenging the contraceptive-coverage benefit are strong. But, in fact, the Supreme Court has roundly rejected the proposition that an otherwise neutral and generally applicable law is unconstitutional simply because it happens to interfere with someone's religious beliefs. Perhaps even more surprising is the fact that this understanding of the First Amendment's intended contours was set forth by the very Supreme Court justice who is commonly thought of as conservative and therefore assumed to be sympathetic to religious-liberty claims—Justice Antonin Scalia.

In *Employment Division v. Smith*, 494 U.S. 872 (1990), the Court confronted a challenge to a statute that denied unemployment benefits to drug users, including Native Americans who consumed sacramental peyote. Justice Scalia, writing for the Court, rejected the claim that the drug-use prohibition violated the Free Exercise Clause as applied to Native Americans who consumed peyote: "The government's ability to carry out aspects of public policy, cannot depend on measuring the effects of a governmental action on a religious objector's spiritual development"; otherwise, every religious objector would "become a law unto himself," a result that Justice Scalia found to be unsupported by both the Constitution and common sense. If a law is neutral and generally applicable, and does not directly target religious activity qua religious activity, it is constitutional. Whether or not an exemption might be desirable, Justice Scalia emphasized, "is not to say that it is constitutionally required."

There is no question that the contraception-coverage benefit is both neutral and generally applicable, and thus accords with the First Amendment. Far from deliberately targeting religious activity, the policy focuses on insurance coverage. And the policy, of course, applies to employers irrespective of their religiosity, or the nature of their religious views. There is simply no support for the claim by the U.S. Conference of Catholic Bishops that the law "targets Catholicism for special disfavor." Indeed, the policy was based on the recommendation of a blue-ribbon panel of medical experts, which in turn was based on substantial scholarship and research.

The stronger claim advanced by opponents of the contraceptive-coverage benefit is that the policy violates the RFRA, a statute designed to overturn legislatively Employment Division and impose a strict-scrutiny test on laws that burden religious exercise. Under RFRA, any federal policy that substantially burdens a person's religious exercise must be justified by a compelling interest, and use the least restrictive means of achieving that interest. Opponents of the contraceptive-coverage benefit argue that a company owner or other employer's religious exercise is substantially burdened by the fact that his or her employees may seek, and access, contraception that the owner/employer finds sinful.

There are numerous problems with this claim—most centrally, the fact that it utterly ignores the religious-liberty interest of the employees, whose health-insurance benefits would be restricted based on their employer's religious beliefs. Indeed, in the Hercules Industries case mentioned above, when the judge sought to balance the harms in deciding whether to grant a preliminary injunction, he weighed the employer's religious-liberty interest against the government's interest in enforcing laws. What is shockingly absent is any consideration of the impact of the decision on the company's 265 employees and their dependents, who have the most to lose in any decision.

This factor—the impact on third parties—is what distinguishes the religious-liberty claims being made here from those made in previous instances where the Supreme Court has permitted a derogation from an otherwise applicable law. For example, in *Wisconsin v. Yoder*, 406 U.S. 205 (1972), the Supreme Court permitted an exemption to school-attendance laws for Amish children. But, in so doing, the Court emphasized that

"there is no intimation" that permitting the children to opt out of public schooling "is in any way deleterious to their health."

But with respect to the contraceptive-coverage benefit, there is an obvious impact on employees' well-being—an opt-out for employers would directly harm employees' health. And the Supreme Court has emphasized that one person's sphere of religious liberty only extends to the boundary of another person's sphere of religious liberty. The common thread in the Court's exemptions-related cases is that the religious exercise protected in each instance "did not, or would not, impose substantial burdens on non-beneficiaries while allowing others to act according to their religious beliefs nor [would they] impose monetary costs on [those] who opposed the religious instruction."

In contrast, exempting employers from the contraceptive-coverage benefit would directly impose both a health and a monetary burden on employees. This differentiates the sought exemption from other religious exemptions—for example, allowing Sikh policemen to have beards or allowing a Saturday-Sabbath observer to collect unemployment benefits if the only jobs she can find require Saturday labor.

In addition, it is wholly unclear whether RFRA even applies to corporations and companies, rather than actual flesh-and-blood human beings, or, as the court in the Hercules Industries case posited, "can a corporation exercise religion?" To answer in the affirmative would certainly open the floodgates to substantial mischief, potentially allowing corporations to flout discrimination laws and other worker protections, zoning policies, and safety regulations by claiming a religious posture. And even if RFRA protections were extended to companies and corporations, it is a highly dubious proposition that purchasing insurance coverage constitutes "religious exercise."

To the extent that a corporate employer can invoke RFRA, the burden on religious exercise is minimal. In the cases where the Supreme Court has found a burden on religious exercise, an individual was prohibited by law from actually exercising his or her religion—keeping the Saturday Sabbath, for example, or using prescribed sacramental substances. In contrast, the employers in the various lawsuits are not being prevented from keeping the Sabbath, participating in communion, or providing religious schooling for their children. And they are certainly not being forced to use contraception or encourage its use; indeed, they remain free to speak out against it. Instead, as the federal district judge noted in the case dismissing an employer's lawsuit, the supposed burden complained of is that an employer will contribute to a health care plan that might, after a series of independent decisions by employees and medical professionals, lead some employees to access contraception that is in some way subsidized by the employer. The link between the employer's subsidization of insurance coverage and the ultimate receipt of contraceptives by an individual employee is so remote as to be meaningless. Indeed, it is difficult to distinguish an employer's supposed interest in how employees use their health insurance from an employer's interest in how employees use their salaries (which are, of course, paid by the employer).

Finally, the contraceptive-coverage benefit is consonant with RFRA because it advances a compelling governmental interest and uses the least restrictive means to achieve it. As noted, the policy furthers a compelling interest in women's health and newborn health. It furthers a compelling interest in combating sex-based inequality—in December 2000, the Equal Employment Opportunity Commission held that Title VII of the Civil Rights Act bars employer-sponsored health-insurance plans that provide prescription-drug coverage but fail to cover contraceptives. It also helps remedy the insurance "penalty" women pay by virtue of being female: Senator Barbara Mikulski, the architect of the legislation underlying the contraceptive-coverage benefit, noted that she hoped that the Women's Health Amendment would remedy the sex discrimination women face when purchasing insurance. And, finally, the policy promotes a compelling government interest in women's autonomy. As a society, we recognize that access to affordable contraception is a cornerstone of women's independence and equality. Justice Sandra Day O'Connor, the first female Supreme Court justice, said it best: "The ability of women to participate equally in the economic and social life of the Nation has been facilitated by their ability to control their reproductive lives."

These are powerful and compelling governmental interests. Where such compelling interests are present, the Supreme Court has consistently rejected religious opt-outs. It bears remembering that groups have often sought exemptions from broadly applicable laws based on religious beliefs. Religious groups have, over time, sought to be exempt from laws banning polygamy, from laws banning child labor, from laws banning racial discrimination, and from laws requiring the payment of taxes. In all of these cases, and in many more, the courts roundly rejected such claims. And with respect to the contraceptive-coverage policy, the highest courts of California and New York confronted challenges to their state's contraceptive-coverage laws, in both cases rejecting religious-liberty challenges to the same narrow religious exemption currently at issue in the federal policy. The California Supreme Court's decision is particularly instructive, holding, "We are unaware of any decision in which the United States Supreme Court has exempted a religious objector from the operation of a neutral, generally applicable law despite the recognition that the requested exemption would detrimentally affect the rights of third parties."

Conclusion

Religious liberty is a core American value, and the delicate balance between the First Amendment's Free Exercise and Establishment Clauses is a uniquely American contribution to global jurisprudence. But in a nation blessed with almost endless religious diversity—with those subscribing to all manner of faiths and none, and innumerable interpretations and manifestations of those beliefs—preferencing one person's religious liberty, or one group of people's religious liberty, without regard to others inevitably results in a diminution of rights.

As a nation, we have, and will continue, to struggle to balance laws and policies protecting the individual and those protecting the community. Where religious liberty is used as a shield, the courts have rightly upheld exemptions to protect religious worship and customs from government intrusion. But the courts have rightly rejected—and should continue to reject—claims where religious liberty is used as a sword to subordinate the rights of others. Indeed, the nation was founded on the principle that all Americans, whether corner-office prince or mail-room pauper, have an equal claim to religious liberty.

Critical Thinking

1. Why might affordable birth control be considered the cornerstone of women's independence and equality?

2. Does the Affordable Care Act violate religious freedom?

3. Describe how providing birth control through the Affordable Care Act might be perceived as a violation of religious liberty.

Internet References

Health Care
www.healthcare.gov

Health Care Law and You
www.healthcare.gov/law

Planned Parenthood
www.plannedparenthood.org

ARAM A. SCHVEY serves as policy counsel at the Center for Reproductive Rights, a global human rights organization dedicated to promoting reproductive rights in the United States and around the world. He previously served as litigation counsel at Americans United for Separation of Church and State and has served as a fellow at the Georgetown University Law Center and Fordham Law School. He also serves on the editorial board for *Human Rights*.

Unit 7

UNIT

Prepared by: Elizabeth Schroeder, EdD, MSW,
Elizabeth Schroeder Consulting

Sexualities and Social Issues

Social issues relating to human sexuality in its broadest definition have evolved, progressed, regressed and been cyclical in nature for over a century. At the heart of whether there is progress or there are setbacks are issues of power and control, and of personal responsibility. Historically, men have been seen as sexual beings, with sex drives that need to be managed and "tamed" by women. This sentiment is pervasive today, with the sentiment "boys will be boys" seemingly excusing men for bad behavior, such as rape on college campuses; sexual harassment in the workplace; nonconsensual, extra-relationship relationships and more. In some cases, this attitude has been taken to an extreme, wherein all men are seen as predators or potential rapists. This societally based lower expectation of men is sexist and denigrating to men.

At the same time, however, the vast majority of people who commit sexual assaults are men. The vast majority of people who proactively traffic and sell girls, women, and children of all genders are men. Intimate partner violence can be committed by someone of any gender against a partner of any gender—yet the vast majority of perpetrators are, again, men. These facts overshadow the many, many good men out there who are sexual beings yet do not use their strength, privilege, or power to manipulate, coerce, or abuse others.

In abusive relationships, it is common for the partner being abused to not leave right away. This leaves a victim of intimate partner violence misunderstood and judged for staying in an unhealthy, unsafe situation. In some cases, that partner is blamed for the abuse itself, with speculations abounding about what she (in cases where the victim is a woman) did to provoke her abuser. Yet there are many reasons why a person of any gender would not leave an abusive relationship right away. The couple may have children. The abusive partner may have taken control of the finances and not let the abused partner work or finish school or do anything else that would enable that partner to have financial independence from the abuser. There may be confusion and conflicting feelings—how could the person s/he fell in love with have turned into this complete monster? Is it possible that the good person s/he knew initially is still in there and

can emerge again, if only s/he changes something? And so on. Relationships are complex and complicated; abusive ones are even more so.

The advent of the Internet, social media, handheld devices, smart phones and whatever is next on the horizon has done so much for human interactions and access to life-enhancing, sometimes life-saving information. Communication has increased, even if that communication is through texting or other technology. More recent technology allows people long-distance to stay in relationships and speak face to face through their computers or even on their smart phones. People who wish to be in relationships but have not met the right person in their lives can go online to any number of dating sites to try to meet someone. People for whom physical intimacy is an issue or who feel isolated socially can have an entire social life online. The positive possibilities continue to be endless.

Yet, as there is so much good that comes from technological advances, there are still those who use it for nefarious purposes. People misrepresent themselves on dating sites. Younger people are still targeted by online predators who troll social media sites. Child porn has exploded, as has sexual trafficking, both of which are facilitated by the Internet. Even consensual, legal porn, which is made by and for adults, is challenging; it is now easy and free to access online, which means younger people, the same young people whose parents do not want them to have school-based sexuality education, are being exposed to material that is not made, or age-appropriate, for them.

Some challenging aspects of technology have to do with intention versus outcome. Some people send their partners sexy, seductive photos via text ("sexting") with the intention that these photos would only be shared between the two of them—until the couple breaks up and one of the partners makes these photos public—known as "revenge porn." The law is slowly catching up with this practice, but currently only a few states in the United States have laws specifically addressing this.

Perhaps a better title for this unit would have been, "Sexualities, Social Issues, and Responsibility." So much of how sexuality is treated in our cultures, in the media, and online have to do with the decisions we make about how it is portrayed and legislated. There is nothing inherently wrong with technology or the Internet—but it can be used for sinister purposes. There is nothing inherently wrong about sharing intimate texts with a partner, but the minute one hits "send," the person has given up all control over what can be done with those texts. If more people behaved responsibly when it comes to sexuality and relationships, we would see a reduction in the vastly negative statistics relating to many of the social issues discussed in this unit.

Article

Prepared by: Elizabeth Schroeder, EdD, MSW,
Elizabeth Schroeder Consulting

The Science of Sex Abuse

Is it right to imprison people for heinous crimes they have not yet committed?

RACHEL AVIV

Learning Outcomes

After reading this article, you will be able to:

- Explain when child pornography first became a concern of federal law enforcement officials.

- Describe at least one impact that the Internet has had on the transmission and propagation of child porn.

- Describe the Adam Walsh Child Protection and Safety Act and how it came to be passed.

On a Saturday night in the summer of 1998, an undercover officer logged in to a child-pornography chat room using the screen name Indy-Girl. Within minutes, a user named John introduced himself and asked her, "Are you into real life or just fantasy?" Indy-Girl said that because of the "legality of it" she had never acted on her fantasies. But she soon revealed an adventurous spirit. She was a bisexual college sophomore, she said, and had learned about sex at an early age. "My mother is very European," she explained.

John, a thirty-one-year-old soldier stationed in Fort Campbell, Kentucky, had been using the Internet for less than a year. He began downloading child pornography after watching a television special about how Internet child porn had become epidemic. He hadn't realized that it existed. In the five months since he'd seen the show, he had downloaded more than two thousand images from child-pornography news groups. In the anonymous chat rooms, he felt free to adopt a persona repugnant to society. He told Indy-Girl that he was a "real-life pedophile," adding, "At least here I can come out and admit it."

"What's the kinkiest you've done?" Indy-Girl asked. John said he'd had sex with a ten-year-old while her parents were skiing, and with a fourteen-year-old at a night club in Germany. Indy-Girl recognized that she was too old for him, which was "depressing," but she offered that her little sister liked older men. "Maybe you could intro me," John wrote. "We could meet somewhere discreet."

John had been in the Army for eight years, serving in Desert Storm and Bosnia, and had graduated from Penn State with a degree in history. He was thinking of leaving the service, in part because he felt picked on by other soldiers. He had been commended for having a memory for technical details, but he was also nervous, nerdy, and eager to please. At all stages of his life, he had been afflicted with the sense that he was just a "wannabe."

Unlike other people John met online, Indy-Girl seemed to like him. After a week of conversations, she asked John if he was "r/l" (real life) about the meeting, and when he said that he was she sent him a soft-focus digital image of a girl who she said was her fourteen-year-old sister. "Now don't be mean when you see it," she warned. "She still has some of her baby fat, she's kinda embarrassed." Undeterred, John described how the three of them would enjoy one another's company: they could have sex in the shower or in a field of flowers. He encouraged Indy-Girl to "talk dirty" and "let your imagination go wild," but she cut him off, explaining, "I'm not the cyber type."

She preferred to discuss the logistics of their meeting, a subject that John approached hesitantly. During the following week, Indy-Girl repeatedly expressed concern that John was avoiding her: "You're usually so fun to chat with . . . and now . . . I feel like just . . . blaaaahhh." She apologized for getting "a bit too gabby" and for "being so weird" and "reading into things." John said it wasn't her—he worked long hours and was tired. He also admitted that he wanted a relationship more than he wanted sex. He hoped to find someone who "could accept me the way I am." "Give it a chance," Indy-Girl encouraged. "If you like her . . . and she likes you . . . things will work out." She added, "It's not like she's gonna die if you don't."

They decided to meet at a park in Elizabethtown, Kentucky, where they could have a picnic or go boating on the lake. Two weeks after their first conversation, John drove three hours to the appointed meeting spot. He brought lacy undergarments in his briefcase. The Military Police Investigations unit, working with the F.B.I., had recruited two young officers to play the roles of the two sisters. They arrived early, spread a blanket on the grass, and waved at John, who was sitting at a picnic table, writing in his journal.

An athletic man with light-brown hair and green eyes, John slowly walked over to the girls, who were playing with a beach ball. He offered them sodas, and they chatted about what they liked to drink—Indy-Girl said she preferred beer—and about how long the drive had taken. It was a "normal conversation," one of the cops later wrote, until John "saw the agents approaching him, and he began backing away." A plainclothes officer whom John had seen standing by the lake, holding a fishing pole and a tackle box, shouted at him to put his hands behind his back.

John waived his right to a lawyer, hoping to end the humiliation quickly. (His mother, for the sake of John's two younger brothers, has asked that I not use the family's last name.) In an interview with the agents, John confessed that he frequently downloaded child pornography, storing it on his hard drive in a folder labelled "2Young." He was sexually attracted to the girls in the photographs, he admitted, but he had never had sexual contact with anyone below the age of eighteen. He insisted that he had invented his sexual exploits to impress Indy-Girl. According to an F.B.I. report summarizing the interview, "Everything that he said on the Internet was a lie."

John pleaded guilty to possessing child pornography and to using the Internet to persuade a minor to have sex, and was sentenced to fifty-three months in federal prison—a relatively light sentence by today's standards. In the past fifteen years, sentences for possession or distribution of child pornography—a federal crime, since images cross state lines—have increased in length by more than five hundred per cent. The average sentence is now a hundred and nineteen months, which is about the same as the average punishment for a physical sex crime.

Child pornography didn't become a priority for federal law enforcement until the mid-nineties, when the Internet, offering a fun-house reflection of the spectrum of human sexuality, exposed a previously invisible population of pedophiles. Chat rooms have spawned an underground subculture in which social status is based on comprehensive libraries of images. Many users consider themselves "collectors," trading pictures until they assemble sets that feature certain children, stars on the Internet, being sexually abused over time.

In a study of child pornography, the historian Philip Jenkins, of Penn State, found that chat rooms foster a kind of "bandit culture." Self-described "Loli fans" see themselves as part of a subversive fraternity, unified by the pursuit of forbidden pleasures. There is a hierarchy of users: newbies, lurkers, traders, and, at the top, the pornographers themselves—"kings of the rooms," as John told me. He said that the most sought-after images were new and made in America, and showed interracial couplings. The more taboos broken, the better. Members reinforced one another's desires, engaging in communal rationalization. "We'd pull at evidence from the dawn of photography to prove that child sexuality was once acceptable," John said. "Then we could say, 'See, it's society—not me!'"

When U.S. obscenity laws were first relaxed, in the fifties, no special stipulations were made for photographs of minors. "If the First Amendment means anything," the Supreme Court wrote in 1969, "it means that a State has no business telling a man, sitting alone in his own house, what books he may read or what films he may watch." But, by 1982, the public seemed to have discovered child sex abuse, both its trauma and its prevalence. The Supreme Court made child pornography an exception to the First Amendment, since "a child has been physically or psychologically harmed in the production of the work."

Early efforts to suppress the American child-porn trade—a small network of adult bookstores and mail-order services—were so successful that within a decade the market was all but nonexistent. But the Internet undid those achievements. Controlling the flow of images is nearly impossible, because pornography is posted online from other nations, which have different definitions of who is a child and what is obscene. In arguing for harsher penalties for viewing child pornography, lawmakers have tended to conflate the desire to view photographs (a crime that can be detected by tracing a computer's I.P. address) with actual sex abuse, which is notoriously difficult to prosecute, since young victims are easily silenced. In 2002, the chief of the F.B.I.'s Crimes Against Children Unit told the House Subcommittee on Crime, Terrorism, and Homeland Security that the online pornography trade had created a "vast network of like-minded people, who believe it is acceptable to engage in sexual fantasies about children, thus lowering their inhibitions . . . and increasing the likelihood that they will actually molest children."

Child-pornography sentencing laws have been passed rapidly, with little debate; it's nearly impossible, politically, to object to harsh punishments for perverts. Melissa Hamilton, a law professor at the University of Houston Law Center, told me that lawmakers have treated pornography possession as if it were an "inchoate crime." She said, "It has become a kind of proxy—a way to incapacitate men who we fear have already molested someone, or will in the future."

In prison, the only friends John made were other child-pornography convicts. "We picked each other out like black beans in a pile of rice," he told me. He adjusted poorly, feeling overwhelmed by a sense of failure. "I was supposed to be the successful child," he told a prison psychologist. In therapy, he refused to share intimate details. "When asked to describe adult relationships with women," the psychologist wrote, "he appeared to be making up details of these as he spoke." On the Internet, John said, "I can be whoever I want to be."

John's father, an engineer, said that he would have disowned his son if he had been the one "standing behind the camera, taking the pictures." But he forgave him for "acting like a schmuck." In 2003, after completing his prison term, John moved into his parents' suburban home and began a three-year term of probation; he was not allowed to use the Internet or to go places where children congregate. He got a job at a bakery but chafed under his legal restrictions, complaining to his case manager, "I am not allowed to use my skills." (After his arrest, he had been "other than honorably" discharged from the Army.) To comply with the terms of his probation, his parents put their computers in one room of the house and padlocked the door.

John's mother was a member of the local Day Lily Club, and spent much of her free time in her garden, where she had seven hundred and fifty varieties of lilies, whose growth she documented in scrapbooks. Warm and self-deprecating, she said that she identified with John's tendency to become compulsively immersed in his hobbies. He'd spent long periods of his life absorbed in role-playing games, like Dungeons & Dragons—he became so caught up in this world that he nearly flunked out of college—and the Society for Creative Anachronism, a club that reënacts aspects of medieval culture. His mother believed that John might have ignored Indy-Girl if only he'd been less "prone to fantasy."

John's imagined sexual encounters had always surpassed his real ones. The first time he saw nude models was in middle school, when he discovered a copy of *Playboy* belonging to his father. He was surprised and disappointed that the models weren't his age. By twelfth grade, he noticed that the girls at school whom he found most attractive were freshmen. But his desires seemed academic, his classmates having nicknamed him Fungus. "If anything, girls wanted me to be their friend—never their boyfriend," he said. When male classmates boasted about their sexual escapades, John made up his own. He paid for the majority of his sexual encounters; he lost his virginity at the age of nineteen to a prostitute at a twenty-four-hour health spa, he said. Pornography became an outlet for assuming an invented role. "You pick exactly which girl you want, when you want her—you control everything," he said. "It was pure pleasure without the stuff of reality."

During John's first year out of prison, his parents were confident that he was "straightening out." He, too, felt that he was on track to acquire the "trappings of success: a wife, a house, children, a beautiful garden." Then the conditions of his supervised release were loosened, permitting him access to the Internet. "It filled some deep hole in me that I didn't even know existed," he said. He visited online forums devoted to medieval culture and war games, and began downloading adult pornography. His downloads became increasingly explicit, but the procession of submissive young females proved monotonous, and he found himself looking on a news group called Youth and Beauty for images that were more extreme. John couldn't quite get himself to believe that he would ever get caught. Crossing the boundary was part of the "mystique," he said.

When he received a letter from Gary, another child-pornography ex-convict, he said, he "fell right back into it." He wrote to Gary about new software that would enable them to view child pornography safely, and marvelled at porn titles as if they were collector's items. In a chummy, rebellious tone, he assured Gary that when their probation terms were over they would cross the border into Mexico and pick up a young brunette or fly to Cambodia and make some "homemade product."

During a routine home visit, John's probation officer spotted questionable images on his computer, and sent the machine to the F.B.I. for a forensic analysis, which revealed twenty images of underage females. Two months later, the letters to Gary were discovered. John pleaded guilty to viewing illicit images and to failing to obtain authorization from his probation officer to have unsupervised contact with his five-year-old niece. (An investigation found no indication that he had behaved improperly toward the child.) At his probation-violation hearing, in 2005, John was sentenced to two more years in prison. In his testimony, he described pornography as an addiction. "I really don't have enough control over it," he told the judge. "I would like to figure out how to make it stop, I really would. I just don't know how to do it yet."

John had been back in prison for a year when, in 2006, Congress passed the Adam Walsh Child Protection and Safety Act, which its sponsor described as the "most comprehensive child crimes and protection bill in our Nation's history." It allows the Federal Bureau of Prisons to keep inmates in prison past their release date if it appears that they'll have "serious difficulty in refraining from sexually violent conduct or child molestation if released." Their extended confinement is achieved through civil commitment, a legal procedure more often used to hospitalize patients who have severe mental illness, usually bipolar disorder or schizophrenia. The law is named after Adam Walsh, a seven-year-old boy who was kidnapped at a mall and decapitated. (His father went on to host "America's Most Wanted.") Since the nineties, twenty states have passed similar statutes, known as sexually violent-predator laws, for offenders who suffer from "volitional impairment"—a legal term that does not correspond to any medical diagnosis. The laws have been passed in the wake of gruesome, highly publicized sexual abductions and murders by men who repeatedly preyed on strangers. The crime is statistically rare—most molestation is committed by family members or friends—but, for nearly a century, has loomed large in the public psyche. One of the first films about a sex offender, Fritz Lang's "M," from 1931, dramatized the plight of this insidious type. "I can't help myself!" the killer cries. "I have no control over this—this evil thing inside of me."

According to the largest study of released prisoners, conducted by the Bureau of Justice, the re-arrest rate for sex offenders is lower than that for perpetrators of any violent crime except murder. But the notion that sex offenders have a unique lack of self-control has been repeated so frequently that it has come to feel like common sense. In 1997, the Supreme Court ruled that sexually-violent-predator state laws are constitutional, because they adhere to the medical model of commitment, by which patients who pose a danger to themselves or others can be prevented from leaving a hospital. To be detained, inmates must have a psychiatric illness or "mental abnormality"—typically sexual in nature—that renders them out of control.

As John's release date approached, his records were examined by the newly established Certification Review Panel, a board of prison psychologists tasked with deciding which prisoners to detain. The panel determined that John had many risk factors: he "self-identified as a 'pedophile,'" evinced a "level of deviant preoccupation," and had "never been married, thus he may have difficulty developing appropriate, intimate relationships with adults." John was transferred from a penitentiary in Pennsylvania to a medical prison in Devens, Massachusetts, for a psychological evaluation. The therapist, Monica Ferraro, wrote that John showed no signs of a thought or mood disorder, though his manner was "inappropriate to content." At times, he laughed at the idea of civil commitment. At other points, he became visibly angry, saying that he was being subjected to "double jeopardy" and would prefer to be executed.

Ferraro gave John a diagnosis of pedophilia, which he discussed candidly during the evaluation. He admitted that he was attracted to kids "hitting puberty," and said that he was unsettled by the realization that all of his sexual partners, the majority of them prostitutes, had been petite, with small breasts. Even when viewing adult pornography, he said, he would "de-age" the models in his mind.

Child-pornography chat rooms had become a "self-reinforcing community," he explained. At first, people in the chat rooms had ignored him or accused him of being a cop. He made up stories about abusing children, because "no one wanted to talk." When Ferraro asked him about his own pornography—during his first prison term, he'd sketched pictures of a man having sex with a young girl—he said that he'd felt isolated and had justified the pictures by telling himself, "This isn't really bad, it's just drawings."

When relying only on clinical interviews, mental-health professionals predict dangerous behavior at a rate not much better than chance. To determine John's risk of committing a new sex crime, Ferraro used an actuarial instrument, the Static-99, and concluded that John was in the "high range of risk." The tool—which was developed through studies of rapists and child molesters, not Internet-pornography offenders—places individuals in classes of risk based on ten factors correlated with recidivism, including age, whether the defendant has ever had a live-in relationship that lasted at least two years, and whether his victims were strangers. (The two undercover cops were considered to be John's victims.) The demand for ways of predicting future criminal behavior has spawned a cottage industry of actuarial instruments, which predict sexual violence about as well as the S.A.T. forecasts freshman grades. Neither correlation is particularly strong. But the instruments confer a stamp of scientific precision on a judgment that psychologists have proved ill-equipped to make.

In early 2007, the Certification Review Panel, after considering Ferraro's report, concluded that John was a "sexually dangerous person." The decision was made without a legal hearing. Two weeks before his scheduled release, John was told that he would remain in prison until his civil-commitment trial, which would be his first opportunity to challenge the panel's decision. He became so distraught that he had to be escorted to a psychologist's office, where he said that he was "ready to curl up in a ball in a corner." The therapist ran through the standard list of questions, asking John if he had delusions or hallucinations or wanted to kill himself. He said no to all of them and shouted, "I want to live! I want to get out of here! I want to go home!" He said that he couldn't control the fact that he was attracted to underage girls, but he knew that he could not act on it. He told the psychologist that he felt morally persecuted, as if he were "wearing a scarlet letter."

Three days later, unable to reach his parents to tell them that he couldn't come home, John cried for much of his therapy appointment. "He presented somewhat dramatically," the therapist observed. "His speech was difficult to interrupt, and he frequently raised his voice when stating, 'And all for a crime I have not yet committed.'"

During the past fifteen years, the American Psychiatric Association has repeatedly objected to the civil commitment of sex offenders. In 1999, a task force created by the organization wrote that "confinement without a reasonable prospect of beneficial treatment of the underlying disorder is nothing more than preventative detention." Six years later, another task-force report asserted that the laws represent a "serious assault on the integrity of psychiatry."

The science of perversion is decades behind the rest of the field. The diagnostic criteria for sexual disorders were tested on only three patients before being added to the *Diagnostic and Statistical Manual of Mental Disorders,* in 1980. No field trials have since been conducted. Most offenders labelled "sexually dangerous" receive a diagnosis of pedophilia, sadism, exhibitionism, fetishism, hebephilia (attraction to pubescents), or "not otherwise specified," a category in the *D.S.M.* reserved for insufficiently studied disorders. Michael First, the editor of the two most recent editions of the *D.S.M.,* told me that there is no scientific research establishing that abnormal desires are any harder to control than normal ones. "People choose to do bad things all the time," he said. "Psychiatry is being coopted by the criminal-justice system to solve a problem that is moral, not medical."

Most sex crimes arise not from illness but from opportunism or disdain for other people's feelings and rights, conditions not easily remedied by medicine. Civilly committed offenders find themselves in what First calls "psychiatry's bottomless pit." They aren't released until a court or a treatment provider concludes that they are no longer dangerous, a risky judgment to make, given the stakes involved in a wrong decision. Although outpatient treatment is modestly correlated with reduced recidivism, the efficacy of institution-based treatment has proved difficult to measure. Treatment varies widely—most programs combine cognitive behavioral therapy with lessons about empathy and anger management—and, in most cases, never ends. In Minnesota, which has one of the largest commitment programs, six hundred and seventy inmates work on correcting distorted thoughts about sex (at a cost of a hundred and twenty thousand dollars per person annually), but in eighteen years only one man has been discharged from the program. (The man was released last year, after concluding a course of treatment that began in 1994.) By 2007, roughly forty-five hundred sex offenders had been civilly committed nationwide, and just over ten per cent had been released.

In 2010, the Supreme Court reexamined sexual-civil-commitment legislation, in *United States v. Comstock,* which was named for Graydon Comstock, the first man detained under the Adam Walsh Act. Comstock, who had been convicted of molesting four boys and downloading child pornography, argued that the federal law allowed the government to reach beyond its "enumerated powers," since civil

commitment has traditionally been regulated by states. By the time the case was heard, four years after Comstock's criminal sentence had expired, Comstock was sixty-seven and was suffering from heart disease, diabetes, and incontinence. He had twice requested to be castrated, thinking that the operation would help his case, but he was told that it wasn't medically justified. The Court upheld the law, but the details of Comstock's case were never discussed in the courtroom, because the decision was narrowly focussed on the scope of the government's authority. "If a federal prisoner is infected with a communicable disease that threatens others," the Court wrote, "surely it would be 'necessary and proper' . . . to refuse (at least until the threat diminishes) to release that individual among the general public, where he might infect others."

A third of the men detained under the Adam Walsh Act had been convicted of child-pornography crimes. Many had disclosed physical sex crimes to prison psychologists while serving their sentences. (Others had had earlier convictions.) Because the therapeutic disclosures have a bearing on public safety, they are not confidential. Shortly after the passage of the Adam Walsh Act, in a memorandum sent to federal public defenders, two lawyers with the National Sentencing Resource Project described therapy as a "trap." They wrote, "No client can safely receive any form of sex offender treatment while in the system."

John waited for his civil-commitment hearings at the Devens prison, and although he had completed his prison term, his daily routine was largely unchanged. He wore the same uniform as other inmates and was subject to the same punishments, schedule, and rules. During a routine shakedown six months after his detainment, guards confiscated an accordion file in his cell containing more than a hundred pages of drawings and notes. A prison psychologist wrote that the papers, "when considered in their totality," suggest that John "believes children are sexual beings who can consent to sex." John appeared to be searching for ways to justify his desires. "Our culture has a fear of (children's) sexuality," he wrote on one page. "Strictly speaking a girl between 13 and 17 is not a child," he wrote on another.

On dozens of pages, he listed books, movies, and art featuring child sexuality, including the Kama Sutra, "Lolita," "Taxi Driver," and the photographs of Robert Mapplethorpe, Sally Mann, Jock Sturges, and Lewis Carroll. "Obscene to who?" he wrote. "Community standard (what community?)."

He also listed the traits of the quintessential sex offender: "social loner," "often balding," "overweight or pot belly," "working a job below their academic achievement." Apparently recognizing himself in the description, John jotted down items necessary for his "disguise kit." He would need makeup to alter his skin tone, a wig, colored contact lenses, fake tattoos, and a mustache. On the next page were more notes on how to escape detection: "Don't become predictable, use widely scattered hot spots"; "Try ultra small flash drives"; "Use proxies (anonymous), wireless? minimal info"; "Avoid uploading—that's how they got ya."

John's civil-commitment hearing began in January 2011, in a federal district court in Boston, after he had been detained in prison for four years past the end of his sentence. (The long delay was due in part to constitutional challenges to the Adam Walsh Act.) The hearing focussed less on what John had done in the past than on what he might do in the future. Psychological experts hired by both the prosecution and the defense agreed that John had pedophilia and would have a hard time avoiding child pornography. Whether this would translate into the sexual abuse of a child was the only significant point of debate.

The case was built on John's own statements—notes and drawings in his cell, his comments to therapists, transcripts of Internet chats, and the letters to Gary—but his sexual history was still impossible to divine. He'd had sex with fifty to two hundred prostitutes, depending on whom he was talking to. It appeared that he'd had one romantic relationship, with an exotic dancer called Dixie Lee Ray, which he described as essentially platonic. Explaining why he'd begun chatting online with pedophiles, he told one of the psychologists who evaluated him, "I joined this subculture just to belong. I don't even know if these were my own fantasies or I was feeding off of these people." He said that he "created a very detailed, elaborate story to be accepted. I created a persona, a character. The more outrageous I could make the story, the more people wanted to talk with me."

The prosecution's expert, Amy Phenix, a forensic psychologist who makes her living testifying at civil-commitment hearings around the country, maintained that the stories John had told Indy-Girl were true, because they were "consistent with his patterns of sexual arousal." She drew heavily on John's admission at his probation-violation hearing, in 2005, that he did not have "enough control." She said that John had roughly a 24.7-percent chance of reoffending within five years, based on her scoring of the Static-99. Phenix co-wrote the coding rules for the Static-99, which has been cross-validated on different samples of sex offenders more than sixty times. She predicted that if John was released he would "reinforce his deviance" by looking at child pornography, but "ultimately that will be insufficient and he will, in my opinion, then seek out children for sexual activity." She explained, "It's just almost like an accident waiting to happen."

The expert for the defense, Robert Prentky, the director of the program in forensic psychology at Fairleigh Dickinson University, said that he had "absolutely no idea where to draw the line between fantasy and reality." He had evaluated hundreds of sex offenders in Massachusetts and had never seen a man civilly committed at the state level without evidence that he had touched a minor. He could not accept the idea that John would have "serious difficulty refraining from engaging in behavior that he has never engaged in."

Prentky spent much of his testimony commenting on his disillusionment with the field. Since the advent of civil-commitment laws, forensic psychology involving sex offenders has become insular and lucrative—the busiest expert witnesses make half a million dollars a year by testifying at hearings—and new research has focussed largely on methods of predicting risk. Prentky said that when he began his career he assumed that it wouldn't be long before scientists uncovered the origins of pedophilia and developed empirically based treatments. But the field had become increasingly politicized, and the disorder remained a "black box." He said, "It feels to me, sadly, that science at this point obfuscates more than it illuminates."

The hearings lasted seven days, over the course of six months, and the judge's decision did not come for another half year. In a supplemental brief filed several months after the proceedings, the federal prosecutor described the defense's argument—that John was inappropriate for commitment because he had no history of physical sex crimes—as "flawed" and "misplaced." To buttress the claim, he summarized the "Butner Study Redux," a widely cited 2009 study in the *Journal of Family Violence* that followed a hundred and fifty-five men who had been convicted of child-pornography crimes. After receiving sex-offender treatment at the Butner Federal Correctional Institute, in North Carolina, eighty-five percent of the men confessed that they had committed physical sex crimes, too. They disclosed a total of seventeen hundred and seventy-seven new victims—roughly thirteen per prisoner.

Two weeks later, on March 8, 2012, Judge George O'Toole found, by "clear and convincing evidence," that John was a sexually dangerous person. O'Toole could not determine whether John had engaged in sexual contact with minors, but he noted that the record clearly established that John had a "long and persistent trajectory of obsession with child pornography—and with sex with children." Without treatment, it was unlikely, he wrote, that John would be able to "control his pedophilia and limit his activity to private masturbation sessions at his home computer."

John was informed that he would be transferred to Butner, which offers "therapeutic confinement" for all civilly committed sex offenders in the federal prison system. He had attempted to enroll in Butner's treatment program seven years before, shortly after returning to prison. But he was told that the program's director, Andrés Hernández, had concluded that he made a poor candidate for treatment, because his records showed "an unwillingness to take responsibility for your sexually deviant behaviors," a common reason for rejection.

Since the passage of the Adam Walsh Act, the Butner program has shifted its focus, and prisoners serving criminal sentences are no longer eligible. Only offenders held under the Adam Walsh act are treated there. The program is still run by Hernández, whose research at Butner, which has been circulating in the legal community since the early two-thousands, has helped shape the legal conception of child-pornography consumers. The Butner research was referenced on the Senate floor in 2003, before a bill was passed that raised mandatory penalties for child-pornography possession, and it was cited five times in the Department of Justice's 2010 National Strategy for Child Exploitation Prevention and Interdiction. Last winter, when the United States Sentencing Commission held a public hearing on child-pornography sentencing, three senior members of Congress wrote a letter summarizing the most recent Butner study, and urging the commission not to underestimate the seriousness of "one of the fastest growing crimes in America."

Former patients at Butner say that they did not realize they were research subjects. Federal civil-commitment hearings have offered a window into the conditions that gave rise to the study's sensational results. Several inmates said that the program's emphasis on confession led them to "remember" crimes that never happened. They disavowed disclosures that were later used as evidence against them.

The program required that its hundred and twelve patients accept responsibility for a life of deviant behavior and thoughts—a philosophy common to most treatment programs. Since sex crimes are vastly underreported, it is reasonable to expect that inmates have committed more crimes than their records reveal. At a professional workshop, Hernández explained that he created a climate of "systematic pressure," so that inmates would "put all the cards on the table," abandoning a "life style of manipulation." Patients were required to compose lists of people they had sexually harmed, which they updated every few months. At daily community meetings, when offenders insisted that they had nothing left to disclose, other prisoners accused them of being in denial or "resistant to change." If they failed to accept responsibility, they were expelled from the program.

For sex offenders, who occupy the bottom of the prison power hierarchy, the Butner unit was a safe haven in the federal prison system. One child-pornography convict, Markis Revland, told the judge at his civil-commitment hearing that when prisoners discover a sex offender among them "they'll go to great lengths to stab that person." He requested treatment at Butner after being raped at knifepoint in a Kansas penitentiary. He was encouraged by the psychology staff at Butner to "get it all out," and came up with a hundred and forty-nine victims. Like other patients, he kept a "cheat sheet" in his cell so that he could remember his victims' ages and the dates that he'd abused them. There was no evidence for the crimes, thirty-four of which would have occurred during a time when Revland was incarcerated. At his hearing, the judge concluded that his crimes were the "product of his imagination, not actual events." After having been held in prison nearly five years beyond the expiration of his criminal sentence, Revland was allowed to go home.

The government has lost roughly half of the more than sixty Adam Walsh cases that have gone to trial so far. Confirming the facts of sexual abuse, the most intimate sort of crime, has always been difficult, with far too many victims keeping quiet about their abuse or not having their stories believed. For offenders, too, the heightened emotional stakes may complicate attempts to get at the truth. Another former patient, Sean Francis, testified that, in order to stay in the "safe confines of Butner," he "fabricated" fifty-four victims and invented and embellished rape fantasies. "Every single human being, if we were to open their head up, has some form or fashion of a deviant sexual fantasy," he said at his hearing. "I don't deny that." But Francis said that he turned himself into a caricature of a sex offender in order to please the "psychological gods that they have working at Butner." Patients would sit in groups and offer one another tips for sprucing up their criminal histories. "We shared victim lists," he testified. "So I would go and I would say, 'Jim, show me what you have. Oh, that—that's really good.' "

A unit composed entirely of sex offenders, like a child-pornography chat room, creates an inverted social structure, where deviant sexuality becomes the norm. Another inmate, Clyde Hall, said that patients who had been formally designated "mentors" encouraged him to confess to more acts of sexual abuse. He submitted his "relapse prevention plan"—which included the complete list of his self-reported crimes—to the psychology staff three times, and, he said, "the third plan came back at me basically with the same note, saying, 'We want more information.' "

"So you're just willing to lie to a psychologist to appease them?" a prosecutor asked another inmate, Michael Riedel, who claimed that he had inflated the number and nature of his sex crimes. "They wouldn't believe me when I said 'one,' " he responded, "so what am I supposed to say?"

Recently, three prisoners at Butner wrote an anonymous thirteen-page report critiquing the Butner study, which they said had been "repeated so many times as to become fact in many places and in many minds." Hernández, too, has publicly expressed concern about the way in which his study has been embraced by politicians and law-enforcement officials, warning that the scientific research is still "in its infancy." But the study, because it confirmed a natural suspicion, has generated its own momentum. "The idea of this one-to-one correspondence— if you are attracted to children, you will act on it—is now a widespread misconception," Michael Seto, a professor of psychiatry at the University of Toronto, told me.

In 2011, Seto reviewed the only six studies he could find that drew on the self-reports of child-pornography offenders and found that the Butner study was a "statistical outlier." The study had provided a politically expedient answer to a social dilemma that, upon further examination, was still ambiguous. In Seto's review, roughly half of child-pornography offenders admitted that they had sexually abused at least one person. The difference between the two groups, Seto said, was that those whose deviant activity occurred only online did not have the antisocial traits, like lack of empathy and impulsiveness, that are common to all types of criminals. They represented a new species, "fantasy offenders," Seto said. "In this weird, disinhibiting space, which lacks the usual social cues, they may do and say things they would never dare in real life."

By the time John was civilly committed, he had become aware of the flaws of the Butner study and was anxious about entering treatment with its author. I met John at the Devens prison last March, in a white cinder-block conference room, shortly before he was transferred to Butner. He wore large, half-rimmed glasses and a prison-issued khaki uniform, his shirt tucked neatly into his pants. He cried frequently, paying little attention to his tears. To describe his thoughts on entering treatment, John paraphrased a line from "The Crucible": "I cannot confess to a lie even if it saves my life." He'd been reading "Les Misérables" when he learned that he would be committed, and he also identified with Jean Valjean. He explained, "We can never escape our past."

John spoke with dramatic hand gestures, modulating his voice like a schoolteacher. During the course of our six-hour conversation, I occasionally had the sense that I was being told a story—it didn't feel untrue, just reshaped, as if he were conforming to narrative conventions for my benefit. He said that his romantic relationships had failed because he wanted to be a "knight in white armor," saving a woman in distress who didn't wish to be saved. He spoke tenderly of Dixie Lee Ray's courageous decision to dump him.

When I asked John why he had made up details about relationships, as one prison therapist had noted, he became quiet. He repeated several times that he didn't know. He wiped away tears and vigorously dried his hand on his pants. "There are some things that are just matters of fact," he offered softly. "People could say of me, 'He was a competent soldier—he knew his stuff.' "

Later, he came back to the question, admitting that none of his relationships had been "tremendous." Intimacy had always felt like an abstraction. "Boy, is that one for the shrinks to get ahold of," he went on. "I know what they'd think: What a

pathetic waste of human flesh. He can't even have a relationship with a woman."

John said that he found solace in the idea that Indy-Girl and her little sister had been fictitious. He liked to think that, even if the girls had been real, he would have decided, at the last minute, not to follow through with the sexual tryst. But he wasn't sure, an uncertainty that nagged at him. He spoke of his online interactions using oddly passive language, explaining that with Indy-Girl he didn't understand how "things got talking." When he looked at photographs of sexually abused children, it barely registered that he was "dealing with people," he said. "In my mind, I was dealing with things. They weren't pictures *of*— they were only pictures. I told myself, 'This is just looking.' "

In May, John was transferred to Butner, and enrolled in the Commitment and Treatment Program for Sexually Dangerous Persons. The program provides milieu therapy, a school of treatment in which patients relearn basic values and skills by immersing themselves in a model community. John and thirty-two other patients lived in the same unit, in unlocked cells that resemble college dorm rooms, and shared two large common areas, where many of the men crocheted. John's roommate, Todd Carta, said that he "cherished" his relationships with his psychologist and the other men in treatment. "I've come to the realization that I'm not the ugliest man in the world," he told me.

Since 2008, all offenders labelled "sexually dangerous" have been housed in one unit at Butner, near the offices of the prison psychologists, and there's a stark divide between the men in treatment and the ones who are still waiting for their civil-commitment hearings. Graydon Comstock, the offender whose case went to the Supreme Court, described a mood of "total paranoia" among the men in pretrial detainment. "We avoided the psychologists," he told me. "Any odd thing you did could go in your records and be used against you. We felt constantly analyzed."

John said that he and the other men in treatment were viewed as "traitors" by the pretrial detainees. "They think if everyone boycotts treatment the system will collapse," he said. John avoided those men, focussing, instead, on fitting in with the program participants, who had been instructed to hold themselves accountable for moral lapses at all hours of the day. At morning community meetings, the men sat in a circle and confessed to bad behavior, forgave themselves, and complimented one another for kind deeds. They opened the meetings by reciting an oath in unison: "Today, I pledge to surrender to the process of change. Today, I pledge to accept responsibility for all my behaviors and actions." They kept arousal logs, documenting magazine articles, television scenes, or dreams that inspired inappropriate sexual fantasies. Improvements in their arousal patterns were assessed through phallometric testing: with a rubber gauge, which measures circumference, around their penises, they listened to audio recordings called "preschool persuasive," "grammar-school coercive," and "female infant."

The Commitment and Treatment Program, which was established in 2007, has been designed as a five-phase treatment regime, but the final stage, which would help inmates reintegrate into the community, has not yet been implemented by the prison. John was encouraged by the fact that the first man to be civilly committed—he had molested four boys, used child pornography, and made obscene phone calls—had moved through the treatment program in eighteen months. But, for much of that time, he had been the only patient in the program. As more offenders have been civilly committed, the pace of treatment has slowed. John said he was at Butner for three months before his therapists set goals for him. His treatment plan established that he would "challenge sexuality myths," "learn how to let go of past resentment," "develop humility," "limit the amount of time spent in solitary activities," "increase his desire for intimacy and meaningful connectedness," and "speak in a slower, lower tone."

At community meetings, John said that he felt bewildered by the "Catholic guilt thing," with people "flogging themselves for every deviant thought they've had since the beginning of existence." He was frustrated that his "thought-process problems" were treated as equivalent to other inmates' "real behavioral problems." "There are a few people here who are obviously incorrigible and shouldn't ever be released," he said.

At one meeting, an inmate pointed out that John was a poor listener, a moving cloud of frantic energy. John reluctantly agreed. "There is definitely something wrong with me," John told me. "But it's not the thing they're locking me up for." He was not surprised when a battery of personality tests revealed that "my social skills are not great, and I'm not a very empathetic person." He increasingly referred to the "hole" in his life, without elaborating. "The reality is embarrassing," he told me. "Being me doesn't ever really seem to get me anywhere."

After nearly 12 years in prison, John had become accustomed to the institutional life style, and he worried about his ability to adjust to the "real world." He wanted to move briskly through the stages of treatment, to prove his health, but no one could tell him when or how this would happen. After taking three orientation classes last summer, he spent the fall waiting to enroll in his next therapy group, "Introduction to the Process of Change."

To pass the time, he worked for several hours a day on his "13th Century Handbook," a time traveller's guide. In the Society for Creative Anachronism, he had been Jan Wedrówka, a Polish nobleman of modest means, and for years he had been chronicling the life of this man, searching prison libraries for details about the crops, architecture, and folk customs of the era. He planned to stay away from the Internet when he was released—a decision inspired by a leader in the Society for Creative Anachronism, who on group retreats cordoned off an area of the campsite and called it Enchanted Ground. "In that space, the twenty-first century does not exist," John said hypnotically. "If you squint your eyes, you can block it out and live the dream. You'll be transported back in time."

Critical Thinking

1. Some people argue that viewing photographs of children helps reduce the chances that they will actually offend against a child. Do you agree? Or do you think having access to these pictures only increases the likelihood that they will act on their feelings?

2. What do you think the penalty for child sexual abuse should be?

3. Currently, there are no supports available for someone who realizes he has pedophilic feelings—he cannot enter a treatment program until he has offended against someone. How should that change? What kinds of efforts can be made to help keep people from acting on their urges in the first place?

Internet References

American Human Association: Children
http://www.americanhumane.org/children
ChildHelp USA
https://www.childhelp.org
Stop It Now: The Campaign to End Child Sexual Abuse
http://www.stopitnow.org

RACHEL AVIV joined *The New Yorker* as a staff writer in 2013. An award-winning journalist, she has written about criminal justice, psychiatry, education, foster care, and homelessness, among other subjects. She has also taught courses in narrative medicine at Columbia University Medical Center, the City College of New York, and at Mount Sinai School of Medicine.

Article

Prepared by: Elizabeth Schroeder, EdD, MSW,
Elizabeth Schroeder Consulting

When Bitter Breakups and Digital Photography Meet: What to Teach Our Kids about Revenge Porn

MARTHA KEMPNER

Learning Outcomes

After reading this article, you will be able to:

- Define the term "revenge porn" and give at least two examples of what could come under that definition.

- Explain how including "selfie" photographs in revenge porn laws can strengthen the case, and how they can lead to victim blaming.

- Describe the provisions of the California law relating to revenge porn.

This month, California became the second state to pass a law that punishes people for posting sexually explicit pictures of someone else (most often an ex) as a way to make that person's life miserable. This form of cyberbullying has been dubbed "revenge porn," and in recent years a number of websites have popped up to profit off the dangerous combination of digital photography and bitter breakups. Victims of revenge porn not only find nude pictures of themselves posted online without their consent, the pictures are often accompanied by names, addresses, and insults—all of which can be seen by friends, relatives, employers, and total strangers.

Some say the only way to stop this damaging trend is to make posting revenge porn a crime, while others argue that the best way to prevent the situation is to put the camera down in the first place. How do we stop revenge porn without blaming the victim, and what should we say to our kids about this new threat to their privacy?

The stories that emerge during discussions of revenge porn are remarkably similar. Young women who had at one point texted or emailed nude pictures of themselves to an ex-boyfriend are shocked and horrified to find the pictures and other identifying information on websites such as YouGotPosted.com or MyEx.com. A college student told *USA Today* that a stranger messaged her on Facebook to tell her that pictures she had sent to her boyfriend of two-and-a-half years were now on that site. One victim told the *New York Times* that she had to give up her job at a restaurant and was stalked by a stranger after nude photos she had sent an ex appeared online. Holly Jacobs, the founder of EndRevengePorn.org, changed her name in an effort to disassociate from pictures and other information about her on a revenge porn site only to find a few months later that the site now had her new name.

These women had few legal options, as existing federal law protects websites that post materials from third parties. In most states, a victim's only recourse would be a civil suit against the ex who posted the images, but these suits can be expensive and embarrassing, and they rarely end in a sizable payout. New Jersey has a law that would allow for criminal prosecution of the person who posted the materials, though it was not passed with revenge porn in mind. California's new law, which was signed by Gov. Jerry Brown last week, is the only law thus far passed specifically to address this issue. It allows for criminal prosecution, but only under a very narrow set of circumstances. Specifically, the law says that distributing private images with the intent to harass or annoy could be punishable with up to a $1,000 fine and six months in jail. However, the law only applies to pictures taken by someone else. Nude "selfies," no matter how they end up online, are not covered by the law.

Many say that this makes the law toothless, at best, as most victims of revenge porn take their own pictures and then email or text them to a partner. Charlotte Law, a mother who became an advocate for revenge porn legislation when pictures of her 25-year-old daughter wound up online, says we really need federal legislation because laws like this are not enough. She told the *New York Times*, "[The California legislation] has been watered down again and again as it has weaved its way through Sacramento."

Hunter Moore, an entrepreneur who started a revenge porn site from his parents' basement and claims to have made $10,000 a month in advertising before shutting the site down in 2011, seems to agree that the California law won't hurt business. Moore told tech magazine *The Register*, "This doesn't stop anything. If you read the bill it is just for peeping toms, not for selfies, which is all revenge porn really is. These stupid old white people are even more stupid to think they can stop it . . . It will just make revenge porn bigger by driving traffic, because people are talking about it."

The author of the law, state Sen. Anthony Cannella (R-Ceres) agrees that it does not go far enough and hopes to expand it in the future. He told the *San Francisco Gate* that he had to exclude "selfies" early on or the bill would have died, in part out of fears of crowding the already over-crowded prison system.

There may be another issue at work when it comes to self-shot photos—victim blaming. Mary Anne Franks, a law professor at the University of Miami who has drafted sample legislation criminalizing the posting of revenge porn, told the *New York Times*, "The moment the story is that she voluntarily gave this to her boyfriend, all the sympathy disappears." Both Professor Franks and Holly Jacobs believe this is akin to commenting on what a rape victim wore on the night of her attack. Jacobs told *USA Today*, "It's the same thing as someone telling someone who's been physically raped that they shouldn't have been wearing that skirt."

While the women (and in some cases men) who have their personal lives shattered by revenge porn are victims in all sense of the word, there are lessons to be learned from their stories that don't amount to blaming the victim. (To use identity theft as an analogy, we don't blame victims of that crime, but we did all go buy paper-shredders once we had learned about it.) As Logan Levkoff, a sexuality educator who often works with high school students in New York City, told RH Reality Check, "I think that young people—and adults—should always use caution before taking naked pictures of themselves. This isn't about blaming a victim, it's about making smart decisions. And until we live in a world where all relationships are respectful, even when they end, and there is always consent, we need to make good decisions."

As parents and educators, I think our responsibility is two-fold. First, we have to remind those growing up in this digital age of what should not but can happen to the pictures you decide to take. We need to teach young people to do a gut check before they hit send. One of the victims quoted in *USA Today* noted that she was uncomfortable sending the pictures to her then-boyfriend, but he pressured her, saying she'd do it if she really loved him, and if she didn't send the picture it was proof that she didn't trust him. "If you really loved me, you would" is still the oldest line in the book, even when it's being applied to modern technology. No one should be pressured into sexual behavior of any kind, including sending nude pictures, and young people should learn to see such attempts at manipulation as a warning sign.

Even when both partners are completely willing participants, it's still important to think through the potential outcomes before engaging in any behavior. In this case, that probably means thinking about the possible end of the relationship. Young people should understand that pictures can never be untaken or unsent. They should consider if they really want this person to have intimate pictures of them forever. Most exes don't share the snapshots with the world, but it could still be uncomfortable to know that someone who is no longer part of your life can look at you naked any time. As awkward as it sounds, it may also help to think about how this person is with other exes—are they friends or do they spread nasty rumors about each other? My high school boyfriend used to curse out his ex all the time and call her horrible names. Even at the beginning of our relationship, when I was sure he'd never ever feel that way about me, this struck me as a bad sign of what could come.

And this brings me to the other thing that I think we have to do a better job teaching young people (and adults, of course): Respect for our friends and lovers should continue even after relationships end. The phrase "Hell hath no fury like a woman scorned" originated in a play in 1697 (and was written by William Congreve, not Shakespeare, as I had always thought), but relationships don't have to end with scorn or fury. Most relationships young people have will end, and we have to help them figure out healthy ways to break up with someone and survive being broken up with. We have to help them understand—through the sadness and anger—that they should continue to respect the person they once cared about and refrain from doing anything hurtful like spreading rumors, calling them names, or posting intimate information for the world to see. This may be hard to learn in our era of bitter celebrity divorces and Twitter fights, but it is an element of basic human decency that we should all try to afford those we once loved. Perhaps it is a simple application of the golden rule: "Do unto others as you would have them do unto you." You may be so mad at a boyfriend that you're willing to send a shot of him pantsless out to the whole school, but how would you feel if your next boyfriend sends a topless "selfie" of you to his football buddies?

Though just last week Hunter Moore showed no remorse in a YouTube video in which he said, "I'm sorry I was smart enough to monetize your mistake," the Web mogul may soon wish he followed the golden rule more closely. In a 2011 interview with Anderson Cooper, Moore was asked if he felt bad about profiting off other people's misery. He replied, "Why would I? I get to look at naked girls all day." This drew the ire of many, including the hacker group Anonymous, which launched the campaign Operation Hunt Hunter and vowed, "We will hold him accountable for his actions." In a more recent interview with *Rolling Stone*, Moore said he was going to return to revenge porn and would freely publish women's addresses along with their naked pictures. In response, Charlotte Law posted Moore's home address on Twitter. Moore is also the subject of more than one law suit and an FBI investigation.

Critical Thinking

1. The UK recently passed a law against revenge porn. Only two states in the United State have similar laws? Should more states pass laws against this practice? Why or why not?

2. What do you think of the fact that the California law covers nude photographs—but not nude "selfies?" Would you change that? Why or why not?

3. Do you feel there is a difference between a teen's photos being posted as part of revenge porn and an adult's? Why or why not? Should the California law or future laws address the age of the person whose pictures are posted without their consent?

Internet References

End Revenge Porn
  http://www.endrevengeporn.org
StopBullying: Cyber Bullying
  http://www.stopbullying.gov/cyberbullying
Women Against Revenge Porn
  http://www.womenagainstrevengeporn.com

MARTHA KEMPNER is a sexual health writer and consultant. She has authored numerous publications for young people, parents, educators, and policymakers. She is also frequently called upon by print, radio, and television media to comment on sexuality issues in popular culture, politics, and research. Martha was previously the Vice President for Information and Communications at the Sexuality Information and Education Council of the U.S. (SIECUS).

Article

Prepared by: Elizabeth Schroeder, EdD, MSW,
Elizabeth Schroeder Consulting

Sex Trafficking and the Sex Industry: The Need for Evidence-Based Theory and Legislation

RONALD WEITZER

Learning Outcomes

After reading this article, you will be able to:

- Define and provide at least two examples of commercial sex trafficking.

- Describe at least two non-U.S.-based cultural considerations relating to the sex industry.

- Describe at least two examples of who sex traffickers tend to, or may, be.

Introduction

Under U.S. law, sex trafficking is defined as "the recruitment, harboring, transportation, provision, or obtaining of a person for the purpose of a commercial sex act."[1] To be punishable, the offense must involve a "severe form" of trafficking involving (1) a person under age eighteen who has been induced to perform a commercial sex act or (2) an adult who has been so induced by the use of "force, fraud, or coercion."[2] Adults who sell sex willingly, with some kind of assistance, are not considered trafficking victims under U.S. la.[3] Trafficking that involves underage persons or adults subjected to force, fraud, or coercion is a serious violation of human rights, and the growing international awareness of the problem and efforts to punish perpetrators and assist victims are welcome developments.

But there is also a parallel story-a robust *mythology* of trafficking. While no one would claim that sex trafficking is fictional, many of the claims made *about* it are wholly

unsubstantiated. This Article offers a critique of the paradigm responsible for this mythology, a perspective that has become increasingly popular over the past decade. This *oppression paradigm* depicts all types of sexual commerce as institutionalized subordination of women, regardless of the conditions under which it occurs.[4] The perspective does not present domination and exploitation as variables but instead considers them core ontological features of sexual commerce.[5] I will contrast this monolithic paradigm with an alternative one that is evidence-based and recognizes the existence of substantial variation in sex work. This *polymorphous paradigm* holds that there is a broad constellation of work arrangements, power relations, and personal experiences among participants in sexual commerce. Polymorphism is sensitive to complexities and to the structural conditions shaping the uneven distribution of workers' agency and subordination. Victimization, exploitation, choice, job satisfaction, self-esteem, and other factors differ between types of sex work, geographical locations, and other structural conditions. Commercial sexual exchange and erotic entertainment are not homogeneous phenomena.[6]

A growing number of researchers have challenged the oppression model's claims, yet their criticisms have yet to gain serious attention from American lawmakers. This Article (1) analyzes the claims made by those who embrace the oppression model, (2) identifies some legal and policy implications of this paradigm, and (3) offers an evidence-based alternative.[7] The analysis pertains to both sex trafficking and to sexual commerce more generally.

The Oppression Paradigm

Many of the leading proponents of the oppression paradigm are affiliated with organizations committed to eradicating the entire sex industry, such as Prostitution Research and Education, Standing Against Global Exploitation (SAGE), Stop Porn Culture, and the Coalition Against Trafficking in Women (CATW).[8] What unites them is their staunch advocacy of the oppression paradigm and political commitment to prohibition of all sexual commerce and adult entertainment.

Oppression writers have been roundly criticized for violating standard canons of social science inquiry and for viewing sex work through a monochromatic lens.[9] Despite this criticism, proponents rigidly adhere to the central tenets of their paradigm, even when confronted with compelling counter-evidence.[10] Moreover, most oppression writers restrict their citations to writings of like-minded authors and ignore research findings that contradict the pillars of their paradigm.[11] Such inconvenient findings are plentiful.[12] Scientific advancement depends on researchers' due diligence in weighing findings and arguments that challenge their own: It is standard practice to situate a study within the related scholarly literature. Oppression writers' neglect of relevant research is a radical departure from conventional scholarly writings. And on those rare occasions when contrasting work is cited, the findings have sometimes been distorted or even inverted by the author.[13]

The oppression model is grounded in a particular branch of feminist thinking: radical feminism. It differs from the religious right's objections to commercial sex, which center on the threat it poses to marriage, the family, and society's moral fiber.[14] The oppression paradigm's central tenet is that sexual commerce rests on structural inequalities between men and women and that male domination is intrinsic to sexual commerce.[15] Women would not be compelled to sell sexual or erotic services if they had the same socioeconomic opportumt1es as men. Moreover, the very existence of prostitution suggests that men have, according to Carole Pateman, a "patriarchal right of access to women's bodies," thus perpetuating women's subordination to men.[16] Another writer declares that prostitution "dehumanizes, commodifies and fetishizes women . . . . In prostitution, there is *always* a power imbalance, where the john has the social and economic power to hire her/him to act like a sexualized puppet. Prostitution excludes *any* mutuality of privilege or pleasure . . . ."[17] Oppression theorists argue that these fundamental harms will endure no matter how prostitution, pornography, or stripping are governed; legalizing these practices (where currently illegal) in order to reduce harms will not lessen the gender inequality that is intrinsic to sexual commerce. Domination will persist simply by virtue of men's paid access to women's bodies.[18]

Champions of the oppression paradigm frequently make extravagant claims about commercial sex as an institution, the participants in paid sex transactions, the nature of sex trafficking, and the effects of different kinds of laws. To drive home the seriousness of the problem, advocates often link prostitution to a host of violent crimes—calling it "domestic violence,"[19] "torture,"[20] and paid rape[21]—and demonizing customers as violent misogynists:

- "Sexual exploitation includes sexual harassment, rape, incest, battering, pornography and prostitution.[22]
- "This naming [as sex predators] is important since it places men who buy sex in the same category as rapists, pedophiles, and other social undesirables."[23]
- "The difference between pimps who terrorize women on the street and pimps in business suits who terrorize women in gentlemen's clubs is a difference in class only, not a difference in woman hating."[24]

Some advocates of the oppression paradigm simply make pronouncements, like the above, without offering any empirical evidence.[25] Other oppression writers, however, try to support their claims with some kind of evidence. Both approaches are present in the oppression-based literature on sex trafficking.

Sex Trafficking
The Politics of Trafficking

In order to further discredit the practice of prostitution and delegitimize systems where prostitution is legal and regulated by the government, oppression writers have fused prostitution with sex trafficking.[26] Donna Hughes claims that "most 'sex workers' are or originally started out as trafficked women and girls."[27] She then calls for "re-linking trafficking and prostitution, and combating the commercial sex trade as a whole."[28] There is no evidence that "most" or even the majority of prostitutes have been trafficked. It is important to recognize that as recently as fifteen years ago, trafficking was not a routine part of the discourse regarding prostitution.[29] Today, several analysts argue that prostitution has been *socially constructed* in a particular way through the trafficking prism and that there is no objective equivalence between the two.[30] Prostitution involves a commercial transaction and trafficking is a process whereby a third party facilitates an individual's involvement in sexual commerce. There is plenty of prostitution by independent operators that does not involve trafficking.[31] And such independent enterprises may be growing with the help of internet-facilitated connections between sex workers and clients.

Some oppression writers are quite candid about their political reasons for linking trafficking with prostitution. Melissa Farley declares, "A false distinction between prostitution and trafficking has hindered *efforts to abolish prostitution . . . .* Since prostitution creates the demand for trafficking, the sex industry in its totality must be confronted."[32] The first sentence reveals that the ultimate goal is not the elimination of trafficking but rather the elimination of prostitution. Regarding the second sentence—asserting that "prostitution creates the demand for trafficking"—there is no compelling reason why prostitution would necessarily "demand" *trafficked* participants (if trafficking is defined as involving deception or force) or even willing migrants, and why it could not draw from a local pool of workers instead. In some places the local pool may be shallow and require migrants to meet demand, but this would not be sufficient to justify Farley's claim regarding prostitution in general.

Despite the problematic way in which oppression writers have constructed trafficking, they have been remarkably successful in rebranding trafficking in a way that implicates all sex work. As one analyst wrote, the prohibitionists have "successfully transformed the 'anti-trafficking' movement into a modern, worldwide moral crusade against prostitution."[33] The prostitution–trafficking connection was fully embraced by the Bush administration, illustrated by the State Department's webpage *The Link Between Prostitution and Sex Trafficking,* which claimed, *inter alia,* that prostitution "fuels trafficking in persons" and "fuel[s] the growth of modern-day slavery."[34] The prohibitionist portrayal of trafficking clashes with an alternative, socioeconomic model that views trafficking as "a complex phenomenon driven by deep economic disparities between wealthy and poor communities and nations, and by inadequate labor and migration frameworks to manage their consequences."[35] Oppression writers often ignore socioeconomic forces and instead focus on individual actors: pimps, traffickers, clients, and female victims.

How is trafficking itself presented in oppression writings? Melodramatically. In an article representative of this literature (and published in this *Journal*), Iris Yen perceives a "pandemic of human trafficking."[36] She writes that sex trafficking is "appropriately" described as "sexual slavery" and that the individuals involved are "essentially slaves,"[37] despite the fact that many of those who are trafficked are not held in slave-like conditions.[38] She claims, without evidence, that "[t]raffickers *routinely* beat, rape, starve, confine, torture, and psychologically and emotionally abuse the women."[39] The magnitude of the problem is said to be "alarming," but the figures Yen cites—14,500 to 100,000 trafficked into the U.S. every year—are incredibly wide-ranging and thus rather dubious.[40] Yen then extrapolates from trafficking to prostitution: "Thus, contrary to the erroneous perception that prostitution is a victimless crime . . . too many victims have paid for their crime of poverty with devastated lives."[41] Bias is particularly evident in her emotive language, e.g., "the ugly truth of the commercial sex industry" and "egregious human rights abuses from the sex trade."[42]

These images of prostitution and trafficking abound throughout the writings of oppression theorists, but their accuracy is belied by their sweeping, unequivocal nature. Each of the above claims has been challenged by other analysts and by a body of research findings cited throughout this Article. The experiences Of trafficked persons, in the migration process and in their working conditions, range along a broad continuum. Some individuals' experiences fit the oppression model well, while others' cluster at the opposite end. Many of those who migrate are responding to push factors such as the lack of economic opportunities in their home countries or the desire to provide a better life for family members, rather than the pull factor of nefarious traffickers.[43]

And there may be other incentives as well. In her summary of research on the motives of migrant sex workers, Laura Agustin writes, "Many people are fleeing from small-town prejudices, dead-end jobs, dangerous streets, and suffocating families. And some poorer people *like* the idea of being found beautiful or exotic abroad, exciting desire in others."[44] In other words, there may be benign motivations for migration, apart from third party deception and coercion. For example, a study of Vietnamese migrants who were working in Cambodian brothels found that their motivations consisted of "economic incentives, desire for an independent lifestyle, and dissatisfaction with rural life and agricultural labor."[45] And a study of Russian women who sold sex in Norway found that the women stressed their own agency:

> [T]he wish to improve the financial status of oneself and one's family emerged as a central theme in the interviews we conducted . . . . In their self-representations, responsibility and individualized experiences came to the fore, and in this way the women distanced themselves from the stereotype of the passive victim . . . . They represented [prostitution] as something that provided both economic and experiential resources that helped them grow as individuals, to act responsibly toward themselves and others, and as a means to ensure independence and equality in their social relationships . . . . They talked about their actions in terms of intentions, choices, and desires.[46]

Given the current state of knowledge, we cannot dismiss such motives and experiences as mere exceptions to the rule. The point here is that there is sufficient empirical evidence, from various parts of the world, to challenge the image of the stereotypical "victim" that is a staple of oppression writings.

Similarly, the traffickers themselves range tremendously—from predatory exploiters to brokers who simply offer assistance, whether for profit or not. As David Feingold points out, "[t]here is no standard profile of traffickers. They range from truck drivers and village 'aunties' to labor brokers and police officers. Traffickers are as varied as the circumstances of their victims."[47] Rebecca Surtees concurs that traffickers are "far more diverse" than conventionally thought. By way of contrast, Surtees reports that most Moldovans in her study were recruited by strangers, whereas 80% of Albanians knew their recruiters, a high percentage of whom were boyfriends, fiances, or husbands.[48] Another European study, based on interviews with seventy-two women, found that most recruiters were friends, acquaintances, or family members. The facilitators made travel arrangements, obtained necessary documents, and provided women with money to purchase necessities.[49] Prostitutes themselves may be involved in recruitment. For example, some Eastern European women who sell sex in Western Europe recruit their girlfriends in the home country to work with them in the West.[50] These intermediaries may have a radically different relationship with workers than do predators, who recruit persons by deception or force and engage in severe economic exploitation of them. Such *variation* is the key to all dimensions of trafficking and prostitution, as the evidence-based polymorphous paradigm holds.

The Magnitude of the Problem: Mythical Numbers

When it comes to estimating the magnitude of any illicit vice (be it drug sales, illegal gambling, or prostitution), it is crucial that analysts carefully examine the quality of the data sources and the procedures used to arrive at figures.[51] Unfortunately, many of those writing about sex trafficking ignore this scientific canon and recapitulate potentially bogus claims regarding the scale of the phenomenon, uncritically accepting figures that should be questioned. With human trafficking, as with drug and arms trafficking and other illicit global enterprises, "the numbers are often highly suspect but nevertheless popularized and rarely critically scrutinized, and . . . there are strong incentives [e.g., for governments, activists, and media interests] to accept and reproduce rather than challenge and critique them."[52]

According to many oppression writers and the government officials they influence,[53] sex trafficking has reached epidemic levels worldwide, victimizing "hundreds of thousands" or "millions" of people every year. But not only is trafficking said to be a *mammoth* problem worldwide, its incidence has also *skyrocketed* in recent years. In her book, *Sex Trafficking,* Kathryn Farr boldly asserts: "The sex trafficking industry is voluminous, and it is expanding at an ever-accelerating rate . . . . [O]ver 1 million are trafficked into the sex industry, and the volume just keeps increasing."[54] Yen agrees that things are only getting worse: Sex trafficking is "mushrooming," child prostitution is increasing at "alarming rates," and "sex trafficking victims are getting increasingly younger."[55]

There are reasons why the problem *may* have grown over time in certain regions—for example, due to' more porous

borders in Europe in the aftermath of the breakdown of the Soviet empire and the growing freedom of movement resulting from the expansion of the European Union after 2004. But this does not mean that the problem is actually increasing worldwide as claimed. Writers who make such assertions provide no solid evidence to support these grandiose claims. In fact, the numbers and trends asserted are impossible to substantiate, given two fundamental evidentiary problems: (1) the clandestine nature of trafficking,[56] and (2) the lack of a baseline from which to measure changes over time.[57] Data are simply not available for drawing macro-level conclusions.[58] While some writers make such claims perhaps naively, simply reiterating others' assertions, other writers acknowledge their political motivations. High numbers are designed to alarm the public and convince governments to commit greater resources to fighting prostitution, to fund rescue operations, and to enhance penalties against traffickers and clients. As two critics suggest, the human trafficking issue has become "a battleground for different positions on prostitution, immigration, and the position and status of women."[59]

Claims regarding a growing worldwide epidemic are contradicted by the U.S. government's own figures. Over the past decade, the State Department's annual *Trafficking in Persons* report has steadily reduced its figures on the magnitude of both transnational and domestic trafficking. In 2002, the maximum transnational figure was 4 million.[60] The following year, the figure was put at 800,000–900,000 victims, falling to 600,000–800,000 in 2004.[61] Subsequently, the estimate has stabilized at 800,000 trafficked across national borders.[62]

These figures on trafficking between countries are "in addition to the far larger yet indeterminate number of people trafficked within countries," according to the 2004 *Trafficking in Persons Report.*[63] Four years later, the State Department was making a similar claim: the 2008 report asserts that "approximately 800,000 people are trafficked across national borders, which does not include millions trafficked within their own countries."[64] These claims are remarkable for their (a) fuzzy elasticity, (b) shock value, (c) implication that the between-nations figures are *not themselves* "indeterminate" and lacking in reliability, and (d) failure to recognize that if something is "indeterminate" it may not be "far larger" than the (already problematic) international figures.

Further undermining the U.S. government's assertions of an "indeterminate" but huge domestic trafficking problem, official domestic U.S. figures have plummeted over the past decade. The TVPA states that "Congress finds that . . . [a]pproximately 50,000 women and children are trafficked into the United States each year."[65] This figure was repeated in the State Department's *Trafficking in Persons* report for 2002.[66] But just one year later, the State Department's figure fell to 18,000–20,000,[67] and in 2004 the figure was further reduced to 14,500–17,500 per year.[68] Apart from the lack of transparency in how officials arrived at these figures, when we compare the 2000 figure (50,000) with the lower figure for 2004 (14,500), we see an *astonishing 71% decrease* in the estimate in just five years. Such dramatic downscaling should give pause to researchers and policymakers alike. More recent reports have substituted vague language for numerical estimates of the domestic situation. The 2008 *Trafficking in Persons* report, for instance, simply declared that "thousands" of people are trafficked into the U.S. every year.[69]

Some researchers have attempted to "resolve" the numbers problem through a meta-analysis of figures from a variety of sources. A recent analysis of 207 estimates concluded that a figure of 5,166 annual victims of all kinds of trafficking "provides a more reliable, although still flawed, estimate of the minimum number of trafficking victims in the United States."[70] But the authors qualify this with numerous cautions. The studies consulted offer estimates that

> range from 1,349 to 46,849 victims of labor trafficking and from 3,817 to 22,320 victims of sex trafficking . . . . [T]he highest estimate from a type of source for any of the identified types of trafficking (labor trafficking, sex trafficking of adults, and sex trafficking of children) is greater than the lowest estimate for that type of trafficking by at least 400 percent, suggesting that there is enormous uncertainty about the national scope of the problem . . . .[71]

Given these serious problems, one might also question the 5,166 figure, which the authors concede is "flawed." As the saying goes, "bad data are worse than no data," and I would question whether any of the 207 estimates were based on what social scientists would consider genuine "data" to begin with. For these reasons, I do not think there is any logic in the analysts' claim that, "[d]espite the limitation of the data, however, this research enables us to say more about the scope and character of human trafficking in the United States than is currently accepted as fact."[72] Instead, their report leads to quite the opposite conclusion: that it is not possible to count the number of victims involved in an illicit, clandestine underground economy at the macro level, nationally or internationally. The wildly varying estimates, based on numerous problematic assumptions, testify to the futility of this exercise. Estimating the size of the problem is only possible at the micro level (e.g., in a city or small region of a country) and then only insofar as the data pertaining to this limited arena are reliable, which is rare.

A related issue is the discrepancy between the claimed magnitude of the problem and the number of victims identified and assisted by authorities. No one would claim that the latter should roughly match the former, given the obstacles to locating victims in black markets, but a huge disparity between the two should at least raise questions about the alleged scale of victimization. The State Department recently reported that only 0.4% of the estimated number of victims worldwide have been officially "identified."[73] And domestically, the Justice Department took issue in 2005 with the "stark difference" between the estimated number of victims trafficked into the U.S. for that year (14,500–17,500) and the number of victims located (611 over the four years from 2001 to 2004).[74] The 2008 *Trafficking in Persons* report provides updated figures: between 2001 and mid-2008, 1,379 trafficking victims in the U.S. were identified.[75] This figure remains but a tiny fraction of the number of persons allegedly trafficked into the U.S. during this time period (14,500 × 7.5 years = 108,750; 17,500 × 7.5 years = 131,250).

Data on the 2008–2010 period show a similarly wide discrepancy between the alleged magnitude of the problem and the number of confirmed cases. Between January 2008 and June 2010, law enforcement authorities investigated 2,065 suspected incidents of sex trafficking (with a suspected "incident" defined as an alleged act of sex trafficking or another crime involving some element of sex trafficking).[76] Only a minority of the reporting agencies (eighteen out of forty-two) engaged in what analysts at the U.S. Bureau of Justice Statistics considered "high-quality" data collection and reporting; confining the analysis to these eighteen agencies, 31% of the alleged sex trafficking incidents (consisting of 218 cases) were confirmed as bona fide trafficking, 37% were not confirmed, and the remainder were pending.[77] Taking into account the challenges involved in identifying and substantiating such cases, the 218 figure is far below what we might expect from the claimed number of victims. For sex and labor trafficking combined, 257 incidents were confirmed,[78] a figure that stands in stark contrast to official claims about the number of victims in the U.S. during this time period: 14,500 × 1.5 years = 21,750. In other words, only 1.2% of the estimated number of victims resulted in confirmed incidents. Again, recognizing the difficulties in locating victims and building cases against perpetrators, the disparities in the numbers presented here should at least raise serious questions about the alleged magnitude of the trafficking problem.

A similarly huge disparity characterizes the official figures in Britain. Despite repeated claims in the British press that there are thousands of trafficking victims in the U.K.—25,000 according to one newspaper report—only fifty-nine persons were convicted of trafficking women into prostitution between 2004 and 2009.[79] An analysis by investigative journalist Nick Davies of the *Guardian* newspaper carefully traced the sources of figures cited in the media and by government officials. Davies found that the original estimates were often much lower than those subsequently presented; moreover, the initial estimates typically contained important qualifications that were ignored in subsequent accounts. Figures presented as maximums were frequently repackaged as minimums and stripped of the cautions attached by the primary analysts.[80] Davies concludes that "the trafficking story is a model of misinformation" and that the issue has become a "moral panic" in Britain.[81] As in the U.S., there have been few substantiated cases, yet the British media and government officials have magnified the problem and generated public alarm via gross distortion of figures that were unreliable in the first place.[82]

In 2006, the U.S. Government Accountability Office (GAO) published a report that was highly critical of the prevailing figures. The GAO highlighted serious "methodological weaknesses, gaps in data, and numerical discrepancies"; determined that "country data are generally not available, reliable, or comparable"; and concluded that neither the U.S. nor other governments had "established an effective mechanism for estimating the number of victims."[83] The GAO added that many countries lump smuggling and illegal migration into the trafficking category, while others separate the figures.[84] Independent analysts concur with these assessments, citing the lack of a standard definition of "victims" as a basis for estimates,[85] the "lack of methodological transparency" and source documentation for the figures,[86] and the practice of extrapolating from a few cases of identified victims who may be quite unrepresentative of the victim population.[87] In some reports, all "migrant sex workers are defined as trafficking victims regardless of consent and conditions of labour, while other reports emphasize abusive conditions of employment or deceptive recruitment policies."[88]

We are left with a hodgepodge of numbers that hardly lend themselves to evidence-based policymaking. The United Nations Educational, Scientific, and Cultural Organization's (UNESCO) Bangkok office was quite blunt in explaining how well-intentioned concerns can trump evidence in this sphere: "When it comes to statistics, trafficking of girls and women is one of several highly emotive issues which seem to overwhelm critical faculties."[89] Unfortunately, numbers gain a life of their own after frequent repetition in the media and publication in government reports. Jahic and Finckenauer state the matter eloquently:

[I]t is in the best interests of groups and NGOs, both national and international, to push these unreliable and most likely vastly overstated estimates . . . . Once the problem has been presented and accepted to be on a certain scale, new information that does not support this notion is dismissed. The estimates have become the "received wisdom". . . .[90]

NGO figures are typically formulated for purposes of advocacy, not derived from careful research. It is well known that research is not the forte of most NGOs involved in assisting victims or of interest groups pushing specific policies. Unfortunately, many scholars recapitulate the NGO and government numbers, ignoring the standard caution against uncritical acceptance of official statistics.[91] A review of over 100 academic journal articles found that the claims of government agencies (especially American) and global organizations (such as the United Nations) were treated as evidence, even though most of these agencies had failed to reveal their data sources or methods.[92] The most quoted ' source was the annual *Trafficking in Persons* report by the State Department; very few of the academic articles were based on independently collected data.[93]

If claims regarding a growing worldwide problem are evidence-thin and inherently unverifiable, data on specific localities can be more reliable. An example is trafficking from Eastern to Western Europe. The breakup of the Soviet empire and declining living standards for many of its inhabitants have made such migration both much easier and more compelling than in the past, and there is no doubt that in the post-Soviet period many women have migrated to Western Europe.[94] But there are two important caveats: First, an increase in *migration* or the subset *assisted migration* (or smuggling) should not be equated with a growing number of *coercively trafficked* persons (i.e., those subjected to what the TVPA calls "force, fraud, or coercion"[95]). Although both of these phenomena have been documented in this part of the world, the available figures on each type of relocation are sketchy at best. Second, an increase in trafficking during the 1990s after the demise of the Soviet empire does not mean that trafficking is growing now throughout that region of the world. States within that region may vary in whether trafficking has (a) stabilized, (b) increased, or (c) decreased in recent years. Regarding (a), a report by the International Organization for Migration concluded that the number of trafficked persons in southeastern Europe who were officially identified and assisted leveled off in the mid-2000s.[96] Market saturation is just one of the reasons why stabilization may occur in any given region. Regarding (b), it is widely reported that trafficking or migration of women from places like Bulgaria and Romania increased in the latter half of the 2000s, whereas in category (c) Albania witnessed a decline in emigration.[97]

In short, changes in the magnitude of trafficking in any part of the world must be documented with the best evidence available; it should not be assumed, as many activists assert, that trafficking is steadily increasing and doing so universally. Some nations, as just noted, appear to have experienced a reduction in trafficking in recent years. Cambodia is another example: A carefully conducted study, funded by the United Nations, reported a decrease in the number of individuals trafficked into the sex trade (from 2,488 in 2002 to 1,058 in 2008) at the same time that the overall number of prostitutes in Cambodia was increasing (from 20,829 in 2002 to 27,925 in 2008).[98] If these figures are even roughly accurate, they suggest that trafficking can decrease over time even where prostitution is increasing.

The numbers problem is also apparent in claims regarding the financial proceeds from trafficking. It is frequently claimed that human trafficking is the second- or third-largest criminal enterprise in the world, after drug trafficking and firearms trading,[99] but it is impossible, to substantiate this claim given the clandestine nature of all three phenomena. Estimates of the profits are similarly dubious. For instance, one author boldly states: "Only 4.2 percent of the world's slaves are trafficked sex slaves, but they generate 39.1 percent of slaveholders' profits."[100] To sustain such precise claims about the proportion who are sex slaves and the profits derived from them would require hard evidence on both dimensions—which absolutely does not exist. Similarly, the source for the claim, made a decade ago, that trafficking is a $5–$7 billion annual business has been dissected and discredited as "guesswork" by Jahic and Finckenauer.[101] Nevertheless, since then the asserted profits from human trafficking have ranged between $7 and $12 billion annually, although some writers put the figure even higher.[102] For the same evidentiary reasons described by Jahic and Finckenauer, these figures are nothing more than conjecture.

Trafficking and Other Sex Work Arenas

I noted above how activists and government officials have conflated sex trafficking and prostitution.[103] But they have also attempted to link trafficking to other kinds of commercial sex. In fact, the campaign against trafficking has steadily expanded its targets over time. Prohibitionists now associate sex trafficking with *all* sexual commerce-prostitution, pornography, and strip clubs. Fusing trafficking with other commercial sex practices arguably makes it easier to condemn and criminalize them which is precisely the prohibitionists' ultimate objective.

Pornography

Oppression writers now link trafficking to pornography. For example, Yen writes: "Pornography is often a stepping stone for trafficked women who eventually end up in prostitution."[104] It is not clear what is meant here by "stepping stone" but it is clear that Yen seeks to associate pornography, prostitution, and trafficking. Donna Hughes's report for the State Department claims that the producers of pornography "often rely on trafficked victims."[105] And Patrick Trueman, chief of the Justice Department's obscenity unit from 1988 to 1992 and now legal counsel for the Family Research Council, provided written testimony at a Congressional hearing, claiming that "pornography

is closely linked to an increase in prostitution, child prostitution, and human trafficking."[106] Echoing this notion at the hearing was Senator Sam Brownback, who declared that "we are seeing people trafficked into the pornography industry for porn."[107] Melissa Farley adds:

> Pornographers are indistinguishable from other pimps. Both exploit women and girls' economic and psychological vulnerabilities and coerce them to get into and stay in the industry. Both take pictures to advertise their "products," suggest specific abuses for johns to perpetrate against women, and minimize the resulting harms.[108]

Or consider Catharine MacKinnon's tautological reasoning and conflation of pornographic materials with persons:

> [T]he pornography industry, in production, creates demand for prostitution, hence for trafficking, because it is itself a form of prostitution and trafficking.
>
> . . . .
>
> [E]ach time the pornography is commercially exchanged, the trafficking continues as the women and children in it are transported and provided for sex, sold, and bought again. Doing all these things for the purpose of exploiting the prostitution of others which pornography intrinsically does-makes it trafficking in persons.[109]

In 2007, over fifty major players in the anti-pornography movement signed a letter to President Bush, urging him to intensify enforcement against pornography. The signatories were alarmed at the "explosive increase in the availability of pornography," which they associated with a litany of dangers: "trafficking in women and children" is "linked to the spread of obscenity" and pornography "corrupts children, ruins marriages, contributes to sex crimes against children and adults, and undermines the right of Americans to live in a decent society."[110] The letter demanded vigorous and expanded prosecution of pornography cases and asked Bush "to make fighting obscenity one of your top priorities."[111] In the mid-2000s, the Justice Department launched a new crackdown on pornography, including greater targeting of adult pornography (previous practice centered on child porn).[112] The Department also created a new Obscenity Prosecution Task Force alongside the existing Child Exploitation and Obscenity Unit.[113]

Strip Clubs

Prohibitionists have also sought to link trafficking to strip clubs. Sheila Jeffreys claims that "trafficking in women by organized crime groups has become a common form of supply of dancers. All over Europe and North America women and girls are brought into the clubs by deception, by force or, initially, by consent."[114] No evidence is offered to support this sweeping charge. Donna Hughes's report on trafficking (funded by the State Department) echoes this claim-that many women are trafficked to perform at strip clubs-despite the fact that Hughes found only six cases of this in the U.S. between 1998 and 2005.[115] Hughes maintains that strip clubs are "attractive to some criminals because they assume that since stripping is legal they will be less likely to be caught trafficking women into these markets."[116] An alternative. and more plausible argument is that most club owners would be averse to hiring trafficked or coerced dancers, for fear of attracting attention from law enforcement and perhaps losing their business license.[117] An interest in maintaining a lawful business is evident in the security measures taken by strip club owners to deal with disorderly customers and thwart criminal activity in the vicinity of the club.[118]

Another attempt, by Farrell et al., to estimate the number of trafficking victims working in U.S. strip clubs is the following:

> We made an *educated guess* that prostitution occurs in a minimum of 25 percent of strip clubs, based on *anecdotal evidence* from qualitative accounts of strip clubs and *news accounts of occasional* police arrests for prostitution in such clubs . . . . [W]e . . . rely upon Raphael and Ashley (2008) to assume that 35 percent of those providing prostitution in strip clubs are trafficked (3,028 $\times$ .35). Thus, we estimate that there are 1,060 sex trafficking victims in strip clubs throughout the United States.[119]

The authors estimated that 606 strip clubs "house prostitution," reported that an average of twenty women work at each club (a total of 12,120 dancers), and "estimate[d] conservatively" that 25% of them sell sex "within the clubs" yielding the 3,028 figure.[120] These are huge assumptions, based on nothing more than guesswork. "Anecdotal evidence" and "occasional" news reports are hardly sufficient to justify the claim that prostitution occurs in a minimum of one-quarter of U.S. strip clubs, just as there is no basis for the estimate that at least one-quarter of the dancers in these clubs sell sex. Moreover, there are many problems with the use of the Raphael and Ashley report cited: (a) it does not address criminal trafficking in persons (despite its title)-instead examining recruitment and current involvement in commercial sex, (b) nowhere does the Raphael and Ashley report state that 35% of those providing prostitution in strip clubs are trafficked, and (c) their report is based on interviews with 100 women working in the sex industry in a single city (Chicago), half of whom were accessed at a Christian-run exit agency-hardly a representative sample and likely biased by the fact that these respondents were clients of a court-mandated rehabilitation program.[121] In sum, the Farrell et al. report's conclusions are entirely lacking in supporting evidence; instead they are based on a set of conjectures and on another report

(Raphael and Ashley) that is misrepresented by the authors and is itself flawed due to its highly skewed sample.[122] Therefore, the estimate of "1,060 sex trafficking victims in strip clubs" is totally lacking in credibility.

Linking strip clubs to trafficking may lead to increased police investigations in the future.[123] In Illinois, activists successfully lobbied the state legislature to pass the Predator Accountability Act in 2006, which allows sex workers to seek civil damages against individuals and businesses that can be tied to their involvement in sexual commerce, even if no criminal charges have been made.[124] The most radical feature of this law is the liability it imposes on businesses. A strip club, escort agency, website, or massage parlor is punishable if it "recruits, profits from, or maintains the victim in any sex trade act," irrespective of whether the "victim" was coerced.[125] In addition, a business that "knowingly advertises or publishes advertisements for purposes of recruitment into sex trade activity" is punishable under this law.[126] The assets of such businesses make them lucrative targets for plaintiffs, and the statute is clearly motivated by prohibitionists' interest in putting a dent in the sex industry.

Targeting Customers

Over time, the focus of the anti-prostitution campaign has expanded to include prostitutes' customers, who are seen as the root cause of trafficking.[127] Today, customers are being vilified as much as traffickers. One writer, for example, declares that clients "are not just naughty boys who need their wrists slapped. They could be more accurately described as predators."[128] A recent government-funded report on clients of prostitutes in Scotland proclaims that "prostitution is best understood as a transaction in which there are two roles: exploiter/predator and victim/prey"; the report advocates putting customers "in the same category as rapists, pedophiles, and other social undesirables."[129] The authors represent two staunch anti prostitution organizations, which guaranteed that their report would reflect the oppression paradigm exclusively.[130]

Oppression writings present the customers of prostitutes (whether trafficked or not) in a one-dimensional, simplistic manner. For example, Yen imagines that "Johns feel their gender and money entitle them to have sex whenever, wherever, however, and with whomever they wish."[131] This sweeping broadside is hardly data-driven. In fact, academic research documents tremendous variation among clients on key axes: demographic background, motivation, and behavior. There are several reasons why customers buy sexual services, and clients vary in the kinds of services they seek and in the settings and conditions under which they engage in this activity.[132] Moreover, research comparing clients with the larger male population finds few differences between them.[133] There is no evidence that most of them, as claimed, feel entitled to have sex "whenever, wherever, however, and with whomever they wish."[134] Some men-both clients and other men—do indeed feel some sense of sexual entitlement,[135] but Yen's all-encompassing claim is a caricature. Similarly, the notion that most clients are violent predators is not borne out empirically. Some act violently and some seek out underage prostitutes, but abusive clients appear to be in the minority.[136] In one study, only 8% of arrested customers had a previous conviction for a violent or sexual offense.[137] Some clients find distasteful the idea of buying sex from anyone who is vulnerable or desperate and say that if they met a trafficked victim they would try to help her escape or contact the police.[138]

A staple of the oppression literature is that "male demand" fuels sex trafficking. It goes without saying that consumer demand is a necessary condition for the survival of any market. What is missing in the "male demand" explanation is consideration of other factors that might lead people to move away from home and relocate in a place where they engage in sexual commerce. Some of these "push" and "pull" factors were mentioned earlier. What is important here is that the "demand" thesis has been used quite successfully by advocates in lobbying government officials to target clients under trafficking statutes. The 2005 Trafficking Victims Prevention Reauthorization Act (TVPRA) authorized $25 million for fiscal years 2006 and 2007 to state and local police departments for expanded targeting of those who "purchase . . . commercial sex acts."[139] Efforts to link customers to trafficking and to fund local enforcement efforts against clients, as the TVPRA does, signal a broader shift toward federalizing prostitution enforcement, traditionally the domain of local authorities.

Sweden's recent experience in combating "the demand" has served as the inspiration for changes in the law or enforcement practices in some other countries, including the United States.[140] It is therefore worth taking a brief look at the outcomes in Sweden. In 1998, Parliament passed unprecedented legislation penalizing the buyers of sexual services but not the sellers.[141] After just a few years in operation, the law was proclaimed a resounding success by activists and by the government.[142] Yet several independent analysts, who have examined the effects of Sweden's crackdown, conclude that it has mainly driven prostitution underground, rendering the activity riskier.[143] And the National Board of Health and Welfare, in three evaluations of the law, concluded that it has not achieved its objectives. The Board's 2007 report states that street prostitution is on the rise after an initial decline and that many other prostitutes use the internet and mobile phones to arrange meetings.[144] Yet the Swedish government continues to claim that the law has reduced both prostitution and trafficking.[145]

If claims that prostitution and trafficking in Sweden have decreased are unsubstantiated, supporters of the law also claim that it has had a salutary symbolic impact: Yen believes that "criminalizing the purchase of sex has positively influenced the cultural values of Swedes . . . . [A] generation of young Swedes has grown up indoctrinated with the belief that prostitution is not socially desirable and is innately harmful to women . . . ."[146] Yet this symbolic dividend seems questionable in light of a commission's conclusion that Swedish men's attitudes toward women have changed little in recent years.[147]

Conclusion

Popular in some academic circles, the oppression paradigm also predominates in the media, in popular discourse, and in legislation in many countries. The mass media are saturated with stories highlighting prostitution's worst cases, and news reports typically center on themes of violence, pimping, crime, disease, and immorality.[148] Regarding trafficking, a recent *Washington Post* editorial typifies the media's widespread endorsement of the dominant discourse: "Thanks to a dedicated band of human rights advocates who have spread the gut-wrenching stories of victims, trafficking is understood today as a global phenomenon exceeding 20 million cases each year. . . ."[149] (The editorial writer seems oblivious to the investigative reporting of one of the *Post's* own reporters, which cast doubt on both the numbers and those who propagate them.[150]) A content analysis of 2,462 newspaper articles on trafficking concluded that the media privilege victimization stories, ignore root causes, and increasingly present the problem as a major organized crime operation and even as a threat to national security.[151] Another content analysis of newspaper coverage of human trafficking in Britain, Canada, and the United States, drawing on 837 articles, found that a very narrow range of viewpoints was presented; that most stories relied exclusively on official sources; and that journalists rarely questioned the idea that the best way to counter trafficking is to build on current policy.[152] Simplistic claims and messages are also evident in documentaries on trafficking (e.g., MSNBC's *Sex Slaves in America)* and feature films (e.g., *Taken*).[153] The net effect of media coverage has been to marginalize alternative viewpoints and critiques of government policy, while legitimizing the views of anti-prostitution activists.

If government officials in most nations view prostitution through the oppression lens, the paradigm has been occasionally questioned in official circles. In the debate on a legalization bill in Western Australia in 2007–2008, the state parliament voted to legalize prostitution because of its harm reduction potential.[154] In the course of this debate, John Hyde, Parliamentary Secretary to the Attorney General of Western Australia, contested the standard prohibitionist claim that legalization would increase the amount of trafficking and prostitution: "New Zealand and Australia have a low incidence of sex trafficking . . . . The size of the Australian sex industry has not expanded in the states and territories that have decriminalised or legalised the sex industry."[155] Hyde also presented a detailed critique of other aspects of the oppression paradigm and of the Swedish system whereby clients exclusively are criminalized.[156]

In a successful challenge to the constitutionality of Canada's three main prostitution laws in 2010, the Superior Court of Ontario downgraded the testimony of three state's witnesses (Melissa Farley, Janice Raymond, and Richard Poulin), who testified in support of the existing laws, because of questions about their objectivity. In addition to ruling that the prostitution laws were unconstitutional because they had the effect of further endangering prostitutes, the judge stated:

> I found the evidence of Dr. Melissa Farley to be problematic . . . . [H]er advocacy appears to have permeated her opinions. For example, Dr. Farley's unqualified assertion in her affidavit that prostitution is inherently violent appears to contradict her own findings that prostitutes who work from indoor locations generally experience less violence. Dr. Farley's choice of language is at times inflammatory and detracts from her conclusions. For example, comments such as, "prostitution is to the community what incest is to the family" and "just as pedophiles justify sexual assault of children . . . men who use prostitutes develop elaborate cognitive schemes to justify purchase and use of women" make her opinions less persuasive. Dr. Farley stated during cross-examination that some of her opinions on prostitution were formed prior to her research, including "that prostitution is a terrible harm to women, that prostitution is abusive in its very nature, and that prostitution amounts to men paying a woman for the right to rape her." Accordingly, for these reasons, I assign less weight to Dr. Farley's evidence. Similarly, I find that Drs. Raymond and Poulin were more like advocates than experts offering independent opinions to the court. At times, they made bold, sweeping statements that were not reflected in their research.[157]

Prohibitionism and, by implication, the oppression paradigm have been challenged by some international bodies as well. In 2007, for example, the Parliamentary Assembly of the Council of Europe passed a resolution on prostitution that included, *inter alia*, the following principles:

> Concerning voluntary adult prostitution, Council of Europe member states . . . must avoid double standards and policies which force prostitutes underground or under the influence of pimps, which only make prostitutes more vulnerable; instead they should seek to empower them, in particular by: . . . refraining from criminalising and penalising prostitutes and developing programmes to assist prostitutes to leave the profession should they wish to do so; . . . ensuring prostitutes have access to safe sexual practices and enough independence to impose these on their clients; . . . respecting the right of prostitutes who freely choose to work as prostitutes to have a say in any policies at national, regional and local level concerning them . . . .[158]

These are three important examples of state and international authorities rejecting—explicitly or implicitly—the oppression framework and the specific claims of its advocates.

Prostitution varies tremendously from place to place and in how it is practiced, organized, and experienced by participants. The same diversity characterizes the arena of trafficking and assisted migration. Migration patterns range from highly coercive and exploitative to cooperative, consensual, and mutually beneficial agreements between migrants and third parties. Some brokers are relatives, friends, or associates who recruit workers and facilitate migration—individuals who have a rather different relationship with workers than those who use force or deception. Such complexities, nuances, and variations are glossed over in the oppression paradigm, a perspective that disregards a wealth of social science research on the sex industry. It is imperative that future anti-trafficking laws be solidly evidence-based, utilizing the best social science data available, rather than being grounded—as most policy has been to date—in a monolithic and simplistic portrayal of sexual commerce.

Instead of funding organizations whose central goal is elimination of the entire sex industry—as the U.S. government has done—or launching crackdowns on currently legal forms of commercial sex—as some activists have demanded—a more sophisticated, evidence-based approach would focus state resources on identifying and assisting victims who have been trafficked by force, fraud, or coercion, and on prosecuting the perpetrators of such crimes. This means intensified targeting of unfree labor in agriculture, domestic service, and industry in addition to the sex trade, as trafficking in the former arenas appears to be much more sizeable than in the latter.[159] In addition, governments and activists should discontinue the fruitless practice of "estimating" the number of victims—numbers that vary wildly, are intrinsically unverifiable, and seem to be propagated for alarmist purposes.

Notes

1. Trafficking Victims Protection Act of 2000 § 103(9), 22 U.S.C. § 7102(9) (2006) [hereinafter, TVPA].

2. *Id.* § 103(8)(A), 22 U.S.C. § 7102(8)(A). Persons convicted of involvement in the trafficking of adults where force, fraud, or coercion is involved or where the victim was under

fourteen years of age are subject to a penalty of a fine and/or imprisonment for any term between fifteen years and life. For victims between the ages of fourteen and eighteen, traffickers are subject to a fine and/or imprisonment for a term between ten years to life. 18 U.S.C. §§ 1591(b)(1)–(2) (2006 & Supp. II 2008).

3. Consensual migration with third-party assistance is often called "smuggling" instead of trafficking. For a good discussion of the differences between trafficking and smuggling, see ALEXIS ARONOWITZ, HUMAN TRAFFICKING, HUMAN MISERY 8 (2009).

4. *See* Ronald Weitzer, *Sex Work: Paradigms and Policies, in* SEX FOR SALE: PROSTITUTION, PORNOGRAPHY, AND THE SEX INDUSTRY 1, 5 (Ronald Weitzer ed., 2d ed. 2010) [hereinafter Weitzer, *Paradigms and Policies*]; Ronald Weitzer, *Sociology of Sex Work,* 35 ANN. REV. SOC. 213, 214 (2009).

5. Published material based on the oppression paradigm will be cited throughout the Article. Key theoretical works include KATHLEEN BARRY, THE PROSTITUTION OF SEXUALITY (1995); ANDREA DWORKIN, PORNOGRAPHY: MEN POSSESSING WOMEN (1981); SHEILA JEFFREYS, THE IDEA OF PROSTITUTION (1997); CAROLE PATEMAN, THE SEXUAL CONTRACT (1988). For a recent defense of the oppression paradigm, see Michelle Madden Dempsey, *Sex Trafficking and Criminalization: In Defense of Feminist Abolitionism,* 158 U. PA. L. REV. 1729 (2010).

6. Such heterogeneity is amply documented. *See, e.g.,* MINDY S. BRADLEY-ENGEN, NAKED LIVES: INSIDE THE WORLDS OF EXOTIC DANCE (2009); JULIA O'CONNELL DAVIDSON, PROSTITUTION, POWER AND FREEDOM (1998); Feona Attwood, *The Paradigm Shift: Pornography Research, Sexualization, and Extreme Images,* 5 SOC. COMPASS 13 (2011); C. Harcourt & B. Donovan, *The Many Faces of Sex Work,* 81 SEXUALLY TRANSMITTED INFECTIONS 201 (2005); Ine Vanwesenbeeck, *Another Decade of Social Scientific Work on Sex Work: A Review of Research 1990–2000,* 12 ANN. REV. SEX RES. 242 (2001); Weitzer, *Paradigms and Policies, supra* note 4; Weitzer, *Sociology of Sex Work, supra* note 4.

7. For other critiques of the oppression literature, see Ronald Weitzer, *The Mythology of Prostitution: Advocacy Research and Public Policy,* 7 SEXUALITY RES. & SOC. POL'Y 15 (2010) [hereinafter Weitzer, *Mythology of Prostitution*]; Ronald Weitzer, *Pornography's Effects: The Need for Solid Evidence,* 17 VIOLENCE AGAINST WOMEN 666 (2011) [hereinafter Weitzer, *Pornography's Effects*].

8. Melissa Farley founded Prostitution Research & Education; Janice Raymond and Dorchen Liedholdt were the co-directors of the U.S. branch of the CATW, now headed by Norma Ramos; Gail Dines created Stop Porn Culture; and Norma Hotaling founded SAGE. Some of the key players are affiliated with universities, e.g., Janice Raymond, Donna Hughes, and Gail Dines.

9. *See, e.g.,* Frances M. Shaver, *Sex Work Research: Methodological and Ethical Challenges,* 20 J. INTERPERSONAL VIOLENCE 296 (2005); Weitzer, *Mythology of Prostitution, supra* note 7; Weitzer, *Pornography's Effects, supra* note 7.

10. *See* Melissa Farley, *Prostitution Harms Women Even if Indoors: Reply to Weitzer,* 11 VIOLENCE AGAINST WOMEN 950 (2005); Ronald Weitzer, *Flawed Theory and Method in Studies of Prostitution,* 11 VIOLENCE AGAINST WOMEN 934 (2005) [hereinafter Weitzer, *Flawed Theory*]; Weitzer, *Mythology of Prostitution, supra* note 7.

11. Janie A. Chuang, *Rescuing Trafficking from Ideological Capture: Prostitution Reform and Anti-Trafficking Law and Policy,* 158 U. PA. L. REV. 1655, 1721 (2010) (noting that these authors have shown "a deep resistance to acknowledging, much less addressing, adverse data"). An example of this is Raymond's article on prostitutes' clients, where not one academic journal article is cited. Janice G. Raymond, *Prostitution on Demand: Legalizing the Buyers as Sexual Consumers,* 10 VIOLENCE AGAINST WOMEN 1156 (2004).

12. See, for instance, these comprehensive literature reviews: Shaver, *supra* note 9; Vanwesenbeeck, *supra* note 6; Weitzer, *Paradigms and Policies, supra* note 4; Weitzer, *Sociology of Sex Work, supra* note 4.

13. For example, Farley claims that prostitutes' regular customers "strongly endorsed rape myths," citing research by Martin Monto and Norma Hotaling to support this statement. Affidavit of Dr. Melissa Farley at 43, Bedford v. Att'y Gen. of Canada, No. 07-CV-329807PD1 (Can. Ont. Sup. Ct. J. 2008) [hereinafter Farley Affidavit]. Monto and Hotaling reported only that repeat customers were more likely than other customers to accept rape myths, not that either group strongly endorsed them. Martin A. Monto & Norma Hotaling, *Predictors of Rape Myth Acceptance Among Male Clients of Female Street Prostitutes,* 7 VIOLENCE AGAINST WOMEN 275, 288 (2001). Moreover, Farley failed to mention the most important finding of this study: clients as a whole were *not* inclined to endorse rape myths. Monto and Hotaling found "low levels of rape myth acceptance" among the large sample of clients studied. *Id.* at 275.

In trying to make the case that indoor prostitution victimizes women to the same extent as street prostitution, Farley claims that a British study found that workers in indoor venues (e.g., private residences and saunas) reported more attempted rapes than street workers. Melissa Farley, *Prostitution, Trafficking, and Cultural Amnesia: What We Must Not Know in Order to Keep the Business of Sexual Exploitation Running Smoothly,* 18 YALE J.L. & FEMINISM 109, 121 n.76 (2006) [hereinafter Farley, *Prostitution, Trafficking, and Cultural Amnesia*] ("[W]omen prostituting in the street more frequently report being slapped, punched, or kicked—while those indoors more frequently report attempted rape."). In fact, the British study reported the *opposite* regarding attempted rape: 28% of street workers said they had ever experienced an attempted rape, compared with 17% of indoor workers. Moreover, Farley failed to mention that street prostitutes were eleven times more likely to have *actually been raped* (vaginally): 22% of the street sample compared with only 2% of the indoor sample had ever been vaginally raped while at work. Stephanie Church et al., *Violence by Clients Towards Female Prostitutes in Different Work Settings,* 32 Brit. Med. J. 524, 525 (2001). This is a clear case of both inverting and ignoring findings that contradict one's arguments.

14. An article in *Christianity Today,* for instance, states: "When sex becomes commerce, the moral fabric of our culture is deeply damaged." Timothy Morgan, *Sex Isn't Work,* Christianity Today, Jan. 2007, at 10, 10; *see also infra* text accompanying note 110.

15. *See* Barry, Dworkin, Jeffreys, Pateman, *supra* note 5.

16. "When women's bodies are on sale as commodities in the capitalist market . . . the law of male sex-right is publicly affirmed, and men gain public acknowledgment as women's. sexual masters—that is what is wrong with prostitution." Pateman, *supra* note 5, at 199, 208.

17. Melissa Farley et al., *Prostitution and Trafficking in Nine Countries: An Update on Violence and Posttraumatic Stress Disorder,* 2 J. Trauma Prac. 33, 34 (2003) (emphasis added). Camille Paglia offers an intriguing counterpoint to Pateman and Farley: "The feminist analysis of prostitution says that men are using money as power over women. I'd say, yes, that's all that men *have.* The money is a confession of weakness. They have to buy women's attention. It's not a sign of power; it's a sign of weakness." Wendy Chapkis, Live Sex Acts: Women Performing Erotic Labor 22 (1997) (quoting Camille Paglia).

18. *See* Kathy Miriam, *Stopping the Traffic in Women: Power, Agency and Abolition in Feminist Debates over Sex-Trafficking,* 36 J. Soc. Phil. 1, 13 (2005) ("[M]en's right to demand access to women is the central conception of male power at stake for the feminist movement to abolish prostitution.").

19. Farley Affidavit, *supra* note 13, para. 16.

20. Farley, *Prostitution, Trafficking, and Cultural Amnesia, supra* note 13, at 112.

21. Janice G. Raymond, *Prostitution Is Rape That's Paid For,* L.A. Times, Dec. 11, 1995, at B5.

22. *An Introduction to CATW,* Coalition Against Trafficking in Women, http://www.catwinternational.org/about/index.php (last visited Sept. 21, 2011).

23. Jan Macleod, Melissa Farley, Lynn Anderson & Jacqueline Golding, Challenging Men's Demand for Prostitution in Scotland 27 (2008).

24. Melissa Farley, *"Bad for the Body, Bad for the Heart": Prostitution Harms Women Even if Legalized or Decriminalized,* 10 Violence Against Women 1087, 1101 (2004). It is not clear what Farley means by the highly-charged term "terrorize" in the context of strip clubs; "pimps in business suits" are presumably club owners and managers.

25. Dempsey, for instance, says that the "harms often suffered by prostituted people are the kind that tend to sustain and perpetuate patriarchal structural inequality," without indicating

what these "harms" comprise. This is because Dempsey defines prostitution as intrinsically harmful, apparently obviating the need to document the harms themselves. Dempsey, *supra* note 5, at 1735.

26. See the report funded by CATW and European Women's Lobby, Monica O'Connor & Grainne Healy, The Links Between Prostitution and Sex Trafficking: A Briefing Handbook (2006), and an article by a CATW leader, Dorchen A. Leidholdt, *Prostitution and Trafficking in Women: An Intimate Relationship,* 2 J. Trauma Prac. 167 (2004).

27. Donna M. Hughes, *Accommodation or Abolition?,* Nat'l Rev. Online (May 1, 2003), http://www.nationalreview.com/articles/206761/accommodation-or-abolition/donna-m-hughes.

28. Donna M. Hughes, *Wolves in Sheep's Clothing: No Way to End Sex-Trafficking,* Nat'l Rev. Online (Oct. 9, 2002), http://old.nationalreview.com/comment/comment-hughes100902.asp.

29. An exception, dating from the 1970s, was Barry's attempt to link prostitution, trafficking, and sexual slavery. Kathleen Barry, Female Sexual Slavery (1979). In the late nineteenth to early twentieth century, prostitution and trafficking were linked in the international movement against "white slavery," but this discourse faded when this movement collapsed. The "white slavery" phenomenon was later found to be largely fictional, and it has been argued that "today's stereotypical 'trafficking victim' bears as little resemblance to women migrating for work in the sex industry as did her historical counterpart, the 'white slave.'" Jo Doezema, *Loose Women or Lost Women? The Reemergence of the Myth of White Slavery in Contemporary Discourses of Trafficking in Women,* Gender Issues, Winter 2000, at 23, 24. The turn-of-the-century campaign had humanitarian motives but, according to Limoncelli, was co-opted by the state: "[S]tate officials selectively used reforms as mechanisms to realize their own interests in maintaining and controlling women's mobility and sexual labor." Stephanie A. Limoncelli, The Politics of Trafficking: The First International Movement to Combat the Sexual Exploitation of Women 3 (2010). A mid-century example is the 1949 United Nations Convention for the Suppression of the Traffic in Persons and of the Exploitation of the Prostitution of Others, *opened for signature* Mar. 21, 1950, 96 U.N.T.S. 271. The Convention conflates trafficking and prostitution, declares prostitution "incompatible with the dignity and worth of the human person," and advocates criminalization of all third-party facilitation of prostitution. *Id.* at 272, 274. The Convention was never widely ratified because its "sweeping conception of prostitution as exploitation would have required states to make such deep legal changes that many felt it was incompatible with their Constitutions and legal codes." Penelope Saunders & Gretchen Soderlund, *Threat or Opportunity? Sexuality, Gender and the Ebb and Flow of Trafficking as Discourse,* 22 Can. Woman Stud., nos. 2–3, 2003, at 16, 19.

30. *See* Melissa Ditmore, *Trafficking in Lives: How Ideology Shapes Policy, in* Trafficking and Prostitution Reconsidered 107 (Kamala Kempadoo ed., 2005); David A. Feingold,

Trafficking in Numbers: The Social Construction of Human Trafficking Data, in Sex, Drugs, and Body Counts: The Politics of Numbers in Global Crime and Conflict 46, 51 (Peter Andreas & Kelly M. Greenhill eds., 2010); Ronald Weitzer, *The Movement to Criminalize Sex Work in the United States,* 37 J.L. & SOC'Y 61 (2010) [hereinafter Weitzer, *Movement to Criminalize*]; Ronald Weitzer, *The Social Construction of Sex Trafficking: Ideology and Institutionalization of a Moral Crusade,* 35 Pol. & Soc'Y 447 (2007) [hereinafter Weitzer, *Social Construction*].

31. One form of prostitution, however, is now defined as criminal sex trafficking in U.S. law: that involving *minors*. Under the 2000 TVPA, anyone under the age of eighteen who is induced to sell sex is categorized as a victim of sex trafficking, irrespective of whether the individual consented or whether third-party facilitation took place. TVPA § 103(8)(A), 22 U.S.C. § 7102(8)(A) (2006).

32. Farley, *Prostitution, Trafficking, and Cultural Amnesia, supra* note 13, at 141–42 (emphasis added).

33. Chuang, *supra* note 11, at 1683.

34. U.S. Dep't of State, The Link Between Prostitution and Sex Trafficking (2004), *available at* http://www.defense.gov/home/features/2008/0608_ctip/docs/Prostitution%20Fact%20Sheet.pdf.

35. Chuang, *supra* note 11, at 1683.

36. Iris Yen, *Of Vice and Men: A New Approach to Eradicating Sex Trafficking by Reducing Male Demand Through Educational Programs and Abolitionist Legislation,* 98 J. Crim. L. & Criminology 653, 654 (2008).

37. *Id.* at 656.

38. Julia O'Connell Davidson, *Will the Real Sex Slave Please Stand Up?,* Feminist Rev., Aug. 2006, at 4.

39. Yen, *supra* note 36, at 659–60 (emphasis added).

40. *Id.* at 658.

41. *Id.* at 660.

42. *Id.* at 660–61, 676.

43. Regarding other push and pull factors in the migration field, see Aronowitz, *supra* note 3, at 11–12.

44. Laura María Agustín, Sex at the Margins: Migration, Labour Markets and the Rescue Industry 45–46 (2007).

45. Joanna Busza, Sarah Castle & Aisse Diarra, *Trafficking and Health,* 328 Brit. Med. J. 1369, 1370 (2004). See also the similar findings in a report for the U.S. Agency for International Development: Thomas M. Steinfatt, Measuring the Number of Trafficked Women and Children in Cambodia: A Direct Observation Field Study 24 (2003).

46. Christine M. Jacobsen and May-Len Skilbrei, *Reproachable Victims? Representations and Self-Representations of Russian Women Involved in Transnational Prostitution,* 75 Ethnos 190, 198–99, 201 (2010).

47. David A. Feingold, *Human Trafficking,* Foreign Pol'y, Sept./Oct. 2005, at 26, 28.

48. Rebecca Surtees, *Traffickers and Trafficking in Southern and Eastern Europe: Considering the Other Side of Human Trafficking,* 5 Eur. J. Criminology 39, 44, 52 (2008). Surtees documents diversity in other areas as well: "The level of organization and number of criminal groups in trafficking differs substantially from one country to another as well as within countries." *Id.* at 47.

49. Judith Vocks & Jan Nijboer, *The Promised Land: A Study of Trafficking in Women from Central and Eastern Europe to the Netherlands,* 8 Eur. J. Crim. Pol'y & Res. 379, 384 (2000). Few of the interviewees were coercively trafficked: "[F]or most of the women, economic motives were decisive. The opportunity to earn a considerable amount of money in a short period of time was found to be irresistible." *Id.* at 383.

50. Interviews with eighty-five Bulgarian women involved in prostitution in Western Europe found that 75% had experienced no coercion in the process of relocating to the West. Girlfriends were the recruiters of 15% of the women, and other recruiters included relatives (8%) and boyfriends (17%). Georgi Petrunov, Sex Trafficking and Money Laundering: The Case of Bulgaria 20–22 (2010).

51. *See* Peter Andreas, *The Politics of Measuring Illicit Flows and Policy Effectiveness, in* Sex, Drugs, and Body Counts, *supra* note 30, at 23.

52. *Id.* at 33.

53. On the influence of anti-prostitution activists on U.S. government officials, and the institutionalization of the former's discourse, claims, and demands in official policy, see Weitzer, *Movement to Criminalize, supra* note 30; Weitzer, *Social Construction, supra* note 30.

54. Kathryn Farr, Sex Trafficking 3 (2005). Farr's sources are activists and certain U.S. government agencies—precisely the sources that critics find highly dubious.

55. Yen, *supra* note 36, at 656, 666–67.

56. Guri Tyldum & Anette Brunovskis, *Describing the Unobserved: Methodological Challenges in Empirical Studies on Human Trafficking,* Int'l Migration, Jan. 2005, at 17, 18 ("[M]ost of the populations relevant to the study of human trafficking, such as prostitutes, traffickers, victims/survivors, or illegal migrants constitute so-called *hidden populations.* . . . [M]embership in hidden populations often involves stigmatized or illegal behavior, leading individuals to refuse to cooperate, or give unreliable answers to protect their privacy.").

57. For well-documented critiques of popular claims regarding trafficking and the thin evidence in support of these claims, see Sophie Day, *The Re-Emergence of 'Trafficking': Sex Work Between Slavery and Freedom,* 16 J. Royal Anthropological Inst. 816 (2010); Sheldon X. Zhang, *Beyond the "Natasha" Story—A Review and Critique of Current Research on Sex Trafficking,* 10 Global Crime 178 (2009); Jerry Markou,

Human Trafficking Evokes Outrage, Little Evidence, WASH. POST, Sept. 23, 2007, at Al; sources cited *supra* note 30.

58. The paucity of solid data is discussed in INT'L ORG. FOR MIGRATION, SECOND ANNUAL REPORT ON VICTIMS OF TRAFFICKING IN SOUTH-EASTERN EUROPE 12 (2005); Anette Brunovskis & Rebecca Surtees, *Untold Stories: Biases and Selection Effects in Research with Victims of Trafficking for Sexual Exploitation,* INT'L MIGRATION, Aug. 2010, at 1; Elzbieta M. Gozdziak & Elizabeth A. Collett, *Research on Human Trafficking in North America: A Review of the Literature,* INT'L MIGRATION, Jan. 2005, at 99; Markon, *supra* note 57; Tyldum & Brunovskis, *supra* note 56; Weitzer, *Movement to Criminalize, supra* note 30; Weitzer, *Social Construction, supra* note 30.

59. Galma Jahic & James O. Finckenauer, *Representations and Misrepresentations of Human Trafficking,* TRENDS IN ORG. CRIME, Mar. 2005, at 24, 32.

60. DEP'T OF STATE, TRAFFICKING IN PERSONS REPORT 1 (2002) [hereinafter DEP'T OF STATE 2002] ("[A]s many as four million men, women, and children worldwide were bought, sold, transported, and held against their will in slave-like conditions.").

61. DEP'T. OF STATE, TRAFFICKING IN PERSONS REPORT 6 (2004) [hereinafter DEP'T OF STATE 2004]; DEP'T OF STATE, TRAFFICKING IN PERSONS REPORT 7 (2003) [hereinafter DEP'T OF STATE 2003].

62. DEP'T OF STATE, TRAFFICKING IN PERSONS REPORT 7 (2008) [hereinafter DEP'T OF STATE 2008].

63. DEP'T OF STATE 2004, *supra* note 61, at 6.

64. DEP'T OF STATE 2008, *supra* note 62, at 7.

65. TVPA § 102(b)(l), 22 U.S.C. § 710l(b)(l) (2006).

66. DEP'T OF STATE 2002, *supra* note 60, at 2.

67. DEP'T OF STATE 2003, *supra* note 61, at 7.

68. DEP'T OF STATE 2004, *supra* note 61, at 23.

69. DEP'T OF STATE 2008, *supra* note 62, at 51. The report claimed that 63% of the victims were trafficked into non-sexual labor situations. *Id.* This is consistent with an increasing focus, under the Obama administration, on victims trafficked into labor arenas outside the sex sector, as reflected in the two most recent *Trafficking in Persons* reports. The 2010 report, for example, stated that "the majority of human trafficking in the world takes the form of forced labor." DEP'T OF STATE, TRAFFICKING IN PERSONS REPORT 8 (2010) [hereinafter DEP'T OF STATE 2010]. The Bush administration took the opposite view. The 2004 *Trafficking in Persons* report, for example, states: "Of the 600,000–800,000 people trafficked across international borders every year, 70 percent are female and 50 percent are children. The majority of those women and girls fall prey to the commercial sex trade." DEP'T OF STATE 2004, *supra* note 61, at 15. And, unlike the Bush administration's conflation of trafficking and prostitution (including legal prostitution), the Obama administration appears to take a different view: "Prostitution by willing adults is not human trafficking regardless of whether it is legalized, decriminalized, or criminalized." DEP'T OF STATE 2010, *supra,* at 8.

70. AMY FARRELL ET AL., REVIEW OF EXISTING ESTIMATES OF VICTIMS OF HUMAN TRAFFICKING IN THE UNITED STATES AND RECOMMENDATIONS FOR IMPROVING RESEARCH AND MEASUREMENT OF HUMAN TRAFFICKING, at vi (2010).

71. *Id.* at iv, vi.

72. *Id.* at iii.

73. DEP'T OF STATE 2010, *supra* note 69, at 7.

74. DEP'T OF JUSTICE, EFFORTS TO COMBAT TRAFFICKING IN PERSONS IN FISCAL YEAR 2004, 5 (2005). Between FY 2001 and FY 2004, the Justice Department prosecuted 131 persons for sex trafficking offenses and obtained 99 convictions. *See* ATT'Y GEN., REPORT TO CONGRESS ON U.S. GOVERNMENT EFFORTS TO COMBAT TRAFFICKING IN PERSONS IN FISCAL YEAR 2004, at 20 (2005).

75. DEP'T OF STATE 2008, *supra* note 62, at 51.

76. DUREN BANKS & TRACEY KYCKELHAHN, CHARACTERISTICS OF SUSPECTED HUMAN TRAFFICKING INCIDENTS 2008–2010, at 3 (2011).

77. *Id.* at 5, 8.

78. *Id.* at 8.

79. Nick Davies, *Sex, Lies and Trafficking—The Anatomy of a Moral Panic,* GUARDIAN, Oct. 20, 2009, at 6. Davies cites a 2005 *Daily Mirror* article, entitled *25,000 Sex Slaves on the Streets in Britain,* a figure repeated in debates in the House of Commons. According to Davies, the headline figure was mythical: the body of the article made no reference to it and instead proffered a much lower figure: 2,000–6,000. Davies's analysis raised major questions about the latter figures as well. *Id.*

80. For instance, one team of researchers reported in 2003 a figure of 3,812 trafficking victims in the U.K. The researchers warned that this figure should be "regarded as an upper bound," and noted that their data was "very poor" and their estimate was "very approximate," subject to "a very large margin of error." But the government and non governmental organizations (NGOs) ignored these cautions and inflated the figures. Davies writes:

> Home Office minister Vernon Coaker ignored the speculative nature of the assumptions behind the figure, stripped out all the caution, headed for the maximum end of the range and then rounded it up, declaring to an inquiry into sex trafficking by the Commons joint committee on human rights: "There are an estimated 4,000 women victims."
>
> . . . .
>
> The Salvation Army went further, [claiming that] "there were *at least* 4,000 trafficked women residing in the UK. This figure is believed to be a *massive underestimation* of the problem." Anti-Slavery International joined them, converting what the Home Office researchers had described as a "very approximate" estimate into "a very conservative estimate."
>
> . . . .

In March 2007, [the Home Office] produced the UK Action Plan on Human Trafficking and casually reproduced the figure of 4,000 without any of the researchers' cautions.

Id. (emphasis added).

81. *Id.*

82. *Id.*

83. GOV'T ACCOUNTABILITY OFFICE, GAO-06-825, HUMAN TRAFFICKING: BETTER DATA, STRATEGY, AND REPORTING NEEDED TO ENHANCE U.S. ANTITRAFFICKING EFFORTS ABROAD 2, 10 (2006).

84. *Id.* at 16 (criticizing the "intermingling of trafficking, smuggling, and illegal migration in official statistics").

85. Gozdziak & Collett, *supra* note 58, at 103.

86. Liz Kelly, *"You Can Find Anything You Want": A Critical Reflection on Research on Trafficking in Persons Within and into Europe,* INT'L MIGRATION, Jan. 2005, at 235, 237.

87. Tyldum & Brunovskis, *supra* note 56, at 24.

88. Gozdziak & Collett, *supra* note 58, at 108.

89. *Trafficking Statistics Project,* UNESCO BANGKOK, http://cms2. unescobkk.org/index.php?id=1022 (last visited Sept. 19, 2011). UNESCO's Trafficking Statistics Project is an ongoing effort to assess the scale of the problem. *See* Feingold, *supra* note 30, at 51–52.

90. Jahic & Finckenauer, *supra* note 59, at 31.

91. John I. Kitsuse & Aaron V. Cicourel, *A Note on the Uses of Official Statistics,* 11 SOC. PROBS. 131, 132 (1963).

92. Zhang, *supra* note 57, at 181, 185.

93. *Id.* at 182.

94. *See, e.g.,* PETRUNOV, *supra* note 50, at 18; Jo Goodey, *Sex Trafficking in Women from Central and East European Countries: Promoting a 'Victim-Centered' and 'Woman-Centered' Approach to Criminal Justice Intervention,* 76 FEMINIST REV. 26 (2004); Louise Shelley, *The Trade in People in and from the Former Soviet Union,* 40 CRIME L. & SOC. CHANGE 231, 232 (2003).

95. TVPA § 103(8)(A), 22 U.S.C. § 7102(8)(A) (2006).

96. INT'L ORG. FOR MIGRATION, SECOND ANNUAL REPORT ON VICTIMS OF TRAFFICKING IN SOUTH-EASTERN EUROPE 12 (2005).

97. According to one report, the top three countries of origin of migrant sex workers in Western Europe in 2008 were Romania, Russia, and Bulgaria. TAMPEP, SEX WORK IN EUROPE: A MAPPING OF THE PROSTITUTION SCENE IN 25 EUROPEAN COUNTRIES 20 (2009).

98. THOMAS M. STEINFATT & SIMON BAKER, MEASURING THE EXTENT OF SEX TRAFFICKING IN CAMBODIA—2008, at 40 (2011). Trafficked victims were defined as individuals who were underage, indebted, or unable to leave the sex trade. *Id.*

99. Zhang, *supra* note 57, at 183 (citing several authors who assert that sex trafficking ranks third behind the drug and arms trades).

100. SIDDHARTH KARA, SEX TRAFFICKING: INSIDE THE BUSINESS OF MODERN SLAVERY 19 (2010).

101. Jahic & Finckenauer, *supra* note 59, at 29 (pointing out that "the author of the estimate was operating with a number of unknowns" and relied on several "rough guesses").

102. Zhang, *supra* note 57, at 183 ("The US government estimated that human trafficking generated $9.5 billion annually. [Donna] Hughes claimed that human traffickers around the world made between $7 and $12 billion annually in profit."). KARA, *supra* note 100, at 19, claims that the exploitation of "trafficked sex slaves generated $51.3 billion in revenues in 2007"; after costs, the yield was "$35.7 billion in profits." His calculations are based on a host of dubious assumptions, which are further undermined by the numerous fallacies elsewhere in his book. For instance, he equates brothel workers with "slaves" and asserts that the "contemporary sex trafficking industry involves the systematic rape, torture, enslavement, and murder of millions of women and children"—offering no sources to support these notions. *Id.* at 13, 15. Similarly, his attempt to discredit the Netherlands' system of legal prostitution is full of errors. He claims, for instance, that police "rarely" conduct visits to legal brothels in Holland "primarily because of bribes paid to the relevant mayor." *Id.* at 104. No evidence, aside from the claim of an unnamed "local expert," is offered as evidence that such bribery takes place. Moreover, contra Kara, the Dutch police *routinely* visit legal sex businesses to check each woman's passport and interview them about their working conditions and links to third parties. (During my research in Amsterdam, I accompanied a team of plainclothes police officers as they made their rounds visiting the window-prostitution rooms in the main red-light district, visits that are conducted frequently.) Kara claims that he saw "pimps" loitering in Amsterdam's red-light district but does not say how he knew they were pimps. *Id.* at 101–03. He equates foreign prostitutes with trafficking victims and claims that trafficking is pervasive in Amsterdam. *Id.* at 101 (stating that the "majority" of foreign prostitutes are "trafficking victims," but citing only an unnamed "local trafficking expert"). He then goes on to say that "[d]espite the lack of conclusive data, observations from local experts indicate that, if anything, sex trafficking in Amsterdam increased after brothels were legalized." *Id.* at 104. Government agencies with expertise on trafficking have reached quite different conclusions. A report by the Ministry of Justice noted that "it is likely trafficking in human beings has become more difficult, because the enforcement of the regulations has increased" since prostitution was legalized in 2000. A.L. DAALDER, MINISTRY OF JUSTICE, PROSTITUTION IN THE NETHERLANDS SINCE THE LIFTING OF THE BROTHEL BAN 84 (2007), *available at* http://wodc.nl/images/ob249a _fulltext_tcm44-83466.pdf. And the government's Rapporteur on Trafficking states:

"It is often said in the media that the lifting of the general ban on brothels [in 2000] has led to more THB [trafficking in human beings]. This is not a correct conclusion.

Before the lifting of the general ban on brothels, THB and other (criminal) abuses were taking place in all sectors of prostitution. Some of these sectors are now under control and can be assumed to have rid themselves of their former criminal excesses, or are doing so . . . . It is possible that THB is increasing in the illegal, non-regulated or non-controlled sectors. If this were to be the case, it still cannot be assumed that the extent of THB is now at the same or even above the 'old' level it was at before the ban on brothels was lifted. It is in fact likely that this is not the case . . . ."

ANNA G. KORVINTJS ET AL., BUREAU OF THE DUTCH NAT'L RAPPORTEUR ON TRAFFICKING IN HUMAN BEINGS, TRAFFICKING IN HUMAN BEINGS: THIRD REPORT OF THE DUTCH NATIONAL RAPPORTEUR 91 (2005) (emphasis omitted). For a detailed discussion of the Dutch and other legal prostitution systems, see RONALD WEITZER, LEGALIZING PROSTITUTION: FROM ILLICIT VICE TO LAWFUL BUSINESS (2012).

103. *See supra* text accompanying notes 26–35.

104. Yen, *supra* note 36, at 673.

105. DONNA HUGHES, THE DEMAND FOR VICTIMS OF SEX TRAFFICKING 26 (2005).

106. *Obscenity Prosecution and the Constitution: Hearing Before the Subcomm. on the Constitution, Civil Rights, and Prop. Rights of the Comm. on the Judiciary,* 109th Cong. 31 (2005) (statement of Patrick Trueman, Senior Legal Counsel, Family Research Council).

107. *Id.* at 11. Senator Brownback cited, as evidence, an article in the *Los Angeles Times,* but that article made no mention of pornography, stating instead that some individuals in the Los Angeles area had been trafficked into prostitution. *Id.;* Steve Hymon, *Probes Link Human Trafficking to Sex, Slave Trade,* L.A. TIMES, Mar. 5, 2005, at B4.

108. Farley, *Prostitution, Trafficking, and Cultural Amnesia, supra* note 13, at 126–27.

109. Catharine A. MacKinnon, *Pornography As Trafficking,* 26 MICH. J. INT'L L. 993, 999, 1004 (2005).

110. Letter from Robert Peters, Pres. of Morality in Media, et al., to President George W. Bush (Sept. 10, 2007), *available at* http://www.moralityinmedia.org/full_article.php?article_no=145. The letter was signed by, among others, Donna Hughes, Patrick Trueman, Morality in Media, Family Research Council, Concerned Women for America, Focus on the Family, American Family Association, American Decency Association, and Citizens for Community Values.

111. *Id.*

112. Julie Kay, *U.S. Attorney's Porn Fight Gets Bad Reviews,* DAILY BUS. REV., Aug. 30, 2005, at Al, *available at* http://www.law.com/jsp/article.jsp?id=1125318960389.

113. Press Release, U.S. Dep't of Justice, Obscenity Prosecution Task Force Established to Investigate, Prosecute Purveyors of Obscene Materials (May 5, 2005); *see also* Richard B. Schmitt,

U.S. Plans To Escalate Porn Fight, L.A. TIMES, Feb. 14, 2004, at Al.

114. SHEILA JEFFREYS, THE INDUSTRIAL VAGINA: THE POLITICAL ECONOMY OF THE GLOBAL SEX TRADE 93 (2009).

115. HUGHES, *supra* note 105, at 22. Hughes received a $108,478 grant from the State Department to write this report. ATT'Y GEN., *supra* note 74, at 33.

116. HUGHES, *supra* note 105, at 22.

117. In interviews with seventy-two Mexican dancers working at strip clubs in San Diego, only one of them reported that she had been coerced into this work. Two-thirds sought out this work by themselves, while 27% were introduced to it by male or female friends. SHELDON ZHANG, SEX TRAFFICKING IN A BORDER COMMUNITY: A FIELD STUDY OF SEX TRAFFICKING IN TIJUANA, MEXICO 140 (2010).

118. A major study found that crime was more prevalent in the immediate vicinity of bars and gas stations than in the area near strip clubs, most likely because of the security measures taken by the strip clubs. Daniel Linz et al., *An Examination of the Assumption that Adult Businesses are Associated with Crime in Surrounding Areas: A Secondary Effects Study in Charlotte, North Carolina,* 38 LAW & SOC'Y REV. 69, 99 (2004). See also the related study: Bryant Paul, Daniel Linz & Bradley Shafer, *Government Regulation of "Adult" Businesses Through Zoning and Anti-Nudity Ordinances: Debunking the Legal Myth of Negative Secondary Effects,* 6 COMM. L. & POL'Y 355 (2001).

119. FARRELL ET AL., *supra* note 70, at 85 (emphasis added).

120. *Id.*

121. JODY RAPHAEL & JESSICA ASHLEY, DOMESTIC SEX TRAFFICKING OF CHICAGO WOMEN AND GIRLS 3 (2008).

122. Jody Raphael is a staunch advocate of the oppression paradigm. See my critique of her writings: Weitzer, *Flawed Theory, supra* note 10, at 939.

123. In Mumbai, India, in 2005 the government banned bar dancing, where women dance seductively but fully clothed at clubs. A survey of 500 dancers found that none had been trafficked, yet the 2005 ban was based in part on the claim that trafficking was rampant. As a result of the ban, 75,000 dancers were thrown out of work. Prabha Kotiswaran, *Labors in Vice or Virtue? Neo-Liberalism, Sexual Commerce, and the Case of Indian Bar Dancing,* 37 J.L. & SOC'Y 105, 110 (2010).

124. 740 ILL. COMP. STAT. 128/1, /5 (2010).

125. *Id.* at 128/15(b)(l).

126. *Id.* at 128/15(b)(3). See the discussion of the statute in Shay-Ann Heiser Singh, *The Predator Accountability Act,* 56 DE PAUL L. REV. 1035 (2007). To date, no lawsuits have been filed under the act. Meribah Knight, *Campaign Against Sex Trafficking is Gaining,* N.Y. TIMES, Aug. 13, 2011, at 21A (Chicago ed.).

127. The very title of Hughes's report, *The Demand for Victims of Sex Trafficking,* seems to imply that customers are intentionally seeking sex with trafficked persons. HUGHES, *supra* note 105.

128. Annie Brown, *Sex Industry in Scotland: Inside the Deluded Minds of the Punters,* DAILY REC. (Apr. 28, 2008), http://www.dailyrecord.co.uk/news/scottish-news/2008/04/28/sex-industry-in-scotland-inside-the-deluded-minds-of-the-punters-86908-20397545 (quoting Melissa Farley).

129. MACLEOD ET AL., *supra* note 23, at 27, 30. The report was funded by the Glasgow City Council, the Scottish Government Equality Unit, and the Glasgow Health Board.

130. The introduction to the report, for example, declares that "misogyny []stimulates and sustains prostitution as a social institution . . . . Acceptance of prostitution is one of a cluster of harmful attitudes that encourage and justify violence against women." *Id.* at 5.

131. Yen, *supra* note 42, at 669.

132. Martin A. Monto, *Prostitutes' Customers: Motives and Misconceptions, in* SEX FOR SALE: PROSTITUTION, PORNOGRAPHY, AND THE SEX INDUSTRY 233, 244–50 (Ronald Weitzer ed., 2d ed. 2010) [hereinafter Monto, *Prostitutes' Customers*]; TEELA SANDERS, PAYING FOR PLEASURE: MEN WHO BUY SEX 38 (2008); John Lowman & Chris Atchison, *Men Who Buy Sex: A Survey in the Greater Vancouver Regional District,* 43 CAN. REV. SOC. & ANTHROPOLOGY 281, 288 (2006); Martin A. Monto & Nick McRee, *A Comparison of the Male Customers of Female Street Prostitutes with National Samples of Men,* 49 INT'L J. OFFENDER THERAPY & COMP. CRIMINOLOGY 505 (2005); Martin A. Monto, *Female Prostitution, Customers, and Violence,* 10 VIOLENCE AGAINST WOMEN 160, 171 (2004).

133. Monto & McRee, *supra* note 132.

134. Yen, *supra* note 36, at 669.

135. *See, e.g.,* Monto, *Prostitutes' Customers, supra* note 132; Eugene J. Kanin, *Date Rapists: Differential Sexual Socialization and Relative Deprivation,* 14 ARCHIVES SEXUAL BEHAV. 219 (1985).

136. There is "no evidence to suggest that more than a minority of customers assault prostitutes" and "most clients do not hold views that justify violence against prostitutes." Monto, *Prostitutes' Customers, supra* note 132, at 243–44; *see also* Lowman & Atchison, *supra* note 132, at 290.

137. BELINDA BROOKS-GORDON, THE PRICE OF SEX: PROSTITUTION, POLICY AND SOCIETY 198 (2006).

138. BRIDGET ANDERSON & JULIA O'CONNELL DAVIDSON, IS TRAFFICKING IN HUMAN BEINGS DEMAND DRIVEN? A MULTI-COUNTRY PILOT STUDY 24–25 (2003); *see also* SANDERS, *supra* note 132, at 53–55.

139. Trafficking Victims Protection Reauthorization Act of 2005, Pub. L. No. 109-164, § 204(a)(l)(B)–(C), 119 Stat. 3558, 3571 (2005).

140. After the Swedish law (described below) went into effect in January 1999, several other countries enacted similar if not identical measures. Finland in 2006 outlawed the act of buying sex from a trafficked woman, and in 2009 Norway and Iceland passed legislation quite similar to Sweden's. In the same year, England and Wales criminalized the act of buying sex from someone who had been coerced into prostitution by a third party, a strict liability offense. In each country, advocates of the measures invoked the Swedish system as a model, and in some cases Swedish advocates personally lobbied politicians in these other nations. Wallace provides some examples of this cross-fertilization and points out that the "reason that so much is heard about the Swedish model internationally is that the Swedish Government is particularly eager to promote it to other countries as the panacea to prostitution and to urge its adoption." BOB WALLACE, OFFICE OF THE PROSTITUTION LICENSING AUTH., (Queensland, Aust1.); THE BAN ON PURCHASING SEX IN SWEDEN: THE SO-CALLED "SWEDISH MODEL" 3 (undated), *available at* http://www.pla.qld.gov.au/Resources/PLA/reportsPublications/documents/THE%20BAN%20ON%20PURCHASING%20SEX%20IN%20SWEDEN%20-%20THE%20SWEDISH%20MODEL.pdf.

141. A Swedish government report describes the logic behind the law:

> [Prostitution] is officially acknowledged as a form of exploitation of women and children and constitutes a significant social problem, which is harmful not only to the individual prostituted woman or child, but also to society at large. [C]ombating prostitution and human trafficking for sexual purposes is central to Sweden's goal of achieving equality between women and men . . . . [G]ender equality will remain unattainable as long as men buy, sell and exploit women and children by prostituting them . . . . Prostituted persons are considered the weaker party, exploited by both the procurers and the buyers . . . . By adopting [the legislation] Sweden has given notice to the world that it regards prostitution as a serious form of oppression of women, and that efforts must be made to combat it.

SWED. MINISTRY OF INDUS., EMP'T & COMMC'NS, PROSTITUTION AND TRAFFICKING IN WOMEN 1 (2004), *available at* http://www.innovations.harvard.edu/cache/documents/1310/131041.pdf.

142. Gunilla Ekberg, *The Swedish Law that Prohibits the Purchase of Sexual Services: Best Practices for Prevention of Prostitution and Trafficking in Human Beings,* 10 VIOLENCE AGAINST WOMEN 1187 (2004). Ekberg served as an advisor on prostitution in the Swedish government and is now co-executive director of CATW-International, based in Brussels.

143. *See* Arthur Gould, *The Criminalization of Buying Sex: The Politics of Prostitution in Sweden,* 30 J. SOC. POL'Y 437, 445 (2001); Jane Scoular, *Criminalising Punters: Evaluating the Swedish Position on Prostitution,* 26 J. SOC. WELFARE & FAM. L. 195, 199–200 (2004); Susanne Dodillet & Petra Östergren, The Swedish Sex Purchase Act: Claimed Success and Documented Effects 19 (Mar. 3–4, 2011) (conference paper), *available at* http://gup.ub.gu.se/records/fulltext/140671.pdf; Victor Clausen, An Assessment of Gunilla Ekberg's Account of Swedish Prostitution Policy (Jan. 2007) (unpublished paper) (on file with author).

144. ANNIKA ERIKSSON & ANNA GAVANAS, SWED. MINISTRY OF HEALTH & SOC. AFFAIRS, NAT'L BD. OF HEALTH & WELFARE, PROSTITUTION IN SWEDEN 2007, at 28 (2008).

145. The Swedish Ministry of Justice reached this conclusion but presented little documentation to support it: "Our assessment shows that the ban on the purchase of sexual services has had the intended effect and is an important instrument in preventing and combating prostitution." SWED. MINISTRY OF JUSTICE, THE BAN ON THE PURCHASE OF SEXUAL SERVICES: AN EVALUATION 1999–2008, at 40 (2010).

146. Yen, *supra* note 42, at 679.

147. Karen Leander, *Reflections on Sweden 's Measures Against Men's Violence Against Women*, 5 SOC. POL'Y & SOC'Y 115, 120 (2006); *see also* Dodillet & Östergren, *supra* note 143, at 20 (reviewing Swedish public opinion of the law).

148. Helga Kristin Hallgrimsdottir, Rachel Phillips & Cecilia Benoit, *Fallen Women and Rescued Girls: Social Stigma and Media Narratives of the Sex Industry in Victoria, B.C. from 1980–2005*, 43 CAN. REV. SOC. & ANTHROPOLOGY 265, 269 (2006).

149. Editorial, *Name, Shame—and Prosecute*, WASH. POST, June 28, 2011, at A14.

150. *See* Markon, *supra* note 57.

151. Amy Farrell & Stephanie Fahy, *The Problem of Human Trafficking in the U.S.: Public Frames and Policy Responses*, 37 J. CRIM. JUST. 617, 621–22 (2009).

152. Girish J. Gulati, Media Representations of Human Trafficking in the United States, Great Britain, and Canada, 10, 16 (2010) (unpublished paper), *available at* http:// papers.ssm.com/sol3/ papers.cfm?abstract_id=1633574.

153. TAKEN (20th Century Fox Home Entertainment 2009).

154. The bill did not become law because the ruling Labor Party lost power in 2008 prior to official proclamation. The current Liberal-National Party coalition government is in the process of drafting a new bill that would legalize certain kinds of prostitution but is more limited than the previous Labor Party bill.

155. WA, Parliamentary Debates, Legislative Assembly, 20 Sept. 2007, 5504 [hereinafter Parliamentary Debates] (John Hyde).

156. Hyde began by refuting claims in an article by Janice Raymond:

> Raymond also said in 2003 that legalisation and/or decriminalisation of prostitution is allegedly a gift to pimps, traffickers and the sex industry. The reality is that Australia does not have a culture of pimps involved in the sex industry [where it is legal] . . . . Raymond also claims that legalisation and/or decriminalisation of prostitution does not control the sex industry; it expands it. The reality is that the size of the Australian sex industry has not expanded in the states and territories that have decriminalised or legalised the sex industry . . . . Another claim is that legalisation and/or decriminalisation of prostitution increases clandestine, hidden, illegal and street prostitution . . . . New Zealand . . . is the only country that has used the decriminalised model that we are adapting in [Western

Australia]—it created a good example of the outcomes of decriminalisation. The only authoritative study of New Zealand has shown that in its early stages there has been no increase in the number of street-based sex workers since the decriminalisation of the sex industry . . . . Another of Raymond's claims is that legalisation and/or decriminalisation of prostitution increases the demand for prostitution. She says it boosts the motivation of men to buy women for sex in a much wider and more permissible range of socially acceptable settings. Again, that is wrong . . . . Raymond [also claims] that legalisation and/or decriminalisation of prostitution does not promote women's health. Nothing could be further from the truth. Most studies in Australia have shown that sex workers enjoyed better sexual health than the general community and much lower rates of HIV-AIDS and sexually transmitted diseases.

Id. at 5504–05. The article to which Hyde is referring is Janice G. Raymond, *Ten Reasons for Not Legalizing Prostitution and a Legal Response to the Demand for Prostitution*, 2 J. TRAUMA PRAC. 315 (2003). A government commission reported that "the number of sex workers in New Zealand has not increased as a result of passage of the [2003 Prostitution Reform Act]." PROSTITUTION LAW REVIEW COMM., REPORT OF THE PROSTITUTION LAW REVIEW COMMITTEE ON THE OPERATION OF THE PROSTITUTION REFORM ACT 2003, at 29, 30–38 (2008); *see also* Gillian M. Abel, Lisa J. Fitzgerald & Cheryl Brunton, *The Impact of Decriminalisation on the Number of Sex Workers in New Zealand*, 38 J. SOC. POL'Y 515 (2009) (reporting a carefully conducted study that concurs with the government report).

Hyde also challenged claims about the success of Sweden's customer-targeted approach. In response to the opposition Liberal Party's use of Gunilla Ekberg's account of the "success" of Sweden's law (Ekberg, *supra* note 142), Hyde countered with Victor Clausen's research (Clausen, *supra* note 143):

> An examination [by Clausen] of 11 of the specific claims that Ms Ekberg has reported shows that much of the article is a presentation of ideological positions. I have no truck with such people who are putting an ideological or a moral position, because such an argument should have population and health considerations, police support and objective information. The main failure in Ms Ekberg's position is that she is not able to specify any sources for her claims.

Parliamentary Debates, *supra* note 155, at 5505. For further analysis of the Western Australia debate, see Ronald Weitzer, *Legalizing Prostitution: Morality Politics in Western Australia*, 49 BRIT. J. CRIMINOLOGY 88 (2009).

157. Bedford v. Canada (2010), 102 O.R. 3d 321, paras. 353–57 (Can. Ont. Sup. Ct. J.) (striking down the criminal code sections that outlawed keeping a bawdy house, living on the avails of prostitution, and communicating in a public place for the purpose of engaging in prostitution). The ruling is currently being appealed by the government.

158. PARLIAMENTARY ASSEMBLY, COUNCIL OF EUR., RESOLUTION 1579: PROSTITUTION: WHICH STANCE TO TAKE? (2007).

159. *See supra* note 69.

Critical Thinking

1. According to this article, the incidence of sexual trafficking in the United States has gone down. To what might you attribute that decrease?
2. Do you think there is a connection between porn, sex work, and sexual trafficking? How might you link the three?
3. What do you think of the assertions in the article that some women (and men) like being thought of as exotic and do not see sexual trafficking as bad as others portray it? How is this similar to and different from "blaming the victim" of sexual assault?

Internet References

ECPAT International
http://www.ecpat.net

The Polaris Project
http://www.polarisproject.org

The Sex Workers Project
http://sexworkersproject.org

RONALD WEITZER has been a Professor of Sociology at George Washington University since 1988. He is a criminologist, and much of his research has investigated police-minority relations in the United States and in other nations (including Northern Ireland and South Africa). He is also an expert on the sex industry, with particular expertise on American policies and law enforcement on prostitution and sex trafficking.

Professor of Sociology, George Washington University. Ph.D., University of California, Berkeley, 1985; B.A., University of California, Santa Cruz, 1975.

Article

Prepared by: Elizabeth Schroeder, EdD, MSW,
Elizabeth Schroeder Consulting

Domestic Abuse Myths

Five mistakes we make when we talk about Rihanna and Chris Brown's relationship.

RAINA KELLEY

Learning Outcomes

After reading this article, you will be able to:

- Describe at least two common myths and misperceptions about domestic abuse or intimate partner violence.

- Provide at least one reason why people who are in abusive relationships may not leave right away.

- Explain why there is no such thing as provocation in a domestic abuse situation; that the person who abused the other person always had an alternative to physical violence.

L ast week, R&B singer Chris Brown was formally charged with two felonies, assault and making criminal threats, in connection with the alleged beating of his pop-star girlfriend Rihanna on February. 8. Though we will never know exactly what happened that night, many of us have seen Rihanna's bruised and bloodied face on the front pages and read horrific details of the alleged attack from the affidavit of a LAPD detective in which he describes contusions on the singer's body. At the same time, rumors are that the 21-year-old singer is back in a relationship with Brown, whom she has accused, according to the affidavit, of biting, choking and punching her until her mouth filled with blood.

While we can argue about how much of all that is true, it really doesn't matter. This sad story doesn't have to be verifiable for it to potentially warp how Rihanna's hundreds of thousands of tween fans think about intimate relationships. We've all heard that this should be a "teachable moment"—a chance to talk about domestic violence with our kids. But children and teens aren't just listening to your lectures, they're listening to

the way you speculate about the case with other adults; they're absorbing how the media describes it; they're reading gossip websites. When you tune in to all the talk about Rihanna and Chris Brown, it's scary how the same persistent domestic-violence myths continue to be perpetuated. Celebrity scandals may have a short shelf life, but what we teach kids about domestic violence will last forever. So rather than "raise awareness," here are five myths that anyone with a child should take time to debunk:

Myth No. 1: It Was a Domestic Argument, and She Provoked Him

We need to remember that any discussion of domestic violence should not revolve around what the couple may have been arguing about, or as one CNN anchor put it: "the incident that sparked the fight." Nor should we be using the word "provoked" when describing this case, as in the Associated Press account that said the "argument" was "provoked" by Rihanna's "discovery of a text message from another woman." Domestic violence has to do with, well, physical violence, not arguments. There isn't a verbal argument that should "spark" or "provoke" an attack of the kind that leaves one person with wounds that require medical attention.

Cable news has to stop referring to this incident as a "violent fight." A "fight" involves two people hitting each other, not—as is alleged in this case—a woman cowering in a car while a man punches and bites her. If Rihanna had called the police beaten and bloodied and alleging an attack of this nature by a stranger, no one would be calling it a "fight." They'd say that a man was being accused of severely beating and choking a young woman half his size.

Myth No. 2: Evolution Makes Us Do It

Steven Stosny, a counselor and founder of an organization that treats anger-management issues believes that the tragic tendency of women to return to the men who hurt them (battered-woman syndrome) is a product of evolution. Stosny was quoted on CNN.com as saying "To leave an attachment relationship—a relationship where there's an emotional bond—meant certain death by starvation or saber-tooth tiger."

Apologies to Mr. Stosny, but that is the most ridiculous thing I have ever heard. This is the kind of argument that really boils my blood because it seems to naturalize the torture of women. Very little is known about the emotional attachments of early humans. And trust me, after 50,000 years, our fear of saber-tooth tigers has abated. In most domestic-abuse cases, we're talking about a situation where one person is wielding power over an individual through pain, fear, and domination. It's not about being scared to leave because of the dangers that await you in the world, it's about being too scared of what's at home to leave.

Myth No. 3: People Make Mistakes. Give the Guy a Break

When singer Kanye West talked about the Rihanna-Brown case with his VH1 audience recently, he asked: "Can't we give Chris a break? . . . I know I make mistakes in life." Kanye's not the only one saying this kind of thing, so let's get something straight: People leave the oven on or fry turkeys in the garage and burn their house down. One may even accidentally step on the gas instead of the brake and run over the family cat. Mistakes resulting in tragic consequences happen all the time. But one cannot mistakenly beat someone up. You do not accidentally give someone black eyes, a broken nose, and a split lip.

Myth No. 4: Brown Said He Was Sorry and They're Working It Out

Experts will tell you that domestic violence is an escalating series of attacks (not fights) designed to increase a victim's dependence on her abuser. According to the police documents released last week, Rihanna told police that Brown had hit her before and it was getting worse. Sorry means you don't do it again. In discussions about abuse, we need to make it clear that sorry is not enough.

Myth No. 5: She's Young, Rich and Beautiful. If It Was Really as Bad as the Media Says, She'd Leave

The secret to the abuser's power is not only making his victim dependent on him, but convincing her that she is to blame for the attack. No amount of money or fame can protect someone from the terrible cycle of emotional dependence, shame and fear that keeps them with abusive partners. Women who are abused look for ways they may have "provoked" an attack, finding fault with their own behavior to explain the unexplainable—why would someone they love hurt them? And it doesn't help when people outside the relationship blame the victim. In this case, Phylicia Thompson, a cousin of Brown's, told "Extra TV" that, *"Chris was not brought up to beat on a woman. So it had to be something to provoke him for Chris to do it."* As the rumors swirl about whether Rihanna is back with Brown, understand that those who are abused do not stay with their abusers because they want to be beaten again, or because they are really at fault; it's usually because they feel trapped and guilty.

You may have noticed the words *power, control,* and *domination* running through my rant. That was purposeful. What we need to remember, and what we need to teach our children, is that yes, you should never hit anybody and you should never let anybody hit you. But, we also need to tell them that love does not guarantee respect and that any relationship they find themselves involved in should be based on both equally.

Critical Thinking

1. What are some of the most common myths about domestic violence?
2. What impact do domestic violence myths have on abusers? On victims? On relationships?

Internet References

Love is Respect
   http://www.loveisrespect.org
National Coalition Against Domestic Violence
   http://www.ncadv.org
National Network to End Domestic Violence
   http://nnedv.org

Article

Prepared by: Elizabeth Schroeder, EdD, MSW,
Elizabeth Schroeder Consulting

Meet the College Women Who Are Starting a Revolution Against Campus Sexual Assault

Vanessa Grigoriadis

Learning Outcomes

After reading this article, you will be able to:

- Explain the significance of carrying a mattress around a college campus as it relates to sexual assault.

- Explain the accusations made against Columbia University in the wake of sexual assault allegations.

- Describe the growing organization happening among some college men who claim accusations of rape discriminate against them because of their gender.

"Want to meet at my dorm? Less carrying for me." Emma Sulkowicz, a.k.a. the international sensation "mattress girl," is emailing from her phone in her Columbia University dorm high up over Morningside Heights, where she lives in a single room within a six-person suite. "My friends and I got the first place in the housing lottery for seniors last year," she says nonchalantly, leading the way through a concrete-block hallway, in purple flip-flops the same color as her painted toes, as well as a light-blue cropped tee featuring a moose with sunglasses over the words FEARLESS LEADER, commemorating a river-rafting trip for freshmen. As you may already know, given how viral Sulkowicz's image has gone in the past few weeks, that's the outdoor-orientation program that preceded Sulkowicz's alleged rape by another orientation leader, which was followed by a Columbia-adjudicated hearing during which the university found her assailant not guilty—a verdict she began protesting, this September, by carrying a mattress around campus until Columbia expels her assailant.

A few years ago, an Ivy League student going public about her rape, telling the world her real name—let alone trying to attract attention by lugging around a mattress—would have been a rare bird. In America, after all, we still assume rape survivors want, and need, their identities protected by the press. But shattering silence, in 2014, means not just coming out with an atrocity tale about your assault but offering what Danielle Dirks, a sociologist at Occidental, calls "an atrocity tale about how poorly you were treated by the people you pay $62,500 a year to protect you." By owning those accusations, and pointing a finger not only at assailants but also the American university, the ivory tower of privilege, these survivors have built the most effective, organized anti-rape movement since the late '70s. Rape activists now don't talk much about women's self-care and protection like they did in the '90s with Take Back the Night marches, self-defense classes, and cans of Mace. Today, the militant cry is aimed at the university: Kick the bastards out.

Taking a seat in a wood-and-wool chair of the blend shared by dorms and doctors' waiting rooms, Sulkowicz starts to tell her tale. At 21, in barely detectable Invisalign braces, she's the type of hipster-nerd who rules the world these days, with the mellow demeanor and direct way of speaking of an Apple genius-bar clerk, except she giggles nervously when worried she's said the wrong thing. The Japanese-Chinese-Jewish daughter of Manhattan psychiatrists, she was a club fencer and an A student at Dalton on the Upper East Side. At Columbia, Sulkowicz thought she'd focus on mechanical physics—she liked the way you could draw a diagram to solve a problem, see the answer—but wound up drawn to visual arts instead. She also joined Alpha Delta Phi, Columbia's co-ed "hipster frat." As she puts it dryly, "Only the most hipster of the hipster kids can get in." That's where she met Paul, a film fanatic and rower. "He was a nice person," she says matter-of-factly, "a cool person who was secretly really crazy."

Toward the end of freshman year, the two students signed up to help lead the next year's outdoor-orientation program, taking a training trip down the Delaware River. There were an odd number of students on the trip, so everyone sat two to a canoe except Paul, who was in a kayak. "He would paddle way out ahead of everyone so that he didn't have to talk to anyone," she says. They had sex twice. He went to Europe for the summer.

When he returned, at the beginning of sophomore year, Sulkowicz was a committee head for orientation. "Paul was really needy," she says. "He asked me to help carry his bags, and I was like, 'I'm organizing food for 400 freshmen.'" One night there was a party for the orientation leaders. In the ivy-covered courtyard outside Wien Hall, Paul kissed Sulkowicz, who says that she was sober except for a sip of gin-and-Sprite. He was buzzed and carrying a handle of vodka. While they were having consensual sex in her dorm room, she alleges that he suddenly pushed her legs against her chest, choked her, slapped her, and anally penetrated her as she struggled and clearly repeated "No."

Sulkowicz didn't report the incident at first. But when two classmates told her that Paul had been abusive to them too—one who had been in a long-term relationship with him, the other alleging he groped her—she pressed charges with the administration. Students tend to be uncomfortable going to the cops, who, despite what plots of *Law & Order* suggest, aren't always great with rape. The preference suits the universities, too, which prefer to handle issues quietly in-house. Under Title IX, a gender-parity law from 1972, universities are required to adjudicate sexual-assault claims to ensure gender equality on campus as a civil right. The Obama White House, taking a strong position on combating campus assault, has reinforced a "preponderance of the evidence" standard in these cases, meaning campus courts need only find it's 51 percent likely the assault occurred to punish the accused. To students like Sulkowicz—who are, after all, putting their good word on the line as well as risking stigma, humiliation, possible retribution from the guy's friends, and diminishment of respect from their own friends—that lower standard can feel like a relief.

Sulkowicz, though, claims that Columbia administrators made errors and acted, frankly, idiotically during the hearing process. One took incomplete notes of her story, writing that she was tipsy that night. Adjudicators "kept asking me to explain the position I was in," she says. "At one point, I was like, 'Should I just draw you a picture?' So I drew a stick drawing." She says one of the three judges even asked whether Paul

used lubricant, commenting, "I don't know how it's possible to have anal sex without lubrication first."

Paul denied the charges. If Sulkowicz is a fencer, she alleges he told the panel, her legs are the strongest part of her body, and he was only a lightweight rower—how could he have pinned her legs down? The anal sex was consensual, he said. He went into detail about how he came on Sulkowicz, and then she grabbed a tissue, wiped the ejaculate off, and "'threw the tissue away,'" she says. "None of which is true—he never came that night. He just stopped and ran away."

Columbia didn't hear Sulkowicz's charges for six months, then found in favor of Paul. "There's three women accusing the same guy here," she says. "Like, we don't have any other motivation other than he assaulted us." When she appealed, a dean refused to overturn the verdict. By Columbia's bylaws, his decision was final.

Today, Paul is still at Columbia, though he's lying low, even keeping his email out of the campus Facebook. The mattress protest is a way for Sulkowicz to both refuse him that anonymity and turn the situation on its head. She'll take the punishment, it says. This is a heavy mattress—an extra-long twin covered with shiny blue bedbug-proof material, bought from a clearinghouse called Tall Paul's Tall Mall, which stocks the same mattresses Columbia orders for its dorms for growing boys. For now, she's not using any hooks or belt loops to carry it—only her hands, or other students' hands (her friends call those "collective carries"). It's a weight Columbia can lift together. "For the record, the best arrangement is four people carrying the mattress, because they each take a corner," says Sulkowicz, smiling. "Then it's really light."

Sulkowicz's mattress project is powerful, indelible; as Hillary Clinton said last week, "That image should haunt all of us." But it is also maybe a little youthful. This is the ethical purview of college students. Strict attention not only to learning and knowledge but also to morality, to right and wrong, when to stand up and when to stay silent, is a large part of why American colleges exist.

"One cannot help but feel terrible about this," Columbia president Lee Bollinger says about Sulkowicz and her mattress in his first interview on the subject. "This is a person who is one of my students, and I care about all of my students. And when one of them feels that she has been a victim of mistreatment, I am affected by that. This is all very painful." Bollinger says that he has spent "as much time on this issue"—meaning sexual assault on campus—"as any issue" over the past year, which includes Columbia's largest expansion in nearly a century, a $6.3 billion, 17-acre satellite campus in West Harlem. In August, he created a new sexual-assault policy, taking a much harder line. Students are now required to have "unambiguous communication and mutual agreement"—that's verbal consent—before sexual acts, or risk consequences. Though an improvement, this hasn't been enough to quell unrest.

Activists of Sulkowicz's generation have long retired the word *victim*, preferring *survivor*. But Sulkowicz calls carrying the mattress "performance art," and we might as well take her at her word. Her daily thoughts, including how the hell she's getting the mattress to class, are about the integrity of her art piece; when this magazine asked to photograph her in a studio in Chelsea, she worried about violating the "rules" for the performance by taking the mattress to a location off-campus.

That she has become the poster girl for the anti-rape movement is an accident of a viral world—she doesn't have a background in activism, and she is not really at the center of this crusade. To find the godmothers, you have to travel to Los Angeles, where Annie Clark, 25, and Andrea Pino, 22, two political-science majors from the University of North Carolina at Chapel Hill, are hard at work in a one-bedroom in Silver Lake, rented off Craigslist, that has become an anti-assault Death Star. Both of them were violently raped as students, and in responding to both cases, UNC seemed to be lax verging on cruel—Clark claims an administrator even said to her, "Rape is like football. If you look back on the game, and you're the quarterback . . . is there anything you would have done differently?" Working with a network of activists, they've helped survivors learn about their Title IX rights and file complaints about violations across the country. Today, 78 American colleges, including Harvard, Princeton, Dartmouth, Amherst, Swarthmore, Brandeis, Emerson, and a slew of West Coast schools from UC Berkeley to USC to UCLA, are under investigation by the Department of Education's Office of Civil Rights.

Though they're at the heart of a national movement now, Pino and Clark were on the sidelines when things started to shake out a few years ago. Online—especially on powerful mainstream blogs like Jezebel—young writers were brewing a cauldron of pop-culture coverage and feminist theory, resuscitating feminism from its post–Monica Lewinsky, *Girls Gone Wild*–era doldrums by coaxing horror stories out of dark crannies and crucifying pop-culture villains. Between Woody Allen, Terry Richardson, Chris Brown, Elliot Rodger, the "legitimate rape" dude, Robin Thicke's "Blurred Lines," and Ray Rice knocking his fiancée out cold in the elevator, they haven't needed to look far. Pop culture was "rape culture," they said, borrowing a term from second-wave feminism as a catchall for America's stew of degradation, objectification, and male entitlement. "Rape culture is an attitude toward women in particular, but not even just to women—to treating all people as sexual objects, nothing more than an opportunity for sex," says Anna Bahr, a Columbia graduate and former editor of *Blue and White*, the school magazine.

Slowly, public discussion of rape among college women began to be normalized, and they started to share.

Amherst student Angie Epifano published the first major, non-pseudonymous "atrocity tale" in 2012, writing about how her rape allegations were denied by her college's sexual-assault counselor; how she became suicidal and was locked up in a psychiatric ward, after which, she alleged, Amherst tried to deny her readmittance; how, when the school agreed to take her back, her dean prevented her from studying abroad ("Africa is quite traumatizing, what with those horrible Third World conditions: disease . . . huts . . . lions!"); how they made her feel like a "broken, polluted piece of shit." She wrote that she did not want to be ashamed anymore. It occurred to her that *she* had no reason to be ashamed. "Silence has the rusty taste of shame," she repeated to herself. "I will not be quiet."

Pino studied policy-framing at school, and she thought about combining Epifano's narrative with developments at Yale, where students had filed a complaint alleging that the school was mishandling rape accusations amid a female-unfriendly atmosphere where frat pledges felt okay yelling things like "No means yes, yes means anal" and "My name is Jack, I'm a necrophiliac, I fuck dead women and fill them with my semen." A mix of the personal and the political, Pino thought, can make a movement. Pino and Clark also had a genius rhetorical idea—they'd take a lesson from the military anti-rape movement, which had beaten a drum about kicking serial, violent rapists out of the armed forces. No one should talk the way activists did in the 1990s—no more date rape. Focus on college men as serial predators, and cite a study that claimed that 6 percent commit three or more undetected rapes and attempted rapes each.

On a staggeringly sunny morning in Los Angeles, Pino and Clark are at their apartment, working away. Best friends, they even dress the same: Today, they're in purple tops, black eyeliner, a surfeit of teeny-tiny diamond-stud earrings, each with a pendant around her neck, plus Clark has slung on her Phi Beta Kappa key—and small ankle tattoos reading ix. This crusade is exciting but not lucrative. Without money to pay rent, they slept in a tent for a little while. Pino became ill and thought she had mono, though Clark didn't have mono and they spent all their time together. Maybe it was the old hummus she'd eaten? At the ER, with her laptop to keep plugging away on activist issues, the doctors gave her prednisone, a no-no because she has PTSD from her rape. "It gave me violent hallucinations, which made me suicidal," she says.

In the end, Pino was diagnosed with a staph infection in her blood, though she looks fine today, doing what she does every day—talking to survivors, advising them on Title IX complaints, and polishing media sound bites about necrophiliacs and the taste of silence and every dirty, repulsive thing. "I got a good one today," says Pino. "My Rapist Was Only Fined $25." On a wall, a whiteboard is filled with the names of schools they're about to target, and a map of the U.S. has tiny colored pins stuck in each state where a college has an investigation. Says Clark, "Like at Penn State, when things aren't connected, it's so easy to say, 'Okay, here are four people doing things wrong. We'll fire them, and the issue goes away.' We reframed the debate as, 'What's happening at one school is a microcosm of what's happening everywhere.' "

Taking a seat at a cardboard box, which functions as their desk, they whip out a laptop. "I wouldn't say we control the media, but we have a good grasp of how the media works," says Pino, shrugging her shoulders.

Drawing bright lines over gray areas is one of the things college students do best—you pay money to learn, among like-minded souls, the contours of the world and your place in it. Over the past couple of decades, the college campus has acquired some aspects of a utopia, too, namely, the free-floating myth of itself as a utopia. But different students have different ideas of what this constitutes. It might be a place to go wild, to do the things you won't get to do as a full-fledged adult; it might be a place to search for a political point of view and dedicate yourself to a cause. It's also seen, primarily by boys, as a sexual utopia, where all you have to do is open the door of a frat party to have mind-blowing sex that catapults you into the pantheon of manhood—as opposed to what college sex is often really like, which on its best nights (after emoji flirting, hits off a five-foot bong from a top bunk, and elegant overtures like "Um-want-to-watch-a-movie-in-my-room") still resembles rutting pubescent chimpanzees.

Is there a rampant hook-up culture on campus today? Of course there is. Does the promiscuity that third-wave feminists heralded as empowerment look a little less attractive when practiced by teenagers with little experience and less maturity? You bet. And frustration with hook-up culture is undeniably a part of the anti-rape movement. In some activists' ideal world, there might be no trial, on campus or elsewhere, but instead a simple presumption of guilt.

In all of the allegations, I'm sure there are a few women who are crying wolf, who are vengeful and looking to punish ex-boyfriends—just a few. A percentage may be misunderstandings—confusing signals, something she wanted and then didn't. Drunkenness doesn't clarify these things, even when they should be clear. The way that college girls, for instance, taught from early life to be polite and well behaved, might say "No" during sex with someone they know isn't the same as with a stranger. It's "No, it's not a good idea," "No, please get off me," and then, often, a numb acceptance.

Survivor-activists like Pino and Clark don't accept this worldview—to them, efforts to understand the problem are nearly useless because they insist, only a small number of college sex offenders can be rehabilitated. "There are people out there who want to say that survivors today are feminism gone wild, railroading men for power," says Dirks, the Occidental sociologist. "And they can rely on talking about kids and alcohol, saying what happened was just drunk sex—and, you know, we've all had great drunk sex!" Research, she says, shows that only a small percentage of college guys truly don't know where the line is—"and, for them, if you tell them to get verbal consent, they don't push so hard." She pauses. "But the rest of them—and I know it's hard to think of our brothers, our sons, like this—are calculated predators. They seem like nice guys, but they're not nice guys. In society, we don't like sex offenders in any other area, but for some reason, if you're in college, we love you and want to protect your rights."

As compelling as this rallying cry about unrehabilitatable offenders is, it's not an assessment of the problem that everyone shares. In the center of this philosophical, and administrative, debate are the universities, which need to protect students, including innocent boys who may not look innocent, as in the Duke lacrosse case. There are good people here who have dedicated their lives to helping young people, and one of the mysteries of this issue is how they created a system that devastates so many of the students who come to them desperate for help. At some universities, it's administrative bloat, middle-management laziness, a habit of shoving assault cases under the rug so they don't become nuisances. At others, too much attention has perhaps been paid to the letter of Title IX and not its spirit, with a sluggishness about giving rape survivors what they want—the accused student out of their dorms, classes, and their lives.

A progressive, politically aware school in Manhattan but also apart from it, Columbia, to my knowledge, isn't accused of covering up sadistic gang rapes that have been exposed at other schools. Most of the cases that I learned about, though each horrid in its own way, involves a female student, perhaps engaged in a hook-up session, being forced into an act against her will. A freshman was raped by a junior who taught her Consent 101 class. A student's rapist was moved back into her dorm by mistake. In one case, an assistant athletic coach whom a student confided in about her assault told the head coach, unbidden, and he berated her for three hours. Camila Quarta says she woke up in the middle of the night and the male platonic friend she had invited to sleep over was fingering her. He begged her not to report him, leaving a letter and David Foster Wallace's *This Is Water* at her door. "He wanted me to have it because I'd shared so many of my political views on the world with him," and he said Wallace's speech was important to his Weltanschauung, says Quarta, a die-hard leftist. "I didn't read it." (Citing privacy laws, Bollinger won't comment on the accuracy of these allegations—it would not only be illegal, he says, but immoral.)

Columbia doesn't have an overt *Animal House* atmosphere—though excessive drinking, often at city bars, has always been part of its social life. Here, the issue around assault built slowly. In 2013, as national headlines sprang up, the university's College Democrats thought it was worth inquiring into Columbia's sexual-assault statistics. They asked Bollinger for data beyond what was mandated by federal requirements—they wanted aggregated, anonymous data about punishments meted out when the accused were found guilty. Otherwise, how could they know if the system was working? As "Prezbo," as Bollinger is called, seemed to ignore their requests, students became suspicious, circulating a petition that gathered over 1,500 names.

Still, this was a relatively quiet collegiate tussle—but Sulkowicz, whose father consulted with a high-profile attorney who knows how to work the press, began to grant interviews. And then Bahr, the magazine editor, published an 8,000-word, two-part article about the three women who had accused Paul of assault. The Columbia campus went nuts—was this what had been going on behind closed doors?

Zoe Ridolfi-Starr, a brunette with a fringe of bangs and a clipped way of speaking that resembles Tracy Flick's, took up the question. The daughter of the two female co-founders of the Northern California Innocence Project—"My favorite baby picture is at my first pro-choice rally, wearing a hat with a pin on it that says ABORTION WITHOUT APOLOGY"—she was an Obama organizer in Nevada at 15, president of her class in San Jose, and then a congressional page with plans to run for public office one day.

But after her first year at Columbia, Ridolfi-Starr was at a fraternity party with two men, one of whom was a student and one who wasn't, when they began assaulting her. "It was dirty and confusing and made me feel sick," she said. Then, at the Democratic National Convention, with the "son of a very important person," it happened again. "I was pretty violently assaulted," says Ridolfi-Starr, audibly drawing in a breath. "I was stranded in North Carolina with no one I knew and no way to get home. The scene at the DNC struck me as extremely grimy, extremely exploitative, with people grabbing power sexually, personally, politically—everything. And then the guy lied about what happened and everybody was laughing about it."

Ridolfi-Starr never brought her assaulters to justice. She studied abroad in Argentina, got away for a while. But now she was back at Columbia. And she was ready to channel her fury over her rapes, along with considerable political expertise, into helping students avoid the same fate. If Pino and Clark are national leaders, Ridolfi-Starr is a star organizer of the Columbia branch of the movement. "Columbia is my home, and I deserve to be safe in my home," she says. "I moved across the country to come to my dream school, and then the institution betrays us. It's hideous."

In general, students were outraged by the unethical ways that the guys and Columbia's administration had acted. But some of them thought survivor accounts were difficult to believe: "They're pigeonholing these guys as autistic, predatory rapist dudes who only think about sex," says a sophomore. And, problematically, no one seemed to understand or agree on what rape means or what qualifies. "I had a friend who was like, 'I had sex with this guy and I was really uncomfortable—I wish I'd said something,' " says Trina Bills, a student who graduated last year. "But she didn't, and so he didn't know. When she finally told him, he said, 'You should've told me. It would've been fine—we just wouldn't have done anything.' The communication aspect of this is real. And everyone communicates differently."

Sulkowicz and Ridolfi-Starr shared a hall as freshmen, but the hipster fencer-artist and the earnest political organizer weren't close back then. "I remember Zoe carried around lollipops in her purse, taking them out to suck on like they were accessories," says Sulkowicz. Ridolfi-Starr laughs. "I always have my little thing," she says. "This year, I'm really into headbands."

Now they had a strong bond. At first, they tried to work with Bollinger and the administration. But, Ridolfi-Starr claims, the school refused to put out a place setting for them, choosing instead to work with student-government leaders. "They don't like us. They don't trust us. They don't want to work with this. Their attitude isn't 'Let us address your needs as students.' It's 'How do we mitigate this situation to protect our reputation?' " She sighs. "Going through the experience in your own life is not a qualification they take seriously."

It was time for direct, nonhierarchical, gyno-friendly, partially anonymous, fuck-Prezbo-up action. Ridolfi-Starr and others founded a radical group called No Red Tape—the mantra is "Red tape won't cover up rape"—and put tape over their mouths at a student-activity fair when they were told to stand 20 feet away. ("It's *our* student center!" says Ridolfi-Starr.) She claims that a dean told another student she was "disruptive" and a "liar"—"Can you imagine, a 50-year-old saying that about a 21-year-old?"—and that on Valentine's Day this year, the same dean kicked No Red Tape out of his office when the group asked about funding for the rape crisis center. "Emma said, 'You mean to tell us that as the dean of our school you don't know how anything is funded?' " says Ridolfi-Starr. "We were sharing some of the worst experiences of our lives with him, and he was in a suit, smirking at us. Then he said, "This meeting is over.' " She shakes her head. "It was so unacceptable."

The administration may not have wanted to listen—but Pino and Clark did. At the time, Clark was advising Hobart and William Smith Colleges on a Title IX investigation, and the two of them were coaching a survivor on talking to the *Times*. It wasn't a long way to New York. Ridolfi-Starr burned the midnight oil, and soon 28 students signed a federal Title IX complaint against Columbia that runs about 400 pages, they estimate. (Columbia has yet to hear whether it will be investigated, and added to that list of 78 schools.)

Now that the Title IX complaint had been filed, media and high-level politicians were ready to give the students a platform. Could Sulkowicz be on the front page of the *Times*? Done. And Senator Kirsten Gillibrand, stung by disappointment about her military-rape bill, was crafting a strong campus-rape bill, asking for more protection for students and higher penalties for colleges, slated to come to the floor in late 2014 or 2015. For certain violations, she wants fines of up to one percent of the universities' operating budget, which can run into the billions.

After a press conference at Gillibrand's office, Ridolfi-Starr talked to her parents. "Right before, I sent them an email like, 'Heads up, you may see something,' because they have, um, a Google Alert for my name. How embarrassing." Her moms were very upset. "You know, they're smart people, feminists, and yet one of the first things they said was, 'This happened in Argentina, didn't it? You've always been too adventurous.' " A "mom response," granted, but "so victim-blaming," she says. "Even if I was assaulted in Argentina, it's not my fault for going to Argentina. And also, like, 'No, I was here, doing the same thing I do every weekend—bar, party, apartment; bar, party, dorm.' " She laughs a little bitterly. "Mom, you probably walked by him when you moved me in."

There was still more courage to summon. One day in May, several people crept into the bathrooms of student buildings and wrote the names of the alleged rapists on the wall—not only Paul but prominent guys like a big campus DJ, an athlete training for the Olympics, and a male student who worked at the Bwog, a campus news blog.[*] Columbia immediately dispatched janitors to wash the graffiti away. The anonymous offenders did it again, two times, and Columbia finally barricaded the third bathroom.

Other students started to ask questions—what was this? This was not taking the university to task in a responsible way—this was vigilantism. Ridolfi-Starr was upset by the blowback: Students were saying it was possible these guys weren't even rapists. She couldn't believe it—she, the daughter of Innocence Project moms, making false accusations? A new flyer appeared from an unknown source, this time explaining which students on the list were found guilty and calling Paul a "serial rapist." The accused student was forced to resign from the blog.

Though some students thought social ostracism made sense, the survivor-activist group lost a little bit of support over Bathroomgate. You can't just disappear a student. Some of these guys had been disciplined—who was to say the punishment was too lenient? To Quarta, whose assaulter was only given a semester off, it wasn't enough. "His family sent him to Europe, and meanwhile I was here working my ass off," she says.

Over the summer, accused male students around the country began to organize, too. They're aware of the political brilliance of the anti-rape movement, the way activists have liberated themselves from litigating individual he-said-she-said cases and moved the burden to universities to foster a safe campus environment, to insist they live up to their own ideals as liberal utopias, where nobody ever has to debate semantics.

At Columbia, a suspended varsity rower from Florida is suing the school, and several others are considering suits as well, alleging their own civil rights are being violated: They wouldn't be coming under fire if they weren't men. (No accused students agreed to speak with *New York*, and a message left for Paul was not returned.) Andrew Miltenberg, an attorney for the rower, says there aren't big settlements in the offing, but the kid's academic record should be expunged of a sexual offense, so he can go to medical or law school, proceed with his life.

On the survivor side, activist lawyer Gloria Allred and others are settling civil cases with universities—at the University of Connecticut, awards ranged from $25,000 and $125,000, though one student received $900,000—but no one at Columbia has signed up with an attorney yet, says Ridolfi-Starr. If you take money from the university, you generally sign a confidentiality clause, and that isn't great for the movement.

On a recent afternoon, I went to see Suzanne Goldberg, Columbia's new head liaison on sexual assault and a law professor best known as co-counsel on the Supreme Court case reversing Texas's sodomy law. Her office, which is hung with a LAMBDA poster featuring Lady Liberty, faces Wien Hall, where Paul and Sulkowicz were kissing that night. Columbia's new policy, says Goldberg, is a good one—"one of the best in the country, with more resources dedicated to supporting survivors and other students affected by gender-based misconduct than most." She pauses. "It's hard for most people to navigate sexual relationships and particularly challenging for young adults." She clicks on a computer to show me a poster hanging in undergraduate dorms, with red, yellow, and green lights. Red means stop: You're drunk, asleep, or passed out, or one person doesn't want to have sex. Yellow is pause: mixed signals. Green: A mutual decision has been made about how far to go and "all partners are excited and enthusiastic!" She looks pleased. "A traffic light is useful. It gives people a vocabulary for having what can be an awkward conversation in a congenial way."

---

[*]This article has been corrected to show that the campus news blog where one of the alleged rapists worked is not editorially affiliated with *Blue and White*.

Sitting here, with this distinguished woman in pearls and a black suit, it strikes me how hard it is to talk about sex, rape prevention, any of this, in a way that fixes what's wrong—this is America, after all, where we're supposed to think about sex constantly, but never talk about it. Shifting our standard of consent from "No means no" to "Yes means yes"—a change being considered on many campuses and recently passed for colleges in the California state legislature—could happen in ten years, like seat belts and laws around secondhand smoke. Or it may be much harder in practice than theory, especially if Pino, Clark, and Dirks are right, that the problem has less to do with communication than with serial predators. Memory is fungible, and especially without the guys' perspective, I can't say whether the survivors' accounts are truthful on every point. A woman who doesn't support other women's rape accusations is an ugly thing. And I can definitely report that whatever happened to them was deeply traumatizing. When Sulkowicz ran into Paul earlier this fall, she says, "I turned around and went the other way. Then I started to cry."

Columbia's new policy still leaves appeals in the hands of undergraduate deans, which No Red Tape finds disagreeable. "My view is the deans are ultimately responsible for the protection and caring of our students, and they should be making the decisions," says Bollinger. "But I'm open to talking about that, just like any other question." In mid-September, at a rally on the steps of Low Memorial Library, where President Bollinger's office is located, as they covered Alma Mater's mouth with red tape and dragged dozens of mattresses onto the steps, this issue was front and center, with students holding signs reading FUCK THE DEANS—plus FUCK RAPE CULTURE, FUCK YOUR COMMITTEE, and FUCK YOUR FAKE CONCERN.

For nearly three hours, survivors—females and males, straight and LGBTQ—talked about their experiences, as observers and a scrum of media bore witness. It started with a Barnard student spitting a poem about howling at the moon, and then calling Columbia out as a place where "future leaders may rape and come back." There was the student assaulted the first day of her freshman year 22 years ago, and a freshman with a red *X* over her bellybutton who said she had been assaulted six days ago. There was a beautiful blonde from Barnard who screamed, "Fuck the administration!" and a heavyset student with magenta hair who described campus response to stories of sexual assault as, "When a pretty girl is raped, it's a tragedy, and when a fat woman is raped, she should be grateful." She pleaded with the crowd not to forget about her.

There were students from Union Theological Seminary, who led the crowd in a civil-rights-era song and talked about Sulkowicz, praising the "courage of a young lady on this campus who cracked shame not only for herself but cracked shame in all of us." There was the male former Amherst student-body president, in his salmon polo shirt, khaki shorts, and duck shoes, who talked about his best friend who was expelled for rape last year. When the speaker didn't defend him, he was ostracized and had to move out of his dorm. "I literally lost all of my friends," he says. "For something about which we're right and they're wrong. Rape culture is what's wrong."

It went on and on, and the sun was hot. Ridolfi-Starr tried to cut things short but then dialed her suggestion back when she realized that the crowd was still swelling. Some were thoughtful: Erik Campano, in gold horn-rims, called for a "compassionate campus," where "my guy friends, who are otherwise men of conscience and intelligence, will not come up to me at a party and ask me who at the party might respond to their advances?" And some were out there: "I had a dream last night," said a Barnard student in black leggings, "that President Bollinger and the deans were in a conference room with naked women on their laps, watching our protest on a screen and laughing at us."

It was like an old-time teach-in, with the survivors teaching the people who hadn't been touched in a nasty, formerly unmentionable way by anyone in their lives what it felt like, but at some point everyone realized something had happened to them that they didn't like, in bed, on a mattress, at least once or twice, and their empathy lifted the survivors' resolve even more. Soon, there wasn't a dry eye. The speeches got angrier, and then they got softer, and the crowd pulled in close, as a third-year student at the engineering school began to speak. "I'm not going to give you the list of assaults, and I'm not going to give you the list of rapes, and I'm not going to give you the names. It's a lot of years." She scanned the group, looking as many people as she could in the eye. "I know what it feels like to be the person in these crowds who doesn't know how to hold this bullhorn yet, and I want to say something for those who are not going to come up here. We believe you. I believe you. So stay." She gripped the bullhorn, demanding their commitment. "Just stay."

Critical Thinking

1. California recently passed a "yes means yes" law—in which students at publicly funded colleges and universities must receive an affirmative statement of consent in order to proceed in a sexual relationship. Do you think this should happen in other states? Why or why not?

2. What do you think the responsibility of a college or university's administration is if a student is sexually assaulted on campus?

3. What should the consequences be for a student who is found guilty of rape? What is an appropriate punishment?

Internet References

Men Can Stop Rape
http://www.mencanstoprape.org

National Sexual Violence Resource Center
http://www.nsvrc.org

Rape, Abuse and Incest National Network
http://rainn.org

VANESSA GRIGORIADIS is a contributing editor at *New York* magazine, *Rolling Stone,* and *Vanity Fair.*

Article

Prepared by: Elizabeth Schroeder, EdD, MSW,
Elizabeth Schroeder Consulting

Reporting Rape and Wishing She Hadn't

How One College Handled a Sexual Assault Complaint

WALT BOGDANICH

Learning Outcomes

After reading this article, you will be able to:

- Understand some of the frustrations faced by some students when they report having been raped by a fellow student.

- See the effect a sexual assault can have on a victim.

Geneva, NY—She was 18 years old, a freshman, and had been on campus for just two weeks when one Saturday night last September her friends grew worried because she had been drinking and suddenly disappeared.

Around midnight, the missing girl texted a friend, saying she was frightened by a student she had met that evening. "Idk what to do," she wrote. "I'm scared." When she did not answer a call, the friend began searching for her.

In the early-morning hours on the campus of Hobart and William Smith Colleges in central New York, the friend said, he found her—bent over a pool table as a football player appeared to be sexually assaulting her from behind in a darkened dance hall with six or seven people watching and laughing. Some had their cellphones out, apparently taking pictures, he said.

Later, records show, a sexual-assault nurse offered this preliminary assessment: blunt force trauma within the last 24 hours indicating "intercourse with either multiple partners, multiple times or that the intercourse was very forceful." The student said she could not recall the pool table encounter, but did remember being raped earlier in a fraternity-house bedroom.

The football player at the pool table had also been at the fraternity house—in both places with his pants down—but denied raping her, saying he was too tired after a football game to get an erection. Two other players, also accused of sexually assaulting the woman, denied the charge as well. Even so, tests later found sperm or semen in her vagina, in her rectum and on her underwear.

It took the college just 12 days to investigate the rape report, hold a hearing and clear the football players. The football team went on to finish undefeated in its conference, while the woman was left, she said, to face the consequences—threats and harassment for accusing members of the most popular sports team on campus.

A *New York Times* examination of the case, based in part on hundreds of pages of disciplinary proceedings—usually confidential under federal privacy laws—offers a rare look inside one school's adjudication of a rape complaint amid a roiling national debate over how best to stop sexual assaults on campuses.

Whatever precisely happened that September night, the internal records, along with interviews with students, sexual-assault experts and college officials, depict a school ill prepared to evaluate an allegation so serious that, if proved in a court of law, would be a felony, with a likely prison sentence. As the case illustrates, school disciplinary panels are a world unto themselves, operating in secret with scant accountability and limited protections for the accuser or the accused.

At a time of great emotional turmoil, students who say they were assaulted must make a choice: Seek help from their school, turn to the criminal justice system or simply remain silent. The great majority—including the student in this case—choose their school, because of the expectation of anonymity and the belief that administrators will offer the sort of support that the police will not.

Yet many students come to regret that decision, wishing they had never reported the assault in the first place.

The woman at Hobart and William Smith is no exception. With no advocate to speak up for her at the disciplinary hearing, panelists interrupted her answers, at times misrepresented evidence and asked about a campus-police report she had not seen. The hearing proceeded before her rape-kit results were known, and the medical records indicating trauma were not shown to two of the three panel members.

One panelist did not appear to know what a rape exam entails or why it might be unpleasant. Another asked whether the football player's penis had been "inside of you" or had he been "having sex with you." And when the football player violated an order not to contact the accuser, administrators took five months to find him responsible, then declined to tell her if he had been punished.

Hobart and William Smith officials said they have "no tolerance for sexual assault" and treat all complaints seriously, offering emotional support, counseling and, when necessary, extra security and no-contact orders. They said the school's procedures offer students a fair hearing and were followed in this case. But they cited privacy laws in declining to answer specific questions.

"Campuses are really frustrated by knowing so much about a given case and how reasonable they were and they can't tell this story," said Brett A. Sokolow, a legal adviser to the school. "It's easy to paint them as the bad guy because they are in a position where they can't defend themselves."

Yet privacy laws did not stop Hobart and William Smith from disclosing the name of the woman—a possible rape victim—in letters to dozens of students. "I'm surprised they didn't attach my picture," she said.

After that disclosure, the woman spoke with her parents and agreed to have The Times use her first name, Anna, as well as her photograph.

The school said it was legally obligated to identify Anna to students who might have been called to testify in a possible criminal proceeding. The district attorney who was assessing the case disagreed, calling the identification "unnecessarily specific and, in my mind, a poor exercise of judgment."

A second female student at Hobart and William Smith, who was sexually assaulted at a fraternity party in October 2012, told The Times that one of her two assailants had had his punishment reduced on appeal because of poor questioning by the school's disciplinary panel. Like Anna, the student said friends of the accused had retaliated against her for reporting the assault.

Colleges nationwide are navigating the treacherous legal and emotional terrain of sexual assault. In May, the federal Department of Education disclosed for the first time the names of colleges—55 in all, including Hobart and William Smith—under investigation for possibly violating federal rules aimed at stopping sexual harassment.

Afterward, Hobart and William Smith's president, Mark D. Gearan, sent letters to the college community, saying the school was confident it had not violated federal law. The school's policies and procedures "reflect our commitment to creating and maintaining an academic environment that is free from sexual harassment and misconduct," wrote Mr. Gearan, a former Peace Corps director and White House aide to Bill Clinton. This summer, a committee of faculty, staff and students is studying whether the school can deal more effectively with sexual misconduct.

Turning to the police may not offer a more equitable alternative. For example, as The Times reported in April, the Tallahassee police conducted virtually no investigation of a Florida State University student's rape complaint against the star quarterback Jameis Winston.

College administrators have their own incentive to deal with such cases on campus, since a public prosecution could frighten parents, prospective students and donors. Until last year, Hobart and William Smith's chief fund-raiser also helped oversee the school's handling of sexual assaults. The two functions are now separate.

While the school explained to Anna that talking to the police was an important option, she said, she decided against it after a school administrator said it would be a longer, drawn-out process. When she changed her mind six months later, the district attorney, R. Michael Tantillo, said he had "virtually nothing to work with" and quickly closed the case.

Although federal officials estimate that up to 20 percent of college students will be sexually assaulted in school, Mr. Tantillo said he rarely heard of such reports at Hobart and William Smith. "I guess that's your job to find out why," he told a reporter.

The Red Zone

Hobart and William Smith, on a hill overlooking Seneca Lake, deep in Finger Lakes wine country, is technically two small liberal-arts colleges—Hobart for men, William Smith for women. Its 2,300 students share the same campus, classes, dorms and overall administration, but receive degrees from their respective schools.

It took one visit for Anna to know this was where she wanted to be. "You could see out on the lake—literally, felt like this is what heaven looks like," she said.

Saying goodbye at the beginning of school, Anna's mother was comforted by a professor who had been in touch with her daughter. " 'She really sounds like something,' " she recalled him saying. "He said: 'This is a very preppy place. I'm going to look out for her.' "

Anna, who considers herself anything but preppy, quickly grasped the challenge. "It was really a culture shock for me," she said. "A lot of the girls, they look alike, and I'm not small and have blonde hair and $500 sunglasses." So she searched for students "who didn't fit into that stereotypical William Smith girl."

There was something else: She had entered what is commonly known as the Red Zone, a period of vulnerability for sexual assaults, beginning when freshmen first walk onto campus until Thanksgiving break.

"Students arrive and you have a new environment, new social circle and the fear that goes with new expectations," said Robert S. Flowers, vice president for student affairs. That can lead to experimentation, including excessive drinking and attendant problems.

For that reason, the school held what students call rape seminars, the first in a program that, Mr. Flowers said, has made Hobart and William Smith a leader in preventing sexual violence.

Anna and her girlfriends often joked about how the national rape estimates might affect them. "They kept repeating the statistics," she said, and "every night we would go out we would be like, 'Oh, who's going to be the one?' "

It took just 14 days to find out, Anna said.

Whether one believes the accuser or the accused, it would be hard to dispute that what happened was a life-altering experience that ruptured Anna's nascent friendships, damaged her health, traumatized her family and derailed her college plans.

Emotionally battered, Anna later took a leave and returned home. "I do not recognize myself—I have become someone that I hate," she said. "It was such a toxic environment that I needed to be home and try and find myself again."

The fraternity houses, where so many parties occur, sit high above the lake. And it was at one fraternity, Kappa Sigma, where sometime between 9:30 and 10 P.M. on September 7, Anna attended one of the year's first big social events—a "highlighter party," where students write on one another's clothes with a marker that glows under black light.

Later there was dancing. Anna and a senior football player she had just met were grinding to the music, rubbing their bodies together.

With so many students packed together in the basement, it became hot, and the football player escorted Anna upstairs, where smaller groups congregated in students' bedrooms. A friend tried to stop her, but she went anyway.

Anna said she had begun the evening drinking shots of rum mixed into Gatorade. She drank one beer at the dance, she said, and then the rest of an opened beer her dance partner had given her.

Around midnight, a fraternity member tried to enter his room, but found it locked. He opened the door with his key and caught a glimpse of what would become a pivotal episode in Anna's case: The senior football player was naked, and Anna was sitting on a bed with her top off, covering her breasts. The visitor quickly left.

About the same time, Anna texted the friend who had tried to intervene earlier; she had asked him to hold her keys because she had a hole in her pocket, and wanted them back. A subsequent message was darker, talking of hookups. "He got ten guys to try and hu with me," Anna wrote and added, "I'm scared." She would later tell the hearing panel that she had exaggerated the number to get her friend's attention.

She texted again for her keys, and then wrote, "He won't leave me."

Her friend tried calling, but got no response. Around 1 A.M., he asked another student to check Anna's room. She wasn't there. "We need to find her ASAP," he texted, adding, "She is so drunk."

Eventually he tracked her to a building called the Barn, a dance hall favored by students who do not belong to fraternities. Inside the dimly lit room, a D.J. played music near a couple of pool tables.

Around 1:25 A.M., after 10 minutes of searching, the friend said, he found Anna "bent over the pool table face down with her back toward the wall." She and the senior football player had their pants down, he said, "and it was clear they were having sex."

Anna "had a scared look on her face," he said, as six or seven people, perhaps five feet away, were "looking and laughing."

Anna's friend, a freshman who was also a football player, approached his teammate and told him that he was being disrespectful and had "crossed the line."

"It wasn't me, it was her," the teammate replied.

The friend walked Anna back to her dorm. On the way, another student saw her crying.

To this day, Anna says she remembers nothing about the Barn, the pool table or what happened there.

The Aftermath

It wasn't long before students in Anna's dorm realized something wasn't right. She was pale and disoriented. After she tried to vomit, classmates changed her clothes and put her to bed. Yet they continued to worry, fearing she had been drugged and raped.

One friend remembered that she had asked a football player earlier if he knew where Anna was. He smirked and made a crude allusion to a sexual act with Anna. "I felt very uncomfortable and got up and left," she said. Anna later identified him as one of her assailants.

Soon word spread that something untoward had happened at the Barn.

"The girls and I decided we should call campus security," one friend said. "We knew something was really wrong."

At 2:10 A.M., Sgt. Anthony Pluretti arrived to find 10 to 15 students outside Anna's room. After talking to her and realizing that she "could not remember how many drinks she had consumed and that she had no idea that she was at the Barn," Sergeant Pluretti called campus paramedics, he wrote in a report.

They recommended that a hospital evaluate her. The closest one with a trained sexual-assault nurse was 20 to 30 minutes away in Canandaigua.

The friend who had walked Anna home from the Barn accompanied her to the hospital. As the hours passed, he later told school officials, she began to talk about what had happened at Kappa Sigma: She was in a room with several boys and girls who left her alone with the football player; three times she refused his request for sex; two other football players entered the room, and she was sexually assaulted.

She did not go into great detail, the friend said, because she was "just beginning to remember what happened."

Around 7:30 in the morning, the nurse told Sergeant Pluretti that she had found "internal abrasions and heavy inflammation" and believed that Anna had suffered a forceful sexual assault. No date-rape drugs were found, but based on tests at the hospital, her blood-alcohol level at the time of the first sexual encounter would have been about twice what is considered legally drunk. While driving Anna back to her dorm, Sergeant Pluretti reported, he pulled over four times so she could vomit.

He tried to comfort her, explaining that the school "would respond in whatever manner that would support her," and that she should not feel rushed or pressured into deciding what to do, including whether to file a police report. She did express a desire to see a counselor after she had slept.

Back at Anna's home, around 2:30 on Sunday afternoon, her mother was entertaining guests when the phone rang. "The caller ID said Geneva, and I knew that was bad," she recalled. The caller identified herself as Maria Finger, a psychologist at the school.

"Are you sitting down?" she asked.

Behind Closed Doors

After a few hours of sleep, Anna gave a statement to the Office of Campus Safety. Other students provided their own statements, including the three accused football players. (They are not being identified in this article because the school cleared them.)

The first football player—who had pleaded guilty to a lesser charge in 2012 after being arrested for fighting and resisting arrest—was given a no-contact order, with a warning: "You should not involve your friends in any manner to breach this order." Yet he twice asked one of the other two players to talk to Anna and check on her. He also texted one of Anna's friends, who then texted her: "He wants me to explain something to you. I don't necessarily believe him, but I wanna tell you his side to see if anything clicks considering that you don't remember some of it."

Now it was the school's responsibility under federal law to evaluate the allegations and, if necessary, hold a hearing.

At 3:14 P.M. on Tuesday, Sept. 17, a three-member panel convened behind closed doors to begin adjudicating Anna's complaint.

Such hearings are usually confidential. But The Times obtained a transcript of the proceedings.

The hearing, not dissimilar to what happens at many colleges, bore little resemblance to a court proceeding. Neither the accuser nor the accused were allowed to have lawyers or family members present. They could bring "advisers," but they would be voiceless advisers, prohibited from speaking.

The panelists could act pretty much as they wished, including questioning Anna about internal college reports and witness statements that she was not shown. Also absent were the usual courtroom checks and balances. The panel acted as prosecutor, judge and jury, questioning students and rendering judgment. All members were supposed to be trained for this delicate assignment.

The chairwoman, Sandra E. Bissell, vice president of human resources, was joined by Brien Ashdown, an assistant professor of psychology, and Lucille Smart, director of the campus bookstore, who the school said had expressed an interest in serving.

Boiled down, the complaint alleged that the senior football player had sexually assaulted Anna at the fraternity house while a second player inserted his penis into her mouth. At some point, a third player was alleged to have held her down. The senior was also accused of raping her later in the Barn.

The panel's initial questioning was based mostly on the investigative work of campus officers who aggressively sought out witnesses, followed leads and conducted interviews. According to the federal Education Department, a sexual-assault investigation typically takes around 60 calendar days. Hobart and William Smith did it in a little more than a week.

The hearing followed almost immediately. While a speedy adjudication can help all parties move on with their lives, in this case it left little time for the panel to study witness statements and prepare a cogent line of questioning. It also left Anna with little time to process events of that night, much less familiarize herself with the statements of others, some of which she had received the day before the hearing.

Anna was questioned first. "It was one of the hardest things I have ever gone through," she said later, adding, "I felt like I was talking to someone who knew nothing of any sort of social interaction; what happens at parties; what happens in sex."

She had to relive that evening through questions that jumped around in time, interrupted her answers and misrepresented witness statements. One question incorrectly quoted one of her friends asserting that at the dance Anna had told her that she wanted to go upstairs and have sex; in fact, the friend had said, Anna told her that the football player wanted to have sex.

At a critical point, Anna was about to describe what happened when she was alone upstairs with the first two football players—only to have the panel abruptly change the subject.

Q. OK, just the three of you?

A. Yeah.

Q. And then what happened?

Q: Can I just ask a question? OK, in your statement you do say that you were trying to text.

This is followed by a lengthy exchange about texting.

Later she was asked how the senior football player had tried to undress her, but the panelists cut her off.

Q. It helps us to understand what took place. You know, I'm going to apologize now because we have to ask difficult questions and I really apologize for that.

Q. And for all of us, as hard as it is, if you could be specific, if you are going to talk about a hand holding you, was his left or his right? And if there's a penis involved, is it flaccid, is it erect?

Q. Because the most detail you give us when you tell us the story, the less questions we have to ask for details. And if you want to break just let us know, we can give a couple of minutes.

Q. And as you start your story about this line of events, I just want to—you know what, can we just back up a little bit before that, because before this line of events starts to happen, there has or has not been any coke brought into the room?

This was followed by a discussion of Anna's allegation that some students in the room were using cocaine.

Two of the three panel members did not examine the medical records showing blunt force trauma—it was the chairwoman's prerogative not to share them. Instead, the panel asked what Anna had drunk, who she may have kissed and how she had danced. It was, Anna said, as if admitting you were grinding—a common way of dancing—"means you therefore consent to sex or should be raped."

The panel asked about the Barn—even though Anna stated that she did not remember being there—and whether the friend who found her there might have misconstrued her dancing as

sex. Anna responded that the pool-table witness had said she and the football player had their pants down. "I don't know who dances like that in public," she added.

It was during this discussion that one panelist asked if the witness had seen the player's penis in Anna's vagina or if he had just seen them having sex. "The questioning is absolutely stunning in its absurdity," Anna's lawyer, Inga L. Parsons, said later.

Anna's panelists were supposed to have "adequate training or knowledge" of sexual violence, according to federal guidelines. Even so, they pressed Anna on why she initially had not wanted a rape exam at the hospital.

"Does anyone really believe that it is pleasant to have rectal, vaginal, vulva and cervical swabs taken?" Ms. Parsons said. "Not to mention photographs of your private parts and dye injected into your vagina?"

A Locker-Room Meeting

The three football players then took their turns before the panel. Their accounts were quite different from their accuser's.

The senior player said Anna had given him a lap dance behind the fraternity bar. Upstairs, he said, she kissed him and then performed oral sex on him for two to three minutes. However, he said, he could not get an erection because he was tired from playing football and "a super long bus ride."

At the Barn, he said, she again pulled his pants down. "My flaccid penis was rubbing up against her vagina," he had told the campus police, adding that he had then realized their conduct "was inappropriate" and pulled up his pants.

The second football player said that while his teammate was in the room, Anna pulled down his pants and gave him oral sex. "I didn't consent," he said. "She's doing it all by herself. My hands are not touching her." After a brief period, he said, he told her to stop. "I zippered my pants up, put my belt on, and I walked out the door."

The third player, who faced the weakest case, acknowledged being in the fraternity room but said he left before the sexual encounter.

Anna's friend who recounted the pool-table scene chose not to testify, but, according to Anna, stands by his account.

Records show that the first two players had lied to campus officers when initially asked about Anna's allegations. The panel, though, chose not to ask about it.

The day after the episode, the senior football player told two campus officers that he could not recall Anna's name, even though he had spent much of the evening with her. The player denied having sexual contact with her during or after the fraternity party.

How the Suspects' Stories Changed

Two football players accused of sexual assault lied to the police and then changed basic parts of their accounts after witnesses contradicted them. The college panel that cleared both players failed to ask them any questions about why they had lied.

Player 1

First contacted by police

Did Not Have Sex

He told the police that he spent a few hours with the accuser but did not have sexual contact with her and didn't know her name.

Official police interview

Had Sexual Contact

He now said he received consensual oral sex from the accuser but was too tired from football to get an erection. Player 2 was not involved, he said.

A few days later

Both Players Were Involved

He said that he was "ready to come clean with the truth" and that Player 2 was in the room and received oral

sex. He said he had lied to protect himself against "false allegations."

Player 2

First contacted by police

Was Not There

He told a college official that he was "not involved in whatever happened" with Player 1.

Official police interview

Was Not There

He told the police in two separate interviews that he was never in the room where the alleged assault took place.

A few days later

Had Sex For "A Few Seconds"

He now told police that he was in the room where the accuser said she was assaulted. He said she gave him oral sex for "a couple of seconds" before he got uncomfortable and left.

Source: The New York Times.

Only after the officers confronted him with reports to the contrary did he acknowledge having "sexual contact"—but not sex—at the Barn, and engaging in oral sex with Anna at the fraternity house.

The second player, during three separate interviews with campus officers, denied even being in the fraternity room. It wasn't until his fourth interview two days after the sexual encounter that he confessed to being in the room with his teammate and having oral sex with Anna.

That same day, the football coach, Mike Cragg, summoned the three accused players, two team captains and the pool table witness for a private locker-room meeting where he heard their recollections, then passed on details of Anna's account, hearing transcripts show.

Two days after that meeting, the senior player changed his account a second time, telling the campus police that he "wanted us to know that he was ready to come clean about the truth," records show. A second player had in fact been with him at the fraternity house, the player said, and Anna had given both oral sex. He said he had lied to protect himself and his teammate from Anna's false allegations.

Mr. Cragg declined to answer questions from The Times. But in a written statement he said, "If I were to learn that a

member of my team had behaved in a manner that violated our code of ethics or community standards, I would want him removed from the team immediately." He added: "I have never and would never encourage any player or players to coordinate stories to avoid disciplinary actions."

While the panel did not ask the players about their changed accounts, it did let the senior give an opening statement.

"I come from a wonderful family with strong Christian values," he said. "I have been blessed with a beautiful mother, grandmothers, nieces and amazing aunts." And he added: "I treat women with the respect and honor they deserve."

The Panel Decides

The panel had to answer several basic questions: Did Anna give consent, was she capable of giving consent, and did the senior player violate the no-contact order either directly or through his friends? The standard of proof, mandated under federal guidelines, was preponderance of evidence—was it more likely than not that the students had sexually assaulted Anna?

Several hours after the last witness, the panel announced its decision clearing all three athletes on all counts.

The next day, the panel chairwoman sent Anna written confirmation of the decision, informing her that if she wished to appeal, she could find directions on Page 13 of the sexual-misconduct policy.

But Page 13 said nothing about appeals. Instead, it contained a section titled "False Allegations." The college admitted its mistake, Anna's mother said.

Anna's lawyer appealed the decision to clear the senior player. Mr. Flowers, the student-affairs administrator, granted the family additional time to file its appeal and reviewed the rape-kit results and hospital records. He upheld the panel's ruling, though he did find a violation of the no-contact order.

In an email response to The Times, the panel's chairwoman, Ms. Bissell, said the members were proud of their service. "A great deal of care and focus goes into this work, including extensive training in advance of our service, as well as refresher training prior to serving on a particular panel," she said.

As students returned after winter break, amid swirling rumors of a gang rape, they were greeted by a new mandate: Everyone had to watch an interactive video designed to educate them about sexual assault. The video contained hypotheticals and a series of questions. Answer them, students were told, or be denied campus housing.

The video generated instant controversy, beginning with its title—"ThinkLuv."

"So right from the start, it's the kind of program that's fun and playful and not something that needs to be taken seriously," said Kelsey Carroll, a recent graduate who founded a student group to combat sexism. "Rape is not about love. It is about violence and power."

The campus paper said the video attempted to educate students "while slut-shaming, generalizing, and even being sexist in the process."

Mr. Flowers defended the video, saying 94 percent of students had called it a positive experience.

On May 2, the day after the federal government announced that Hobart and William Smith was among the schools under investigation, the school sponsored an event used on other campuses called "Walk a Mile in Her Shoes," in which men walk around campus in high-heeled shoes to raise awareness of sexual assault. Campus meetings were also held to discuss the issue.

"I think the school has been receiving a lot of pressure from the press, alums and certainly from students to act," Ms. Carroll said. "As a campus we know it's not the case that rapes and sexual assaults are not happening on campus—it's that they aren't reported or the reporting system is failing."

Mr. Tantillo, the district attorney, said that after prosecuting a campus rape case 7 years ago, he had worked with the school to improve its handling of sexual-assault reports. He praised what he said was the thoroughness of its investigation of Anna's case.

But he also understands the questions that might lead a woman to stay silent. "Is this going to be publicized? Is everybody going to know about this? Am I going to be ostracized? Is this going to affect me for the rest of my life? Am I going to lose friends? Are people going to believe me?"

If a woman does decide to come forward, he said, she should do so immediately. "If you wait hours, days or weeks, that gives people plenty of time to get their stories together, to engage other witnesses to support them, and it makes it much, much more challenging."

Looking Back

Disappointment is a recurring theme among many students who ask their schools to adjudicate their sexual-assault complaints.

"Most of the students I work with say, 'Had I known how bad the school process was, I would not have reported at all,'" said Annie E. Clark, who counsels assault victims on their rights.

One reason for this disappointment is that many college hearing panelists lack even the most basic training, said Senator Claire McCaskill, a Missouri Democrat who has investigated the quality of campus rape investigations. The senator recently surveyed 440 colleges and universities and found that one-third had failed to properly train officials adjudicating claims.

A lack of transparency in student hearings makes it difficult, if not impossible, for students to evaluate the way their schools adjudicate complaints. "They are a little like snowflakes—they are all different," said Ms. McCaskill, a former sex-crimes prosecutor.

The police have their own shortcomings, she said, citing the flawed inquiry in the Jameis Winston case in Florida.

The Geneva police hardly distinguished themselves in Anna's case. Detective Brian E. Choffin, relying primarily on his reading of school records, sent the prosecutor an error-filled report.

Detective Choffin mischaracterized witness statements, put the words of one student in the mouth of another, and stated that he "never saw any discrepancies or alterations" in what the two football players told the authorities, even though they had initially lied about having sexual contact with their accuser. And while Anna's blood-alcohol tests had been done many hours after she last had a drink, he also stated unequivocally that her level "would not make a person impaired to the point of blacking out."

The detective defended his report, which disputed much of Anna's account, calling it "thorough and based on facts."

Looking back, Anna said she knows only too well the price of pursuing her complaint—physical threats and obscenities on her dormitory door, being pushed in the dining hall and asked to leave a fraternity party. Her roommate moved out with no explanation.

Mr. Flowers said the school continued to strengthen programs to stop sexual violence. Over the last 2 years, he said, seven students have undergone disciplinary hearings for sexual assaults; four were expelled.

Against her parents' wishes, Anna plans to return to Hobart and William Smith in the fall.

"Someone needs to help survivors there," she said.

Critical Thinking

1. Is it better to report the crime directly to the police rather than to the school?
2. If a woman gets drunk, shouldn't she be responsible for what happens to her?
3. What should the school have done differently, if anything?

Internet References

Create Central
www.mhhe.com/createcentral

The Herald
hwstheherald.com/wordpress/2014/02/20/federal-sexual-assault-investigation-questions-answerdsort

U.S. Department of Education
www.ed.gov/news/press-releases/us-department-education-releases-list-higher-education-institutions-open-title-1

Article

Prepared by: Elizabeth Schroeder, EdD, MSW,
Elizabeth Schroeder Consulting

Receiving Online Sexual Requests and Producing Online Sexual Images: The Multifaceted and Dialogic Nature of Adolescents' Online Sexual Interactions

JOYCE KERSTENS AND WOUTER STOL

Learning Outcomes

After reading this article, you will be able to:

- Understand that researchers and the public have become increasingly concerned with the intersection of adolescent behavior in cyberspace and adolescent attitudes and behaviors toward sex.

- Understand that some research indicates that there is a wide prevalence of "sexting" among adolescents; other research disagrees.

- Understand that translating research findings into information for the public can be a challenging task.

- Understand that it is difficult to make comparisons across research studies because they often differ in how they define "sexting."

Introduction

The Internet is playing an increasingly central role in the exploration and expression of adolescents' sexuality. Adolescents engage in various online sexual activities: they search for information about sex (Suzuki & Calzo, 2004), they engage in implicit and explicit sexual conversations and make obscene and flirtatious comments (Subrahmanyam & Šmahel, 2011) and they produce and send sexual self-images (Lenhart, 2009). Research suggests that the Internet provides adolescents with opportunities to explore and express their sexuality (Valkenburg & Peter, 2011). However, adolescents' online sexual activities may also entail adverse consequences which might be detrimental to their sexual development. Adolescents may feel bothered by receiving online sexual requests from other online individuals. Feeling bothered can be an indication for having experienced harm online. Looking back, adolescents may also negatively evaluate their own online sexual behaviour. A negative evaluation can be an indication that adolescents' online sexual behaviour has led to unintended consequences. In the understanding of the adverse consequences of adolescents' online sexual interactions, many factors come into play. This study examines the incident characteristics and the characteristics of adolescents who received online sexual requests and who produced online sexual images, thereby focusing on requests perceived as bothersome and sexual behaviour evaluated as negative. Identifying which incident characteristics and characteristics of adolescents are related to adverse consequences of online sexual interactions, is a prerequisite to design personalized tools for adolescents that will enable them to recognize and counter online sexual interactions that might entail adverse consequences.

Prevalence of Receiving Online Sexual Requests and Producing Online Sexual Images

Receiving online sexual requests refers to receiving requests to talk about sex, questions about private parts and requests for sexual intercourse or to undress in front of a webcam. Prior research predominantly investigated the prevalence of unwanted online sexual requests, i.e., online sexual solicitations (e.g., Ybarra, Espelage, & Mitchell, 2007). The three *Youth Internet Safety Surveys* conducted in the United States show a decline in receiving unwanted sexual solicitations: from 19% to 9% between 2000 and 2010. These studies also investigated the impact of the solicitations. The percentage of adolescents who reported feeling distressed declined from 5% in 2000 to 3% in 2010 (Jones, Mitchell, & Finkelhor, 2012). These studies did not encompass questions about wanted sexual solicitations, i.e., developmentally normal and/or consensual sexual requests as a part of adolescents' sexual exploration (e.g., Subrahmanyam & Šmahel, 2011). The *EU Kids Online* survey, a representative sample of children aged 9–16 years in 25 European countries, investigated the prevalence of receiving and seeing online sexual messages and found that 15% of the surveyed children had received or seen sexual messages on the Internet and that 4% of the surveyed children reported being bothered by these messages (Livingstone, Haddon, Görzig, & Ólafsson, 2011). However, the questions about sexual messaging included items about seeing posts from others and seeing other people perform sexual acts, i.e., the survey did not limit sexual messaging exclusively to online interactions, but included passively seeing sexual content from others. To our knowledge, no study has investigated the prevalence of receiving online sexual requests and how many adolescents perceived this as bothersome.

Producing online sexual images refers to making and sending sexual images of someone else and sexual self-exposure in front of a webcam. Prior research primarily investigated the prevalence of producing and distributing online sexual self-images and sexual images of peers through the Internet or by mobile phone. In research, this behaviour is labelled as "sexting" (Lounsbury, Mitchell, & Finkelhor, 2011; Ringrose, Gill, Livingstone, & Harvey, 2012). Since sexting is a relatively new practice, studies on sexting are still scarce. The prevalence rates found in the—predominantly North-American—studies differ considerably, ranging from 2 to 20% (Livingstone et al., 2011; Mitchell, Finkelhor, Jones, & Wolak, 2012). Lounsbury et al. (2011) state that methodological inadequacies—for example, lack of consensus on definitions—account for the large differences in the studies they reviewed. No prior research has investigated how adolescents evaluated having produced online sexual material. Therefore, we asked:

RQ1: What is the prevalence of (a) receiving online sexual requests and (b) producing online sexual images?

RQ2: How many adolescents (a) perceive receiving online sexual requests as bothersome and how many adolescents (b) evaluate producing online sexual images as negative?

Incident Characteristics

Insight in the context of adolescents' online sexual interactions is important to understand why these interactions may entail adverse consequences. The concerns about adolescents' online sexual interactions primarily address two issues: (1) male perpetrators sending online sexual requests to minors for the purpose of sexual abuse and exploitation and (2) adolescents' inability to realistically estimate the risks of their own online sexual behaviour. Sender characteristics (age, gender, and familiarity) are important to gain insight in the context of online sexual interactions. However, adolescents who receive online sexual requests may also engage in sending these requests. This can indicate that sending and receiving sexual requests is reciprocal, for example to initiate a romantic relationship, or that sending sexual requests is related to adolescents' developing sexuality.

Little is known about the incident characteristics of receiving online sexual requests and producing online sexual images. The aforementioned *Youth Internet Safety Surveys* found that more males than females were identified as senders of online sexual requests and most youth whose contact with senders was limited to the Internet were not certain of the sender's age. Furthermore, the proportion of senders of sexual requests personally known increased between 2000 and 2010 and most senders were identified as same-aged peers (Jones et al., 2012; Wolak, Mitchell, & Finkelhor, 2006). This tendency to communicate within the context of existing relationships is consistent with findings from the *EU Kids Online* survey (Livingstone et al., 2011). A survey conducted in the United States found that sexting occurs most often in the following contexts: solely between two romantic partners, first between partners and then shared with others and between adolescents hoping to enter a romantic relationship (Lenhart, 2009). Findings from a qualitative study indicate that sexual images are being used as "a form of 'relationship currency' with boys asking for them and with 'pressures' upon girls to produce/share such images" (Ringrose et al., 2012, p. 13). To date, no study has investigated the relation between sexual requests perceived as bothersome, evaluating producing online sexual material as negative and incident characteristics. To our knowledge, no study has investigated adolescents' own role—either as sender or receiver—in online sexual interactions or investigated the motives for engaging in online sexual behaviour. To understand why online sexual requests and producing online sexual images may and may not entail adverse consequences, we asked:

RQ3: What are incident characteristics of sexual requests perceived as bothersome and behaviour evaluated as negative, in terms of (a) the characteristics of the communication partner, (b) the own role of adolescents in communication and (c) motives for exposing?

Investigating incident characteristics provides insight into the way receiving online sexual requests and producing online sexual materials are embedded within a broader communicative context and existing offline and online relations.

Characteristics of Adolescents

Prior research primarily investigated the socio demographic characteristics of adolescents who receive online sexual requests and who produce online sexual images (e.g., Jones et al., 2012; Lenhart, 2009; Livingstone et al., 2011). An overall picture of adolescents who receive requests and produce images is missing (e.g., Ringrose et al., 2012). Prior research revealed that adolescents' online victimization can be associated with the frequency of Internet use, online disinhibition, a lower level of psychological wellbeing, a lower level of self-control and being cyberbullied (e.g., Barak, 2005; Bossler & Holt, 2010; Ybarra et al., 2007). Producing online sexual images is categorized as risk-taking behaviour. Prior research revealed that risk-taking behaviour can be associated with the aforementioned characteristics (e.g., Grasmick, Tittle, Bursik, & Arneklev, 1993; Livingstone & Helsper, 2007). Parental mediation generally refers to parental management of children's media use. Parental mediation of adolescents' Internet use might reduce the likelihood of online risks and might decrease online risk-taking behaviour (Pardoen & Pijpers, 2006; van den Eijnden & Vermulst, 2006). To develop an integrative perspective that helps us to understand why online sexual interactions may and may not entail adverse consequences for adolescents, we asked:

RQ4: What are the characteristics of (a) adolescents who reported bothersome online sexual requests and (b) adolescents who evaluated their behaviour negatively?

We compared the characteristics of these adolescents with the characteristics of adolescents who were not bothered and who did not evaluate their behaviour as negative. Knowing who is vulnerable online and why and conversely, who is not, is a prerequisite for the protection and ultimately the empowerment of vulnerable adolescents.

Method
Sample and Procedure

For this cross-sectional study a sample was taken from *Youth & Cybersafety*, a 4-year Dutch research project on online risks for children (2009–2013) commissioned by the Dutch Ministry for Education, Culture and Science.[1] The questionnaire on online sexual risks and online sexual risk-taking behaviour was developed in co-operation with *Rutgers WPF*, a Dutch knowledge centre on sexual and reproductive health and rights. The questionnaire was developed on the basis of feedback from 25 adolescents and tested in a pilot study for validity and reliability and to refine question wording, sequence and questionnaire length. 442 adolescents participated in the pilot study. In total, 4538 adolescents filled in the online questionnaire. Validity checks for nonsensical answers resulted in the removal of 85 respondents of our dataset. The data analysis was based on 4453 completed questionnaires filled in by respondents attending secondary schools (51.2% male). The age range of the adolescent sample was 11–18 years ($M = 13.9$, $SD = 1.48$). Younger adolescents (11–14 years) were over represented. Data were collected between January 2011 and April 2011. Parental consent and adolescents' assent were obtained before participation.

Adolescents were not directly recruited; we randomly sampled secondary schools. Schools exclusively providing special or practical education that were excluded from the sample, since pupils attending these schools require a different research approach. Schools were sent a letter asking them to participate in the *Youth & Cybersafety* research project. Seventeen secondary schools from three different levels—pre-vocational education (vmbo), higher general secondary education (havo), and pre-university education (vwo) participated. Each participating school received a report in which the findings from the school were compared with the overall findings. A detailed account of the recruitment and sampling procedures can be found elsewhere (Kerstens & Stol, 2012).

Data were collected using an online survey. The questionnaire was filled in at school during class in the presence of researchers and supervisors. We redesigned classrooms in order to create privacy for each respondent. Each respondent was provided with a unique number code making it impossible to link answers to identifying information of the participant. At the start of the questionnaire, participants were notified that (1) the questionnaire would be about the internet and online sexual risks; (2) that the investigators had no chance to identify who had given the answers; and (3) that they could stop at any point in time if they wished.

Measures
Prevalence and Adolescents' Perception

Receiving sexual requests. Participants were asked if they had received online sexual requests: questions about sex, and requests for sexual intercourse, questions about private parts, requests to undress in front of a webcam. Response categories were 1 (*never*), 2 (*once*), and 3 (*several times*). Participants who reported receiving online sexual requests were asked how they perceived the incidences. Response categories were 1 (*pleasant*), 2 (*common*), and 3 (*bothersome*).

Producing sexual images. Since not all adolescents are familiar with the term "sexting", the term 'sexting' was not used in the questionnaire (e.g., Ringrose et al., 2012). Two types of producing and distributing sexual images were investigated. Participants were asked (1) if they had made sexual images of someone else within the past 12 months: photo or video of intimate body parts, masturbation and sexual intercourse. Response categories were 1 (*never*), 2 (*once*) and 3 (*several times*). Participants were asked (2) if they had exposed their breasts and/or private parts in front of a webcam within the past 12 months. Response categories were 1 (*never*), 2 (*once*) and 3 (*several times*). Participants who reported having exposed their breasts and/or private parts in front of a webcam were asked how they evaluated their exposure in retrospect. Response categories were 1 (*pleasant*), 2 (*common*), and 3 (*bad*).

Incident Characteristics

Gender of sender and webcam partner. To measure the gender of the sender of sexual requests and webcam partner, we asked participants to indicate whether they knew the gender of the sender. Measures of knowing the gender of the sender of sexual requests and the webcam partner were 1 (*male*), 2 (*female*), and 3 (*don't know*).

Estimated age of sender and webcam partner. Measures of knowing the age of the sender of sexual requests and the webcam partner were 1 (*more than 5 years younger*), 2 (*more than 2 years younger*), 3 (*approximately the same age*), 4 (*more than 2 years older*), 5 (*more than 5 years older*), and 6 (*don't know*).

Familiarity with sender and webcam partner. To measure the familiarity with sender and webcam partner, we asked participants if they knew senders and webcam partners in real life. Response categories were 1 (*I know the other person well in real life (for example, from school)*, 2 (*I have met the other person in real life, but I don't know him/her very well*), and 3 (*I know the other person only via the Internet*).

Receiver's role in online communication. Participants who reported having received online sexual requests were asked if they had sent online sexual requests themselves.

Characteristics of Adolescents

Frequency of Internet use. Participants were asked to indicate how many hours per day on average they were active on the Internet, for example engaging in activities such as gaming, sending emails, or chatting.

Online disinhibition. Online disinhibition—a lower level of behavioural inhibitions in the online environment—may be particularly significant when considered in the context of sexual risks and sexual risk-taking behaviour on the Internet (Whittle, Hamilton-Giachritsis, Beech, & Collings, 2013). Online disinhibition was measured using a 7-item scale based on studies on the online disinhibition effect (Suler, 2004) and a study by Schouten, Valkenburg, and Peter (2007). The items were rated on a 5-point Likert scale from 1 (*agree entirely*) to 5 (*disagree entirely*). The Cronbach's alpha was 0.86.

Parental mediation. We measured adolescents' perspective on parental mediation by asking questions about the four basic strategies of parental mediation: supervision (parent is present while using the Internet), restrictive mediation (parent sets rules), monitoring (parent checks records afterward), and active mediation (parent communicates on Internet use and safety). The items were rated on a 3-point Likert scale: 1 (*(almost) always*), 2 (*sometimes*) and 3 (*never*).

Psychological well-being. Psychological well-being can be defined as "people's positive evaluations of their lives" (Diener & Seligman, 2004, p. 1). Psycho social well-being was measured using a 12-item scale based on the study by Vandebosch, Van Cleemput, Mortelmans, and Walrave (2006) in which items from the *Self-Description Questionnaire* by Ellis, March, and Richards and the *SHIELDS Questionnaire* by Gerson were implemented. The items were rated on a 5-point Likert scale from 1 (*agree entirely*) to 5 (*disagree entirely*). The Cronbach's alpha was 0.85.

Self-control. Low self-control is an individual trait associated with risk-taking behaviour. Grasmick, Tittle, Bursik, and Arneklev (1993) developed a 24-item scale to measure self-control. We abbreviated the original scale to 13 items. The six sub-components of the original scale—impulsivity, simple tasks, risk-taking, physical activities, self-centeredness, and temper—were represented. The 13 items were rated on a 3-point Likert scale from 1 (*(almost) never*) to 3 (*often*). The Cronbach's alpha was 0.74.

Cyberbullying. We asked respondents if they had been the target of one or more negative actions conducted by others via Internet or mobile phones within the past three months: spreading malicious rumors, posting threats or embarrassing information, deliberate exclusion, and/or posting embarrassing photos or videos on the Internet. If respondents answered affirmative at one or more of the questions and evaluated these actions as offensive, we labeled them as cyberbully victims: a dichotomous variable (0–1).

Results
Prevalence and Adolescents' Perception

How prevalent are incidences of receiving online sexual requests and producing online sexual images (*RQ1*) and how did adolescents perceive and evaluate the incidences (*RQ2*)? Of the overall sample, 25.4% of the adolescents reported having received one or more online sexual requests. Table 1 depicts the percentages of participants who received specific sexual requests. Percentages are presented according to gender, age, and educational level. Among all sexual requests,

asking general questions about sex had the highest prevalence, whereas requests to undress before the webcam had the lowest prevalence. Female participants did not differ from male participants, although female participants more often received requests to do something sexual. Levels of receiving online sexual requests differed according to age and educational level. As adolescents get older, they are more likely to receive online sexual requests. Adolescents attending pre-university education received fewer requests.

Table 2 depicts the perception of receiving online sexual requests. Percentages are presented according to gender, age and educational level. The majority of the adolescents who received online sexual requests perceived the incidences as pleasant or common (71.2%). Less than one-third of the adolescents (28.8%) perceived the incidences as bothersome. Of the overall sample, 7.0% of the participants reported bothersome incidences (*n* = 312).

Percentages of reported bothersome incidences differed according to gender, age and educational level. Female participants and adolescents attending pre-vocational education reported more bothersome incidences, and younger adolescents reported more bothersome incidences than older adolescents.

Table 1   Percentages of Incidences of Online Sexual Requests (*n* = 4,453)

	Questions about sex	Requests for sexual intercourse	Questions about breasts and/or genitals	Requests to undress on webcam	One or more of the mentioned requests
Gender	*	NS	**	**	NS
Boys	23.3%	15.9%	10.3%	7.5%	25.4%
Girls	20.6%	16.1%	14.1%	10.7%	25.3%
Age	**	**	**	**	**
≤ 12 years	9.9%	6.7%	6.0%	5.6%	12.7%
13–14 years	18.6%	13.3%	11.5%	8.2%	22.7%
15–16 years	35.1%	26.8%	17.2%	13.1%	37.7%
≥ 17 years	38.2%	26.8%	17.1%	11.8%	40.5%
Educational level	**	**	**	**	**
Lower pre-vocational education	23.8%	19.2%	13.7%	10.7%	28.5%
Higher general secondary education	23.5%	17.2%	12.9%	9.5%	26.6%
Pre-university education	18.8%	11.6%	9.8%	6.9%	20.9%
Total	**22.0%**	**16.0%**	**12.1%**	**9.1%**	**25.4%**

**P<0.01, Chi-Square, *P<0.05, Chi-Square; NS difference is not significant.

Table 2   Perception of Having Received Online Sexual Requests ($n = 1,108$)

	Pleasant	Common	Bothersome
Gender **			
Boys	28.3%	59.6%	12.1%
Girls	9.9%	44.8%	45.3%
Age **			
≤ 12 years	11.3%	46.4%	42.3%
13–14 years	16.4%	51.2%	32.4%
15–16 years	21.7%	55.2%	23.0%
≥ 17 years	33.3%	53.9%	12.7%
Educational level **			
Lower pre-vocational education	14.7%	49.1%	36.2%
Higher general secondary education	23.2%	54.7%	22.1%
Pre-university education	23.7%	55.8%	20.6%
Total	**19.4%**	**52.4%**	**28.2%**

**P<0.01, Chi-Square.

Table 3 depicts the percentages of participants who indicated having produced online sexual images: exposing breasts and/or private parts in front of a webcam and making photos or videos of intimate body parts, masturbation, and/or sexual intercourse. Percentages are presented according to gender, age, and educational level. A minority of the participants reported having produced online sexual images (3.0%).

Percentages of producing online sexual images differed according to gender and age: male adolescents produced more online sexual images than female adolescents and older adolescents produced more online sexual images than the younger ones.

Table 4 depicts how adolescents evaluated having exposed breasts and/or private parts in front of a webcam in retrospect. Percentages are presented according to gender, age and educational level. 32.4% of the participants felt bad about their behaviour. Of the overall sample, 0.5% of the participants felt badly about their sexual exposure ($n = 22$).

Some cells had an expected count less than 5; therefore, statistic tests to find out whether differences are significant were not possible. However, more females than males, more young adolescents than older adolescents and more adolescents attending lower pre-vocational education felt bad about their online sexual behaviour. The most frequently reported negative consequences were sexual harassment, bullying and negative comments—offline as well as online—and general regret.

Incident Characteristics

Research question 3 asked what specific incident characteristics are related to receiving online sexual requests and exposing breasts and/or private parts in front of a webcam, in terms of (1) the characteristics of the communication partner, (2) the role of the adolescent him-herself in online communication and (3) motives for exposing. Table 5 depicts the percentages of incident characteristics of receiving online sexual requests between participants who perceived these requests as bothersome and those who did not. Percentages are presented according to gender and age of sender, familiarity with sender and the receiver's role in online sexual communication.

If we compare online sexual requests that are perceived as pleasant or common with sexual requests that are perceived as bothersome, it appears that sexual requests perceived as bothersome more often originated from males or from senders whose sex is unknown, from senders more than 5 years older than the recipient and from senders solely known from the Internet. The role of the receivers of online sexual requests was also significant: being passive in online sexual communication, i.e., not sending online sexual requests to others is related to perceiving online sexual requests as bothersome. The results indicate that anonymity in online sexual communication makes it more likely that online sexual requests are perceived as bothersome.

Table 3 Percentages of Incidences of Producing Online Sexual Images ($n = 4{,}453$)

	Exposing breasts and/or genitals on webcam	Making photos or videos of intimate body parts, masturbation, and/or sexual intercourse	One or more of the mentioned activities
Gender	NS	**	**
Boys	1.7%	2.6%	3.7%
Girls	1.4%	1.2%	2.3%
Age	**	*	**
≤ 12 years	0.7%	1.0%	1.7%
13–14 years	1.3%	1.7%	2.7%
15–16 years	2.4%	2.5%	4.1%
≥ 17 years	2.8%	4.0%	5.6%
Educational level	NS	**	**
Lower pre-vocational education	1.3%	1.6%	2.4%
Higher general secondary education	2.3%	3.0%	4.7%
Pre-university education	1.3%	1.5%	2.6%
Total	**1.5%**	**1.9%**	**3.0%**

**P<0.01, Chi-Square, *P<0.05, Chi-Square; NS difference is not significant.

Table 4 Evaluation in Retrospect about Exposing Breasts and/or Private Parts in Front of a Webcam ($n = 68$)

	Pleasant	Common	Bad
Gender			
Boys	44.7%	28.9%	26.3%
Girls	23.3%	36,7%	40,0%
Age			
≤ 12 years	16.7%	33.3%	50.0%
13–14 years	36.7%	36.7%	26.7%
15–16 years	32.0%	28.0%	40.0%
≥ 17 years	57.1%	28.6%	14.3%
Educational level			
Lower pre-vocational education	43.5%	17.4%	39.1%
Higher general secondary education	20.8%	50.0%	29.2%
Pre-university education	42.9%	28.6%	28.6%
Total	**35.3%**	**32.4%**	**32.4%**

Table 5　Prevalence of Incident Characteristics of Receiving Online Sexual Requests for Adolescents Who Perceived This As Pleasant or Common (*n* = 796), and for Those Who Perceived This As Bothersome (*n* = 312)

	Perceived as pleasant or common	Perceived as bothersome
Gender of sender **		
Male	38.2%	64.7%
Female	50.1%	9.9%
Gender unknown	11.7%	25.3%
Total	**100.0%**	**100.0%**
Age of sender **		
Peer (about the same age)	81.3%	53.8%
>5 years older	4.5%	12.2%
Age unknown	14.2%	34.0%
Total	**100.0%**	**100.0%**
Familiarity with sender **		
Well acquainted, also offline	69.8%	27.9%
Little acquainted	17.3%	23.4%
Acquainted only online	12.8%	48.7%
Total	**100.0%**	**100.0%**
Receiver's role in online sexual communication **		
Active: sent sexual requests to others	54.0%	18.3%
Passive: did not sent sexual requests to others	46.0%	81.7%
Total	**100.0%**	**100.0%**

** P<0.01, Chi-Square.

Table 6 depicts the percentages of incident characteristics of exposing breasts and/or private parts in front of a webcam between participants who felt bad about their behaviour in retrospect and those who did not. A negative evaluation of sexual behaviour is related to reported negative consequences. Percentages are presented according to gender and age of sender, familiarity with sender and motives of participants.

Some cells had an expected count less than 5; therefore, statistic tests to find out whether differences are significant were not possible. However, participants more often felt bad about their behaviour when the webcam partner was male and when the webcam partner was known only from the Internet. A positive evaluation of sexual behaviour more often occurred when the webcam partner was a peer. It is not surprising that a negative evaluation is related to negative motives for engaging in sexual behaviour in front of a webcam.

Characteristics of Vulnerable and Risk-Taking Adolescents

Research question 4 asked (1) what are the characteristics of adolescents who received online sexual requests and perceived this as bothersome and (2) what are the characteristics of adolescents who produced online sexual images and felt bad about it in retrospect. Table 7 depicts the characteristics of participants who received online sexual requests and perceived this as bothersome and participants who did not. The analysis includes 6 characteristics: socio demographic characteristics, Internet use,

Table 6   Prevalence of Incident Characteristics of Exposing Breasts and/or Private Parts in Front of a Webcam for Adolescents Who Felt Bad about Their Behaviour in Retrospect ($n = 22$) and Those Who Did Not ($n = 46$)

	No bad feelings in retrospect $n = 46$	Bad feelings in retrospect $n = 22$
Gender of the webcam partner		
Male	39.1%	50.0%
Female	54.3%	27.3%
Gender unknown	6.5%	22.7%
Total	**100.0%**	**100.0%**
Age of the webcam partner		
Peer (about the same age)	89.1%	54.4%
>5 years older	2.2%	0.0%
Age unknown	8.7%	45.5%
Total	**100.0%**	**100.0%**
Familiarity with the webcam partner		
Well acquainted, also offline	58.7%	22.7%
Little acquainted	15.2%	13.6%
Acquainted only online	26.1%	63.6%
Total	**100.0%**	**100.0%**
Motives for exposure		
Positive motives (excitement, enjoyment)	93.5%	59.13%
Negative motives (social pressure, coercion)	6.5%	40.9%
Total	**100.0%**	**100.0%**

parental mediation, individual characteristics, negative online experiences and initiative in online sexual communication.

Table 7 reveals that receiving online sexual requests and perceiving this as bothersome ($n = 312$) is associated with being female and being younger, a higher level of online disinhibited behaviour, a lower level of psychological well-being and being cyberbullied. Conversely, a greater likelihood of receiving online sexual requests and perceiving this as pleasant or common ($n = 796$) is associated with being male, a lower level of parental mediation and a high frequency of Internet usage. Age is strongly associated with a positive perception: as adolescents get older, the likelihood of perceiving online sexual requests as bothersome decreases. A lower level of self-control is associated with receiving online sexual requests, regardless of a positive or negative perception.

Adolescents who take initiative in online sexual interaction are less likely to perceive receiving online sexual requests as bothersome.

Table 8 depicts the characteristics of participants who produced online sexual images. The columns of Table 8 show the results for (1) exposing breasts and/or private parts in front of a webcam and a negative evaluation; (2) exposing breasts and/or private parts in front of a webcam and no negative evaluation and (3) making photos or videos of intimate body parts, masturbation, or sexual intercourse. We included the following characteristics: socio demographic characteristics, Internet use, parental mediation, individual characteristics and negative online experiences. Exposing breasts and/or private parts in front of a webcam and feeling bad about this ($n = 22$) is associated with a higher level of online disinhibited

Table 7 Logistic Regression Analysis for Variables Predicting Receiving Online Sexual Requests for Adolescents Who Perceived This As Bothersome (*n* = 796) and Adolescents Who Perceived This As Pleasant or Common (*n* = 312)

Predictor	Perceived the requests as bothersome		Perceived the requests as pleasant or common	
	OR	95% CI	OR	95% CI
Socio demographic characteristics				
Girl	4.04 *	2.96–5.51	0.75	0.59–0.94
Age	1.04	0.95–1.13	1.31 *	1.22–1.40
Internet use				
Frequency	1.09	1.00–1.20	1.14 *	1.06–1.23
Online disinhibition	1.28 *	1.09–1.50	1.10	0.96–1.26
Parental mediation				
Parental supervision while using the Internet	1.03	0.78–1.35	0.91	0.72–1.16
Rules about Internet use and activities	0.95	0.72–1.25	0.79	0.63–0.99
Monitoring Internet use (afterward)	1.03	0.89–1.19	0.91	0.81–1.03
Communication on Internet use and safety	0.98	0.87–1.11	0.89	0.80–0.98
Individual characteristiscs				
Psychological well-being	0.72 *	0.59–0.88	1.12	0.94–1.34
Self-control	0.42 *	0.28–0.62	0.24 *	0.17–0.33
Negative online experiences online				
Was bullied online	2.70 *	1.97–3.69	1.32	0.92–1.88
Initiative in online sexual communication				
Produced sexual images (photo,video,cam)	1.48	0.83–2.64	2.03 *	1.23–3.37
Sent sexual requests	1.33	0.92–1.92	17.84 *	13.88–22.94
$\div^2$	254.65		1335.08	
Nagelkerke R^2	0.15		0.46	

Note: *n* = 4453. Results of girls were compared with boys (reference group). *P<.05,*P<.01**.

behaviour and being cyberbullied. Conversely, a greater likelihood of reporting no negative feelings after exposing breasts and/or private parts (*n* = 46) is associated with a high frequency of Internet usage and a lower level of self-control. Age is strongly associated with a positive evaluation: as adolescents get older, the likelihood of feeling bad about sexual exposure in front of a webcam decreases.

Making photos and videos of intimate body parts, masturbation and/or sexual intercourse (*n* = 83) is associated with being male and being older, a high frequency of Internet use, a higher level of online disinhibited behaviour and a lower level of self-control.

Discussion

This article investigated adolescents receiving online sexual requests and adolescents engaging in producing online sexual images. Our purpose was to enhance our understandings of the complex nature of these online sexual interactions in terms of (1) their perception and evaluation, (2) incident characteristics and (3) the characteristics of adolescents involved. The findings suggest that a more nuanced view on adolescents' online sexual interactions is required. Prior studies on online sexual risks primarily framed adolescents either as victims—passively being at risk and vulnerable—or as perpetrators—actively engaging

Table 8 Logistic Regression Analysis for Variables Predicting Exposing in Front of Webcam for Adolescents Who Felt Bad about This ($n = 22$) and Adolescents Who Did Not ($n = 46$) and for Variables Predicting Making Sexual Photos or Videos ($n = 83$)

Predictor	Sexual exposure feeling bad		Sexual exposure no bad feelings		Making sexual photos or videos	
	OR	95% CI	OR	95% CI	OR	95% CI
Socio-demographic characteristics						
Girl	1.32	0.50–3.45	0.79	0.41–1.54	0.53 **	0.32–0.88
Age	1.19	0.99–1.43	1.34 *	1.03–1.73	1.18 **	1.02–1.36
Internet use						
Frequency	1.37	0.99–1.88	1.43 **	1.14–1.78	1.35 **	1.15–1.58
Online disinhibition	2.74 **	1.74–4.32	1.37	0.98–1.91	1.43 **	1.12–1.83
Parental mediation						
Parental supervision	0.63	0.20–2.06	0.42	0.13–1.33	1.45	0.90–2.34
Rules about Internet use	1.10	0.43–2.84	0.85	0.43–1.72	0.9	0.54–1.50
Monitoring Internet use (afterward)	1.22	0.76–1.96	0.96	0.67–1.39	0.89	
Communication on Internet use	0.64	0.41–1.00	1.00	0.75–1.33	0.95	0.77–1.18
Individual characteristiscs						
Psychological well-being	0.93	0.48–1.81	1.06	0.64–1.74	1.01	0.70–1.45
Self-control	1.32	0.39–4.51	0.14 **	0.06–0.34	0.16 **	0.09–0.31
Negative online experiences						
Was bullied online	4.61 **	1.65–12.93	0.81	0.24–2.72	1.47	0.70–3.07
$\div^2$	47.34		70.06		105.88	
Nagelkerke R^2	0.18		0.15		0.14	

*Note: N = 4453. Results of girls were compared with boys (reference group). *P<.05,*P<.01**.

in risky and deviant behaviour. This strict distinction conceals the multifaceted, dialogic and developmentally normal nature of adolescents' online sexual interactions.

Our findings indicate that receiving online sexual requests is quite common among adolescents. Requests for information about sex had the highest prevalence. This is in line with previous research (Ward, 2004). The levels of receiving requests did not differ considerably for male and female adolescents, although female adolescents more often receive requests to do something sexual. The likelihood of receiving sexual requests increases when adolescents get older. An increased interest in sexuality and sexual relationships is developmentally normal for adolescents (Subrahmanyam & Šmahel, 2011). Producing online sexual images is relatively rare. Older adolescents are more likely to produce sexual materials than younger

adolescents. This finding is in line with other studies (Lenhart, 2009; Livingstone et al., 2011). Male adolescents send more sexts than female adolescents. Findings in other studies, however, are inconclusive.

One-fourth of the adolescents who received an online sexual request perceived this as bothersome. Looking back, one-third of the adolescents who exposed breasts and/or private parts in front of a webcam felt bad about their behaviour. Adolescents reported negative consequences such as sexual harassment, bullying and negative comments—offline as well as online. The finding that female and younger adolescents more often perceive sexual requests as bothersome is in line with previous research (Jones et al., 2012 Livingstone et al., 2011). The degree of sexual interest and subsequent sexual activity increases with adolescents' age (Cubbin, Santalli, Brindis, &

Braveman, 2005). Therefore, receiving sexual requests might be developmentally inappropriate for younger adolescents. Female adolescents use the Internet for communication purposes more often, which increases the likelihood of experiencing the downsides of communicating online (Mitchell, Finkelhor, & Wolak, 2003).

Online sexual requests originating from senders who are male and whose age and sex are unknown were more often perceived as bothersome. Requests originating from peers and senders adolescents were well acquainted with and were more often perceived as pleasant or common. Although anonymity might be beneficial for adolescents who send sexual requests (Valkenburg & Peter, 2011), our findings suggest that this is not the case for adolescents who receive these requests. The same picture emerges for adolescents who exposed themselves in front of a webcam. Not surprisingly, a negative assessment of this behaviour is related to negative motives such as social pressure and coercion. Previous research has shown that sexting is often coercive (Ringrose et al. 2012). Interestingly, being passive in online communication is associated with a negative perception. Receivers of requests who send sexual requests themselves are less likely to perceive these as bothersome. Trust, reciprocity and equivalence are essential for adolescents in exploring their sexuality and engaging in romantic relationships (Subrahmanyam & Šmahel, 2011). Therefore, negative experiences are more likely to occur when adolescents interact with people relatively unknown and when an intrinsic motivation for engaging in sexual interaction is missing. Our findings suggest that incident characteristics play an important role in explaining why sexual communication is perceived as bothersome or not.

There are striking similarities in the profiles of vulnerable adolescents; i.e., adolescents who perceived receiving sexual requests as bothersome and adolescents who evaluated their online sexual activities as negative. Likewise, the profiles of adolescents who have did not perceive these requests as bothersome and who did not evaluate their activities as negative show significant similarities. Therefore, it is possible to give an overview of risk factors and protective factors. Firstly, bothersome and negative experiences do not stand alone. There is a strong relation with other negative online experiences, such as being cyber bullied. Secondly, there is a strong relation between adolescents' Internet usage and receiving sexual requests or engaging in sexting. An above average score on online disinhibition increases the likeliness of being involved in bothersome and negative incidences. Conversely, very frequent Internet use increases the likeliness of being involved in non-problematic incidences. Therefore, it seems that being frequently online is a protective factor.

Possibly, learning-by-doing helps adolescents to early recognize and counter negative online situations. Thirdly, adolescents with low self-control are more likely to engage in both sexual communications as well as in producing online sexual material, whether this leads to bothersome incidences or not. However, adolescents who also score low on psychological well-being are more likely to perceive incidences as bothersome, although the direction of this relation is unclear. Lastly, age and taking initiative in online interactions are both very important factors in protecting adolescents from harm. The older adolescents get, the more they developmentally are interested in sex and the more they voluntarily become involved in online sexual communications and activities. Conversely, younger adolescents who are passively confronted with sexual requests from others feel intimidated or bothered. Therefore, this group needs special attention.

Our study has several limitations that need to be addressed in future research. First, our data is cross-sectional which allowed us to identify relations between variables, but it did not allow us to investigate temporal sequence or causality. Second, we did not investigate long-term effects, neither of receiving online sexual requests nor of producing online sexual images. Third, the sample size of the models explaining sexting (Table 8) is quite small. Therefore, caution needs to be used in the interpretation of the findings and the inferences to the population. Although the represented models describe the variables that significantly correlated with sexting, a more elaborated rationale for studying psychological variables in relation to sexting is needed to understand psychological processes which shape youth's motivations and experience with this type of online activity.

Conclusion

The binary conceptions "being at risk-risk-taking", "victim-perpetrator", "online-offline" do not grasp the reality of adolescents' multifaceted and dialogic online sexual interactions and the ways in which these interactions are integrated within and shaped by adolescents' offline lives. However, the online environment differs from its offline counterpart in terms of the extent to which people are disembodied or anonymous and the extent to which people may interact with a known or unknown other. Furthermore, adolescents are no homogeneous group, neither online nor offline. In addition, adolescents are constantly developing themselves, gaining experience, acquiring skills and building resilience. A personalized rather than general approach in which the adolescent is central, and that fosters the empowerment of adolescents is more likely to entail an outcome in the interest of adolescents.

Note

1. This research project was undertaken in accordance with the Code of Research established by the HBO-council (Andriessen, Onstenk, Delnooz, Smeijsters, & Peij, 2010).

References

Andriessen, D., Onstenk, J., Delnooz, P., Smeijsters, H., & Peij, S. (2010). *Gedragscode praktijkgericht onderzoek voor het hbo; Gedragscode voor het voorbereiden en uitvoeren van praktijkgericht onderzoek binnen het Hoger Beroepsonderwijs in Nederland* [Dutch Code of conduct for research in applied sciences]. Delft: Elan Strategie & Creatie.

Barak, A. (2005). Sexual harassment on the Internet. *Social Science Computer Review, 23*, 77–92. http://dx.doi.org/10.1177/0894439304271540

Bossler, A. M., & Holt, T. J. (2010). The effect of self-control on victimization in the cyberworld. *Journal of Criminal Justice, 38*, 227–236. http://dx.doi.org/10.1016/j.jcrimjus.2010.03.001

Cubbin, C., Santelli, J., Brindis, C. D., & Braveman, P. (2005). Neighborhood context and sexual behaviors among adolescents: Findings from the National Longitudinal Study of Adolescent Health. *Perspectives on Sexual and Reproductive Health, 37*, 125–134. http://dx.doi.org/10.1363/3712505

Diener, E., & Seligman, M. E. P. (2004). Beyond money: Toward an economy of well-being. *Psychological Science in the Public Interest, 5*, 1–31. http://dx.doi.org/10.1111/j.0963-7214.2004.00501001.x

Eijnden, R.J.J.M. van den, & Vermulst, A. (2006). *Online communicatie, compuslief internetgebruik en het psychosociale welbevinden van jongeren* [Online communication, compulsive Internet use and psychosocial well-being among youth]. In Jaarboek IVCT en samenleving 2006. De digitale generatie (pp. 25–44). Amsterdam: Boom.

Grasmick, H. G., Tittle, C. R., Bursik Jr. R. J., & Arneklev, B. J. (1993). Testing the core empirical implications of Gottfredson and Hirschi's general theory of crime. *Journal of Research in Crime and Delinquency, 30*, 5–29. http://dx.doi.org/10.1177/0022427893030001002

Jones, L. M., Mitchell, K. J., & Finkelhor, D. (2012). Trends in youth internet victimization: Findings from three youth internet safety surveys 2000-2010. *Journal of Adolescent Health, 50*, 179–186. http://dx.doi.org/10.1016/j.jadohealth.2011.09.015

Kerstens, J., & Stol, W. P. (2012). *Jeugd en Cybersafety: Online slachtoffer- en daderschap onder Nederlandse jongeren* [Youth & Cybersafety: Online victimization and perpetration among Dutch youth]. Den Haag: Boom Lemma uitgevers.

Lenhart, A. (2009). *Teens and sexting: how and why minor teens are sending sexually suggestive or nearly nude images via text messaging*. Washington, D.C.: Pew Internet & American Life Project.

Livingstone, S., Haddon, L., Görzig, A., & Ólafsson, K. (2011). *Risks and safety on the Internet: The perspective of European children. Full Findings*. LSE, London: EU Kids Online.

Livingstone, S., & Helsper, E. (2007). Taking risks when communicating on the Internet: The role of offline social-psychological factors in young people's vulnerability to online risks. *Information, communication and society, 10*, 619–643. http://dx.doi.org/10.1080/13691180701657998

Lounsbury, K., Mitchell, K. J. & Finkelhor, D. (2011). *The true prevalence of sexting*. Crimes Against Children Research Centre, University of New Hampshire, Durham, New Hampshire.

Mitchell, K. J., Finkelhor, D., Jones, L. M., & Wolak, J. (2012). Prevalence and characteristics of youth sexting: a national study. *Pediatrics, 129*, 13–20. http://dx.doi.org/10.1542/peds.2011-1730.

Mitchell, K. J., Finkelhor, D., & Wolak, J. (2003). The exposure of youth to unwanted sexual material on the internet: A national survey of risk, impact, and prevention. *Youth & Society, 34*, 330–358. http://dx.doi.org/10.1177/0044118X02250123

Pardoen, J., & Pijpers, R. (2006). *Mijn kind online: Hoe begeleid je als ouder je kind op internet?* [My child online: guidelines for parents to mediate their children's Internet use]. Amsterdam: SWP.

Ringrose, J., Gill, R., Livingstone, S., & Harvey, L. (2012). *A Qualitative Study of Children, Young People and 'Sexting'*. London: NSPCC.

Schouten, A. P., Valkenburg, P. M., & Peter, J. (2007). Precursors and underlying processes of adolescents' online self-disclosure: Developing and testing an "Internet-attribute-perception" model. *Media Psychology, 10*, 292–314. http://dx.doi.org/10.1080/15213260701375686

Subrahmanyam, K, & Šmahel, D. (2011). *Digital Youth: The Role of Media in Development*. New York: Springer.

Suler, J. R. (2004). The online disinhibition effect. *CyberPsychology & Behavior, 7*, 321–326. http://dx.doi.org/10.1089/1094931041291295

Suzuki, L. K., & Calzo, J. P. (2004). The search for peer advice in cyberspace: An examination of online teen bulletin boards about health and sexuality. *Journal of Applied Developmental Psychology, 25*, 685–698. http://dx.doi.org/10.1016/j.appdev.2004.09.002

Valkenburg, P. M., & Peter, J. (2011). Online communication among adolescents: An integrated model of its attraction, opportunities, and risks. *Journal of Adolescent Health, 48*, 121–127. http://dx.doi.org/10.1016/j.jadohealth.2010.08.020

Vandebosch, H., van Cleemput, K., Mortelmans, D., & Walrave, M. (2006). *Cyberpesten bij jongeren in Vlaanderen* [Cyberbullying among youth in Flanders]. Brussel: viWTA.

Ward, L. M. (2004). Wading through the stereotypes: Positive and negative associations between media use and black adolescents' conceptions of self. *Developmental Psychology, 40*, 284–294. http://dx.doi.org/10.1037/0012-1649.40.2.284

Whittle, H., Hamilton-Giachritsis, C., Beech, A., & Collings, G. (2013). A review of online grooming: Characteristics and concerns. *Aggression and Violent Behavior, 18*, 62–70. http://dx.doi.org/10.1016/j.avb.2012.09.003

Wolak, J., Mitchell, K., & Finkelhor, D. (2006). *Online Victimization of Youth: Five years later*. Alexandria, VA: National Center for Missing & Exploited Children Bulletin - #07-06-025.

Ybarra, M. L., Espelage, D. L., & Mitchell, K. J. (2007).
The co-occurrence of Internet harassment and unwanted
sexual solicitation victimization and perpetration: Associations
with psychosocial indicators. *Journal of Adolescent Health,
41*, S31–S41. http://dx.doi.org/10.1016/j.jadohealth.
2007.09.010

Critical Thinking

1. At what point does a behavior qualify as an "epidemic"?
   How do we measure it?

2. What are the consequences of sexting for an adolescent?
   Are adolescents capable of considering these consequences
   before engaging in this behavior?

3. How might researchers better communicate their findings to
   the media and the public?

4. What responsibility does the media have in communicating
   with the public? What is the public's responsibility?

Internet References

Cyberbullying Research Center
www.cyberbullying.us
Do Something
https://www.dosomething.org/facts/11-facts-about-sexting
The National Campaign
www.thenationalcampaign.org/resource/sex-and-tech

JOYCE KERSTENS is a senior researcher at the Cybersafety research
Group (NHL University). Her research activities have mainly focused
on policy and evaluation research in the field of safety and security.
WOUTER STOL is chairholder in Cybersafety at NHL University of
Applied Sciences and the Police Academy, and professor in Police
Studies at the Open University. He served as the chief of police in
Amsterdam until 1992. He has written about 100 publications; the
main theme of his research is safety and information and communica-
tions technology.

Cyberpsychology: Journal of Psychosocial Research on Cyberspace, 8(1), article 8. doi: 10.5817/CP2014-1-8.

Prepared by: Elizabeth Schroeder, EdD, MSW,
Elizabeth Schroeder Consulting

Article

Sexting at School: Lessons Learned the Hard Way

LISA E. SORONEN, NICOLE VITALE, AND KAREN A. HAASE

Learning Outcomes

After reading this article, you will be able to:

- Identify reasons made for taking teen sexting seriously.

- Understand the position cited and analysis used in examining penalties for teen sexting.

- Evaluate the ways in which teen sexting affects the lives of teens who participate.

A 16-year-old boy asks his 15-year-old girlfriend to send him a naked photo of herself. She does so via text message, thinking that the photo will remain private and will show him how much she cares about him. Three weeks later, the couple breaks up, and her boyfriend forwards the text message to his friends, who quickly spread the image throughout the school. The girl is teased for months afterward, her grades plummet, and the formerly sunny teen refuses to go to school or to socialize with other students.

As many school attorneys and administrators know, this case is far from isolated. "Sexting," the practice by which teens forward sexually explicit images of themselves or their peers via text messaging, has become increasingly common nationwide. According to a frequently cited survey from the National Campaign to Prevent Teen and Unplanned Pregnancy, one in five teens has sent or posted nude or seminude photos of themselves online or via text message. Twenty-two percent of teens have received a nude or semi-nude photo of someone else. The study found that while most of the images are exchanged between boyfriends or girlfriends, 15 percent of teens have forwarded images to someone they only know online.

The potential detrimental effects that sexting can have on students are vast. Educators, child psychologists, and prosecutors agree that most teens do not understand the implications that sexting may have on their futures. While sexting often originates as a private exchange between a teen and his or her love interest, relationships can quickly deteriorate. Before long, the seemingly private images can be distributed throughout the school. These incidents can be highly embarrassing for students and, in some extreme cases, can have deadly consequences. At least two female students have committed suicide after the sexually explicit photos of themselves sent to a boy were disseminated to classmates. As discussed below, criminal prosecution—including being required to register as a sex offender—is another possible long-term negative consequence of sexting.

This article discusses a number of legal and practical issues related to sexting in schools. Specifically, this article discusses searching cell phones, what steps administrators can and should take upon discovering sexting, anti-sexting policies, and preventing sexting through education.

Searching Cell Phones

School administrators typically find out about sexting through the rumor mill. Of course, the only way administrators can determine if sexting actually has happened and who is involved is to ask students or to "see for themselves." In the ideal world, students will readily admit to being involved in sexting upon being questioned by administrators. In the real world, administrators may feel they need to search cell phones as part of a sexting investigation. Depending on the facts, searching a student's cell phone without a warrant may violate the Fourth Amendment. Likewise, it is at least arguable that searching open text messages on a cell phone without consent violates the Stored Communications Act. To avoid Fourth Amendment and Stored Communications Act issues, school administrators may always seek consent of a student and his or her parents before searching a cell phone as part of a sexting investigation.

Fourth Amendment Concerns

The U.S. Supreme Court held in *New Jersey v. T.L.O.* that school officials may search students as long as the search is reasonable; that is, the search must be justified at its inception and reasonable in scope. According to the Court:

> Under ordinary circumstances, a search of a student by a teacher or other school official will be "justified at its inception" when there are reasonable grounds for suspecting that the search will turn up evidence that the student has violated or is violating either the law or the rules of the school. Such a search will be permissible in its scope when the measures adopted are reasonably related to the objectives of the search and not excessively intrusive in light of the age and sex of the student and the nature of the infraction.

In no reported cases to date has a student challenged administrators searching his or her cell phone in a sexting investigation. However, in *Klump v. Nazareth Area School District*, a federal district court denied a school district's motion to dismiss on the basis of qualified immunity in a case involving a search of a student's cell phone. A teacher confiscated Christopher Klump's cell phone because he displayed the phone in violation of a school policy that prohibited the display or use of cell phones during school hours. The teacher and the assistant principal called other students in Christopher's phone directory to see if they were also violating district policy and accessed his text messages and voicemail.

Christopher asserted that these actions constituted an unreasonable search in violation of his Fourth Amendment rights. The court found that confiscation of the cell phone was justified because Christopher was caught violating the district's policy prohibiting the use or display of cell phones during school hours. However, the search of the cell phone violated Christopher's Fourth Amendment rights because: "They had no reason to suspect at the outset that such a search would reveal that Christopher Klump himself was violating another school policy; rather, they hoped to utilize his phone as a tool to catch other students, violations." The search of the cell phone, therefore, was not reasonable in scope.

It is not too difficult to imagine a fact pattern involving sexting where a school district could argue persuasively that an administrator's search of a student's text messages and pictures was justified at its inception and reasonable in scope. For example, let's say Christopher Klump showed an administrator an inappropriate picture a classmate texted him. As part of an investigation, the administrator should determine whether the named classmate actually sent Christopher the picture. It would seem a search of the classmate's text messages sent to Christopher Klump would be justified at its inception and reasonable in scope. Likewise, simply asking the classmate to present his cell phone to the administrator and calling the number in Christopher's phone associated with the text probably would be all the proof an administrator would need.

School administrators can take a few steps to make it more likely that searches of cell phones in sexting investigations pass Fourth Amendment muster. First, as described in the paragraph above, in some instances administrators can rely on information provided by technology—rather than just rumors—to determine whose phone to search and where to look. Second, while common sense indicates that sexting is a violation of school rules, explicitly prohibiting it in a school district policy or a student code of conduct will make it clear. Third, providing notice in the school district's cell phone policy that the administration may search cell phones if it has reasonable suspicion that a search will reveal that school rules have been violated, may also support a district's argument that a search was reasonable.

If school administrators ask school resource officers (SROs) to search a student's cell phone, the more demanding probable cause standard may apply. Likewise, if school administrators ask the police to search the student's phone, the probable cause standard likely will apply to the search.

In some instances, administrators may need to search to find a cell phone; for example, let's say Christopher's classmate in the example above denies having a cell phone at school. The time Christopher received the text message or a call to the student's parents about whether he generally brings a cell phone to school may cast doubt on the student's claim that his phone is not with him. If administrators search for the phone, they should consider T.L.O.'s requirement that the search be permissible in scope when determining where to look.

Stored Communications Act Concerns

In *Klump v. Nazareth Area School District*, Christopher Klump also argued that the school district violated Pennsylvania's version of the federal Stored Communications Act (SCA) by accessing his text messages, phone numbers, and call records. It is a violation of the federal SCA (which is very similar to Pennsylvania's statute) to: "(1) intentionally access without authorization a facility through which an electronic communication service is provided; or (2) intentionally exceed an authorization to access that facility; and thereby obtain, alter, or prevent authorized access to a wire or electronic communication while it is in electronic storage in such system."

The district court concluded that a call log and phone number directory are not "communications" under the statute, so searching them did not violate Pennsylvania's SCA. However, concluding that Christopher's "voice mail at least would have been stored by his cell phone provider and not in the cell phone itself," the court did not dismiss the unlawful access claims related to the voicemail or text messages.

While not argued in this case, under the federal SCA courts have held that open emails of which a recipient maintains a copy do not meet the definition of "electronic storage."

"Electronic storage" is defined as: "(A) any temporary, intermediate storage of a wire or electronic communication incidental to the electronic transmission thereof; and (B) any storage of such communication by an electronic communication service for purposes of backup protection of such communication." An open email is not in "temporary, intermediate storage"; instead, it is in "post-transmission storage." Open emails that users store on an Internet Service Provider's (ISP) system are not backup copies; backup copies are made by ISPs to protect the email from technical problems before it is transmitted.

Under this rationale, Christopher's opened text messages contained on his phone would not be in "electronic storage." Instead, they would be in post-transmission storage and are not "backups" maintained by his cell phone company to protect its system integrity. In other words, had the court analyzed this case by applying the definition of "electronic storage," it likely would have concluded Christopher's open text messages did not fall under the SCA.

The federal SCA allows users to authorize access to communications otherwise protected by the statute. To avoid possibly violating the SCA school districts may seek authorization from the student and his or her parents before searching a student's cell phone. If consent is denied, the federal SCA allows the government to compel the content of electronic communications from providers of "electronic communication service" and "remote computing service," which includes cell phone companies, after obtaining a search warrant, subpoena, etc.

Sexting Has Been Discovered . . . Now What?

When sexting arises in the school setting, it can have broad practical and legal implications. When school administrators discover sexting, they should consider at least the following: (1) telling the parents of all the students involved; (2) reporting the sexting to the police; (3) reporting the sexting as suspected abuse or neglect; (4) minimizing exposure to child pornography charges; (5) whether, who, and how to discipline the students

involved; and (6) preventing the harassment and bullying of students involved in sexting. The rather dramatic story of a Virginia assistant principal charged with possession of child pornography and failure to report suspected child abuse after he asked a student to send him a seminude picture in the student's cell phone as part of a sexting investigation, illustrates what can happen when a school administrator fails to take the steps listed above.

Assistant principal Ting-Yi Oei explained that after he viewed an inappropriate picture contained in a student's cell phone, he showed the picture to the principal, who instructed him to transfer it to Oei's computer "in case we needed it later." Oei did not know how to do this, so the teen texted the picture to Oei's cell phone and told Oei how to forward it to his work email address. Oei could not identify the person in the photograph, concluded it was probably not a student at the school, told the principal what happened, and assumed the matter was closed.

Two weeks later, the boy caught with the photo was suspended for pulling down a girl's pants in class. Oei told the boy's mother about the sexting when he told her about the suspension. She was outraged that he had not informed her of the picture earlier and complained to the police. They conducted an investigation, and Oei showed them the photograph on his cell phone after he could not find it on his computer.

A month later, Oei was charged with failure to report suspected child abuse. The commonwealth (district) attorney dropped that charge but later charged him with possession of child pornography. The circuit court dismissed the child pornography charge finding that the picture—which at worst maybe showed a nipple—did not meet the definition of "sexually explicit visual material," pursuant to Virginia's child pornography statute.

Tell the Parents of All Students Involved

School administrators should notify parents promptly upon discovering that their child is the subject of, is in possession of, or has sent inappropriate pictures for many reasons. First, contacting parents immediately should demonstrate that the pictures were viewed for investigative purposes only, dissuading parents from pursuing child pornography charges. Second, as the Ting-Yi Oei incident illustrates, some parents want to know about sexting as soon as possible. Any concern regarding a parent's potential overreaction is outweighed by the district's duty to act in place of the parents while their children are at school. Parents should be told of this dangerous behavior, and administrators should follow abuse and neglect reporting statutes if they fear a parent's reaction might be violent.

Tell the Police

State law or school district policy may require school districts to report to the police certain crimes that have happened on school grounds. It may come as a surprise to school administrators that sexting in some states in some instances may be a crime. In fact, students in a number of states have been charged criminally and convicted of violating child pornography laws by sexting. For example, students likely could be prosecuted for sexting under Ohio's Illegal Use of Minor in Nudity-oriented Material or Performance statute, which prohibits "[p]hotograph[ing] any minor . . . in a state of nudity, or creat[ing], direct[ing], produc[ing], or transfer[ing] any material or performance that shows the minor in a state of nudity. . . ." Under the Ohio statute, it appears that both the girlfriend and the boyfriend from the example at the beginning of this article could be convicted. The girlfriend photographed herself nude and transferred the picture; the boyfriend further transferred the picture. The Ohio Legislature is considering adopting a statute specifically aimed at minors sexting.

Prosecutors across the country have taken various approaches to sexting. Parties who have been charged include the "victim," the recipient, and the disseminator. Prosecutors in some instances may not charge anyone at all or may recommend that those charged participate in a diversion program. Few reported cases discuss whether, and under what circumstances, students can be criminally prosecuted for sexting. . . . In this case, a school district discovered sexting and informed the district attorney. The parents of the girls depicted in the photographs successfully challenged the district attorney's threat to criminally prosecute them unless they participated in an education and counseling program. This case has been appealed to the Third Circuit.

District attorneys have been heavily criticized for prosecuting children engaged in sexting—particularly when the result is the child prosecuted being required to register as a sex offender. As one district attorney points out, child pornography laws were intended to prosecute child sexual predators, not minors who may not even know what child pornography is. Miller is a great example of backlash against district attorneys prosecuting sexting cases.

To respond to myriad concerns raised by sexting, in 2009, lawmakers in at least 11 states have introduced legislation addressing the issue, according to the National Conference of State Legislatures. At least two other states—Kentucky and Virginia—are expected to consider legislation in 2010. . . . To summarize, a number of states have adopted (Vermont, North Dakota) or proposed (Ohio, Pennsylvania) legislation that specifically addresses sexting as a crime separate from child pornography with lesser penalties. Other states have created (Nebraska) or proposed to create (New York) an affirmative defense to child pornography statutes for sexting in some circumstances. Two states have proposed to create (New Jersey, Pennsylvania) educational diversionary programs for students charged or convicted of sexting. Two other states (Colorado, Oregon) have amended their Internet sexual exploitation of a minor statutes to include texting. Finally, two states have proposed to educate students about sexting (New York, New Jersey).

Given that sexting is a new phenomenon and that most child pornography statutes were adopted before cell phones were widely used and sexting was a national problem, school attorneys in most instances will not be able to determine definitely whether a crime has been committed. For this reason, school districts are well-advised to inform the police of sexting so that they can conduct a criminal investigation. However, any school administrator who knows the facts of *Miller v. Skumanick* as described by the district court—where the district attorney threatened to charge the girls depicted in the photographs with felonies that could result in a long prison term, a permanent record, and registration as sex offenders—would think twice before telling the police about sexting. School administrators should not assume all district attorneys will prosecute all sexting cases or that school administrators will be unable to influence the district attorney. Sexting is a new crime. For this reason, many district attorneys likely would welcome input from school district officials on how to handle these cases. Particularly if the district is going to discipline the students involved, the district attorney may be amenable to not charging the students criminally depending on facts of the case.

It is always a good idea for school district officials to try to foster cooperation with local police and the prosecutors. The best time to approach the district attorney's office about this issue is before sexting occurs on campus and before a district attorney has had the chance to decide that prosecuting sexting cases will be the new "tough on crime" tactic. Likewise, part of building a good relationship with the district attorney's office may be asking for input on how the district should punish sexting and inviting the district attorney to participate in the district's sexting education and prevention efforts.

Report Sexting as Suspected Child Abuse and Neglect

A sexted image may constitute child abuse or neglect, depending on the state's definition of these terms and what is exactly depicted in the photograph. All states have child abuse and neglect reporting statutes which apply to school districts. Most, if not all, statutes include in the definition of child abuse and neglect sexual crimes against a child. For example,

Virginia's definition of an abused or neglected child includes one: "[w]hose parents or other person responsible for his care commits or allows to be committed any act of sexual exploitation or any sexual act upon a child in violation of the law." Virginia's Department of Social Services states that child abuse occurs when a parent: "[c]ommits or allows to be committed any illegal sexual act upon a child including incest, rape, fondling, indecent exposure, prostitution, or allows a child to be used in any sexually explicit visual material."

Ting-Yi Oei admitted that he did not think about the sexting incident in terms of whether it violated Virginia's child abuse and neglect reporting statute. It is unlikely Oei could have been successfully prosecuted under this statute for at least three reasons. First, he did not know the identity of the girl, though her identity was determined later. Second, he did not know she was only 16. Third, the circuit court ruled in Oei's possession of child pornography case that the picture was not "sexually explicit visual material." Had Oei known the girl's identity and age, and had the picture been more revealing, Oei likely would have had a reporting obligation under Virginia law.

In short, depending on the state's definition of abuse and neglect and depending on the visual depiction in the sexted photograph, school districts may have an obligation to report sexting under child abuse and neglect reporting statutes.

Minimize Exposure to Child Pornography Charges

School administrators should take steps to avoid being accused of possession of child pornography by prosecutors or disgruntled parents. This may simply involve turning over confiscated evidence of sexting to the police immediately. In fact, Oei may have avoided being charged altogether had he taken possession of the boy's phone and turned it over to the police promptly, like the school officials in Miller, instead of receiving and maintaining the photo on his own phone.

School administrators should also take steps to avoid charges of disseminating child pornography. As described later in this article, a lawsuit has been filed against a Washington state school district which rather cryptically accuses school officials of showing sexted photographs of a student to "other adults" in violation of Washington's dissemination of child pornography statute. The district denies doing so in its answer. Regardless of what actually happened in this case, it illustrates that a school administrator who discovers sexting should not share the images with other school employees much less non-employees.

The Utah legislature, likely in response to the Ting-Yi Oei incident, has passed a law to ensure that school employees and others cannot be liable "when reporting or preserving data" in a child pornography investigation. . . .

Discipline the Students Involved

As the case described below illustrates, school districts should consider disciplining all students involved in the sexting—the student featured in the image, students who received the image (unless they deleted it immediately), and students who disseminated the image—equally if possible.

The parents of a Washington state high school student are suing the school district for violating Washington's sexual equality statute for only punishing their daughter in a sexting incident. The parents admit in their complaint that their daughter took a naked picture of herself which was circulated among other students. The school district suspended her for one year from the cheer squad for violating the athletic code. Her parents alleged that the school district violated Washington's sexual equality statute by punishing only her and not the football players who possessed and viewed the picture of her. The school district responded that it did not discipline the football players because it did not know who sent, received, or forwarded the pictures. The daughter refused to tell the district because she did not "want to get anyone in trouble."

Whether the sexual equality claim is successful, plaintiffs do have a fair point that the boys who received and did not immediately delete the photograph of their daughter—or, worse yet, forwarded it—also should have received punishment. While a court likely will not be sympathetic to the daughter's refusal to inform the district of the football players who received and forwarded the picture of her, it likewise might not be sympathetic to the school district's failure to investigate further without her help.

Preventing Bullying and Harassment

Eighteen-year-old Jessica Logan committed suicide after being bullied and harassed after her ex-boyfriend forwarded to other students nude photos she took of herself and sent to him. Her parents are suing the school district, who was aware of the sexting, claiming that the district did not do enough to stop her from being harassed. Whether their claim against the district will be successful, it illustrates that districts should take measures to prevent harassment before and following a sexting incident.

Preventing bullying and harassment at school generally is a difficult task. At minimum, those involved in a sexting incident should be specifically instructed not to harass the "victims" of sexting. Likewise, before a sexting incident occurs, parents and school staff should be informed that sexting may occur, discipline will result, and harassment is prohibited. If an incident occurs, these messages might have to be reiterated. Finally, if harassment or bullying related to a sexting incident occurs, the district's anti-harassment/bullying policy should be followed and harassers should be disciplined.

Anti-sexting Policies

Adopting anti-sexting policies may be one approach school districts can take to prevent sexting. Obviously, no anti-sexting policy will stop sexting altogether, no matter how carefully written or widely circulated. However, an anti-sexting policy will put students and their parents on notice that sexting is unacceptable and has serious consequences.

School districts may take a variety of policy approaches to prevent sexting. Districts may revise existing policies addressing acceptable use, student codes of conduct, cell phones, harassment and bullying, or other similar subject areas, to prohibit sexting. School districts may ban cell phone use during school or cell phone possession at school altogether to prevent sexting. Some boards may decide that they need a separate policy addressing sexting.

Districts adopting a comprehensive anti-sexting policy should consider including the following elements. First, an anti-sexting policy should clearly state that the mere possession of sexually explicit digital pictures on any device is prohibited regardless of whether the state's child pornography law is violated. Second, the policy should state that all involved in sexting, unless they deleted images right away, will be punished. For example, student handbook language should prohibit "sending, sharing, viewing, or possessing pictures, text messages, emails, or other material of a sexual nature in electronic or any other form on a computer, cell phone, or other electronic device." Third, the policy should inform students that their parents and the police may be contacted and sexting may be reported as suspected child abuse or neglect. Fourth, the policy should put students on notice that administrators may search their cell phones if they have reasonable suspicion a student has been involved in sexting. Fifth, the consequences for sexting should be clearly stated but should include discretionary wording that allows administrators to adjust punishments up or down as appropriate. Finally, the policy should prohibit harassment and bullying related to sexting incidents and should punish nonconforming behavior.

Education as Prevention

Education professionals—including school lawyers—should make parents, staff, and students aware of the existence of and dangers of sexting. School districts should consider a variety of actions to raise awareness of and increase education about sexting. Districts may partner with other community organizations or public offices to provide staff trainings on bullying, cyber-bullying, and computer/Internet safety, including sexting and safety on social networking sites. This can include in-school assemblies for students, professional development for staff, training for school board members, distribution of school rules and policies through student handbooks, newsletters/correspondence to the community, meeting with parent groups, and resources on the school webpage and public forums.

Any education around sexting can and should be aimed at the whole community when possible. This means including students, board members, and staff as well as parents and community members. While the majority of recent press has involved middle and high school students, education regarding computer/Internet/technology safety should include younger children as appropriate. A variety of websites and documents provide information about sexting for students, parents, and educators.

Conclusion

The world of social interaction through new technologies is evolving at break-neck speed. Because young people are trendsetters—particularly when technology is involved—schools are affected by these changes. Disturbing, new technology trends like sexting have significant legal implications for school districts that may not be immediately obvious even to an experienced school administrator or school lawyer. However, sexting has been a growing problem long enough to give us the Ting-Yi Oei incident, Washington state case, and the Jessica Logan case, all of which are full of lessons learned about sexting. School attorneys must pass these lessons learned on to their clients.

Critical Thinking

1. Think more broadly about teens' sexting. Is it healthy or unhealthy? Natural or dangerous? What are the larger implications of sexting behaviors?

2. Should parents monitor what their children are posting? Do children know what their parents' expectations are of them online?

3. Are there proper limits on electronic communication for children as they develop their digital citizenship skills? Is this the job of schools? Parents? Places of worship?

Internet References

Psychology Today on teens' sexting

http://www.psychologytoday.com/blog/teen-angst/201103/sexting-teens

ABC News and "Sexting Teens Going Too Far"

http://abcnews.go.com/Technology/WorldNews/sexting-teens/story?id=6456834

Pew Internet and American Life Project and teens' sexting research

http://www.pewinternet.org/Reports/2009/Teens-and-Sexting.aspx

Safeteens.com provides sexting tips:

http://www.safeteens.com/teen-sexting-tips